CAMBRIDGE STUDIES IN P

D1683209

Value and justification

COLLEGE FOR HUMAN SERVICES
LIBRARY
345 HUDSON STREET
NEW YORK, N.Y. 10014

CAMBRIDGE STUDIES IN PHILOSOPHY

General editor SYDNEY SHOEMAKER

Advisory editors J. E. J. ALTHAM, SIMON BLACKBURN, GILBERT HARMAN, MARTIN HOLLIS, FRANK JACKSON, JONATHAN LEAR, WILLIAM G. LYCAN, JOHN PERRY, BARRY STROUD

JAMES CARGILE *Paradoxes: a study in form and predication*
PAUL M. CHURCHLAND *Scientific realism and the plasticity of mind*
N. M. L. NATHAN *Evidence and assurance*
WILLIAM LYONS *Emotion*
PETER SMITH *Realism and the progress of science*
BRIAN LOAR *Mind and meaning*
J. F. ROSS *Portraying analogy*
DAVID HEY *Supererogation*
PAUL HORWICH *Probability and evidence*
ELLERY EELLS *Rational decision and causality*
HOWARD ROBINSON *Matter and sense*
E. J. BOND *Reason and value*
D. M. ARMSTRONG *What is a law of nature?*
H. E. KYBURG, JR. *Theory and measurement*
M. ROBINS *Promising, intending and moral autonomy*
N. J. H. DENT *The moral psychology of the virtues*
R. A. DUFF *Trials and punishments*
FLINT SCHIER *Deepter into pictures*
ANTHONY APPIAH *Assertion and conditionals*
ROBERT BROWN *Analyzing love*
ROBERT M. GORDON *The structure of emotions*
FRANÇOIS RECANATI *Meaning and force*
WILLIAM G. LYCAN *Judgement and justification*
GERALD DWORKIN *The theory and practice of autonomy*
MICHAEL TYE *The metaphysics of mind*
DAVID O. BRINK *Moral realism and the foundations of ethics*
W. D. HART *Engines of the soul*
PAUL K. MOSER *Knowledge and evidence*
D. M. ARMSTRONG *A combinatorial theory of possibility*
JOHN BISHOP *Natural agency*
CARL GINET *On action*
CHRISTOPHER J. MALONEY *The mundane matter of the mental languages*
MARK RICHARD *Propositional attitudes*

Value and justification

The foundations of liberal theory

Gerald F. Gaus

The right of the University of Cambridge to print and sell all manner of books was granted by Henry VIII in 1534. The University has printed and published continuously since 1584.

Cambridge University Press

Cambridge

New York   Port Chester   Melbourne   Sydney

Published by the Press Syndicate of the University of Cambridge
The Pitt Building, Trumpington Street, Cambridge CB2 1RP
40 West 20th Street, New York, NY 10011, USA
10 Stamford Road, Oakleigh, Melbourne 3166, Australia

© Cambridge University Press 1990

First published 1990

Printed in the United States of America

Library of Congress Cataloging-in-Publication Data

Gaus, Gerald F.
Value and justification : the foundations of liberal theory /
Gerald F. Gaus.
p. cm.
Includes bibliographical references.
ISBN 0-521-37525-8, ISBN 0-521-39733-2 (pbk)
1. Values. 2. Emotions (Philosophy) 3. Justice (Philosophy)
4. Liberalism. I. Title.
BD232.G38 1990
121'.8—dc20 89-27088

British Library Cataloguing in Publication Data
Gaus, Gerald F.
Value and justification: the foundations of liberal
theory. – (Cambridge studies in philosophy)
1. Ethics I. Title 170

ISBN 0-521-37525-8 hardback
ISBN 0-521-39733-2 paperback

In memory of Stanley Benn

Contents

Preface

This book is intended to be a contribution to axiology, moral theory, and political philosophy. However, those interested in these fields are apt to find much of the material unfamiliar. It is perhaps advisable to alert readers at the outset of the ways in which this book is unlike most others in these fields.

Most obviously, in the second chapter I offer a fairly detailed analysis of emotions. In the course of this analysis, I explore problems in the philosophy of mind as well as the psychology and neurophysiology of emotions. Students of ethics and political philosophy may be tempted to skip these discussions, supposing that they are not important for the arguments concerning morality and justification that are presented in Part II. But they really are foundational: the theory of emotion is the basis for the theory of value. I will try to show that once we have resolved some of the issues concerning, say, the intentionality of feeling states in the context of the theory of emotion, many puzzles are resolved, and pitfalls avoided, in the theory of value. And, once we have a good grasp of the nature of value, we are in the position to approach some of the problems of contemporary moral and political philosophy in a new light.

Although laying the foundations of a theory of justice in a theory of emotions may seem odd today, it would not, I think, have struck Hobbes or Hume so. For, in many ways, my project is in the spirit of their great works: I seek to show that the foundations of moral and political theory lie in certain important features of human psychology. Political theorists – especially those trained in political science departments – will probably find this approach congenial. That political theory rests on an understanding of human nature is a fundamental presupposition of that sort of political theorizing exemplified by John Plamenatz. But, although political theorists have remained true to this insight of Hobbes and Hume, they have generally sacrificed the rigor of those great philosophers. The status of the claims made by today's political theorists about human nature are as difficult to evaluate as they are interesting. Often they seem little more than possible stories about the nature of human beings or, as they are sometimes described, "visions" of human nature. To be sure, political theorists in recent years have relied more on psychological theories; as do I, many political theorists have discussed the work of Piaget and Kohlberg, for instance. But, typically, all this remains at a very general and abstract level. In this work, I draw on the psychology of emotions, attitude theory, and studies of values. Those working in these fields have collected enlightening data and have developed some relatively well-supported theories, which provide a rich source for moral and political philosophers.

Nevertheless, although I try to learn from attitude theorists and psychologists of emotion as well as from philosophers of mind, my aim here is to develop theories of value and moral justification, not to contribute to these other fields. But, even when I am concentrating on the theories of value and justification, my approach may seem somewhat alien to contemporary moral and political philosophers because I provide extensive citations to the relevant literature, especially in axiology. I have discovered that some of my colleagues are nearly scandalized by this. A friend who is a moral and political philosopher – and who shall remain nameless – has told me that my references are a sign of bad upbringing. But no student of value theory can fail to be surprised by the good work that was done – especially by Austrian and American axiologists – in the first half of this century, contributions that have been almost entirely forgotten. When reading recent publications dealing with ethics on problems of value, I have often felt that philosophers were proclaiming that they had once again invented the wheel – and often enough one that had been rounder forty years ago. So I have cited much of this earlier work because I have learned much from it. However, I also hope that others will learn from it, and I intend my notes as guides, suggesting where they may find useful discussions. I conceive of philosophy as a cooperative endeavor, encompassing those who have worked before, one's contemporaries, and our students; my citations are a sign of my debts and my assistance for those who may want to study these problems in depth.

Writing this book has been a cooperative experience in another way. During the years I have been working on these problems, I was fortunate enough to be Stanley Benn's colleague in the Philosophy Department of the Research School of Social Sciences at the Australian National University. We had worked together from 1979 to 1982, coediting a book on *Public and Private in Social Life*. After completing that explicitly cooperative project, we each set about writing books in moral theory. Almost all the core ideas in the first eight chapters of this book were discussed – well, actually argued about – in our daily philosophical lunches, which more than once finally concluded in the early evening. Problems were raised, solutions proposed, rejected, and revised in such a way that it was often unclear who was writing which book. I cannot even begin to say which of these ideas are "mine" and which were first raised by Stanley, except for the key arguments in §§17.2–17.4 and 22.2–22.3, which were certainly inspired by his paper on "Freedom, Autonomy, and the Concept of a Person."[1] At one point, our agreement on basic issues was close enough to write a paper jointly, entitled "Practical Rationality and Commitment,"[2] presenting a theory of rational action that provides a foundation for both our theories. And yet, for all that, our views remain opposed on the most basic of issues: a fundamental aim of this book is to defend a "subjectivist" account of value, something Stanley consistently rejected. In his *A Theory of Freedom*, he honored me by telling the world why I am wrong; yet, in a note that bespeaks of our cooperative experience, he indicates that his response to my theory is partly of my devising.[3] And, that, perhaps, was the greater honor.

Indebtedness is not characterized by scarcity. As enormous as is my debt to Stanley Benn, room enough remains for others. Fred D'Agostino, as a colleague and friend at the Australian National University (ANU) and later when he moved to the University of New England, has been a constant source of encouragement, which was often more needed than he might have thought. His own work on justification originally spurred me to

1 *Proceedings of the Aristotelian Society* (1975–6): 103–30.
2 *The American Philosophical Quarterly* 23 (July 1986): 255–66.
3 *A Theory of Freedom*, pp. 79–82.

think about these matters. Fred was also kind enough to read more than one draft of the manuscript for this book, providing both sound advice on philosophical matters and correcting the all-too-abundant errors. J. Roland Pennock read Part I and much of Part II in an early draft; he has an uncanny sense for weak arguments, and I almost always found it necessary to respond to his queries. In addition, Professor Pennock has fought a valiant battle for the English language against my prose; the reader can only reflect with dismay what this book must have been like before his assistance. My thanks, too, to Ralph Kennedy for his useful comments on an early draft. John W. Chapman was also kind enough both to read a draft and discuss my general approach. But my great debt to him remains as a teacher. His lesson, that political philosophy traces back to theories of human nature, informs this book, though, to paraphrase Bernard Bosanquet, it has returned to him in a form that he will not be able to recognize.

At the ANU we were lucky enough to have visits by distinguished philosophers, who often spurred me to think about issues that I had blissfully ignored. Among them, Loren E. Lomasky was kind enough to argue with me about most topics – from practical rationality to the nature of liberalism – and I always benefited. He also read the penultimate draft of the entire book, and was all too honest in his responses; I hope some day to pay him back in kind. My colleague at the ANU, Philip Pettit, provided useful insights (even though he is a consequentialist). Our lunch, in which I somehow ended up defending David Gauthier's *Morals by Agreement*, had, as the reader will see, far-reaching consequences. John Kleinig exposed me to relentless questioning one summer afternoon in New York, which led me (after a rest) to go home and think harder about some things. Two Ph.D. students at the ANU were also a great help. Stephen Buckle, who was writing a thesis on natural-law theories of property, taught me a great deal. Daniel Skubik, also a student in our department, was kind enough to read an early draft of Part I and immediately pointed out a contradiction.

A draft of the book was completed at the University of Queensland. David John Gow displayed great patience in helping me formulate the argument of Chapter IX; as a favor, he talked slowly using small words, as is befitting when a statistician talks to a political philosopher. I also greatly benefited from discussions with Sharon Beattie and Simon Jackman. My deep thanks are extended to the Department of Government of the University of Queensland, which was extraordinarily generous in providing the facilities that I needed to revise.

This long project was completed at the University of Minnesota, way up north in Duluth. Loren Lomasky enticed me from the warmth of Australia to the winter of northern Minnesota with the claim that, given the heated philosophic exchange in Duluth, I would not notice the difference. Well, I have noticed *some* differences, but he was right about the quality and liveliness of Duluth philosophy. I would like to thank my colleagues in both the political science and philosophy departments for making the University of Minnesota, Duluth, such an interesting place to work.

I have been lucky enough to have had research assistants who helped me do many things quicker, and with less pain, than would otherwise have been the case. I am especially grateful to Ra Foxton, who helped me begin, and Mary Callahan, who helped me finish. Along the way, C. T. O'Connell, David Braddon-Mitchell, and D. Bryne provided valuable help.

My first attempt at formulating the theory of value and justification, "Subjective Value and Justificatory Political Theory," was published in *NOMOS XXVIII: Justification*. Much, I think, was right in that argument, but a great deal was wrong; in any case, the position articulated in this book is rather different. My account of friendship and justice, which is important to the argument of §17 of this volume was first presented in a panel where I commented on an essay by Martin Golding; this short piece was published in the *Bulletin of the Australian Society of Legal Philosophy*.[4] The account of practical rationality – which I have partially revised – was published in *The American Philosophical Quarterly* and was expanded upon in an article in *Ethics*.[5] The argument for the rationality of moral action and our commitment to moral justification was first presented in "The Commitment to the Com-

4 "On Community and Justice: A Reply to Professor Golding," vol. 9 (October 1985): 197–204.
5 "Practical Rationality and Commitment" and "Practical Reason and Moral Persons," vol. 100 (October 1989), pp. 127–48.

mon Good."[6] My essay "A Contractual Justification of Redistributive Capitalism" reproduces parts of Chapters VIII and IX.[7]

Various formulations of my argument – from the stage where it was a glimmer in my eye to more or less what appears here – were presented to the American Political Science Association, the International Political Science Association, the Australasian Association for Philosophy, the Department of Economics of Wake Forest University, the Department of Traditional and Modern Philosophy at the University of Sydney, the Philosophy Colloquium at the University of Minnesota, Duluth, and, of course, to the Department of Philosophy, Research School of Social Sciences of the Australian National University. My thanks to all the participants, and to all those who have helped whom I have been unable to mention.

G.F.G.

6 In *On Political Obligation*, edited by Paul Harris (London: Routledge & Kegan Paul, 1990), pp. 26–64.
7 *NOMOS XXXI: Markets and Justice*, edited by John W. Chapman and J. Roland Pennock (New York: New York University Press, 1989), pp. 89–121.

I

The nature of the theories

1 THE THEORY OF VALUE

1.1 Some basic features of the concept of value

Some things we like, or find interesting, or useful; other things we abhor or find distasteful. We judge some objects and activities to be valuable or disvaluable, and sometimes we work hard to appreciate that which we believe to be of value. We compare the value of a multitude of things, activities and states of affairs, and these comparisons are central to our deliberations about what we should do. We pursue what is of value, avoid or attack what is disvaluable; we plan our lives around our most cherished values. And we constantly argue with each other about what really is and is not valuable, yet nothing surprises us less than others valuing that in which we can find little or no value.

These, then, are some of the central characteristics of the practice of valuing. As has been noted by others, compared to issues concerning right action and obligation, recent ethical philosophy has paid scant attention to the problems of valuing.[1] Even utilitarian theory, which would seem inevitably focused on a theory of value, has been largely preoccupied with what Rashdall called the "consequential or teleological criterion" of right action.[2] Indeed, today it is common to understand "utilitarianism" as meaning much the same as "consequentialism"; that is, it has come to be interpreted as a doctrine about rightness with only minimal, or vague, commitments to a theory of value.[3] Not that

1 See, e.g., Joel J. Kupperman, "Value Judgements," p. 506.
2 Hastings Rashdall, *The Theory of Good and Evil*, vol. II, p. 121. On consequentialism, see also G. E. M. Anscombe, "Modern Moral Philosophy."
3 "The central thesis of utilitarianism, in its most general form, is that actions are to be judged solely by their consequences and are not right or wrong

contemporary ethics actually does without theories of value; utilitarians are apt to reduce all questions of value to a matter of "preferences" or "desires,"[4] and the contemporary followers of Aristotle seem to equate what is valuable with what is good for humans. And, of course, John Rawls has made much of the idea of a "plan of life" as establishing "the basic point of view from which all judgments of value relating to a particular person are to be made."[5] I shall have something to say about these proposals later on,[6] but it is worth noting here that none of them have emerged from analyses that closely attend to the main features of our practice of valuing. To a remarkable extent, contemporary ethics has employed theories of value and goodness with little attention as to whether they adequately capture our concept of value and the practices that it informs.

Let us begin, then, by considering the nature of our concept of value. Among philosophers who have considered the problem, the following are perhaps the most widely recognized characteristics of value discourse and practice:

(a) Value language is grammatically complex, having a verb form (where someone *values* something), an adjectival form (where something is said to be *valuable*), and an abstract noun form (where something is said to be *a value*). Let us call these, respectively, *valuing*, *valuableness*, and *a value* (or *values*).
(b) Valuing, judgments of valuableness, and values provide reasons for action and choice.[7] They guide choices and enter into deliberation by providing at least a partial ordering of persons, acts, rules, institutions, experiences, objects, etc.[8]
(c) We argue about values, judgments of valuableness, and whether cer-

in themselves." D. H. Monro, "Utilitarianism," p. 444. This tendency to focus on utilitarianism as a theory of right action is particularly striking if one considers some of the major works of contemporary utilitarian theory, such as David Lyons, *Forms and Limits of Utilitarianism*, and Donald H. Regan, *Utilitarianism and Co-operation*. See J. Griffin, "Modern Utilitarianism."
4 On the place of preferences in utilitarian theory, see Amartya Sen and Bernard Williams, "Introduction" to *Utilitarianism and Beyond*. I consider the notions of desire and preference at length in §7.2.
5 John Rawls, *A Theory of Justice*, p. 409. See §14.3 in the present volume.
6 See §§7.3, 14.3, 15.3.
7 See Joseph Raz, *Practical Reason and Norms*, p. 25; E. J. Bond, *Reason and Value*. Michael Slote, however, argues that the link between recognition of value, or valuing, and reasons for action is not "axiomatic." *Goods and Virtues*, p. 124. See also Neil Cooper, *The Diversity of Moral Thinking*, p. 95.
8 See John Laird, *The Idea of Value*, p. 357; Robert Nozick, *Philosophical Explanations*, p. 429; Kurt Baier, "What is Value?," pp. 58ff.

tain valuings are correct. We often charge that another's values, value judgments, and valuings are wrong, ill-founded, or somehow inappropriate.[9]

(d) Values, judgments of valuableness and valuings are impersonal: "value-grounding considerations are not respecters of persons. . . . [I]f *X*'s contention that *V* is a value is correct and well-founded, then *V*'s status as a value is just as compelling for *Y* as for *X*."[10]

(e) Not only do we often agree to differ about values, value judgments, and valuings, but in some cases we also believe that people can disagree or differ on questions of value and yet each can quite properly and correctly maintain that neither is in any way mistaken. It is often said that "one man's meat is another man's poison" and that "there is no arguing about tastes."[11]

(f) Valuing and value judgments are in some way grounded in the properties or characteristics of the thing valued or judged to be valuable.[12]

(g) Values are often said to be chosen.[13]

(h) Every person experiences situations in which his values, valuings or value judgments conflict.[14]

(i) Value is typically divided into the intrinsic and instrumental; it is also often divided into types such as aesthetic, hedonistic, economic, moral, etc.[15]

(j) Value is both positive and negative, that is, it concerns both goodness and evil.[16]

(k) Valuing is somehow related to the affective and/or conative side of life.[17]

---

9 See Nicholas Rescher, *Introduction to Value Theory*, pp. 10, 56; Lawrence C. Becker, *On Justifying Moral Judgments*, p. 22: Kupperman, "Value Judgements," pp. 514–15.

10 Rescher, *Value Theory*, p. 11.

11 See Bond, *Reason and Value*, p. 97; C. I. Lewis, *An Analysis of Knowledge and Valuation*, p. 526; Becker, *Moral Judgments* pp. 21–2. However, the Austrian axiologist Christian Ehrenfels maintained that tastes could indeed be disputed. "The Ethical Theory of Value," p. 376.

12 See Elliot Cohen, "The Epistemology of Value," pp. 179–80; Samuel Hart, *Treatise on Values*, p. 54.

13 See Eva H. Cadwallader, "The Main Features of Value Experience," p. 232; Nozick, *Philosophical Explanations*, pp. 447, 558ff.; Rollo May, "Values, Myths, and Symbols," p. 270.

14 See Cadwallader, "Value Experience," pp. 232-3; Nozick, *Philosophical Explanations*, pp. 446–50.

15 See Derek Wright, *The Psychology of Moral Behaviour*, pp. 197–8; Aurel Kolnai, "Aesthetic and Moral Experience" and "Contrasting the Ethical with the Aesthetical"; Laird, *The Idea of Value*, p. 88.

16 See Bond, *Reason and Value*, ch. 7; Nozick. *Philosophical Explanations*, p. 420; Bernard Gert, *The Moral Rules*, ch. 3.

17 See Becker, *Moral Judgments*, p. 25; Rescher, *Value Theory*, pp. 9–10.

Some of these claims can be disputed, and others could be added; indeed, as we progress, I will both criticize some of them and point to a number of other features of value practice and discourse. But in general, and subject to some disagreements at one point or another, (a)–(k) enumerate the main claims made by philosophers regarding the concept of value. To some it may seem that this is simply an enumeration of things that philosophers of very different persuasions have said about the concept of value. How, one might say, could we possibly hope to make sense of such a list of claims? But if some theory could do so, if it could bring order to this enumeration and account for these seemingly unrelated claims in a coherent fashion, then such a theory could lay claim to integrate the insights of a number of philosophers who have thought about the problem of value.

"Conceptual clarification," Joel Feinberg has written, "is the most distinctively philosophical of enterprises."[18] I aim to present in this book a theory of the concept of value. However, in contrast to many conceptual analyses, I hope not only to explain our most basic intuitions about value but also to make sense of the claims that previous philosophers have made. Philosophy, it is often said, is not a cumulative discipline; each philosopher must, as it were, start from scratch or at least very nearly so. This seems to me a mistake. Philosophers of earlier generations devoted a good deal of attention to the problems of value; keeping their claims before our minds, and trying to integrate their findings, will, I think, help us to avoid a number of mistakes.

1.2 Theories of concepts

My attempt to explicate the concept of value will, then, pay at least as much attention to what previous axiologists have claimed as to what seems intuitively correct to reflective agents. But I still have not explained just what a theory of the concept seeks to do. Clarifying a concept, or presenting a theory of a concept, can take radically different forms. Keeping (a)–(k) in mind, we can usefully distinguish three understandings of the aims and nature of a theory of our concept of value.

The first conceives of a theory of value as simply descriptive, in the sense that it aims only to fully describe (a)–(k) and other

18 Joel Feinberg, *Harm to Others*, p. 17.

relevant features, telling us, for instance, what sorts of reasons for action value judgments imply, or what are the accepted uses of notions like "economic value." At its most basic, this descriptive project is more lexicographical than philosophical because it does not seek in any obvious way to explain, criticize, or defend some understanding of value. On a more philosophic level, this essentially descriptive endeavor may take the form of a "semantic map" or "model" of the concept of value.[19] Such a semantic model might not only seek to describe the main features of the concept, but also to show how they are related to each other and how the concept relates to other normative notions, psychological or metaphysical beliefs, understandings of agency, the nature of social life, various practices and even institutions. These relations, of course, will by no means be exclusively, or perhaps primarily, logical; they may usefully be called "ideological" in one sense of that much-abused term. The resulting model or map would then provide an account of the internal relations among various features of the concept and its external relations, embedding it in a particular form of ethical life.

But, for all that, this sort of conceptual cartography remains essentially descriptive. And, like any map, it is a fault of such a semantic map if it fails to include some significant feature and to relate it to the rest in a consistent way. Insofar as it does fail in this manner, its claim to describe and explain is not fully justified. However, because linguistic and social practices are complex, and especially because in a plural culture such as ours such practice-oriented concepts are apt to reflect conflicting sets of presuppositions and beliefs, it is often impossible to construct conceptual maps that coherently relate and explain all the relevant features of a concept. Stanley Benn and I discovered this in our work on the notions of the public and private.[20] Our Western, liberal, understanding of publicness and privateness seems unable to be coherently described by a single model (or, to continue the map metaphor, all the significant features cannot be placed on the same map). Although discourse relating to the public and private can be largely understood in terms of an "individualist" model,

19 On semantic models, see S. I. Benn and G. F. Gaus, "The Public and Private: Concepts and Action." See also Benn, *A Theory of Freedom*, ch. 16.
20 S. I. Benn and G. F. Gaus, "The Liberal Conception of the Public and Private."

some crucial features (for example, the public interest) only make sense in terms of an "organic" model, which draws on a different, and it seems incompatible, theory of social life. Thus, we concluded, in a fundamental sense the liberal notion of the public and private suffers from an incoherence. Now this conclusion is, I think, useful and informative on the explanatory-descriptive level: if our interest is simply in explaining and describing (charting) the nature of a concept and the practices and discourse it informs, we may well conclude that it is incoherent in some fundamental way. But this will hardly do if, as agents, we are interested in a reasonable way to employ these concepts, make arguments drawing on them, and so forth. That one is appealing to inconsistent presuppositions when drawing on the full range of liberal public/private discourse provides a rational believer-agent with reason to rethink his conceptual commitments.

All this is relevant to the concept of value. The question whether values are in some sense "objective" or "subjective," to give just one example, has dominated much of modern ethics. And by this time both objectivists and subjectivists have had significant success in molding value discourse to reflect their ways of thinking. It would be surprising indeed if, after centuries of disagreement, any straightforwardly subjectivist or objectivist account could embrace all the significant features of value discourse and practice. Even a cursory examination of (a)–(k) suggests that features such as (c) and (d) incline toward an objectivist outlook and (e) and (k) are apt to be more in tune with subjectivism. I do not rule out a priori the possibility that some "mixed" – subjectivist and objectivist – theory may be able to account for all the features in a consistent and persuasive way; perhaps the whole debate can be avoided by some all-embracing account. Nevertheless, it should not be too surprising if we discover that a coherent and reasonable conception of value does not include every significant feature of value discourse.

Some seem to believe that, once a theory begins rejecting or omitting significant features of a concept, analysis has been forsaken in favor of *stipulation*, our second sort of "theory."[21] On this

21 This seems to be the position of Grenville Wall, "Against Subjective Intrinsic Value," p. 40. Cf. also Feinberg's remark in relation to the concept of "harm" that "insofar as it is ambiguous, we must select among its normal senses the one or ones relevant for our normative purposes, and insofar as it

view, one either stays true to the concept in its full complexity or one is simply stipulating that, in one's personal vocabulary, "value" just refers to whatever characteristics are accepted; or perhaps it even refers to something entirely different than (a)–(k). Now, although they have legitimate uses in developing certain sorts of technical theories, purely stipulative definitions do not engage our theoretical interest in the notion normally denoted by the term. If an account employs the words "valuable," "valuing," or "a value" in unfamiliar ways to perform functions not normally associated with value, it will not relate to our preexisting interest in the concept of value. And, perhaps more importantly, it will fail to engage our practical interest as agents, that is, valuers. We all care for some things, make judgments of valuableness or worthlessness, wonder whether our valuings are sound and take action to promote our values. As rational agents, we are concerned with the internal consistency of these related practices and activities, whether they presuppose false theories (for example, false ontological theories), etc. And, perhaps most importantly, we seek to eliminate errors in our own practical activity by coming to better understand its rational grounding and its rationale; we may thus, for instance, eliminate errors in our value judgments by better grasping just what they are judgments of. If a theory of value strays too far from the sorts of practices and activities depicted by (a)–(k), it is not likely to be of much assistance in these matters.[22]

Stipulative definitions are objectionable on another count. Suppose a stipulative theory accepts (a)–(d) but, without showing good reason, omits or rejects all the other features. Its use of "value" will then have some relevance to our normal notion, and so may at least engage some of our practical value-related interests. However, as Lawrence C. Becker has argued, because it arbitrarily rejects or omits significant features of what we understand by "value," such a stipulative account fails as a philosophic enterprise, that is, as a "reasoned explanation of things."[23] Becker

---

is vague in those senses, it should be made more precise – the task that requires some degree of stipulation, not simply a more accurate reporting of current usage." *Harm to Others*, p. 32.

22 The extent to which accounts of value can diverge from our normal notions about value is nicely brought out by T. Y. Henderson, "A Substantial Theory of Value."

23 Becker, *Moral Judgments*, p. 9.

thus requires that a theory of moral life – in which he includes value – must provide reasons for either accepting or rejecting "the existing intuitions, practices, and institutions of moral experience. . . . When a theory does either in an arbitrary way, one is justified in judging it objectionable in direct proportion to the importance of the issue (the 'given') at stake."[24] In contradistinction, a theory that provides reasoned explanations of its positions engages our theoretical concerns relating to the concept of value; and it guides intelligent practice by providing good reasons for either continuing to accept, or revise, the existing practice.

This, too, has direct relevance for the theory of value. Technical decision theory and economic theory, especially welfare economics, often employs a largely stipulative notion of "value." In these theories, to say that someone values ϕ-ing is just to say that he or she has a reason to do it; or, alternatively, to value X over Y might be understood in terms of preferring X to Y, where "preferring" means something like "has more reason to choose" or is disposed to choose (and actually does when the choice situation arises).[25] This clearly departs from our ordinary notions of preference and value. "In ordinary speech, I *can* decide (or choose) to do something different from what I should prefer to do, as for instance when I do something reluctantly from a sense of duty. 'To prefer,' in that case, is roughly speaking 'to like better'; and when we act dutifully we often do what we like least."[26] In a similar way, we sometimes do something even if we do not value it, but because we think it is the right thing, or the just thing, or the rational thing to do. Valuing certainly provides reasons for choice and action, but to simply equate valuing with choice or rational action misses and obscures a good deal, making it impossible to even sensibly ask why one might have reason to do one's moral duty when one does not particularly value the dutiful action or its consequences. Now in the context of a technical theory of rational choice none of this is apt to be particularly troublesome; its concern is what is done, or what is decided upon, and not in distinguishing various sorts of reasons from others (for example, the reason to act morally). But much ethical

---

24 Ibid.
25 See S. I. Benn and G. W. Mortimore, "Technical Models of Rational Choice," p. 161.
26 Ibid., p. 160.

theory, especially utilitarian ethics, has adopted this essentially stipulative use of value and employed it as if it were an adequate theory of our normal conception of value.[27] And, as we will see, that is indeed troublesome.

The theory advanced in Part I of this book is thus neither a semantic model nor is it stipulative; it takes our existing concept of value as its starting point and aims to defend a well-grounded and coherent version of that concept and the practices it informs. This method thus shares much with conceptual "reconstructionism," according to which "[c]onceptual analysis aims at clarification and systematization of concepts and is not bound to reflect usage where that usage is confused and likely to mislead."[28] But, unlike most proponents of reconstructive conceptual analysis, I make no attempt to engage in conceptual clarification divorced from normative theory.[29] On this point, I agree with von Wright:

> The idea of a sharp separation of normative ethics and meta-ethics seems to me to rest on an oversimplified and superficial view of the first and on an insufficient understanding of the nature of the second. The view of normative ethics as (some sort of) moral legislation, perhaps in combination with a criticism of current moral standards, is one-sided. So is the view of normative ethics as casuistry. "Normative ethics" is not a suitable name for any *one* thing. Those, who use the name, tend to heap under it a number of different philosophic and moralistic activities. *One* of these activities, thus classified as "normative," I would myself call *conceptual* investigation; and I would not know how to distinguish it sharply from the allegedly non-normative conceptual analysis belonging to meta-ethics.[30]

If all that is proffered is a semantic model of a concept – "people talk and act in these internally related ways, which are in turn related to a particular set of beliefs" – then, I suppose, the conceptual investigation really is largely without any significant normative implications. (Even here, however, it may be found that some concept is thoroughly muddled, and that certainly has implications for practice.) However, if one is reconstructing a con-

27 See Sen and Williams's "Introduction," pp. 11–14. Cf. John C. Harsanyi, "Morality and the Theory of Rational Behaviour."

28 Joseph Raz, quoted in Felix E. Oppenheim, *Political Concepts: A Reconstruction*, p. 180. Ch. 9 of Oppenheim's book presents a detailed defense of reconstructionism. See also R. B. Brandt, *A Theory of the Good and the Right*, pp. 2ff.

29 See, e.g., Oppenheim, *Political Concepts*, pp. 187–9; Joel Feinberg, *Social Philosophy*, pp. 1–2; Alan R. White, *Rights*, p. 1.

30 Georg Henrik von Wright, *The Varieties of Goodness*, p. 3.

cept and claiming not just that this reconstruction makes the concept internally consistent, but also that good reasons exist for accepting some features of it and rejecting others and, further, that the concept is practical insofar as it guides action and deliberation, then it does indeed seem impossible to deny that this is a normative project too.[31]

1.3 Grounds for accepting the theory

In Part I, then, I propose a theory of value that I call the *Affective-Cognitive Theory*. Put very roughly, and thus inaccurately, the main claims of the theory are that *valuings* are dispositional emotions, that *value judgments* concern the appropriateness of certain sorts of valuings, and that *a value* or "*a person's values*" are either important and abstract valuings or patterns of valuings. The general concept of "value" is thus explicated in terms of: (i) valuings, (ii) value judgments, and (iii) the idea of "a value" or "a person's values." I think G. E. Moore would have called this a subjective account of value,[32] though I will argue later (§10) that it possesses a number of features typically identified with objectivist accounts. For the most part, however, I will avoid describing the theory as either "subjectivist" or "objectivist," because these are particularly ambiguous labels, sometimes referring to ontological theses, sometimes to epistemological claims, and yet at still other times referring to the agent-relativity or neutrality of value reasons.[33]

Why accept the Affective-Cognitive Theory? Thus far, I have been discussing the first ground for embracing it: that it provides a reasoned explanation and defense of the main features of the concept of value. Not that it eschews revision: as we will see, I am generally critical of feature (g) – the idea that values are chosen – though it seems intelligible enough in relation to adopting certain sorts of ideals (see §14). More radically, I argue against a strong version of the claim that value judgments are not "respecters of persons"; that is, I am critical of the claim that, if *V* is a

31 See Ronald Dworkin's theory of interpretation in *Law's Empire*.
32 See G. E. Moore, "The Conception of Intrinsic Value," pp. 253–4.
33 This point is made by Stanley Benn, *A Theory of Freedom*, ch. 4. As I have since discovered, my earlier use of the labels "subjectivist" and "relativist" to describe the theory invited confusion. See my "Subjective Value and Justificatory Political Theory."

sound value judgment, it (in principle) provides all with reasons for actions [feature (d)]. The ways in which value judgments are impersonal or personal is complex, and I will not try to summarize them here. Suffice it for now to say that, though I hold that all value judgments are impersonal in one sense, they also, perhaps in more important ways, are tied to particular valuational perspectives (§§10, 12). (Moral value, I acknowledge, is impersonal in a stronger sense, but, once again agreeing with von Wright, I argue that it is a derivative sort of value;[34] see §22.2.)

So the first ground for accepting the Affective-Cognitive Theory is that it unites and makes coherent the main features of our concept of value (subject to some "reconstruction"), and so demonstrates the rational foundations of our value-based practices and activities. This, then, points to my second claim for the theory: it generally endorses our current valuings. More specifically, the theory rarely leads to conclusions of the sort "Although *X* is often valued, it cannot soundly be valued." Now in itself, to endorse current valuings is not particularly difficult; it is easily done, for example, by embracing the widely held view that something is valuable simply because it is desired (see §7.2). On that view, what is valuable is, essentially, what is valued (desired), and so one cannot value that which is not valuable. But, pretty clearly, this traditional view has great difficulties accounting for the nature of value discourse:[35] we *do* argue about what is really valuable; suppose that people – including ourselves – can make mistakes; and assume that value judgments have some sort of public, impersonal status. The attraction of the Affective-Cognitive Theory is that it both presents an account of the main features of the concept of value and confirms the diverse valuings characterizing our pluralistic culture. The Affective-Cognitive Theory endorses this diversity without appealing to skepticism about values, undermining the point of value discourse, or denying that value judgments have an impersonal and public nature. As such, the Affective-Cognitive Theory can be aptly described as a nonskeptical liberal theory of value.

But some may object that confirming the diverse, and in some

34 Wright, *Goodness*, p. 18. This is not to say that I follow von Wright's account of moral goodness. See also I. M. Loring, *Two Kinds of Values*.
35 The shortcomings of this theory are stressed by Bond, *Reason and Value*, ch. 3.

sense conflicting, valuings characterizing our liberal culture is no virtue. A radical (and I do not necessarily mean "leftist") critic of liberal society will see no reason to embrace a theory that confirms the valuings that he so detests. He is likely to criticize liberal culture as consumerist, or bourgeois, or philistine, or nihilistic; in place of the multitude of corrupt or unsound valuings characterizing our Western liberal culture, the critic may offer some much more specific and harmonious vision of the truly valuable. I do not intend to deny the intelligibility of this alternative project; if, say, some Platonic theory of value could be established, such a wide-ranging critique would be well grounded. My claim here is much more modest: that, though such revolutionary accounts of value may marshal various grounds for accepting them, they forgo the possibility of an important rational pull on believer-agents: that the theory articulates the foundations of their valuings. Rational agents, deliberating whether to embrace an account of a practical activity in which they are engaged, consider a variety of reasons; one of these is whether the theory helps make sense of their activity. Perhaps agents can be rationally convinced to accept a theory that tells them their activity is radically misguided but, because such revolutionary accounts cannot depict themselves as foundational to the agents' practice, their task is more difficult.

The third ground for accepting the Affective-Cognitive Theory is its psychological soundness. Part I draws a great deal on the psychology of emotion, attitudes, and values; I argue that a considerable body of evidence supports the main claims of the Affective-Cognitive Theory. Different theories of value are built on different foundations; some seem to rely on metaphysical claims, some on epistemological claims, and many others on psychological claims. It is certainly incumbent on any theory to show that its foundational claims are sound, and that alone would justify the psychological discussions of Part I. But the fourth ground for accepting the theory is also relevant. Psychologists studying attitudes and values have assembled a large body of data and have formulated and tested theories relating to how people evaluate things, but to a truly remarkable extent philosophers have developed theories of value with little or no cognizance of this work. With a few notable exceptions, philosophers concerned with value questions have been more attracted to the technical theories of economists than the work of psychologists; and, when they have focused on the psychology of valuing, their interest is more apt to be in general theories of personality and self-realization rather than the more empirically oriented attitude theories.[36] The Affective-Cognitive Theory thus claims to integrate a philosophically sound theory of the concept of value with a large body of relevant psychological literature.

The theory thus rests on four main claims: (i) its soundness as a theory of value; (ii) its coherence with actual valuings; (iii) the soundness of its foundational psychological claims (and, it might be added, the absence of any unsound metaphysical or ontological foundational claims); and (iv) its ability to integrate a body of experimental and theoretical work on the psychology of emotion, attitude, and values with the sound philosophical theory. Competing theories must show themselves at least as sound in these ways. It is thus, for example, not sufficient to present a theory that explains and defends our understanding of value if it relies on unsound or dubious foundational claims or if it is unable to make sense of findings concerning how people evaluatively respond to objects.

2 MORAL JUSTIFICATION

2.1 Morality and value

The theory of value defended in Part I of this volume maintains that value judgments are indeed impersonal, but it shows that these impersonal judgments about valuableness do not necessarily provide everyone with reasons for action. Again, to put the point roughly, I shall hold that value-based reasons for action are essentially (to borrow a phrase from Derek Parfit) "agent-relative."[37] This conclusion, I believe, undermines the most powerful argument for consequentialist ethics: once we show that a value-based

---

36 The major exception to both these rather broad generalizations is, of course, R. B. Brandt. See his *A Theory of the Good and the Right*, pt. I. Brandt, however, takes a very strong learning theory approach, which I reject (see, e.g., §3.3), and emphasizes desires and wants, again something I criticize (§7.2). In contrast to Brandt, I focus on the recent work relating to the affective foundation of attitudes, that can be viewed as something of a counterrevolution to the cognitive revolution that has been so important in recent psychology. See, for instance, §8.2.

37 Parfit, *Reasons and Persons*, p. 143. See §12 in this volume.

reason to act for Alf is not necessarily a reason for Betty to act, the intuition that both Alf and Betty always have reason to promote impersonal value begins to evaporate. But, if a consequentialist ethic based on the agent-neutrality of value-based reasons to act must be rejected, what is to take its place? On its own, Part I may seem to endorse a sort of egocentrism: if value-based reasons are so strongly agent-relative, why not simply promote one's own valuings as best one can without a concern for the values of others? In the past, those who have proffered theories of value that, in some way, have relativized value reasons to individual points of view have sometimes also adopted versions of ethical relativism.[38] And, recently, James S. Fishkin's study of ethical subjectivists has demonstrated that such moral agents typically base their skeptical ethical position on a "subjectivist" account of value.[39] Does, then, the Affective-Cognitive Theory of value lead us toward some version of ethical relativism or skepticism?

Part II of this book explores what sorts of moral reasons we possess. The Affective-Cognitive Theory of value allows us to grasp the complex yet intimate tie between value systems and moral beliefs. I shall argue that the value systems of almost all agents rationally presuppose the validity of certain moral principles, and rest on a conception of others as moral persons. Although the value-based reasons to act implied by our value systems are essentially agent-relative, these systems presuppose the rationality of impersonal moral principles. Put simply, I maintain that our value systems rest on the presupposition that, in addition to value-based, agent-relative reasons, we also possess moral reasons to act.

This tie between values and morals is, I believe, usually overlooked in contemporary ethics, which has focused on the distinction between deontological and teleological justification. If we accept this as the fundamental division between ethical theories, we will tend to ask whether the right is to be defined as that which promotes the good, or whether the right is in some sense prior to the good. Now in one sense my account accepts this way

38 See, e.g., Gardner Williams, "Hedonic Individual Ethical Relativism."
39 See his *Beyond Subjective Morality*, esp. pp. 35–45. I have discussed Fishkin's analysis and the way it relates to "the taste model of value" in my "Subjective Value and Justificatory Political Theory."

of approaching the problem, for I shall show in Chapter VII that both relations between the right and the good obtain. But, in another way, the relation of morality and value defended here is more complex than this simple division can accommodate. We will see that our value systems presuppose moral principles, but our commitment to these moral principles derives from their foundational place in our valuational perspectives. What is valued and what is morally right are intertwined in complex ways.

The argument of Chapter VI, in which I explicate this relation between values and morals, upholds what I call *Value-Grounded Rationalism*. I contrast this to what I take is the orthodox view of practical rationality: that one always has reason to do that which best promotes one's values. I will argue that this "orthodox" view is at bottom radical, for it undermines the rationality of our value systems. The value systems of almost all rational valuers presuppose that others are *moral persons*. That is, our value systems rest on the supposition that other agents are able to put aside their values and take up the moral point of view: they can have reasons to act morally even at a cost, *all things considered*, to their own values. Through a discussion of psychopathy, I show just how basic is this conception of others, and how it would play havoc with our value systems to reject it. The "orthodox" view, however, requires that we reject this conception of others as rationally putting aside their values. I shall thus conclude that embracing the orthodox view and its consequences requires rational agents to radically revise their valuational perspectives, probably to an extent that is psychologically impossible. Agents such as ourselves, then, have reason to reject the orthodox view because it badly articulates the concept of practical rationality upon which our view of the world is premised. And, once we have rejected the orthodox view in favor of Value-Grounded Rationalism, one of the main problems of nonconsequentialist ethics is resolved: we can have reason to act morally even when doing so does not advance what is rationally valued.

2.2 *Public justification*

The first fundamental claim of the theory of justification, then, is that our value systems commit us to the supposition that moral action (that does not, all things considered, best promote one's values) is rational. We believe that others are moral persons, those who can rationally act from the moral perspective, and we also believe that we are such persons. Now because moral persons can rationally put aside their values, it follows that they can be provided with good reasons to do so. That is, to say that such moral action is rational is to say that agents who act morally can do so for good reasons. To justify a moral principle to such agents is, then, just to show that they have good reasons for acknowledging it. Moral justification thus aims to provide moral persons with reasons for embracing principles of action that can rationally require them to put aside their value-based reasons to act.

I focus on the justification of a *public morality*. Although I allow that moral justification can occur within groups of various levels of intimacy, my concern is moral justification within our Western plural culture, where we often confront each others as strangers. One part of morality in such a society is what I call the public morality; it is that part of our moral code that seeks to regulate the actions of moral persons, considered not under any specific description such as "Alf," "University Lecturer," or "Democrat," but simply as moral persons or, we might say, abstract members of the general public. I do not claim that this is all of morality, but it does seem that this is the part of morality of most interest to political and social philosophy. For it is public morality that makes the claim to provide all members of the public with reasons to act morally, and so abstracts from specific descriptions in order to articulate the general code that underlies all social life. Those who insist that a "subjective" theory of value such as the Affective-Cognitive Theory undermines morality are most likely to have public morality in mind. The critic might allow that, even under a "subjectivist" account of value, moral principles might survive in a small like-minded community sharing many values; our critic, however, is apt to be skeptical that the Affective-Cognitive Theory of value can ground a public morality among strangers who are characterized by a diversity rather than a community of valuing. Hence, the justification of a public morality seems the greatest challenge to my account.

A public morality, then, is that part of our morality which seeks to regulate the actions of all members of the public. Now I will also argue that a justified public morality is one that provides all moral persons who are members of the public with reasons for accepting it. Moral persons, I have said, are those who can rationally act on moral principles even at a (net) cost to their values; they act morally because they have good reasons to do so, that is, it is rational for them to do so. A *publicly justified* morality, then, is (roughly) one that provides all moral persons with good reasons to accept it. I shall show that only a publicly justified morality satisfies the demands of our value systems. Our valuational perspectives are based on the assumption that we can make moral demands on all moral persons and, further, that these moral persons have reason to act in accordance with our moral demands. But they will only have reason to act in accordance with our moral demands if the morality can be publicly justified, that is, is a morality that everyone has reason to embrace. A morality that was not publicly justified would be one that some moral persons had no reason to embrace; thus, we would admit that some moral persons could ignore it and we would have no ground for complaint.

Chapter VII examines two ways in which a public morality can be publicly justified, that is, in which a morality that *applies to all* can be *justified to all*: deontologically and teleologically. To justify a morality deontologically is to show that everyone's value system is based on certain moral principles: the rationality of everyone's value system, the deontological argument contends, requires that certain moral principles provide everyone with reasons to act. Deontological justification of a public morality, then, consists simply is showing that we are all rationally committed, because of the nature of our value systems, to certain moral beliefs or, one might say, "intuitions." However, not all public justification is deontological. One way to show that a rational moral person is committed to accepting a moral rule is to show that he is already committed to it by virtue of his value system, but another way is to show that it is part of a public morality that advances the values of all in a reasonable way: a morality that promotes a common good. I call such justification *constrained teleological justification*. It is a form of teleological justification insofar as it shows that morality is justified because it advances value. If Alf wants to justify a moral code to Betty, he can do so by showing her that it advances her values: it is teleologically justified in relation to her value system. But the nature of the teleological argument is constrained by the requirement that the code must be teleologically justified to all others – that is, it must be publicly justified and, so, advance the values of everyone.

2.3 *Contractualism*

Chapters VIII and IX seek to make the ideas of deontological and constrained teleological justification more concrete by offering a contractual justification of a liberal public morality. Contractualism, I argue, is a particularly helpful way to think about moral justification as it readily accommodates two important insights: (i) that the deontological phase of justification is logically prior to, and can be distinguished from, the constrained teleological phase; and (ii) that constrained teleological justification is a search for a common good.

The first insight is developed in Chapter VIII, which describes the state of nature. Although since Rawls's *A Theory of Justice*, contractual arguments are common enough – if by no means uncontroversial – in contemporary moral and political theory, state of nature arguments are, it is safe to say, far more suspect. But the idea of the state of nature, I will suggest, allows us to articulate the insight that our value systems presuppose certain fundamental moral principles. These principles are not justified on the grounds that they *advance* our values, but because our valuational perspectives *presuppose* their validity. Their justification is, then, deontological. In one sense, deontological justification is logically prior to teleological justification. Before the latter can commence, we must know which values are rational and which are irrational. To show that ill-grounded values will be promoted by some code of public morality, I shall maintain, is hardly a rational justification of that code. Now if this is true, and if some of our values presuppose moral principles, we shall want to know whether those grounding moral principles can be deontologically justified. If they can be so justified, the values that presuppose them can be rationally included in the teleological phase of justification. Consequently, before we embark on constrained teleological justification, we shall want to know what, if any, moral principles can be deontologically justified.

I suggest that the idea of a state of nature, as for instance presented in Locke's *Second Treatise*, allows us to develop the idea of deontologically justified morality. In Locke's contractual theory, the law of nature is prior to the social contract and constrains the outcome of the contract. The structure of his argument reflects the two stages of moral justification. The state of nature articulates those moral principles that are deep commitments of everyone's value system; based upon these, the contractual argument advances a constrained teleological argument for a moral code. Chapter IX presents one formulation of such a contractual argument. I try to show there that certain sorts of ideological positions are favored by the contractual situation, and I think it is accurate to call these, in a broad sense, "liberal."

Although I employ the idea of a social contract, I stress throughout that I do not rely on the moral bindingness of consent or promise-keeping. I offer an interpretation of the contract tradition that focuses on the notion of the common good; the contract defines a public morality that advances the values of all. The contract metaphor is useful because, given the defense of agent-relative, value-based reasons to act, we suppose that each person has a different set of reasons for action. Given this essential agent-relativity of value reasons, constrained teleological justification seeks to uncover some moral code that is acceptable from all perspectives. It is here that the contractualist puts the question in a helpful way: What morality would all rational agents agree to? But "agree to" here is a proxy for "have reasons to acknowledge or accept"; our ultimate concern is what morality all moral persons have reason to embrace; we assume that fully rational agents would accept or agree to such a morality. The importance of the contract device, then, is that it stresses that a morality must be acceptable to each and every valuational perspective, even though they differ in many ways.

2.4 Remarks on the task of moral theory

This section has largely been a sketch of the argument of Part II of this volume. My aim has not been to lay the methodological basis for the theory of justification, but, rather, to orient the reader by providing a broad overview of the topics to be discussed and the arguments that I advance. This is to be contrasted with my analysis of theories of value in §1, where my concern was indeed to provide a methodological basis by explaining what I take a theory of value to be, and on what grounds such theories are to be evaluated. There are a number of reasons for saying little here about the method of moral theory. For one thing, the topic of Part II – a contractual theory of justice – will be more familiar to most readers than a theory of value, and so there is perhaps less need to explain what such a theory is. More importantly, the foundations for the theory of justification lie in the theory of value. Part II does not start afresh, but builds on the conclusions of the Affective-Cognitive Theory of value. Lastly, and most pragmatically, in the structure of the book, Part II is a rather long way from this introduction; it seems best to defer a number of issues relating to the methodology of moral and political philosophy until we confront the problems of moral justification.

However, it may be helpful at this stage to contrast my view of moral theory to two other approaches, both of which have been associated with John Rawls. In *A Theory of Justice*, Rawls made much of the idea of "reflective equilibrium." This idea, like so much of his theory, is far more complex than a first or second reading might indicate; I certainly shall make no attempt to provide a definitive interpretation here.[40] However, one straightforward interpretation deserves mention. On this view, Rawls's reflective equilibrium is, at bottom, a quest for coherence in an individual's moral life; and the aim of moral theory is to render an individual's own moral system unified and coherent. Thus, employing the idea of reflective equilibrium, an individual considers his personal judgments on a number of issues and compares these to some set of moral principles which are, for various reasons, appealing. Our moral agent will then compare his personal judgments and these higher-level principles, seeing that in this case or that the abstract principles conflict with the concrete judgments. He will then have to bring these into equilibrium; either by abandoning the personal judgment or altering the principle to accommodate it.

I assume that this view is familiar to most readers: it conceives moral theory as an essentially personal activity aiming to make one's own moral life coherent and unified by adopting some general moral principles. Now, despite its popularity, it is not at all clear whether this was ever Rawls's overriding concern.

40 For thorough treatments, see Norman Daniels, "Wide Reflective Equilibrium"; Fred D'Agostino, "The Method of Reflective Equilibrium."

Throughout *A Theory of Justice*, he stresses that the aim of moral theory is interpersonal justification. As he depicts it, the aim of a theory of justice is to justify a "public conception of justice," that is, to "reach a reasonably reliable agreement in judgment in order to provide a common conception of justice."[41] The theory of justification developed in Part II of this volume has much in common with this second Rawlsian project: it is not focused on our individual moral structures except in so far as they affect the sorts of reasons that we can give others and they can give us.[42] It is thus essentially a theory of interpersonal justification. My aim, like that of Rawls, is to formulate a public conception of justice that provides the foundation for a common moral life among those pursuing diverse values.

But, although this second understanding of Rawls's project is much closer to my account than the first, two important differences still separate our theories of interpersonal justification. Firstly, although the search for a public consensus is at the heart of both theories of moral justification, this search for shared moral principles characterizes only what I call the deontological phase of justification. For Rawls, this seems the only relevant form of justification in political philosophy, but in my account it is only a part of public justification. Because we are not only committed to specific basic moral principles, but also to a conception of others as moral persons, we are also rationally committed to the idea of a justified public morality that articulates the common good. Hence, moral justification can proceed both deontologically and teleologically. Secondly, as I will point out in various places, Rawls's theory of justification – and I think this is especially clear in his latest works – is pragmatic is a fairly radical sense. The aim of his theory is "free agreement": the "practical social task" of resolving our actual disagreements is "primary."[43] That is, Rawls

41 See Rawls, *A Theory of Justice*, pp. 44–5, 577ff. I am indebted to Fred D'Agostino for impressing upon me the importance of interpersonal justification aiming at actual agreement in Rawls's work. I have greatly benefited from D'Agostino's "The Method of Reflective Equilibrium." See also John Gray, "Contractarian Method, Private Property, and the Market Economy."

42 These two views of moral justification are distinguished by Stanley Benn in his "Persons and Values." In contrast to Rawls and myself, Benn stresses personal moral coherence as the aim of moral theory, indicating that "too much" has been made of interpersonal justification (p. 21).

43 See Rawls, "Justice As Fairness: Political Not Metaphysical," p. 230; "Kantian Constructivism," p. 519.

aims at something very much like actual consensus among real moral agents. Although he is somewhat obscure on this point, I believe my aims are ultimately less pragmatic than are his. As I understand it, justification aims only at providing reasons; it will persuade fully rational agents, but may well fail to move less than fully rational persons. Because there may well be many such people, it is not to be expected that moral justification will lead to anything like actual consensus. So the aim of moral and political philosophy is to provide reasons; whether this induces actual agreement on a public conception of justice is not, on my view, a concern of moral or political philosophy. This, I think, will be seen to have profound consequences, for, in relation to Rawls's theory, this understanding of moral justification elevates the importance of the theory of practical rationality in moral philosophy. In place of "What moral principles can we all agree upon?" I ask "What moral principles do we all have reason to accept?"

ONE

A theory of value

II

Emotion

The core claim of the Affective-Cognitive Theory of value is that value and the emotional side of life are intimately related. This in itself is not particularly controversial; it is a view widely shared by "subjectivists" and "objectivists" alike.[1] The Affective-Cognitive Theory of value, however, advances a much more controversial thesis: that intrinsic valuings *are* emotional dispositions. Yet, although controversial, it is by no means radically new; indeed, in one version or another it has been one of the dominant theories in twentieth-century axiology.[2] However, emotional theories of value are only as strong as the accounts of emotion on which they are based, and I believe that these accounts have been inadequate. My aim in this chapter, then, is to defend the outlines of an empirically (psychologically) and conceptually sound theory of emotion, which will provide the foundation for the analysis of value in the remainder of Part I.

Exploring the theory of emotion in some detail, this chapter examines such difficult problems as the intentionality of emotional states, the way in which emotion rests on beliefs, and how emotional states can be said to be rational or irrational. Confronting these problems at the outset of a work on value theory and moral justification – which, by the last chapter discusses the social contract and liberal theory – will no doubt seem surprising

---

1 For a general survey that brings out the importance of emotion and affect to a wide range of value theories, see W. H. Werkmeister, *Historical Spectrum of Value Theories*.

2 A number of theories stress the foundational role of emotion or affect. In one way or another, I believe that the following all qualify: David W. Prall, "A Study in the Theory of Value"; Wilbur Marshall Urban, *Valuation: Its Nature and Laws*; John R. Reid, "A Definition of Value"; C. I. Lewis, *An Analysis of Knowledge and Valuation*. For a more recent formulation, see Ian Davison, *Values, Ends, and Society*. See also E. J. Bond, *Reason and Value*.

to many readers. It is certainly highly atypical. Nevertheless, these preliminary investigations are necessary for the arguments of later chapters. A number of perplexing problems concerning values and valuations can be resolved, and many fatal errors avoided, by going deeper into value theory than is common today. Hence, whereas recent books in moral theory usually devote at most one or two chapters to value theory, all of Part I of this book analyzes value. But my thorough treatment of valuing, value judgments, and values rests on a theory of emotion. Consequently, we must begin by exploring some questions unfamiliar to students of moral and political philosophy. As the argument of the book unfolds, it should become apparent how these investigations provide the foundation for the theories of value and of justification.

3 TWO THEORIES OF EMOTION

3.1 The internal sensation theory

Let us approach the analysis of emotion by asking "How are emotions recognized and named?"[3] What has been called the "traditional theory" answers "By introspection" or "By immediate knowledge of internal sensations."[4] Although this view is typically attributed to Descartes and Hume,[5] it was most fully developed in the psychologies of the late nineteenth and early twentieth centuries. According to William McDougall, for example, each "emotional experience" has a "distinctive quality . . . given it by the complex of relatively intense bodily impressions." These "bodily impressions," he went on to say, are the result of the various changes "in the respiration and the beating of the heart, in the degree of contraction of the muscular walls of thousands of small arteries and of the whole intestinal tube, and changes in the secretions of the many glands (the tears, sweat, saliva, and gastric juice) including many internal secretions." Consequently, in most cases the emotional excitement "has some quality which enables us to apply to it one of the many names by

3 For a general survey of positions, see Paul Thomas Young, "Feeling and Emotion," pp. 753ff.
4 See, e.g., Errol Bedford, "Emotions"; George Pitcher, "Emotion."
5 See Anthony Kenny, *Action, Emotion and Will*, ch. 1; William Lyons, *Emotion*, pp. 2–17.

which we refer to such states of excitement, such names as fear, or anger, or lust, or curiosity, or compassion, or scorn, or contempt, or pride, or elation, or disgust, or horror, or any one of a large array of such names."[6]

William James's formulation of this general view is much better known. James began his analysis with what he called "the *coarser* emotions, grief, fear, rage, love." In an often-quoted passage (I will break tradition by not quoting it in full), he presented the heart of what has become known as the James-Lange theory of emotions: "Our natural way of thinking about these coarser emotions," according to James, is that the perception of some fact "excites the mental affection called the emotion, and that this latter state of mind gives rise to the bodily expression." James, however, reversed this order; as he saw it, "*the bodily changes follow directly the perception of the exciting fact, and . . . our feeling of the same changes as they occur* IS *the emotion.*" Emotions, then are the inner perception of "organic changes": if we remove from our consciousness of an emotion "all the feelings of its bodily symptoms, we find we have nothing left behind." And, because the bodily "changes are so infinitely numerous and subtle," emotions are various and shade into each other.[7] The analysis of the "subtler emotions" – the "moral, intellectual, and aesthetic feelings" – is somewhat more complicated. James acknowledges that "aesthetic emotion, *pure and simple*, the pleasure given us by certain lines and masses, and combinations of colors and sounds, is an absolutely sensational experience, an optical or auricular feeling that is primary, and not due to the repercussion backwards of other sensations elsewhere consecutively aroused." Nevertheless, James held that aesthetic response – pure "intellectual or moral rapture" – is not properly called emotional at all "unless there be coupled a bodily reverberation of some kind" such that "we actually laugh at the neatness of the demonstration or witticism . . . thrill at the case of justice, or tingle at the act of magnanimity."[8]

Such somatic-viscera change theories of emotion have been the

6 William McDougall, *The Energies of Men*, pp. 149–51. He distinguished these internal sensations accompanying emotions from "feelings" (ibid., p. 156). On this, see K. T. Strongman, *The Psychology of Emotion*, pp. 16–17.
7 William James, *The Principles of Psychology*, vol. II, pp. 449–53 (emphasis in original).
8 Ibid., pp. 468–71.

target of extensive, and generally damaging, critiques. Although it would be going too far to say that they are simply of historical interest, they are certainly out of favor with most contemporary psychologists.[9] One of the theories that has supplanted them is the "central neural theory," according to which subjective feelings of emotion are not the internal perception of bodily changes, but are rather "mental feelings" resulting from the interaction of the thalamus and the cortex.[10] Important differences are to be found within this general group of theories; indeed, I will argue later that, properly understood, some neural theories can provide the basis of a sound theory of emotion (§4). However, many neural theories agree with the older somatic-viscera accounts on a crucial point: they reply to the question "How does one recognize and name distinct emotions?" by pointing to an immediate awareness of the "subjectively quite distinct"[11] inner state that characterizes each emotion. The formulations I have in mind do not sharply (if at all) distinguish emotions from feelings or sensations – all are essentially similar sorts of subjective experiences. As have others, we can treat both somatic-viscera accounts and "mental feeling" theories as instances of the Internal Sensation Theory, the "traditional view" of emotions.[12]

One mental sensation theory is particularly interesting from our perspective because it explicitly identifies such an experience as a "valuative sensation." According to George Edgin Pugh, "innate (or primary) human values are built into the human mind as part of our genetic inheritance." These "innate built-in values," he says, "are experienced as good or bad valuative sensations, such as tactile pleasure or pain, comfort or discomfort,

---

9 The classic critique of James's theory is that of Walter B. Cannon, "The James-Lange Theory of Emotion: A Critical Examination." For a detailed analysis of Cannon's criticisms, see George Mandler, *Mind and Emotion*, pp. 94–101. Mandler discusses a contemporary Jamesian, M. A. Wenger, on pp. 101–2. For other discussions of Cannon's critique, see Lyons, *Emotion*, p. 16; Melvin Konner, *The Tangled Wing*, pp. 138ff. For recent studies of bodily changes and emotion, see Stephanie A. Shields and Robert M. Stern, "Emotion: The Perception of Bodily Changes"; Nico H. Frijda, *The Emotions*, ch. 3. For a recent philosophic treatment of James's theory, see Robert M. Gordon, *The Structure of Emotions*, pp. 87–94.

10 See Cannon, "The James-Lange Theory"; Howard Leventhal, "A Model of Emotion," pp. 4–5; Konner, *The Tangled Wing*, p. 209.

11 See, for example, Konner, *The Tangled Wing*, p. 209.

12 See, for example, Pitcher, "Emotion," p. 326.

joy or sorrow, and good or bad taste. These primary human values include both the 'emotions' and what have traditionally been known as 'biological drives.' "[13] Such valuative sensations are said to be experienced and recognized as "qualitatively distinct."[14] If James and McDougall think of emotions as throbbings and constrictions, Pugh sees them as akin to "tactile pleasure and pain."

Several lines of criticism have been advanced against the Internal Sensation Theory in one or the other of its forms.[15] Following Wittgenstein, some have questioned whether emotion terms could be sensibly used to describe such essentially private happenings; I take up that issue very briefly in §4.2. Philosophers have also tended to be skeptical of the very idea of "mental feelings," though I think Michael Stocker is right that this skepticism leads to considerable difficulties.[16] At present, however, I wish to pursue a different – and I think sounder – criticism: that internal sensation theories are conceptually inadequate as they do not account for the appropriateness conditions informing emotions. In particular, they cannot make sense of two basic ways in which an emotion can be inappropriate: (i) *absurd* and (ii) *ill-grounded*. I consider each in turn.

(i) All internal sensation theories allow that in some sense "perception of the exciting fact" (to borrow James's phrase) results in particular sensations that we name by such words as "joy," "anger," etc. Like all reasonable theories of emotion, then, they acknowledge that cognition is an "initiator of emotional experience."[17] To employ an example of McDougall's: it is a characteristic of humans that, when perceiving a threatening object on one's hand such as a tarantula, one experiences not joy, but the "quite intense" excitement of "that peculiar quality we call fear."[18] But what if one experiences this feeling when perceiving

---

13 George Edgin Pugh, *The Biological Origin of Human Values*, pp. 10,30. F. A. Hayek criticizes Pugh's theory in *Law, Legislation, and Liberty*: vol. 3, *The Political Order of a Free People*, "Epilogue: The Three Sources of Human Values."

14 Pugh, *Human Values*, pp. 113–7. See also his "Values and the Theory of Motivation," pp. 60ff.

15 For a summary of problems with this theory, see William P. Alston, "Emotion and Feeling."

16 See his "Psychic Feelings: Their Importance and Irreducibility."

17 See Leventhal, "A Model of Emotion," p. 11.

18 See McDougall, *Energies of Men*, pp. 148–9.

an object that is not perceived as threatening such as, say, a rabbit? It happened to McDougall:

> Yesterday I was walking alone in an English beech-wood, a place than which none could be safer or more peaceful; suddenly a rabbit, than which no creature could be less dangerous, started up from the undergrowth about my feet; and, absurd as it may seem, I experienced instantaneously a faint shock of excitement which had quite recognizably the quality of fear.[19]

As McDougall recognizes, it does indeed seem absurd to say that one fears something one believes to be utterly harmless. But an internal sensation account has difficulty explaining why it is absurd. To be sure, an internalist can acknowledge that it is most odd to be afraid of that which is perceived to be harmless; in this context, though, "odd" does not capture the absurdity of saying that McDougall is afraid of the rabbit, that he fears it, or even that he experiences fear at the sight of the rabbit. We can grant that it is sometimes intelligible, if still unusual, to fear rabbits; we would all understand if President Carter, having been attacked by a rabbit, is now afraid of them. But it is very different to fear that which is perceived as *utterly harmless or of no threat or danger whatsoever*; that is not simply unusual, but absurd or senseless.[20] It is so because fear presupposes a belief that the feared object is in some way a threat or danger. Whatever feelings or sensations one has, it seems very hard to make sense of calling them "fear" if they are directed at something believed to be utterly harmless. Of course, one may not know precisely what one is afraid of – one may well have only a general sense that something is amiss. But this sort of anxiety is not groundless. Quite the contrary: normal anxiety seems to be grounded on the belief that "a danger, a problem, a test situation or an opportunity has been encountered, but its precise nature is as yet unknown."[21] One believes that one is in danger or that something is wrong, but has yet to perceive the specific nature of the threat. But, quite clearly,

19 Ibid., p. 150.
20 See O. H. Green, "Emotions and Beliefs," p. 28. Cf. Gordon, *The Structure of Emotions*. p. 56. Gordon, however, believes that such absurd reactions are not inappropriate emotions, but not emotions at all. This, I think, obscures the puzzle: the reaction seems, say, to be one of fear, yet it cannot really be.
21 Charles Rycroft, *Anxiety and Neurosis*, p. 12.

this does not imply that the anxiety is altogether independent of beliefs that render it appropriate or inappropriate.

When confronted with a genuinely absurd – totally inappropriate – emotion, we try to render it somehow intelligible. We do not rest content by remarking something like "How unusual to be afraid of things one considers utterly harmless!" One route we might take in the case of McDougall and his rabbit fear is to suggest to him that he was actually startled and not really afraid at all. We might support this suggestion by pointing out that it is widely agreed that facial expressions differ when experiencing fear and when being startled; and, if we saw him, we might say that his expression was akin to the latter rather than the former; or we might point out to him that his own description of his state, that he felt a "faint shock," is atypical of those reporting how it feels to be startled.[22] McDougall, then could be misdescribing his feeling (§4.2.1). But let us say he insists that he really was afraid and we have no reason for doubting him other than the inappropriate object of his fear. It would still be absurd, however, until we uncovered some belief of his that showed rabbits to be in some sense threatening, or to stand for something else that is. This, of course, is just what psychoanalysis often seeks to do, by pointing to some unconscious belief that would (if sound) render the fear appropriate and sensible. As Freud said, anxious reactions that have no apparent relation to danger are "quite beyond our comprehension."[23] To make them comprehensible, he maintained that the ego is reacting to a perceived danger situation, such as castration by one's father.[24] Regardless of what one thinks of the success of the psychoanalytic explanation, the project of uncovering beliefs to render prima facie inappropriate (absurd) emotions somehow intelligible accords with the view of emotions as somehow grounded on, or presupposing, appropriate beliefs.

(ii) Psychoanalysis does not simply aim to uncover an unconscious belief that renders intelligible the previously unintelligible fear. Having shown the patient why rabbits are a target or a focus of fear, the analyst aims at undermining the fear by showing that it is not well grounded.[25] To employ our previous example: as-

22 See Carroll E. Izard, *Human Emotions*, p. 12.
23 Sigmund Freud, *Introductory Lectures on Psychoanalysis*, p. 447.
24 See Sigmund Freud, *Inhibitions, Symptoms and Anxiety*, pp. 227–33.
25 See Ronald de Sousa, "The Rationality of Emotions."

sume we discover that the real target of McDougall's fear is his father (whom he feared would castrate him) and the rabbit is (to use Amélie O. Rorty's term) merely serving as a "front" for that "target."[26] In a sense, we have made the fear intelligible: we know what he sees as the danger and, presumably, why he associates the danger with the rabbit. But, once the patient sees this, we expect the fear to vanish because at least some of the relevant beliefs are recognized to be ill-grounded. And it does indeed seem that emotions tend to dissipate when their grounding beliefs are acknowledged (by the agent) to be ill-grounded or false.[27] Perhaps, though, by a type of self-deception, one can continue to hold a belief recognized as false, and so persist in an emotion grounded on that belief. In that case, the emotion would still be inappropriate; though the emotion is appropriate to the belief, the belief is inappropriate given standards of evidence, principles of logic, etc. The inappropriateness of the emotion then stems from the inappropriateness of belief.

Emotions are conceptually dependent on certain beliefs in a way that escapes internal sensation accounts. If one "feels" the relevant way, then, according to the internalist, one just does experience the emotion. And that appears wrong. It may seem, however, that the internalist can at least make sense of the sort of ill-grounded emotion I have just mentioned: the internalist may claim that emotion *E* is ill-grounded if it is triggered by ill-grounded beliefs. This would not affect our example because in our original case McDougall does not have any false beliefs – he just has an odd reaction to standard beliefs. More fundamentally, though, the very idea of an ill-grounded sensation is problematic. As George Pitcher tells us: "If my headache is caused by the belief that my fortune has been lost, no one would be tempted to judge my headache unreasonable [or absurd] on the grounds that my belief is so."[28] Because the internalist sees emotions as only causally dependent, and not logically or conceptually dependent, on beliefs, he or she seems unable to account for the absurdity or unreasonableness of some emotions.

---

26 Amélie O. Rorty, "Explaining Emotions," pp. 106ff.
27 See Roger Trigg, *Pain and Emotion*, p. 50; Gordon, *The Structure of Emotions*, p. 78; Colin Radford, "How Can We be Moved by the Fate of Anna Karenina?," pp. 67–9. Cf. Rorty, "Explaining Emotions."
28 Pitcher, "Emotion," pp. 329–30.

3.2 *The cognitive-arousal theory*

Thus far, I have been arguing that internal sensation accounts of emotion cannot make sense of two basic ways in which an emotion can be inappropriate: absurd and ill-grounded. (I am not claiming that these are the only senses in which an emotion can be inappropriate, though I do believe that they are the least contentious; see §6.3). In this respect, the conception of emotion proffered by internalists is inadequate as it does not account for crucial features of emotion discourse and related practices (see §1.2). However, it is widely thought that the most damaging critique of internalism has been empirical rather than conceptual.

In what has been described as "now almost classic experiments,"[29] Stanley Schachter and his colleagues appear to provide strong evidence that, contrary to internalist claims, people do not recognize and name emotions simply by introspection. In perhaps the most famous of these experiments, conducted by Schachter and Jerome E. Singer,[30] subjects were told they were engaged in an experiment to test the effects on vision of an injection of "Suproxin" – "a vitamin compound." In fact, they were injected either with epinephrine (adrenalin) or a saline solution (a placebo). Subjects were then divided into three groups: (i) some subjects were informed that "Suproxin" sometimes has "side effects" (those actually associated with epinephrine) such as shaking hands, pounding heart, flushed and warm face; (ii) some were told nothing about the "side effects"; (iii) some were misinformed about the "side effects," being told that they might experience numbness, headaches, etc. (these are not effects of epinephrine). Subjects were then placed in a room with a "stooge," who was instructed by the experimenters to act either euphorically or angrily. During the period with the stooge, the subjects were observed through a one-way mirror; afterward, they completed reports about their moods.

Schachter and Singer found that the misinformed and ignorant subjects who received epinephrine were significantly more likely than the informed subjects to act in ways similar to the stooge. Put in with an angry stooge, they were more likely to act angrily;

29 See Konner, *The Tangled Wing*, p. 217.
30 Schachter and Singer, "Cognitive, Social, and Physiological Determinants of Emotional State."

placed with a euphoric stooge, they were more apt to act euphorically and to describe themselves as happy. This seems to support the thesis that one names and recognizes one's emotional state "in terms of the cognitions available to him." On Schachter's view, emotion is a general "stirred-up" physiological state that one labels and interprets according to one's beliefs about the situation. Those who were not informed or were misinformed about the basis of their stirred-up condition interpreted it as anger when they were placed with an angry stooge, who pointed out many reasons why anger is appropriate; when placed with a playful stooge, they were more likely to label their aroused state as happiness. In contrast, those who were informed that the injection was apt to cause the sort of physiological arousal they actually experienced were significantly less prone to interpret their state in terms of anger or euphoria. Already possessing a relevant belief, they had an explanation of their excitement and, so, did not appeal to their beliefs about the appropriateness of emotion.

3.3 Three versions of CAT

The Cognitive-Arousal Theory (CAT) of emotions – which is probably still the favored view of most psychologists[31] – seems straightforward: one is experiencing an emotion if one is physiologically aroused, and one has beliefs (cognitions) that allow one to label this arousal as an emotion appropriate to the circumstances. We might characterize the theory thus understood in a more formal way as:

CAT(1): Alf is in emotional state *E* if and only if:
(i) Alf is physiologically aroused; and

31 See, for example, the long and sympathetic discussion by Strongman, *The Psychology of Emotion*, ch. 4. Perhaps more important is that those who offer alternative accounts invariably begin by criticizing the Cognitive-Arousal Theory in general, and Schachter's work in particular. See Izard, *Human Emotions*, pp. 30ff.; Leventhal, "A Model of Emotions," pp. 8ff. However, recently criticism of Schachter and Singer's experiments by psychologists has increased; see Frijda, *The Emotions*, pp. 222–3. Philosophers, too, are generally sympathetic, though they also favor the appraisal theory of Magda B. Arnold; see her *Emotion and Personality*. I discuss appraisal theory in §6.2. As we shall see, some versions of appraisal theory are also Cognitive-Arousal Theories. For representative positions by philosophers, see Lyons, *Emotion*, pp. 114–23, 132ff; Alston, "Emotion and Feeling." For a critical philosophic treatment of Schachter and Singer's theory that relates it to James's, see Gordon, *The Structure of Emotions*, ch. 5.

(ii) Alf believes that *E* is appropriate in his present situation.[32]

Whereas the Internal Sensation Theory has difficulty with the idea that an emotion can be appropriate or inappropriate, CAT(1) focuses on appropriately labeling one's aroused state. As Schachter and Singer write, "Cognitions arising from the immediate situation as interpreted by past experience provide the framework within which one understands and labels his feelings. It is the cognition which determines whether the state of physiological arousal will be labeled 'anger,' 'joy,' 'fear,' or whatever."[33] Not surprisingly, then, Schachter and Singer's theory has been described as an "arousal-label" theory of emotion.[34] However, a little reflection on the point of their experiment reveals that they are not ultimately concerned with CAT(1).

The experiment centered on manipulating three main variables: (1) whether the subject was physiologically aroused; (2) whether, if aroused, the subject had an explanation of his arousal; and (3) whether the subject had anger- (or euphoria-) appropriate cognitions available. For the present purposes, it is important that much of Schachter and Singer's theory relies on what happens when (2) is varied but (3) is not; that is, when some subjects injected with epinephrine have been informed about its actual effects while others are ignorant or misinformed, but all had available cognitions that made emotions appropriate (for example, they are all asked to complete an insulting questionnaire in the presence of an angry stooge). The finding, of course, is that a subject who is expecting the effects of epinephrine is, for instance, less apt to "interpret his state in terms of the cognitions provided by the stooge's angry behavior."[35] But this raises a problem for CAT(1). All such subjects were aroused, and all subjects (within, say, the anger group) were confronted by cognitions that

32 Cf. Schachter and Singer's remark that "emotional states may be considered a function of a state of physiological arousal and of a cognition appropriate to this state of arousal." "Determinants of Emotional State," p. 380. An alternative formulation of clause (ii) is Alf believes he is in a circumstance of type *T*, where *E* is appropriate to *T*. This change would not affect the following discussion.

33 Schachter and Singer, "Determinants of Emotional State," p. 380.

34 Warren Shibles, *Emotion*, p. 129. Gordon seeks to relate this concern with "labeling" to Schachter's early work. *The Structure of Emotions*, p. 106.

35 Schachter and Singer, "Determinants of Emotional State," p. 393.

rendered emotional labels appropriate. According to CAT(1), in this case all should be labeled "angry" because (1) all are aroused, and (2) all are in a situation in which anger is obviously appropriate. But the whole point of the experiment is that some aroused subjects with appropriate cognitions do not get angry.

One might attempt to rescue CAT(1) by arguing that, though epinephrine-informed, ignorant, and misinformed subjects were all confronted by the same situation, their beliefs about the appropriateness of anger differ. Those subjects informed about the likely effects of the drug, it could be pointed out, tend to remark to the angry stooge such things as "Take it easy, they probably have a good reason for wanting the information [requested on the insulting questionnaire]."[36] So perhaps they do not believe that anger is appropriate; and, if beliefs about the appropriateness of a certain emotion differ between informed and ignorant groups, CAT(1) is consistent with the latter and not the former being angry. But this interpretation trivializes Schachter and Singer's study. They interpreted a subject's remark such as "Take it easy, they must have a good reason for asking" (for example, "Which members of your family need psychiatric care? – where "none" is unacceptable) as behavioral evidence that the subject was not angry. If, instead, it becomes evidence that the subject does not think anger is appropriate, Schachter and Singer no longer have independent evidence that anyone in the study actually became angry. That is, if what they took as behavioral evidence of anger is interpreted as evidence concerning beliefs about the appropriateness of anger, they only show that informed and misinformed/ignorant subjects had different beliefs, not that they had different emotions.

One could seek to defend the relevance of CAT(1) to Schachter and Singer's work in yet another way. What is important, it could be argued, is that some subjects actually did label their arousal as "anger" or "happiness" and that these subjects acted angrily or happily, but aroused subjects who did not label their arousal as emotional did not act emotionally. Although this interpretation may seem consistent with the idea of an "arousal-label" theory of emotion, it is neither true to the experiment nor is it a plausible account of emotion. It is not true to the experiment because, in

36 Ibid., p. 386.

the case of anger, Schachter and Singer's subjects generally refused to label their mood as "angry" until the experiment was over;[37] what is important from Schachter and Singer's perspective is that those subjects *acted* angrily. This leads to a more general point. Despite the talk of labeling, it is clear that a theory would not be plausible if it required one to consciously label a state of arousal as *E*, before one felt and acted in the ways characteristic of *E*.[38] Certainly we want to allow that people can feel and act angry without ever saying to themselves "My arousal is anger." The important point is not, then, that those who say "My arousal is anger" act and feel in angry ways, but that some aroused people who find themselves in anger-appropriate situations act and feel angry and, further, will come to label themselves as being "angry" if asked. The real question is why only some aroused subjects who find themselves in, say, circumstances appropriate to anger, acted angrily.

To answer this question, Schachter and Singer move from talk of labeling to *explanations* of arousal. The epinephrine-informed subjects, they argue, had a better explanation of their aroused state: that they had been injected. Schachter and Singer rely here on what they call "evaluative needs."[39] A person who finds himself aroused without having an explanation requires (needs) some account and, so, looks to the environment for one. Thus, according to the evaluative needs thesis, a person will settle on an emotion explanation if he was not accurately informed of the probable effects of the drug. This, then, is to move away from a simple appropriate labeling account to some sort of causal hypothesis about the source of one's feelings. The informed subjects have a ready hypothesis about the cause of their arousal – they were injected. Consequently, they did not have to look elsewhere to explain why they were aroused. Anger (or euphoria) would have been appropriate, but they were not angry because they did not attribute their arousal to the anger- (or euphoria-) evoking features of their situation. But the ignorant, and especially the misinformed, subjects[40] had no other available hypothesis, so they at-

37 The subjects, who were students, were apparently reluctant to acknowledge that they were angry at their teachers. Ibid., pp. 391–2.

38 See Kenny, *Action, Emotion, and Will*, p. 15.

39 Schachter and Singer, "Determinants of Emotional State," p. 381. See Mandler, *Mind and Emotion*, pp. 90–91.

40 Schachter and Singer speculate that ignorant subjects were more likely to

tributed their agitation to the emotional situation in which they found themselves. The whole thrust of Schachter and Singer's experiment thus depends not simply on labels appropriate to the situation, but on causal hypotheses about the basis of one's agitation. This leads to a second version of the Cognitive-Arousal Theory:

CAT(2): Betty is in emotional state *E* if and only if:
(i) Betty is physiologically aroused; and
(ii) Betty believes that her arousal is caused by the *E*-evoking features of her present situation.

CAT(2) certainly seems more adequate from the point of view of Schachter and Singer's study. William Lyons seems to agree that this formulation captures the crux of their study; after reviewing their experiment, Lyons apparently endorses a version of CAT(2), insisting that the subjects of feelings "always attempt to label their feelings by reference to the *cause* of their feelings. So, as regards feelings in the context of emotions, correctly or incorrectly, we label feelings as emotional just so long as we *believe* that the feelings are *caused* by our evaluation of the situation as being a situation appropriate to such and such an emotion."[41] Again, we need to be careful: the recurring references to labeling notwithstanding, Schachter and Singer's theory is not primarily about how we label aroused states, but about how we feel and act. As I have just suggested, one can act angrily and feel anger without any conscious labeling of one's state as "anger."

It seems wrong, however, to insist that individuals can only experience an emotion if they entertain a causal hypothesis about the origins of their feelings. If you insult me and I get angry, it seems both odd and unnecessary to attribute to me a belief about the cause of my arousal, and it certainly seems misplaced to focus on such a belief as fundamental to the emotion. The objection here is not simply that one need not have such a belief before one's mind in order to experience an emotion, for beliefs can affect behavior without being consciously before one's mind.[42] Rather, the point is that conscious or nonconscious, such a causal belief can-

hit upon the injection hypothesis to explain their arousal than were the misinformed subjects. "Determinants of Emotional State," p. 390.

41 Lyons, *Emotion*, p. 133 (emphasis in original).

42 See §7.2.3 for an argument that nonconscious beliefs can provide the basis for reasons to act.

not be necessary. Say that I am presently absorbed in a heated argument and, thus, I am unaware that I am aroused or even that I am angry at someone. Afterward, if someone points out that I was angry I may be surprised and resist the idea, though I can be brought to see that I was indeed angry by pointing out to me that I was abrupt, talked rather more loudly than usual, and so forth. It does not seem to make a great deal of sense in such a case to attribute to me (during my argument) any belief, conscious or not, that someone is the cause of an arousal of which I am not aware. Certainly this is an odd way to explain emotions; emotional people, we are to believe, are necessarily making conjectures about the causes of their physiological condition (see §8.1). CAT(2) is plausible in the context of Schachter and Singer's study only because their subjects were first aroused and then left to explain this agitation. This points to the way in which their experimental design fails to capture the normal emotion sequence in which beliefs lead to arousal, feelings, etc.[43] By starting with an unexplained arousal (in their ignorant and misinformed subjects) Schachter and Singer render CAT(2) far more plausible than it really is.

Although, as I have said, Lyons seems attracted to a version of CAT(2) – at least when discussing the labeling of feelings – he is ultimately concerned with defending a different theory, a version of:

CAT(3): Charlie is in emotional state *E* if and only if:
(i) Charlie has *E*-relevant beliefs; and
(ii) These beliefs [in (i)] cause Charlie to be aroused.

On Lyons's formulation, the "beliefs"[44] relevant to CAT(3) are "evaluative"; consequently, for him *E* "is to be deemed an emotional state if and only if it is a physiologically abnormal state *caused by* the subject of that state's evaluation of his or her situation."[45] CAT(3) thus seems more reasonable than CAT(2); according to CAT(3), beliefs about one's circumstances cause

43 See Mandler, *Mind and Emotion*, pp. 91–92; Shibles, *Emotion*, p. 129.
44 Lyons in particular, and evaluative (or appraisal) theory in general, is typically unclear as to whether evaluations are beliefs. See §6.2 in this volume. Lyons, *Emotion*, p. 129.
45 Lyons, *Emotion*, pp. 57–8. Emphasis added. This, of course, is not a restatement of CAT(3), because it only concerns the criteria for being in an (any) emotional state; it does not serve to distinguish emotional states. See ibid., ch. 6.

arousal, but it is not necessary to hold *beliefs about* the causes of arousal. But note that, despite Lyons's sympathy with Schachter and Singer's work, CAT(3) undermines their classic study. It seems hard to deny that the cause of the subjects' arousal was the epinephrine injection:[46] a central aim of the study was to arouse subjects and then see under what conditions they explained their arousal in terms of emotions. But, according to CAT(3), because the arousal was not caused by their *E*-relevant beliefs, none of the subjects were in an emotional state! CAT(3) implies that Schachter and Singer only showed that people can act *as if* they were angry/euphoric and mistakenly come to believe that they are. But, in the end, none of the subjects was really emotional.

CAT(3) is thus less plausible than it first appears. In order to accept it, one must deny either (1) that Schachter and Singer's angry and happy subjects were aroused by, and only by, the epinephrine injection; or (2) that they were genuinely emotional. To deny (1) appears inconsistent with Schachter and Singer's pulse-rate data, which indicates that no injected group was significantly more aroused than others.[47] Some may be attracted to denying (2); those who were injected, one might say, were not really angry or happy because their state was drug induced. This suggestion is not without merit; after all, if entirely independent of the appropriate circumstances, some drug induced the entire experience of a particular emotion, we would, at the very least, be tempted to deny that the resulting state was a full-fledged, paradigmatic instance of the emotion.[48] And, as I will argue a little later (§5.4.1), we may well want to say that the emotion in this case is inappropriate. But this is far from saying that anyone who is aroused by adrenalin injections cannot experience genuine emotions; although the subjects' arousal was induced by epinephrine, it seems much too strong to say that their emotional states were. It seems much sounder to say that certain sorts of arousing drugs

46 Lyons seems to recognize this; perhaps that is why at this point in his book he focuses on labeling and CAT(2), which is consistent with their work. See ibid., pp. 132–3, including the references to the causation question in Schachter and Singer's study.

47 Schachter and Singer, "Determinants of Emotional State," p. 388. Informed subjects had the highest pulse rate; they did, however, report themselves to be slightly less aroused than did the ignorant and misinformed subjects, but these differences are modest.

48 See Gordon, *The Structure of Emotions*, pp. 49ff., 99ff.

predispose one to emotional responses than to say that they prevent genuine emotions.

4 AFFECTS

The dispute between the Internal Sensation and Cognitive-Arousal theories turns on two points: (i) Does naming and recognizing emotions fundamentally depend on a characteristic subjective feeling that distinguishes emotions, or are emotional states primarily characterized by undifferentiated physiological arousal? (ii) Is naming and recognizing emotions simply a matter of introspection, or does it turn on beliefs that render an emotion appropriate or inappropriate to a particular situation? One might think that these ultimately involve the same point, or at least that the answer to one question implies that to the other. I shall argue that this is not so; at least in the ways I have put the issues, the internalist position on point (i) – subject to some modifications (§6.4) – can be conjoined with the cognitivist position on point (ii). That is: recognizing and naming (the fundamental) emotions turns on characteristic subjective feelings *and* beliefs. The resulting theory is aptly called the Affective-Cognitive Theory of emotions.

4.1 Some evidence for discrete affects

Cognitivists have stressed that no particular set of feelings or visceral changes characterize emotions. As Lyons says, "feelings such as throbs and twinges are not invariably associated with emotions and much less with particular emotions."[49] But, as I have tried to show (§3.1), internalists are not committed to some sort of somatic-viscera theory; more recent accounts have focused on special subjective experiences quite distinct from, though perhaps related to, somatic-visceral changes. Is there, then, any evidence, that such "mental feelings" exist and are not, as the cognitivist would have it, simply a function of belief?

The work of Paul D. MacLean provides evidence of such feelings.[50] For our purposes, most important are his reports of clin-

49 Lyons, *Emotion*, p. 133.
50 For a general survey of his work and his theory, see Paul D. MacLean, "Sensory and Perceptive Factors in Emotional Functions of the Triune Brain."

ical cases involving certain types of epileptics. In a 1952 paper, he reported on several patients experiencing neural discharges in the limbic portion of the frontotemporal region.[51] Most interesting for us is the patient who reported a "feeling of sadness and of wanting to cry." What is so interesting is that the patient apparently was aware that there was no reason to be sad and that the sadness was not an appropriate response to his environment. Indeed – and this is the crucial point – he did not seem to be sad *about* anything at all. He simply felt sad. In all these cases, MacLean stresses that the reported feelings are "out of context." To use his terminology, the "affect" – the subjective feeling aspect of an emotion[52] – is experienced apart from the conditions that make it appropriate and, apparently, which direct it upon some particular person or object in the world.

In later papers, MacLean reports that "[n]euronal discharges in or near the limbic cortex of the temporal lobe may trigger a broad spectrum of vivid, affective feelings."[53] Among these, he distinguishes three groups: the *basic*, *specific*, and *general* affects. Basic affects are related to "internal states associated with basic bodily needs – namely, the needs for food, water, air, sexual outlet, sleep, and those associated with various emunctories." The specific affects include tastes, odors, and other sensory as well as somatic sensations. The general affects – those associated with the emotions – include fear, terror, sorrow, joy, and affection.[54] MacLean maintains that only "a limited number" of general affects can be identified. Although "[s]ymbolic language makes it possible to identify many variations of these affects,"[55] he believes that these variations are all built up from some small number of general affects.

51 Paul D. MacLean, "Some Psychiatric Implications of Physiological Studies on Frontotemporal Portion of Limbic System (Visceral Brain)."
52 MacLean suggests this distinction in "Sensory and Perceptive Factors in Emotional Functions of the Triune Brain," p. 11.
53 Ibid., p. 20. See also pp. 12-13. In addition, see MacLean's "The Hypothalamus and Emotional Behavior," esp. pp. 660-1, pp. 671ff.; "The Triune Brain, Emotion, and Scientific Bias," esp. pp. 337–8.
54 Although MacLean includes these last two "positive affects," his work does not stress them because he suggests that they have not been the focus of as much research as the "negative" affects. For an easily accessible survey of work on the "positive" affects, see Konner, *The Tangled Wing*, chs. 11, 13. I discuss the distinction between positive and negative affects in §6.2.
55 MacLean, "The Hypothalamus," p. 661.

MacLean, then, provides some important evidence that people can experience and identify affects even when, as in clinical settings, they are perceived as entirely inappropriate. This helps to undermine an important cognitivist argument against internal sensation accounts. William Lyons, whom I have identified as advocating a version of the Cognitive-Arousal Theory (§3.3), holds that if, as the internalist maintains, some special "lovey" feeling always accompanied love,

> one would have grounds for saying that one was in love without knowing or believing that there is any person whom one loves, or having any other grounds for believing that one was in love. But in fact it seems impossible to assert that one is in the grip of such and such an emotion just by introspecting the quality or type of one's present feeling.[56]

Two preliminary points need to be made. First, even given his own thesis, what Lyons says cannot be quite right: he starts out by asking whether we "invariably connect" a particular feeling with a particular emotion, but his argument here seems to assume that the feeling *is* the emotion. Put differently, he begins by asking whether a specific feeling is a necessary element of an emotion, but he criticizes the view that the feeling is sufficient for the emotion. This is just the error that internal sensation theory typically makes: identifying the feeling element with the entire emotion. Secondly, Lyons's understanding of feelings is (like Ryle's),[57] extremely visceral, emphasizing "twinges" and "throbs." MacLean's research, however, casts doubt on the necessity of visceral or somatic sensations for general affects. Although some patients report such viscera-somatic sensations (our sad patient, for instance, also reported a "sensation of hunger"), and they do seem to contribute to the "vividness of the emotion," MacLean concludes that the evidence supports the hypothesis that affective experience can occur without any visceral or somatic feelings.[58] However, given these clarifications, his clinical

56 Lyons, *Emotion*, p. 133.
57 See Gilbert Ryle, *The Concept of Mind*, ch. IV. Lyons is discussing Ryle here.
58 MacLean, "The Hypothalamus," pp. 661–2. See also his "Implications of Microelectric Findings on Exteroceptive Inputs to the Limbic Cortex." Cf. Frijda's conclusion that "Autonomic awareness is not a prerequisite for emotional experience or emotional behavior. It contributes to intensity and quality of experience, although it probably is not the cue for distinguishing the different emotions of fear, anger, joy, and so on." *The Emotions*, p. 23.

evidence supports the thesis that Lyons believes to be so implausible: people can apparently feel, and recognize themselves as feeling, angry, sad, fearful, joyous, and, apparently, even affectionate, without believing the relevant emotion is in any way appropriate to the situation, without entertaining beliefs that ground the feeling and even without having any person or situation in mind. In the absence of any environmental cues or grounding beliefs, it seems that people can identify an affect as that characteristic of a particular emotion.

MacLean's neurological approach to affect and emotion partially converges with the differential emotions theory of such psychologists as Silvan S. Tomkins and Carroll E. Izard.[59] Although Tomkins's work was seminal, because Izard's is more recent I shall focus on his formulation. His theory seeks to bring together various perspectives with the aim of achieving a unified theory of emotion; he too thus draws on neuroscience as well as physiology and more traditional psychological approaches to the study of emotion, particularly studies of emotional expression.[60] And, most important right now, he focuses on studies of the emotional experience – "felt emotion." Employing self-reporting methods based on adjective checklists or scales,[61] he reports that ten discrete emotional experiences emerge: interest, enjoyment, surprise, distress, anger, disgust, contempt, fear, shyness and guilt.[62] This enumeration does not perfectly converge with MacLean's general affects. Most significantly, interest, which is fundamental to Izard's theory, is not mentioned by MacLean; and MacLean has uncovered several rather different sorts of affects – for example, a feeling of individuality, a feeling of truth, and a feeling

59 See Silvan S. Tomkins, *Affect, Imagery, Consciousness*; Izard, *Human Emotions*. For critical discussions of this approach, see Strongman, *The Psychology of Emotion*, pp. 88-90; Frijda, *The Emotions*, pp. 60, 86, 233ff.; John Sabini and Maury Silver, "Emotions, Responsibility and Character," p. 167.

60 See Izard, *Human Emotions*, pp. 109–23.

61 Izard has employed two main scales. The Differential Emotions Scale (DES) tries to uncover an individual's experiences of various emotions. Comprised of thirty emotion names (see Appendix A in the present volume), it either instructs the respondent to rate himself (i) on a five-point scale concerning the intensity of his emotion at the time, or (ii) a five-point scale regarding the frequency with which he experiences the emotion. The other scale, the Dimensions Rating Scale (DRS) aims to tap various dimensions of emotional experience such as pleasant, tense, active, etc. Ibid., pp. 123–9. See §6.2 in this volume.

62 See Appendix A for DES categories and reliability statistics.

of familiarity – that do not play a role in Izard's account. (They may diverge less than this suggests, however, because MacLean uses these rather special affects to explain our sense of what is "true and important,"[63] and that obviously is related to what we find interesting. But see §5.1.) Such discrepancies underscore the tentative status of all enumerations of fundamental emotion affects as well as just how far we are from a unified neurological-based and psychological-based theory of affects and emotions. Nevertheless, the extent to which MacLean's and Izard's enumerations of fundamental and experientially discrete affects do converge is, I think, impressive and encouraging for a discrete affects theory of emotion.

4.2 *Some objections and additional evidence*

4.2.1 Innate public expressions

A number of objections might be raised to this analysis. Anthony Kenny, for example, draws on Wittgenstein's remarks on private language to criticize internal sensation accounts.[64] I cannot pause here to engage this complicated debate.[65] However, without responding to the details of the Wittgensteinian analysis, it is important to consider just how we could ever develop a common discourse regarding such private inner events. Consider the following possibility: What if humans were constructed in such a way that each fundamental affective experience was causally connected to some public expressive act? This of course, would not assuage the objections of the Wittgensteinians, who would want to be told how we could ever know that the same experience lay behind the public expressions of different people. But, if we had, say, a neurological theory which held that affective experience could be located in different areas of the brain, and that there were pathways which tightly linked these events to certain public expressions, many of us would, I think, be rather less worried

63 See MacLean, "Emotion and Scientific Bias," p. 339. See also his "Implications of Microelectric Findings" and "Sensory and Perceptive Factors in Emotional Functions," pp. 20–21.
64 Kenny, *Action, Emotion and Will*, p. 13. See Ludwig Wittgenstein, *Philosophical Investigations*, §§243–58, 583.
65 For a useful criticism of Kenny's analysis see J. R. S. Wilson, *Emotion and Object*, chs. II–IV.

about this general line of objection. Equipped with such a theory, we would have some reason for believing that what Alf identified as "anger" was what Betty also felt. For the use of "anger" would be checkable by the public performance, and our neurological theory would give us some reason for thinking that similar affective experiences were being named. Again, this would not even begin to convince someone like Kenny, but for many it would be evidence in favor of the discrete affects theory.

A number of theories hypothesize just such a causal link between affective experiences and facial expressions. I shall not go into the details of these theories here, though it should be noted that they disagree regarding how complex a model is required to adequately map these causal relations.[66] But all such theories maintain that facial expressions are intimately linked to fundamental affective experiences; unless one voluntarily overrides the automatic response system, the fundamental emotion-affects manifest themselves in distinct facial expressions.[67] Moreover, impressive cross-cultural evidence supports the claim that these expressions of affect are at least partially innate. Subjects in widely varying cultures – including isolated peoples in New Guinea – have agreed as to what facial expressions are characteristic of particular emotions. Happiness, surprise, fear, disgust, and sadness are among those that have been most widely identified in this way.[68] This finding is particularly relevant to Izard's theory because his basic emotions, including interest, have been shown to manifest themselves in such pancultural facial expressions.[69]

This innate, certainly pancultural, connection provides the public foundation for learning to name the fundamental affects.

66 See, e.g., Leventhal, "A Model of Emotions"; Izard, *Human Emotions*, pp. 55ff.; Tomkins, *Affect, Imagery, Consciousness*, vol. I, pp. 224ff.

67 This is perhaps slightly misleading; such theories often maintain that the particular facial expressions manifest themselves in distinctive affective experiences. The claim that the facial expression causes an affective experience seems too strong; there is good evidence that one can experience an affect without a facial expression. See Frijda, *The Emotions*, pp. 233–7.

68 See Paul Ekman, "Biological and Cultural Contributions to Body and Facial Movement in the Expression of Emotions," p. 97; Paul Ekman, Wallace V. Friesen, and Phoebe Ellsworth, *Emotion in the Human Face*, pp. 153–73; Frijda, *The Emotions*, pp. 60–9.

69 See Izard, *Human Emotions*, pp. 7–8, 84, 215–216. Frijda disputes some of these claims in *The Emotions*, p. 68.

(For those unable to experience the affect but who can employ emotion concepts based simply on public expressions, see §17.4.) However, once the affect concept is learned on the basis of this and other public expressions, it is possible to sensibly say that one is experiencing the affect even if the public expression does not occur. Roger Trigg has argued: "If the sensation is 'exactly like' those occurring in obvious cases of pain, it is pain."[70] So too, if an affect is exactly like that occurring in a full-fledged emotion, it is the affect. Consequently, if someone experiences the affect without the expressions, and indeed even out of the appropriate context, we can still accept his testimony that, for example, he "feels angry" (unless, of course, we have independent reason to conclude that he does not grasp the concept or that he is deceiving us). And this is why we can accept the testimony of MacLean's patients despite the absence of most of the normal features of emotional experience.

To be sure, all this only directly concerns the fundamental affects that are so intimately connected to facial expression; more subtle and complex affective states do not have the same strong ties to public expression. I see no reason to resist the conclusion that communicating the nature of these latter sorts of states may be extraordinarily difficult.[71] And, because we have problems publicly naming these subtle and complex states, we should not be surprised that our discourse about them is typically confused and obscure; it is perhaps one of the chief aims of literature to convey, or at least intimate, the nature of these states. But even these complex affective states have ties to public expression. Both MacLean and Izard believe that they are somehow built up from the more fundamental ones[72] (for instance, "smug" has been characterized as a complex of contempt and happiness).[73] If these fundamental affects have a public dimension, then descriptions of more subtle states grounded on them will also have some relation, albeit complex, to public expression.

70 Trigg, *Pain and Emotion*, p. 32. Although Trigg's methodological dictum strikes me as entirely sound, I express some reservations about his account of pain in §9.3.
71 This is acknowledged by MacLean. See his "Psychosomatics," pp. 1728–729.
72 See MacLean, "Sensory and Perceptive Factors in Emotional Functions," p. 13; Izard, *Human Emotions*, ch. 3. But cf. Frijda, *The Emotions*, pp. 72–3.
73 See Ekman, "Body and Facial Movements in the Expression of Emotions," p. 97.

4.2.2 *Infant and animal data*

A thoroughgoing cognitivist, however, might claim that all MacLean shows is that our learned notions about appropriate labeling of aroused states can be triggered by certain types of neural discharges. MacLean's patients, it may be argued, learned to associate arousal in particular types of circumstances with a particular emotional concept, and what they recall as a result of the neural discharges are past experiences of being aroused conjoined with the appropriate, learned, emotional label. But it is hard to see how this will do as a general account of MacLean's findings. His patients were not recalling past experiences, nor were they for the most part imagining general or paradigmatic cases of the various emotions.[74] Typically, they had no relevant beliefs or scenarios in mind, yet they were able to identify a feeling as that characteristic of a particular emotion. At the very least, the Cognitive-Arousal theorist seems forced to allow that, independently of particular beliefs and situations, we can come to identify an affective experience as characteristic of a particular emotion.

The learning explanation does not accord well with observations of infants.[75] Babies less than three months old display a variety of facial expressions characteristic of emotions in contexts similar to those in which adults display them. Because at this stage of development imitation of adults is sporadic, the more plausible hypothesis is that these emotional expressions are innate. Combined with the hypothesized connection between facial expressions and feeling states (§4.2), this provides support for the claim that neonates experience emotional affects.

Cognitive-Arousal Theory looks even less plausible if animal studies are taken seriously. To be sure, as MacLean realizes, methodological objections confront the study of affective experiences in animals.[76] It is often claimed, for instance, that animal studies are restricted to claims about behavior and so can say nothing about the feeling states of animals. MacLean's response

74 But see, e.g., the patient who was afraid that someone was behind him, but became even more afraid when he checked and discovered that there was no one there. See MacLean, "Some Psychiatric Implications."

75 This paragraph draws on the studies cited in Frijda, *The Emotions*, pp. 68–9.

76 See MacLean, "Hypothalamus," pp. 559-60, and "Psychosomatics," pp. 1727–9.

to this line of criticism is entirely sound, emphasizing that in this respect human and animal studies are not radically different. The study of human feeling relies on verbal and nonverbal behavior (for example, facial expressions) as grounds for inferring feeling states; although cross-species research poses additional problems, they are not of an entirely different order. Moreover, because MacLean's theory relates affective experience to certain brain structures, and these structures are common to mammals, his theory provides a theoretical rationale for drawing on animal as well as human studies.

Assuming, then, that not only human studies, but animal studies too can tell us something about feeling states, MacLean reports that "electrical stimulation in the frontotemporal region in animals . . . elicits autonomic and behavioral effects comparable to those observed in psychomotor epilepsy."[77] Angry, defensive, and fearful reactions were among those observed. Now these cannot be welcome findings from the perspective of Cognitive-Arousal Theory. If, as the cognitivist observed at the beginning of this subjection, MacLean's patients only demonstrated that learned "emotional experiences" could be triggered in humans out of context, the similarity of human and animal responses is, to say the very least, surprising. Perhaps such findings can be interpreted in a way that is compatible with the cognitivist account, but pretty clearly the task is a challenging one.

5 AFFECTS AND OBJECTS

5.1 Intentional objects

Internalists such as Pugh (§3.1) seem correct that a variety of "feelings," "sensations," or, as I say, "affects," can be identified by a subject independently of environmental cues and beliefs about appropriateness; indeed, it would seem that they can be recognized apart from any emotion-relevant beliefs about one's situation. The error of internal sensation theory is in identifying these sensations or affects with emotions or emotional states. The challenge confronting a discrete affects theory is, then, to relate affects to emotions in a way that is both intuitively plausible and avoids the conceptual problems of internal sensation accounts.

77 See MacLean, "Hypothalamus," p. 674.

Although he is typically understood as a strong cognitivist, Spinoza provides a valuable insight. According to him, joy (or pleasure), sorrow (or unpleasure), and desire are the primary affects. It has been suggested that Spinoza can be interpreted as offering a theory of emotions based on the first two, joy and sorrow.[78] Emotions, on this account, arise when such affects are joined with ideas about objects and, in particular, with ideas about the objects that cause the affect. Thus, for instance, according to Spinoza "*Love* is nothing else but joy accompanied with the idea of an external cause, and *hatred* is nothing but sorrow with the accompanying idea of an external cause."[79] This thesis – that in contrast to mere sensations, emotional feelings are somehow related to, or directed toward, objects of some sort – is widely accepted. Anthony Kenny, for example, insists that "emotions, unlike sensations, are essentially directed to objects. . . . It is not in general possible to ascribe . . . a sensation to a particular emotional state without at the same time ascribing an object to the emotion."[80] Thus, it would seem, we may simply feel a sensation, but someone who is angry is angry *at* or *about* someone or something.

All this seems essentially correct, and today it is generally recognized as such. The difficulty, though, is that, once we go beyond the insight that emotions are somehow directed to objects, and try to specify the nature of this direction and these objects, a host of problems arise. Franz Brentano introduced into modern philosophy the notion that mental phenomena have "reference to a content, direction toward an object,"[81] but philosophers have expressed a variety of worries about the ontological commitments of such "intentional objects," the relation between 'inten*t*ionality' and 'inten*s*ionality,' what account of propositions is implied by allowing, as intentional objects, "things that don't exist," etc.[82]

78 See Jonathan Bennett, *A Study of Spinoza's Ethics*, pp. 267ff. See also Lyons, *Emotion*, pp. 38-40. MacLean agrees that desire is an affect; see "Sensory and Perceptive Factors in Emotional Functions," p. 13. I deny this, arguing that the concept of desire derives from affects and beliefs; see §7.2.

79 Spinoza, *Ethic*, pp. 221ff. See esp. pt. 3, props. XIII, XXX.

80 Kenny, *Action, Emotion, and Will*, p. 60.

81 Franz Brentano, *Psychology from an Empirical Standpoint*, p. 88.

82 This is evident in Wilson, *Emotion and Object*, e.g., p. 57. As Wilson recognizes, it is not clear that the inten*t*ionality of mental states is significantly related to the inten*s*ionality of propositions; they are clearly not the same, and it is important not to confuse them. See John R. Searle, *Intentionality*, pp. 22ff., ch. 7.

Nevertheless, it is common enough for philosophers, especially when analyzing emotion, to rehearse such objections, but, in the end, conclude that something like the idea of an intentional object is necessary to make sense of emotions.[83] I wish to take a slightly different course. Rather than pointing out why the intentionality of emotions is such a problematic but nevertheless necessary notion, I intend briefly to suggest why it may be rather more straightforward, or at least no more theoretically worrying, than is the intentionality of belief. However, I can only sketch the broad outlines of an account of intentionality here; even a partial, much less a general, theory of intentionality would require a volume in itself.[84] My concern at present is only to sketch an account of the intentionality of emotions that is complete enough to (i) indicate why it does not commit one to odd ontological entities or nonstandard accounts of propositions; and (ii) illuminate the status and presuppositions of emotional states and characterizations of people as "emotional."

5.2 *The content of emotional states*

One reason why reference to the intentional objects of emotional states is apt to raise the specter of Meinongian objects[85] is a failure to properly distinguish two "types" of "intentional objects": (i) the "object" as the content of the emotional mental state; and (ii) the "object" as a thing, event, or relation in the world.[86]

Let us first consider the object *qua* content of the emotional mental state. I take it that in an obvious and intuitive sense, to say that a mental state is intentional is to say that it is *about* something.[87] Like a report of a belief, a report of an emotion refers to what the mental state is about. So, if Betty describes herself as being in emotional state *E*, it should always be appropriate for Alf to ask her to fill out that description by telling us just what

83 See, for instance, Trigg, *Pain and Emotion*, pp. 9–19. Wilson, in his *Emotion and Object*, is perhaps the most successful in resisting this.
84 Even Searle's book does not purport to present a general theory. *Intentionality*, pp. vii, 35. Although on many crucial points my analysis departs from his, it should be manifest that I draw extensively on his work.
85 It is worth noting that Meinongian objects really do play an important role in Meinong's theories of emotion and value. See his *On Emotional Presentation*. See also J. N. Findlay, *Meinong's Theory of Objects and Values*.
86 See Searle, *Intentionality*, p. 17.
87 Ibid., pp. 1–4.

she is *E* (for example, angry) about. If it is said "McDougall is afraid," we can then ask just what the fear concerns, that is, "the rabbit."[88] Now it is standardly assumed that this intentionality of emotional states derives from their association with beliefs. It has been claimed, for instance, that this was Aristotle's view:

> Including the thought of outrage among the essential components of anger . . . enables Aristotle to argue that an angry man is necessarily angry at some individual like Cleon (1378a 33–34). Aristotle's reasoning is clear enough. Anger is directed at some individual, because anger involves thought or belief about some outrageous individual. Beliefs have objects and, since beliefs are a necessary ingredient in anger, it follows that angry men are necessarily enraged at someone or other.[89]

Beliefs are necessarily object-directed and, thus, feeling conjoined with belief is also directed to an object. This same general thesis, that the intentionality of emotion stems from that of belief, informs the quote from Spinoza at the beginning of §5.1; for him, it was the idea of the *cause* of the feeling that provides intentionality to emotion. Perhaps, then, the intentionality of emotional states can be explained by the relatively simple thesis that the intentionality of belief transfers to any belief-feeling complex. Simply put, we might say: Belief (intentionality) + Feeling = Feeling-Belief (intentionality).

But clearly this will not do. If I have a headache, and I also believe that Alf is the cause of my headache, it does not follow that my headache is about Alf. The problem is that a headache, though certainly a feeling of sorts, does not admit of a content.[90] Unless the belief attaches to a feeling that is in some sense an intentional feeling, the belief transference model is obviously inadequate. Some feelings, such as headaches, tactile pleasure, etc., just do not seem oriented to objects, but affects such as anger, fear, etc., almost always are.

An alternative, and superior, strategy is to explain the intentionality of emotions using essentially the same model as we employ to account for the intentionality of belief, rather than making

88 I consider contentless "moods" in §5.4.3.

89 W. W. Fortenbaugh, *Aristotle on Emotion*, p. 14. Cf. Searle, *Intentionality*, pp. 29–36.

90 Brentano held that all mental phenomena, including pain, have intentional objects. *Psychology*, pp. 90–1. I disagree, holding that only some mental states are intentional. See Searle, *Intentionality*, pp. 1–2. See my comments on Trigg in §9.3.

the intentionality of emotions derivative of belief. That is, according to the transference account, some theory explains the intentionality of belief and, in turn, the intentionality of belief is then used to explain the intentionality of belief-feeling complexes; instead, I propose that the same general sort of theory can be used to directly explain the intentionality of emotions and beliefs. Let us begin, then, with the theory that explains the intentionality of belief. Now it is plausible to analyze the intentionality of belief in terms of a propositional content and what may be called a psychological mode or attitude;[91] indeed, this is implied by the notion that a belief is a "propositional attitude." If, for instance, Alf believes that it is raining, his mental state can be analyzed as [Believe (It is raining)];[92] a propositional content – It is raining – in a particular psychological mode – Belief. So should Alf fear that it is raining, he has a structurally similar intentional state, *viz.*, [Fear (It is raining)]; the propositional content is the same, but the mode or attitude has changed.

On this analysis, emotion affects do not always have beliefs as their objects. Consider:

(1) [Fear (The pope is never infallible)]
(2) {Fear [Believe (The pope is never infallible)]}
(3) [Fear (I believe that the pope is never infallible)]

My main concern is to emphasize that (1) is not essentially the same as (2) or (3); when Alf fears that the pope is not infallible, the content of his fear is not his belief that the pope is infallible as in (2) and (3). What he is afraid of in (2) and (3) is that *he believes* the pope is never infallible. Certainly that is clear in (3). I also want to argue that much the same is true of (2), which can be understood as structurally similar to:

(2′) {Disgust [Enjoy (Betty suffered a significant loss)]}

(2′) is a second-order emotion, that is, an emotion directed at another emotion; one is disgusted that one enjoys Betty's loss. Note too that it is not a special feature of belief propositional attitudes that type (2) intentional states seem, at least roughly, able to be recast in terms of type (3):

(3′) [Disgust (I enjoy that Betty suffered a significant loss)]

91 Cf. Searle, *Intentionality*, p. 6.
92 See ibid.

The contents of type (3) states are propositions about propositional attitudes. They are thus first-order propositional attitudes. In contrast, (2)-type states seem properly described as second-order attitudes, those directed at other propositional attitudes. Nevertheless, whether or not these are equivalent can be left aside here; what is crucial for our purposes is that (1) is distinct from (2) and (3).

It may seem that this analysis must be wrong. One may plausibly maintain that emotional states must have as contents beliefs about the state of the world, for how could Alf fear that the pope was never infallible unless he believed that there is a pope? Now I too will insist that emotions are grounded on beliefs, so I certainly do not want to suggest that emotions are conceptually independent of beliefs. But the question at present is whether the *content* of emotional states must include beliefs, and it is fairly clear that not all emotions necessarily do. Certainly we can have emotions about fictional characters, as one who is reading Tolkien (or listening to Wagner) may be disgusted by the greed of Dwarves. It is difficult to see how the content of this emotion involves any beliefs about the state of the world.[93]

But, one might say, even this involves a belief: that "Dwarves are greedy for precious metals." To be sure, this is not a belief about the state of the world; it is a belief about Dwarves, and it is this belief that makes sense of one's disgust. Leaving aside the difficulties with such fictional beliefs,[94] let us accept that in this case one's disgust is grounded on such a belief. But this still will not do as a general account, if it is meant to imply that one cannot have an affective attitude toward a proposition unless one believes it. For one can have contempt for something just because it is false, for example, [Contempt (The earth is 4,500 years old)]. More than this, though, one can be emotional toward propositional contents without any concern whether they are true or false; an idea can strike one's fancy or bore one, and this entirely independent of any assumption about its truth or falsity. The claim, for instance, that no great philosopher's surname begins with the letter "G" strikes me as being of this latter sort. Perhaps

93 Some argue that all fictional emotions are thus irrational; I consider this argument briefly in §5.4.2.
94 Searle mentions the problems with fictional discourse on p. 18 of *Intentionality*.

a less eccentric example is presented by a novel – not the characters or events portrayed but the novel itself – which can certainly be boring, interesting, or frustrating without any concern whether it is true or false in any particular respect.

This second example also points to an apparent difference between believing and many affective psychological modes: namely, a number of affects – for example, fear, enjoyment, or interest – do not seem to require a propositional content at all (and, if the content is not propositional, it cannot be the object of believing). That is, one might fear that Alf is going to hit you, but you might also simply fear Alf. These seem to be different mental states; one can certainly fear "Alf is going to hit me" without fearing Alf, and vice versa. To be sure, whether this distinction is ultimately sustainable will depend on how a theory accounts for nonpropositional contents such as "Alf." Obviously, if one insists that somehow "Alf" implies or stands for a body of propositions, and in that sense is ultimately propositional, the distinction will not be seen as significant. However, I will assume the more or less standard view that emotions really can have nonpropositional contents in a significant sense.[95]

To sum up: I have argued that, instead of understanding the intentionality of emotions as derivative of the intentionality of belief, they can be seen as intentional in much the same way as beliefs. Believing and affects are both psychological modes directed to certain contents. I have not argued, however, that believing is itself an affect, or that affect and belief intentional states are precisely the same. MacLean points to this more radical thesis. I mentioned earlier (§5.1) that some of his epileptic patients experienced, out of context, "a feeling of what is real, true and important." Such patients seem to feel a free-floating (see §5.4.1) "aura" such that any thoughts that occur to them strike them "as if this is what the world is all about . . . [this is] the absolute truth."[96] I shall not explore this suggestion that believing is itself a sort of affect;[97] if it be one, it is tied to our concept of rationality in ways in which affects such as fear and enjoyment are not.

95 See, e.g., Irving Thalberg, "Emotion and Thought," pp. 47–8.

96 MacLean, "Emotion and Scientific Bias," p. 342. In §4.1 I suggest another explanation: that this affect may be related to interest.

97 Meinong, too, believed that knowledge and believing were concerned with feeling, but he maintained that these feelings differed in important ways from "value feelings." See his *Emotional Presentation*.

I have insisted that the contents of emotional states are not necessarily beliefs. But, again, I do not deny that emotional states are grounded on various beliefs or that they may be directed to objects or events in the world, about which we have various beliefs. The next two subsections take up the relation between an emotional state (a content in a certain affective mode) and one's beliefs and the world.

5.3 Items in the world

It is a serious mistake to think that the content (propositional or not) of an emotional state fully captures the idea of the object of an emotion. That would be to suggest that emotions are somehow necessarily directed at mental phenomena. Emotions are typically directed at objects, events, etc. in the world; most emotional states are best understood as focusers of one's attention on certain objects in the environment.[98] This seems to be essentially Izard's view. According to him, emotional states are not disrupting influences but ongoing modes of organizing consciousness and attending to one's environment.[99] Thus, for Izard, interest-excitement is perhaps the most important of all emotions because it directs attention to those things in our environment that are complex and novel, and so is fundamental to learning.[100]

What, then, qualify as objects of emotion in this (second) sense? J. R. S. Wilson's analysis is useful here; he uses the "term 'object' to apply to [what he calls] items in the world of any category, and not just to particular persons or things." The following, for example, qualify as items in the world:

(i) events: a person can be overjoyed at the return of his son, or horrified by a catastrophe;
(ii) states or conditions of persons or things: a person can be annoyed by the untidiness of the garden, or worried about his wife's illness;
(iii) attributes or qualities of people: a person can be overawed by someone's intelligence, or envious of someone's happiness;

---

98 J. R. S. Wilson also recognizes that emotional reaction involves focusing one's attention. As opposed to someone who is consciously trying to focus his attention on a musical work because it is difficult, he tells us that a person who is emotionally responding to it finds his attention riveted to it. *Emotion and Object*, p. 83. See also Gabriele Taylor, "Justifying the Emotions," p. 391.
99 Izard, *Human Emotions*, p. 211.
100 See Izard, *Human Emotions*, chs. 8, 9. See also Tomkins, *Affect, Imagery, Consciousness*, vol. I, pp. 347ff.

(iv) relationships: a person can be jealous of his wife's friendships with another man;
(v) actions or behavior: a person can be ashamed by the way he treated his parents, or embarrassed by someone's bad manners.[101]

As Wilson points out, this sense of "objects" of emotion is ontologically unobjectionable. If we follow him in restricting the objects of emotion to items in the world, we can say that an emotion has an object (i) if the content is propositional, it succeeds in referring to items in the world; or (ii) if the content is nonpropositional, there is an item in the world corresponding to the content.

Emotional states, then, have objects in two senses. When Alf is angry that Betty was unfaithful, his mental state has an object *qua* content (Betty was unfaithful); but Alf's anger is not directed to the proposition "Betty was unfaithful," but to an event in the world, that is, her act of infidelity. However, whereas on my analysis all emotional states have contents, many are not directed at items in the world. Some examples of objectless emotions are: fantasy emotions (such as my disgust at the greed of Dwarves [§5.2]), emotions the propositional content of which fails to refer because the proposition is false (for example, my joy that Walter Mondale was elected to the presidency in 1984), and emotions whose content concerns future events, things, etc.[102] But this is not to say that emotions concerning fantasy, events that did not occur and future events are all on a par, one as valid as another because they all lack objects *qua* items in the world. To see why, we need to consider the notion of a grounding belief.

5.4 *Grounding beliefs*

It is generally agreed that emotions are somehow grounded in beliefs about the object to which they are directed, but not only is it disputed as to just what constitutes an "object," but also philosophers disagree about what it is for a belief to "ground" an emotion. "Grounding belief" is sometimes taken to be simply a "justifying belief": that is, in order for Alf to, say, appropriately be "afraid of snakes," he needs to have certain beliefs according to which snakes are somehow threatening. More strongly, some

101 Wilson, *Emotion and Object*, pp. 53–4.
102 See ibid., p. 57.

argue that these justifying beliefs must also have a causal role in bringing about the emotional state.[103] I begin (§5.4.1) by examining what I call the "standard case," in which Alf's emotional state is indeed directed to an item in the world; I argue here for an account according to which the beliefs that warrant the emotion are also causal factors in bringing it about. §5.4.2 then looks at the three cases I mentioned above in which the emotion is not directed to an item in the world; I try to show that the analysis of the standard case allows us to distinguish these cases in an intuitively appealing way. Finally, I briefly suggest in §5.4.3 how this analysis also provides a theoretical basis for distinguishing emotions from both moods and appetites.

5.4.1 The standard case

The thesis that emotions are caused by beliefs about their objects is appealing. For one thing, it captures the role of emotions in the life of an organism. A being capable of emotions monitors its environment for various cues; a cue that is hit upon then causes a certain affective response that directs consciousness, attention (and action; see §9.2) along a particular path. Emotions translate cognizance of one's environment into certain distinct modes of attention. To deny either the focusing or causal dimension would seem to lead to a distorted view of the role of emotions in the life of an organism. In addition, the causal relation is also deeply embedded in the language of emotions: an object is said to "evoke" or "elicit" an emotional "response."

Let us take a standard case of anger: Betty, who works with Alf, is angry at him. He asks what he has done to warrant anger, and she points out that his estimate on an important contract was wrong; it is his fault that the firm lost the contract and, as his supervisor, she is angry at what she says is his error. We have thus far shown (i) that Betty is angry; (ii) that the object of her anger is Alf and; (iii) (let us assume) that her beliefs about him warrant her anger. What can Alf say? Well, he might attack her beliefs [that is (iii)] in various ways, claiming either that they are not sound or that they do not really warrant anger (§6.1). But Alf might do something quite different: he might respond to her by

103 See, for instance, Bennett, *Spinoza's Ethics*, p. 274; Wilson, *Emotion and Object*; Bijoy H. Boruah, *Fiction and Emotion*, pp. 22–5.

saying: "Just like every time after we've been working hard, you're angry because you haven't slept enough, and you've been looking all day for someone to get angry at." The cause of her anger, he is saying, is not his faulty estimate, but her lack of sleep. What are we to say about Alf's reply?

Some theorists would insist that, strictly speaking, it is not relevant: regardless of the cause of Betty's emotional state, if it is directed at an appropriate object, it is an appropriate emotion.[104] To be sure, these theorists may well admit that such causal claims can have a derivative place in attempts to show that an emotion is inappropriate, but only as a roundabout way of demonstrating that, after all, one's beliefs about the object do not warrant the emotion. When Alf points out that Betty is angry because she has not slept enough, this may simply be part of a case that aims to convince her that he really has not done anything to deserve her anger. But on this view, even if he establishes his causal claim, his maneuver may fail; what if she replies "You're right about me being angry today; it was great luck for me that I hit upon an appropriate target like you to take it out on!"? Now even if Betty is right that Alf is an appropriate object of anger, something apparently is still amiss. It is what is wrong with Tolstoi's Countess Rostoff, who apparently had a physiological need to express an emotional cycle every few days – anger, melancholy, peevishness, mirth – and who was fortunate enough to have a family that so arranged things as to find her suitable objects.[105] Phenomenologically, we rebel at the idea that our emotional life might be so arranged that our emotions only coincidentally find appropriate targets.

I shall say that such emotions are *free-floating*. They recall Freud's description of anxiety neurosis, where a "*quantum of anxiety in a freely floating state* is present, which, where there is expectation, controls the choice of ideas and is always ready to link itself with any suitable ideational content."[106] That E is free-floating is always a reason – different from either absurdity or unsoundness (§3.1) – to criticize it. This is, I think, a basis for crit-

104 See Kenny, *Action, Emotion, and Will*, pp. 71–5. Cf. CAT(1) in §3.3 of the present volume.
105 I borrow this example from A. O. Rorty, "Explaining Emotions," p. 116.
106 Sigmund Freud, "On the Grounds for Detaching a Particular Syndrome from Neurasthenia under the Description 'Anxiety Neurosis,' " p. 39.

icisms of emotional states as physiologically induced (for example, a hormonal imbalance):[107] it is not that normal emotions have no physiological foundation, but they are also anchored in beliefs about the object.[108] To identify the beliefs as causal is thus to say that they are necessary conditions; they are certainly not the complete set of necessary and sufficient conditions (see §14.2). Consequently, if Betty comes to accept the criticism that her emotion is free-floating in this way, and simply happened to link itself to an appropriate object such as Alf, it seems that she is normally expected to cease being angry (or whatever) at him. "Leave me alone, you're in a nasty mood" or "You don't really love her, you're just euphoric today" both point to free-floating emotions and, further, imply that their linking to a particular object is fortuitous *and so* should be severed. Given all this, continuing to be, for example, angry with Alf is, I would suggest, inappropriate.[109] (The reply "Yes I'm in an angry mood, too bad for you that you were the first anger-appropriate person I met" functions not as a justification of my anger with you, but as a proclamation that I will not be moved by this appropriateness consideration.) Moreover, a general psychoanalytic perspective provides a deeper rationale for judging free-floating emotions to be inappropriate, even when they hit appropriate targets. To the

107 See Rorty, "Explaining Emotions," pp. 116–17.

108 This seems to leave the Affective-Cognitive Theory open to the same objection that I advanced against CAT(3) in §3.3. CAT(3), I argued, held that to be in emotional state *E*, Alf's arousal must be caused by beliefs relevant to the appropriateness of *E* in those circumstances. But, because the subjects' arousal was caused by epinephrine, it follows that according to CAT(3) no one was in an emotional state. But the Affective-Cognitive Theory is not open to this objection because it does not characterize affect as simple arousal. So, on my view, that Schachter and Singer aroused their subjects does not mean that they induced affective states. Arousal certainly leads to increased alertness, making emotional response more likely, but it does constitute the "feeling" aspect of emotion. If Schachter and Singer had managed to induce free-floating emotions, then I would hold that the emotional states were deviant.

On the relation between arousal and emotional states, see Mandler, *Mind and Emotion*, p. 117. It is a matter of dispute whether emotional experience requires physiological arousal. For evidence *against* the necessity of arousal, see Leventhal, "A Model of Emotion," pp. 10–1; see also note 58 in this chapter. Schachter argues *for* the necessity of such arousal in "The Interaction of Cognitive and Physiological Determinants of Emotional State," pp. 163ff. For a useful discussion, see Frijda, *The Emotions*, ch. 3.

109 Cf. Stuart Hampshire, *Freedom of the Individual*, pp. 94–5.

extent we assume that these emotions are caused by unconscious beliefs about some object, focusing the emotion on another object clearly does seem inappropriate (see §6.3).

5.4.2 Objectless emotions

So in the standard case, one's beliefs about an object cause one to experience an emotion directed at that object.[110] Now the problem with my joy that Walter Mondale was elected president in 1984 is that it is founded on a false belief that he was indeed elected. The emotion is based on the (false) supposition that he really was and that is why it is an unsound emotion. Its unsoundness does not stem from the mere fact that its content "Walter Mondale was elected president in 1984" does not refer to an item in the world. I might be a Republican who enjoys contemplating utterly ridiculous and fantastic events: the thought that Mondale was elected might strike me as hysterically funny. In that case, the emotion would not be unsound even though Mondale was not in fact elected because the emotion does not rest on the supposition that he was in fact elected.

Like my joy that Mondale was elected president in 1984, my disgust at Dwarves does not refer to any item in the world. This has led Colin Radford to insist that emotions directed at fictional characters are incoherent. If, literally, there are no Dwarves, then there is simply nothing to be disgusted at; so being disgusted at them seems to involve a fundamental inconsistency.[111] Inasmuch as we do not believe that there are Dwarves, we cannot entertain emotions about them. But we can now see the problem with Radford's claim: the mere fact that a content of an emotional state

110 Irving Thalberg has argued that one cannot claim that a belief about an object causes an emotion because the specification of the emotion requires that we identify the content of the emotion, and this will call on just those beliefs that are said to cause it; this, Thalberg argues, renders the causal claim vacuous. According to him, the causal theorist makes two claims: (1) Beliefs $(b_1 \ldots b_n)$ cause emotion E; but also (2) $E \rightarrow (b_1 \ldots b_n)$. Thalberg believes that this violates the principle that "you must be able to gather evidence of the effect which is logically independent of your evidence of its putative cause." "Emotion and Thought," p. 51. Thalberg's argument has been effectively criticized by O. H. Green in his "Emotion and Belief" (esp. p. 38) and Boruah, *Fiction and Emotion*, pp. 23–4. In any event, because I have insisted that the contents of emotional states need not be beliefs, Thalberg's criticism is not directly relevant.

111 Radford, "The Fate of Anna Kerenina."

does not refer to an item in the world does not render it irrational.[112] The irrationality of my joy at Mondale's election stems from its basis on a false belief; if I wrongly believe that Dwarves really exist, then of course my disgust is similarly irrational. But if my disgust does not presuppose any such existential beliefs about Dwarves, then it need not be irrational. It should be stressed that, though my disgust need not suppose that Dwarves exist, it still is based on other beliefs about Dwarves, and about these I may be wrong.[113] Based on your greater knowledge of fantasy literature, you may be able to convince me that I've been too quick to be disgusted by Dwarves; "After all, their preoccupation with precious metals leads them to fashion things of great beauty." Here we take a body of literature and tales as providing evidence relating to fictional characters. However, in some cases, for example, "whims," one's emotional state seems to have very little in the way of grounding beliefs at all. Thomas Nagel imagines someone with a whim that there should be parsley on the moon (Derek Parfit confirms that this is "an excellent whim").[114] The idea, we might say, catches one's fancy: the content of the emotional state causes the affect (amusement, interest, etc.).

Sound emotions about *future events* are not grounded on false beliefs nor do they avoid relying on existential claims. Indeed, emotions about the future are grounded on existential beliefs: that is, a necessary condition for their rise is belief that something will, or is apt to, exist.[115] This is, I would venture, the reason why of all the types of objectless emotions I have discussed we are most uncomfortable with the claim that future-oriented emotions do not have objects. Not only do they have content – they are about something – but they are also based on beliefs that a relevant object will exist. But we can capture this characteristic

112 For other, related, criticisms of Radford's view, see Michael Weston, "How Can We Be Moved by the Fate of Anna Kerenina?" pp. 81–93; Boruah, *Fiction and Emotion*, ch. 2. Boruah's book provides an excellent analysis of the debate concerning fictional emotions.

113 For a broadly similar account, see Boruah, *Fiction and Emotion*, chs. 1, 5.

114 See Derek Parfit, *Reasons and Persons*, p. 123. Nagel and Parfit explain whims in terms of desires; I argue that desires derive from affect and belief in §7.2.

115 The account defended here thus avoids Kenny's criticism that future objects cannot cause emotions because they do not yet exist. *Action, Emotion, and Will*.

of future-oriented emotions by pointing to the existential presuppositions on which they are grounded, thus avoiding appeal to nonexisting-but-potentially-existing objects.

5.4.3 Emotions, moods, and appetites

It has often been argued that not all emotional states (or emotion-types) have objects,[116] and in the sense of object *qua* item in the world, I have agreed. But it also seems that some emotions do not have objects in the sense that they are contentless; that is, they do not seem to be about anything at all. One who is merely "feeling blue" may not be depressed *about* anything. To be sure, philosophers tend to overemphasize the extent to which depression is contentless in this way; often, perhaps typically, someone who is depressed is depressed about something. But I do not deny that some depressed conditions have this diffuse quality. Some theorists distinguish such "moods" from emotions, others feel uncomfortable doing so;[117] it should be clear that the account I have offered provides a rationale for making the distinction. A mood, in contrast to an emotion, is a contentless affective state. Moods are much like free-floating emotions before they happen to hit a target: one just feels a certain way.

My analysis also allows us to see why it is a mistake to see anxiety as essentially objectless. The view that anxiety is objectless is plausible because the absence of a definite object seems to characterize anxiety. But cases of normal anxiety do indeed have *content*, though they are not directed to specific *items in the world.* "An anxious person," it has been said, "is not anxious about what has happened, nor even what is happening, but *about* what may happen."[118] So [Anxious (Something could still go wrong)] is by no means contentless: and that is why normal anxiety is neither a mood nor a free-floating affect. On the other hand, free-floating anxiety is just that; the problems with it are the general problems of free-floating emotions (§5.4.1).

---

116 As Wilson makes clear, the claim that each emotion type has its typical object is distinct from the thesis that each instance of the emotion has a particular object. *Emotion and Object*, ch. V.

117 A. R. White (quoted in Wilson, *Emotion and Object*, p. 24) and Taylor ("Justifying the Emotions," p. 329) do so; A. O. Rorty seems to resist this move in her "Introduction" to *Explaining Emotions*, p. 1 (but see her p. 3 on conceptual reconstruction). See also Frijda, *The Emotions*, pp. 59–60.

118 See Rycroft, *Anxiety and Neurosis*, p. 7 (emphasis added).

Some theorists also distinguish emotions from an appetite such as hunger. Given the account presented here, a primary distinction between hunger and a standard emotion is that the affect related to hunger is caused by somatic changes; it "rises from within": hunger as an appetite is not caused by beliefs about objects (see §7.2). Of course, these are not sharp distinctions. Some appetites such as the need for sexual outlet and hunger do often have an emotional character,[119] sometimes being triggered by beliefs about objects rather than by internal cues, as when I am hungary for a piece of Black Forest cake, even after I have eaten a large meal. And many moods, though diffuse, do tend to focus on some types of objects rather than others. But, though often blurry, if not simply vague, we do make distinctions between appetites, moods, and emotions. My account provides a rationale for the distinctions while also indicating why they are rough and tentative.

6 APPROPRIATENESS CONDITIONS

6.1 *Appropriate beliefs and objects*

The much criticized Internal Sensation Theory, I have argued, seems right on an essential point: at least with regard to the fundamental emotions, types of emotional states are characterized by unique feelings (that are not simply a function of arousal plus belief). The flaw of the Internal Sensation Theory is not, as the cognitivists would have it, that it relies on discrete feeling states, but that it identifies these states, or the internal perception of them, with emotions and/or emotional states. The cognitivists are right that emotions (almost always) involve beliefs. I have argued, then, that an emotional state is constituted by an affect directed at a content and, further, that the emotional state – in particular, the affective response – is grounded in (that is, justified and caused by) certain beliefs. (The exception here are those emotions in which a nonbelief content itself evokes a response.) I now make two further claims: in order to qualify as being in emotional state *E*,

(i) The grounding beliefs must be *E*-appropriate;
(ii) The content of the emotional state must be *E*-appropriate.

119 On lust and gluttony, see Konner, *The Tangled Wing*, chs. 12, 15.

Let us turn to (i). The basic idea is straightforward. If Betty fears Alf, she must not only must have her fear grounded in beliefs about him, but by certain relevant beliefs, that is, he is threatening or dangerous. It will not do for her to claim that she fears him because he is so thoughtful and harmless; that is an absurd sort of fear (§3.1). Now it is tempting to think that all emotions are like fear insofar as the grounding beliefs appropriate to the emotion are fairly specific – for example, "*X* is a danger." But despite attempts to do so,[120] using fear as a model in this way is deceptive, for the beliefs that appropriately ground fear are more well defined than most.[121] The beliefs that appropriately ground enjoyment, for instance, are much more open-ended. Indeed, we would probably be at a loss to enumerate them, except under such formalistic descriptions as "in some way good or enjoyable." One can enjoy something because one sees it as complex or simple, old or new, delicate or rough-and-tumble, etc. We might be more successful at formulating beliefs that *cannot* appropriately ground enjoyment: for example, "I enjoy it because it causes me nothing but pain" and, much more controversially, "I enjoy it because it causes you nothing but pain."[122]

In relation to the appropriateness of their grounding beliefs, then, we would do best to envisage emotions on a spectrum, ranging from the very specific to the open-ended. Toward the specific end of the spectrum we not only have fear, but also specialized emotions like "pity," "vanity," "resentment," and "indignation" – all these presuppose fairly specific sorts of beliefs about the object of the emotion. In contrast, the open-ended emotions are those such as enjoyment, distress, or, simply, liking and disliking. I follow Roger Trigg here in understanding these last two as emotional states.[123] As he argues, if liking or disliking becomes sufficiently intense, then they are obviously emotional (for example, joy, distress); so to deny that liking and disliking are

120 See O. H. Green, "The Expression of Emotion," p. 553. See also Lyons, *Emotion*, pp. 99–104.
121 For differing comparisons of the appropriateness conditions for fear and love, see Lyons, *Emotions*, pp. 79–80; Robert Brown, *Analyzing Love*, pp. 110–16.
122 The former is (roughly) one description of masochism; the latter, sadism. It seems to me that masochism raises real problems as to whether the enjoyment claim is intelligible; sadism is all too intelligible. See §10.4.
123 Trigg, *Pain and Emotion*, pp. 55ff.

emotions, it must be argued that they are too mild to qualify as emotions. At some point, a nonemotion would then become an emotion by crossing an intensity threshold. Unless one insists that emotions must somehow be turbulent and obviously unsettling, I see no reason to accept the threshold view; it does not seem wrong or radically revisionist to say that before a person becomes joyous, but is only liking something, he is emotionally responding to it.

However, we need to distinguish here occurrent from dispositional emotional states.[124] Ascriptions of emotions may refer to a particular emotional experience at a particular time (the occurrent sense) or a disposition to experience the emotion toward a certain object or type of object. In the occurrent sense, to "like ice cream" is to experience an affective state with "ice cream" as its object. But with no ice cream in sight, and no thoughts of ice cream dancing in my head, someone may ask me whether I like ice cream. If I say "yes," I am not reporting an occurrent emotion, but my disposition to experience the emotion of liking toward ice cream. So my affirmation that I do indeed like ice cream would refer to a dispositional emotion. (I return to dispositional emotions in §8.1.)

The first claim, then, is that emotions must be grounded in appropriate beliefs. I think it is fairly uncontroversial that the same line of analysis supports the second claim, that the content must be appropriate.[125] [Fear (The unmitigated benefit will accrue to me)] is also absurd (§3.1). Generally, if believing a proposition is an inappropriate grounding for an emotion, that proposition is also an inappropriate content. However, I will not belabor all this. Neither will I argue for the obvious claim that if there are appropriateness conditions on the objects of emotion *qua* content, so too will there be on the objects *qua* items in the world.

More interesting is that the existence of appropriateness conditions indicate one, albeit limited, way in which it is accurate to

124 On this distinction, see Lyons, *Emotion*, pp. 53–7; Trigg, *Pain and Emotion*, p. 116; Rorty, "Introduction," p. 2.

125 Gordon presents an analysis of appropriateness conditions in *The Structure of Emotions*, esp. chs. 3, 4. However, it is not clear that all the states he analyzes (e.g., some instances of "afraid") are properly deemed emotional. On this point, see Frijda, *The Emotions*, p. 101.

describe emotions as cultural artifacts.[126] Because emotions are not simply names for feelings, but require that the affect must be directed at an appropriate content and be grounded on appropriate beliefs, different cultures and languages may (i) recognize different appropriateness conditions relating affect, content, beliefs and emotional concepts; or, (ii) distinguish emotions that are not recognized by other cultures or, conversely, be without emotion concepts that are present in other cultures. Moreover, it follows from this that, in principle, in our own culture a person might be experiencing some affect caused by beliefs about, and directed at, an object, but because no emotion concept exists to cover that belief-affect-content-object conjunction, he is not in a recognizable emotional state. Two considerations however, limit the relativistic implications of these contingencies. Firstly, as I have pointed out already (§4.2), evidence indicates that the fundamental human emotions are panculturally recognized, and this includes not just facial expressions but, necessarily, some agreement about the characteristics of the grounding beliefs and objects of various emotions. Moreover, we have reason to think that some innate causal link exists between perception (of some types of objects) and affects, and it is more than likely that these will somehow be accommodated within our "culturally defined" emotional concepts.[127] So even though under cultural influences of various sorts these primitive emotions evolve in complex and diverse ways, we have reason to expect a fundamental shared core among most conceptions. Secondly, however, at least in our Western culture and its associated languages, the existence of open-ended emotions such as joy/distress and like/dislike ensures that most every object-oriented affect will be an emotion in at least one sense. Let me explain.

MacLean believes that all affects are characterized by a negative/positive dimension.[128] And Silvan Tomkins, upon whose work Izard builds, divided his main treatise on emotion into two

126 Clifford Geertz takes a much stronger view of emotions as cultural artifacts. See his *The Interpretation of Cultures*, pp. 79–81. I return briefly to this issue in §9.3.
127 See, e.g., Carl Sagan, *The Dragons of Eden*, pp. 148–9; Konner, *The Tangled Wing*, ch. 10; Frijda, *The Emotions*, pp. 271–7.
128 MacLean, "Sensory and Perceptive Factors in Emotional Functions," p. 12.

volumes: *The Positive Affects* and *The Negative Affects*.[129] Intuitively, this positive/negative dimension seems right; with the possible exception of startle/surprise, we do not have difficulty in deciding which of the fundamental emotions involve a positive attitude (joy, interest-excitement) and which seems to imply a negative one (fear, terror, sorrow, anger).[130] Both MacLean and Izard account for this positive-negative polarity of emotions by appealing to something very much like C. D. Broad's much-criticized[131] "hedonic tone" thesis. According to Broad, feelings (among other things) possess both hedonic and nonhedonic qualities, the hedonic being a quality of pleasantness or unpleasantness.[132] Interestingly, Izard and his colleagues have actually provided experimental support for the claim that people readily classify their emotional experiences on the dimension of pleasantness. Employing a "Dimensions Rating Scale" that asked subjects to describe their emotional experiences – how they felt – in terms of seven factors, including pleasantness,[133] Izard found that subjects widely agreed that the experiences of joy, surprise, and interest were generally very pleasant but that distress, anger, and fear were very low indeed on the pleasantness scale.[134]

Such findings can be interpreted in different ways; at a minimum, they show that people can agree on the pleasantness/unpleasantness of emotional experience. However, it is not my in-

---

129 Tomkins, *Affect, Imagery, Consciousness*. The exception to the positive/negative classification is surprise-startle, which Tomkins viewed as a "resetting" affect. Ibid., vol. I, p. 337, ch. 13. Cf. Trigg, *Pain and Emotion*, p. 57.
130 See Patricia S. Greenspan, "A Case of Mixed Feelings: Ambivalence and the Logic of Emotion," pp. 229ff.
131 For criticisms, see Trigg, *Pain and Emotion*, pp. 119ff.; Richard B. Brandt, *A Theory of the Good and the Right*, pp. 35–8.
132 C. D. Broad, *Five Types of Ethical Theory*, pp. 229ff. See also Wisdom, "God and Evil," pp. 18ff. MacLean writes: "Affects differ from other forms of psychic information in so far as they are subjectively recognized as being imbued with a quality that is either agreeable or disagreeable. There are no neutral affects." "The Hypothalamus," p. 660.
133 Izard, *Human Emotions*, p. 125.
134 Ibid., pp. 222, 263, 279, 289, 332, 367. It perhaps should be noted that at one juncture Izard seems skeptical of the positive/negative distinction, but there he interprets it as "good that one has the emotion"/"bad that one. . . ." This is clearly a different matter. Ibid., pp. 8–9. For my purposes, the greatest problem with Izard's study is that his pleasantness scale ranges from zero upward; thus, rather than rating an unpleasant experience negatively, subjects had to place it very low on the positive pleasantness scale. But cf. Frijda, *The Emotions*, p. 254.

tention to insist on resurrecting the hedonic tone theory. What I do want to insist upon is that the overwhelming majority of emotions, if not all, can be described – not fully, but partly – as a type of liking or disliking of something. (Although, of course, emotional experience is very often a complex mixture of liking and disliking.) This sense of liking (or disliking) is related to, but distinguishable from, that which is simply a low-level enjoyment or distress. The sense of "liking" I have in mind here is more akin to "having a favorable attitude toward" than to "enjoy or be pleased by"; it is not a type of particular emotional state but a generic notion that applies to positive emotional states. I thus call it *generic liking*. Now my point here is that, at least in our language and culture, even if one cannot make out a claim that one appropriately experienced a certain emotion toward something, one can usually with little difficulty make out a claim that one (generically) likes or dislikes it, for the appropriateness conditions for such a claim are extremely modest. So Alf may not be able to show that fear of Betty is sound, because he cannot point to anything threatening about her; he may not be able to make out claims about anger or resentment either. But it is much harder to show that he lacks grounds for disliking her. I do not believe it is impossible that he may lack grounds; the more we point out that her traits are just the sort he is attracted to, the more we may be puzzled about his claim that he dislikes her. It is thus not, it seems to me, simply a report of an internal feeling of his ("I feel dislike"), but rather is best understood as a very general and vague emotion claim.

6.2 Emotions and evaluations

It is very widely held that in some way emotions presuppose evaluations.[135] Certainly some do. Indignation, for example, requires that the indignant person has certain beliefs about the object of the emotion that can properly be called "evaluative." For someone to be indignant about another's transgression of some rule, it is necessary that the indignant person believes that the other should not have violated the rule, that the other knew, or could

135 See, for instance, Lyons, *Emotion*, ch. 3; Pitcher, "Emotion"; Trigg, *Pain and Emotion*, p. 57; Greenspan, "Ambivalence and the Logic of Emotion," p. 248.

reasonably have been expected to know, that the rule should not be violated and that it was possible for the other not to violate it. A similar analysis would apply to other "moral emotions" such as guilt and remorse.[136] But what I shall call "the evaluative theorist" does not simply maintain that some emotions presuppose evaluations: he insists that all do. As I pointed out in §3.3, William Lyons is such a theorist; in essence, he sees all emotions as physiological arousals caused by evaluations. I earlier described these evaluations as "evaluative beliefs," but, as with evaluative theorists in general, it is somewhat difficult to grasp precisely what he means by "evaluation." Although he sometimes asserts that it is noncognitive, at times it seems employed in such a way as to indicate a belief such as "*X* rates highly on scale *S*."[137] Let us begin with the "evaluative belief" variant.

According to a causal evaluative belief theory, then, evaluative beliefs must precede the emotional feeling/experience, for they cause it. Now I suppose it is always possible to insist that if Alf experiences a positive emotion toward something he must have first favorably evaluated it, even if he was not aware of doing so. But in many cases this strikes me as making the phenomenon fit the theory rather than vice versa. Consider, for instance, the following story told by Melvin Konner:

> When my firstborn daughter was six weeks old we went to the pediatrician with her for the usual scheduled visit. My general impression as a scientist – that newborn babies all looked the same and were quite unappealing, much less appealing, say, than a Barbie doll, or a pony – was confirmed by my experience as a father. Not only that, but this one was one of those that did not sleep. (I became convinced at the time that colicky babies are a small coterie of otherworldly spirits sent to certain new fathers to punish them for prior unnamed sins.)
>
> Anyhow, there we were, the three of us, in the bosom of medical wisdom, and I wanted an answer to a question. So I held the baby up to the light, squinted at the physician out of one bloodshot eye, and made my statement starkly and clearly: "Tell me, Doctor" (I said). "You've

136 I examine such emotions in §17.3.2. See Gabriele Taylor, *Pride, Shame, and Guilt*.

137 Typically, evaluative theories begin by suggesting that evaluations are beliefs, or at least very much like beliefs, but then extend the analysis to include attitudes, desires, etc. See, for example, Pitcher, "Emotion," pp. 334–5. Lyons tells us that emotions "are not really cognitive," and later calls them "evaluative attitudes" (*Emotions*, pp. 59, 63). Yet he talks of rating objects according to "reasonably objective" scales, but one does not, he says, gain knowledge through such ratings (p. 59).

been in this business a long time." (I now glanced meaningfully at the baby.) "She's ruining my life. She's ruining my sleep, she's ruining my health, she's ruining my work, she's ruining my relationship with my wife, and . . . and . . . and she's ugly." (Here the reader may well imagine that my usual professorial reserve was doing battle with other forces on the strained and tiny field of the vocal cords. And yet, swallowing hard, I managed to compose myself for my one simple question and peroration.)

"Why do I like her?"[138]

Clearly, Konner is not questioning whether his love for his daughter is really appropriate. The point of the story is that we all know why his love is appropriate: she is his daughter. At least in our culture, this is pretty much all the grounding belief that is required.[139] Yet Konner is pointing to the absence of any beliefs that are manifestly positively evaluative. On all the relevant evaluative criteria, negative evaluations seem to be implied. But these do not undermine his positive emotion; he does not love her because he has positively evaluated her, but rather his loves constitutes his positive valuation. Perhaps some might want to say that "she's my baby" is a positive evaluative belief, but then it is hard to see just what "a positive evaluative belief" is supposed to mean. If it means any belief that grounds a positive evaluation, then of course the Affective-Cognitive Theory requires that all positive emotions be grounded on such "evaluative beliefs." But this renders the evaluative theory truistic. If, on the other hand, it is claimed that some beliefs identifiable beforehand as "evaluative" must precede an appropriate emotional response, then the evaluative theory is dubious (see further §8.2). The question is whether it is more accurate and informative to say that Konner likes her because he has positive evaluative beliefs about her, or whether to say that he sees something good about her is just another way of saying that he does indeed like her.

The thesis that emotional responses are always caused by evaluative beliefs makes sense in the context of a strongly cognitivist theory that understands emotional states as undifferentiated physiological arousals caused by (or somehow informed by) par-

138 Konner, *The Tangled Wing*, pp. 291–2.

139 Some maintain that love is special, and is not based upon beliefs. For a defense of the relevance of beliefs to love, see Gabriele Taylor, "Love." Taylor, however, appears to defend an evaluative account of the grounding beliefs. See further §14.2.1 in this volume.

ticular beliefs. I have argued that emotional responses to objects exhibit a positive/negative, pro/con dimension, and cognitivist theories generally agree. But, because they also hold that emotions are only differentiated by the accompanying beliefs, they (understandably enough) derive the pro/con character of emotions from the nature of the relevant beliefs. Positive evaluative beliefs are said to give rise to positive emotions, negative evaluations to negative emotions. However, once we recognize that emotions are characterized by affective experiences with, as it were, an inherent positive or negative character, we need not posit evaluative beliefs at the root of all emotions.

Somewhat surprisingly, the claim that the evaluative character of emotions derives from the felt characteristics of the emotional experience is supported by Magda B. Arnold, probably the foremost proponent of the evaluative approach among psychologists. She conceives of an emotion as a felt action tendency[140] caused by an intuitive, generally "hidden," appraisal of the situation. In essence, such appraisals are intuitive likings or dislikings. The difficulty with this approach – an instance of noncognitive evaluative theory – is that, though she believes that these largely unconscious likings and dislikings cause emotional responses, she acknowledges that it is "all but impossible" to distinguish the appraisal from the emotion.[141] Because, then, this intuitive liking/disliking is so difficult to distinguish from the emotional feeling, it seems plausible to hypothesize that it is an aspect or dimension of affective experience. Affective experience, we can say, has an evaluative dimension: appraisal is a constituent rather than (necessarily) a cause of affects.

A deeper objection to theories according to which all emotional responses are caused by evaluations – especially the evaluative belief variant – is the place they assign to emotion in human life. According to such theories, emotions are physiological responses to evaluations, preparing the organism for action, but in no way

140 Theories that depict emotions as felt action tendencies have particular difficulty making sense of fictional emotions, which are typically emotions without action. See Boruah, *Fiction and Emotion*, pp. 104–7.

141 Arnold, *Emotion and Personality*, vol. I, p. 177; vol. II, ch. 2. For discussions of Arnold's theory, see Izard, *Human Emotions*, pp. 31–2; Strongman, *The Psychology of Emotion*, pp. 22–4, 81; Frijda, *The Emotions*, pp. 70–2, 180, 195, 202, 206, 237–9, 269.

helping to inform it about its environment.[142] In contrast, the Affective-Cognitive Theory understands emotions as ways of orienting us in our environment by rendering some features attractive or unattractive.[143] To a significant extent, the appeal of this theory depends not just on the type of evidence supplied by MacLean and Izard, and its ability to perform the tasks that we demand from a theory of emotion, but on whether one believes that emotional reactions do indeed perform this orienting role.

I have been arguing that emotions possess an evaluative dimension. This would seem to conflict with John McDowell's recent influential discussion of temperance. He writes:

> The temperate person need be no less prone to enjoy physical pleasure than the next man. In suitable circumstances it will be true that he would enjoy some intemperate action which is available to him. In the absence of a requirement, the prospective enjoyment would constitute a reason for going ahead. But his clear perception of the requirement insulates the prospective enjoyment . . . from engaging his inclinations at all. Here and now, it does not count for him as any reason for acting in that way.[144]

Because McDowell seems to accept that to hold something to be good is to acknowledge a reason to act,[145] his denial that a prospective enjoyment necessarily provides a reason implies that the enjoyment need not be seen as good. He thus appears to deny the claim of the Affective-Cognitive Theory that to have a positive emotion about something implies a positive evaluation of it as, in some sense, good.

A quick way to overcome – or, rather, to avoid – this challenge would be to concentrate on the *prospective* nature of the enjoyment: the emotional experience lies in the future. That is, one might reply that McDowell's temperate person can deny that anything is good about the object of enjoyment because he has yet to enjoy it. But this seems unconvincing (see §10.3); McDowell's temperate person would, I think, hardly be apt to see the object in a more favorable light if he actually partook of the

---

142 See Izard, *Human Emotions*, pp. 31ff.; Trigg, *Pain and Emotion*, p. 42.

143 For other defenses of this view, see Izard, *Human Emotions*, pp. 141ff.; Pugh, *The Biological Basis of Human Values*. See also John McDowell, "Non-cognitivism and Rule-following," pp. 142–3.

144 "Are Moral Requirements Hypothetical Imperatives?" p. 27.

145 See Michael Slote, *Goods and Virtues*, pp. 109–12. This raises the problem of "internalism" and "externalism," which I take up in §§10.2, 16.2.

intemperate enjoyment. Admittedly, I am not quite sure about this, because I find McDowell's temperate person puzzling. "Sure I enjoy it, but what is good about it?" does strike me as absurd: to see it as enjoyable *is* to see how it is in some way good. However, we can make sense of a temperate sort of person's outlook in three ways. (i) The temperate person might be saying that in another context he would enjoy the thing, but not in the present one. (ii) Alternatively, he may acknowledge that he would now gain some enjoyment from it, but in this context the enjoyment is outweighed by other, negative, evaluations of it.[146] (iii) Lastly, the temperate person might be saying that he would be distressed to find himself enjoying such a thing. Just as the masochist takes pleasure in the knowledge that he is in pain,[147] the temperate person may be distressed by the knowledge that he was enjoying an object that he had reasons to stay away from. All three possibilities are consistent with the thesis that insofar as one does enjoy something, one sees it in a favorable light. [According to (iii), one sees in a negative light the fact that one views it in a positive light.] I very much suspect, however, that McDowell has none of these in mind. In any event, in later chapters I shall analyze our concerns not to "give in to" or "act upon" emotions in terms of (i), (ii), or (iii). Consequently, I will show that we need not resort to the puzzling position of McDowell's temperate person.

6.3 *Stronger appropriateness conditions*

It may be helpful to bring together the various claims I have made in this chapter about the appropriateness of emotions. In order for Alf's emotion *E* to be a fully appropriate emotion, at least four conditions must be met:

(i) Alf must experience the *E*-relevant affect(s).[148]

146 McDowell's distinction between "silencing and overriding" is captured by the difference between (i) and (ii). It is thus clear that McDowell does not have (ii) in mind. "Are Moral Requirements Hypothetical?" p. 26.

147 See Trigg, *Pain and Emotion*, p. 154. As he stresses, to enjoy the fact that one is in pain is not to enjoy pain.

148 This does not require that every emotion has a unique affect or complex of affects. It is possible that E_1 and E_2 both are characterized by the same affect, *A*, but E_1 requires that *A* be produced by one set of beliefs and E_2 requires that *A* be produced by a different set of beliefs. Anger and indignation could, I suppose, be like this.

(ii) His emotional state must have an *E*-appropriate content.
(iii) His emotional state must be grounded in *E*-appropriate beliefs.[149]
(iv) His *E*-appropriate grounding beliefs must themselves be well-grounded, true, etc.

Some philosophers have proposed another condition:

(★) Alf must exhibit/experience *E* at a level that is proportionate to the attributes of its object.

In support of (★), it can be pointed out that we often criticize a person for being "excessively" or "unreasonably" emotional.[150] Should we, then, accept (★) as an additional requirement for a fully appropriate emotion? I believe we should not.

We have already rejected the proposal that an emotion such as fear, which has fairly definite appropriateness conditions, can serve as a general model for all emotions. The appropriateness conditions for emotions range from the specific to the open-ended (§6.1). Now the proportionality requirement implies that some level *l* of emotion *E* is uniquely appropriate to object *X*. But this presupposes fairly specific appropriateness conditions for *E*, and this is just what many emotion concepts are lacking. If Alf can appropriately enjoy a movie because it stars Harrison Ford, Betty because it is action-packed and the good guys win, and Charlie because it reminds him of the movies of his youth, the claim that level *l* of enjoyment is uniquely appropriate for all looks dubious indeed.[151] So, at best, (★) is only applicable to emotions near the specific end of the appropriateness continuum.

Now one might try to rescue the proportionality condition by relativizing it to an individual's set of well-grounded beliefs: given Alf's well-grounded beliefs about Harrison Ford and his acting in this picture, l_a is uniquely appropriate for Alf, and l_b and l_c are appropriate, respectively, for Betty's and Charlie's well-grounded belief sets. But what would it mean to criticize Alf for exceeding l_a? Given the Affective-Cognitive Theory, the criticism would take the form of something like "Alf's beliefs about Harrison Ford and his role in this movie do not justify him enjoying

149 Fantasy emotions may not meet this condition insofar as they are not grounded in any beliefs at all. But the *E*-appropriate content does evoke them, so a modification of (iii) would suffice.
150 See, e.g., Pitcher, "Emotion," p. 340; Ewing, "The Justification of Emotions," p. 64; Boruah, *Fiction and Emotion*, pp. 35–6.
151 See Mary Warnock, "The Justification of Emotions," p. 56.

this movie as much as he does." This would be a criticism of Alf's emotional nature: compared with some standard, he enjoys the movie too much. People do indeed make these sorts of criticisms of others,[152] but we should be cognizant that, unlike (i) – (iv), they are criticisms of a person's affective disposition rather than the rationality of the emotion. If Alf has some flaw, it is not that he has false beliefs or misunderstands the notion of "enjoy": his problem (if it is one) is that he is the sort of person who responds too favorably to this movie. It is hard to see what is irrational about that. Moreover, it seems simply wrong to maintain, as this reformulation of condition (*) implies, that given identical well-grounded beliefs, all persons should reasonably be expected to experience the same level of emotion. We certainly allow that, in a way that does not imply a flaw on anyone's part, people differ in their emotional sensibilities; indeed, evidence suggests that they do so from birth.[153] Consequently, it is only when emotional reactions radically depart from some norm that they are the targets of such criticism.

When we do observe a radically disproportionate emotional reaction, it is generally more fruitful to investigate whether the person has nonstandard, perhaps hidden, beliefs, than to criticize his affective disposition. Consider for example, Hans, who is radically disproportionately afraid of some animal – say, he is afraid of being bitten by a horse. One possibility is to say that, while the danger of being bitten might, in suitable circumstances, justify a little fear, a lot of fear is disproportionate, and, so, inappropriate. The alternative is to investigate whether Hans has some nonstandard beliefs that he relates to horses and which

152 Such criticisms of emotional responses often take the form of "moral criticisms" in the sense that the criticism is not internal to a particular emotion concept – "this is not a well formed case of *E*" – but provides other reasons why *E*, or this level of *E*, is not good in these circumstances. See Edward Sankowski, "Responsibility of Persons for Their Emotions"; Sabini and Silver, "Emotions, Responsibility, and Character." Joel Feinberg seems sometimes to have a similar sort of criticism in mind in his "Sentiment and Sentimentality in Practical Ethics," esp. pp. 21–2, 30. Ewing considers such external criticisms on p. 66 of "The Justification of Emotions."

153 See Stella Chess, "The Role of Temperament in the Child's Development." She and her colleagues scored children's temperament into nine categories in a longitudinal study (starting at two to three months of age) at three-month intervals for the first eighteen months of life, at six-month intervals until the age of five, then yearly. Chess found "significant degrees of consistency from one age period to another."

evoke such a terrible fear. And this, of course, is what Freud purported to discover with respect to little Hans – the animal phobia was grounded on castration beliefs and an association of his father and horses.[154] Hans's fear of horses thus violated condition (iv), for many of the grounding beliefs were unsound. But the real problem was a disassociation between the beliefs grounding the fear and its content; although the (unconscious) castration beliefs were *causal* factors in bringing out the fear of horses, their lack of relevance to horses implies that the grounding beliefs do not *justify* the content of the emotion. We cannot see how a rational agent with those beliefs about castration (assuming for the moment they were well-grounded) would be appropriately afraid of horses: condition (iii) is thus violated as the grounding beliefs must not only cause, but justify, the emotional state (see §3.1).

It would probably be going too far to claim that all seemingly disproportionate emotions will violate (i)–(iv); still, I very much suspect that radically disproportionate ones will. So, by rejecting (*), we do not reject all criticisms of emotions as disproportionate. However, one type of disproportionate emotion worthy of note meets the requirements of (i)–(iv). Imagine someone who greatly fears funnel-web spiders, rightly believing that they are aggressive and that their venom is extremely toxic. All this appropriately grounds a considerable fear. But assume the person does not know that an antivenin has recently been formulated, and, thus the probability of death from a funnel-web has considerably decreased. It might be said that the current fear is disproportionate because, if the individual was fully informed, he would not be as afraid as he is. This is precisely the move we often make when we believe someone's emotional reaction to be disproportionate to the object: we call attention to features of the object of which he is not aware that tend to decrease the emotional response. ("Do you know what she did to her last lover?") The beliefs the person entertains are appropriate grounds for his emotional response, but the response is based on a partial and incomplete grasp of the relevant features of the object.

In place of (*), then, we can add to our requirements for a fully appropriate emotion:

(v) Alf's grounding beliefs must be *E*-complete given his perspective: that is, they must be pragmatically complete.

154 See Freud, *Inhibitions, Symptoms, and Anxiety*, pp. 254ff.

This condition is obviously much more demanding than (i)–(iv);[155] perhaps it is often not met. Now in one respect the requirement of completeness, even if demanding, is not problematic; it does not pose any more difficulty than the requirement that a juror base a decision on all the relevant evidence. One can probably never be certain that all relevant factors have been considered, and at some point the information costs of further investigation might be such that one has good reason to stop looking for further factors. A person does not need to be certain that his grounding beliefs are complete – that he knows everything that is relevant to *E* – in order reasonably to be emotional towards *X*. However, it is always a relevant criticism of his emotional state that it is incomplete insofar as it ignores some feature which, if considered, would change his response. And it is a further, and more serious, criticism of one's emotion if it is knowingly or by intention incomplete, for example, the wife of a mafioso who sets out to have incomplete emotion-grounding beliefs by avoiding knowledge of her husband's "business activities."

Nevertheless, the notion of a complete set of *E*-relevant beliefs about something is problematic. It certainly does not even in principle require that one know all the *E*-relevant propositions about an entity. People emotionally respond to things under certain descriptions, and the nature of the description that regulates their response will influence what *E*-relevant propositions are relevant for pragmatic completeness. Say a metallurgist and a motor racing enthusiast are both fascinated by object *X*, the former under the description "formed of an exciting new alloy" and the latter "a great sports car." Now clearly what grounds the metallurgist's interests will be different than the those of the racing enthusiast; he may care nothing about its aerodynamics but much about its strength and molecular structure. But, given the perspective of each, both will be open to completeness arguments; the metallurgist's interest might wane if he discovers that the alloy is economically unfeasible to produce, the racing fan by the knowledge that the "car" is just a shell, with no chassis or engine. Just what constitutes an (in principle) *E*-complete set of be-

155 Patricia S. Greenspan would reject it. "[A]n emotion is appropriate," she tells us, "as long as there are adequate reasons *for* it, whatever the reasons against it." "Ambivalence and the Logic of Emotions," p. 237 (emphasis in original).

liefs about an object thus depends on the description under which one conceives of the thing. Nevertheless, despite these difficulties, charges of incompleteness are important in discourse about emotions; it is thus crucial to include something like condition (v) if we are to grasp discourse about the appropriateness or inappropriateness of emotions.

Thus far, I have been in the main concerned with the conditions for describing one's affective experience as a fully appropriate instance of emotion *E*, but some philosophers have also claimed that one can be inappropriately nonemotional. That is, some argue that the appropriateness conditions of emotions are such that one can go astray not only by being inappropriately emotional, but by not being emotional when it is appropriate to be emotional.[156] Given the analyses thus far, the crux of my position on this issue should be manifest. If Alf does not experience the relevant emotion because he has false (or ill-grounded) or pragmatically incomplete beliefs, it seems intelligible to say that his lack of emotion is based on a cognitive defect and so is in a way inappropriate. Because he misconceives the object, he inappropriately responds to it. But, if he has no such cognitive problems, but his complete set of sound beliefs just does not evoke in him the relevant affect,[157] any criticisms we make of him will be a very different sort. We may say that he is hard-hearted (or too soft-hearted), but, again, we are criticizing his affective nature. We can indeed do that, but I will show later (§10) that he would not be rationally defective to ignore these criticisms, but he would indeed be so defective to ignore the appropriateness requirements I have endorsed here. And, as I will argue, claims about rational defects possess a sort of objectivity that renders them fundamental in ethical theory.

156 See Taylor, "The Justification of Emotions"; Hastings Rashdall, *The Theory of Good and Evil*, vol. I, p. 156.
157 See Lawrence A. Blum, *Friendship, Altruism, and Morality*, pp. 201–3.

III

Valuing

In the previous chapter, I defended an "affective-cognitive" theory of emotion. As I warned at the outset of the chapter, a number of difficult issues in the theory of emotion were dealt with. But my investigations have pointed the way toward a more adequate account of emotional life than the hitherto dominant cognitivist approach. I shall not seek to summarize all my conclusions; nevertheless, three claims stand out. Firstly, I argued that emotions are based upon "feelings" or, as I have said, "affects." Moreover, I have maintained that these affects constitute evaluative responses to objects. Secondly, I indicated that, though internal sensation theories are right to focus on such "feelings" as central to emotional experience, they are wrong to identify these with emotional states. For emotional states have contents – often propositional – and they are founded on beliefs. And this gives rise to the third claim: because emotions have cognitive as well as affective elements, we can describe appropriateness conditions for the various emotions. And this means emotional states can be rationally criticized in different ways.

I now turn to relating this understanding of emotional life to valuing, in the sense of "caring for," "prizing" or "cherishing" something. The aim of this chapter, then, is explicating the sort of attitude or stance toward an object or person that can be described as valuing it.[1] One of the basic claims of the Affective-Cognitive Theory *of value* is that this activity of valuing is conceptually prior to ascriptions of valuableness or talk of abstract values. Put grammatically, the claim is that the verb (valuing) is

1 John Dewey stressed that "valuation" has two senses: "caring for," which I focus on here, and appraisal or evaluation in relation to some standard. I consider the latter in §§8.3 and 10.2. See Dewey's "Some Questions About Value."

fundamental; the adjective (valuableness) and the abstract noun (a value) are derivative [feature (a), §1.1]. I try to show in the remainder of Part I that those who fail to recognize this priority are apt to go astray. Those who take value to be primarily an adjective are typically led to a distracting search for the property or quality of "valuableness"[2] (Chapter IV), and those who stress the abstract noun[3] are too apt to see particular valuings as instantiations of general abstract commitments (Chapter V).

7 WHAT VALUING PRESUPPOSES

7.1 *The affect presupposition*

In an important sense, all our concepts have a practical bent,[4] but a concept such as valuing is, quite clearly, especially concerned with action, deliberation, and choice [feature (b), §1.1]. When analyzing such essentially practical concepts it is, I think, useful to begin with what may be called a (broadly) Kantian approach, inquiring into the presuppositions of the concept and the practices it informs. If we wish to grasp a practical notion, before we become too involved in complexities it is helpful to be clear about what sorts of conditions, beliefs, and outlooks are necessary for the concept to take hold. In particular, I wish to begin here by following Kant and asking what sorts of beings could develop and use the concept, and engage in the sort of practices it regulates. In examining the concept of duty, it will be recalled, Kant argued that neither a holy will nor a completely determined will would entertain such a practical concept; the very notion of a duty, he believed, presupposed that duty holders are capable of both autonomy and heteronomy. In a similar manner, then, we might begin an analysis of valuing by considering what characteristics necessarily pertain to valuers as such. What sort of entities can value?[5]

Given the deep cleavages among value theorists on most issues,

2 See, e.g., John R. Reid, "A Definition of Value," p. 673; Risieri Frondizi, "Value As a Gestalt Quality," p. 177.
3 See, e.g., Nicholas Rescher, *Introduction to Value Theory*, pp. 8ff., 57.
4 I argue this in S. I. Benn and G. F. Gaus, "Practical Rationality and Commitment."
5 For a similar approach – which, however, arrives at very different conclusions – see Donald Walhout, *The Good and the Realm of Values*, p. 40.

it is perhaps surprising to discover widespread agreement that only entities capable of feelings, emotions, affective response, and so forth, could develop value concepts. Santayana articulates this intuition thus:

> [A]part from ourselves, and our human bias, we can see in . . . a mechanical world no element of value whatever. In removing consciousness, we have removed the possibility of worth. But it is not only in the absence of all consciousness that value would be removed from the world; by a less violent abstraction from the totality of human experience, we might conceive beings of a purely intellectual cast, minds in which the transformations of nature were mirrored without any emotion. . . . No event would be repulsive, no situation terrible. . . . In this case, as completely as if consciousness were gone altogether, all value and excellence would be gone.[6]

It is fairly obvious how this intuition lends itself to a "subjectivist" interpretation, according to which emotion in some sense creates value or worth. But the thesis that only creatures who feel or have emotions would develop value concepts is consistent with a wide range of accounts, including those according to which value is in some way a property of objects. John McDowell, for example, has recently argued that value concepts would not take root in creatures incapable of affective response, yet he still insists that, in ways analogous to color, value can be understood as a property of objects.[7] Just as blind people would not develop color concepts, one might say, an affectively flat species would not develop value concepts. Indeed, following Meinong, such objectivist-inclined theorists may conceive emotional response as providing a special sort of knowledge of values without in any way creating those values.[8] This is true even if value is understood as a simple, nonnatural property; G. E. Moore, for instance, seems to allow that feeling could be a necessary condition for the cognition of goodness.[9] Indeed, as Nicolai Hartmann shows, the affect presupposition is even consistent with a Platonism of sorts.[10]

---

6 George Santayana, *The Sense of Beauty*, pp. 17–18.
7 John McDowell, "Non-cognitivism and Rule-following," p. 142. See also A. W. Price, "Varieties of Objectivity and Values." See §10.1 in this volume on "the color analogy."
8 Alexius Meinong, *On Emotional Presentation*, ch. 12. See also J. N. Findlay, *Meinong's Theory of Objects and Values*, chs. IX–X.
9 G. E. Moore, *Principia Ethica*, pp. 130–1 (sec. 79).
10 Nicolai Hartmann, *Ethics*, vol. I, p. 177. See J. N. Findlay, *Axiological Ethics*, pp. 67ff.

As the passage from Santayana illustrates, however, the affect presupposition is fundamentally at odds with a thoroughgoing rationalistic account of value according to which (i) nonerroneous belief simply mirrors the world, and so in no way reflects human affect, interest, will, etc.; and (ii) to value *X* correctly is just to have such a belief that *X* possesses value. Now to be sure (i) enjoys considerable currency; however, those who strongly endorse (i) do not typically accept (ii). Many contemporary followers of Hume, for instance, hold that belief reflects a world unrelated to human purposes and interests,[11] but they also insist that to value something requires more than simply holding a belief: some desire or attitude is necessary as well (see §7.2). Alternatively, I think it is at least prima facie plausible to hold (ii) if (i) is rejected, that is, to hold that valuing is essentially a matter of belief, but belief itself somehow reflects the human interest in the world. And some value theorists do insist that belief is inherently informed by affect or is in some sense related to human interest.[12] However, to explain valuing as essentially a sort of believing, when belief is understood along the lines of (i) above, does indeed raise serious problems for a theory of value. Most fundamentally, it is difficult to account for the motivational aspects of valuing if to value something is simply to hold a disinterested belief about the world. And it will not suffice for such a rationalist to simply affirm that value beliefs imply reasons for action and guide choice [see feature (b), §1.1]. Our aim is to provide a reasoned explanation (or critique) of the main features of the concept of value, not just to reassert them (§1.1); it is thus incumbent upon such rationalists to explain how and why some disinterested beliefs about the world provide motivating reasons for action. And that seems a fairly daunting task (see §16.2).

None of this demonstrates that a thoroughgoing rationalistic account of valuing is doomed to failure. It does, however, provide reasons for accepting Santayana's suggestion that an affect presupposition is more plausible than a "purely intellectual cast" presupposition. Not only, I think, do our intuitions indicate that the coldly intellectual species would not be capable of valuing, but we have rather more specific reasons (relating to motivation and

11 For a criticism of this view, see Benn and Gaus, "Practical Rationality."
12 See, e.g., George Schrader, "The Status of Value," pp. 196–204.

action) for thinking that purely rationalistic accounts of valuing are problematic. The real challenges to the affect presupposition, I would venture, arise not from the possibility of a passionless and disinterested intellect presupposition, but from two other more familiar presuppositions: the *desire* presupposition and the *need* presupposition. I now consider them in turn.

7.2 *Desire presuppositions*

At least within modern axiology, the chief rival to the affect presupposition is the will or desire presupposition. F. C. T. Moore, for instance, has recently offered a desire-based account of value that takes as its starting point the notion of a "pure will," abstracted from the "forms of our actual experience of willing."[13] Moore thus begins his theory of value by suggesting a will presupposition: unless wills exist that can introduce change into the universe, and to which the universe can either conform or fail to conform, a notion of valuing could not arise. Only beings capable of willing could entertain our concept of value.

Now, like Ryle, I find the faculty of will and the capacity for willing more than a little elusive.[14] But the concepts of wanting and desiring are hardly any easier to grasp; despite their fundamental place in contemporary ethics as well as philosophy of mind and action theory, they are particularly vague and amorphous. For example, Derek Parfit explicitly stretches "the word 'desire' to cover intentions, projects, and other aims."[15] E. J. Bond, though, distinguishes two senses of desire or want (he uses these synonymously, whereas others distinguish them.)[16] In the broadest sense, he tells us that "desire" is a "motivational propensity"; in a narrow sense, it is an "inclination" requiring "no effort of will." "It is in the motivational sense of 'want,' " he writes, "that every act of every person is done to satisfy some want of his or hers."[17] But even in this sentence yet another notion of desire is implied; although Bond depicts desires as propensities to act, he ends the sentence talking of satisfying desires, yet we do not normally think of *satisfying* propensities. We act in accord-

13 F. C. T. Moore, *The Psychological Basis of Morality*, p. 6.
14 Gilbert Ryle, *The Concept of Mind*, pp. 62ff.
15 Derek Parfit, *Reasons and Persons*, p. 117.
16 See David A. J. Richards, *A Theory of Reasons for Action*, p. 36.
17 E. J. Bond, *Reason and Value*, p. 11.

ance with propensities, but we satisfy things like appetites; appetites can give rise to propensities to act, but it is strange to talk of satisfying the propensity rather than, say, the hunger. "Satisfaction" language is more in tune, then, with desire characterized as cravings for certain objects. Other uses abound too: for example, desire is often enough explained in terms of preferences or of pro and con attitudes.

It is impossible in the present context to consider carefully all the significant ways in which "desire," "want," etc. are employed. Nevertheless, because the concept of desire looms so large in contemporary ethics and especially in theories of value, it is incumbent upon us to examine the notion of desire in some depth in order to determine whether any or all of the various formulations can provide a presupposition of valuing that is independent of the affect presupposition. I consider here four interpretations of "desire": (i) what I call the "craving-satisfaction model," (ii) the propensity to act formulation, (iii) the "stretched" interpretation of "desire" as "goal" or "end," and (iv) the preference account.

7.2.1 Craving-satisfaction

Although it is not generally recognized, probably the most important concept of desire in value theory is that premised upon the craving-satisfaction model. Value, it is often claimed, is to be defined as the satisfaction or assuagement of desire.[18] Now let us forget for a moment the dominant "Humean" theory that every action necessarily includes a desire,[19] and instead ask in what sorts of cases does it make most sense to say that an agent is acting to satisfy a desire, and then we will see whether we can plausibly extend this analysis to all rational action. A paradigmatic case, I would venture, is the desire of a hungry person for food. Here is a desire of which it is clearly appropriate to say that it is "as-

18 See, e.g., Christian Ehrenfels, "The Ethical Theory of Value," p. 372; DeWitt Parker, *The Philosophy of Value*, p. 14; Moore, *The Psychological Basis of Morality*, ch. 2, pp. 87–8. Perhaps the most famous desire-based account of value is that of Hobbes. See *Leviathan*, pp. 48–9 (ch. 6). See also Spinoza, *Ethic*, p. 217 (pt. 3, prop. IX); but see also pp. 293–4 (pt. 4, prop. VIII).
19 Bond says that this is the favored view today, citing, as proponents, Bernard Williams, J. L. Mackie, Richard Taylor, Gilbert Harman, and Roger Beehler in his *Reason and Value*, p. 3.

suaged" or "satisfied." In the case of hunger, as well as thirst and sexual desires, the agent is uncomfortable or unsettled and he has certain beliefs as to what will relieve the discomfort or settle him; together, these lead him to focus his attention and direct his behavior in such a way as to attain the satisfying object. Reflection, I believe, readily reveals that we all have experienced such desires.

Moreover, this analysis of the paradigm case can be extended to cover a wider range of actions. Even in cases where no unpleasant somatic or other disagreeable "bodily sensations" are present, the model can be applied by depicting the desirer as suffering from a longing that can be assuaged – a sort of mental discomfort or agitation that can be relieved by obtaining the desired object. The very notion of *assuaging* desires, I believe, implies some such notion. If, then, all cases of desiring are not just like being hungry, it may seem that they can be assimilated to the model of separated lovers, pining for each other. And, if we assume that people who seek something they would enjoy are, like the lovers, unsettled by not possessing it, the basic paradigm case might be extended to cover a wide range of goal-directed actions. Nevertheless, even allowing these sorts of extensions, it does not seem plausible to stretch the paradigm case so as to include all rational actions. Often enough we act without any felt discomfort whatsoever, not even the agitation of not achieving a goal. For example: if someone asks me the time of day, my response does not seem motivated by anything like a discomfort or a craving.

So it seems manifest that, even allowing for all plausible extensions of the paradigm case, the craving-satisfaction model is not broad enough to encompass all action. If no trace of a craving remains, what is left to be assuaged, and what does it mean to say that "satisfaction" occurs? Well, it might be pointed out that "satisfaction" is a complex (or vague) notion, including not only relief from discomfort but some positive gratification or experience as well. (Presumably that is why we typically endeavor to satisfy our desire for food rather than simply to extinguish it.)[20] Moreover, it has been argued that one can feel this positive sort of satisfaction without the preceding discomfort; according to one analysis, for example, a person can feel positively satisfied

20 See George Edgin Pugh, *The Biological Origin of Human Values*, pp. 215–18. I am indebted to Loren Lomasky for pointing out to me the distinction between satisfying and extinguishing desires.

when his expectations are met.[21] So, perhaps, desires might be construed as aims or expectations that, when met/achieved, result in some particular, positive, sort of satisfaction. But a little reflection shows that such a theory is either a false descriptive theory of action or a form of hedonistic prescriptive theory.[22] It is a false descriptive theory if it maintains that an agent always experiences this positive satisfaction when aims, goals, purposes, etc. are achieved. Very often, perhaps usually, such successes do not usher in any such feelings. We must, then, reject the claim that the assuagement of any desire (understood simply as achieving any aim) necessarily leads to some felt satisfaction.[23] Note, however, that the link between *craving fulfillment* and *satisfaction* is not open to this objection. Sometimes, to be sure, relieving a craving does not result in a positively satisfying experience, as when a hungry person with a bad cold eats but, because he can taste nothing, gets no joy from it. But insofar as satisfaction covers relief from discomfort as well, something that relieves a discomfort is ipso facto satisfying. Of course, no satisfaction at all (either positive or negative) will be found if the object sought is not one capable of providing relief. However, as it would appear Hume recognized, such desires can be criticized as irrational inasmuch as they rest on false beliefs.[24] An object is sought because it is believed that it will relieve the felt discomfort, but this belief is false, as when a person with a peptic ulcer seeks food to relieve somatic discomfort. And that is why attaining it is not satisfying. Nevertheless, it is still correct to say that, on the craving-satisfaction model, the assuagement of a rational desire is necessarily satisfying.

Now someone defending the positive satisfaction account of what it is to satisfy a desire may try to exploit this distinction between rational and irrational desires by arguing that all *rational* action aims at pleasurable, enjoyable, satisfying, etc. experiences. But, if that is the claim, satisfaction is not the inevitable result of obtaining a desired object; rather, satisfaction is then a substan-

21 See Theodore Benditt, "Happiness." See also John Laird, *The Idea of Value*, p. 147.

22 See Bond, *Reason and Value*, pp. 44–5.

23 This claim is indeed sometimes made; see Parker, *Philosophy of Value*, pp. 11–2.

24 Cf. Hume's two senses in which "any affection can be call'd unreasonable." *A Treatise of Human Nature*, p. 416. (bk. II, pt. III, sec. III).

tive aim by which the rationality of action is judged. This form of the satisfaction model thus collapses into a sort of prescriptive hedonism (§8.1).

Thus far, I have argued that the craving model (and its pining extension) provides an intelligible account of what it means for a desire to be satisfied, though it cannot plausibly be so stretched as to include all rational action. But, as should be fairly evident, such craving-satisfaction can be analyzed simply in terms of (i) affects, that is, discomforts or felt needs (see §4.1 on basic affects); (ii) beliefs that a certain *X* will assuage the discomfort; (iii) the focusing of thought and attention on how to obtain *X*, and perhaps contemplating *X*; and (iv) beliefs that some course of action, ϕ, is an appropriate way to obtain *X* (see §9.2). To take an example: if someone is experiencing pangs of hunger, has a belief that eating food will be satisfying, and further believes that going to the market is an appropriate and efficient way of obtaining food, we have an adequate craving-satisfaction explanation of the trip to the market. I am not claiming here that desiring is not necessary; rather, my claim is that if we take the idea of craving and satisfaction seriously, the claim that one acts so as to satisfy desire can be analyzed into affects, beliefs, attention focusing, and appropriate action. What remains to be labeled a "desire"?

7.2.2 Propensities to act

One quick answer is a "motivational propensity," a second conception of desire.[25] A standard reply to my account of market-going behavior would presumably be that, without a special motivational propensity to go to the market, the discomforts, beliefs, and attention focusing, will not lead to action. And that is why a desire is necessary for every action. Now certainly I do not want to deny that, unless one has a propensity to go to the market, one will not do so, if this simply means that one will not do what one has no propensity to do. But the question is whether

25 For a psychologically sophisticated explication of this account of desires, see R. B. Brandt, *A Theory of the Good and the Right*, pp. 24–35. Brandt, however, does not depict desires as primitives: ". . . enjoyments are basic to acquiring normal desires or valences . . . and not the other way around" (p. 89). Brandt, too, thus stresses "affect" in his account of rational action. However, because he adopts a motivational account of pleasure (pp. 35–42), his theory of rational action differs greatly from my own.

this propensity is an independent condition, or whether the affect-belief-attention complex provides a motivation. If the latter, then desire *qua* propensity, though necessary in some sense for action, is derivative. And it seems that it is derivative.[26] Consider the following two cases:

(A) The affect-belief-attention complex is present, but the agent has no propensity to act.
(B) The agent has a propensity to act, but this propensity is not grounded in any affects or beliefs.

One way to defeat my claim that desires *qua* propensities are derivative is to show that case (A) is simply an example of insufficient conditions for rational action; that is, because an independent and necessary condition is absent, it should not be puzzling or seem crazy that no action occurs. So, to use our paradigm hunger case, Betty feels the relevant uncomfortable sensations, believes that the discomfort could be assuaged by eating, and believes that she can obtain food by going to the market. Yet, she has no propensity to do so. Drawing on the analysis of §6.2, we could make sense of her absence of propensity in one of three ways. Betty may, in fact, believe that, given other beliefs and affects, she would not find the food satisfying. Perhaps she is a deeply religious person who is fasting, and the thought of eating "makes her sick." This is to say, then, that she does not really believe the food will be satisfying. Or, another possibility is that, though the food would be satisfying, Betty, being a religious person, would be very distressed by the fact that she was enjoying a forbidden object, and the distress here outweighs the satisfaction (see §8.4). Thirdly, and most mundanely, it might be that, again while the food would be satisfying, the costs of going to the market, or perhaps the costs of simply interrupting her present activity by eating, outweigh the satisfaction to be gained by eating. But assume that none of these possibilities characterize this case: despite (i) that Betty is feeling hungry, (ii) her belief that she would find eating satisfying, (iii) her belief that market-going is an appropriate, efficient, and available way to obtain food and, (iv) the absence of any countervailing costs of either eating or going to the market, she nevertheless experiences no propensity

26 E. J. Bond also argues that desires are derivative in this sense. See his *Reason and Value*, esp. chs. 1–3.

to go to the market or to eat. This, I submit, is by no means an unproblematic case of the absence of an independent, necessary condition for action. It strikes one as a sort of defect or craziness; indeed, it calls to mind Freud's description of a neurotic as one who has arrived at a remarkable and inexpedient attitude to life.[27] Moreover, a good indication that practical rationality has indeed broken down here, and we thus find the absence of motivational propensity incomprehensible, is that a psychoanalytic explanation would be appropriate and enlightening. By uncovering unconscious beliefs, fears, etc. that provide the person with reasons for not eating, the psychoanalyst could transform apparently crazy – certainly wildly maladaptive – behavior into a case of conflicting reasons for action. Her reasons to eat would then be overridden by her reasons to act implied by unconscious beliefs. Now all this suggests that a propensity to act is not somehow an independent feature to be superadded to the belief-affect complex, but is constituted and implied by the complex. That is why case (A) is crazy: all that is needed to act is present, but somehow the act does not occur.

Case (B) is, roughly, the opposite: the propensity to act exists apart from any grounding beliefs or affects. However, we cannot make (B) simply, as it were, the mirror image of (A); those who base their accounts of rational action on desire often hold that beliefs are necessary too:[28] one's description of the act as, for example, "market-going" itself involves beliefs. Let us say, then, one has simply a propensity to ϕ, acknowledging that some beliefs may be involved in understanding one's act as ϕ-ing. If propensities to act are independent and nonderivative, these freestanding propensities should not strike us as odd or surprising. Indeed, given the widely accepted Humean model of rational action, according to which desires are primitive and the basis for all action, it would seem that such freestanding propensities, so far from being puzzling, would be a standard feature of many rational actions. Yet we do find them puzzling. To see why, it will be helpful once again to draw on psychoanalysis, which concentrates on seemingly incomprehensible behavior and attitudes.

27 Sigmund Freud, *Introductory Lectures on Psychoanalysis*, p. 314 (Lecture 18).
28 But see Stuart Hampshire, *Freedom of the Individual*, ch. 2; Richards, *Reasons for Action*, pp. 32ff.

Freud's analysis of an obsessional neurotic focuses precisely on the apparently freestanding nature of his propensity to act. As Freud says, the obsessional has impulses that lead him to perform "actions the performance of which give him no enjoyment, but which it is quite impossible for him to omit."[29] If we understand desire as an "impulse or force"[30] acting on the agent, or even a tendency to perform an action, then it seems that those with freestanding desires suffer from the essential problem of the obsessional: they have a tendency to do things that are unrelated to any expectation of satisfaction, enjoyment, or any other explanatory belief. It is only because we generally know well enough why hungry people have a propensity to seek food and thirsty people are apt to drink that a tendency to act often calls for no further explanation. But when we do encounter apparently freestanding propensities we seek to render such compulsions comprehensible by uncovering their grounding in affects and beliefs.

But perhaps a desire theorist can, after all, deal with crazy propensities. Drawing on R. B. Brandt's notion of "cognitive psychotherapy,"[31] it may be held that a motivational propensity is irrational if it is extinguished when the agent reflects on all the relevant information and his other desires (I shall leave aside here problems with specifying what constitutes "relevant"). This (rough) idea of an irrational desire would seem (i) to allow a desire theorist to criticize some propensities as crazy without (ii) adopting an affect-based account. Moreover, this would not commit the desire theorist to saying that desires logically derive from beliefs; the test concerns simply the ability of desire to withstand reflection on certain sorts of information. But Brandt's proposal seems, at best, problematic. He is drawing here on therapeutic situations in which a patient possesses a desire to, say, smoke, and this desire is extinguished by recalling the adverse effects of smoking. In these cases, people come to therapists because they seek to eliminate some troublesome desire. Or, in more standard psychoanalytic cases, people seek treatment because they are sub-

29 Freud, *Introductory Lectures*, p. 297 (Lecture 17).
30 David Milligan suggests that this is a typical, though in his opinion inadequate, conception of desire. *Reasoning and the Explanation of Action*, p. 22.
31 Brandt, *A Theory of the Good and the Right*, ch. VI. See also R. M. Hare, *Moral Thinking*, pp. 101–6. We must remember, however, that Brandt himself does not maintain that desires are primitives. See note 25 above.

ject to obviously inappropriate emotions (§3.1). Now, to be sure, it often happens that, once cognizant of the irrational nature of their emotion, it evaporates. But (i) that the recognition of an emotion or valuing as irrational tends to extinguish it is very different from Brandt's claim (ii) that any desire that is extinguished after contemplation of relevant information is irrational.

Consider: on Brandt's account, Alf's desire to go to the dentist would be irrational if it is extinguished by his contemplation of himself sitting in the dentist's chair watching the drill descend into his mouth as it screams away at a high pitch. It may well be that even if he thinks of all the good things that will happen if he does go to the dentist – and the possible bad things like toothaches that will be avoided – the thought of that drill descending is enough to extinguish in him any propensity to go to the dentist. This would hardly show that his initial desire was irrational. Indeed, knowing in calmer moments that going to the dentist is the rational course of action, he may resolve to refuse to contemplate all the "relevant information," knowing full well that if he thinks about that screaming drill he will never get himself through the door of the dentist's office. He will rationally refuse to engage in "cognitive psychotherapy" because he knows that it will extinguish a rational desire.

To sum up thus far: I have argued that the conception of a desire as something that can be satisfied is intelligible on a craving-satisfaction model, but (i) this model cannot be extended to all rational action, and (ii) in these cases, desire can be analyzed in terms of affects, beliefs, objects of attention, and appropriate actions. I have also maintained that (iii) in the sense of propensity to act, desire is rationally derivative, requiring grounding in affects and beliefs. Now whether desire is understood as craving-satisfaction or propensity to act, it seems that a desire presupposition for value theory is unnecessary. Or, rather, we might say, that desire is "so entirely dependent on feeling" that an account of value in terms of desire is "after all, reduced to feeling,"[32] or

32 Ehrenfels, "Ethical Theory of Value," p. 373. This is a particularly significant statement, because he was the foremost proponent of a desire-based theory of value among the Austrian axiologists. See also Wilbur Marshall Urban, *Valuation: Its Nature and Laws*, p. 38. Cf. Hume's remark that " 'Tis from the prospect of pain or pleasure that aversion or propensity arises towards any object." *Treatise*, p. 414 (bk. II, pt. III, sec. III).

at least feeling and belief. The affect presupposition thus implies such desire presuppositions.[33]

7.2.3 *Attaining goals*

Someone upholding the importance of desire as an independent component of action might at this point challenge the craving interpretation of satisfaction. David A. J. Richards, for example, begins an analysis of desire with those paradigmatic desires for food, drink, and sex, but then goes on to say that "desires, importantly, have objects, objects which, when achieved, attained, or realized, *satisfy* the desire, which does not imply having a certain sensation or distinctive quality of feeling."[34] Now my argument thus far has tried to show that this widely accepted doctrine is far more problematic than it may first appear; once all traces of discomfort or craving are removed, it becomes very difficult to see just what it is to satisfy or assuage a desire. Again: What is left to be satisfied?

Although I believe that the intuitive appeal of desire satisfaction language is parasitic on the craving model – and that is why hunger, thirst, and sex are paradigms – one might try to articulate a nonexperiential conception of satisfaction along the lines of Parfit's "stretched" conception of desire, including intentions, projects, and aims. To satisfy such a desire would be, I take it, to achieve an aim, goal, or purpose. Strictly speaking, talk of "satisfaction" or "assuagement" still seems out of place, for one does not really satisfy, but achieves or fulfills, aims; employing W. D. Ross's distinction, we can say that desires (or wants) thus

33 I have endeavored to analyze desire in terms of affect and belief. In contrast, some seek to explicate enjoyment (an affect) in terms of wanting (desire). According to motivational theories of enjoyment, to enjoy an activity is simply to want to do it, to want to go on doing it, and to want to do nothing else instead. Leaving aside the difficulty of providing an adequate account of rational wanting that does not itself presuppose affect, motivational theories of enjoyment still are inadequate. They cannot, for example, distinguish a compulsive hand-washer from a binge drinker trying to reform himself. Because each has some want not to be doing what he is doing, it would follow that neither is enjoying himself. In fact, though, the drinker may well be having a good time while it lasts whereas, as Freud said, the obsessional really does not seem to obtain any enjoyment from his compulsive behavior. See Ryle, *The Concept of Mind*, p. 108.

34 Richards, *Reasons for Action*, p. 33 (emphasis in original). See also J. N. Findlay, *Values and Intentions*, pp. 179ff.

understood are *fulfilled* rather than *satisfied*.[35] So a desire presupposition for valuing would, on this interpretation, claim that unless we were creatures who sought goals we could not have developed the concept of valuing. Although this seems innocuous enough, it is, I think, crucially ambiguous. The notion of goal-seeking can be construed either *broadly*, so as to be the same thing as intentional or purposive behavior; or *narrowly*, so as to be restricted to project-making or end-seeking (where the ends are longer term or complex).

Alan Gewirth is among those who formulate an account of valuing based on the broad interpretation, depicting wants or desires as simply intentions, "so that in every action an agent acts more or less reflectively in accordance with his wants."[36] So, according to Gewirth, if Alf intends to ϕ, he wants to ϕ – he regards ϕ-ing as having some point or purpose. And, Gewirth insists, this in turn implies that Alf has some pro-attitude toward ϕ-ing, and "from this conativeness it follows that the purposes for which he acts seem to him to be good. Hence, he implicitly makes a value judgement about this goodness."[37] The argument thus seems to rest on the analysis of the relations among three concepts: (i) wanting, (ii) pro-attitudes, and (iii) value judgments (or seeing things as good). Let us consider more carefully each of the elements of his analysis of wanting and valuing.

(i) *Wanting*. Gewirth, as I have indicated, tells us that he employs "wanting" in the "intentional sense." To say that Alf wants to ϕ is, then, to say that he intends to ϕ. And, because all action is in some sense intentional, it follows that all action is concerned with satisfying (or, rather, fulfilling) wants, or performed in accordance with desires. Now this seems truistic, yet also misleading. An action, as opposed to a piece of automatic behavior, is necessarily intentional in the sense that the agent is intending to do this rather than that. Intentional action, we might say, is done for some reason.[38] So, if the claim that one always acts to "satisfy" or "fulfill" a desire reduces to the claim that action is nec-

35 Ross's distinction between want fulfillment and want satisfaction has been recently employed by Joel Feinberg in *The Moral Limits of the Criminal Law*, vol. 1, *Harm to Others*, pp. 84–5. See W. D. Ross, *Foundations of Ethics*, p. 300.
36 Alan Gewirth, *Reason and Morality*, p. 38.
37 Ibid., p. 49.
38 See G. E. M. Anscombe, *Intention*, pp. 9ff.

essarily intended, then it seems true, given the definition of action. But, if this is all that is meant, then why talk of desires and wants at all? All that needs to be said is that action is necessarily intended insofar as it is performed for some reason. Saying that we act so as to fulfill or satisfy our wants, or in accordance with our desires, seems to suggest either (a) something in addition to reasons are necessary for action, or (b) the reason for acting is of a certain sort, that is, to satisfy a craving. But Gewirth's use of "wants," so far as I can see, involves neither (a) nor (b), but simply the claim that action, so far as it is action, is intended. Although I think it is confusing to bring in the language of "desire" and "wants" here, in principle anyone who understands the nature of action (as opposed to mere behavior) must also accept this version of the thesis "no wants, no action."

(ii) *Pro-attitudes*. But perhaps this is too quick, for Gewirth stresses that wanting involves a "pro-attitude," which itself possesses three features. (a) If Alf has a pro-attitude, we are told, he attends to, or focuses upon, his purposes. "This attending need not be completely exclusive in its objects, nor need it be very intense in quality; but still, in a relative sense, it involves focusing on E [the purpose] sufficiently to constitute an awareness of E in contradistinction to other objects."[39] Because Gewirth appears committed to allowing any recognized reason for action as a "purpose" – to have a purpose in ϕ-ing is just to grasp the reasons for ϕ-ing – this notion of a pro-attitude implies that, when Alf does something, (to some extent) he attends to, or focuses upon, his reasons for doing it. But this seems far too strong a requirement for action, or even rational action. To be sure, cases in which Alf does attend to his reasons for acting are important instances of rational action: he deliberates about them, and acts with his reasons firmly before his mind. But, if this condition were necessary for rational action, one could not act rationally out of habit, for to act out of habit is to act without attending to, or focusing upon, the reasons for so acting. But it seems wrong to deny that habitual action can be rational. Certainly we can act on the basis of reasons without actually having them before our mind or attending to them. We have excellent reasons for not taking the quick way down from the tops of tall buildings, but we

39 Gewirth, *Reason and Morality*, p. 40.

seldom have these reasons before our mind when we take the elevator rather than the window. Of course, habitual action can be irrational. Rationality breaks down when, through inattention, a person mistakes the cues that trigger the performance that has become habitual, or allows the habit to govern action when the routine he has formed is inappropriate to the full range of the relevant reasons for acting. Someone accustomed to turning right at a certain crossroads each morning on the way to work acts irrationally when, through inattention, he fails to turn left when he is going on holiday. As a condition for efficient action, forming a habit may be perfectly rational, but it must include cultivating an overall monitoring capacity to prevent the routine taking over when, exceptionally, one has reasons to follow a divergent program. An absentminded person fails to organize his attention in such a way that his acts are those to which he is committed by what, on reflection, he would recognize as an overall regulative belief, for example, that today is the day for going on holiday, not for going to work.

So it is only in this very weak sense that one must attend to one's purpose when acting rationally out of habit: one must be able to attend to the cues that indicate the habit's appropriateness or inappropriateness. Some philosophers, though accepting that habitual action may be rational, make it a condition of an act's rationality that the agent be able to give at least an ex post facto account of the beliefs that ground his reasons for acting. But this too seems an overly strong requirement. A craftsman may know very well how to meet the various contingencies encountered in his practice, based upon true beliefs concerning the properties of his materials acquired through long experience, and yet be quite unable to articulate those beliefs. There may be abundant evidence, despite that incapacity, that he understands what he is about, that he can recognize his beliefs when they are put to him, and that if need be he can give his work his full attention, rationally suiting his performance to a conscious grasp of the problem. What seems crucial, then, is that one who acts rationally knows what he is about: he is focusing on, and attending to, ϕ-ing, not necessarily his reasons for ϕ-ing or the purposes informing ϕ-ing.

(b) Intentional action, then, seems necessarily to presuppose the first element of Gewirthian pro-attitudes in only an extremely extended sense. The second element of his account of pro-attitudes is their "directive or vectorial character." Other things equal, the agent tends to "move himself toward the attainment" of his purpose.[40] This once again suggests the motivational propensity account of desire (§7.2.2), and I shall not rehearse once again the difficulties with that version of desire theory. What is important here is that Gewirth's claim that "wanting involves a tendency to move oneself" translates into the claim "reasons to act are motivating." Consider. According to Gewirth, to want to ϕ is to intend to ϕ, and to want to ϕ involves a pro-attitude towards *one's purposes* in ϕ-ing such that one moves oneself to attain them. Now if, as I said, we can substitute "reasons" for "purposes," this pro-attitude towards one's reasons simply means that one tends to act on one's reasons. That is, if the pro-attitude is nothing but the tendency to move oneself to attain one's purposes, then it is equivalent to the claim that one's purposes are motivating; and if purposes are reasons, then Gewirth is claiming here that reasons for action move those who hold them to act. As I have argued elsewhere, this seems to me an entirely sound claim, but it concerns the motivational character of reasons and, as we will see in Part II, it is not necessarily about valuing.[41]

(c) But Gewirth's third feature of pro-attitudes goes beyond this. Not only, he indicates, does Betty have a pro-attitude toward her purposes *qua* tendency to achieve them, but she "has some favorable interest in or mind-set" toward attaining her purpose, "as against being indifferent or hostile to it." It is here the ambiguity between the broader and narrower sense of "purposes" becomes troublesome. On the narrower sense of purpose, for example, where Betty has ends or purposes that are part of her long-term plans – to become a movie star, to help humanity or whatever – it is certainly true that she takes some positive interest in her purposes or has a favorable mindset toward them. Gewirth, though, insists that one must view *all* one's purposes (that is, reasons to act) favorably: interference with *any* action whatsoever, he tells us, causes "at least momentary annoyance or dissatisfaction. It follows from this that there are no indifferent ac-

40 Ibid.
41 See Benn and Gaus, "Practical Rationality." See also Chapter VI in the present volume.

tions, 'indifferent' meaning that the agent does not care at all whether he performs the action or not."[42] Here, I think, Gewirth confuses two fundamentally different points. To say that one resents interferences with one's action, or sees interferences as an insult, is to be distinguished from the claim that one always values or prizes the reasons one has for action. The first does not imply the second. I shall later (§24) argue that the first claim is, essentially, valid: agents of a certain sort do indeed resent unjustified interferences with their self-directed activity. But this is not at all the same as looking "favorably" at one's reasons. One can, and often does, have reasons to act that one would rather not have, and would be happy if they could vanish. Consequently, one can welcome an interference with one's action that stops one from performing a burdensome duty, even while resenting it *qua* interference with one's agency. Thus, I may find my reasons to discuss philosophy with an obstinate student burdensome, and wish that such discussions were not a requirement of my role as teacher. And, if an inconsiderate colleague barges into my room and ends this burdensome discussion, I may well feel a distinct relief. The only way one must look at one's reasons (purposes) in a favorable light is seeing them for what they are: reasons to act in one way rather than another. Gewirth seems right to this extent: a rational person cannot be totally indifferent when faced with reasons, that is, he must be motivated to act in accordance with them.[43]

(iii) *Value judgments.* Based on his analyses of wanting and pro-attitudes, Gewirth concludes that "I do X for purpose E" implies a value judgment "E is good."[44] The conativeness of action implies a judgment of value. "Good" here is to be understood as having "the common illocutionary force of expressing a favorable, positive evaluation. . . . [T]o say that they are good is to give expression to these attitudes." And so, Gewirth claims, every agent implicitly makes a judgment of goodness expressing these attitudes toward his own purpose.[45] We are now in a position to reject this claim. Because we seriously qualified claim ii(a), and

42 Gewirth, *Reason and Morality*, p. 40.
43 This problem raises basic questions concerning practical rationality; I consider these in more depth in §16.
44 Gewirth, *Reason and Morality*, p. 49.
45 Ibid., pp. 51–2.

rejected altogether ii(c) – except insofar as it reiterates ii(b)'s claim that reasons to act motivate – we need not accept the claim that one must "prize" one's purposes.[46] Only in the weakest of senses need one attend to these purposes when acting; and one need not view them in a favorable light. One need only see them as reasons to act that move to action.

It is useful to stress again how much more plausible Gewirth's conclusion becomes if one takes a narrower interpretation of "purposes." Our longer-term and more general aims are important parts of our value systems and, certainly, are generally prized or cherished. But, pretty obviously, in this narrow sense, "purposes," "goals," etc. cannot stand in for the notion of "desire"; I know of no one who explicitly equates desire with long-term goals. Moreover, it does not seem very helpful to say that only a species capable of seeking such goals would develop the concept of valuing; the notions of one's regulative goals or ends and one's values are pretty much synonymous.[47] To say that only goal-seeking creatures could value or entertain values, if not precisely empty, does not seem too enlightening. In any case, I aim to explain long-term goals in terms of what we find of value rather than vice versa; I hope to demonstrate that my procedure leads to a more enlightening conception of values (Chapter V).

7.2.4 *Preferences*

One other common interpretation of "desire" should be mentioned, though given what has already been said it need not long detain us. Sometimes, especially in utilitarian theories, the notion of a preference is treated as a sort of substitute for desire, as for example in R. M. Hare's *Moral Thinking*.[48] Admittedly, the language of preference is not identical with that based on desire, for example, backward-looking preferences seem to make more sense than do desires for things that are in the past; still, at least in some ethical theories, preferences play essentially the role traditionally occupied by desires. One might, then, translate "Betty

46 Ibid., p. 52.
47 See, for instance, Charles Fried, *An Anatomy of Values*, p. 11, but see also p. 51, where ends are said to "express" values.
48 See R. M. Hare, *Moral Thinking*, pp. 17, 185, 215, and the "Desire" entry in the index. On p. 17 Hare indicates that "preference" may be a more comprehensive notion.

wants *X*" as "Betty prefers having *X* to not having *X*";[49] to provide her with *X* is thus said to *satisfy* her preference. (Once again, describing this as a sort of satisfaction is a bit misleading; it seems more appropriate to say that we act in accordance with the preferences of others, or that we give them what they prefer.) But consider: either Betty has a reason for preferring having *X* or she does not. If she does have a reason, then the preference can be said to derive from this reason. And if "preference" is understood as disposition to choose, this account implies that preferences are tendencies to choose for various reasons. But, if this is so, then it seems that preferences are just a special case of dispositions to rational action, that is, actions where one chooses among alternatives.

It has been suggested, however, that to value *X* *is* simply to have a reason for preferring having *X* to not having *X*, or for preferring *X* to something else.[50] Valuing, on this view, does not simply provide the basis for some reasoned choices [as it surely does: feature (b), §1.1]: *valuing is equated with reasoned choice.* But such a conception fails for much the same reason as the attempt to identify valuing with intentional action: it is mistaken to assume that one values something simply because one chooses it, or prefers its existence to its nonexistence. One may have nonvalue reasons for making the choice, as when a person chooses to buy a certain painting (rather than one that he believes to be superior) because he promised his deceased, art-loving – though not knowledgeable – father that he would acquire it if the opportunity arose. His reason here is a promise, and I see no need to complicate and distort the account by bringing in valuing, either of the picture or of keeping promises. Action aimed at promoting what is valuable is certainly a central, and indeed fundamental, type of rational action. However, as we will see later, the assumption that it is the whole of reasoned action both misses the point of principled action and misguidedly questions the rationality of much moral activity. In Chapter VI, I offer an alternative theory of rationality in action that allows for reasons to act, the *telos* of which is not the promotion of value and which thus firmly grounds the rationality of moral, principled action.

49 Ibid., p. 95.
50 S. I. Benn, *A Theory of Freedom*, p. 80. Benn suggests a less rationalistic characterization on p. 65.

COLLEGE FOR HUMAN SERVICES
LIBRARY
345 HUDSON STREET
NEW YORK, N.Y. 10014

However, those who use preferences as a rough equivalent of desire usually depict them as primitives in the sense that they need not be based on reasons: one just prefers *X* to not-*X*, for no reason at all. What, though, could it mean to say that a preference is not based upon reasons? Well, it may mean that Betty just likes *X*, though she is unclear why she likes it, or that she finds it somehow satisfying to possess in a way that she cannot articulate. But, as should be clear by now, both of these are essentially affective claims; if they do indeed point to the proper interpretation, "desire" once again derives from affect.[51] The other obvious possibility is that the preference is simply a propensity to choose: when confronted with a choice between *X* and not *X*, Betty finds herself choosing *X* for no reason at all. The arguments I presented relating to propensities to act apply here too: without any reason at all for choosing, Betty's propensity is apt to strike us as puzzling, not to say crazy. This is so even with apparently trivial choices, as for example if she always chooses chocolate over vanilla ice cream, though she does not enjoy chocolate more, does not find its color more pleasing, is not seeking to ingratiate herself with her chocolate-loving sweetheart, she doesn't even do it to save decision-making costs. She just always picks chocolate, for no reason whatsoever. This, I suggest, is much closer to a paradigm of neurotic, than of rational, action.

7.3 Needs presuppositions

I have been arguing that, in the types of cases in which it is an intelligible and useful notion, "desire" derives from affects and beliefs. An explanation of rational action cannot be built upon desire as a primitive element; desires that are ungrounded in affects and beliefs provide a model of irrational rather than rational action. Given this, I think we have good reason for rejecting the commonly held view that desiring is somehow the key to explaining valuing. If I am correct about the way in which desire enters into explanations of rational activity, desiring always points back beyond itself, to beliefs and affects.

Although not so popular as desire presuppositions, it is often

51 Hare acknowledges the "intimate conceptual relation between the cognitive, affective and conative states," though, no doubt, he would resist my analysis of the last in terms of the first two. *Moral Thinking*, p. 94.

held that value and valuing are ultimately best explained by reference to needs or interests. Although this view is typically inspired by Aristotelian ethics, which articulates value in terms of human flourishing and what is needed for it,[52] a need-centered account is not necessarily Aristotelian. Morton A. Kaplan, for example, argues from the perspective of systems analysis that "What is good for the system involves a relationship between environmental possibility and system needs. What is valued by the system depends upon its cognition of these relationships."[53] For Kaplan, it would seem that the essential presupposition of valuing is that the valuers are homeostatic systems and, consequently, have certain needs; the recognition of these system needs is the foundation for what is valued. Generally, then, the need presupposition asserts that only creatures capable of recognizing such needs, conditions for well-being, or interests would develop the concept of value or would be able to value things.[54]

This claim is plausible; from an evolutionary perspective, our status as beings with needs and conditions for well-being no doubt had much to do with the development of valuing. Still, it is not really obvious that creatures that value must be creatures with needs; it is a bit fanciful, perhaps, but we might speculate that angels, despite their lack of needs, could value and disvalue. If contemplation and appreciation imply a sort of valuing (see §10.1), and if one can appreciate without needing, valuing without needing seems intelligible enough. But leaving angels aside, the notion of a creature that can "recognize its needs" is open to two possible interpretations, both of which are objectionable as a basis for a theory of value.

According to the first interpretation, to "recognize a need" is to have a *felt need*. So, on this interpretation, something can only be properly valued by Betty if it fulfills a felt need of hers or (which is somewhat different) if it is "directly felt" by her as a

52 For a critical examination of such theories, see Gilbert Harman, "Human Flourishing, Ethics, and Liberty."
53 Morton A. Kaplan, *Justice, Human Nature, and Political Obligation*, p. 83.
54 Sometimes a much less plausible need thesis is suggested: all that is presupposed by valuing is that valuers have needs and be capable of behavior that satisfies these needs. Cognition, recognition, or consciousness is not required. On this view, amoebas value. For indications of this view, see Laird, *The Idea of Value*, pp. 301ff. See also Kaplan's remark about "dispositional behaviors" on p. 83 of *Justice and Political Obligation*.

fulfillment of a need.[55] An argument that I will more fully explore later on (§8.1) is relevant here: such an account is far too egocentric or, at best, too anthropocentric. A multitude of things are valued without any belief that they satisfy needs or contribute to human well-being, and it is not commonly assumed that this implies some mistake. To be sure, many of the things humans value are valued because they are good for the species, some group or individual. But not all: many environmentalists, for instance, value the preservation of some species or ecosystem quite regardless of whether these things in any way make humans better off. Indeed, some environmentalists are quite prepared to sacrifice general human well-being for the sake of these valued environmental objects (§15.3). I see no reason to revise the concept of value so as to rule out such environmental (or aesthetic)[56] valuations as being inherently confused. Unless we are given very good reasons for accepting such a revision of our understanding of value, we should reject any equation of the valuable with the needs or welfare of humans.[57]

So the first criticism of *felt needs* as a basis of valuing is that it is too narrow (the only way to avoid this is to stretch the notion of "need" beyond its plausible limits).[58] However, to the extent "felt needs" are indeed a foundation of valuation, they can be accommodated within an affective theory. As we saw in §4.1, MacLean identifies "basic affects" – "internal states associated with basic bodily needs" – and the "specific affects" relating to somatic sensations. More generally, though, insofar as a "felt need" is based on some discomfort, psychological agitation, or imbalance, it seems clear that such needs can be characterized as types of affective states.

Often, perhaps typically, though, it is insisted that "[n]eeding . . . is *not* a psychological state, but rather a condition which is as-

55 For a theory that at least partially characterizes value in this way, see Walhout, *Realm of Values*, pp. 56–7, 80.
56 For an argument that "our concern for the safety and condition of works of art" is not entirely derived from considerations of human benefit, see S. I. Benn, "Personal Freedom and Environmental Ethics," pp. 413ff.
57 The benefit dimension of value is, I believe, overemphasized by Kurt Baier and Nicholas Rescher. See Baier, "What is Value?"; Rescher, *Value Theory*, pp. 9–11.
58 Walhout, a need theorist, is aware of this and, so, expands value judgments beyond need to include objects that fulfill "variety" capacities. *Realm of Values*, pp. 41, 56.

cribed 'objectively' to the person who is its subject."[59] One way to articulate a thoroughgoingly nonpsychological, nonexperiential account of need is to (i) define "Betty needs *X*" as "Betty will suffer harm if she lacks *X*," and (ii) give an account of harming her according to which in at least some instances "*H* harms Betty" can be fully explicated without any references to her psychological states, for example, pain experiences, disappointments, somatic sensations, etc.[60] Whatever the merits of such a strategy as an explication of "needs," it is hard to see how it can provide the foundation for a theory of valuing. To be sure, it may well be preferred as an account of what is *valuable* for Betty, but our concern at present is her valuing of *X*. Now on the sort of radically nonexperiential account I have sketched, it is not at all clear why Betty's recognition that she needs *X* would lead her to value it in the sense of caring for it, liking it, prizing it, or cherishing it. After all, she simply has a belief that "Without *X*, *H* will occur"; and, though *H* does not relate to any tactile, somatic, or emotional affect of hers, she acknowledges that it fulfills the objective criteria of being "a harm." At least thus far in the account (and this is as far as I will now take it), it seems that she may rationally have no concern about, or interest in, either *H* or *X* (see §8.3). Moreover, I believe that those who have employed such impersonal and objective accounts of need have generally not been concerned with explaining what people value, but what is good for them, whether they value it or not.[61]

In any event, it seems to me that Brian Barry is essentially correct that "need" is a derivative category. "Betty needs *X* to achieve goal *G*" seems the most useful way of explicating needs, and that implies, as Barry says, that need is derivative: the most interesting justificatory questions center on *G*, the goal or end.[62] Although David Miller criticizes Barry's formulation, his own account seems to concur – despite his efforts not to – with this

59 David Miller, *Social Justice*, p. 129.

60 Ibid., pp. 130–4. Miller is considering "intrinsic" not "instrumental" needs here.

61 Ibid., pp. 129ff. Cf. David Braybrooke's remark that "what counts here is meeting the need, not the subjective value anyone puts on meeting it." *Meeting Needs*, p. 42.

62 Brian Barry, *Political Argument*, p. 49. But cf. Braybrooke, *Meeting Needs*, pp. 29–32. Miller acknowledges that Barry is correct regarding "instrumental" needs. *Social Justice*, p. 127.

conclusion.[63] Miller, who defends (i) in the explication of need *via* harm (see above), characterizes harming Alf as "whatever interferes directly or indirectly with the activities essential to his plan of life." And, because Miller sees Alf's "plan of life" as articulating a coherent picture of what Alf finds of value, Miller does seem to ultimately understand Alf's "needs" as those activities that are necessary to pursuing/achieving what Alf values.[64] So needs, once again, are explicated in terms of ends or valuings and not vice versa.

To conclude: I have distinguished felt needs and objective (unfelt) needs accounts. Felt needs, I argued, can be accommodated within a suitable affective theory. To concentrate simply on felt needs, however, results in an overly narrow account of valuing, implying that one somehow only values that which is felt to be good for oneself or for human beings in general. Not all needs, of course, are felt, and I have by no means suggested that unfelt needs do not exist. But insofar as needs have no relation whatsoever to feeling, I have expressed doubts as to how they give rise to the active caring for a thing we associate with valuing. Furthermore, it seems to me that Barry is right in conceiving the justificatory force of (unfelt) need as derivative of the end it promotes: and that suggests that the notion of value may be logically prior to need, at least to the extent need is a justificatory category (see further §26.5).

8 INTRINSIC VALUING

8.1 Hedonism and the Affective-Cognitive Theory

In the previous section, I considered three widely endorsed answers to the question "What sort of creatures are able to value?" My aim was to show that the answers "creatures that desire" and "creatures that recognize their needs" are problematic and/or not really basic. Having provided some reasons to be wary of embracing its traditional rivals, the initial plausibility of the affect presupposition is reinforced. However, even if we accept the superiority of the affect presupposition to its traditional rivals, it by

63 Miller, *Social Justice*, pp. 121ff. For a criticism of Miller's criticism of Barry, see William Galston, *Justice and the Human Good*, pp. 162ff.
64 Miller, *Social Justice*, pp. 133–5.

no means follows that a thoroughgoing affective theory of value is called for.[65] As I emphasized in §7.1, a wide variety of value theories have embraced some version of the affect presupposition while still denying that value is to be explained primarily in terms of affect or feeling. Often, I pointed out, affect, feeling, or emotion is understood as a sort of faculty through which we gain knowledge of a special sort of property – value – which is held to be in some sense objective. Granted all this, however, if the affect presupposition is accepted, then it does indeed seem that we have good reason to explore theories that focus on affect. The most straightforward and simple way to take account of the affect presupposition is to characterize value in terms of affective response. Perhaps the concept of value presupposes a species capable of affective experience because value, like emotion, is essentially concerned with feeling. If this is the crux of value, we avoid the problems associated with an epistemology according to which feelings perceive a quality – value (§10.1). Nor do we need to rely on the queer and elusive entities that J. L. Mackie says are characteristic of objectivist accounts.[66] If these are not necessary to explain feelings and emotions, we may be able to do without them in analyzing value. It thus seems worthwhile to inquire to what extent the thesis that value is somehow to be analyzed in terms of affects allows us to elucidate the main features of the concept of value. Only if this simple and straightforward hypothesis should prove inadequate to the task do we need to resort to more complicated accounts.

Now among the affect-centered accounts, probably the simplest and most widely known are those premised on what I shall call the hedonistic thesis, *according to which only agreeable, pleasurable or satisfying experience is intrinsically valuable, and, so, only such experience can be properly valued for its own sake.*[67] Affective expe-

65 This point is made by Lawrence C. Becker, *On Justifying Moral Judgments*, p. 52.

66 J. L. Mackie, *Ethics: Inventing Right and Wrong*, pp. 38–42.

67 The classic proponent of the hedonistic thesis is, of course, Jeremy Bentham. See his *An Introduction to the Principles of Morals and Legislation*, ch. X, sec. X. For a much more sophisticated analysis premised on the hedonistic thesis, see Lewis, *Knowledge and Valuation*, pp. 382–9, ch. XIII. I have grouped together here theories articulated in terms of pleasure and those cast with reference to satisfaction, though these are sometimes distinguished (e.g., ibid., pp. 397ff.). See also Laird, *The Idea of Value*, pp. 147–9. For an analysis of hedonism, see Bond, *Reason and Value*, ch. 6.

rience is the heart of the concept of value because only pleasure or satisfaction is in itself valuable; everything else is only valuable to the extent it gives rise to such experiences. (*Mutatis mutandis*, much the same can be said of disvalue in relation to painful or dissatisfying experiences.)[68] But, despite its long-standing appeal, the hedonistic thesis is seriously flawed. Perhaps the most familiar criticism is that it simply cannot account for many of our valuations: we sometimes value things that do not in any way give rise to pleasurable experiences. As is often pointed out, one might greatly value in itself – that is, not as a means to any other valued thing – a dramatic performance that is extremely disturbing and unsettling and not at all agreeable or pleasant.[69] It is rather less obvious whether the performance can be said to be "satisfying." As should be clear by now, "satisfaction" is a particularly amorphous notion, sometimes referring to an experience of some sort, sometimes to meeting a need, and at others to simply acting intentionally. But, in the context of affect theory, those who use "satisfaction" seem to have in mind some sort of mental feeling that includes, but goes beyond, pleasure. Yet it is unclear just what it is; if it is a sort of contentment at having one's expectations met (§7.2.1), then it seems that the valued dramatic performance need not be satisfying. Finding it a disappointing (dissatisfying) performance is certainly a reason to disvalue it, but one's positive valuing of it may not in any way arise from a feeling of contentment but, say, from its power to rivet one's attention or somehow grip one.

Whatever the satisfaction version of hedonism asserts, it must accept the hedonistic thesis that, because only satisfaction (or pleasure) has value in itself, one can rationally value a performance, event, object, etc. "as a means only to this . . . end."[70] David Wiggins rightly criticizes this thesis:[71]

---

68 Things are slightly more complex than this suggests: the hedonist can allow that one might positively value the absence of pain or disvalue that which thwarts pleasure. See, for instance, J. S. Mill, *Utilitarianism*, pp. 10–1. (ch. II, para. 2).

69 See Frondizi, "Value as a Gestalt Quality," p. 164; Victor Kraft, *Foundations for a Scientific Analysis of Value*, pp. 65–6; Joel J. Kupperman, *The Foundations of Morality*, pp. 85–6; Kenneth H. Simonsen, "The Value of Wilderness," pp. 260–1.

70 See Lewis, *Knowledge and Valuation*, p. 434.

71 David Wiggins, "Truth, Invention, and the Meaning of Life," p. 346. His

[O]ne cannot say without radical misconception that these states are all that is intrinsically valuable. For (a) many of these conscious states have intentional objects; (b) many of the conscious states in which intrinsic value supposedly resides are strivings *after* objects which are not states, or are contemplations *of* objects which are not themselves states; and (c) it is of the essence of these conscious states, experienced as strivings or contemplations or whatever, to accord to their intentional objects a non-instrumental value.

The problem, then, is that the hedonism puts self-gratification (or, rather, the gratification of selves) altogether too much at the heart of value; it fails to recognize that "in a significant sense, value-experience is object-directed while pleasure is self-directed."[72]

I suggest that the hedonistic thesis goes wrong on two points: it starts out with the wrong aspect of the concept of value, and it is based upon the wrong sort of affect. These errors are related. Because hedonism identifies affective experience with the intrinsically *valuable*, it is led to treating all objects as instrumentally valuable. And it is led to this error because it is built upon an essentially nonintentional sort of affect: pleasure (§5.1). Although, as Brentano recognized, pleasure can be intentional[73] – one can take pleasure *in* something – it still seems true that the model underlying hedonism is an essentially nonintentional sort of feeling, that is, an undirected pleasant experience. ("Satisfaction" does seem an intentional notion, but most satisfaction theorists do not recognize the implications of this.)[74] Now the important insight of twentieth-century axiologists such as Meinong and Scheler was that the feelings that are critical in value experience are intentional feelings, that is, those essentially directed out on objects.[75] This insight allows us to escape hedonism's error of maintaining that only feelings are intrinsically valuable. Rather, we can now say that all intrinsic valuing of objects in-

---

criticism extends beyond hedonism to all theories which insist that only states of consciousness have intrinsic value. See, e.g., Hastings Rashdall, *The Theory of Good and Evil*, vol. I, p. 65.

72 Aurel Kolnai, "Aesthetic and Moral Experience," p. 186.

73 Franz Brentano, *Psychology from an Empirical Standpoint*, pp. 89–91. See also Roger Trigg, *Pain and Emotion*, pp. 10ff.

74 See, however, Bond, *Reason and Value*, chs. 6, 8.

75 For Meinong, see his *Emotional Presentation*, pp. 114–15, and Findlay, *Meinong's Theory of Values*, pp. 269ff.; Scheler, *Formalism in Ethics and Non-Formal Ethics of Values*, pp. 257ff. See also Howard O. Eaton, *The Austrian Philosophy of Values*, pp. 223ff.

volves an intentional feeling. The affective basis of the concept of value is then focused on the nature of *valuing* rather than what is *valuable*.

The idea of an intentional feeling is not in any way odd or mysterious: we have already seen that emotions are characterized by intentional feelings (§5.1). The question arises, however, whether the intentional feeling related to valuing is a distinct sort of feeling – a special feeling of valuableness – or whether the feeling (or feelings) underlying valuing is of a more common and familiar sort. The question is not a new one: Adam Smith distinguished the moral systems of, on the one hand, his own and that of Hume and, on the other, Hutchinson, with reference to this general point. Some, says Smith, hold that "the principle of approbation is founded upon a sentiment of a peculiar nature . . . distinct from every other." In contrast to this moral sense theory of Hutchinson, Smith describes a second position as maintaining that "in order to account for the principle of approbation, there is no occasion for supposing any new power of perception which had never been heard of before: Nature, they imagine, acts here, as in all other cases, with the strictest oeconomy [*sic*], and produces a multitude of effects from one and the same cause."[76] The Affective-Cognitive Theory thus follows the route of Smith and Hume, seeking as it does to avoid any special feeling of value: the intentional feelings that characterize intrinsic valuings are those of emotions. Given our analysis of emotions, we have good reason for following Smith and Hume rather than Hutchinson: not only are emotions intentional feelings, but we also saw that it is widely agreed that emotions are somehow closely tied to evaluations (§6.2). So, given that we already have a class of intentional feelings that are bound up with evaluations, it hardly seems necessary to posit a special sort of value feeling. Consequently, we can say that, roughly (and, so, somewhat inaccurately), one values something intrinsically if and only if one experiences a positive emotion toward it; one intrinsically disvalues it if and only if one experiences a negative emotion toward it.

As stated, this characterization of intrinsic valuing is not quite right; as J. N. Findlay has noted, "not every passing twinge of

76 Adam Smith, *The Theory of Moral Sentiments*, p. 321 (pt. VII, sec. III, ch. 3).

agreeable feeling inspired by a situation amounts to valuation or in6 volves an attribution of value, but only one that represents a moderately stable posture of soul."[77] Essentially, the problem is that, though valuing seems a dispositional concept, we have seen that emotion concepts are both occurrent and dispositional (§6.1). That is, whereas "Betty values *X*" implies a relatively stable disposition on her part in respect to *X*, ascriptions of emotions to her may either refer to a particular emotional experience at a particular time (the occurrent sense) or a dispositional emotion. Thus, for instance, "Betty is raging at *X*" is occurrent; "Betty hates *X*" seems (generally) dispositional, and "Betty is angry at *X*" can easily be either (though perhaps it is more often used in the occurrent sense). Now all this suggests that valuings are manifestations of dispositional rather than (directly) of occurrent emotions.[78] And intuitively this seems right: though to say that Betty experienced rage at Alf is apt to tell us little, if anything, about her valuings,[79] to say that she loves him or hates him indicates a stable evaluative stance.

Although this seems generally right, the distinction between occurrent and dispositional emotions is, as is so often the case regarding such distinctions, not as clear-cut as it may first appear. To be sure, it does seem clear-cut if we consider two paradigm cases: (a) Betty's very uncharacteristic rage at Alf's forgetfulness, where she herself is more than a little surprised at her reaction and (b) her enduring love of him. Case (a) seems close to an isolated single-instance reaction, and (b) does indeed describe a stable posture of the soul. But what are we to say of (c), Betty's regular anger at Alf when he comes home late? Unlike (b), in which throughout long periods she can rightly be described as loving him, in (c) she is not angry at him throughout long periods, but instead has regular episodes of anger. Perhaps (c) should be described as an emotional disposition, to be con-

77 Findlay, *Axiological Ethics*, p. 7. See also Lewis, *Knowledge and Valuation*, p. 410. This may not be as crucial in what might be called the "Japanese concept of value." See Robert Edgar Carter, "Comparative Value Theory." Stanley Benn and I have considered some of the problems associated with cross-cultural comparisons of concepts in "Public and Private: Concepts and Action."
78 See Ian Davison, *Values, Ends, and Society*, pp. 29–30.
79 Rage is a particularly striking example because it often leads people to act out of character and harm that for which they care. See Melvin Konner, *The Tangled Wing*, ch. 9.

trasted with (b), a dispositional emotion. However, such categorizations are not my concern. Rather, the important point is that a theory of value, especially one that is to provide the foundation for public justification and a theory of right (Part II of this volume), will be primarily concerned with emotions of type (b) and, I think, type (c). Let us call both "dispositional emotions." I do not assert that cases like (a) tell us nothing about Betty's evaluations – at one point, she certainly negatively values Alf's forgetfulness – but (a) is pretty uninformative about Betty as a continuing valuer and how she responds to the world. Because in ethics and political philosophy, and as agents trying to reflect on the soundness of our own and others' projects and plans, our focus is on personalities that have some relatively stable orientation to the world, theories of value typically pay little heed to cases such as (a). This seems a sound approach. So long as we do not ignore the possibility of important one-off valuations (for example, of rare events), or so stress stability that only lifelong or entire adult life valuings are noticed, this focus on dispositional emotions is appropriate.

We can say, then, that Betty intrinsically values (or disvalues) X if and only if she has a positive (or negative) dispositional emotion toward X.[80] Observe how this avoids the two difficulties of hedonism that I noted above. First, dispositional emotions are diverse: one can be disposed to enjoy something, but one can also be interested in it, disgusted by it, afraid of it, or hate it. All these imply valuings and disvaluings. Thus, one may certainly value dramatic works which, just because of the features that make them disturbing, are also fascinating, interesting, and riveting. Interest-excitement's status as perhaps the most fundamental of emotions carries over into the analysis of valuings: being interested in, or fascinated by, an object is a fundamental type of valuing. The Affective-Cognitive Theory thus partially converges with R. B. Perry's theory of value, which takes as its basis a "motor-affective" notion of interest.[81] But, for Perry, in-

80 Of course, one can be ambivalent, that is, have mixed emotions. See §§8.2, 14.1. One can also have second-order valuings critical of first-order ones; see §§5.2, 6.2, 8.4.

81 See R. B. Perry, *General Theory of Value* and *Realms of Value*. For a recent defense of his theory, see Gene G. James, "Is Value a Gestalt Quality?" C. E. Izard acknowledges the "pioneering ideas of Perry" on interest in *Human Emotions*, p. 230.

terest is the sole foundation of all valuings and, indeed, disvaluing; consequently, he characterizes all disvalue as a "negative interest" – an interest in prevention or undoing.[82] The theory of emotions I advanced in Chapter II, however, assumes a multiplicity of discrete affects (both positive and negative) that can provide the foundation for emotions and hence, intrinsic valuings. Anger, fear, anxiety, hatred, disgust, distress, etc. all constitute negative valuings: we thus need not attribute both positive and negative dimensions to interest. Following Izard, I conceive of interest-excitement as a positive affect, grounding positive valuings.

Turning to the second difficulty of hedonism, it should be manifest that the Affective-Cognitive Theory does not in any way imply that a rational agent only instrumentally values objects. When, say, Betty is angry at Alf, she is *not* necessarily angry at him because she believes that he causes negatively valued feelings in her. Indeed, we had occasion to reject a theory of emotion just because it required beliefs about such causes (§3.3). The Affective-Cognitive Theory thus allows in principle for any sort of object to be valued or disvalued without any beliefs about causal relations between the object and feeling states.

8.2 Affects and attitudes

A virtue of the Affective-Cognitive Theory is that it integrates philosophical analysis of the concept of value with psychological investigation into evaluative states and processes. As social psychologists have often recognized, theories of attitudes are concerned with valuing and what people find of value.[83] Attitude theory, that is, explains the activities of prizing and disapproving, that is, valuing. The notion of a pro/con stance toward an object – or, to use the psychological term, positive or negative valence on objects, states of affairs, etc. – is at the heart of both valuing and attitudes.[84] I thus take "attitude" and "valuing" as synonymous – this is by no means an innovation.[85]

82 Perry, *Realms of Value*, p. 77.
83 "The object of an attitude is of *value* to the individual." Muzafer Sherif, *An Outline of Social Psychology*, p. 207.
84 See Norman T. Feather, "Human Values and the Prediction of Action," pp. 277–80. Among philosophers, R. B. Brandt makes most use of the notion of

At the most general level, it is manifest that the Affective-Cognitive Theory converges with most contemporary attitude theories, for it is very widely agreed that, though in some sense attitudes are cognitive, "affect is the most essential part of the attitude concept."[86] Until relatively recently, however, this fundamental role of affect was more of a vague, general, theoretical commitment than a hypothesis to be tested.[87] However, as we will see presently, recent work in the psychology of attitudes has begun to take the role of affect in determining attitude as a topic for investigation. But, in any event, it is clear that despite the general dominance of cognitive approaches in social psychology, affect has remained central to attitude theory; and it seems even more apt to be the focus of research as this dominance of cognitivist analyses is increasingly challenged.[88]

So at the most fundamental level it is certain that the Affective-Cognitive Theory accords with the mainstream of attitude theory. More interestingly, though, this theory converges with some attitude theories at a much more specific level. Consider, for instance, the much discussed, and empirically well-supported, attitude theory of Martin Fishbein and Icek Ajzen.[89] According to them, affective response is a function of one's salient beliefs[90]

---

valence, which he uses as yet another equivalent of "desire." Because, like many psychologists, I explain valences in terms of affect and belief, once again we see that desire is not primitive (§7.2). See Brandt's *A Theory of the Good and the Right*, ch. II.

85 Cf. J. N. Findlay's remark that pro- and con-attitudes are "new-fangled equivalents of valuing and disvaluing." *Axiological Ethics*, p. 6. Lawrence C. Becker suggests the same equivalence on p. 52 of his *Moral Judgments*. See also W. H. Werkmeister, *Man and His Values*, pp. 102–3.

86 Martin Fishbein and Icek Ajzen, *Belief, Attitude, Intention, and Behavior*, p. 11.

87 For instance, despite the impressive body of evidence they marshal for their theory, Fishbein and Ajzen devote little attention to showing that attitudes are actually affective. See ibid., pp. 217, 277.

88 This point is emphasized by Robert P. Abelson *et al.*, "Affective and Semantic Components in Political Person Perception," p. 619.

89 See Fishbein and Ajzen, *Belief, Attitude*, pp. 340–3; Martin Fishbein, "A Consideration of Beliefs and Their Role in Attitude Measurement," p. 257; Richard P. Bagozzi and Robert E. Burnkrant, "Attitude Organization and the Attitude-Behavior Relationship," pp. 913–29.

90 A significant finding reported by Fishbein and Ajzen is that attitude is determined by a relatively small number of beliefs. Arranging beliefs hierarchically according to the subjective probability that the object really does have the relevant attribute, Fishbein and Ajzen report that the five or six most probable beliefs have the predominant role in determining attitude; after, say,

about the attributes of an object and one's evaluation of each of those attributes. More precisely, where A is the attitude, b_i is the subjective probability that the object possess attribute i, e_i is the evaluation of attribute i, then:

$$\text{(equation 1) } A = \sum_{i=1}^{n} b_i e_i$$

Fishbein and Ajzen tell us that "evaluation" (e) is used synonomously with "affect";[91] consequently, we can interpret their theory as maintaining that the overall affective response (A) to an object is a function of one's beliefs about its attributes (b_i) and one's affective response to those attributes considered individually (e_i). So, in order to arrive at the overall valuing of an object, we simply sum up the valuings of each of the most salient attributes.

Insofar as attitude is understood as an affective response that is a function of a person's beliefs about an object, the Affective-Cognitive Theory shares much with Fishbein and Ajzen's summation theory. But they do not seem identical. The Affective-Cognitive Theory does not postulate that a person affectively responds to each attribute of an object (or each of his beliefs about it). Rather, I have proposed that overall evaluation is a result of the affective response to the object and the relevant grounding beliefs. So, it may seem that the Affective-Cognitive Theory points toward:

$$\text{(equation 2) } A = \sum_{i=1}^{n} b_i$$

According to equation 2, we need not consider individual trait evaluations, but only a person's beliefs about an object. But equation 2 is generally an inferior predictor of attitudes to equation 1.[92] Are, then, individual trait evaluations necessary to an adequate theory of valuing?

Equation 1, however, is not always a better predictor of attitudes: equation 2 is as good a predictor when all the evaluations

---

the tenth belief, marginal importance quickly diminishes. *Belief, Attitude*, pp. 223–4.

91 Ibid., p. 11n. But see p. 342, where they are included among beliefs.

92 Ibid., p. 227.

(e_i) are either purely positive or purely negative.[93] This suggests a hypothesis. Let us say that attitudes can either be (i) pure or (ii) ambivalent.[94] A pure attitude (or valuing) occurs when a person has either a purely positive or a purely negative affective response to an object. In this case, a person's attitude can be seen as his affective response to his set of beliefs about an object (equation 2). But when a person is ambivalent, that is, responds with both positive and negative affects, this simple equation is misleading. A person does not simply affectively respond to his set of relevant beliefs; he responds positively to some beliefs, and negatively to others. His total response will be ambivalent; if asked to depict his overall attitude toward the object, it will be (roughly) a summation of his negative and positive reactions. Now if this is right, we would expect Fishbein and Ajzen's evaluation variable to increase predictive power in cases of ambivalent evaluations, but not for pure evaluations. If the attitude is either purely positive or negative, then affective response (valuing) will be simply a function of the number and strength of beliefs one has about an object; in this case, one *is* responding to the total set of beliefs. However, in cases of ambivalence, one is responding to some of the beliefs positively and others negatively; thus, the supposition of equation 1 that one affectively responds to each belief separately will record this differential response. And, importantly, it allows in the calculation for negative reactions to cancel out positive reactions and vice versa.[95]

The claim, then, is that equation 1 is a superior predictor to equation 2 because it is sensitive to ambivalent reactions: in cases of ambivalence, valuing is not simply a function of salient belief because some of one's beliefs point one toward approval while others point toward disapproval. In these cases, the assumption that one affectively responds to each belief allows us to identify such mixed responses. But when responses are pure, the evalu-

---

93 Ibid., p. 227n.

94 See §14.1.

95 That is: according to equation 2, the more beliefs a person strongly holds about an object, the stronger will be his affective response. Say Betty has six such beliefs, all inducing a positive affective response. According to equation 2, if we add a seventh belief, the affective response will be increased. But say that Betty responds negatively to this seventh belief; instead of increasing her positive response, it will decrease her (net) positive response. Equation 2 could not capture this; equation 1 does.

ation variable does no work: in these cases, one's attitude is indeed simply a function of one's beliefs about the object, as equation 2 indicates.

The Affective-Cognitive Theory, then, seems compatible with Fishbein and Ajzen's attitude theory.[96] But it also is compatible with more complex accounts. Fishbein and Ajzen's theory is the leading example of what is known as a "single-component" attitude theory: attitudes possess only a single component insofar as they are exclusively a matter of intentional affect for or against some object – this overall affect being a summation of individual affective evaluations. Some attitude theorists dispute this; though these psychologists agree that attitudes are indeed affective, they insist that attitudes are complex constructs with additional components.[97] Some recent studies have supported a two-component view, according to which a person's attitude toward an object is *composed* of his affective response to it *and* beliefs about it. Interestingly, Richard P. Bagozzi and Robert E. Burnkrant have reanalyzed some of Fishbein and Ajzen's data, with the result that a two-component, affective-belief, model seems clearly superior.[98] Of particular interest from our perspective is the work of Robert P. Abelson and his colleagues. In two studies examining the role of affect in the overall evaluation of aspirants for Democratic and Republican presidential nominations in 1976, they employed an affect checklist that has much in common with the affects I enumerated in the last chapter. They sought to discover to what

96 Depending on the way in which the evaluation variable (e) is interpreted, Fishbein and Ajzen's theory is also consistent with what I have called evaluation theories of emotion (§6.2). However, that e does not increase predictive power in cases of pure affective response supports the Affective-Cognitive Theory: in these cases, we need not suppose evaluation occurs.

97 See, e.g., Milton J. Rosenberg and Carl I. Hovland, "Cognitive, Affective, and Behavioral Components of Attitudes"; Virupaksha Kothandapani, "Validation of Feeling, Belief, and Intention to Act as Three Components of Attitude." These are both instances of three-component views, including not only affect and belief but also intention to act. For considerations against including the last, see Bagozzi and Burnkrant, "Attitude Organization," pp. 914–15. Bagozzi and Burnkrant also cast doubt on Kothandapani's findings on p. 915.

98 Bagozzi and Burnkrant, "Attitude Organization," esp. p. 923. But see William R. Dillon and Ajith Kumar, "Attitude Organization and the Attitude-Behavior Relation: A Critique of Bagozzi and Burnkrant's Reanalysis of Fishbein and Ajzen"; Richard P. Bagozzi and Robert E. Burnkrant, "Attitude Organization and the Attitude-Behavior Relation: A Reply to Dillon and Kumar."

extent the various candidates made the respondents feel afraid, angry, disgusted, frustrated, sad, uneasy, unhappy, hopeful, proud, sympathetic, or, whether they liked or disliked them.[99] As with the Affective-Cognitive Theory, it was assumed that these affects are naturally either positive or negative (§6.2). Respondents were also asked to select from a list those traits they believed the candidate possessed, for example, honest or (more broadly) "would appoint good advisors." Two interesting results emerge: (i) negative and positive affective response are relatively independent, that is, no strong tendency was found to experience either all negative or all positive affects toward a single candidate (whereas trait ascriptions were more apt to be uniformly negative or positive. I consider this difference in §14.1). (ii) Affective response was a strong predictor of overall evaluation, but it was not identical with it, and trait ascriptions added to the predictive power of the model.

At this juncture, the second result is relevant. The two-component view suggests that a person's overall attitude to an object is a function of (1) one's direct affect response to it, and (2) commitments relating to it that derive from other things that one values or cares for. I will defer until §9.2 discussion as to how a valuing can be a rational commitment, but the fundamental idea is straightforward: sometimes one evaluates a thing favorably, acts toward it in preservative and caring ways, etc., not because one is attracted to it, but because it is a means to, or in some other way related to, something to which one really is affectively attracted. So, on this interpretation, the nonaffective component of the attitude are those rational, derivative, valuings to which we are committed by other, directly affective, valuings.[100]

Two considerations support this interpretation. (i) The traits used in the study do indeed seem very likely to relate to a variety of commitments and abstract values (§13) of the individual: for example, courageous, honest, knowledgeable, open-minded, immoral, selfish, reckless, and prejudiced. It is very likely that, given a person's various intrinsic valuings, he would be committed to some positive or negative valuing (in this derivative sense) of people with such attributes, regardless of his direct affective re-

99 Abelson et al., "Affective and Semantic Components," pp. 620–2.
100 This is not entirely accurate; see §9.3.

action. Even if one finds a politician very appealing, one's general disvaluing of "selfishness" may cause one to lower one's overall evaluation of him beyond the extent to which it diminishes one's direct affective response. (ii) Happily, this is precisely the interpretation that some proponents of multi-component views have themselves suggested. Milton J. Rosenberg, who has been one of the foremost theorists of the multi-component view, explicitly saw the "cognitive" component of attitude as the extent the object of the attitude was perceived as instrumental to some important value.[101] These "values" are the sort of abstract commitments – for example, to the welfare of others, prestige, personal independence – that we will consider in §13. For now the important point is that multi-component theorists endorse the thesis that attitudes can be composed of direct affective responses to the object (intrinsic valuings) and evaluations derived from other valuings (extrinsic valuings). The two-component view, then, maintains that Alf's overall valuing of *X* will be a function of his intrinsic valuing of (his direct affective response to) *X* and other valuings of his that relate to *X*.

To sum up: my aim in this section has been to show that the Affective-Cognitive Theory's account of valuing is compatible with current research into attitudes. Fishbein and Ajzen's summation model seems a good account of intrinsic valuing, and the two-component view provides a persuasive explanation of total (intrinsic and extrinsic) valuing. The central claim of the Affective-Cognitive Theory is that our valuings are affective responses to objects based on our beliefs about them; we have seen that this claim is empirically well supported.

8.3 Beliefs about goodness

I have argued in several places that evaluation is not a necessary precondition for affective response. Contrary to the evaluative theory of emotion (§6.2), I have maintained that emotional responses *are* evaluations but are not necessarily based on them. And I have just argued in relation to Fishbein and Ajzen's theory

101 See Milton J. Rosenberg, "An Analysis of Affective-Cognitive Consistency" and "Cognitive Structure and Attitudinal Affect." For a more recent analysis along these general lines, see Shelly Chaiken and Mark W. Baldwin, "Affective-Cognitive Consistency," esp. pp. 3–4.

that the evaluation variable is not necessary to predict pure affective responses.[102] But, although direct affective response is not necessarily based on prior evaluations, it certainly can be. Typically, when we value something we appraise it according to some standard; we judge it to be in some way excellent. As Rescher puts it, "evaluation is thus generally 'principled,' i.e., based on criteria that take account of objective features of the items (real or assumed) that are being evaluated. Value has, therefore, an objective basis and can be assessed by impersonal standards or criteria that can be taught to an evaluator through training."[103] The relation between valuing, value judgments, and standards is a central problem of axiology. The complete Affective-Cognitive account of these matters cannot be presented until we discuss value judgments in the next chapter. However, three claims can now be made:

(i) Direct affective valuings – intrinsic valuings – can be based on beliefs relating to standards.
(ii) These standards need not be about the ability of something to evoke an emotional response or the suitability of the emotional response.
(iii) Believing that something is good with respect to such standards is not a sufficient condition for being described as intrinsically valuing it, nor does it imply that one is rationally committed to valuing it.

I consider each in turn.

(i) Nothing said by way of criticizing evaluative theories of emotion (§6.2) was meant to imply that emotions cannot be based on prior evaluations based on standards. Indeed, I explicitly acknowledged that an emotion such as indignation necessarily presupposes some evaluative beliefs about the object of the emotion (§6.2; see also §17.3.2). More generally, however, most if not all emotions can be based on such evaluations. Following von Wright, we might say that something can be evaluated as good of its kind, technically or instrumentally good, medically good, and so forth. Let us focus here on the (oft-discussed) evaluation of an object as good of its kind, that is, *X* is an object of type *K* and, as a *K*, *X* is good.[104] For simplicity's sake, let us say further that the criteria for evaluating *X* as a good *K* are such that we

102 In any case, Fishbein and Ajzen depict *e* as itself an affective response.
103 Rescher, *Value Theory*, p. 56. See also Neil Cooper, *The Diversity of Moral Thinking*, ch. 5; Bernard Gert, *The Moral Rules*, pp. 52–5.
104 See Georg Henrik von Wright, *The Varieties of Goodness*, esp. pp. 19–20.

can rank various objects as better or worse *K*'s; we have in this sense a standard for judging whether one object of type *K* is better or worse than another.[105] Given this, we can see that such evaluations are beliefs about the object; they are beliefs that *X* is an object of type *K*, and that given the criteria of goodness for objects of type *K*, *X* is a good *K*. I see no good reason why we should deny to such evaluations the status of beliefs (§6.2). If I can be excused for once again reintroducing von Wright's example into the literature, to say that a knife is good seems reducible to a set of beliefs about the knife: that the object is properly described as a knife, that it has certain properties, and that these properties satisfy the criteria of goodness in knives. And, this being so, such evaluations fit into my schema for intrinsic valuings *through the belief variable*.

(ii) This leads to my second claim: because such evaluations are properly conceived of as beliefs about the object, they are not in themselves necessarily affective or about affects. They need neither be based on prior affective responses, more fundamental affective responses, or predictions of future affective responses. The belief that a knife is a good knife is quite clearly nonaffective, and any theory that insists that it is affective is obviously defective. In this regard, then, Rescher is quite right: evaluations (in the sense we are considering) are based on impersonal criteria that can, in principle, be taught, and do not require any personal affective response.

(iii) Neither of the first two claims seem particularly controversial. However, my third claim is often denied. I maintain that the sort of evaluative beliefs we have been considering – of which "*X* is, as a *K*, good" is a paradigm – do not imply valuings (or, indeed, value judgments). Lawrence Becker disagrees: to "valuate" *X* as a good *K*, he tells us, is to see *X* as good in at least one respect (that is, as a *K*). Further, he apparently wants to say, this implies some valuing of it. Thus, in this context he refers to our "horrible fascination" or "grudging or disturbed admiration" for a "rack [i.e., instrument of torture] as good of its kind."[106] He thus seems to believe that any "good of its kind" judgment implies some, perhaps weak, attitude that it properly

---

105 This is not to say, however, that judgments concerning goodness are essentially comparative. See §11.

106 Becker, *Moral Judgments*, pp. 34–6.

called a valuing of it. (Even though, he adds, one may not think it as good "on balance," and so, on the whole, one may disvalue it.)

This is wrong. To say that *X* is a good rack – has technical goodness as an instrument of torture – does not, I think, imply anything at all by way of valuing it. At most, this evaluative belief implies that if I am choosing racks on the basis of their technical excellence, I have reason to choose this rack over those that rank lower on the relevant standard. But compare this to "I find *X* to be a valuable rack," "I value *X* as a rack," or "I value the rack *X*." Although no doubt such valuings are often related to a belief about technical goodness, they go beyond a mere belief about technical excellence by implying some personal attitude toward such excellence. Consequently, one way to distance oneself from an evaluation of technical goodness is to be explicit that one does not value that sort of technical excellence. "That may well be a good rack, but I place no value at all on being good in that way" is both a sensible and informative thing to say. (Note that, in contrast, it is confusing to transpose the goodness and valuing terms in this sentence: for example, "Of course I value that rack, but I see nothing good in that sort of valuing" is, I think, puzzling. If it means anything, it is a way of calling into doubt one's own valuations as perhaps unsound.)[107]

So, according to the Affective-Cognitive Theory, the belief that *X* possesses goodness of some sort may ground an intrinsic valuing of it. That a dramatic performance achieved a high standard of excellence may ground one's interest; that a wine is a particularly fine variety may be a basis for enjoying it. The notion of a direct affective valuing thus by no means implies that all intrinsic valuings are somehow unthinking and unreflective affective reactions. However, as made explicit by this third claim, the Affective-Cognitive Theory does insist that merely believing that *X* is good (in the sense of fulfilling the criteria of goodness for its type set by impersonal standards), is not itself to value *X*, nor does it somehow logically commit one to valuing *X* (see §6.3). Let me briefly consider two types of goodness ascriptions that may seem to belie this claim.[108]

107 See §10.4.

108 I do not consider a third sort of goodness that many may be apt to think

(a) The notion of *medical goodness* points to a much closer tie between the belief that X is characterized by a certain sort of goodness and the valuing of it. To take an extreme example: say that X is a life-saving medical treatment, Alf recognizes that X is such a treatment and so possesses medical goodness and, further, that he rightly believes that X is necessary to save his life. Are these sufficient grounds for concluding that he values X or that any rational person would do so? Well, certainly we do indeed tend to have doubts about his rationality if he does not value the treatment at all. How can anyone who is rational evaluate something as medically good and yet place no value on it at all? But upon reflection it becomes clear that our doubts about Alf do not arise because his position is somehow conceptually incoherent. John Kleinig points to our chief worry in this sort of case:

> There is something of a presumption that people wish to live, not simply because of some inborn "will-to-live," but because continued life is a prerequisite to almost all our valued projects. It is not immediately intelligible to us that a person would voluntarily choose to die. Choices are made in the pursuit of valued ends; choosing death seems to go contrary to this, since it involves a denial of the prerequisite for valued ends.[109]

But this is to imply that we do not expect Alf to necessarily intrinsically value X – that is, value it in itself – but to value it just because it is a pre-condition for other valuings. I consider such extrinsic valuings in the next section (§9); what is of importance at present is that if, as a matter of fact, Alf's life is such that continued life will not in any way contribute to the promotion of his other values, then it does not seem rationally incumbent on him to value X at all. Sometimes, however, we are apt to think that health is valuable in itself; or, at least, that the absence of health, involving as it does pain and suffering, is necessarily disvaluable. I believe that this second position is plausible, and will consider it more closely below. Indeed, it seems that one who places no value on (that is, does not value) that which can prevent him from suffering does indeed suffer from a defect in practical rationality (§§9.2, 9.3). But this is to again bring in affect. In the

---

of in this context: moral goodness. Like von Wright, I believe it to be a derivative notion. See *The Varieties of Goodness*, pp. 17–18. See §23.2 in this volume.

109 John Kleinig, *Paternalism*, p. 131.

absence of any possibility of pain and suffering, and in the absence of any instrumental value attached to continued living, one whose life was filled with gloom and despair could, I submit, be perfectly rational to not value *X* in any way at all.

(b) Sometimes, however, "goodness" does seem to be used in ways such that it really does seem crazy to say that something is good but one does not value it, or see any reason for valuing it. I do not think it is unintelligible for someone to object that "Alf does not value the life-saving treatment because, after all, he doesn't really think that it is good for him; if Alf really thought that the treatment was good, he would value it." The difference between this sort of use of "good" and that which I have been considering up to now has been recognized by prescriptivists.[110] In the case of medical goodness, "goodness" has a specific content in the sense that its proper use is determined by fairly definite, impersonal standards. But, as I have argued, a belief that something is good in this sense does not rationally require that one value it or approve of it. In this second case, on the other hand, it does indeed seem that if one says something is good, one approves of it or values it; indeed, this use of "good" seems primarily aimed at conveying approval (cf. Gewirth's use of "good" in §7.2.3). But "goodness" now cannot be plausibly explicated in terms of beliefs that *X* is a good *K* according to the criteria regulating the evaluation of *K*'s. Rather, "good" is used in a way which includes precisely that element of approval which we have been analyzing as "valuing"; as such, it includes a personal stance toward the *X* and is thus not based simply on impersonal criteria.

Although, as should become manifest, I depart from prescriptivism on most matters, I follow it to this extent: if "goodness" is used in a specific way based on impersonal criteria, the belief that "*X* is good" is "rejectable," that is, one need not necessarily value that sort of goodness;[111] if "goodness" is used in such a way as to imply approval, it is not based simply on a set of beliefs centering on impersonal criteria. To avoid confusion, I shall call the sort of "goodness" based simply on judgments implied by impersonal criteria "beliefs about goodness." These "beliefs about goodness" are thus to be contrasted to the more gen-

110 See Cooper, *The Diversity of Moral Thinking*, ch. 7. See also §16.2 in this volume.
111 Ibid., p. 126.

eral sort of "goodness" implying approval, which I include as a species of value judgments (§10).

8.4 *Unworthy emotions and their objects*

According to the Affective-Cognitive Theory, having a dispositional emotion toward X is sufficient for intrinsically valuing X. But it has been suggested that this cannot be right because we can, and often do, experience emotions such as love toward that which is quite worthless.[112] As Franz Brentano wrote:

> Should we say that whatever is loved or is capable of being loved is something that is worthy of love and therefore good? Obviously this would not be right, and it is almost impossible to comprehend how it could be that some have fallen into such an error. One person loves what another hates. And . . . the miser is reduced to heaping up riches irrationally and even to sacrificing himself in order to acquire them. And so we may say that the fact that a thing is loved is no indication that it is worthy of being loved – just as we may say that the fact that something is affirmed or accepted is no indication that it is true.[113]

It is of course true that people can value that which is not truly valuable; this sort of valuational error will be the particular focus of §10.4. Brentano, however, seems to have something more in mind, for he adds as a further comment to the last quoted sentence, "it may frequently happen that one loves something that *one admits* to be unworthy of such love."[114] This might mean that one could love something while seeing it as worthless, that is, as not good, and that conflicts with what I said in §6.2. And this suggests that one might love something without valuing it. We need to be clear here, however, about the distinction between two senses in which one might feel an emotion such as love toward something while acknowledging the object's unworthiness.

(i) One might, as Brentano says, love something despite recognizing that it is *unworthy of love*; this indeed would be a sort of irrational loving. In terms of my analysis in Chapter II, the lover would recognize that his beliefs about the beloved's attributes indicate that love is inappropriate toward the beloved, yet this recognition does not undermine the emotion. This is a case

112 See Laird, *The Idea of Value*, p. 171.
113 Franz Brentano, *The Origin of Our Knowledge of Right and Wrong*, p. 19.
114 Ibid. (emphasis added).

of what A. O. Rorty calls "*akrasia* of the emotions":[115] one persists in the emotion despite an awareness that it is inappropriate toward that object. As we saw (§3.1), it is difficult to make sense of these sorts of inappropriate emotions; as when McDougall was afraid of what was harmless, the person persists in describing himself as *E*, and acting in *E*-appropriate ways, but acknowledges that necessary conditions for an appropriate *E* are absent. Like Rorty, I find psychoanalytic explanations very plausible in these cases, for the psychoanalyst resolves the inconsistency by uncovering the underlying, appropriate, target of the emotion (again, see §3.1). In any case, in relation to this notion of an unworthy object of emotion, it seems as problematic to ascribe the emotion to the person (without, say, a psychoanalytic account) as it is to ascribe valuing. (It is also worth noting that this seems to be an unstable position. In experiments that artificially induced an affect – through hypnosis – that seemed inappropriate given a person's beliefs, there was a marked tendency to change beliefs to obtain some sort of consistency.)[116]

(ii) This notion of an unworthy object of emotion must be distinguished from another, in which the person's beliefs about the object render the emotion appropriate (and so in this sense *X is* worthy of *E*), but the person is also convinced that in some other sense *X* is unworthy or not valuable. Advocates of this view are apt to point to cases such as the love of parents for a severely retarded child; the parents, it is claimed, certainly love the child, but do not think he is valuable, and they do not value him. I find this puzzling. Apparently, as loving parents they cherish their child in the sense of fostering, nursing, holding him dear, and, in a significant sense, clinging to him. Only one sense of "cherish" given by the *Concise Oxford Dictionary* remains, and that is the one which our critic will not allow: to value him. The sole rationale I can perceive for excluding this last sense of "cherish" is that the child is, presumably, not admirable, and it is supposed that one must admire what one values. But, even if the child is not to be admired (and in this case that is not clear), it seems that only an overly aesthetic understanding of value would erect that into a bar to valuing. One can, for example, greatly value every-

115 Amélie O. Rorty, "Explaining Emotions."
116 See Rosenberg, "Affective-Cognitive Consistency."

day delights that it would be inappropriate to admire – for example, a smilc from onc's four-month-old daughter.

A related objection to my sufficiency claim is the *disvalued emotion argument*. Proponents of this argument are apt to point to those drug addicts or sadists who recognize the "loathsome and irrational" nature of their enjoyments.[117] Consequently, it is said, the addict or sadist places no value on them; indeed, it is plausible to say he disvalues them. So, the argument concludes, if Betty disvalues possessing emotion *E*, then obviously she does not value *E*'s object, and so having a positive emotion toward an object is not sufficient for valuing it. Now this, I suppose, is one way of describing such cases; I certainly see no knockdown argument against it. Nevertheless, it strikes me as implying that the valuations of such drug addicts or sadists are altogether too tidy and coherent. There is nothing wrong, the argument seems to suggest, with the things they value, they just have "impulses" that override what they value. But isn't it more accurate to say that, for instance, the sadist values certain activities, while at the same time detesting these valuations or finding them loathsome?[118] On my account, then, the sadist has what Rescher calls a second-order valuing (in this case disvaluing); the would-be reformed sadist values certain aggressive sexual activities but he disvalues his valuing of them.[119] I do not think this is simply a neat way out of the sort of difficulties posed by reform-minded sadists. Rather, unlike the disvalued emotion argument, it points to a deep conflict in the sadist's valuings; his higher order valuings (based, say, on a self-ideal), clash with his first order valuings. All is not well with his value system (see §14). It is not just a question of alien impulses upsetting a perfectly coherent system of valuings.

9 EXTRINSIC VALUING AND RATIONAL ACTION

9.1 Intrinsic and instrumental valuing

My aim in this section is to distinguish those valuings grounded on direct affective responses (that is, dispositional emotions)

117 See Michael Slote, *Goods and Virtues*, pp. 15–16.

118 This is a different side of the case mentioned by Michael Stocker, "Values and Purposes: The Limits of Teleology and the Ends of Friendship," pp. 764ff.

119 See Rescher, *Value Theory*, p. 23n. See §5.2, examples (2′), (3′), in the present volume.

from other ways in which one can be said to value something. Because directly affective valuing offers a plausible interpretation of the notion of intrinsic valuing, I shall employ the traditional distinction by referring to these other valuings as *extrinsic* valuings. However, readers familiar with this axiological terminology should be aware that my analysis of extrinsic valuing has little in common with most traditional accounts. In particular, it departs from C. I. Lewis's famous analysis of extrinsic value, which upheld the hedonistic thesis, insisting that only experience could be valuable in itself (§8.1). Consequently, he held that the value of objects could only be *extrinsic*, of which there were two sorts. *Inherent* extrinsic value was ascribed to objects that are somehow capable of directly giving rise to intrinsic value (for example, aesthetic objects); objects have *instrumental* extrinsic value if they are "an instrumentality to some other [valuable] object."[120] Roughly, Lewis's aim was to distinguish those things that we value because they directly give rise to experience (for example, a tree as an object of contemplation and appreciation) from those that are valued just because they are a means to other valued things (for example, lumber as a resource). This difference, then, is essentially that between agreeable and useful *things*.[121]

Because I reject the hedonistic thesis, I obviously do not follow Lewis in ascribing only extrinsic value to objects; I have stressed, in fact, the contrary thesis: that objects can be valued intrinsically.[122] Nevertheless, one of the key ideas underlying Lewis's analysis still seems applicable: extrinsic valuing is in some way ultimately based upon, yet distanced from, affective response. Instrumental valuing would seem the most obvious and clear-cut example of an extrinsic valuation. It seems reasonable to say that we (purely) instrumentally value *Y* if we judge that it is an efficient or necessary instrument to produce some intrinsically valued object, *X*. On this account, the valuing of *Y* is based upon, but does not itself manifest, an affective response: it is thus an extrinsic valuing.

120 Lewis, *Knowledge and Valuation*, p. 391.
121 Eaton, *The Austrian Philosophy of Values*, p. 94. Lewis, however, defined "utility" somewhat more widely. *Knowledge and Valuation*, p. 385.
122 Perhaps the contrast is not perfect, because I am discussing valuing, and Lewis is often (but by no means always) concerned with valuableness. However, as we will see in the next chapter, I make a similar claim with regard to valuableness.

But at this point we must introduce a complication. The traditional sharp distinction between intrinsic and instrumental value makes sense if, as does Lewis, one upholds the hedonistic thesis, for then only mental states of a certain sort have intrinsic value while all objects, events, etc. only have value in so far as they bring about these states. But when we characterize intrinsic valuing as interest, enjoyment, and so forth aimed at an object, the distinction breaks down, for one can intrinsically value something just because of its instrumentality. This was stressed by John Dewey. In *Democracy and Education*, for example, Dewey harshly criticized the idea that "aesthetic appreciation" (which he understood as an intrinsic valuing) was somehow "confined to such things as literature and pictures and music." Rather, he argued, valuing in the sense of having an "attitude of prizing a thing, finding it worth while, for its own sake, or intrinsically" could be directed at industrial or mechanical objects, scientific endeavors, etc.[123] A similar point is put rather differently in *Reconstruction in Philosophy*, where Dewey argues that:

> No one can possibly estimate how much of the obnoxious materialism and brutality of our economic life is due to the fact that economic ends have been regarded as *merely* instrumental. When they are recognized to be as intrinsic and final in their place as any others, then it will be seen that they are capable of idealization, and that if life is to be worthwhile, they must acquire ideal and intrinsic value.[124]

Put in terms of the Affective-Cognitive Theory, Dewey's main point is intelligible and sound: beliefs regarding an object's instrumental or technical goodness, or concerning its economic efficiency, can ground a dispositional emotion toward it. That is, one can intrinsically value instruments *as* instruments. Although related, this idea is distinct from the much discussed idea of *functional autonomy*, according to which, for example, *Y*, originally valued nonintrinsically simply as an instrument to achieving *X* can, over time, itself become intrinsically valued.[125] Dewey's challenge to a sharp distinction between intrinsic and instrumental valuing is, I think, more radical: the ground for intrinsically valuing *Y*, he says, just is the cognizance that it has instrumental

123 John Dewey, *Democracy and Education*, ch. 18, esp. pp. 235–6, 248–9.
124 John Dewey, *Reconstruction in Philosophy*, p. 171. See L. Duane Willard, "Intrinsic Value in Dewey."
125 See Gordon W. Allport, *Pattern and Growth in Personality*, pp. 226ff. See also Mill, *Utilitarianism*, ch. V.

goodness. He appeared to believe that the dominant understanding of instrumental goodness tended to block an intrinsic valuing of it, and in this regard he saw his educational program as aiming at reforming the dominant understanding. Still, once we realize that valuing not only takes the form of aesthetic interest, but a wide variety of practical interests and enjoyments, I do not think that it is at all counter-intuitive to say that even today people often, perhaps typically, intrinsically value things for their instrumental and technical goodness. A craftsman's prizing his tools is, of course, an obvious example, but the same point applies to one's fondness for a trusty car, the engineer's interest and joy in a solution to a technical problem, and the manager's fascination for organizational reforms. If Izard is right in thinking that, rather than being rare, emotions inform most consciousness, it seems hard to avoid Dewey's thesis that intrinsic valuing and instrumental thinking are not at all mutually exclusive.

Moreover, this sort of intrinsic valuing of *Y* for its instrumental goodness in no way presupposes that the thing for which *Y* is an instrumentality is itself in any way valued. That is, once we realize that we can intrinsically value something because of its instrumental goodness, it becomes obvious that such valuing does not depend on a prior valuing of that which the instrument produces. [See here claim (ii) in §8.3.] As von Wright says, "[t]o attribute instrumental goodness to something is *primarily* to say that *it serves some purpose well*."[126] I maintain, then, that one can (intrinsically) value something because it serves some purpose well without valuing this purpose. Recall Becker's rack (§8.3). Becker, I argued, was wrong to suggest that seeing a rack as a good rack somehow implies that one must value it. But I agree with him to this extent: one can have a "grudging admiration" for its technical excellence despite not valuing, and indeed actually disvaluing, the rack's purpose. And, unfortunately, Becker's example is by no means fanciful. In his analysis of personality integration and disintegration in Nazi concentration camps, Bruno Bettelheim points out that not only the persecutors, but the persecuted as well, put great value on – took pride in – the exercise of their professional or technical skills, irrespective of the purposes to which they were put.[127] Although in these cases the in-

126 von Wright, *Goodness*, p. 20.
127 Bruno Bettelheim, *The Informed Heart*, pp. 205ff., 260ff.

dependent intrinsic valuing of instrumental or technical goodness is related to a failure to take proper cognizance of other valuations, such instrumental or technical valuings are not necessarily based on this sort of overly narrow, and so distorted, view. I suppose that those participating in large enterprises are at times culpable of being selectively attentive in this way, but, often enough, the participants are well aware that they neither particularly value nor disvalue the organization's purposes, yet cooperation is still achieved by widespread interest in technical problems and joint endeavors aiming at solving them.[128]

9.2. *Purely derivative valuings*

9.2.1 Derivative valuings as reasons for action

My first claim, then, is that intrinsic valuings are much more common than are often thought; one can value something intrinsically, just because of, say, its instrumental goodness. However, this first claim does not assert that all valuings are intrinsic; as I indicated above – and like nearly all other value theorists – I wish to allow that in some cases one might value *Y* in a purely derivative way. The problem, though, is providing a clear explication of just what it is to value something in this manner. One of the things I aim to show here is that, though it is almost universally accepted that some valuings are wholly extrinsic or derivative, it is problematic as to just how these valuings are to be understood.

Let us begin with what seems to be almost a truism of value theory: *Y* is simply instrumentally valued by Alf if it is valued just because it is a means to some other valued object, *X*. In this sense, it is typically assumed that to say that something is purely instrumentally valued is to say that it is not intrinsically valued.[129] We are now in a position, however, to see that there are two possibilities:

(A) Alf has a dispositional emotion toward *Y* grounded on the belief that it is instrumental to *X*, which itself is valued.

128 Of course, cooperation is also achieved by making it an instrument to money. But my point is that, to the extent participants are not concerned simply with earning money, intrinsically valuing various instrumental projects, relations, etc. is apt to be crucial.
129 See, e.g., Robert Audi, "Axiological Foundationalism," p. 167.

(B) Alf has no dispositional emotion toward *Y*. He intrinsically values *X* and has a belief that *Y* is a means to *X*.

Our interest here, of course, is (B); as we have seen, (A) can be described as an instance of intrinsic *and* instrumental valuing. Before going on to look more closely at (B), however, it is important to ask whether the distinction between (A) and (B) is simply an artifact of the Affective-Cognitive Theory, or whether it reflects an important difference in the phenomenology of valuing. I believe we can and do distinguish someone who cares for or is interested in some instrumentality from he who is cognizant of an object's instrumental importance, but takes no interest in it and does not enjoy it. As I said, the craftsman intrinsically values his tools, but not all instrumentalities are so responded to. Car engines are instrumentally valuable to arriving at one's destination, and one can recognize this is to be so, without, in one sense at least, taking up any discernible "valuing attitude" toward them at all. The distinction between (A) and (B), in fact, is an enlightening one that value theorists have typically overlooked. Sometimes we do take up an identifiable "valuing stance" toward something because it is instrumentally valuable ("Thank God the engine is so reliable!"); often enough, however, though we are cognizant of something's instrumental role, only someone with commitments to some value theory would say we unproblematically value the thing. These latter sorts of cases, the sort described by (B), seem difficult to describe as having an attitude toward the object *Y* at all except insofar as one recognizes that, given a valuing of *X*, certain actions and policies in respect to *Y* are appropriate. Such purely derivative valuings, it seems, are recognitions that the valuing of *X* rationally commits one to certain actions in respect to *Y*.

To see this better, let us say that one intrinsically values movies of type *K*, that one has an opportunity to see a movie of this sort on a certain night, and that one rightly believes that one needs a ticket to see the movie on that night. Now it seems unlikely, and certainly not at all necessary, that one will intrinsically value the ticket, or even possessing it. Will one instrumentally value it in any way? Well, it seems that one "values" it only in the following sense: one recognizes that, given one values seeing such movies, one has a reason to obtain a ticket. It is important to stress in this regard that, given that one does (rationally) value going to the movie, one has a reason to obtain a ticket without positing any independent desire to possess the ticket: the intrinsic valuing is enough to generate a commitment to obtain it. Moreover – and this is a much more controversial claim – given my account of intrinsic valuing, one is committed to obtaining a ticket even without positing *any extra, independent, desire to go to the movie.* As I argued in §7.2, affect and belief, but not desire, are fundamental to (primitives in) the explanation of action. Given this, if one has the relevant dispositional emotion and set of beliefs, one has a motivating reason to perform those actions to which the emotions and beliefs commit one.

Extrinsic valuings, then, are reasons to act implied by one's intrinsic valuings. The language of "implication" is appropriate here. If proposition p implies q, someone who assents to p, but refuses to acknowledge (even when it is pointed out to him) his commitment to q displays epistemic irrationality; similarly, if R is a reason to ϕ implied by valuing X, then someone who refuses to acknowledge his reason to ϕ (even when it is pointed out to him) demonstrates practical irrationality. Confronted with such an agent, we must conclude that he has failed to understand what is involved in valuing X, what R is, or what it means to ϕ. Or perhaps he is not speaking truthfully, or he has some sort of cognitive or rational defect (for example, he is psychotic). So, should Betty proclaim that she values going to the movie but insists that she has no reason at all to obtain a ticket, we will indeed believe her to be practically irrational until she shows how these are practically consistent. Perhaps she values going to the movie but is unable to go for some reason; perhaps she has a key to the back door and so does not need a ticket. But these possibilities are relevant because they are ways of showing that she is not really crazy; they resolve the practical inconsistency. But if she simply claims "Oh, how I would enjoy the movie, how lucky that I have nothing to do tonight, yes I need a ticket to see it, but how does any of this give me a reason to obtain a ticket?" we would assume that she is either crazy or joking.

9.2.2 Valuing and practical rationality

In general, my concern throughout this book is with what fully rational agents will value and what reasons for action they will recognize. To some extent, then, this focus will help avoid the problems associated with the distinction between "internal" and "external" reasons for action, that is, between reasons that an agent recognizes and reasons that he in some sense "objectively has."[130] Nevertheless, it will be helpful to introduce a distinction. I shall say that an agent has *a reason to* ϕ if the agent has (for the relevant purposes) a complete and sound set of beliefs and his valuings are not rationally flawed (see §10.4), and ϕ-ing is an appropriate action given those beliefs. In contrast, I shall say that an agent is *rationally committed to* ϕ*-ing* if, given his beliefs and valuings, ϕ-ing is an appropriate action. Reasons to act, then, are a proper subset of rational commitments to act: a person with a complete and fully rational set of beliefs, and well-grounded and appropriate valuings, who has a reason to ϕ is also rationally committed to ϕ-ing. But one can be rationally committed to ϕ-ing without having a reason to ϕ: if a building is not really on fire, but Alf believes it to be, he is still rationally committed to fleeing – his beliefs and values imply that fleeing is the appropriate action. But, in the sense I am using the term, he does not have "a reason" to flee.

I thus understand "reasons to act" and "commitments to act" as implications of one's beliefs and values: the former are the implications of sound values and beliefs, the latter of whatever values and beliefs an agent has, be they sound or unsound. This way of thinking about rational action precludes attributing to Alf a reason (or a commitment) that is not implied by any of his beliefs and values. Thus, if there is a fire in the building but Alf does not know about it, I shall not say that he has an external reason to act of which he is unaware. Rather, I will say that a fully rational Alf with relevantly complete information would have a reason to flee the building. Although this may seem odd to some, upon reflection, it seems a more useful way of locating his problem. His problem, after all, is not that he somehow fails to recognize a reason he has: it is that his beliefs about the building's safety are importantly incomplete and so do not generate a reason to act. Of course, sometimes he can indeed fail to recognize that, given his sound beliefs, he has a reason to run (say, he somehow does not know that fleeing the building is appropriate), but that

130 See, e.g., Bernard Williams, "Internal and External Reasons."

obviously is a different problem. Given this basic contrast between reasons for action and commitments to act, we can distinguish the following cases.

(i) A fully rational valuer would, roughly: (a) have a value system without errors; and (b) recognize all the reasons for action (for example, to ϕ) that follow from his value system. Again, I will say that such a person *recognizes that he has reason to* ϕ.

(ii) Of course, real valuers are not like this. They can, for instance, make valuational errors (§10.4). Given these unsound valuings, however, they might still correctly grasp what actions (for example, ϕ) are appropriate vis-à-vis these unsound valuings. Henceforth, let us describe such a person as *recognizing his commitment to ϕ-ing*.

(iii) But one could have an unsound extrinsic valuing even given perfectly sound intrinsic valuings: Betty might wrongly believe she needs money at the door to see the movie when, in fact, all sales are tickets-in-advance and she can no longer purchase admission at the door. In such a case, we can say that her beliefs commit her to bringing money with her, but *this commitment is ill-grounded because it is based on a false belief.* (Cf. Hume's notion of an irrational desire, §7.2.1.)

(iv) One may also fail to appreciate that one's valuings commit one to certain courses of action. If Alf loves Betty, he is committed to certain caring and protective actions. But he may be confused about what loving involves; despite the fact that he loves Betty, and recognizes that he does so, he may fail to grasp that caring and protective actions are appropriate. In this case, Alf *does not recognize that his valuings commit him to these actions.*

(v) Yet another way in which a valuer may fall short of full rationality is, even when he has no false valuings or false relevant beliefs, his beliefs may be incomplete. For instance, Alf may be unaware that the movie is playing tonight; if his beliefs were complete in the relevant respects, then he would have a reason to obtain a ticket. In this case, (like iii) the flaw in his practical rationality stems from an epistemic problem.

However, unless I am specifically concerned with the possibility of errors in valuation, my main concern will be an ideally rational agent who is cognizant of all the reasons for action implied by his valuings and having all the relevant and sound beliefs. My ideal of a fully rational agent thus shares much with R. B.

Brandt's, who also uses "rational" to refer agents who act on the basis of all relevant available information.[131] As Kurt Baier notes, this is an extremely demanding ideal: considering the tremendous amount of relevant and available information, it seem impossible for an agent to ever know that he has obtained it.[132] Certainly, as agents, we cannot wait for assurances that we are fully rational before we act; that would only lead to paralysis. We act in accordance with our action commitments the best we can. Yet, the notion of a fully rational agent is a regulative ideal in the sense that, when we are shown that in a particular respect we depart from such an ideal, rationality demands that we conform to the ideal by adjusting our beliefs or values. A fully rational valuer, then, is a generally unobtainable ideal, but because it remains a regulative ideal of intelligent practice it will be enlightening to focus on it.

These comments are very sketchy indeed, though I believe they are sufficient for the present purposes. After all, the idea that valuings imply reasons for action is scarcely controversial (see feature (b), §1.1). However, as we proceed in Parts I and II, I will develop this intuition about the nature of reasons for action in a variety of ways, showing, for example, the extent to which it lends support to various brands of "externalism" (§§10.2–10.4, 16.2); its consequences for objectivity in value (§12); and, indeed, the requirements it provides for an adequate theory of the rationality of moral action (Chapter VI) and justification in ethics (Chapter VII). However, I shall consider these matters as they arise, and refrain from presenting at the outset a doctrine of rational action.[133] At present, then, I wish only to insist that it is fundamental to our conception of a rational agent that he recognizes that his valuings – the things he cares for, cherishes, etc. – provide him with commitments to act.

131 Brandt, *A Theory of the Right and the Good*, pp. 11–13.

132 Kurt Baier, "Rationality, Reason, and the Good," p. 194.

133 I do so in "Practical Rationality and Commitment." I now believe, however, that too much emphasis was placed there on *beliefs about* affective states and this led to ignoring the rational implications of emotional states themselves.

9.2.3 Emotion and rational action

It is sometimes objected, though, that emotions cannot rationally commit one to actions; they are natural facts that have no particular relevance to rationality. This certainly is wrong.[134] To be sure, affects or feelings alone, in the absence of any beliefs whatsoever, could not provide reasons for action, but I have not claimed that they do. But it seems completely implausible to say that one who is experiencing fear, and believes that the fear is grounded in the threatening characteristics of a tiger and that running away will remove the danger, has no reason whatsoever to run. Emotions, we can say, generally rationally imply policies for action.[135] Of course, one may have reasons not to run, and perhaps some other action such as shooting it is a better response to the tiger. But all that is consistent with saying that emotions imply (context-dependent) reasons for action. What would we say of someone who recognized that he was in a state of fear, that this fear was grounded in the threatening attributes of the tiger, that only running would remove the threat, and, further, acknowledged that he had no reason not to run and, yet, insisted that he could see no reason at all to run? Various avenues could be pursued to make sense of his denial that he has a reason to run away. Perhaps he believes that his fear is not well-grounded and, so in that sense irrational (§3.1); or perhaps he has a second-order disvaluing of being fearful, and this leads to countervailing reasons to act (§8.4). But, if such possibilities are not borne out, and he simply insists that he has no reason to run away – "What does running away have to do with being afraid of the man-eating tiger?" he asks – we can only conclude that he either is crazy in the very specific way of dissociating emotion and beliefs from action,[136] or that he fails to grasp what it means to fear something. (It would not, we should note, in any way resolve our puzzlement if he insisted that he had no reason to run away because he lacked

134 For related arguments, see R. G. Swinburne, "The Objectivity of Morality," esp. p. 16; Kurt Baier, *The Moral Point of View*.

135 See Findlay, *Values and Intentions*, p. 169.

136 Indeed, it is not implausible to see such attitudes as characteristic of some form of schizophrenia. Schizophrenics are typically unable to properly conceptualize emotions, and they seem to suffer from a cognitive defect such that they do not cognize – or at least see as a reason for belief or action – relations of consistency or inconsistency. See Michael Argyle, *The Psychology of Interpersonal Behaviour*, p. 211.

a desire to run, while still acknowledging that he was experiencing the appropriate fearful mental state, grounded on the appropriate beliefs. Insofar as a desire does enter in here, its absence would be as problematic as the denial of a reason to run. See §7.2.2.)[137] Some types of valuings, to be sure, do not imply much in the way of reasons for action. Grief about the past or nostalgia may have little relevance for present or future action.[138] Although emotions and valuings are practical notions, some are much less so than others. But, even in these cases, reasons to act are sometimes implied: one who grieves over past deeds is often committed to some form of restitution or compensation. And, even where nothing can be done, it seems a genuine grief almost, if not quite always, implies a sort of counter-factual commitment of the sort "Could I do it again, I would not. . . . " or "Could I change the past. . . . "

That one intrinsically values *X* will, then, provide one with commitments to act. Can we say anything more specific about these commitments? Many have believed that one, and only one, commitment is ultimately implied by intrinsic valuings: to maximize the total amount of (intrinsic) value (see §16.1). Indeed, consequentialist ethics is premised on just this assumption.[139] However, we will see later that popular versions of this thesis are implausible (§12), and in any case a more complex view is possible, according to which a variety of actions may be appropriate, depending on the grounds of one's valuing.[140] Most basic – and these probably apply to all (positive) valuings of objects that have some kind of well-being[141] – are commitments not to damage, to preserve and to protect. The very description of someone as (intrinsically) "valuing *X*," to the extent it can be captured by phrases such as "cherishing *X*" or "caring for *X*," implies both a dispositional emotion toward *X* and a readiness to take action to protect or promote its welfare. This is nicely captured by the two senses of "caring for something," as a loving of it and a protecting of it. But more specialized responses can be appropriate, too.

137 The mere belief that "being eaten by a tiger is bad" is not, however, sufficient to motivate. See again the case of Alf and his belief about medical goodness in §8.3.
138 See Lyons, *Emotion*, p. 96; Rorty, "Introduction," p. 2.
139 See, e.g., Kupperman, *Morality*, p. 94.
140 See Robert Nozick, *Philosophical Explanations*, pp. 451ff.
141 See Benn, "Environmental Ethics," p. 413.

An object that is valued because, say, it is sublime may well call for a reverence or a sort of respect.[142] In this vein, Aurel Kolnai suggested that we can value something because it possesses a type of nobility or dignity;[143] if one does value something on this ground then, apart from any concern with the maximization of goodness, it would be inappropriate, for instance, to ridicule it, to use it to weigh down garbage or to wrap fish in it.[144] Someone who professed to intrinsically value *X* but saw no reason to refrain from harming it, or who professed to value it because it was noble but saw no reason not to treat it in ignoble ways, would again leave us puzzled and searching for some way to make sense of what he says. Perhaps he acknowledges that these things are worthy of being valued in these ways, but cannot himself see any value in them (§§10.1–10.2); or perhaps he values *X* instrumentally and needs, like fuel, to destroy it in order to use it. But without some such account we cannot make sense of his value claims.

So far from being aimed only at the maximization of overall value, value-based commitments to action demonstrate a certain egocentricity, and it is perhaps this insight that is the partial truth at the core of hedonistic theories. Although an art collector certainly need not value a painting because it makes him feel good, he may, quite rationally, devote himself to *his* appreciation of it rather than maximizing overall appreciation. So too, one who finds something to be dangerous and is afraid of it will be committed to removing himself; whether he also is committed to assisting others in fleeing is more problematic. One who flees without regard for others is a coward, but it is far less clear that this in itself shows that he is failing to see that his disvaluing (that is, fear) commits him to assisting others, and so he is acting irrationally. In contrast, someone who is fearful but can see no reason to flee is irrational (unless some account can be provided showing how in this case fleeing is inappropriate). It may well be that un-

142 On respect and value, see Carl Cranor, "Toward a Theory of Respect for Persons," pp. 314ff.; Robin Attfield, "The Good of Trees," p. 52. It thus seems to me wrong to maintain, as does Cooper, that "pure aesthetic judgments" have no practical implications *if* this means that aesthetic valuings (as opposed to beliefs about aesthetic goodness) have no action commitments. *The Diversity of Moral Thinking*, p. 95. See §§10.1–10.3 in the present volume.
143 Aurel Kolnai, "Dignity."
144 See Benn, "Environmental Ethics," p. 414.

less other valuings are brought to bear – for example, one's concern for others, valuing nobility, etc. – one's value-based commitments to act will very much center on one's own relation to the valued or disvalued thing (see §12).

To be sure, in an important sense just what actions are required by valuings is culture bound. In a culture in which warrior virtues predominate, the appropriate thing to do may be to laugh at fear rather than to flee. But as this example shows, culturally varied responses often derive from different background values and beliefs. If warriors value bravery and honor above all else, they will have reason to laugh at dangers that a less warlike culture does not possess. Or, perhaps the warriors believe that laughter is an effective way to intimidate the enemy, a belief not shared by other cultures. Without denying the importance of cultural influences in determining what counts as an appropriate response to value, we should thus not be too quick to conclude that, say, it is just a brute fact that though in some cultures it is appropriate to flee in the face of fear others insist on very different responses. Given a grasp of a people's beliefs, other valuings, and environmental conditions, we may well be able to see the rationality of their different responses: that is, see why, given their life, it is the appropriate thing to do.[145]

These remarks are only suggestive; my primary concern here is to show that sound valuings do indeed imply reasons to act rather than to discover the specific reasons various valuings imply. Now given that our intrinsic valuings do indeed imply that we are committed to act in various ways, we might simply say that *all* such reasons constitute extrinsic valuings. Thus it would follow that we extrinsically value our car engine simply in the sense that we recognize a reason to care for it. Although this suggestion is not deeply flawed, it is perhaps too simple. One might, I suppose, translate "it is inappropriate to ridicule that which is intrinsically valued as noble" as "one who intrinsically values something as noble is rationally committed to extrinsically disvaluing ridiculing it." But that seems, at least to me, strained. Typically, we refer to reasons for action as an extrinsic or (purely) instrumental valuing when our valuing of one thing leads us to

145 See Arthur M. Diamond, Jr., "Stable Values and Variable Constraints"; Marvin Harris, *Cows, Pigs, Wars, and Witches: The Riddles of Culture.*

act toward another object in some of those ways characteristic of intrinsic valuing: we see reason to protect and promote it, we do not part with it without compensation or for some good reason, etc. In short, the dispositional emotion toward *X* not only leads us to treat *it* in preservative and attentive ways but, as it were, provides reason to take similar sorts of action with regard to *Y*.

9.3 Foundational valuings

Throughout the analysis of extrinsic valuings, I have been assuming that, ultimately, all such valuings are grounded on intrinsic valuings. This is very much in the spirit of traditional axiology: affective evaluations of objects are the first link in all chains of valuings. Put somewhat more formally, I have been assuming that all foundational valuings are intrinsic valuings.[146] Following other analyses of axiological foundationalism, I shall say that Alf's valuing of *X* is foundational if and only if it is not grounded on any other valuing, but it provides a grounding for other valuings.[147] So, an intrinsic valuing can be foundational because one can have a dispositional emotion toward *X* which, though grounded on various beliefs, including beliefs about goodness (§8.3), is not grounded on any other emotions; but this valuing may itself ground a series of other valuings. We have seen, though, that not all intrinsic valuings are foundational: in case A of §9.2.1, one intrinsically values *Y* because it is instrumental to *X*. But need all foundational valuings be intrinsic? Is being intrinsic a necessary condition for being a foundational value?

I have indicated that the traditional answer given by axiologists, at least those who admit foundational values,[148] is affirmative. This can at least be questioned. Recall our analysis of a hungry person (§7.2.1). He experiences a negative affect – what MacLean calls a "basic" affect (§4.1) – has certain beliefs that food will assuage it, that a course of action, ϕ, will result in get-

146 This is a common assumption. See, e.g., Elliot D. Cohen, "The Epistemology of Value," pp. 179–80.
147 See Audi, "Axiological Foundationalism," p. 165; Mark Pastin, "The Reconstruction of Value," pp. 389ff.
148 According to strong coherence theories of value, no purely foundational values exist, for every value is to some extent grounded on other values. See Audi, "Axiological Foundationalism," pp. 168ff.; Pastin, "The Reconstruction of Value," pp. 390ff.

ting food, that ϕ is possible, that no better alternative presents itself, and so on. Now if (i) his hunger is not an intentional state, (ii) he values the food, and (iii) this valuing does not presuppose any dispositional emotions, then valuing the food is a foundational, but not an intrinsic, valuing. For if (i)–(iii) holds, he is without any intentional affect (attitude) towards food, and so does not intrinsically value it. Yet it qualifies as a foundational value, for it is a valuing not grounded on other valuings and (we can assume) grounds other valuings. Let us, then, consider (i)–(iii) in turn.

(i) It is sometimes said that hunger is an intentional state. When we are hungry we are, after all, hungry *for food*: "food" is thus the object of our hungry state. One problem, to which I have already pointed (§5.4.3), is that, like sex, hunger partakes both of an emotion and an appetite. Sometimes we are hungry for a particular food and nothing else will do. We can allow that such a hunger is intentional. But it seems wrong to say that we are always hungry for food. When working, we may identify the unpleasant and distracting somatic sensation as hunger and yet respond by taking a hunger suppression pill or take an injection of a drug that relieves the sensation. That our thoughts turn to ways to relieve the somatic sensation does not make it an attitude or an intentional feeling (see §5.2). Any way to rid oneself of the sensation may do. And this, of course, is even more obvious with, say, affects concerning nausea and feelings related to the emunctories.

(ii) Even if this is accepted, it can still be argued that no valuing is involved in these cases. But this would imply that paradigmatic craving-satisfactions such as the desire for food, drink, and sex do not concern valuings. Surely a hungry person does value food, and a nauseous person values that which he believes will bring him relief. Certainly they have reasons to pursue these things: "Yes, drinking that will relieve my nausea, but what has that to do with whether I drink it or not?" strikes us as fundamentally crazy. To be sure, this valuing is essentially like what I have called an extrinsic valuing: it is the recognition of a reason to act, and does not imply any cherishing or caring for the thing. One need not have any liking for, or interest in, antacids (though as the discomfort becomes severe or prolonged, one may begin to take a genuine interest in them).

(iii) Perhaps, though, this overlooks some other intrinsic valuing that always enters into such cases. Roger Trigg's analysis of pain suggests how this might be so. According to him, someone who is in pain not only has a pain sensation, but also a dislike (an emotion) of that sensation.[149] So one does intrinsically disvalue the pain; the sensation alone, without the emotional component of the pain experience, would not ground a valuation or a reason to act. We might generalize this to all sensations: any nonintentional somatic (etc.) sensation *S* only grounds a valuing if one also has an emotion directed at the sensation. It is difficult to evaluate this thesis. Philosophers sometimes put great weight on the way in which prefrontal lobotomy affects pain experiences – patients are described as no longer minding the pain, or at least, no longer wanting to rid themselves of it – but, as Trigg himself points out, the clinical evidence is confusing and contradictory; if it establishes anything, it is that patients are less anxious about their pain.[150] In any event, it is not manifest what would be the value implications of a finding that patients no longer had any propensity to rid themselves of pain. Although some seem to argue that this would show that they were not really in pain,[151] and Trigg would suggest that they were experiencing an indifferent "pain sensation" that they did not dislike,[152] others would insist that this absence of "aversion" does not obviate the badness of their pain.[153] On this last view, their actions (that is, not taking steps to rid themselves of pain) are irrational because of their failure to make the cognitive connections between taking certain actions and ridding themselves of pain. Such patients would exhibit the sort of craziness I depicted in case (A) in §7.2.2: all the grounds for action are present yet action fails to occur. And, indeed, some evidence indicates that prefrontal lobotomy patients do sometimes suffer from the cognitive failure to draw causal connections between events.[154]

149 Trigg, *Pain and Emotion*, esp. pp. 35–7.
150 Ibid., ch. VII.
151 See Brandt, *A Theory of the Good and the Right*, pp. 38–42.
152 Trigg, *Pain and Emotion*, pp. 134ff.
153 "Suppose I were taken into a psychological laboratory and given anesthetic *A*, which would destroy desire but leave me sensitive to feeling. Suppose I were made to feel an intense pain. It is evident to me that it would be an evil." William Savery, "A Defense of Hedonism," p. 15. See also his fable on pp. 17–18.
154 See Trigg, *Pain and Emotion*, p. 137.

These issues are perplexing. I cannot adequately deal with the problems of properly interpreting the effects of such surgical procedures, much less the experimental data and clinical evidence concerning abnormal reaction to pain on which Trigg draws. Nevertheless, I want to point to three grounds for resisting applying his analysis to all basic and specific affects (§4.1) and for accepting the traditional view that the feeling of pain is itself disagreeable.[155] (a) It is, I would venture, a much more difficult task to demonstrate that people have an intentional attitude toward their feelings or sensations than that they value the food, drink, or medicine. It is much more certain that a hungry person has reason to eat than that he experiences an emotion of dislike directed at his internal somatic states. On the view I am proposing we are not committed to accounting for this reason by appealing to this uncertain emotion. (b) The generalization of Trigg's argument places a great deal of weight on the emotion of dislike, for it is that which, when turned inward, yields the complete experience of pain and, by extension, all negative basic and specific affects. Now we have seen that "like" and "dislike" are employed both as names for specific emotions and as generic evaluative terms (§6.2). Although Trigg seems to employ "dislike" as a name for specific (and occurrent) emotion, the ambiguity between the specific and the generic helps make the argument more persuasive. For to say that one dislikes pain, though Trigg means it to refer to a specific intentional state of disliking a sensation, also brings to mind that pain is a negative affect: that is, to say one dislikes pain is just to say that the sensation of pain is felt as bad. (In this respect, Trigg's theory is open to criticisms similar to that which I directed at Magda Arnold's in §6.2.) (c) Lastly, Trigg's account, which makes emotions the source of the negative and positive felt characteristics of internal sensations, is inconsistent with MacLean's hypothesis according to which these internal affects are not only themselves experienced as positive and negative, but are in some way more fundamental than the emotion-related affects.[156]

155 This could be relaxed by acknowledging that pain is the intimate union of sensation and feeling, so long as this feeling is not an intentional affect (or an attitude) aimed at one's sensation. See Ferdinand Sauerbach and Hans Wenke, *Pain: Its Meaning and Significance*, pp. 76ff.
156 See Paul D. MacLean, "The Hypothalamus and Emotional Behavior," pp. 660–1.

I shall not, however, further insist on all this. If Trigg is right, emotional responses are even more important to value-based reasons for action than I have depicted them. As long as disliking is itself an affective state, and is no mere motivational propensity, the Affective-Cognitive Theory can accommodate a generalization of Trigg's analysis to all basic and specific affects. In that case, all foundational valuings would indeed be intrinsic valuings.

IV

Value judgments

The previous chapter advanced an analysis of *valuing*. Valuing, I argued, can be understood as a dispositional emotion. To value something (intrinsically) is to possess a dispositional emotion toward it; to value it purely derivatively is to have a reason to preserve, protect, promote it (and so forth) based upon such an emotion. Like hedonism, then, the Affective-Cognitive Theory rests the theory of value on our affective natures. This distinguishes my account from most contemporary theories of value, which place desire at the heart of valuing and valuableness. But the Affective-Cognitive Theory departs from hedonism in two fundamental ways: the feeling states on which my analysis lies are generally intentional; and affect is employed to explain valuing rather than, directly, valuableness. It is now time to turn to the analysis of valuableness.

One of the main claims of the Affective-Cognitive Theory of value is that the analysis of valuing provides the best foundation for explicating the notion of a value judgment – a judgment concerning the valuableness of an object. This separates the Affective-Cognitive Theory not only from hedonism but from "objective" accounts of value that take the property of "valuableness" as their point of departure. In short, the Affective-Cognitive Theory claims that the analysis of value judgments is best based on the account of valuing, not vice versa. The aim of this chapter is twofold: to present this account of value judgments and show how it is superior to theories that begin with the claim that valuableness is a property of objects.

A central theme of this chapter is the sense in which value judgments are "objective." This is an extraordinarily complicated issue; it sometimes concerns an ontological thesis, sometimes it involves a claim about the truth or falsity of value judgments, sometimes it is about whether value judgments can be criticized, and sometimes it describes a position concerning the relation of value judgments and reasons for action. I try here to sort out these various senses: in §§10 and 11, I consider in what way value judgments can be described as impersonal and how they require some personal approval. §12 then considers several interpretations of the "objective point of view," arguing that the Affective-Cognitive Theory helps articulate a sound and intelligible conception of objectivity in value theory. The analysis of this chapter does not affirm either unqualified "objectivism" or "subjectivism" in value theory. Not too surprisingly, value judgments partake of both.

10 SIMPLE VALUE JUDGMENTS

10.1 The color analogy

Disputes between "subjectivist" and "objectivist" theories of value often focus on the relation between judgments about an object's valuableness and the properties of that object. One sort of extreme subjectivist position insists that a sentence such as "*X* is valuable," despite its appearance, is not about the properties of *X*, but someone's approval of *X*: it tells us nothing about the characteristics of *X*, except that someone approves of it.[1] At the other extreme is the type of objectivist who maintains that "*X* is valuable" is simply a proposition about *X*'s possession of a particular sort of property, valuableness, and has no necessary relation to anyone's actual approval of *X*. I believe that both these views are wrong, but it is also fairly clear that, as Mill would say, though exaggerated and distorted, they are also partial truths. My aim here is to consider in just what ways value judgments imply personal approval and how they are impersonal propositions about the properties of objects.

Because the Affective-Cognitive Theory obviously leans toward a personal approval account, let us begin with the "objectivist" challenge to such accounts, according to which value is a property of objects. Although some versions of this brand of ob-

1 This is indeed an extreme position. Even C. L. Stevenson stressed that one has reasons for approving, and that these reasons relate to features of that which is approved. *Facts and Values*, pp. 83ff.

jectivism seem to cast humans simply in the role of perceivers of the totally nonanthropomorphic value attributes of objects, a more plausible version (and one consistent with the affect presupposition; §7.1) has been recently resurrected. Consider David Wiggins's formulation:

There is an analogy. . . . We may see a pillar-box as red because it is red. But also pillar-boxes, painted as they are, count as red only because there actually exists a perceptual apparatus (e.g. our own) which discriminates, and learns on the direct basis of experience to group together, all and only the *de facto* red things. Not every sentient animal which sees a red postbox sees it as red. Few or none of them do. But this in no way impugns the idea that redness is an external, monadic property of a postbox. "Red postbox" is not short for "red to human beings postbox." Red is not a relational property. . . . All the same, it is in one interesting sense a *relative* property. For the category . . . corresponds to an interest which can only take root in creatures with something approaching our own sensory apparatus.[2]

Such an account of value (I will call it the "color analogy") can allow that only creatures capable of affective response would develop a concept of value. On this view, though value concepts are grounded in the affective makeup of humans, any individual can employ these concepts in a perfectly competent and full-fledged way without having the relevant affect himself. According to this interpretation of the color analogy, then, it is the case that, though (a) color concepts are grounded in human sensibilities determined by our species' sensory apparatus, (b) having correct beliefs about the color of objects does not require a perceptual experience on the credent's part (the blind can have correct beliefs about the color of objects). So too, then, though (a′) value concepts are grounded in human affective sensibilities, (b′) having correct beliefs about the value of an object does not require any personal affective experience on the credent's part.

Critiques of the color analogy can take various forms. One might look harder at the traditional notion of a secondary property to see whether color really is usefully conceived of as a nonrelational property; or, to take a very different tack, one might propose a counter-model. The Austrian axiologist Victor Kraft

2 David Wiggins, "Truth, Invention, and The Meaning of Life," pp. 348–9. For a critique of Wiggins, see E. J. Bond, *Reason and Value*, ch. 8. John McDowell also believes that "[t]he phenomenology of value experience in general suggests a visual model for our dealings with value." "Aesthetic Value, Objectivity, and the Fabric of the World," p. 5.

argued in this second way, proposing that value predicates are better understood on the model of "useful" than of "red."[3] However, I wish to take yet another route, asking why so many value theorists have been attracted to the color analogy in the first place. What do advocates of the color analogy hope to establish *if* they succeed in showing that we should use color concepts as a model for understanding value?

Wiggins tells us the attraction of the analogy is that it points to how "objectivity and anthropocentricity" can be combined, and apparently "objective" here refers to "the externality which human beings attribute to the properties by whose ascription they evaluate things."[4] But it seems to me that the deep motivation for employing the color analogy is not just to show how value-related properties are external; such externality is itself stressed in order to show that value judgments (i) have truth-values and (ii) the truth or falsity of a value statement is uniform across individuals, and (iii) one can know the truth of a value statement without direct perception or experience of value. C. I. Lewis was rather clearer about this:

> Protagoras was right in recognizing that in point of relativity there is no difference between the value of a thing and the color of it. But he was wrong in supposing that either the color of the object or the value of the object depends on the individual and particular experience of it. . . . [A] thing may be green, and may be valuable, even though it should not appear so to any individual whatever; and the fact that it may appear so, does not make it so.[5]

So, like color judgments, value judgments are impersonal in the sense that the truth of "*X* is valuable" does not vary with speakers or depend on any particular person's experience of *X*. Furthermore, it seems clearly implied that it is *not* a necessary condition for Alf's assenting to "*X* is valuable" that he has had a personal experience of *X*'s value, any more than he must have a sensory experience of *X*'s greenness in order to be entitled to assent to "*X* is green."

---

3 See Victor Kraft, *Foundations for a Scientific Analysis of Value*, pp. 36–7. He actually conceived of "usefulness" as a type of value predicate, so that argument is from a particular case (of value) to a general account, rather than an analogical argument.

4 Wiggins, "The Meaning of Life," p. 349.

5 C. I. Lewis, *An Analysis of Knowledge and Valuation*, p. 532. Wiggins's position is somewhat unclear; some of the things he says later in the essay point to a rather different, and not obviously consistent, position.

My suggestion, then, is that the fundamental aim of (at least most) advocates of the color analogy is to show that value judgments are impersonal in this sense. Without such impersonality, it is thought that value judgments are no more than personal likings or reactions, and this is thought to be a subjectivism of the most objectionable sort.[6] My reply to all this is somewhat complicated, for I neither outright reject nor embrace the quest for impersonality. Rather, I distinguish two senses of impersonality. Letting "*X* is *V*" stand for all judgments of intrinsic[7] valuableness, we can distinguish *Strong* and *Weak Impersonality* as follows. *Strong Impersonality* claims that:

(i) "*X* is *V*" always has a truth-value.
(ii) This truth-value is nonrelative, that is, uniform across individuals. In particular, it is not relative to an individual's experience of *X*'s value.
(iii) For Alf to be entitled to assent to "*X* is *V*," it is not necessary that he has had some personal experience of *X*'s value.
(iv) Those who rationally assent to "*X* is *V*" on the basis of a personal experience of *X*'s value and those who rationally assent to it on other grounds have in all relevant respects equal knowledge of *X*'s value.

Weak Impersonality accepts claims (i)–(iii) of Strong Impersonality but denies (iv), claiming instead:

(iv′) Those who rationally assent to "*X* is *V*" on the basis of personal experience have a fuller knowledge of *X*'s value than do those who assent to "*X* is *V*" on other grounds.

I shall argue, then, (a) that the color analogy strives to support Strong Impersonality, but (b) Weak Impersonality is more plausible, and (c) Weak Impersonality is consistent with, indeed implied by, The Affective-Cognitive Theory.

To see this, consider the ascription of amusingness to *X*.[8] Amusingness, I take it, is a sort of valuableness, but, even should one be prone to deny this, we shall see that the analysis of amusingness casts light on serious types of value judgments. A person

6 This line of criticism is developed by James S. Fishkin, *Beyond Subjective Morality*. I have focused on Fishkin's study of "subjective" morality in my "Subjective Value and Justificatory Political Theory."
7 I briefly consider extrinsic value ascriptions in §10.5.
8 I am drawing here on Philip Pettit, "The Possibility of Aesthetic Realism"; Roger Scruton, *Art and Imagination*. Wiggins refers to amusingness on p. 349 of "The Meaning of Life."

who believes a joke to be funny because he has been informed by an expert authority that it is so has a (true) belief that the joke is amusing, but his grasp or appreciation of its amusingness seems privative compared with he who believes it to be funny because he finds it to be so. The difference is not simply that the two have arrived at the belief by different epistemological paths; the purely testimonial credent seems to have a less complete or intimate grasp of the joke's amusingness. In absence of direct access to a joke's funniness, the testimonial credent knows *that* the joke is funny, but he is lacking, as it were, knowledge *of* its funniness. And if he does not "see" how it is funny, his asserting that "*X* is amusing" is a sort of puzzled, uncomprehending, assertion.

This issue has ramifications far beyond ascriptions of amusingness, being central to understanding the nature of aesthetic characterizations. Just as with amusingness, it seems that one must "see" aesthetic "properties" for oneself. Writes Roger Scruton:

> If ϕ is a visual property, say, then it is not true that I have to see ϕ for myself in order to know that an object possesses it: there are circumstances where the opinion of others can give me a logically conclusive reason for saying that ϕ is there, as indeed a blind man can have knowledge of colors. In aesthetics you have to see for yourself precisely because what you have to "see" is not a property: your knowledge that an aesthetic feature is "in" the object is given by the same criteria that show that you "see" it. To see the sadness in the music and to know that the music is sad are one and the same thing. To agree in the judgement that the music is sad is not to agree in a belief, but in something more like a response or an experience; in a mental state that is – unlike belief – logically tied to the immediate circumstances of its arousal.[9]

The Affective-Cognitive Theory has no difficulty explaining why testimonial evidence is insufficient for "full knowledge" of aesthetic and amusingness characterizations. The point is not that the testimonial credent has a privative or weaker *belief* than does he who has direct access, that, for instance, "*X* is amusing," but that the testimonial credent *only* has a belief. To once again use the schema introduced in §5.2, though the testimonial credent's state can be characterized as [Believe (*X* is amusing)], he who has direct access also has the state [Amusement (*X*)]. To say, then, that the latter person "sees" or "grasps" how *X* is amusing is just

9 Scruton, *Art and Imagination*, p. 54. See also Pettit, "Aesthetic Realism," p. 26.

to say that he has an amused mental state of which *X* is the content.

Now either colors are like this or they are not. That is, assume that an analysis of our "knowledge" of colors would conclude that someone who perceives that "*X* is green" has a mental state such that he "grasps" – and he does *see* – *X*'s greenness, and this puts him in a privileged position vis-à-vis someone who has only testimonial evidence of *X*'s greenness. Pace Scruton, the blind would then not have full knowledge of colors. If this is so, the color analogy does not support Strong Impersonality because condition (iv) is violated; if the color analogy is interpreted only as supporting Weak Impersonality, then I have no deep objections to it. Assume, then, that given some analysis of color it is said that color is not like amusement; all that matters is that one has title to assent to "*X* is green," and it is irrelevant that some have perceived (*X* is green) and some merely believe it. In that case, Strong Impersonality is rescued, but then it can be argued that, pace Wiggins and Lewis, color is not analogous to value. For I have argued that at least some actual value concepts (not just analogous concepts) do indeed admit of a significant distinction between those who believe that *X* is such as to be the appropriate content of a certain intentional state and those who have apprehended *X* in that mode.[10]

Before proceeding, we need to pause to consider an important objection. I have been arguing that the "objectivist" – or, one might say, the "realist" – position in value theory is best understood *via* the color analogy. But it might be objected that this implies a distorted view of the sort of value properties to which the objectivist/realist is committed. It is widely agreed that a realist account of value properties maintains that they supervene upon nonvalue properties. G. E. Moore – who provided one of the first analyses of supervenience in his essay on "The Conception of Intrinsic Value" – argued that "if a given thing possesses any kind of intrinsic value in a certain degree, then not only must that same thing possess it, under all circumstances, but also anything *exactly like* it, must, under all circumstances, possess it in exactly the same degree."[11] Moore's idea seems to be something like this:

10 See A. W. Price, "Varieties of Objectivity and Values."
11 G. E. Moore, "The Conception of Intrinsic Value," p. 261. See also Jaegwon Kim, "Supervenience and Nomological Incommensurables," p. 149.

if *X* possess *V*, then anything just like *X* will possess *V*. Now call the set of properties that make something exactly like *X*, *X-ish* properties. Moore held that *V* supervenes upon *X-ish* properties because it is conceptually or logically impossible for something to possess *X-ish* properties and not also *V*. But more than this: although *V* is said to be irreducible to *X-ish* properties, in some sense *X-ishness* explains or accounts for the presence of *V*.[12] And Moore seems to think that this was not only true of value but of color attributions: "To say, of 'beauty' or 'goodness' that they are 'intrinsic' is only, therefore, to say that this thing which is obviously true of 'yellowness' and 'blueness' is obviously true of them."[13] But (and this is the objection), it seems that "redness or being red is not a supervenient . . . characteristic, but rather a paradigm of one that is not. Nothing is red because it is square, or round, or oblong, or flexible, or shapeless."[14] So, by focusing on the color analogy, it may be said that I have misconstrued the claim of those realists who uphold the existence of value properties: "value" is not like "red" but is a property that supervenes upon other, nonevaluative, properties of things.

The notion of supervenient value or ethical properties is, I think, far more obscure than a first look indicates. Moreover, it has been shown that notions of supervenience developed in the philosophy of mind are not straightforwardly applicable to ethical and valuational questions, so we cannot simply borrow those relatively sophisticated notions.[15] However, in principle I have no strong objection to the currently popular appeal to supervenience; indeed, my attempt in this chapter to show that sound valuings are grounded in appropriate beliefs about the object of valuing can be interpreted as showing that valuableness is supervenient upon those properties. And that is the problem: both my account as well as the more objectivist approach of Lewis and Wiggins can appeal to some notion of supervenience.[16] Mere superveni-

12 See Jan Narveson, "The How and Why of Universality," p. 8; Kim, "Supervenience"; William G. Lycan, *Judgement and Justification*, pp. 205–7.
13 Moore, "Intrinsic Value," p. 269. R. M. Hare also seems to see both value and color as supervenient properties. See Narveson, "How and Why of Universality," n. 5; George Marcus Singer, "The Generalization Principle," pp. 53–8. I consider Hare's views more closely in §18.1.
14 George Marcus Singer, "The Generalization Principle," p. 58.
15 See Lycan, *Judgement and Justification*, p. 205; David Zimmerman, "Moral Realism and Explanatory Necessity," pp. 83–90; Kim, "Supervenience."
16 Hence the often-repeated statement that "the *general* claim that moral facts

ence is, then, too general a notion to distinguish strongly objectivist from more subjectivist theories. What is crucial for our purposes is the distinction between Strong and Weak Impersonality: if a theory upholds the Strong Impersonality of value judgments, it does not matter for what follows whether it asserts that value properties are supervenient upon some other set of properties or whether they are more like color properties. It is the claim of Strong Impersonality that I wish to refute.

10.2 Externalism and internalism in value theory

I have argued, then, that at least concerning aesthetics and the comic, secondhand privative judgments can be validly distinguished from firsthand judgments arising out of direct access. I am not claiming that one is unwarranted in asserting secondhand judgments: given good grounds, one can rationally believe certain characterizations. But these characterizations are about a certain content in a particular psychological mode, and if one has not experienced that state one's grasp of it is incomplete. I have not demonstrated, however, that this distinction applies to all judgments of intrinsic value. Many, like William James,[17] believed that it is widely, if not universally, applicable, but I see no way to show that (especially because "intrinsic value" is a theory-laden term) without appeal to the Affective-Cognitive Theory. And that would be to beg the question. However, an argument can be advanced that provides a somewhat more indirect defense of the distinction: *viz.*, to the extent the distinction is accepted, we can account for both externalist and internalist positions in value theory. This does not show that the distinction is needed to make sense of all judgments of (intrinsic) valuableness, but it provides an independent reason (apart from the defense of the Affective-Cognitive Theory) why we should push the distinction as far as possible. Let me explain.

"Externalism" and "internalism" refer in this context to two groups of theories concerning the relation of "moral obligation"

supervene on nonmoral facts seems obvious to both cognitivists and noncognitivists alike." Lycan, *Judgement and Justification*, p. 206. Cf. Zimmerman, "Moral Realism," p. 84; Narveson, "How and Why of Universality," p. 8.

17 See James Campbell, "William James and the Ethics of Fulfillment," pp. 225–7.

and "motivation." Following some suggestions in W. K. Frankena's important paper on "Obligation and Motivation in Recent Moral Philosophy," we might distinguish *Minimal*, *Strong* and *Complete Externalism* as follows:[18]

> *Minimal Externalism*: "Alf has a moral obligation to ϕ" does not logically/conceptually imply that "Alf is motivated to ϕ."
>
> *Strong Externalism*: "Alf recognizes (assents) that he has a moral obligation to ϕ" does not logically/conceptually imply that "Alf is motivated to ϕ."
>
> *Complete Externalism*: "Alf sees for himself that he has a moral obligation to ϕ" does not logically/conceptually imply that "Alf is motivated to ϕ."

Roughly, Minimal Externalism is a thesis that obligations exist whether or not people are motivated to act on them; Strong Externalism is a thesis that people can logically assent that they have moral obligations even if they are not motivated to act on them; lastly, Complete Externalism is a vaguer thesis that, somehow, people can possess what Frankena calls "moral insight" – see their obligations for themselves – without being in any way disposed to perform them.

Although externalism is usually understood as a doctrine about duty or obligation, and this is how I have characterized it, it is also applied to the relation between judgments about the goodness/value of *X* and acting to choose it, promote it, etc.[19] Philippa Foot, for example, has argued for a Strong Externalist position with regard to goodness. Judgments of goodness, she holds, are typically based on impersonal criteria reflecting general

18 William K. Frankena, "Obligation and Motivation in Recent Moral Philosophy," pp. 60–1, 69. On internalism and externalism, see also Thomas Nagel, *The Possibility of Altruism*, ch. II. A related "internalism" and "externalism" debate is whether reasons necessarily motivate. Although this is sometimes seen as the same debate as that which I consider in the text, it is possible to combine an externalism (with respect to obligation) with an internalism (with respect to reasons). For example, one might argue (i) that "Alf recognizes he has an obligation to ϕ" does not imply "Alf is motivated to ϕ" (strong externalism with respect to obligation), and (ii) "Alf has a reason to ϕ" implies "Alf is motivated to ϕ" (internalism with respect to reasons), but (iii) "Alf recognizes that he has an obligation to ϕ" does not imply "Alf has a reason to ϕ" because (say) he does not have a desire to ϕ [and so, (i) and (ii) are consistent], E. J. Bond is concerned with both senses of internalism and externalism in his *Reason and Value*. I consider their relation further in §16.2.

19 See Frankena, "Obligation and Motivation," pp. 56–7.

human purposes that are not necessarily the purposes of every individual. Thus, she says, "Good riding is the kind of riding likely to achieve the characteristic purposes of the rider, not those which a particular individual may happen to have."[20] And, Foot indicates, because judgments of goodness are impersonal in this way (i) a person can competently employ them without any feeling for such goodness or a purpose that such goodness advances but (ii) when so used they have no necessary relevance for that person's choices. As she puts it:

> A man has reason to read an interesting book just so far as he thinks it will interest him, or if he expects the reading to be pleasing or profitable in some other way. The idea that one should have good works of art around just because they are good works of art, and even if one can get nothing from them, must depend on hopes of improvement in one's taste.[21]

To begin to evaluate this brand of externalism, I wish to call on a distinction I introduced earlier between beliefs about goodness and value judgments (§8.3). I do not claim that this distinction is anything like universally observed in value discourse, but it is, I think, grounded in it. Now I shall take as a paradigm of beliefs about goodness those fitting the schema "*X* is a good *K*"; as I argued earlier, though such beliefs can ground valuings, one is not committed to valuing something just because it is ranked high, or ranked as good, according to some standard. Instruments of torture, horse-riding skills, racing cars, and the candidates of some political parties can all be evaluated as "good" according to some standard[22] without any implication that they are appropriately valued, except by someone so described as to care about such goodness. The Strong Externalist position seems unassailable here because (i) a person can be perfectly competent at evaluating something such as a riding performance as "good" on the relevant standard without (ii) having any "use for" such goodness, the purpose it serves, or pro-attitude toward it. Con-

---

20 Philippa Foot, *Virtues and Vices*, pp. 144–5.

21 Ibid., p. 151.

22 J. O. Urmson distinguishes "good of its kind" from "good from a point of view" judgments, and it may be argued that the political-candidate case is an instance of the latter. Although "good from a point of view" judgments are more akin to value judgments than simple "good of its kind" judgments, I do not think much turns on the point here. Urmson, *The Emotive Theory of Ethics*, ch. 9.

sequently, just because Alf appraises or evaluates[23] *X* as good according to standard *S*, it does not follow that he is logically required to act or that he is motivated to do so.

Value judgments are more complicated. We should try to keep in mind that, quite literally, to judge whether something is value-*able* is to judge whether it is worthy of being, value-*d*. Just as something is desirable if it is appropriate to desire it, something is valuable if it is appropriate to value it. How, then, might we conclude that it is appropriate to value *X*? Well, we may rely on what has been called a "summary judgment": various experts, authorities, or perhaps, popular opinion provide one with grounds for rationally believing that it is properly valued.[24] But one need not be trusting and rely on authorities; a more reflective sort of judgment relates (i) the properties or characteristics of *X* to (ii) some value concept, with the conclusion, (iii) that (i) appropriately grounds a type of valuing described in (ii). To use Foot's example, to judge a book interesting is to say that it has certain qualities (for example, if it is a work in philosophy its topic/arguments and/or conclusions must have some novelty, insightfulness, etc.) and that, given the concept of "interest," these qualities appropriately ground an interest in the book. Although less obviously, so too is the judgment that something is, say, beautiful. To judge that something is beautiful is to judge that, based on complex criteria, it has certain characteristics (for example, harmony, unity, order), and these characteristics make an aesthetic appreciation of, or interest in, the object appropriate. In short, to say that something is beautiful is to say it is a worthy object of that attentive attitude called "valuing" or, more particularly, an aesthetic attitude.

Now, when one makes a value judgment, it is not an entirely independent question whether one happens to have any "use for" the thing. As I argued in §5.4.1, beliefs that warrant a certain emotion are also causal factors in producing the emotional state. So, given the analysis of valuing in terms of the Affective-Cog-

---

23 I shall not distinguish these terms. They are, however, distinguished by P. H. Nowell-Smith in his *Ethics*, pp. 170–1; and the distinction is discussed by Ronald D. Milo, *Immorality*, pp. 168–9. My distinction between beliefs about goodness, impersonal value judgments, and personal value judgments accommodates Nowell-Smith's main point.

24 See Lawrence C. Becker, *On Justifying Moral Judgments*, pp. 26–8. See §10.4 in this volume.

nitive Theory of emotion, to say that *X* has characteristics that properly ground valuings implies both (i) believing *X* to have these characteristics justifies the valuing (emotion) and (ii) those characteristics tend to evoke the valuing (emotional) response. Thus, according to Affective-Cognitive Theory, a judgment that something is (intrinsically) valuable implies that sound beliefs about it evoke a valuative response. When, then, I judge *X* to be of value I am committed to all this. And, at least presumably, I have reason to believe that knowledge of *X* will evoke the emotional response on my part too. But this makes the Strong Externalist challenge less plausible with respect to value judgments. Again, to use Foot's example, if I judge a book to be interesting, I claim that it properly grounds interest in it – and grounding beliefs, we have seen, are both justifying and causal (§5.4). If you believe that it is interesting, then you are rationally committed to believing that interest in it is justified and that it tends to evoke interest; you thus have grounds for believing that acquaintance with it would evoke in you a rational (that is, appropriate) interest in it. And it seems very plausible indeed to conclude that *all that* does provide you with *a* reason to acquaint yourself with the book. Think how very odd it would be to reply to "Here is a book that you are apt to find interesting, and is rational to find interesting" with "But what reason does that give *me* to read it?" This seems more confused than tough-minded.

A Strong Externalist like Foot has a reply, however. "A man," I quoted her as saying, "has reason to read an interesting book just so far as he thinks it will interest him." Although an "interesting book" may be one that as a rule evokes interest, I may be deviant. So Foot implies that Strong Externalism also characterizes what I have called value judgments. It is here that our analysis of testimonial and nontestimonial value judgments is helpful: a belief that the book is interesting does not imply that one finds it interesting. This points to a contrast between two types of value judgments.[25] *Impersonal value judgments*, let us say, assert that, given the relevant (impersonal) criteria, *X* is worthy of being valued. A *personal value judgment*, in contrast, asserts that *X* is valuable based on (i) apprehending *X* in the relevant affective mode

25 For arguments on behalf of related distinctions, see Milo, *Immorality*, pp. 166–73; Urmson, *The Emotive Theory*, pp. 66–7.

and (ii) a conviction, or at least an assumption, that this emotional response is appropriate (§6.3). A personal value judgment, then, is not simply a report that one experienced a certain emotional state with respect to *X* but, if it is to be a judgment that *X* is valuable – worthy of being valued – it is implied that this was a fully appropriate response to *X*. One, for instance, judges a book to be interesting because one finds it to be and, at the very least, one has no reason to doubt that one's interest in it is appropriate. As one value theorist has described such judgments, "[t]he person who asserts the value is not making a simple statement; he is not neutrally confirming the value discovered by other people, he is recreating it, recognizing this value as an individual convinced at the same time that it is general."[26]

The upshot of this distinction is fairly clear: the Strong Externalist thesis cannot be rebutted with respect to some instances of impersonal value judgments. Take Mackie's example of one who says "That is a good sunset, but the beauties of nature leave me cold."[27] To say that a sunset is "good" is not, I think, just to say that it ranks high on some sunset standard (is simply a belief about goodness); it is to say that it is a beautiful sunset, and beautiful things evoke a certain emotional reaction. But one who says that a beautiful sunset leaves him cold is saying that he does not himself see the beauty of the sunset: in a significant sense, *he* does not *find* it beautiful. Some "internalists" might argue that to believe a sunset to be beautiful is necessarily to be attracted to it, but in this case one has a belief that it is beautiful but, because one is "cold" to such beauty, one is not attracted to it. And I think Mackie is quite right to object to the maneuver that puts the affirmation of goodness/beauty in inverted commas, as if one does not really believe it to be beautiful.[28] As Aurel Kolnai observes: "The expert or even the more reflective sort of man will habitually, and often very keenly, distinguish between what he holds to be 'beautiful' (or 'good' as a work of art) and what peculiarly enchants and prepossesses *him*, that is, be on his guard against automatically erecting his taste into (his) judgment."[29]

26 Ludwig Grunberg, "Rationality and the Basis of the Value Judgments," p. 127.
27 J. L. Mackie, *Ethics*, p. 55.
28 Ibid.
29 Aurel Kolnai, "Contrasting the Ethical with the Aesthetical," p. 338. See also Milo, *Immorality*, p. 169.

Nevertheless, one can understand the impulse behind the "inverted commas move," for in this case the judge cannot really find the beauty in that which he judges to be beautiful.

However, externalism is not plausible with regard to personal value judgments (that is, Complete Externalism does not characterize value judgments). Intuitively, this seems clear: to proclaim "I find the book interesting," but then ask "but what motivation do I have to (say) continue reading it?" is manifestly strange. The Affective-Cognitive Theory provides a solid theoretical foundation for this intuition. As I argued in the previous chapter, to value something is to have a certain attitude toward it and to be rationally committed to certain courses of action with respect to it; furthermore, this affect-content-belief complex that constitutes the valuing provides a motivation for acting.[30] Valuing motivates action. But affective theories of value also explain why someone who values something can be said to "see" the value of it, that is, experience it as a content in a certain affective mode. Of course, not all affective responses constitute seeing the value of a thing: one who inappropriately responds to an object (§10.4) cannot be said to "see" its value. Moreover, it seems possible to "see" the value of something without valuing it. I argued earlier (§8.1) that fleeting emotions do not constitute valuing because valuing points to a settled disposition; and it seems right in this context, too, to say that a fleeting grasp of the value of something does not constitute valuing of it. But one who is disposed to grasp or appreciate something and who acts appropriately[31] can indeed be said to value it. The affective response, which gives one the insight the purely testimonial credent does not have, is also the basis of one's valuing it.[32] I take it that this is essentially Scruton's view; as he says regarding amusingness: "In one sense it is absurd to ask of something said to be amusing: And what is good about *that* (although there may be other reasons for disapproving of it). . . . In liking something for its amusing quality one is liking it for an intelligible reason."[33] Scruton nicely points to the connections within affective theories of value of (i) seeing

30 Hence my account of personal value judgments is internalist with respect to reasons. See note 18.
31 That is, in accordance with one's commitments. See §9.2.2.
32 See Kraft, *Scientific Analysis of Value*, pp. 86–7.
33 Scruton, *Art and Imagination*, p. 246.

or grasping the amusingness of a joke, (ii) thinking the joke to be good (that is, valuable), and (iii) liking the joke (that is, valuing it). Given this analysis, it is manifest why externalism is implausible with respect to personal value judgments.

It should be emphasized that the distinction between personal and impersonal value judgments is not at all ad hoc. It is deeply embedded in the Affective-Cognitive Theory of emotion. Any emotion *E*, it will be recalled, is only appropriate in relation to certain beliefs and content (§6). Whether or not any object is an appropriate target of *E* is a matter of public, impersonal judgment; anyone who grasps the concept of *E* can make that judgment. However, one who does not experience the relevant affect will not himself find that set of properties to be (we might say) "affectively provocative."

Let me briefly consider a possible objection to the idea of an impersonal value judgment.[34] Surely, one might say, it is senseless to talk of an impersonal value judgment that a book is interesting; depending on people's background knowledge and values, different books will be interesting. What interests a moral philosopher will not be what interests an artist. Care needs to be exercised here. An impersonal value judgment is a judgment that a valuing is appropriate toward some object; whether or not the artist finds a work in moral theory interesting does not tell us much about whether it is impersonally valuable – that is, whether it is appropriate for someone to be interested in it. The problem is that the appropriateness conditions for interest are so broad that the impersonal value judgment that "Book *X* is worthy of interest" tells us little as to whether the book's value will be accessible to *us*. For that we need something different: personal value judgments by people with similar background beliefs and values. If, for instance, a fellow contractualist moral philosopher has found value in a work, I have good grounds for suspecting that I too will be able to appreciate its value. So impersonal value judgments – especially concerning valuing attitudes that do not have well-defined appropriateness conditions – are often not very useful guides as to whether we will find the thing of value. But I hope it is clear that this is consistent with the view I have been developing.

34 I am grateful to J. Roland Pennock for calling my attention to this point.

Strong Externalism, then, characterizes some impersonal value judgments: namely, where one has grounds for concluding that, although *X* is worthy of being valued, one cannot grasp or appreciate its value – one cannot intrinsically value it oneself. However, this argument does not endorse Strong Externalism with respect to all impersonal value judgments. A sound judgment that a piece of music is impersonally beautiful standardly provides good grounds for people to believe that they will find it to be so. Moreover, that one believes that one will find it to be of value provides one with a rational commitment to act – it commits one to a certain course of action.[35] I hasten to add that one may have conflicting action commitments based on other values and nonvalue considerations. The nature of these conflicts and other commitments will occupy us later. My point now is simply that the sound belief that one is apt to find something of value does provide one with *a* commitment to act.

Consider a variation of an example provided by E. J. Bond.[36] Say I am very modestly acquainted with some sorts of classical music, but have heard very little Brahms. I have been told by several friends, though, that Brahms's First Symphony is something I would find particularly worthwhile or beautiful; it has a sort of excellence that would, they think, be accessible to me. Now this is a sort of impersonal value judgment: Brahms's First Symphony is said to have particular sorts of excellences. But it is also pointed out to me that these sorts of excellence are, in my friends' opinion, ones I might grasp. If I accept that my advisers have a certain expertise in this area, then it seems undeniable that I also believe that they have provided me with reason to listen to Brahms.

It is not easy to specify just how extensive are the reasons for action implied by sound impersonal value judgments. Are they, say, on all fours with those implied by our actual valuings? Let me approach this issue by suggesting a lower and an upper limit on the sort of reasons implied, and then I shall say something about the very broad area that remains. Now, as the Brahms case

35 Recall that, as I use the terms, only if one's beliefs are sound and complete in the relevant ways, and if one's valuings are appropriate, does one have a reason to act; whether or not one's beliefs and valuings are flawed, however, one can still be said to be rationally committed to act. See §9.2.2.
36 Bond, *Reason and Value*, pp. 35ff.

indicates, at a very minimum, a sound impersonal judgment that something is valuable normally provides a reason to acquaint oneself with the thing, explore it, and so on to see if one will also find value in it.[37] If one accepts the sound impersonal judgment "The book is interesting" then one has reason to, say, select it if one is about to buy a book. But the externalist is right that this commitment to act is undermined if one has good grounds to believe that one is not apt to find the thing of value. Thus, if I know that all classical music "leaves me cold," impersonal judgments of experts on classical music will have no necessary implications for action. (Of course, one may devote oneself to developing a taste for it; I consider such higher-order valuings in §14.2). As Bond says, someone who is tone deaf or is "constitutionally unable to appreciate Brahms" has no reason to expose himself to Brahms.[38] It is not merely that a person fails to recognize a commitment that he has, or even that he would recognize such a commitment but for certain rational defects; rather, the point is that he is both perfectly rational and has no such commitment. Does he, however, have a commitment to protect, preserve, or promote music that he believes to be impersonally valuable but the value of which he cannot grasp? I shall examine a little later some arguments seeking to affirm that he does indeed have such reasons (§12), but it is hard to see how he would necessarily be rationally defective for denying that he was committed to such actions. True, he acknowledges that but for some defect in hearing he too could appreciate the music, but it is unclear how this implies that he is now committed to act toward it in preserving and caring ways. Foot and other externalists proffer a challenge in these sorts of cases that cannot be simply ignored: precisely where is the rational defect in acknowledging that Brahms is worthy of being valued, but as someone who is left cold by Brahms, denying that Brahms provides you with any reasons at all to act? (I take up this issue from a slightly different perspective in §16.2.) Some internalists might insist that this is to misun-

37 This role of impersonal value judgments – as providing evidence for what one will find of value – is often described in terms of potential value. See Harold N. Lee, "The Methodology of Value Theory," pp. 162–3; Gene G. James, "Is Value a Gestalt Quality?" p. 219. See also Joel J. Kupperman, *The Foundations of Morality*, p. 23.

38 Bond, *Reason and Value*, p. 38.

derstand what it means to believe that Brahms is *valuable*. But this is to beg the question; it is precisely the action implications of value beliefs that is at issue between internalists and externalists. Someone accepting the Affective-Cognitive Theory is able to give an account of such value beliefs – that certain affective intentional states are appropriately directed at certain contents/objects – and he quite rightly wants to know why he is irrational to entertain the belief but acknowledge no commitments to act. He cannot be shown to be irrational, I submit, because he is not.

So much for what I have called the lower limit. As an upper limit, I suggest that a sound impersonal judgment that *X* is valuable does not have as strong implications for one's actions as actually valuing *X*. There are many more things worthy of being valued than I can possibly value; when deliberating about action, my focus must be on things I actually value – whose value I appreciate – and not on the innumerable things that are worthy of being valued but are not actually valued by me. I cherish, love, and care for things with which I am acquainted in various ways, and the fact that I actually do cherish something has consequences for my action. To claim that I should treat equally with respect to action those things I would cherish (if I knew them) and those that I actually do cherish seems quite implausible. The similarity here to "desired" and "desirable" is strong: though recognizing that *X* is desirable may well have consequences for my action, it certainly does not have as strong implications for my action as does my actual desiring of *X*.

Between these two limits lie all sorts of possibilities. Sometimes an impersonal value judgment may have highly significant consequences for action: for example, a wilderness area that an environmentalist has never visited and knows relatively little about may be at risk, and impersonal judgments concerning its value may motivate him to take action. At other times, only the minimal commitment may be in order. Such differences derive from the relation of the impersonal value judgment to one's valuings. Say one appreciates music of a certain type, and, though one has not yet grasped Brahms, many of the things one has been told are admirable in Brahms are in many ways akin to things one already appreciates in other music. In this case, one's beliefs about what is valuable in Brahms are very close to those things that one finds of value in other pieces; one might thus be described as on the brink of grasping Brahms. In other cases, the impersonal value judgment might relate in other ways to one's valuings. The environmentalist mentioned above, for instance, has a general or abstract valuing of certain things (for example, ecosystems) and the impersonal value judgment shows him that *X* is an instantiation of this general valuing. (I consider this relation in some depth in §13.) I do not wish to insist on any limited number of ways that impersonal judgments might relate to current valuings; I wish only to emphasize that an account of the action implications of impersonal judgments will center on their relations to actual valuings – even if these take the form of character ideals that value becoming the sort of person who can appreciate the valuable thing. (See §14.2.)[39]

The chief objection to my claim that impersonal value judgments are motivating is posed by the "Humean" doctrine that, for Alf to have a reason to ϕ he must have a desire which ϕ-ing somehow satisfies. I have held, however, that Alf can have a reason to expose himself to Brahms given a well-grounded belief that an impersonal value judgment provides evidence that he will value Brahms. No desire on Alf's part to foster a taste for Brahms or to further enjoy him is necessary. Moreover, I have held that Alf has a *reason* to expose himself to Brahms and that such a reason is *motivating*.[40] Given my general critique of the role of desire in explaining (and motivating) action (§7.2), this departure from the Humean view is, perhaps, not surprising. What may well be surprising, however, is that not only the presence of a desire, but the presence of an affect as well, is unnecessary to ground such reasons. My strategy thus far has been to show that affect, not desire, is basic in explaining a wide variety of actions. But here, and much more radically in Chapter VI, I want to extend this affect-based account of valuing and value-based reasons for action to ground rational action that is not directly concerned with promoting what one presently values. The argument of Chapter VI will be somewhat complex, but this first extension,

39 Of course, if seeking out a particular value would distract one from other important valuings, the cost to one's other sound valuings provides a reason not to pursue the distracting value.

40 David A. J. Richards allows that Alf can have a reason to ϕ without a desire, but the reason would then only move to action if one has, for instance, a desire to be rational or reasonable. *A Theory of Reasons for Action*, chs. 5, 6, 13, 14.

grounding reasons to act on sound impersonal value judgments, is pretty straightforward. The belief that one would value or disvalue something – that one would have a certain emotional disposition toward it – can motivate; one does yet not experience an affect, but the motivating belief is about prospective affects. This is not to say, as does the hedonist (§8.1), that one is acting to gain or to escape from the *affect*: one acts to gain or to escape from *objects* to which one would react in these ways. Intuitively, it seems clear that one is rationally committed to act in these cases; an externalist, who admits that he has excellent grounds for believing that he would be interested in a book, but sees no motivating commitments to read it, is indeed puzzling. If one has a difficulty here, it is not because my account generates intuitively implausible reasons for action, but (I suspect) because one is entertaining a model of action according to which some propelling power is necessary to, as it were, get the Humean machine moving. Apparently this at least was Hume's own view. Unless some desire or affect is present *before the action*, the agent could never get moving; and, if that were true, the mere belief about prospective emotions could not, presumably, motivate. But I see no reason to adopt this mechanistic outlook on action: Humean sentiments notwithstanding, it seems clear that a belief about prospective emotions or affects can indeed motivate. I shall not object, however, if committed Humeans insist that this belief necessarily generates a desire,[41] as long as it is acknowledged: (i) that the belief is sufficient to produce the desire, and (ii) that the desire, without the grounding belief, would not explain this type of rational action (§7.2.2).

10.4 *How value judgments can be criticized*

It is commonly said that "subjectivist" accounts of value, because they focus on personal reactions, tastes, desires, or whatever, somehow undermine the possibility of intelligible disagreement about value. If "*X* is valuable" translates into something such as "I have a taste for *X*" or "*X* appeals to me," then, it is said, Alf can assert that *X* is valuable and Betty that it is not, and yet they do not really disagree: "I (Alf) have a taste for *X*" is entirely con-

41 See Bond, *Reason and Value*, pp. 39–40, for a Humean account along these lines.

sistent with "I (Betty) do not." Alternatively, it is sometimes charged that theories that emphasize the "valuing process" are somehow inclined to explicate "valu*able*" as "is valued."[42] It is important to see why such criticisms do not apply to the Affective-Cognitive Theory.

It should be obvious enough why these criticisms miss the mark with respect to impersonal value judgments, at least of the more reflective sort. Whether or not *X* is, say, impersonally exciting depends on *X*'s characteristics, and how these relate to our understanding of excitement. To be sure, there will be disagreements, indeed, perhaps some that cannot be resolved. Concepts such as "exciting" are open-textured and subject to disputes on a variety of points; if we cannot agree on the criteria for properly describing something as exciting, then of course we will have some seemingly unresolvable disputes about whether a particular *X* is or is not exciting. But this is not a difficulty peculiar to the Affective-Cognitive Theory of value; it is a very general problem concerning the public nature of concepts and conceptual disputes (see §1.2).

Somewhat more problematic are what I have called "summary" impersonal value judgments (§10.2). Rather than being of the form "*X*, by virtue of some set of features, is *V*-able," such summary judgments rely on authorities or popular opinion, resulting in something like "Given the testimony of those who know, *X* is *V*-able." Disputes in these cases may be even more difficult to resolve; different "experts" may give different opinions, and as long as one remains at the summary level such disputes may be most intractable. (One way to resolve them is to focus on the experts' qualifications and experience.) Again, however, this is a much more general problem, in this case concerned with the matters of expert judgment, which would arise in nearly any account of value. At present, what is important is that disputes among authorities are precisely that: real disputes as to whether a certain thing is properly the object of valuing. I take it that it is clear that the Affective-Cognitive Theory provides a basis for genuine disputes here as well.

---

42 For criticisms along these general lines, see Fishkin, *Subjective Morality*, chs. 1, 4, esp. p. 145; Grenville Wall, "Against Subjective Intrinsic Value"; Becker, *Moral Judgments*, pp. 50–3; George J. Harrison, "Values Clarification and the Construction of Good." See also Brenda Cohen, "Positive Values."

But it might be thought that the possibility of genuine disputes regarding impersonal value judgments just drives the essential subjectivity of value judgments back one stage further. For if personal value judgments are matters of taste, and if "there is no disputing tastes" [feature (e), §1.1] then regarding (what is on my account) the really basic type of value judgment, real value disputes are indeed conceptually impossible. "If I bite an apple," C. I. Lewis wrote, "I cannot be in error about the good or bad taste of the present bite." Hence, "Value as immediately found is subject to no critique."[43]

Given the analysis of the appropriateness conditions for emotions, it should be clear why this is not the view implied by the Affective-Cognitive Theory. Because personal value judgments are related to valuing (§10.2), and valuing to emotion (§9), and emotions can be appropriate or inappropriate (§6), it is not difficult to grasp how the appropriateness conditions provide a foundation for criticizing personal value judgments. To see this, assume that Betty claims to find *X* exciting; drawing on the analysis of the appropriateness conditions for emotions, her claim "*X* is exciting (because I find it to be so)" can be criticized on at least five grounds.

(i) *Betty must experience the* E-*relevant affect*. Her claim that she was excited can be called into question. This would not be to dispute whether *X* is worthy of being the object of excitement, but rather that she apprehended *X* in the appropriate (excited) mode. Such criticisms are made often enough: that is, when we doubt whether a person has really been moved in the way he claims to have been. Thus one may call into question the claim of one's companion that he found the movie fascinating, when he spent most of the time looking at his watch; or if a mother of an infant purports to be interested in a tedious film, we might ask her whether or not she was simply enjoying the relative calm and sanity of the theater.

(ii) *Betty's emotional state must have an* E-*appropriate content*. It might, secondly, be objected that *X* is not an appropriate content/object of excitement. "The day was uneventful" and "watching paint dry" are not appropriate in this sense. This appropriateness

43 Lewis, *Knowledge and Valuation*, pp. 410–85. Cf. John Locke, *An Essay Concerning Human Understanding*, p. 272 (bk. II, ch. xxi, sec. 58).

condition takes on importance in disputes about masochism and sadism – that is, whether "pain" is an appropriate object of enjoyment. If we understand masochism in a straightforward way, the case against it as a coherent valuation is compelling: "my pain" just is not a conceptually appropriate content for the intentional attitude, enjoyment. Given our understanding of enjoyment and what it is to be in pain, to simply enjoy one's own pain is as intelligible as fearing what is utterly harmless.[44] In order to make sense of masochism, then, we need to employ, for instance, some theory about guilt and a craving for punishment, such that one enjoys the fact that one is in pain. [Enjoy (that I am in pain – and so am being punished)] is thus to be distinguished from [Enjoy (my pain)]. Now unlike some,[45] I do not think sadism is in this respect on all fours with masochism. "To see others suffer does one good," Nietzsche wrote, "to make others suffer even more: this is a hard saying but an ancient, mighty, human, all-too-human principle."[46] Whatever we take Nietzsche to mean by the "transvaluation" of values, it is certain that he is not just turning values upside down; his point is that like it or not, deny it or not, men do take pleasure in inflicting suffering on others, and we have no trouble understanding or grasping what that might mean. We may well be disgusted or appalled by such valuings,[47] and I will later argue (in a most un-Nietzschean way) that all but psychopathic humans have nonvalue reasons to refrain from inflicting such suffering on others. Nevertheless, the sadist's valuing does not strike us as irrational or incoherent in the way that does the masochist who simply asserts that he enjoys his own pain.[48]

44 If one accepts Roger Trigg's analysis of pain (§9.2 in this volume) as a sensation conjoined with an emotion, one might, I suppose, say that the masochist has the pain sensation but conjoins this with a liking, rather than a disliking. In fact, the analysis of masochism I present in the text follows Trigg, *Pain and Emotion*, pp. 154ff. See §§6.1, 6.2 in the present volume.
45 Following Franz Brentano (§8.4 in this volume), one might say that such an emotion is "incorrect" or has an "inappropriate object." See, e.g., Michael J. Zimmerman, "On the Intrinsic Value of States of Pleasure"; G. E. Moore, *Principia Ethica*, p. 209.
46 Friedrich Nietzsche, *On the Genealogy of Morals*, p. 67 (essay II, sec. 6).
47 That is: [Disgust (Friedrich enjoys inflicting suffering)]. In fact, moralists do tend to use terms such as "abhor" in describing their attitude toward such valuings. See S. I. Benn, "Wickedness."
48 "Thus there are serious objections to placing on equal footing desires to

(iii) *Betty's emotional state must be grounded in* E-*appropriate beliefs.* Her excited state, though having an appropriate content, may not be appropriately grounded in two ways. (a) Perhaps she was euphoric and aroused all day, and indeed would have found watching paint dry exciting, but she was lucky enough to focus on something, *X*, that is properly described as "exciting." This criticism, then, does not doubt whether *X* is exciting, but whether Betty really was excited *by it.* (b) It could also be objected that the beliefs that grounded her excitement were inappropriate. If, for example, *X* is Betty's job, and the grounding beliefs were "It isn't dangerous" and "It is secure," her claim that it is exciting is open to criticism on this ground.

(iv) *Betty's* E-*appropriate grounding beliefs must themselves be well grounded, true, etc.* If, once again, *X* is "Betty's job" and her grounding beliefs are that at any time she may be sent to remote parts of the world to report on political upheavals, conditions (ii) and (iii) would be met. But if she is wrong, and her editor had assigned her only to report on epistemology conferences, Betty's excitement would violate this appropriateness condition. As I indicated earlier (§5.4.2), this is also the condition according to which we can distinguish, among those emotions or (roughly) valuings that do not have an object *qua* item in the world, those that are rationally flawed from those that are not. It is important to stress that the mere fact that one's emotional state does not have an object *qua* item does not show it to be somehow ill-grounded; and *mutatis mutandis*, so too with personal value judgments.

(v) *Betty's grounding beliefs must be* E-*complete, given her perspective, that is, they must be pragmatically complete.* Arguments from completeness are fundamental to value discourse and criticism. One technique of journalism – as, for instance, regarding apartheid – is to undermine someone's positive valuation of something by bringing to light aspects of it that render the valuation inappropriate. By demonstrating the true (that is, complete) nature of the thing, one seeks to show that the prior evaluation is in-

harm oneself and desires to harm others. . . . Although it would be irrational for me to cut off my own arm just because I felt like doing it, it need not be irrational for me to cut off the arm of another just because I felt like doing it. It would, of course, be monstrous of anyone to do that, but it would not be irrational." Bernard Gert, *The Moral Rules*, p. 41.

appropriate because it is based on a mistaken or inadequate conception of it.[49] To return to our example: if Betty judges her job as a reporter exciting because she may be sent anywhere in the world to cover political upheavals, and this is true, her judgment will not be subject to criticism along the lines of (iv); but if, though this may happen, it is extraordinary and most of her time is actually spent at epistemology conferences, her judgment may be unsound in the way depicted in (ii) above. But, even if she is sent overseas often enough to make the excitement appropriate, if her excitement is nevertheless based on her failure to realize just how much time she has to spend at epistemology conferences, her judgment may still be subject to challenge as being founded on a distorted and partial view of the object (that is, her job).

Readers may well have noted that these criticisms include, but go beyond, the charge that what is asserted to be valuable on the basis of direct experience is not really impersonally valuable. That is, if Betty claims "*X* is exciting (because I find it to be so)," criticisms (ii)–(v) all provide grounds for questioning whether her excitement is appropriate given the nature of *X* and the public conception of excitement. But the claim that she finds *X* to be exciting is a *stronger* (not a *weaker*) claim than that it is (impersonally) exciting: thus criticisms (i) and (iii)(a) in particular focus not on *X*, but on Betty's claim that *she found X* to be exciting.

Suppose Betty finds that she is unable to answer one or more of the charges implied by (i)–(v) – indeed she acknowledges the force of the criticisms; she can reply in one of three ways. (a) She may try to show that our understanding of excitement should be revised; perhaps her job is not clearly exciting based on the usual criteria, but it is related to those criteria in ways that suggest a plausible extension of the concept. Such extensions and modifications of value concepts occur constantly; for example, if fear is grounded on possible harm, the rise of the notion of psychological harm expanded the instances of appropriate fear. (b) She may simply retreat to a psychological, rather than a value, claim. "Well, it may not be exciting, but I sure felt excited." But this

49 "A value judgement is wrong if the object does not possess the quality to which the judgement refers or if it has additional pertinent characteristics not taken into account in the evaluation." Kraft, *A Scientific Analysis of Value*, p. 141.

move has its costs, for not only is one abandoning value discourse, but it is not at all clear that such a response grounds a reason for acting. I earlier (§9.2) rejected the claim that, as mere natural facts, emotions cannot imply reasons for action; but mere reports of affective experiences, with no grounding in appropriate beliefs, really do not typically yield reasons for actions. Thus, for instance, MacLean's patients who experienced free-floating affects (§4.1) did not appear to think action was appropriate, and in this they seem right. (c) More interestingly, one may retreat in a way that preserves a value claim, albeit of a more general and vague sort. If Betty cannot sustain the claim that she appropriately found *X* exciting, she may well be able to appropriately claim that she *likes X*. This is a significant move in value discourse. When one finds that a specific valuation – that is, exciting – cannot be supported, one can retreat to more open-ended, vague, or general valuations. Put in terms of the analysis of §6.1, one can retreat from the specific end of the belief-appropriateness continuum toward the open-ended extreme. Consequently, value discourse is apt to be far more fruitful when the value ascriptions have well-defined appropriateness conditions; it is much easier to have useful discussion as to whether something is fear-inspiring, terrifying, shameful, or appropriately resented than whether it is unlikable or simply disvaluable. Axiologists and moral theorists have been cognizant of this feature of evaluative terms: general terms such as "good" or "valuable" seem remarkably devoid of real content and, consequently, it is most difficult to show that they are being misapplied.[50]

This is not to say that it is in principle impossible to show that anyone is ever wrong when it is said that "*X* is (intrinsically) valuable." If nothing can be pointed to concerning *X* that could ground any positive emotional disposition, even these general judgments can be defeated. But it seems more important to realize that "valuable" is not simply, as some would have it, a generic term for a variety of specific evaluations.[51] It also functions as a general and vague residue claim that provides besieged valuers with an easily defended, if not quite impregnable, fall-back

50 See ibid., p. 13; Neil Cooper, *The Diversity of Moral Thinking*, ch. 7. See §§6.2, 8.3 in the present volume.
51 "*Value* is the generic noun for any positive predicate." Holmes Rolston III, "Values in Nature," p. 114.

position. The Affective-Cognitive Theory explains why this is so (§6.2).

In one sense, however, the theory of value defended here does endorse the dictum that there is no disputing tastes or, more accurately in this context, that "one man's meat is another man's poison." In Chapter II (§6.3) I rejected the very strong requirement that one can be deemed irrational for being inappropriately nonemotional when one meets conditions (i)-(v), but nevertheless fails to experience the *E*-relevant affect. Although others can certainly disvalue such failures (that is, have emotional dispositions toward them), I argued that they are not the type of failures of rationality that the appropriateness conditions articulate. Indeed, given the different background values (Chapter V) and affective natures of individuals, we have strong grounds for believing that fully rational and informed individuals will not necessarily find the same things to be of value.[52] A professional book that a microbiologist finds interesting will not appeal to many others. Consequently, it does not follow from the mere fact that one does not find value (disvalue) in that which is impersonally valuable (disvaluable), that one is open to criticism that one has misunderstood the value concept or has false or incomplete beliefs. I have indicated that the value judgments of a rational person will be undermined or altered by acknowledging the criticisms detailed in §10.4. But I do not see how this is necessarily the case with his "failure" to affectively respond.

10.5 Extrinsic value judgments

The analysis of impersonal and personal value judgments has focused on judgments of intrinsic value (§8). Extrinsic value judgments, at least in this context, are more straightforward. In §10.1, I stressed that, in the case of intrinsic value, one can come to believe that something is valuable without being able to grasp that value. One way to make this point is that, for example, [Believe (*X* is interesting)] is a very different mental state from [Interest (*X*)]. However, I also maintained (§9.2) that purely extrinsic valuings can be explicated in terms of a set of requirements

52 For evidence concerning different affective reactions to the same events, see Randy J. Larsen, Ed Deiner, and Robert A. Emmons, "Affect Intensity and Reactions to Daily Life Events."

for rational action based on affects, emotions, and beliefs. In essence, to value something extrinsically is to have certain beliefs about what is appropriate given one's intrinsic valuings or certain nonintentional affects (§9.3). But that is to say that extrinsic valuings are essentially matters of belief; and, if that is so, no distinction can be made between believing *X* to be of value and grasping its value.

Still, a distinction can be made between (i) extrinsic value judgments derived from impersonal (intrinsic) value judgments and (ii) those derived from personal (intrinsic) value judgments. Although both can be criticized in a variety of ways (for example, the soundness of the grounding intrinsic value judgment, if the extrinsic value is a means, whether it is efficient etc.),[53] our argument thus far implies that the motivational implication of these two types of judgment will differ in ways roughly corresponding to that between personal and impersonal intrinsic value judgments (§§10.2, 10.3). It would, however, be tedious, and in any event it seems unnecessary, to provide these extensions here: I shall content myself with claiming that, because one is motivated to act on personal and impersonal intrinsic value judgments, one is also motivated to act on the extrinsic judgments that derive from them.[54]

11 COMPARATIVE VALUE JUDGMENTS

It has long been disputed among value theorists whether or not value (or goodness) is an essentially comparative concept. Most contemporary philosophers – including Roderick Chisholm and Kurt Baier[55] – characterize the very concept of value in terms of betterness or preferability: to say that something is valuable is just to claim that it is better than, or preferable to, something else, or perhaps, to its negation or to a world in which it is ab-

53 Even theorists such as C. I. Lewis, who held that reports of immediate value experience could not be criticized, acknowledged that value judgments informed by beliefs were open to critique. See *Knowledge and Valuation*, e.g., p. 410. See also Locke, *Essay*, pp. 276ff. (bk. ii, ch. xxi, secs. 64ff.).

54 Bond stresses that instrumental valuations motivate in his *Reason and Value*, e.g., p. 48.

55 See Roderick M. Chisholm, "Intrinsic Value." Baier distinguishes "value assessments" (which are comparative) from simple "melioration claims" (which are not) in "What is Value?" p. 48.

sent. The other position – and I would include among its proponents theorists as diverse as R. B. Perry and Franz Brentano – maintains that an analysis of worth is logically prior to an analysis of betterness. As Perry saw it, "whatever the definition of generic value," *X* is better than *Y* only if *X* is of more value, and one can only determine that once one knows what value is and the relative degrees to which *X* and *Y* possess it.[56] As such, this latter group of theorists typically insist that "preferential" sentences are to be distinguished from the more basic, "valuative," sentences.[57]

Comparative accounts are subject to serious criticism.[58] However, my concern here is not to rehearse the difficulties with comparative conceptions, but to emphasize that the Affective-Cognitive Theory is noncomparative; in the previous section, I analyzed value judgments in a way that shows that they are not essentially about comparisons or preferences. This is not to deny, however, that we often value something just because it rates high on some standard or is better than others in its class; the analysis of beliefs about goodness (§8.3) shows how such considerations ground valuings. Rather, the crucial (negative) claim of noncomparative accounts is to *deny* that "Alf values *X*" just *means* that he judges *X* to be better than something else, or he prefers *X* to something else.

In order to be adequate as theories of value, however, noncomparative accounts must show how simple valuings and value judgments give rise to comparative valuings and value judgments, and, further, how these relate to deliberation and choice [feature (b), §1.1]. I divide this task into two parts. In §11.1, I analyze comparative valuing, that is, what is involved in valuing one thing more than another. §11.2 then considers whether these comparative valuings can be said to be impersonally appropriate or inappropriate; or (and this is a somewhat different point) in what sense one thing can be, impersonally, more valuable than another.

56 R. B. Perry, *General Theory of Value*, pp. 599–600. See also Franz Brentano, *The Origin of the Knowledge of Right and Wrong*, pp. 25ff. See R. M. Chisholm's *Brentano and Intrinsic Value*, pp. 52–4, where he explicates Brentano's theory of "intrinsic value" in a way that rather suggests a comparative notion.
57 See Willis Moore, "The Language of Values," p. 13.
58 See Michael David Rohr, "Is Goodness Comparative?"

11.1.1 A neo-Millian account

What, then, does it mean to say that Betty values *X* more than *Y*? An obvious candidate, and one in the spirit of the Affective-Cognitive Theory, is that her affective response to *X* is somehow greater than that to *Y*. "Greater" is itself ambiguous in this context, but "more intense" seems a natural interpretation. Remember that, unlike the hedonist, we are not concerned with the amount of satisfaction or pleasure that one receives, but with the degree of one's affective response to objects.[59] "Strength of response," or "intensity of affect," seems to capture this notion of greater or lesser response to things. Moreover, this interpretation underscores the convergence of the Affective-Cognitive Theory with attitude theories, where attitude measurement is often conceived of as measuring the "intensity of feeling" for or against an object;[60] it also draws support from those sociobiologists who argue that the function of felt differences in intensity of affect is to "permit and encourage quantitative comparison."[61] Certainly it is generally agreed that affective or emotional experience does manifest variation in felt intensity; we have, of course, been assuming so throughout.

So variation in intensity of affect provides us with a natural, and from our perspective theoretically appealing, conception of "valuing more."[62] If Betty values *X* and *Y* purely intrinsically, and, further, her intentional affect is not complex, for example, she is simply interested (*or* afraid, *or* angry), then it seems rea-

59 Bentham's calculus, of course, includes a variety of characteristics that contribute to "greaterness," e.g., fecundity, certainty, propinquity, purity, etc. Jeremy Bentham, *An Introduction to the Principles of Morals and Legislation*, ch. IV. For alternative analyses of the dimensions of value, see Parker, *The Philosophy of Value*, pp. 104ff.; Perry, *Realms of Value*, pp. 53ff.; Nicolai Hartmann, *Ethics*, vol. II, pp. 55ff.

60 See, e.g., Louis Guttman and Edward A. Suchman, "Intensity and a Zero Point for Attitude Analysis," pp. 269ff. However, it should be acknowledged that attitude is sometimes simply understood as "amount" of affect for or against.

61 George Edgin Pugh, *The Biological Origin of Human Values*, p. 111. See §3.1 in the present volume.

62 Because, as we will see presently, my account does not stress intensity, I will not consider the difficulties that confront accounts stressing it. For a discussion of these in relation to the Austrian economists, see Howard O. Eaton, *The Austrian Philosophy of Value*, pp. 185ff.

sonable to say that she values (or disvalues) X more if she feels more interested in (or more afraid of, or more angry at) X than Y. But this provides an appealing conception of "valuing more" only so long as we restrict the comparison to intensities of a single sort of affective response. The intuitive appeal of the proposal is undermined when there are a variety of distinct affects. It is plausible to conceive of each affect as varying in intensity, and for any affective experience it seems that this intensity scale articulates an intuitive conception of degrees of valuing; but it is by no means obvious how different degrees of intensity of different affects can be mapped on to a common intensity scale. Gordon W. Allport pointed to this general problem long ago. In criticizing those who conceived of attitudes as all capable of being placed on a single, bipolar, degree of affect for or against scale, he stressed the qualitative differences in attitudes; two people with the same degree of affect toward an object, Allport maintained, could have qualitatively different attitudes toward it.[63] Nevertheless, however qualitatively distinct attitudes may be, an agent deliberating about what to do must be somehow able to compare and order them.[64] If it was really impossible to compare them – if most valuings were literally noncomparable – what we value would be of little help in deciding what to do. And that would be to fundamentally misconceive the practice of valuing.

To be sure, contemporary philosophers such as Isaiah Berlin, Stuart Hampshire, and Bernard Williams do indeed stress the incommensurability of values. But it is by no means always clear just what this claim of incommensurability involves.[65] Williams suggests that at least three plausible and important claims can be implied:

(1) No currency exists in terms of which each conflict of values can be resolved.
(2) It is not true that for each conflict of values some value, independent

63 Gordon W. Allport, "Attitudes," pp. 819–20. See also Martin Fishbein, "Attitude and the Prediction of Behavior," pp. 477–8. By "qualitative difference," however, Allport seemed to have in mind nonaffect differences.
64 See John Laird, *The Idea of Value*, pp. 353ff.; Hastings Rashdall, *The Theory of Good and Evil*, vol. I, p. 174, vol. II, chs. 1, 2; Robert Nozick, *Philosophical Explanations*, p. 429.
65 See James Griffin, "Are There Incommensurable Values?" Joseph Raz defends the intelligibility of the idea in his "Value Incommensurability: Some Preliminaries." See also Raz, *The Morality of Freedom*, ch. 13.

of any of the conflicting values, can be appealed to in order to resolve that conflict.
(3) It is not true that for each conflict of values some value can be appealed to (independent or not) in order to resolve that conflict rationally.[66]

I shall return to claim (1) below; depending upon its interpretation, it strikes me as either quite right or quite wrong. But, as we shall see, I have no real quarrel with either claims (2) or (3). And I, too, maintain that, ultimately, some "value conflicts" may be resolved in a way that is, in a fundamental sense, nonrational. But, still, if we are to talk of a "resolution" or "choice" in any intelligible sense at all – and not simply paralysis or a random[67] outcome – we need to have some idea of what is involved when a person resolves such an incommensurable conflict. We must provide some account as to how these qualitatively different values are to be related.

On the Affective-Cognitive Theory, this at least partially translates into the problem as to how qualitatively different affects are related. One way to relate them is suggested by Freud (at least in his earlier papers). If, as he seemed to believe, all affects can be understood as manifestations of psychic energy,[68] it is reasonable to conjecture that the relative strengths of affects (be they of the same general type or quite different) will vary with the quantum of energy they manifest. And this would seem to rescue the simple (bipolar) view of attitudes as amount of affect for or against something. But, whatever other problems characterize such energy models,[69] we certainly have reason to doubt that motivational strength, much less the intensity of valuing, re-

66 Bernard Williams, "Conflicts of Values," p. 77. See also Stuart Hampshire, "Public and Private Morality." For Berlin, in addition to his well-known *Four Essays on Liberty*, see his essay on "Montesquieu" and his "The Question of Machiavelli." For an analysis of Berlin's pluralism, see Robert A. Kocis, "Reason, Development, and the Conflicts of Human Ends: Sir Isaiah Berlin's Vision of Politics." Williams's and Hampshire's views are criticized by Stanley Benn in his *A Theory of Freedom*, ch. III. Although our views here are very different, I have been deeply influenced by Benn's analysis.
67 Cf. G. J. Warnock's critique of the claim that we "choose" our values. "On Choosing Values." See also Charles Taylor, "What Is Human Agency?" pp. 118ff.
68 See David Rapaport, *Emotions and Memory*, pp. 24, 28–33. See also William Lyons, *Emotion*, pp. 25–32.
69 I have considered a different problem in my *Modern Liberal Theory of Man*, pp. 136–48.

lates in any obvious way to the amount of psychic energy manifested by an affect. It is not at all obvious that one cannot be extremely interested and excited by something yet, when deliberating what to do, act on a relatively modest fear. Say I am the sort of person who tends to be afraid of, or worried about, physical injury; I may well decide to forgo valued activities rather than incur such injuries, or even run a significant risk of doing so. On the other hand, others tend not to act on their fears, but will systematically choose to engage in interesting or exciting activities, regardless of their fears.

Some people are timid and others are courageous. It may be that the timid person experiences intense fear and the courageous one does not. To some extent, this is doubtlessly so. But it is widely agreed that one cannot really be courageous if one does not experience fear, or only experiences it to such a small degree that it is relatively insignificant. Rather, one who is brave is one who experiences fear, and disvalues the fearful thing, but, as it were, heavily discounts this disvaluing in his deliberations. This notion of "discounting" can be articulated in two ways. Like Michael Slote, we might say that, though the courageous man can be said to value his safety, it does not provide him with a reason to act.[70] Although I have insisted that valuings and disvaluings do provide reasons, we can well describe the courageous man as one who pays little heed to personal safety in his deliberations, and so it can be said that it provides him only with weak reasons to act. Alternatively, we may say that the courageous man places little value on personal safety.[71] It is not clear, however, that these are really incompatible accounts. For, in this context, to value *X* more than *Y* simply is to give *X* greater weight in one's deliberation. In deliberating about what to choose or to do, the value of *X* is, in some sense, a more weighty or powerful consideration than that of *Y*. And this explains why comparative valuing can be analyzed in terms of a preference for *X* over *Y*:[72] if *X*'s value

70 Michael Slote, *Goods and Virtues*, p. 124.

71 See John McDowell, "Are Moral Requirements Hypothetical Imperatives?"; Ronald Dworkin, "What Is Equality? Part 1: Equality of Welfare," pp. 210–1.

72 According to Brentano, "more" in "loving more" "has nothing to do with comparative intensity. It refers to a peculiar type of phenomenon to be found within the sphere of emotions – namely, to the phenomenon of *preferring*. Acts of preference – emotive acts that relate and compare – are familiar

is a more weighty or powerful consideration in deliberation than Y's, then, if one was forced to choose from the set $\{X, Y\}$, conceived simply as a choice between valuables, one would choose X over Y.

But all this seems overly metaphorical.[73] Just what is meant when it is said that X's value is "more weighty" in deliberation than Y's? One way to explain the weightiness of reasons is through coherence considerations. For example, given some system or web of beliefs, we might say that the more weighty belief is that which is more central to the overall structure or more consistent with the other beliefs in the structure or, perhaps, the rejection of which would cause the most overall damage to the structure.[74] I will consider the nature of coherence of value systems in §14, but it is worth noting now that it has been said of both emotion[75] and value[76] that they are far less subject to consistency requirements than are beliefs. And, as we saw in the studies of Abelson et al., a person's affective responses to another seem remarkably independent and diverse, displaying little tendency to be either consistently positive or negative (§8.2). These points are thus far only suggestive, but they do indicate that we should perhaps be cautious about treating value systems in the same way as belief systems, especially with regard to coherence and consistency requirements.

I wish to explore another account of value weightings, one that I think is implicit in J. S. Mill's discussion of higher and lower pleasures. In this discussion, Mill apparently allows that, if we are comparing pleasures of the same type, "amount" of pleasure is the criterion of "more valuable."[77] Let us say, then, that, when deliberating about whether to pursue one or the other of two such pleasures (valuables), the value reasons for action implied by each should be "weighted" according to the amount of pleasure. That

---

to us all." *Right and Wrong*, p. 26. See also Linda McAlister, *The Development of Franz Brentano's Ethics*, pp. 99–100.

73 This point has been impressed upon me by Stanley Benn.

74 See S. I. Benn and G. F. Gaus, "Practical Rationality and Commitment." For a general introductory account, see W. V. Quine and J. S. Ullian, *The Web of Belief*.

75 See Patricia S. Greenspan, "A Case of Mixed Feelings: Ambivalence and the Logic of Emotions."

76 See, e.g., Neil Cooper, *The Diversity of Moral Thinking*, p. 288.

77 As a hedonist, Mill concentrated on valuableness rather than valuing. See §8.1 in this volume.

seems clear enough. However, when comparing pleasures of different qualities, Mill thinks this quantitative weighting will not do. It is here that he offers "preferred" as an interpretation of "more valuable":

> Of two pleasures, if there be one to which all or almost all who have experience of both give a decided preference, irrespective of any feeling of moral obligation to prefer it, that is the more desirable pleasure. If one of the two is, by those who are competently acquainted with both, placed so far above the other that they prefer it . . . and would not resign it for any quantity of the other pleasure which their nature is capable of, we are justified in ascribing to the preferred enjoyment a superiority in quality so far outweighing quantity as to render it, in comparison, of small account.[78]

I will return later (§11.2) to the claim that such "preferences" provide the basis of impersonal comparative value judgments. At present, what is of interest is that Mill postulates an apparently primitive – that is, not supported by reasons – preference for higher over lower pleasures.[79] He seems to resist the idea that people prefer higher pleasures because – for the reason that – they are higher or better: this is apparently the point of his denial that they are chosen out of a feeling of obligation. And, unlike preferences between pleasures of the same type, it is not grounded on some judgment of relative amounts or intensity. It simply is a fact, Mill tells us, that, confronted with a choice, almost all who are acquainted with higher and lower pleasures opt for the former. Interpreting him in this way also makes sense of his analysis of those who concentrate on lower pleasures: rather than charging them with making an error, ignoring good reasons, or having false beliefs (that is, having unsound grounds for their preferences), he argues that their natures have been corrupted. Having lost the capacity to appreciate the higher, their recourse is to pursue the lower.[80] The important point here is that Mill sees this as a question of psychological constitutions and the effects of hostile environments;[81] and, given that the choices are not reasoned, that is the only sort of account of good and bad choices open to him.

This sort of choice does not, then, primarily reveal whether

78 J. S. Mill, *Utilitarianism*, p. 12 (ch. II, para. 5).
79 See Dorothy Mitchell, "Mill's Theory of Value," pp. 110–1.
80 Mill, *Utilitarianism*, p. 14 (ch. II, para. 7).
81 See my *Modern Liberal Theory*, pp. 25–32, 122–39.

one has reasoned well or ill; it reveals the kind of person one is.[82] This is not to say that the choice is random or undetermined;[83] though subject to challenge from self-conscious ideals (§14.2.3), it has a type of necessity about it. One choice rather than another strikes the agent as right. As Hampshire quite rightly says, "[i]f the agent reflects, he will say: 'The necessity is not principally a matter of reason, in the sense of calculation; it is more a matter of reflective feeling and of perception, and of a feeling and a perception which I am prepared to stand by and to endorse.' "[84]

We are now in a position to interpret the often-repeated claim that people differ regarding the "weights" they "place" on values and disvalues.[85] I am proposing that these weights are neither somehow simply a function of the value's role in the overall system (see §14.2) nor arbitrarily chosen. Rather, they reflect relatively stable dispositions to see a certain level of affect *A* as equivalent, for choice, to a certain level of *B*. Of course these dispositions are subject to change, and from one period of life to another they are apt to alter. But a considerable amount of relative stability is required for anything approaching a personality or an emotional character. These dispositions can be viewed in different ways: if we are considering two positive affects, they can be understood as sorts of indifference substitution functions; when comparing positive and negative affects, they are perhaps better understood as cost or price functions.[86] A timid man may consider even a little fear too high a price to pay for great excitement and interest; that is, the latter does not compensate him for the former. The suggestion, then, is that this subjective exchange rate will reflect itself in variable "weightings" of his fear- and excitement-based valuings. He does not, then, choose to value, say, a secure job in the public service more than an interesting one in journalism: it is a manifestation of the way he "sees and feels."

It should be manifest that calculating such exchange rates does not require any "common currency" in the sense of a third value

82 Rem B. Edwards points toward a more rationalistic interpretation of Mill in his *Pleasures and Pains*, pp. 111–6.
83 See Taylor, "What Is Human Agency?" pp. 118ff. See also Nozick, *Philosophical Explanations*, pp. 294ff.
84 Stuart Hampshire, "Morality and Conflict," p. 157.
85 See, for example, Gert, *The Moral Rules*, p. 51; Bruce B. Wavell, "The Rationality of Values."
86 I am drawing here on Kenneth E. Boulding, "Prices and Values."

or third sort of affect.[87] Furthermore, we can go on to develop, as it were, a relative price structure of the individual's affective economy, and this would still not imply that all affects are being compared to the super-value, price.[88] Price, expressed in some common unit, is a theoretical construct designed to simplify the calculation of exchange rates across commodities or, in my analysis, affects.

11.1.2 Deliberation and reasons

Some preferences, that is, between various levels of affects, are thus in a fundamental sense nonrational. The transformation functions[89] describing these preferences, viewed in one way at least, are not best conceived as criteria to be employed to rationally resolve value conflicts, but more as descriptions of a person's disposition to resolve them in one way rather than another. In this sense, I accept variants of Williams's incommensurability theses (2) and (3). (If "currency" in his thesis (1) means "price structure," then I reject it; if it means some special commodity, for example, pleasure, I accept it.) But notice the level on which this unreasoned preference occurs; like Mill, I take actual choices as (imperfect) indicators of much more abstract preferences, that is, between different levels of different affects. The primitive preference, then, is not between one specific object and another (or one state of affairs and another); these actual comparative valuings can indeed be supported by various reasons.

This point is worth emphasizing, for it provides a way to reconcile the primitive, that is, nonreasoned, nature of some preferences with the claim that comparative valuings are the outcome of reasoning and deliberation. Consider an example discussed by David Milligan. Mary Casson is a career adviser, and Kevin Granger a client. Mary, of course, will try to discover Kevin's "abilities and interests."

87 In addition to Williams, "Conflicts of Values," pp. 77–8, see also Taylor, "What Is Human Agency?" p. 105; Loren E. Lomasky, *Persons, Rights, and the Moral Community,* pp. 141–6. For an analysis of this argument for incommensurability, see Griffin, "Incommensurable Values," pp. 43ff. Once again I am indebted here to Stanley Benn; see his *Theory of Freedom*, ch. 2.
88 See Pugh, *The Biological Origin of Human Values*, p. 119, for an alternative formulation of this point.
89 See Boulding, "Prices and Values."

In the light of this information she tries to list the various conditions which would have to be satisfied by an acceptable career, and after discussion decide how important each condition is. She considers possible careers and the degree to which each satisfies the conditions. Thus she may decide that one job is more exciting, while another is more secure; excitement is a reason for choosing the first and security for choosing the second. From weighing up these reasons, she comes to a final judgement, a judgement supported by reasons.[90]

Milligan thus recognizes – and does so even more explicitly in his following paragraph – the distinction between simple and comparative valuings. First, based on her insight into Kevin, Mary concludes that both excitement and security would ground valuings of the competing occupations; she then must decide on the "relative importance" of these factors. Although Milligan insists that Mary reasons about this relative importance (she can, for instance, be criticized for doing it badly by ignoring relevant considerations), he also acknowledges that it involves comparisons based on the interests, values, and tastes of Kevin.[91] Knowing what Kevin cares for and what sort of person he is, Mary can reason as to whether he would value more the excitement of journalism or the security of a job in local government. Assume, then, that Mary reasons that, though Kevin would find value in both, overall he will find greater value in journalism.

She may do so by constructing an argument similar to one she might use to defend her conclusion against criticism. She has discovered that he has skills in writing and dealing with people and that he enjoys an outdoor life which provides excitement. He would prefer a job near home and is more concerned about security than the possibility of high pay. No job will meet all these demands, but the reasons in favor of journalism seem to outweigh those against, more than they do for other possible jobs.[92]

What Mary can do for Kevin, he can do for himself. Consequently, his choice between journalism and the local public service is not an unreasoned, primitive, choice. But this is all consistent with it being a primitive, unreasoned, feature of his

90 David Milligan, *Reasoning and The Explanation of Action*, p. 84.
91 Milligan tells us that this second decision depends on the "tastes, interests or values *of the judge or* of the person for whom the decision is to be made." Ibid. (emphasis added). It is all too true that career advisers often recommend on the basis of their own values and tastes, and that is what makes career advice generally so unhelpful.
92 Ibid., p. 85.

character that his transformation function between excitement and fear is such that for him, unlike Timid Tom, the excitement of journalism more than compensates for the loss of security. When Mary reasons whether journalism or local government is best for Kevin, she accepts his character and personality as background conditions, that is, givens that do not themselves call for reasoned justification. (But see §14.2 on character ideals.) Giving reasons for a particular comparative valuing underdetermines the choice; it is only against the background of the person's personality and character that the reasons determine a choice.[93] And aspects of that character will be beyond rational defense; if challenged on, say, why he seems willing to accept significant insecurity as the cost for excitement, Kevin may well have to rely on "reflective feeling" that he is prepared to stand by.

11.1.3 The derived component

I have been dealing at some length with the complexities associated with comparing qualitatively distinct affects so as to yield a choice between valued things. This in itself is sufficiently daunting that studies such as those of Abelson et al. (§9.2) rely instead on very simple and uniform (across subjects) rules for aggregating affective responses into overall attitude measures.[94] The hypothesis implied by the foregoing is that affect would be even a more powerful predictor of attitudes if individualized weightings were considered.[95]

Abelson's studies, however, serve to recall yet another complexity of valuing: valuings are apt to be both intrinsic and de-

93 For a related argument, see Adam Morton, "Character and the Emotions."
94 "[E]ach respondent (in both studies) was assigned a positive affect score for each candidate, as the simple count of the number of positive affects mentioned; a negative affect score was assigned correspondingly. (This procedure was chosen in preference to weighted factor scores because of its simplicity and uniformity across candidates.)" Robert P. Abelson et al., "Affective and Semantic Components in Political Person Perception," p. 623.
95 It is possible that in reporting their affective response some weighting for importance already implicitly occurs. This is not likely in Abelson et al.'s studies, however, because respondents did not report intensity of affect, but simply "yes" or "no" to the affect checklist. In other studies of attitudes, it has been found that weighting trait evaluations by importance does not improve the predictive power of the model because respondents seem to take account of weightings in making the evaluations. See Fishbein and Ajzen, *Belief, Attitude*, p. 228.

rivative (that is, two components). To this extent, one's value-grounded choice between *X* and *Y* will not only depend upon the relative intensities of one's affects toward them and one's personal transformation functions, but upon a variety of other valuings that are relevant to this choice. And, of course, these other valuings themselves have to be compared if their relative importance for the choice is to be assessed.

11.2 Are there impersonal comparative value judgments?

11.2.1 A negative conclusion

It should be fairly clear why there are no public, impersonal, appropriateness conditions for claiming that, though *X* and *Y* are both appropriately valued, it is appropriate to, and inappropriate not to, value *X* more than *Y*. As I have analyzed it, comparative valuing (or degree of valuing) can be accounted for in terms of (i) affect intensity, (ii) transformation functions between affects, and (iii) derived valuings. None of these have impersonal appropriateness conditions. In §6.3, I explicitly rejected the suggestion that in order to be correctly characterized as having a fully appropriate emotion *E*, Alf must exhibit/experience the *E*-relevant affect at a level that is in some sense proportionate to the *E*-relevant attributes of the object or state of affairs toward which he is emotional. This precludes, then, appropriateness conditions for the intensity of affect. And, once intensity can appropriately vary, it is difficult to see how a case can be made for appropriateness conditions for transformation functions. Indeed, what would be involved in the latter is even more obscure than in the former. Apparently, it would require an impersonal standard such that level *l* of affect *A* is equivalent for choice purposes to level *k* of affect *B*. But, even if we accepted this (and it seems rather dubious), it still would not establish the impersonality of comparative value judgments because, as long as intensity of affect is without appropriateness conditions, fully rational people embracing the same transformation functions might still arrive at different comparative valuings of *X* and *Y*.

The case for impersonal value judgments becomes yet more problematic when we bring derived valuings into the equation. If one can rationally not find value in that which is impersonally valuable (§§10.2, 10.3), Alf can, rationally, intrinsically value, say, good relations with other countries and his compatriot Betty might rationally not do so. Consequently, as in the studies conducted by Abelson and his colleagues (§8.2), when evaluating Carter and Reagan, Alf has a derivative valuing endorsing (let us assume) Carter over Reagan that Betty, quite rationally, does not possess.

I reject, then, the claim that there are impersonal criteria for claiming that, though *X* and *Y* are both intrinsically valuable, any fully rational person will, in his deliberations, take *X*'s intrinsic value as a more weighty reason for action than *Y*'s. As the analysis in §11.1.2 showed, though reasons can be given for comparative valuings, these reasons are only determinative given a character. This general view gains support from Eric Matthews's analysis of disputes about tastes:

> The proverb says that there is no arguing about tastes, but this is not strictly correct. It is easy to imagine a perfectly genuine argument between two men about [the relative merits of blondes and brunettes]. . . . [T]he men would be trying to persuade one another to see things differently, and they would give reasons in support of their respective preferences which they would hope to have some weight with the other party. Blondes might be recommended on the grounds of their coolness and poise, brunettes, perhaps, on account of their air of warmth and sensuality. The grain of truth in the proverb, however, is that there is a sense in which this would not be a *serious* argument. . . . It would always be open to the man who preferred brunettes, say, simply to deny the appeal of coolness and poise, or to say that these qualities did not excite him as much as warmth and sensuality. In saying this, he would in no way impair his claim to be considered a rational man, since it is no part of our concept of rationality that the rational man is more excited by qualities of coolness and poise.[96]

11.2.2 Moore's suggestion

In important ways, the position I have advocated is akin to Brentano's. As we saw (§8.4), he held that to be valuable is to be worthy of being loved, but he denied that, given two things both of which are worthy of being loved, one could be worthy of a more intense love than another. To be worthy of love, he maintained,

96 Eric Matthews, "Objectivity, Values, and History," p. 215.

was to be worthy of love of the highest degree (that is, intensity).[97] Thus, although for very different reasons, he too rejected worthiness or appropriateness conditions for intensity of response. In his review of Brentano's *Origin of Our Knowledge of Right and Wrong*, G. E. Moore suggested that if, given this conclusion, "more valuable" could not be explicated as "worthy of more love" it could still be analyzed as "more worthy of love."[98] I want to explore briefly this neglected suggestion.

It will be recalled that an impersonal value judgment is a judgment that, given the attributes of *X* (or testimony of experts), *X* is worthy of being valued; or, more precisely, it is an appropriate target of a certain sort of valuing. Taking up Moore's suggestion, then, we might analyze "*X* is more valuable than *Y*" as "*X* is more appropriately valued than *Y*." I shall leave aside here worries as to whether our normal understanding of the concept of "appropriateness" is open to this sort of variation;[99] the really important point is that we can, indeed often do, distinguish *X* and *Y* by the richness of their value-grounding features. Consider once again impersonal value judgments about the interestingness of a book (§§10.2, 10.3). Let us now make the judgment comparative, so that one book (*X*) is judged to be more interesting than another (*Y*). Certainly one way to support this comparative judgment is to point out that *X* is so much richer in those features that make a book interesting. Although acknowledging that *Y* is also an interesting book, it may be shown that *X* has all the interest-relevant features of *Y* plus a wealth of other interesting attributes. This is a version of the principle of inclusiveness so stressed by value theorists:[100] if *X* possesses all the value-relevant traits of *Y*, plus others as well, we have grounds for saying that *X* is more worthy of being valued than is *Y*.[101] Of course, inclusiveness is a relatively straightforward basis for a compara-

97 Brentano, *Right and Wrong*, pp. 25ff.
98 See McAlister, *Franz Brentano's Ethics*, p. 99. Moore's review was in *The International Journal of Ethics* (now *Ethics*) 14 (October 1903), pp. 115–23. This was not Brentano's proposal; see note 72 in this chapter.
99 One line of criticism is implied by Alan Gewirth's discussion of the principle of proportionality in his *Reason and Morality*, pp. 120ff.
100 For various formulations of this principle, see: Brentano, *Right and Wrong*, pp. 28–9; Perry, *General Theory*, pp. 645ff.; Charles Fried, *An Anatomy of Values*, pp. 96–7; John Rawls, *A Theory of Justice*, pp. 412ff. But see also DeWitt H. Parker, *The Philosophy of Value*, pp. 171–3.
101 Organic whole analysis can complicate this argument. See §§13.2, 14.2.

tive value judgment because it does not require any determination of the relative importance of different value-relevant attributes. If *Y* has some interest-relevant qualities lacking in *X*, but overall *X* is much richer in features that ground interest, we may still be warranted in claiming that *X* is more worthy of being valued. But we now need some way to compare the relative importance of those features lacking in *X* but present in *Y* to those which *X*, but not *Y*, possesses.

Sometimes the relative importance of the various traits will be part of our shared, public, understanding of the appropriateness conditions for a particular valuing attitude. It is no mystery why this should be so: just as we can make impersonal judgments that something is appropriately valued in a certain way, we can make impersonal judgments that one thing possesses traits that render it a superior target for a particular valuing attitude. Often these comparative judgments will not be particularly controversial. That a novel is action-packed is an appropriate ground for interest in it; but, if compared to another novel that is somewhat slower moving but which possesses a complex but intelligible plot, a range of diverse and realistic characters, a striking theme, and surprising yet comprehensible twists and so on, at some point it will become very difficult indeed to sustain an *impersonal claim* that the former is as worthy of interest as the latter. At some point, repetition of the claim "It *is* fast moving" is no longer a counter-argument, but an admission that there is little else to be said in its favor.

Nevertheless, often enough the shared public understanding of what is valuable will not provide the basis for selecting one thing over another as more worthy of being valued. In these cases, no impersonal comparative value judgment can be made. (And, of course, in other cases it will be a matter of dispute.) However, this is less of a problem in relation to those valuings for which there are well-defined appropriateness conditions (§6.1). Not only do such well-defined appropriateness conditions allow for fruitful value discourse and argument (§10.4), but it seems more likely that we will be able to say that one thing fulfills these conditions to a lesser or fuller extent than another. In contrast, one would expect comparative judgments of "generic" valuableness to be exceedingly difficult to make: the range of possible grounding features is apt to be very diverse, and the appropriateness conditions will be open-ended. This analysis appears intuitively sound: it does seem that we are more apt to have fruitful discourse about questions such as "Which is more worthy of interest (or indignation, or fear or even love)?" than "Which is more worthy of being valued?" Which *is* more worthy of being intrinsically valued, a striking sunset or an advanced computer? Put thus, the question hardly makes sense. As David Milligan rightly points out: "We compare two objects or two activities in respect of a shared characteristic which each may have to a different degree. Is this stone heavier than that one? Is this book longer than the other?"[102]

It is just these sort of value comparisons that are apt to have impersonal status; and it is these that the Affective-Cognitive Theory incorporates. To be sure, in particular situations one may have to choose, say, to divert a resource (for example, one's time) to either appreciating striking sunsets or mastering an advanced computer. But the claim that there is an impersonal, relatively stable comparative value judgment between sunsets and computers seems, if not entirely unintelligible, not particularly enlightening or compelling. And, indeed, when parties to such disputes insist that such impersonal value judgments can be made – for example, a dispute between an environmentalist and a technologist about the relative merits of sunsets and computers – the disputants are generally unyielding, the dispute fruitless. Typically, the argument is not really about impersonal value judgments at all: it is a manifestation of divergent comparative valuings.

Just as impersonal (simple) value judgments have action implications (§10.3), so too do impersonal comparative judgments, and for essentially the same reasons. Because our chief practical interest in making impersonal value judgments is an indicator of what we will find of value, and in informing our fellows what they will see value in, we have obvious interests both in ranking things by their richness in value-grounding features and in taking these rankings as reasons for action. But, just as a person may, rationally, not value that which is impersonally valuable, so too may his comparative valuings conflict with impersonal comparative value judgments. Even though, for instance, an impersonal value judgment would judge most French red wines as more wor-

102 Milligan, *Reasoning and Action*, p. 76.

thy of being valued than South Australian reds – because they are richer in the relevant qualities – one may be very strongly attracted to the distinctive tannin taste of South Australian wines. Only if responding too intensely to tannin, or if failure to respond to the relevant features of French wine, were defects of rationality could we with certainty say that the preferrer of South Australian wines was rationally at fault. And, of course, I have rejected this (§6.3).

Still, criticisms of others' comparative valuings as rationally defective are possible. Throughout we have been assuming that the simple valuings that are being compared are faultless; but often enough, when we criticize another's preferences it is on the grounds that he has false or pragmatically incomplete beliefs about one or both options. That is, one might under- or overvalue a thing in the sense that one has not taken account of relevant features or wrongly believes it to possess certain features. If, to again use Matthews's somewhat objectionable example, blondes are not cool or poised, then the preference can be criticized as being grounded on a defect of reason. Indeed, it is on the presupposition that one or the other error has been made that fruitful discussion is apt to proceed; we point to value- and disvalue-relevant features, trying to show that there is more (or less) to the thing than has been thought. But, even if that gets us nowhere, the Affective-Cognitive Theory does not imply that those who value more highly that which is less worthy have no reason to change their ways. Sound impersonal value judgments imply prima facie reasons for action, at least to acquaint oneself with what is valuable (§10.3). Given his value system, our wayward valuer may have more or less reason to engage in courses of action that would allow him to gain access to those features (of the more worthy thing), the value of which now eludes him. Only if he has grounds for concluding that he cannot find value in those features (for example, he is tone deaf) will the greater worthiness of one thing have no relevance whatsoever for his action.

12 REASONS AND OBJECTIVITY

12.1 Objectivity as impartiality

Derek Parfit and Thomas Nagel have distinguished *agent-relative* from *agent-neutral* reasons for action. An agent-relative reason necessarily refers to the person for whom it is a reason, that is, "*R* is a reason for Alf"; in contrast, an agent-neutral reason is a reason for anyone (though some may be so situated as to be unable to act on it).[103] In *The Possibility of Altruism*, Nagel held that agent-neutral reasons "represent the values of occurrences, acts, and states of affairs themselves, not their values *for* anyone."[104] Here, at least, it seems that Nagel equated reasons for action and valuing; valuing or values, for him, *did not imply* reasons to act but, rather, recognition of a reason to act *constitutes* a valuing (see §§7.2.4, 16.1). However, it is important to clearly distinguish (i) sound valuing and value judgments from (ii) the reasons for action those valuings or judgments imply.[105] My concern here, then, is with agent-neutral reasons to act: if all value-based reasons to act are agent-neutral, then Alf's (sound) valuing of *X* implies not only a reason for him, but also a reason for anyone (who is able to do anything about it) to act to preserve, promote, or protect *X* or secure it for Alf. If, however, value-based reasons to act are agent-relative rather than agent-neutral, that Alf soundly values *X* only provides reasons for Alf to act. (I will consider judgments of valuableness presently.) As I conceive of them here, then, agent-neutrality and agent-relativity are opposing doctrines about the sorts of reasons implied by "Alf (soundly) values *X*."

In *The Possibility of Altruism*, Nagel argued that only insofar as one acts on reasons that are, or derive from, agent-neutral reasons, does one fully recognize the reality of others. To act on an agent-neutral reason is, he said, to act from an objective point of view. Nagel, and indeed many others, especially utilitarians, thus point to a doctrine of objectivity as impartiality. Abstracting from the many specific arguments,[106] what we might call the generic argument runs as follows: if one insists that only one's own valuings provide one with reasons to act, one is preferring one's

103 See Thomas Nagel, *The View from Nowhere*, pp. 152ff.; Parfit, *Reasons and Persons*, p. 143.
104 Nagel, *The Possibility of Altruism*, pp. 119–20. In this work, Nagel used the terms "objective" and "subjective" reasons; he notes his adoption of Parfit's alternative terminology on p. 152n of *The View from Nowhere*.
105 Nagel now makes this distinction. See *The View from Nowhere*, p. 152n.
106 See, e.g., Nagel, *The View from Nowhere*, ch. VIII; Rashdall, *The Theory of Good and Evil*, vol. I, pp. 43–8; Henry Sidgwick, *The Methods of Ethics*, pp. 420–1; R. M. Hare, *Moral Thinking*, ch. 5; Nicholas Rescher, *Introduction to Value Theory*, p. 11; T. G. Roupas, "The Value of Life," pp. 170–1, 179; Robin Attfield, "The Good of Trees," p. 50; Edward C. Hayes, "Social Values."

own valuings simply because they are one's own, and this indicates a sort of egoism or self-centeredness.[107] It is being partial toward one's own perspective. Consequently to take up an "objective point of view" is to acknowledge that the points of view of others are equally real: one must give equal weight to the valuings, or at least the sound valuings, of all. And this endorses impartiality in the sense that you are not partial to your own valuings by insisting that only they provide you with reasons to act; you must be impartial between your own (sound) valuings and those of others. So, from the objective point of view, every (sound) valuing implies agent-neutral reasons; in principle, it provides anyone with reasons to act.

Notice first how intrusive, at least in principle, is this conception of objectivity. Every (sound) extrinsic valuing based on any appetite, every (appropriate) interest in any object, every rightly valued experience, provides every agent with a commitment to act.[108] To accept this interpretation of an objective point of view requires that partiality in favor of one's own valuings is only appropriate insofar as one is so strategically placed that, after considering the (sound) valuings of all others, one concludes that (in some sense) it is best if one acts on those valuings that happen to be yours. This is indeed an extreme commitment, for it requires a disassociation from your own valuings, viewing them, for the purposes of your own action, as simply one set of valuings among others.[109] It is thus not surprising, then, that theorists who accept this conception of objectivity expend considerable effort, and display great ingenuity and sophistication, in showing that, suitably interpreted or modified, such impartiality need not lead

107 See esp. Becker, *Moral Judgments*, pp. 56–7.

108 Bond, I think, is right that at one point Nagel believed that "[n]ot just the agent's *future* as well as his present desires create reasons for him, but the desires of *every* person create reasons for every person. Where there is a desire, present or future, mine or yours, there is a reason." Bond, *Reason and Value*, p. 7.

109 Throughout *The Possibility of Altruism*, Nagel makes a great deal of recognizing that one is simply one person among others, something which, suitably interpreted, I endorse in §12.2. But, on Nagel's interpretation, this notion leads to the sort of problems relating to personal integrity that Bernard Williams so stresses (though not in relation to Nagel). See Williams's "Persons, Character, and Morality." The relation between integrity and impartiality is discussed by Nancy Davis, "Utilitarianism and Responsibility."

to such radical disassociation from the things for which one cares.[110]

It is not my intention to consider such modifications and interpretations here, for I wish to suggest that the basic conception itself is deeply flawed. Much of its traditional plausibility stems from a stark contrast between egoism and altruism. A universal egoism implies that each has reason to promote his own, and only his own, interests or pleasure: such reasons are thus agent-relative. Confronted with this egoistic doctrine, the proponent of impartiality has traditionally argued that if the egoist acknowledges that (i) the satisfaction of his own interests or pleasure is good and (ii) that every agent sees the satisfaction of his own interests or his own pleasure as good, then (iii) the egoist is appealing to an impersonal conception of goodness (in general) but (iv) if there is such general goodness – the satisfaction of interests or pleasure in general – the egoist is arbitrarily insisting that only his interests or pleasure provide him with reasons to act. Hence, as Rashdall concluded, "it is rational for him to pursue his neighbor's pleasure as well as his own, and to prefer the larger amount of pleasure to the smaller, even though the larger pleasure be the pleasure of others, and the smaller his own."[111] As I will argue shortly, this is not anything like a conclusive argument against a thoroughgoing agent-relativism; important for my immediate purposes, however, is that it loses most of whatever force it does possess once we understand value judgments in the way I have suggested in this chapter. Consider, for instance, the following case:

> (A) Alf directly experiences ("grasps") the sublimity of Niagara Falls, and so judges it to be sublime. Betty acknowledges that Niagara Falls is appropriately (impersonally) judged to be sublime, but it leaves her cold. "A lot of water falling off a cliff," she says.

We should note, to begin with, that not only does Alf have reasons to act in relation to Niagara Falls, but also that these are by no means merely reasons for selfish acts. To be sure, he has reason to visit the falls, but, even if he has no further prospects of visiting it, he nevertheless has reason, say, to oppose hydroelectric schemes that would divert almost all the water from the falls. We

110 See, e.g., Samuel Scheffler, *The Rejection of Consequentialism*; Philip Pettit and Robert Goodin, "The Possibility of Special Duties."
111 Rashdall, *Good and Evil*, vol. I, p. 48.

already rejected the hedonistic thesis that all such valuings are simply means to gratifying mental states (§8.1); suffice it here to emphasize that to care about or cherish something one has been moved by is not to care about it simply as a means to being moved. Consequently, one who no longer can be moved by actually seeing it can continue to care for it and to act in the appropriate ways.

But the proponent of objectivity as impartiality insists that Betty, too, has reasons to act. Now she may be said to have such reasons (i) just because Niagara Falls is impersonally valuable, or (ii) because it is impersonally valuable *and* someone, namely Alf, actually values it. However, (i) has already been rejected (§10.2). The challenge of an externalist like Foot – "What do I care about the sublimity of the falls?" – remains unanswered. To say that such a challenge exhibits a partiality toward one's own valuings hardly seems decisive, for Betty's reply is that she values those things that strike her as valuable. She is only "partial" to her own valuings insofar as she finds some things to be of value and others not. She, indeed, has a convincing reply to the charge of "partiality": "Does impartiality demand that I treat things in which I see no value as if I saw value in them?" Betty is not being partial in the sense of "partial to her own interests," but in the sense of "partial to what she finds of value." But this hardly seems objectionable, for it is the very essence of valuing that one is partial to what one values.

It could, of course, be pointed out that Betty acknowledges that the falls is impersonally valuable, and so she too should value it. But we explored just what it means to say something is impersonally valuable: for example, that the appropriateness conditions for "sublime" are such that it is appropriate to feel the falls to be sublime. The mere fact that Betty recognizes these conditions does not mean she is moved by the falls; affective constitutions and grounding values (see Chapter V) differ, and Betty's are such that, even with a sound and pragmatically complete set of beliefs, she is not moved or struck with awe by Niagara Falls. I conclude that her mere recognition that it is appropriate to value the falls does not commit her to valuing it. And if she does not value it, and has no reason to believe she would, she is not committed to acting toward it as if she valued it.

(ii) The spirit of the impartiality thesis, however, is to maintain that it is not simply the impersonal value of the falls that implies commitments to act for Betty, but Alf's valuing it as well. If she insists that she has no reason to assist him in his projects and actions based on his valuing, it is charged that she fails to recognize his reality, or is being egocentric or selfish. This is a difficult issue; I will argue in Part II that she can be provided with various reasons to take cognizance of his valuing and act in certain appropriate ways. So I certainly do not deny that, when all is said and done, she does (in all likelihood) have reasons of her own to act because of his valuation. But it is not simply a matter of treating his value judgments as if they were her own. Ultimately, she does have a perspective according to which she finds some things of value and others not, and it is implausible to insist that she must treat valuings that she cannot grasp as of equal importance for her actions. Admittedly, she believes that being awed by the falls is appropriate and she knows that he is awed by it, so she is prepared to acknowledge that his valuing is rational. But she is not awed by it – she sees no value in it: "Lots of water, too much noise and you just get wet when you try to have lunch outside. Ho hum." This is the way Betty sees the world; to be sure, Alf, equally rationally, sees it in another way, but why must her view of the world give way to his, requiring her to act as if she saw something interesting in lots of water falling off a cliff? To be impartial between what you grasp as valuable and what others grasp as valuable requires a practical denial of one's valuational experiences.

It may seem more difficult to defend agent-relativity in case (B):

> (B) Alf and Betty have been admitted to hospital with serious burns, having been rescued from a fire. "I understand how *my* pain provides *me* with a reason to take an analgesic," she says, "and I understand how his pain gives *him* a reason to take an analgesic; but how does *his* pain give *me* any reason to give him an analgesic? How can *his* pain give *me* or anyone else looking at it from outside a reason?"

"This question," Nagel insists, "is crazy."

> As an expression of puzzlement, it has that characteristic philosophical craziness which indicates that something very fundamental has gone wrong. This shows up in the fact that the *answer* to the question is *obvious*, so obvious that to ask the question is obviously a philosophical act. The answer is that pain is *awful*. The pain of the man groaning in

the next bed is just as awful as yours. That's your reason to want him to have an analgesic.[112]

Nagel has something specific in mind when charging Betty with "craziness." Philosophers, he indicates, have often arrived at skeptical or subjectivist conclusions about value because they have combined (i) a presumption that the burden of proof lies with proponents of value objectivity, realism, etc. with (ii) a standard of proof and rationality that places inordinate stress on logical consistency. The upshot of (i) and (ii) is that proponents of the objectivity of values have been burdened with showing that denial of objectivity is self-contradictory. But Nagel wants to argue all this is unreasonable: we cannot help believing some things (for example, the objectivity of some values), and there is no need to provide justification for that which we cannot help but believe. It is, Nagel thus says, neither reasonable nor credible to deny the objectivity of value.[113]

The problem with this argument in relation to pain – which Nagel takes as a fundamental case – is that it is by no means simply philosophers who ask questions similar to Betty's.[114] If Nagel's antiphilosophic argument is to be persuasive, competent nonphilosophic reasoners would (i) have to believe that it is equally obvious that Betty has a reason to alleviate her own pain and Alf's, or (ii) they would have to react in a puzzled, uncomprehending manner to her question; because the answer was so obvious, they would not grasp why she was asking the question. If (i) or (ii) holds, then Nagel might be right that the seriousness with which philosophers treat Betty's question is a professional craziness. But, although Nagel seems to believe that Betty's is a very strange question, it seems to me that neither (i) nor (ii) is plausible. In ordinary discourse, we are not puzzled by those who ask why they should care about the pain of others. We might be shocked at their insensitivity, their hard-heartedness or whatever, but this very shock is based on grasping just why they are

112 Nagel, "Objectivity," p. 109. Case (B) is a very slight modification of Nagel's example. See also his *View from Nowhere*, pp. 156–63.
113 Nagel, "Objectivity," pp. 104–5, 109.
114 There are indeed adult relativist ordinary moral reasoners who affirm Betty's position, though it could be argued that they are infected with philosophical craziness because they tend to be college students. See Fishkin, *Subjective Morality*, pp. 37ff.: L. Kohlberg and R. Kramer, "Continuities and Discontinuities in Childhood and Adult Moral Development," pp. 109ff.

asking the question. They (typically) want some self-interested reason for acting: "What is in it for me?" Contrast this to our reaction to someone who asks why *his* own pain provides any reason for *him* to act. This would indeed tend to evoke a puzzled and confused reaction, for it really is a crazy question. Given our understanding of rationality and sanity, someone who fails to see how his own pain provides motivating reasons to act exhibits a paradigmatic sort of craziness.[115]

Although Nagel is suspicious of arguments from consistency, his analysis does point to such an argument.[116] He suggests that Betty is really reasoning as follows: (1) pain is itself bad, and so there is a reason for everyone to alleviate it; hence (2a) my pain is bad, and so there is a reason for me to alleviate it and (2b) Alf's pain is bad, and so there is a reason for him to alleviate it; but (3) Alf's pain is bad, yet there is no reason for me to alleviate it. Nagel's thesis – step (1) – is that pain itself is bad, and so everyone has a reason to alleviate it, wherever it may occur. Step (3) is thus inconsistent with (1): if you accept (1), then it really would be irrational to assert that you have no reason to alleviate your neighbor's pain. (This is essentially a restatement of Rashdall's argument; see above.) Now the response of the Affective-Cognitive Theory is that it is false to claim that (2a) is necessarily based on (1).[117] It may be – some, like Nagel and Rashdall might, I suppose, disvalue their own pain on the basis of the general principle articulated by (1) – but it need not be. Our understanding of what it is to be in pain is such that Betty's pain provides her with a reason to do something about it without any appeal to the impersonal value judgment about the evil of pain articulated by (1). This is so even if we accept Trigg's analysis of pain.[118] Given our notions of pain and disliking, the intentional

115 "[W]hereas everybody has adequate reason to follow precepts following which favorably affects his life, not everybody has reason to follow precepts following which favorably affects other people's lives. . . . [F]or it would seem to be impossible for a normal person to be entirely unconcerned about himself, but possible for him to be unconcerned about many other persons. It seems that total indifference towards or unconcern about one's own fate is characteristic of psychotics." Kurt Baier, "The Practice of Justification," p. 40. See also Foot, *Virtues and Vices*, chs. XI, XII.

116 For a detailed analysis of Nagel's arguments against agent-relativity, see Eric Mack, "Moral Individualism: Agent-relativity and Deontic Restraints."

117 See Foot, *Virtues and Vices*, p. 154; Mackie, *Ethics*, pp. 141–4.

118 See §9.2.

state [Dislike (my pain)], and the corresponding value judgment, can be perfectly adequately grounded on beliefs that have nothing to do with (1): namely, the belief that *I* am in pain. Any analysis of the appropriateness conditions for [Dislike (my pain)] that included anything like (1) would be highly dubious indeed.

12.2 Objectivity as decentering

I have criticized objectivity as impartiality on three counts: (i) it implies, at least on the theoretical level, a radical weakening of the tie between one's actions and one's valuings: the (sound) valuings of others are always intruding on one's decisions as to what is the thing to do; (ii) if we focus on intrinsic valuings along the lines of case (A) – our above case about Niagara Falls – it is implausible to claim that one should be impartial as between what one finds to be of value and what others do; (iii) if we focus on valuings of the sort pointed to by case (B) – Nagel's example about Alf and Betty in the hospital – it cannot be successfully argued that denial of impartiality leads to inconsistency, irrationality, or philosophical craziness. With respect to reasons for action, absolute impartiality between one's own (sound) valuings/personal value judgments and those of others is thus far too demanding a conception of objectivity. Nagel, in a general way, seems to concur, for his most recent work stresses that only some values demand such impartiality. Let me briefly sketch his revised position.

"The first stage of objectification of the mental," Nagel has recently written, "is for each of us to be able to grasp the idea of all human perspectives, including his own, without depriving them of their character as perspectives. It is the analogue for minds of a centerless conception of space for physical objects, in which no point has a privileged position."[119] This seems right. However, Nagel still strives for a more thoroughgoing objectivity in which one does not merely recognize a multiplicity of perspectives, none of which is essentially privileged, but one in some sense views things abstracted from any particular perspective at all. Nagel believes that this sort of objective stance, a type of Archimedean perspective outside all actual perspectives whatsoever,

119 Nagel, *The View from Nowhere*, p. 20.

will reveal "what is of value in itself, rather than *for* anyone."[120] And, with respect to values that are objective in this sense, agent-neutrality and, hence, impartiality are still in order. But Nagel now allows for other sorts of genuine values, which can be seen from this objective standpoint to have value from particular, personal, standpoints. Nagel has in mind, say, desires that are in some way "adopted" or reflect choices. "Their value to us depends on our individual aims, projects and concerns, including particular concerns for other people that reflect our relations with them; they acquire value only because of the interest we develop in them and the place this gives them in our lives, rather than evoking interest because of their value."[121] Such personal values, Nagel believes, can be recognized and understood from the objective point of view, and so it can be acknowledged that they are reasons for those who entertain them. But to understand such reasons is not, he says, to accept them (from the objective perspective). These personal interests and desires, then, provide primarily agent-relative reasons.

Certainly the upshot of this analysis – that objectivity sometimes sanctions agent-neutral, sometimes agent-relative, reasons – is more plausible than the consequences of objectivity as strict impartiality. But the idea that to see things objectively is to see them from no perspective at all, to stand outside all actual perspectives, is itself puzzling. I at least find it extraordinarily difficult to grasp,[122] especially as an account of value.[123] I shall not, however, pursue a critique of it, but offer instead a more accessible conception. This alternative conception takes seriously what Nagel described as "the first stage of objectification of the mental": the notion of a multiplicity of perspectives, none of which is essentially privileged. One who achieves objectivity in this relatively modest sense overcomes what Piaget calls egocentrism:

120 See Thomas Nagel, "Subjective and Objective" in his *Mortal Questions*, p. 206. This point is also central to ch. VIII of *The View from Nowhere*.
121 Nagel, *The View from Nowhere*, p. 168.
122 "We cannot occupy the independent perspective that platonism envisages; and it is only because we confusedly think we can that we think we can make any sense of it." John McDowell, "Non-cognitivism and Rule-following," p. 150.
123 Nagel proffers this as an account of our knowledge of other minds and of value. It strikes me as more plausible with regard to the former. Cf. Nagel's remark that "one should pursue the kind of objectivity appropriate to the subject one is trying to understand." *The View from Nowhere*, p. 27.

the inability to recognize one's own point of view as one among others.[124] As Piaget depicts it, mental, including emotional, development is largely a process of moving from egocentrism to what he calls decentering, an ability not only to grasp that others too have perspectives, but to take up those perspectives by considering how things look to them.[125] And Piaget is explicit that this is nothing less than a movement toward objectivity; "Objectivity presupposes a decentering – i.e., a continual refocusing of perspective. Egocentrism, on the other hand, is the undifferentiated state prior to multiple perspectives."[126] There is nothing mysterious, or even difficult to grasp, about being objective in this way. Moreover, not only is it intuitively accessible, but impressive evidence indicates that it is a normal social-cognitive achievement in humans and, indeed, one that has been shown to have consequences for moral thinking (see §17).[127]

To achieve such objectivity, one must recognize in what sense one's perspective is simply one among others. Furthermore, if, as Nagel suggests, part of being objective is to grasp that one's position is not inherently privileged, to be objective in this way while retaining the capacity to be objectively critical of others requires criteria on which to found criticism that do not merely derive from one's own perspective. The Affective-Cognitive Theory of value supplies such criteria while providing an interpretation of what it means to be one valuer among others. A valuer who accepts the Affective-Cognitive Theory will (i) value particular things and make personal value judgments, (ii) understand in what way the different valuings and value judgments of others are symmetric with his own but, (iii) still have the resources to criticize their valuings and personal value judgments,

---

124 See, e.g., Jean Piaget, *The Moral Judgment of the Child*, pp. 35–7.

125 See Lawrence Kohlberg, "Justice as Reversibility."

126 Jean Piaget, "The Growth of Logical Thinking from Childhood to Adolescence," pp. 440–1.

127 For a general survey pointing out strengths and weaknesses of this research, see Lawrence A. Kurdek, "Perspective Taking as the Cognitive Basis of Children's Moral Development: A Review of the Literature." For a survey of theory and research on decentering in general (not simply in relation to moral development), see Hugh Rosen, *Pathway to Piaget*, ch. 7; see also ch. 2 on egocentrism. See also Dennis Krebs and Janet Gillmore, "The Relationship among the First Stages of Cognitive Development, Role-taking Abilities, and Moral Development"; Norman Buckley et al., "Egocentrism, Empathy, and Altruistic Behavior in Young Children."

not simply from his own perspective (for example, as things that disgust *him*), but also by appealing to impersonal considerations.[128]

Objectivity, then, does not require abstracting oneself from any and all actual perspectives (whatever that might mean) but, rather, it demands that one broadens one's perspective so as to embrace the appropriate meta-ethical theory which relates one's own perspective to that of others. In short, the first demand of objectivity is, if I am right, to accept the Affective-Cognitive Theory as a general theory that embraces one's own particular value perspective. (The second demand of objectivity is to engage in justification; see Chapters VI and VII.) The objective valuer does not seek to stand outside his own perspective, but to make it more adequate by coming to a proper understanding of his place in the larger scheme of things. Ultimately, one can only grasp anything from one's own perspective, in the sense that the resources for understanding and theorizing must draw on one's system of beliefs and valuations. To grasp valuing objectively is to have within one's system the resources (for example, a certain sort of general theory) that allows one to see *some other parts* of one's system of beliefs and values (for example, particular valuings) as nonprivileged vis-à-vis those of other people. But one cannot stand back from one's perspective in toto: that is to go beyond objectivity to, quite literally, self-annihilation.

My claim, then, is that the Affective-Cognitive Theory articulates a conception of objectivity in value that is intuitively accessible and psychologically sound (that is, people really do seem able to view their perspectives as one among others). This leads to another claim: this conception of objectivity endorses the agent-relativity of reasons for action based on sound valuings (or personal value judgments). From my perspective, I value certain things and make various personal value judgments, and these provide me with rational commitments to act. Do they necessarily provide all others with such commitments? Well, from an egocentric position, one might simply insist that they do.[129] But,

128 Gilbert Harman writes: "Nothing prevents us from using our values to judge other people. . . . But we only fool ourselves if we think our values give *reasons* to others who do not accept those values." This is quite right, but it does not preclude the sorts of impersonal criticism discussed in §10.4 of this volume. Harman, "Human Flourishing, Ethics, and Liberty," p. 321.

129 This seems to be the case with those "ordinary" moral reasoners whom

if we realize that our position is not privileged, we will reject that option. Three obvious alternatives present themselves. We might embrace (i) strict impartiality, (ii) some Nagel-like mixed view, according to which some valuings provide agent-neutral reasons, and some do not, or (iii) strict agent-relativity.[130] I have already canvased the first option and found it to be wanting: it is one thing to acknowledge that my perspective is not privileged, but quite another for *me* to treat, with respect to *my* action, the emotional dispositions of *others* on par with my *own*. I find no value in those things; to deny that I have reason to pursue them is not to insist that my position is privileged, but only that it is *my* position which provides the grounds of *my* action. But the same difficulty informs the second option insofar as it admits agent-neutrality: cases arise when it insists that I must treat things that I do not find of value (but which other people do) as if I did. The reasons implied by valuings and personal value judgments, I conclude, are inherently agent-relative. Impersonal value judgments, however, are different. They do partake of agent-neutrality; or, more accurately, they carry with them a presumption of agent-neutrality, albeit one that can be defeated (§§10.2, 10.3). That *X* is impersonally valuable does, at least prima facie, imply a reason for anyone to act. But, if one has grounds for believing that such value is not accessible to you, this reason is undermined; that is, the presumption that it provides a reason is defeated so that one has no reason at all to act. It is not merely that you cannot recognize that you have such a reason: rather (i) you are not rationally committed in this case to acting, and (ii) the absence of commitment cannot be attributed to any rational defect or incomplete beliefs (§9.2.2). Whether this is best described as a type of agent-neutrality or agent-relativity, the important point is that the value judgment does not imply that every fully rational agent will necessarily recognize a reason to act. The core insight here is that one's value-related reasons all stem from one's dispositional emotions, judgments that relate to those emotions or judgments that

Fishkin describes as "subjective universalists." *Subjective Morality*, pp. 35–7, 141ff. Nagel quite rightly calls this "false objectification." *The View from Nowhere*, pp. 86–9.

130 There are, of course, more complicated possibilities, e.g., discounting the importance of others' valuations. For another defense of the thoroughgoing agent-relativity of value reasons, see Mack, "Moral Individualism."

give one good reason to think one is apt to respond to something emotionally. The objective and rational valuer, recognizing the essential symmetry between himself and another, will also see that the valuings and value judgments of another provides that other with similar, essentially agent-relative, reasons.[131] But it is altruism to promote things that are of value to others just because others value them, and pace Nagel, objectivity is a much weaker requirement than altruism.[132]

131 This provides some support for those "ordinary" moral reasoners who strive to achieve what Fishkin calls "cosmic" neutrality. *Subjective Morality*, pp. 61–9.

132 It may be thought that the position I have endorsed leaves the Affective-Cognitive Theory open to an analogue of Derek Parfit's critique of self-interest theory. To simplify greatly, he suggests that the traditional self-interest theory of rationality is untenable because it combines (i) a claim that all reasons for action are agent-relative (relating to the agent's own interest) with (ii) a claim that, with respect to his own life, the agent should exercise "temporal neutrality," in particular he is to treat the interests and desires of his future self on par with those of his present self. Parfit (again, to greatly simplify his conclusion) indicates that if one goes for the temporal neutrality in (ii), it is hard to justify rejecting, as does (i), agent-neutrality. Doesn't the Affective-Cognitive Theory also combine agent-relativity of value reasons with temporal neutrality within an agent's life? Isn't the acknowledgement that impersonal value judgments can motivate tantamount to accepting what our future self might value should be motivating for our present self? No. I reject temporal neutrality, as we shall see in §14.3. I have not argued that the belief that one will come to see the value of something in the future necessarily provides one with reasons now to pursue it; indeed, I will deny it. All that is implied by accepting that impersonal value judgments can be motivating is that the belief that one's present self – the self as one now conceives it – would grasp the value of something providing one's present self with reasons to pursue it. See Parfit, *Reasons and Persons*, secs. 51ff., esp. pp. 134–44.

V

Values and value systems

13 VALUES

In the previous chapter, I argued that analyses of emotion and valuing provide the foundation for understanding value judgments. Once we grasp what is involved in valuing something, we can see the point of the claim that some things, but not others, are appropriate or worthy objects of a particular type of valuing. We are apt to go astray, though, if we take the idea of a value judgment as our point of departure in developing a value theory, for then it is all too likely that we will seek some special sort of property – valuableness, goodness, or whatever. It is, I suppose, possible to make sense of value judgments by focusing on the (supervenient) property of valuableness; but this approach tends to obscure the intimate relation between value judgments, valuing and motivation, with the consequence that externalism appears even more of a challenge than it is. In any event, even if one insists on seeing value judgments in terms of a supervenient evaluative property, it is a property that can only be grasped once we know what it is to value something.

Just as some insist that value theory is best conceived as a study of an evaluative property, others maintain that abstract values are the key. Consider, for example, Nicholas Rescher's "full exposition" of a specific evaluation such as "Smith's friendship was of the greatest value for the advancement of Jones's career." According to Rescher, the exposition must include:

1. The *value object* that is being evaluated (Smith's friendship).
2. The *locus of value* (the advancement of one's career).
3. The *underlying values* that are at issue ("financial security").[1]

It is revealing that Rescher describes the "locus of value" as the

1 Nicholas Rescher, *Introduction to Value Theory*, p. 8.

"particularizing factor that intervenes in an evaluation between an abstract *value* and the particular, concrete thing under consideration."[2] He apparently believes that particular evaluations are always based on some abstract underlying value, even though mediated by a "locus." Jones, then, is said to prize Smith's friendship because it advances his career, but, in turn, his career "is of value to Jones presumably because such items as 'success,' 'financial security,' 'the respect of his peers,' and the like, are among his values."[3]

In this section, I examine both the concept of "a value" and the ways in which such values relate to particular valuings. Rescher's analysis is objectionable as a general account of values and valuings, I will argue, on two related counts. First, we employ the notion of "a value" in at least two ways, and Rescher's analysis cannot accommodate both; in contrast, the Affective-Cognitive Theory can. Secondly, I will maintain that we have no good reason to accept the claim that particular valuings, to be fully explained, must *always* be shown to be derived from, or somehow "in the service" of, abstract values. In sum, I argue that Rescher (and, we will see, a number of others) has mistakenly converted a particular value-valuing relation into a general account.

13.1 Abstract valuings

The concept of "a value," particularly "a value of Alf's," is most at home in sociological and social psychological discussions. Although the notion of "a person's values" is now part of common parlance, this itself is in no small measure due to the popularization of sociological and social psychological ways of thinking. In this section, therefore, I will focus – not exclusively, but largely – on the senses of "a value" employed by these disciplines.

Values have sometimes been understood by social psychologists and, indeed, by philosophers as a type of attitude or something quite similar. Kurt Baier, for example, writes: "Having values is . . . like having convictions about, or like valuing (in the sense of cherishing, treasuring, prizing) something: it is what might be called an essentially appraisal-dependent attitude. That

2 Ibid.
3 Ibid.

I believe or value something consists in my having a certain attitude or behavioral disposition."[4] Some social psychologists are even more straightforward in seeing values as a type of attitude, that is, attitudes that are (i) more important than others and (ii) directed at more abstract contents or in some way more general.[5] Certainly no theoretical barrier bars having attitudes toward abstract notions. As Fishbein and Ajzen note, "Judgments can be made with respect to any concept [content/object] whatsoever. The concept may be a physical object, an institution, a trait, an attribute, a behavior, etc. Such concepts can be described in detail or in a more general fashion."[6] So the term "a value" is sometimes simply reserved for one's most general and important attitudes because these may be most useful in providing insights into, say, a person's personality or his political and social outlook.[7] And it is this sort of description or profile of a person's important prizings that is a basic aim of those who talk about values. Clearly, though, on this conception no deep theoretical gulf divides (ordinary) valuings and values.

Without doubt, Rescher's explanation will often be the preferred method in these sociological or social psychological investigations; the central and general attitudes may be treated as the *explicans* that accounts for a variety of particular attitudes or valuings. This research strategy is in no way objectionable, though we shall see later that thus far the evidence is consistent with a rather more complex picture. But all this is quite distinct from the claim that in normal value discourse a particular valuing has not been fully explained until it has been shown to be in some way derived from an abstract value. Granted, we do sometimes account for our valuings in this way. As in Rescher's example, we might value the particular (someone's friendship) because it promotes some other valued state (financial security);[8] or we might

4 Kurt Baier, "What is Value?" p. 54.
5 See M. Brewster Smith, "Personal Values in the Study of Lives," pp. 101ff.; Ben Reich and Christine Adcock, *Values, Attitudes, and Behaviour Change*, p. 20. Although he does not refer to "value" in this context, Solomon E. Asch's analysis of "sentiments" is a good example of this approach. *Social Psychology*, pp. 569ff. See also Gordon W. Allport, "Values and Our Youth," p. 164.
6 Martin Fishbein and Icek Ajzen, *Belief, Attitude, Intention and Behavior*, p. 54.
7 See Asch, *Social Psychology*, ch. 19.
8 It is this instrumental "property" that Bentham described as "utility." Un-

value the particular because it instantiates, that is, is an instance of, an abstract value such as friendship.[9] But it seems arbitrary to insist that all particular valuings must either promote or instantiate an abstract value. I can see no reason to accept the claim that one can explain a specific and/or relatively unimportant attitude only by showing that it flows from one's central and important ones. Nothing in attitude theory suggests it must be so. Intuitively, it seems more the mark of a fanatic to let one's abstract or general commitments determine all one's attitudes. It certainly strikes me as implausible to insist that, if I value a smile from my infant daughter, the full exposition of this valuing must, necessarily, turn on the claim that it promotes or instantiates an abstract value such as "being loved by my children," "happiness in babies" or whatever.

Sometimes abstract valuings do indeed provide the grounds of particular valuings. At other times, however, the particular valuing may well be unrelated to any abstract value. Moreover, as I will argue later (§13.3), in some cases particular valuings may be more soundly grounded than the abstract value and, so, it will be more accurate to say that the specific valuing, or a set of particular valuings, explains the abstract value (rather than vice versa). I see no good theoretical or intuitive reason to exclude any of these relations; indeed, we shall see that it is misguided to do so.

13.2 Valuational criteria

I have argued that, if values are seen as a type of attitude, then, though they may well be a chief focus of interest, no good reason indicates that all valuings (attitudes) must be somehow derived

like some later utilitarians, he did not use "utility" to refer to all value, but reserved it for "that property in any object, whereby it tends to produce benefit, advantage, pleasure, good or happiness." *An Introduction to the Principles of Morals and Legislation*, ch. I, sec. III.

9 As Bernard Williams points out, even a consequentialist ethic must allow that "there are some types of things which have non-consequential value, and also some particular things that have such value because they are instances of those types." "A Critique of Utilitarianism," p. 83. John Finnis places great stress on this relation while being very critical of the instrumental or consequential relation between general values and particular valuations (and actions). See his *Natural Law and Natural Rights*, pp. 111–25. See also S. I. Benn's analysis of rational participation in politics based on standing up for, or affirming, one's values even when one cannot effectively advance or promote them. "The Problematic Rationality of Political Participation."

from abstract values. Many social psychologists, however, have insisted on a much sharper distinction between attitudes and values. Milton Rokeach, whose study of human values has had wide impact in the field, writes:

> An attitude differs from a value in that an attitude refers to an organization of several beliefs around a specific object or situation. A value, on the other hand, refers to a single belief of a very specific kind. It concerns a desirable mode of behavior or end-state that has a transcendental quality to it, guiding actions, attitudes, judgments, and comparisons across specific objects and situations and beyond immediate goals to more ultimate goals.[10]

Rokeach and those sharing his general view accept the contrasts between attitudes and values with respect to (i) generality and (ii) importance, but also insist that (iii) attitudes refer to objects though values do not[11] and (iv) values are standards of evaluation though attitudes are not.[12]

Rokeach's research has focused on thirty-six values; eighteen of these are described as "terminal" (that is, involving ends) and eighteen – labeled as "instrumental" – are perhaps best described as personality traits and ways of acting. The left column of Table 1 lists these values.[13] Rokeach assumes that these values are all universally held; consequently, humans are conceived as "differing from one another not so much in terms of whether they possess particular terminal or instrumental values, but in the way they organize them to form value hierarchies or priorities."[14] Rokeach thus claims that these thirty-six values – which cannot be reduced to a smaller number of factors – provide the basis for a person's thousands of attitudes, from those toward peace to detergents. "Whatever the attitude, it is an expression or manifes-

10 Milton Rokeach, *The Nature of Human Values*, p. 18 (textual references deleted). See also Rokeach's *Beliefs, Attitudes, and Values*, ch. 7.

11 This is particularly emphasized by Robin M. Williams, "Change and Stability in Values and Value Systems," pp. 16–17.

12 See Rokeach, *The Nature of Human Values*, pp. 4, 13, 18; Norman T. Feather, *Values in Education and Society*, pp. 4, 9, 10; Robin Williams, "Values and Value Systems," pp. 15–16, 20, 28. See also M. Brewster Smith, "Personal Values," pp. 102ff.

13 Rokeach's survey form presents subjects with eighteen terminal and eighteen instrumental values arranged alphabetically, instructing respondents to rank order them. See his *Nature of Human Values*, Appendix A. See Table 1 in the text of the present volume.

14 Milton Rokeach, "From Individual to Institutional Values," p. 49.

Table 1. *Rokeach's values and their association with some attitudes.*

Values	Attitudes toward: King's assassination	Blacks	Poor	Student protests	Vietnam War (adults)	Vietnam War (students)	Communism	Church activism	Personal importance of religion	Total
Terminal Values										
A comfortable life	★	★	★	★	★			★	★	7
An exciting life		★			★					2
A sense of accomplishment		★	★	★					★	4
A world at peace	★		★							2
A world of beauty		★			★	★	★			4
Equality	★	★	★	★	★		★	★		7
Family security	★	★		★				★	★	5
Freedom										0
Happiness		★	★							2
Inner harmony		★								1
Mature love		★			★					2
National security	★	★	★	★	★			★		6
Pleasure		★							★	2
Salvation	★	★	★	★	★	★	★	★	★	9
Self-respect										0
Social recognition						★	★		★	3
True friendship				★						1
Wisdom		★	★	★				★		4

Adapted from: Rokeach, *The Nature of Human Values,* p. 119. Copyright The Rokeach Value Survey, 1982, Consulting Psychologists Press, Palo Alto, California. Used with permission.

tation of and should therefore be significantly related to some subset of terminal and instrumental values."[15] This, then, would seem to pose a direct challenge to the Affective-Cognitive The-

15 Rokeach, *The Nature of Human Values*, p. 95. See also pp. 18, 103–6, 117.

Table 1. *Continued.*

Values	King's assassination	Blacks	Poor	Student protests	Vietnam War (adults)	Vietnam War (students)	Communism	Church activism	Personal importance of religion	Total
	Attitudes toward									
Instrumental Values										
Ambitious		★				★			★	3
Broad-minded		★		★			★			3
Capable					★				★	2
Cheerful			★							1
Clean	★	★	★	★			★	★		6
Courageous								★		1
Forgiving								★	★	2
Helpful			★	★			★		★	4
Honest									★	1
Imaginative	★	★		★			★	★		5
Independent			★				★		★	3
Intellectual	★	★		★		★		★	★	6
Logical	★	★			★				★	4
Loving	★		★			★	★		★	5
Obedient	★	★	★	★		★	★		★	7
Polite	★	★		★						3
Responsible			★	★	★					3
Self-controlled			★				★			2
Number of values	13	21	16	16	10	7	12	11	16	122

Adapted from: Rokeach, *The Nature of Human Values,* p. 119. Copyright The Rokeach Value Survey, 1982, Consulting Psychologists Press, Palo Alto, California. Used with permission.

ory of value: valuings (attitudes) are not basic, but rather derive from some small number of fundamental values. Rescher's "full exposition" seems vindicated.

I shall defend three claims relating to Rokeach's work:

(i) Despite his insistence on a sharp contrast between attitudes and values, his notion of a value can be embraced in the value-as-general-attitude account.
(ii) If his theory is so interpreted as to maintain a sharp attitude/value distinction, the notion of "a value" loses central features such as importance and generality.
(iii) His reports of empirical findings relating values and attitudes do not provide much support for his claim that attitudes are in the service of values; the findings are consistent with several alternative accounts of the value-attitude relation.

13.2.1 The first criticism of the sharp distinction

My first claim, then, is that despite Rokeach's and others' insistence on a sharp attitude/value distinction, his conception of a value can be subsumed under the (somewhat older) notion of a value as a general (or abstract) and important valuing (attitude). Certainly the distinction between attitudes as "object-directed" and values as not having an object is no bar to doing so, for it does not withstand scrutiny. As I have already emphasized, an attitude theory such as Fishbein and Ajzen's allows for diverse contents of attitudinal states, from specific objects to abstract ideals. We must take care not to confuse the thesis that an intentional state such as valuing (that is, having an attitude toward) necessarily has an object *qua* content with the claim that this state necessarily refers, or somehow corresponds, to an object *qua* item in the world (§§5.2–3). Rokeach's values (see Table 1) are certainly general (and often vague), but I see no reason why "a comfortable life," "equality," "social recognition," or "cheerfulness" are not entirely suitable contents of attitudinal states.

Rokeach and his followers, we saw, offer another fundamental contrast:[16] values, but not attitudes, function as standards of evaluation. M. Brewster Smith, who was a precursor of Rokeach in this regard, argued that even highly general attitudes only concern what is "desired" or "preferred" and not, as with values,

---

Rokeach could allow slightly more than his thirty-six as fundamental values, but he believes that the number of basic values is "in the dozens." Ibid., p. 18.

16 Rokeach actually points to seven contrasts in *The Nature of Human Values*, pp. 18–19. I believe that I deal with the most fundamental in the text.

what is "desirable" or "preferable."[17] This might lead one to suspect that, for Brewster Smith and Rokeach, values function as impersonal standards (§10.2) or beliefs about goodness that generate impersonal rankings (§8.3). And this is reinforced by Rokeach's characterization (in the quote above) of values as "beliefs." But in much the same manner of my account of valuings, Rokeach's values concern what is (in some sense) personally affirmed. Values, Rokeach and others acknowledge, are both cognitive *and* affective.[18] So values are certainly not conceived as mere criteria that allow one to judge whether something is a good instance of its kind, or impersonally valuable; like attitudes, they have personal affective components. The claim of Rokeach and those who share his view, then, must be that, though both attitudes and values are affectively based, only values are able to serve as standards. Rokeach has a number of things in mind when saying that values are standards, but these are generally fairly straightforward, for example, a standard leads us to take positions on social issues, provides a basis for various choices, provides a foundation for judging, praising, etc.[19] It is difficult to see why attitudes cannot function in this general manner. Most importantly, it is widely accepted that one's attitude toward one thing can provide the grounding for an attitude toward another. If so, then one's valuing of, say, private automobiles can lead one to take a stand on public policy issues (for example, negatively value certain urban transportation plans), praise the actions of automobile associations, choose certain residential areas, and so on. This much seems undeniable.

But can't it still be said that this concerns only what one "prefers" rather than what is "preferable"? Or, to employ the language of value, it concerns only one's comparative valuings rather than impersonal comparative value judgments? To this extent I concur: the mere fact that Alf rationally values, say, private cars more than public transport does not imply that private cars are impersonally more valuable (§11.2.1); and, further, he might rationally value more that which is less worthy of being valued (§11.2.2). But it is nevertheless mistaken to posit a sharp distinc-

17 M. Brewster Smith, "Personal Values," pp. 102–3.
18 See Rokeach, *The Nature of Human Values*, pp. 6–7; Feather, *Values in Society*, pp. 4–5; Robin Williams, "Values and Value Systems," pp. 15–16.
19 See Rokeach, *The Nature of Human Values*, pp. 13ff.

tion between what is soundly valued and what is judged to be valuable. That Alf soundly values private cars more than public transport does indeed imply that he sees cars as being of more value, that is, he personally finds them to be more valuable. From the perspective of his own deliberations and choices, his sound comparative valuing provides him with good reasons to forgo the opportunity of using or promoting public transport in order to ensure use of his own car. The comparative valuing is thus evaluative in the relevant sense.[20]

13.2.2 The second criticism of the sharp distinction

One might seek to sustain a sharp attitude/value distinction by (roughly) depicting (i) attitudes as likings and dislikings and (ii) values as the reasons that support those likings/dislikings. Attitude and value sentences would thus have different forms: whereas attitude sentences would conform to the schema "Alf likes/dislikes *X*," value sentences would have the general form "*V* is a reason for Alf to like/dislike *X*."[21] This strikes me as one of the most plausible ways to defend a very sharp distinction; moreover, it provides a rationale for Rescher's "full exposition" thesis, for he is then making a formal claim about the structure of value sentences. I see no conclusive argument against using "value" in this way: if one wants to reserve the notion of "a value" for reasons for valuings and/or value judgments, so be it. However, four problems confront such a usage.

(i) *Organic wholes.* Rokeach, as we have seen, wishes to retain the intuition that we have some personal affective stance toward our values. This becomes difficult to do if every reason warranting a valuing is deemed a "value." One way to do so is to embrace Fishbein and Ajzen's summation model as a truly general account. It will be recalled (§8.2) that, according to them, a per-

20 Rokeach provides yet another contrast between attitudes and values: values refer to end-states or modes of behavior whereas many attitudes (e.g., toward work and private automobiles) do not. "From Individual to Institutional Values," pp. 48–9. Two comments: (i) even if accepted, this criterion, like generality and importance, would only serve to distinguish the subset of values from the general class of attitudes; (ii) it is not clear that many relatively minor attitudes could not be described as "terminal" – e.g., a world in which private cars abound.

21 I am ignoring here the distinction between internal and external reasons. See note 18 in Chapter IV and §16.2.

son's attitude toward *X* is a summation of his evaluations of *X*'s salient attributes; and each of these evaluations is, at least on one interpretation, affective. Now, although the success of Fishbein and Ajzen's simple summation model may suggest that philosophers have perhaps been overly worried about "Gestalt" or "organic whole" valuations – that is, where the overall valuation is not a summation of individual attribute evaluations – it does seem that a theory of value should at least allow the possibility of such organic valuations. "It is certain," G. E. Moore wrote, "that a whole formed of a good thing and an indifferent thing may have immensely greater value than the good thing itself possesses. . . . And it seems as if indifferent things may also be the sole constituents of a whole which has great value, either positive or negative."[22] Now if such organic whole valuations actually occur, we are committed to one of three views. (a) In such cases, we might say that the presence of an otherwise indifferent feature is a reason warranting the valuation but not itself a value. This seems plausible, but it is inconsistent with the view we are considering. (b) Alternatively, one might insist that in such cases the indifferent feature is a value, but one which is not cared for as such. This is consistent with the values-as-valuational-criteria thesis, but sacrifices the intuition that values are affectively charged. (c) Lastly, it could be maintained that in this case the value is the whole set (organic whole) of features. This is consistent with the valuational criteria thesis and retains the affective intuition; however, it appears inconsistent with Rokeach's insistence (in the above quote) that, in contrast to attitudes that involve "an organization of several beliefs around a specific object," a value concerns "a single belief of a very specific kind."

(ii) *Importance.* If one adopts the valuational criteria interpretation, one can no longer maintain, as Rokeach does, that values are necessarily important. If my reasons for valuing a steak is that it is tender, medium rare, and thick, my grounding "values" are not particularly important. It really is most difficult to see how the reasons warranting attitudes can all be seen as values while still conceiving of values as necessarily important to a person's overall outlook, personality, etc. It is perhaps revealing that Ro-

22 G. E. Moore, *Principia Ethica*, p. 28. See also Hector-Neri Castañeda, "On the Ultimate Subjects of Value Predication," p. 27.

keach nevertheless seems tempted to do so. He tells us – and it is certainly a fascinating finding – that choices of dishwashing detergents have a statistically significant relation to a subset of his thirty-six values. But his theory, as well as some of his specific remarks in this discussion, rather suggests that he thinks all such "inconsequential" attitudes can be wholly explained as being "in the service of" some of his thirty-six values.[23] This seems most unlikely (see §13.2.3).

(iii) *Generality*. Given what has been said, it should be manifest that values *qua* valuational criteria need not be particularly general or abstract. Thickness in steaks is a valuational criterion, albeit a fairly specific one.

(iv) *Attitudes and values*. Even if one does insist on a sharp distinction between values and attitudes along these lines, it still must be acknowledged that attitudes can also be values. If Alf's attitude towards *X* can serve as a reason for his attitude towards *Y*, it would function as a value in the sentence "*V* is a reason for Alf to like/dislike *Y*." The earlier example of liking private automobiles and attitudes toward residential areas illustrates this point.

13.2.3 Correlations between attitudes and values

I have argued, then, that if values are affective, general, and important, and also serve as grounds for various other attitudes (valuings), no sharp divide separates attitudes and values. "A value" is then used to mark off an attitude (valuing) that has features of generality, importance, and so forth that make it of particular interest in describing and understanding a person's valuational perspective or "plan of life" (§§14.2–3). On the other hand, if one does insist on a sharp attitude/value distinction as, say, between valuings and reasons for the valuings, all values cannot then be described as affective, general, and important. Now as I pointed out earlier, Rokeach seems not only to dispute this, but provides evidence that, in fact, all (or at least very nearly all) of our attitudes can be explained as complex combinations of instantiations of, or ways to promote, some subset of the thirty-six fundamental values.

---

23 Rokeach, *The Nature of Human Values*, pp. 116–17. See §13.2.3 in this volume.

That, at least, is his theory. However, the hypothesis upon which he concentrates is much more modest: any attitude should be significantly related to some subset of his thirty-six values.[24] And, as Table 1 shows, a number of attitudes are indeed significantly related to (ways in which respondents rank order) his thirty-six values. But, although this data is indeed generally consistent with his theory relating values and attitudes, the data (and, indeed, the hypothesis he discusses) is consistent with a variety of theories. In essence, he shows that we have good reason to believe that abstract values and particular attitudes are nonrandomly related; and, though very important, this does not provide particular support for the claim that all attitudes are in the service of abstract values. At least two other types of relations, which I shall explore in this chapter, are also consistent with the hypothesis and data:

(i) Abstract values often sum up a person's value orientation, that is, his disposition to value particular sorts of things. In this sense, a person's particular attitudes may be more basic than his abstract values (§13.3).
(ii) A person's value system is characterized by a tendency to coherence among his many valuings, both specific and general (§14.2).

Both (i) and (ii), we will see, also lead one to expect that abstract values and various attitudes will be nonrandomly related. Again, I am not denying here that Rokeach's (and Rescher's) analysis sometimes, perhaps often, captures the value-valuing relation; my claim is simply that no good reason supports insisting that it is the only relation.

A closer look at Rokeach's data seems to confirm the suspicion that, though indeed some attitudes flow from abstract values, in other cases the attitude-value relation is rather more obscure. For instance, Rokeach's and Rescher's analysis seems vindicated by the finding that attitudes toward blacks and the poor are most significantly related to a commitment to equality.[25] On the other hand, why those who stress a comfortable life as a value tend to have negative attitudes toward blacks but positive attitudes toward the poor is much more obscure.[26] Again: why women who stress politeness should prefer Plymouths to Fords or Chevrolets

24 Ibid., p. 95.
25 Ibid., pp. 100, 103.
26 Ibid., p. 103.

is by no means clear.[27] My purpose here is not to criticize the findings reported by Rokeach, but to emphasize that, though he provides evidence that attitudes and values are systematically related, the nature of these relations often remains elusive. This helps confirm the intuition that a variety of types of relations may be required if we are adequately to grasp the coherence of value systems.

13.3 Value orientations

Let us turn from Rokeach's value survey to the older, but extremely influential, Allport-Vernon (and Lindzey) measure of values. Both the actual test instrument and the underlying theory differ greatly from Rokeach's approach. The theoretical foundation is drawn from Eduard Spranger's *Types of Men.* Spranger analyzed personalities in terms of six value ideals or value orientations: the theoretical, the economic, the aesthetic, the social, the political, and the religious. He depicted these types of individuality or character-types as "ideal types" rather than "photographs of real life."[28] Each type is thus based on a central value direction that also determines the relative importance of the other directions within the ideal type. Thus, for instance, the "theoretic attitude" is described as the "attitude aiming at objectivity, the attitude which identifies and differentiates, generalizes and individualizes, conjoins and separates, reasons and systematizes." According to Spranger, the dominance of this attitude leads to a devaluing of the "subjective" side of life (for example, aesthetics), a lowered concern for politics, and an individualism that is inconsistent with a "social nature."[29] It perhaps goes without saying that his analysis is very much in the spirit of my own account of comparative valuing: both insist that, in a fundamental sense, value weightings are a constituent of broad personality or character types (§11.1).

Based on Spranger's types, Allport and Vernon developed a forty-five item test.[30] What is significant for our purposes is that,

27 Ibid., p. 117.
28 Eduard Spranger, *Types of Men: The Psychology of Ethics and Personality*, p. 104.
29 Ibid., pt. II, ch. 1.
30 Allport and Vernon developed the test in 1931; see the 1960 version of G.

in contrast to Rokeach, the Allport-Vernon test does not ask the respondent to identify directly with a fundamental value; rather, through a series of items tapping attitudes and opinions on specific matters, the test seeks to build up value profiles corresponding to Spranger's types. These values are not commitments to abstract notions but are general descriptions of patterns of particular valuations.

Allport and Vernon are drawing on a distinct and important notion of a person's "values." When we say, for instance, that "sensory delights are Alf's chief value," we by no means need imply that he actually has any attitude toward "sensory delights"; more likely is that his many particular valuations and the grounds that give rise to them are best summed up as a sensory-delights value orientation. Rescher's "full exposition" does not capture the role of such value ascriptions. These value orientations do not necessarily warrant or endorse particular valuings; Alf does not value a particular tender steak because it instantiates, or promotes, "sensory delights." That is reversing the logical priority. It is because Alf is the sort of person who consistently values such things that we are warranted in attributing to him this value orientation.

The obvious point I wish to make, then, is that social psychologists have employed the concept of "a value" in at least two distinct ways. Values are sometimes seen as abstract and general attitudes that yield various lower-level attitudes and at other times as descriptions of clusters of fairly specific valuings. The Affective-Cognitive Theory accommodates both these senses and so to that extent is a more adequate theory of value than that implied by Rokeach's or Rescher's analyses. A more important point follows. Although these two conceptions of value are distinct, it is reasonable to suppose that many values will partake of the nature of both. We may come to stress some of Rokeach's thirty-six values because those abstract values articulate our characteristic valuing pattern or orientation. For instance, one reason for subscribing to "true friendship" as an abstract value is that one comes to see that in a variety of contexts one values

W. Allport, P. E. Vernon, and G. Lindzey, *A Study of Values*. See also G. W. Allport, *Pattern and Growth in Personality*, pp. 453–7; Derek Wright, *The Psychology of Moral Behavior*, pp. 197–8; Reich and Adcock, *Values, Attitudes*, pp. 21–3.

friendship and the welfare of one's friends. One's subscription to the abstract value in such cases comes as a sort of self-discovery; given one's various valuings in a number of personal relations, one comes to see friendship as a regulative value. This recalls the account Mill gives in his *Autobiography*. Although Tocqueville's *Democracy in America* brought home to him that his "political ideals" had shifted away from "pure democracy," Mill also points out that by that time "I was now well prepared for speculations of this character."[31] A number of his lower-level attitudes (which, of course, are grounded in beliefs) had already changed, preparing the way for a value change. But, having discovered that one possesses a certain sort of value orientation, one may then come to value the abstract ideal itself; the ideal then not only articulates the pattern of, but organizes and extends, one's particular valuings. In contrast to Rescher's full exposition, then, it would seem that particular valuings sometimes ground abstract values and sometimes are grounded by them and, perhaps most typically, the abstract and particular are in a dynamic relation in which they shape each other.

14 VALUE SYSTEMS

14.1 *Ambivalence and conflict*

Earlier (§11.1.1) I indicated that valuings and value judgments are less subject to consistency requirements than are beliefs. This requires defense, especially because a number of philosophers have employed epistemological models as a basis for analyzing value systems;[32] and, even more strongly, some have insisted that valuing simply *is* a matter of belief (see §7.1). Prima facie, the parallel between belief and value is strong.[33] Just as it would be irrational to hold the beliefs that *p* and that not-*p*, it would seem irrational to judge *X* both valuable and not-valuable. If {*X* is worthy of being valued}, then it must be that [not {*X* is not worthy

31 John Stuart Mill, *Autobiography*, p. 134 (ch. VI, para. 9).
32 See, e.g., Robert Audi, "Axiological Foundationalism"; Mark Pastin, "The Reconstruction of Value"; Robert Nozick, *Philosophical Explanations*, p. 414.
33 For a useful discussion of Brentano's views on the analogies and disanalogies between judgment and emotion, see Chisholm, *Brentano and Intrinsic Value*, pp. 54–7.

of being valued}]. But, of course, "value" functions as a generic term (§10.4), so Alf might believe both that *X* is worthy of interest and that it is not worthy of enjoyment, and so in this sense consistently maintain that *X* is both valuable and not-valuable. More importantly, he might be ambivalent about *X*; he might, that is, both value it (and judge it to be valuable) and *dis*value it (and judge it to be *dis*valuable).[34] He may thus judge Betty worthy of both love and hate and, indeed, both love and hate her. Mixed feelings toward *X* are possible, both psychologically[35] and logically, in a way that "mixed beliefs" about *p* are not. One cannot, say, simply believe *p* to be both true and false or, to make the parallel closer, both believe and disbelieve *p*. To be sure, one can weigh contradictory evidence, and (as one may when a member of a jury) swing back and forth between believing and disbelieving *p*. But one is rationally at fault to believe and disbelieve *p* simultaneously (see §18.2), whereas it does not seem to be such a defect to simultaneously value and disvalue *X*.

Betty can, then, combine characteristics that render loving and hating simultaneously appropriate. If love-grounding characteristics necessarily excluded the presence of hate-grounding features such ambivalence would be rationally objectionable. But that is not so. Alternatively, if rational emotional responses were necessarily "all things considered" or "on balance" responses such that one was committed to weighing up the positive and negative features of *X* so as to arrive at a single overall affective-evaluative response, then too we might say that one who simultaneously responded both positively and negatively was rationally defective in some way. But, again, there seems little reason to think this is so; one can have a pragmatically complete set of beliefs (§§6.3, 10.4) but yet, quite rationally, respond separately to *X*'s positive and negative features. And, as Abelson et al.'s studies indicate, this seems to be what people do; rather than demonstrating consistently positive or negative affective responses (which would be consistent with the single, overall, response the-

34 The distinction between this and the former case is that between a judgment that something is not worthy of being valued, and a judgment that it is worthy of being disvalued. It is, then, a distinction between that which is worthless and that which is bad. As I depict it, one who is ambivalent simultaneously sees something as both good and bad, as both of value and disvalue.
35 See Patricia S. Greenspan, "Ambivalence and the Logic of Emotion."

sis),[36] Abelson's subjects were apt to report a variety of both positive and negative affects directed at a single political figure (§8.2).

This, then, is one intelligible sense in which a person may be said to experience a value conflict: one can both (intrinsically) value and disvalue the same thing. Typically, however, those who talk of value conflicts or the admissible (rational) inconsistency of value systems have something rather different in mind. Neil Cooper, for instance, insists that "[t]he totality of facts must be logically consistent, but the totality of values does not have to be, for if values or ideals are incompatible with one another, this is not a problem for the world, even for a "world of value"; it is a problem for the moral agent, but one of which he is not expected to provide a definitive resolution."[37] The notion of the *incompatibility* of values is often employed to make the Berlinian point that "ends collide": we cannot realize all that is of value and, so, we must necessarily choose to promote some values over others.[38] I want to suggest that this conception of value conflict can be recast, far more prosaically to be sure, in terms of opportunity costs: given the states of affairs that are actually realizable (as opposed to imaginable utopias), promoting, protecting, or instantiating one thing a person values has severe opportunity costs in terms of promoting other valued things. Understood thus, the concern of pluralist philosophers such as Berlin is not altogether different than that of economists, as both are ultimately concerned with the question "Since, in order to have *X*, one must forgo *Y*, which will one choose?" But it needs to be stressed that

36 Fishbein's summation theory, which does not presuppose such balanced judgments, has been shown to be a superior predictor of attitudes to theories which postulate that individual affects are somehow balanced or made congruent. See Lynn R. Anderson and Martin Fishbein, "Prediction of Attitude from the Number, Strength, and Evaluative Aspects of Beliefs about the Attitude Object: A Comparison of Summation and Congruity Theories"; Martin Fishbein and R. Hunter, "Summation *Versus* Balance in Attitude Organization and Change." However, for considerations supporting a tendency toward such evaluative consistency, see George A. Miller, *Psychology*, pp. 296ff.; Wright, *The Psychology of Moral Behavior*, pp. 110–1; Reich and Adcock, *Values, Attitudes*, ch. 7.

37 Neil Cooper, *The Diversity of Moral Thinking*, p. 288.

38 See Isaiah Berlin, "Does Political Theory Still Exist?" p. 8. See also Robert A. Kocis, "Reason, Development, and the Conflict of Human Ends." Cf. Robert Nozick's brand of value pluralism in his *Philosophical Explanations*, pp. 446ff.

it is not simply decisions about personal gratification or consumption that involve such opportunity costs; even one who intrinsically values the environment may find that the cost, say, of protecting a river and the life it supports is to forgo the possibility of promoting human welfare through recreational uses of the river.

One may, of course, endeavor to avoid these opportunity costs by striving for states of affairs in which, somehow, all of one's valuings are harmonized or integrated. Or, one may take an inner route to harmony and seek to cultivate valuings that are all easily co-realized. The former course articulates the sort of rationalism Berlin so often criticizes – a conviction that in a properly ordered world all good things can be had to the fullest extent – and the latter points to a certain sort of stoicism. But, though some may be adverse to incurring opportunity costs when pursuing values, it is difficult to envisage any general case for insisting that value systems be characterized by such a harmony. Indeed, it is just because value-based actions do – inevitably, it seems – involve these sorts of opportunity costs that it is useful to understand comparative valuings in terms of trade-offs or rates of indifference substitution (§11.1). When one values *X* more than *Y* one is not typically just rating it higher according to some standard (for example, its capacity to "confer benefits on people");[39] one is exhibiting a settled disposition to forgo opportunities to promote *Y* in order to advance, secure, or protect *X*. Comparative valuings, then, manifest dispositions to incur opportunity costs relating to one valued thing so as to promote another. So, often enough, to say that values conflict, and thus agents must "choose" to promote one rather than another, is to point out that value-seeking action entails opportunity costs vis-à-vis other values the promotion of which one must now forgo. Once more belief seems a poor model for grasping value. Admittedly, a reasonably sophisticated account of theoretical rationality could integrate some conception of opportunity costs: when confronted by rival theories, both of which are apt to lead to some insights (for simplicity's sake, let us assume that each is partially correct), a scientist who devotes himself to one will incur opportunity

39 This is Kurt Baier's suggestion; see his "What is Value?" p. 47. See also Rescher, *Value Theory*, pp. 6–62. For a criticism of this benefit-oriented conception of value, see §7.3 of this volume.

costs in relation to the other. Nevertheless, a fundamental difference remains between standard believing and standard valuing. Valuing is programmatic and action-guiding in a way that ordinary descriptive beliefs are not. One's valuings translate into commitments to act (§9.2), to change the world in some ways and to resist change in others; and, when one acts in this way rather than that, one incurs opportunity costs. Or, to employ the more traditional language of ethics, one sacrifices (insofar as one does not promote or preserve) one valued thing for the sake of another. And it is because of this that value discourse, and deliberation about value-based action, is so centrally concerned with conflict, choice, rankings, weightings, etc.

14.2 The coherence of value systems

Thus far I have been stressing the ways in which valuings and value judgments can, rationally, be inconsistent or in some sense conflict. But a rational individual's valuings, value judgments, and values are certainly not atomistic, unrelated, unorganized, or incoherent. Although the analysis of value systems shows the possibility of rational conflict, value systems are also characterized by various types of coherence.

14.2.1 Valuational consistency

The first factor tending toward coherence – and perhaps the most controversial – I shall call the *principle of valuational consistency* (see further §§10.1, 18.1). According to this principle, if *X*'s possession of *f* is a rational ground of Alf's valuing of *X*, *Y*'s possession of *f* is also a ground for his valuing of *Y*. This principle has also been described as the "universality of value judgments," that is, "Whenever something has value (disvalue), there must be something about it *in virtue of which* it has it. However, it then appears that *anything else* having the same attribute must, *ceteris paribus*, also have value (disvalue)."[40] We need to be clear here, however, about what it means to say that *X*'s possession of *f* is a reason for valuing *Y* as well. Impersonally, of course, if feature *f* appropriately grounds an emotion such as interest, then anything's possession of *f* will, prima facie and other things equal, be a reason

40 Elliot D. Cohen, "The Epistemology of Value," p. 180.

to value it in the sense of take an interest in it; but I have argued that one is not irrational if one nevertheless is not interested in things that possess *f*.[41] However, I want to argue that matters are very different if one is the sort of person who finds *f* interesting, at least in regard to *X*. For a fully rational person who claims that his interest in *X* is grounded solely in *f* but then discovers that he does not value *Y* despite its possession of *f* has, at least on the face of it, a genuine quandary. It is my claim that he is mistaken about either his valuings of *X* and *Y* or the grounds of his valuing of *X*. As such, when confronted with this sort of violation of the principle of valuational consistency, a fully rational agent will so revise his value claims in order to make them consistent with the principle.

Consider Michael, who praises the socialist's "frank and human egotism [*sic*]; he lives for himself, openly and without fine-sounding phrases."[42] Michael, let us assume, thus thinks that frank and human egoism grounds admiration. But if, when confronted with the frank and human egoism of his son, Michael criticizes such egoism as ingratitude (it is, then, disvaluable), he is confronted by a violation of the principle of valuational consistency. Not that it would be difficult for him to alter his value claims in such a way that he achieves consistency. He can circumscribe his claims about frank and human egoism as to make it only appealing in other people's children. (It is an indication that the principle is psychologically well grounded that people do seem to circumscribe their values in this general way.)[43] One way to rationally do so is to appeal to some variant of Moore's principle of organic wholes, such that "egoism that is inconsistent with due consideration of one's parents" is disvaluable, rather than valuable.[44] Organic whole accounts, then, allow one to over-

41 See §§6.3, 10.2, 11.2, 12.2.

42 Michael Bakunin, "Federalism, Socialism, and Anti-Theologism," p. 119.

43 See Robin Williams, "Values and Value Systems," p. 18, on "universality of application."

44 It may be objected that I have overuniversalized this: couldn't Michael simply disvalue egoism in *his* children, without worrying about what is the proper place of egoism in parent-child relations in general? But, if his child's egoism properly grounds Michael's disvaluing of the child, it must be because such egoism is, given the concept of ingratitude, an appropriate grounding characteristic. And this implies that, ultimately, Michael's disvaluing of his child's ingratitude will draw on notions as to what appropriately grounds ingratitude that will not simply concern him and his children, but which will

come apparent valuational inconsistency by recasting the grounds of one's valuings so as to include that which distinguishes *X* from *Y*. But the very familiarity of this sort of response – "Well, in him that sort of outspokenness is simply blustering because he has no real ideas of his own" – underscores the force of a charge of valuational inconsistency: one is loath to acknowledge that something which grounds liking in one case is irrelevant or actually disvalue-grounding in another, without being able to point to any relevant difference between the two.

But it may well be objected that no *rational* defect is involved. If the beliefs grounding an emotional reaction have a causal role in bringing about an affective response (§5.4.1), then it is merely a psychological trait of Michael's that he responds to frank and human egoism differently when it is manifested by his own children and when it is manifested by others. Thus, it has been suggested, one may value at one time that which one disvalues at others.[45] Or, more moderately, what is found exciting at one time may fail to excite one at a later date. To begin, let us leave aside the possibility that one's valuings have undergone a change, such that one once found *X* exciting because it possessed *f*, but now one no longer sees any appeal in *f*, and so in *X*. Such changes no doubt occur throughout life and do not seem particularly problematic.[46] Further, let us leave aside the possibility that, on a particular day, or week, or month, one is, as it were, affectively flat (or especially aroused). One may thus fail to find value in, say, a favorite piece of music because one is depressed or sick. But valuings are dispositional, not occurrent (§8.1); the issue, then, is not whether *f* evokes the relevant response on each and every occasion, but whether one is disposed to respond to *f* in a consistent way.

Assume, then, that one values *X* just because it possesses *f*, but

be universal. This is a central point in discussions of an emotion such as loyalty; some, such as Andrew Oldenquist, insist that loyalties are grounded on *one's* relation to *one's own* country and not on any universal criteria as to what properly grounds anyone's loyalty to their country. But, if this was true, the very concept of loyalty would seem parochial because its appropriateness conditions would only relate to oneself and one's compatriots. This seems false. See Oldenquist, "Loyalties." I am indebted here to Daniel Skubik.

45 See, e.g., A. Campbell Garnett, "Intrinsic Good," p. 86.

46 See Michael Slote, *Goods and Virtues*, ch. 1. See §14.3 of the present volume.

one sees no appeal in *Y* (or *X* at a later time) even though it too possesses *f*. Now if that is so, it then becomes difficult to make out the claim that *f* is the cause of the affective-emotional response: presumably identifying *f* as the cause of the response is intended to point to a regularity between the *f* and the response, but now it is asserted that *f* only sometimes leads to the relevant response. But, if that is so, we have good grounds for disputing the claim that *f* causes the response in relation to *X* because no clear causal regularity exists. If *f*'s grounding role in the case of *X* itself is to be maintained, *f* needs to be embedded in a more comprehensive account that includes other features of *X*, such that there is a relevant difference between *f* in *X* and in *Y*. And so we are led back to an organic whole reply to the charge of valuational inconsistency.

Yet, it may still be asked whether our valuer has demonstrated any *rational* defect. However, if he cites *f* as his ground for valuing *X*, but it is really {*f*,*g*}, then he has clearly made an error about the grounds of his valuing. So if, say, Alf claims that he always enjoys a dinner at Betty's flat because she serves seafood ("I love seafood!"), but he disliked a later feast of calamari, his earlier claim was mistaken. Perhaps he only enjoys shellfish; or perhaps it is having a seafood dinner alone with Betty that he enjoys, and Charlie was present at the calamari feast.

The obvious reply here is that one's belief that an object possesses *f* only causes an affective response in some circumstances but not in others. So one's claim to value *X* by virtue of its possession of *f* is not inconsistent with one's denial that one values *Y*, or even *X* at a later time because they are experienced in different circumstances. A number of value theorists have accepted this reasoning, and so have maintained that (personal) value judgments are best understood as conforming to the schema "*X* has value for Alf in circumstances *C*."[47] I believe this common insistence on reference to particular circumstances is misguided. This is not because value judgments do not make implicit references to circumstances; to call a painting beautiful assumes that, under certain lighting conditions, experienced or sensitive viewers will see a certain sort of value in it. But it is much more ac-

47 See, e.g., Jorge J. E. Gracia, "The Ontological Status of Value," p. 396; C. I. Lewis, *An Analysis of Knowledge and Valuation*, p. 512ff.; Howard O. Eaton, *The Austrian Philosophy of Values*, p. 230 (on Meinong's theory).

curate to say that value judgments typically assume some notion of standard circumstances. To say that Alf enjoys watching baseball assumes that he is not in pain, is not too tired, snow is not falling while he is watching from the bleachers, etc. Now one could say that what he really values is "watching baseball when he is not in pain, when it is not snowing, etc.,"; and there would be little harm in that, except that it may then well be impossible to state what one values accurately, because the background conditions are apt to be indefinitely numerous (for example, no nuclear wars are occurring, no terrorists are in the stands, oxygen is present). The claim that one values something is made against a background of assumed normal conditions, and little is to be gained by attempting to build all these into the value claim.

However, we have a deeper reason for resisting the suggestion that all value claims are circumstance specific in this way. As Hart and Honoré point out, a condition for an event is identified as a cause if it is an "abnormal" condition which, together with normal ("mere") conditions, brings about the event.[48] These normal or mere conditions cannot of course, be fully specified; nevertheless, they are assumed when identifying the abnormal condition as the cause. So, when we say that a certain belief or set of beliefs cause an emotional reaction, it must be remembered that, like other causal statements, a large set of "mere" conditions is assumed. Now if the normal conditions do not hold – if some of the conditions for the emotional response are atypical – then, as Hart and Honoré suggest, these should be assigned a causal (as opposed to background condition) role. And that means that they can be evaluated as one of the grounding (causal) beliefs of the emotion, and thus are subject to appropriateness conditions. Consequently, if someone experiences an emotion only under particularly odd conditions, the emotion is apt to be inappropriate. If, say, Alf fears snakes, but only on Tuesday, or in the company of a blond woman, it seems that his fear is not fully appropriate because it is grounded on beliefs that seem irrelevant to danger.

The principle of valuational consistency, then, seems sound. But it may well be questioned whether it applies to those dispo-

48 See H. L. A. Hart and A. M. Honoré, *Causation in the Law*, pt. I, esp. chs. II, V.

sitional emotions that seem uniquely directed at specific individuals, that is, love and friendship. Armed with the principle of valuational consistency, Charlie may advance an odd argument against Betty: "You love Alf because he is quick-witted, honest, and considerate; but I am all of these things to an equal degree. Valuational consistency thus demands that you love me equally!" As Robert Brown has noted, this is clearly wrong: Betty can rationally continue to love Alf even after she acknowledges Charlie's equality on these counts.[49] But why?[50] I cannot enter into this important issue deeply, but it seems that the key to a proper understanding of love and friendship is to see them as temporally extended, such that the grounding for love at one stage of the relationship differs from that at others. In the early stages, the beloved may well be loved simply because she instantiates a set of qualities to which one is attracted; perhaps she is believed to be unique in doing so, but at a relatively early stage in the love's career, one may well have been just as attracted to another person displaying those qualities.[51] But, as love develops, it has its own history; gratitude, shared memories, and experiences may ground the love in a way that it is impossible for another to have those historical and relational qualities possessed by the beloved. And that is why a long-standing love may weather drastic personality changes (for example, those resulting from disease) where a newer love would wither along with those traits that grounded the love. But still, though this may point the way to an adequate analysis of some friendships, it is not adequate for an understanding of love. For even with a new love, in which Betty may be equally attracted to Alf and Charlie because they display those characteristics she finds appealing, she is not apt to love both equally. We say in such a case that she finds it difficult to make up her mind, but the point is that she aims to decide on

49 Robert Brown, *Analyzing Love*, pp. 41–3. Yet we would not be surprised if a rejected suitor advanced precisely this argument – there is something in it.

50 One view is that love is unlike other emotions, and is not based on beliefs at all. Gabriele Taylor, however, has effectively criticized this radical proposal. See her essay on "Love."

51 Brown seems to believe that this would imply that one loves the qualities, or the person as the exemplar of those qualities, rather than the whole person himself. *Analyzing Love*, p. 44. This seems to confuse the grounding beliefs with the content of the emotional state. See §§5.2., 5.4 of this volume.

one. Love typically – not always, but usually – is based on the supposition that one is of unique importance to the beloved and vice versa. If a loving involves suppositions of unique importance and exclusive mutual commitments, the principle of valuation consistency will be of little relevance.

14.2.2 Central valuings

A second factor tending toward coherence in valuing has already been mentioned (§13.2.1): the way in which one valuing can be the grounds of other valuings. An attitude toward *X* can also serve as a grounds for an attitude toward *Y*, and *Y* for *Z*, etc. Fishbein and Ajzen note this:

> On a day-to-day basis we automatically acquire an attitude toward some new object when we learn its associations with other objects, attributes, or qualities toward which we already have attitudes. These attitudes (that is, attribute evaluations) are themselves a function of beliefs linking the attribute to other characteristics and evaluations of those characteristics. The latter evaluations are again based on beliefs and evaluations, etc.[52]

As a consequence, a person's valuings will tend in certain directions. Having acquired a favorable attitude toward unionism, this may lead to a valuing of the Labor party which, in turn, may ground valuings of other Labor policies or, perhaps, certain sorts of constitutional changes that will benefit Labor.

This provides an interpretation of the "centrality" of a valuing. A valuing, we can say, is more central the more it grounds, directly or indirectly, other valuings. Consequently, to abandon a central valuing would cause severe damage to the fabric of one's value system: giving up such a valuing would undermine its status as a grounds of other valuings, and so one may have to reject a great deal when one gives up a central valuing. By "giving up" I have in mind some sort of rejection or reversal, as when one finds what was formerly valued can be no longer, or it may even be an object of hate. Such is often the case with converts. However, someone who converts to a religious or a political cause very often replaces one central valuing with another, so that a new system emerges from the ruins of the old. But the merely disillusioned, who find what they once cherished is now worthless, suf-

52 Fishbein and Ajzen, *Belief, Attitude*, p. 217.

fer real disintegration, with nothing, at least immediately, to form a nucleus for a new system. Bruno Bettelheim's description of the nonpolitical middle-class prisoners in Nazi concentration camps brings this home. Having a self-conception (see §14.2.3) and system of values built on law-abidingness, their jobs and their positions within their families, they suffered shock and personality disintegration when "all of a sudden every thing that had made them feel good about themselves for so long was knocked out from under them."[53]

It is, I think, commonly assumed that a valuing that is central in this way is an important value in the sense that it is heavily weighted in deliberations (§11.1). This is mistaken. "Giving up" a value or valuing must be distinguished from "forgoing its realization for the sake of other valuings": a value may be very difficult to give up, but one may still regularly forgo realizing it in favor of other valuings. To see this, let us assume that it is only because I value unionism that I value the Labor party and, further, it is only because I value the party that I value constitutional reform. So unionism is, at least in this set, the foundational or central valuing. But I may confront a choice between contributing to my union or to famine relief. Now if I do the latter I am forgoing an opportunity to advance my valuing of unionism, but I am not necessarily rejecting unionism and, thus, I am not necessarily undermining my valuings of the Labor party or constitutional reform. Moreover, when I forgo the opportunity to contribute to unionism, it does not follow that, ipso facto, I am forgoing the opportunity of promoting, say, constitutional reform (perhaps in the present circumstances, nothing much can be done to promote the reform, at least by the unions). It does not follow, then, that just because values V_1 and V_2 are grounded on V (the central value) that forgoing the opportunity to advance V is also to forgo the opportunity to advance V_1 and V_2. And, thus, it is not the case that, in deliberation, a more central valuing is necessarily more weighty because all the valuings based upon it are also brought to bear (as derivative valuings; see §§8.2, 9.2, 11.1). They need not be. So it is wrong to equate "more central" with "more important" with this being understood as "more weighty a consideration in deliberating about action." This is im-

53 Bruno Bettelheim, *The Informed Heart*, p. 121.

portant, for it provides a real obstacle to attempts by coherence theorists to show that judgments of comparative value are simply a function of the centrality of the valuing in relation to the whole system. To employ the familiar web metaphor: we cannot say that a valuing is rationally given more weight in deliberation if and only if it is more central to the web of value.[54]

14.2.3 The unity of personality

The first two factors making for coherence in value systems are more or less formal insofar as they derive from the concept of value. The third feature is a psychological principle, though idealists understood it as the principle of rationality.[55] It has been described variously, as an impulse to coherence,[56] personality integration,[57] ego organization,[58] and patterned individuality.[59] It is what is grossly lacking in schizophrenics; according to one psychiatrist, when talking to a schizophrenic it is "as if one was talking to a series of complexes or mental processes, not to a person; as if one was presented with all the parts of the body dissected from each other with no unity to bind them into a single body."[60] Because value systems are subsystems of personality,[61] indeed the core of personality, their unity and coherence is also the unity of personality. A person must be able to embrace his valuings as his own, in the sense that he can see how they are intelligible as the

---

54 The web metaphor is, of course, most familiar with respect to analyses of belief systems; see, e.g., W. V. Quine and J. S. Ullian, *The Web of Belief*, but see pp. 134ff. on value. The coherence criterion of comparative value is most closely associated with idealist philosophy, but, unlike many contemporary theorists, the idealists generally insisted that greater coherence was associated with some "felt perfection," and thus that which was more central was typically depicted as more affectively charged. The coherence and affective criteria were thus united. See, for instance, Bernard Bosanquet, *The Principle of Individuality and Value*, ch. VIII, and *Some Suggestions in Ethics*, ch. III. For a contemporary coherence approach to value with closer links to web accounts of belief, see Benn, *A Theory of Freedom*, ch. 4.

55 See my *Modern Liberal Theory of Man*, pp. 34–5.

56 See John W. Chapman, "Toward a General Theory of Human Nature," pp. 297–9; Charles Fried, *An Anatomy of Values*, ch. III, p. 97. Like the idealists (see note 54 of this chapter), Fried relates this impulse to reason.

57 See Bettelheim, *The Informed Heart*.

58 See Heinz Hartmann, *Essays on Ego Psychology*, e.g., pp. 63ff.

59 See Allport, *Pattern and Growth in Personality*, chs. 1, 12, 16.

60 Anthony Storr, *The Integrity of the Personality*, p. 68.

61 See Allport, *Pattern and Growth in Personality*, pp. 294ff.

valuings of a single individual. To be sure, such unity is always imperfect – there may well remain pockets of one's life quite isolated from the rest, and which may always seem alien – but, if one achieves anything like a personality, one's valuings cannot ultimately be understood atomistically.

All this is regrettably vague, but this seems inescapable, at least at present, because the nature of the unity of personality is not clearly grasped. But nothing I have said is inconsistent with the Affective-Cognitive Theory, for our understanding of what we are has obvious and important implications for what we find affectively charged or valenced. It has been useful to analyze valuings largely as if affective experiences were isolated and independent, but the theory certainly does not presuppose it. A person with, say, a value system generally focused on academic matters[62] will not find exciting or interesting the same things as a businesswoman or a sportsman, and not simply because they do not share the same grounding valuings (§14.2.2). It is because, rather, that in choosing one coherent way of living the charms and fascinations of other ways of living are lost.[63] But, as Bettelheim points out, though the integrated personality may thus in one sense incur a cost – the charms of some ways of living may remain quite opaque – the benefit is the possibility of effective choice:

> Basically, reaching a decision on any matter and solving any conflict depends on a man's ability to eliminate, first, all solutions clearly not in line with his values and personality. Then very few solutions remain possible and to choose the correct one is relatively simple. A person who is not well integrated, who does not follow a consistent set of values, cannot correctly test a vast number of choices against his values and interests, and then cannot cut the problem down to manageable size. Such a person feels overpowered by any new need for decision.
>
> Strangely enough, when a person faces many possibilities that are equally attractive it is theoretically an expression of freedom to choose one of them; but psychologically he does not experience it that way. If anything, it leaves him vaguely dissatisfied. On the other hand, to know definitely that you do not want this one or this one, and then to select that one as being best or most appropriate for you, is a satisfying experience. Though less actual choice making may be involved, it leaves the individual with a feeling of accomplishment and well-being.[64]

62 This example could be put in terms of Spranger's "theoretic attitude." *Types of Men*, 109–29. See §13.3 of this volume.
63 I am indebted here to Stanley Benn. See his *Theory of Freedom*, ch. 4.
64 Bettelheim, *The Informed Heart*, p. 78.

One aspect of this unity can, however, be analyzed in a more precise manner: the pursuit of character ideals. Recall J. S. Mill's criticism of Bentham, which in many ways marked the emergence of the focus on personality and development that has characterized liberal ethics and political theory in the last one hundred and fifty years.[65] "Man is never recognized by him," complained Mill, "as a being capable of pursuing spiritual perfection as an end; of desiring, for it own sake, the conformity of his own character to his standard of excellence."[66] One can value being a person of a certain sort, either in a general sense (a hero, a scholar) or in rather more specific senses (the sort of person who does not get drunk on Saturday nights). These ideals, especially the more general ones, provide a conscious and explicit type of unity to a life and to a value system. One sets oneself the task of becoming a certain type of person, and that means one with a particular pattern of valuings.

I take it that these ideals are values in at least one of the senses in which I have characterized them, namely abstract and important valuings (§13.1). After all, one does not randomly choose to pursue an ideal of character; if it is not somehow imposed on you, you presumably find it somehow exciting, interesting, noble, beautiful, etc. One thus values the ideal and the type of life it articulates, and, in turn, the ideal is comprised of a pattern of valuings. We can say, then, that such an ideal is a second-order valuing (§8.4): it is essentially valuing being a type of person with a particular configuration of more specific valuings. This brings to mind the accounts of philosophers such as Charles Taylor, who depict these ideals in terms of second-order desires, that is, desires to have (or not have) certain other desires.[67] Many who employ the language of second-order desires seem to believe that a rational person's second-order desires will necessarily outweigh in deliberation conflicting first-order desires. Dropping the language of desire (§7.2), it certainly is mistaken to understand first- and second-order valuings in this way. The relation is altogether

65 I argue this in my *Modern Liberal Theory*; see p. 270.
66 J. S. Mill, "Bentham," p. 95.
67 Charles Taylor, "What is Human Agency?" esp. p. 110. Cf. Taylor's remark that "If we examine my evaluative vision more closely, we shall see that I value courageous action as a part of a mode of life; I aspire to be a certain kind of person." Ibid., p. 107. See also Harry G. Frankfurter, "Freedom of the Will."

more complex. A person is only attracted to an ideal – comes to value it – because it is supported by, and makes sense given, some of his first-order valuings. Otherwise – if indeed it was totally ungrounded in any of the things he values – it would be more akin to a child's commitment to be a firefighter, an astronaut, or whatever seemed attractive on a particular day (though even these are based on some current valuings). So character ideals are best conceived as second-order *valuings*, supported by some subset of one or more specific valuings, though also aiming at bringing about new valuings or giving up some current ones.

But there is another complexity. I see no reason why an ideal's status as a *second-order* valuing should imply that it must, for choice purposes, outweigh the reasons for action implied by conflicting first-order valuings. If someone values an ideal that is, all things considered, at odds with the great majority of the things that he values, it certainly does not seem the hallmark of rationality to deliberate in such a way that the ideal always holds sway over all else that is valued. Even if we relax the assumption, and suppose that the ideal conflicts with some relatively isolated, but intensely held, valuings, it is not always obvious that rational deliberation must endorse only the ideal: for example, if one's ideal is that of a certain type of family man, and this calls for the attempt at eradicating, and certainly outweighing for choice purposes, strong homosexual valuings. And this recalls Karen Horney's insistence that one's idealized image of oneself must be practical and realizable; if it is radically at odds with one's actual capacities and interests, neurosis is apt to result.[68]

Character ideals, as well as more specific second-order valuings, are indeed important in shaping a coherent value system. But we need to resist the temptation to assume that abstract values always, rationally, determine particular valuings (§13.2). As I suggested at the close of the discussion of values, one's abstract valuings must be grounded upon one's value orientation, and this is so even when those values are reformist in nature.

68 Karen Horney, *Neurosis and Human Growth*. For applications of her work to the problem of value organization, see W. H. Werkmeister, *Man and His Values*, p. 23; Donald Walhout, *The Good and the Realm of Values*, pp. 8, 229–30. See also S. I. Benn, *A Theory of Freedom*, ch. 9.

The idea of a value system is usefully distinguished from several related concepts that are prominent in contemporary ethics: human good, a person's good (and, somewhat differently, his conception of the good), and a plan of life. Let us begin with the idea of human good. Very often what is valuable is equated with what is good for humans; I have already, in the discussion of the need presupposition (§7.3), indicated why this is an overly narrow conception of value. More interesting is the attempt to identify Alf's good with something like the successful promotion of what he values; a person's good, then, is often taken to be defined in terms of what he values. Thus it might be said that a person flourishes if his values are realized. This seems to be an especially important strain in self-realization ethics, where what is perceived as valuable is that which satisfies or realizes the self, and this self-satisfaction constitutes the person's good.[69] Now I certainly do not wish to deny that what is good for a person (or what advances his good) is closely bound up with what he values, but it is surely going too far to equate the two notions. To do so commits one either to endorsing a type of egoism or accepting an ill-grounded optimism. Rashdall believed self-realization theories to be essentially egoistic: "a reasonable being," he wrote, "aims at what his Reason tells him to be not merely *his* good, but part of *the* good."[70] Properly interpreted (but see §12.1), this seems right. If we employ "self-satisfaction," "self-realization," or "a person's good" in anything like the normal sense, one who values only his own satisfaction or good would

69 Instances of value, wrote Bosanquet, "meet our nature's want or need, that is, amply and enduringly, at many points, without leading up to failure and self-contradiction." *Ethics*, p. 55. Thus, "Value is the power to satisfy" us. *Individuality and Value*, p. 297. On self-satisfaction, self-realization, and goodness, see T. H. Green, *Prolegomena to Ethics*, bk. III. Many of these same themes arise in Aristotelian ethics, in which idealist self-realization theory is rooted. See, e.g., Walhout, *The Realm of Values*; John Finnis, *Natural Law and Natural Rights*; David L. Norton, *Personal Destinies: A Philosophy of Ethical Individualism*.

70 Hastings Rashdall, *The Theory of Good and Evil*, vol. I, p. 36; see also pp. 38–43. Cf. Nozick's remark that "there is the possibility of a conflict between your good (which lies in exercising your most valuable characteristic), and the overall value, to which you might make your greatest contribution by exercising another characteristic of yours, one special to you." *Philosophical Explanations*, p. 517.

indeed be a sort of egoist; even when acting altruistically, his own satisfaction would be his ultimate aim. But let us assume that this is not what the self-realizationists want to say. Instead, it is plausible to interpret them as allowing that one might intrinsically value all manner of things, and then characterizing a person's good as the successful protection or advancement of these intrinsically valued things. It is here the charge of ill-grounded optimism is relevant, for such a view seems unable to cope with the likelihood that at least some of us will confront circumstances in which what is good for oneself will diverge from promoting or protecting that for which one cares.[71] If the promotion of a person's values calls for radical self-sacrifice, perhaps even the sacrifice of his life, we fail to appreciate the cost of the agent's actions if we depict him as achieving his good when he stands by these valuings. What is good for Alf must somehow promote his welfare or interests, benefit him, promote his flourishing, etc.; and, though these cannot be done for a valuer without regard to what he values, I see no reason to believe that promoting his values is always necessarily consistent with these sorts of benefiting, much less constitutive of them.[72]

The disjuncture between promoting one's values and one's good is especially striking when one must sacrifice one's personal integrity in order to promote some important value. Such cases seem particularly salient in political life. In order to promote some highly valued goal such as world peace, the revolution, or whatever, people engaged in political life often enough find themselves committed to courses of action that they despise, and, worse still, see themselves turning into people who engage in these sorts of acts in a complacent manner.[73] And, yet, to refuse to incur such a cost would mean that one's cherished values will

---

71 Idealists like Bosanquet sought to accommodate such situations. See, e.g., his *Psychology of the Moral Self*, p. 97. I have considered his analysis in my *Modern Liberal Theory*, pp. 105–6, though I am now more skeptical about the possibility of a convincing account of self-sacrifice in the context of a coherence theory.

72 Gilbert Harman is clear that what constitutes flourishing for a particular person is relative to what he values; what is less clear is whether Harman realizes that a person can act to promote his values at the expense of his flourishing. "Human Flourishing, Ethics, and Liberty," pp. 312–13.

73 S. I. Benn, "Private and Public Morality: Clean Living and Dirty Hands," pp. 167-9.

not be promoted. Hence, the way in which Hoederer criticizes the young and idealistic Hugo in Sartre's "Dirty Hands":

> How you cling to your purity, young man! How afraid you are to soil your hands! All right, stay pure! What good will it do? Why did you join us? Purity is an idea for a yogi or a monk. You intellectuals and bourgeois anarchists use it as a pretext for doing nothing. To do nothing, to remain motionless, arms at your sides, wearing kid gloves. Well, I have dirty hands. Right up to the elbows. I've plunged them in filth and blood. But what do you hope? Do you think you can govern innocently?[74]

If Hoederer is right, Hugo's chief political values demand that he becomes the sort of person that he now despises. To say that this advances his good altogether misconstrues what is demanded of him, for it is his good that he must sacrifice.

What one values, then, must be distinguished from one's good, well-being, or flourishing. And because what people value may not be consistent with their good – or, indeed, anyone's good – the notion of a person's good or the human good, like the concept of need (§7.3), is in some ways too restricted a concept to serve as a foundation for a theory of justice.[75] Although justification and justice is the concern of Part II of this book, it seems appropriate at this juncture to note the way in which contemporary liberal theories of justice stress the foundational role of a concept of the personal good or the human good. Thus, for instances, in his *Justice and the Human Good*, William A. Galston tells us that "[i]t is evident that every theory of justice rests on some view of the good";[76] he then proceeds to enumerate the elements of "the human good": existence, development, happiness, and reason. But people also value things such as the environment (§§7.3, 15.3), and at least in some cases this valuing is not derivative of any commitment to the human good. It seems arbitrary to disregard such valuings when considering what are the proper principles regulating social life (see §22.1). So long as liberal theories rely on an implicit assumption that all that matters to people is their own good, or even the good of humans, they are rightly open to the criticism that they are arbitrarily restrictive. It is sometimes argued, however, that, though disputes about what is

74 Quoted in ibid., p. 160.
75 In other ways, however, it is too broad a notion, because one may not value what is good for one, or good for others. See §§8.3, 19.
76 William A. Galston, *Justice and the Human Good*, p. 55.

valuable do occur, "[i]t is not farfetched to assert that most political disputes take place in the context of widespread agreement about what is desirable, valuable, or good," and so politics can be understood as the competition of interests within a largely agreed-upon understanding of what is valuable.[77] And, so, it may seem that focusing on what is good for people, or in their "interests," is adequate as a basis for a theory of justice. But this really is pretty farfetched. Thirty years or so ago, it was perhaps widely believed that Western democracies were characterized by a wide-ranging value consensus, but that hardly seems convincing in the era of environmentalists and animal liberationists. Moreover, Rokeach's study of Americans' values indicates differences in the ordering of fundamental values between men and women, the poor and rich, the well- and less-educated, whites and blacks, and between various age groups.[78] And, interestingly, there is considerable evidence that differing weightings of equality and liberty are associated not only with predispositions to accept different political ideologies, but the likelihood of engaging in political activism.[79]

It may be thought that I have simply confused two distinct concepts: a person's good and a person's conception of the good. The former is indeed what is good for the person, but the latter concerns what he sees as good, and thus need not be restricted to, or even consistent with, his good. This is a real distinction; I have no deep objections to substituting the idea of a person's conception of the good for the concept of his values/valuings,[80] if we interpret that to mean what he believes to be, and finds to be, of value. The problem is that these quite distinct concepts – what is good for a person and what he sees as good – are repeatedly confused or, once again, misleadingly identified with each other. Rawls is a case in point. He tells us that "in a well-ordered society citizens' conceptions of their good" are derivative of their conceptions of what is good because a person's good consists in "the execution of a rational plan of life" and the plan of life "es-

77 Ibid.
78 Rokeach, *The Nature of Human Values*, ch. 3
79 Ibid., chs. 6–7.
80 It does, though, wrongly suggest that when people arrive at divergent personal value judgments they are offering competing theories of the same concept (§1.2); it thus suggests that the disputes are essentially conceptual rather than valuative.

tablishes the basic point of view from which all judgments of value relating to a particular person are to be made."[81] So a plan defines a person's conception of the good (value), and successfully executing this plan is, essentially, his good. I will not repeat here my objections to this familiar equation; suffice it to say that, though a person's value system can, roughly, be said to be much the same thing as his conception of the good, I see no reason to believe that successfully pursuing these value commitments is necessarily constitutive of his good.

A word concerning the concept of "a plan of life" is in order. We might distinguish such a plan from a person's value system in the following way: the plan concerns the organization of commitments to act that flow from one's value system. As I said earlier (§9.2), valuings imply action commitments; one who adopts a plan of action has organized his activity in light of his comparative valuings, resources, and circumstances. Understood thus, plans do not directly determine or organize what one values[82] but rather how one's value system translates into efficient action in particular circumstances. To be sure, if a rational plan[83] can give little scope to action relating to some valuing, that valuing may fade – one who can never get to see baseball games may find his interest waning. But what I want to insist upon here is that plans concern action and only indirectly organize one's valuings.

Although the notion of a plan is useful in understanding how valuings can ultimately lead to organized ways of acting, some serious difficulties confront the claim that a plan must encompass an entire life in the sense that "[f]uture aims may not be discounted solely in virtue of being future. . . . The intrinsic importance that we assign to different parts of our life should be the same at every moment of time."[84] This doctrine of "temporal neutrality" has recently been criticized, in very different ways, by

81 John Rawls, *A Theory of Justice*, pp. 395, 433, 409.
82 Fried seems to assign to plans a much more basic role in the organization of one's value system. See his *Anatomy of Values*, chs. II, III; see pp. 34–6 on his distinction between ends and action. Rawls too, of course, attributes a fundamental organizational role to plans. See *A Theory of Justice*, secs. 63–66.
83 I shall not provide any analysis of what constitutes rationality in a plan; it obviously must be consistent with one's value system and in some sense efficient given one's circumstances. Much of what Rawls says in *A Theory of Justice*, secs. 63-64, is relevant here (but see next paragraph).
84 Rawls, *A Theory of Justice*, p. 420. For a sustained defense of this notion of "temporal neutrality," see Thomas Nagel, *The Possibility of Altruism*, pt. 2.

Derek Parfit and Michael Slote.[85] Rather than summarizing their arguments, however, let us reconsider, with this issue in mind, the case against strict impartiality presented in §12.1. It is not, I argued, an objectionable type of partiality to treat differently that which one soundly values and that which others soundly value but in which you see no value. The very essence of valuing, I claimed, was that one favors what one values over that in which one can see no value. This also seems to apply to one's future and past valuings.[86] According to the doctrine of temporal neutrality, we are to treat something that we know we will come to see value in as equally important to that in which we now see value. But that surely is odd, for if we cannot now see value in it, we cannot really grasp how it is important; and, if it remains obscure to us in what way it has value, it hardly seems an objectionable sort of partiality to at least concentrate on that which we can now appreciate. And by "concentrate" I do not simply mean attend to in a contemplative or appreciative sense, but to give pride of place in one's deliberations. This is not counter-intuitive. Slote, I think, is quite right that "[h]uman life seems . . . to possess a natural, though socially influenced, development of different times or stages of life."[87] We expect adolescents to focus on those things that they can savor; an adolescent who actually gave equal weighting to "his" valuings for social conservatism and financial security, which he had grounds for believing he would develop in his fifties, would strike us as pathological, not rational. But this is not to say that one cannot be criticized for being imprudent. Leaving aside the obvious fact that most of us actually do presently value our future well-being (and so can be criticized for not acting consistently with this general valuing), many of the things we presently find disvaluable – pain, hunger, poverty – will provide reasons for us to avoid these things in the future. It is important to realize that denying temporal neutrality does not commit one to any endorsement of living for the present; that one presently sees the disvalue in X, and one knows that X will occur

85 Derek Parfit, *Reasons and Persons*, pt. 2; Slote, *Goods and Virtues*, ch. 1.
86 This is by no means a novel strategy; both Nagel and Parfit fundamentally rely on essentially the same argument applying to both interpersonal considerations and intertemporal issues within one life. For a criticism of this general strategy, see Lomasky, *Persons, Rights*, pp. 22ff.
87 Slote, *Goods and Virtues*, p. 13.

in twenty years, provides one now with a reason to act so as to prevent or diminish *X*.[88] All I am denying is that one is rationally committed to treating equally in one's present deliberations those things one sees value or disvalue in and those things one knows will be valued or disvalued sometime in the future. I am not even denying that such future valuings may call for some attention in present rational deliberation, insofar as they are a species of impersonal valuings, and ones that the agent knows he will come to appreciate (§10.3).

15 CONCLUSION TO PART I

15.1 *The Affective-Cognitive Theory: revisions and retentions*

Beginning with a very simple and straightforward thesis, that valuings are essentially emotions, I have developed a complex account of value that distinguishes what is valuable from what is valued, what can be impersonally described as valuable and what is personally discovered to have value, how discourse about value judgments can focus on errors and be characterized by real (that is, not illusory) disagreement, and why, given two rational people with the same sound set of beliefs relating to *X*, one may rationally value it but the other may, without rational defect, fail to see anything of value in it. I have tried to show that these complexities and distinctions are not ad hoc, but are the sound elaborations of our initial simple suggestion. Surely this is what we aim at when trying to explain a complex phenomenon such as valuing and value discourse; a complicated practice can be accounted for by a simple hypothesis, but this is not necessarily to simplify the practice itself. Hedonism, in contrast, offers a simple basic explanation of value, but it is generally unable to show how this simple root notion gives rise to many of the complexities characteristic of our understanding of value. Although I do not claim that the Affective-Cognitive Theory embraces all the main features of our concept of value (§1.1), it is clearly superior in this respect to a theory such as hedonism.

I shall not attempt to summarize the argument of Part I, or

88 Even if one knows one will not disvalue it then? I am not sure, but I suspect so.

even to review the way in which the Affective-Cognitive Theory accounts for all the features of the concept of value enumerated in §1.1. However, it might be helpful to point out my chief defenses and criticisms of our current conception of value. One of my main aims has been to show how two pairs of prima facie inconsistent features of our current conception can be reconciled. Although (i) valuing is related to the affective-conative side of life [feature (k)], and (ii) we often believe that people can value very different sorts of things without error on anyone's part [feature (e)], nevertheless (iii) value judgments are about the properties of objects [feature (f)] and (iv) we can sensibly argue about value judgments and we can err both in valuing and in making judgments of value [feature (c)]. By showing how an adequate understanding of value readily admits all four features of our current practice, the Affective-Cognitive Theory defends its essential coherence.

Another important concern of Part I, and it will also be a focus of Chapter VI, was to determine to what extent externalism is sound or, alternatively, to what extent the externalist challenge can be met (§10.2). The externalist insists that a rational agent can accept a value judgment while denying that it has any necessary implications for his action, thus calling into doubt this fundamental feature [(b)] of our current practice. We have seen that, though this externalist position is unassailable regarding some impersonal value judgments, it is not sound regarding all of them nor is it sound in relation to what is personally found to be of value. Here too, then, the Affective-Cognitive Theory defends the heart of our current conception of value against an important philosophic challenge.

However, the Affective-Cognitive Theory calls for some revision of our current understanding of value. I have been critical of the idea that values are chosen or that we choose how to resolve value conflicts [feature (g)]. To be sure, to the extent that we consciously aim to become the sort of person who values some things rather than others (§14.2.3), it can be said that we choose our values. But although we do not arbitrarily choose what to value – we really do discover things to be of value – there is, as we have seen, an important sense in which the resolution of value conflicts [feature (h)] is nonrational (§§11.1, 14.1). One ultimately "chooses" to resolve value conflicts in one way or another because of the sort of person one is, just as one ultimately chooses to value some things rather than others because of one's background values and affective nature.

But clearly the main revision called for by the Affective-Cognitive Theory concerns feature (d): that values, judgments of valuableness, and valuings are impersonal and so are not respecters of persons. I argued in §12 that, at least in the way that this is normally understood, the conception of objectivity in valuing and action upon which this feature depends is implausibly strong. On the face of it, this may appear a radical revision; it certainly is fundamentally at odds with the view of value informing consequentialist ethics. However, a good deal of liberal ethics and political theory has either rejected this impersonality feature or at least abjured appeal to it. Social contract theory, including Rawls's, Alan Gewirth's brand of rationalism, and Bruce Ackerman's neutrality principle, all suppose that value-based reasons to act can be accorded only an agent-relative status from the perspective of moral and political theory. The Affective-Cognitive Theory generally supports such theories. Moreover, in Part II I will follow them in arguing that, because value-based reasons for action are largely agent-relative in this way, principles of right are required to supply reasons of a more impersonal and universalistic character. But, because my defense of agent-relativity does not derive from any skepticism about the possibility of public discourse concerning, or knowledge of, values, or indeed from any attempt to avoid axiological investigations, my endorsement of agent-relativity is more firmly grounded (and thus the Affective-Cognitive Theory is able to reply to, and critique, the essentially consequentialist conception of the objectivity of valuing – §12). Furthermore, because my defense of agent-relativity is firmly rooted in a theory of value, we are better able to grasp the nature and limits of agent-relativity. Having rejected views that assimilate the "good" to a person's good or human flourishing (§14.3), we can see that the agent-relativity of value is distinct from the claim that a rational person acts only to achieve what benefits him or somehow promotes his good. And we have seen that value-based reasons for action are not thoroughly agent-relative: impersonal value judgments do supply weak prima facie agent-neutral reasons to act (§§10.3, 12.2).

Although this chapter closes the focus on value, an important feature of the concept of value cannot be adequately explored until we consider the theory of right in Part II. Although we have distinguished some types of value [feature (i)], that is, intrinsic, extrinsic, and instrumental (§§8–9), the analysis of moral value must await the analysis of moral justification in Chapter VII.

15.2 The open-question argument

Before going on to consider the problem of justification in moral and political philosophy, however, it is appropriate to consider two remaining objections to the Affective-Cognitive Theory of value. I begin with what is perhaps the most frequently raised objection: that an account of value along the lines I have presented commits the "naturalistic fallacy." Such objections typically focus on Moore's "open-question" test;[89] it might thus be argued:

(i) If the Affective-Cognitive Theory is sound, "*X* is valuable" means "*X* is the object of a dispositional emotion."
(ii) But it is always significant to ask "Is the object of the dispositional emotion valuable?"
(iii) Because (ii) is always a significant question, the claim in (i) – that "*X* is the object of a dispositional emotion" *means* "*X* is valuable" – cannot be true.

This would be the most persuasive form of the argument; it is worth stressing, however, that (i) is false. Furthermore, because the Affective-Cognitive Theory is not essentially a theory about the meaning of words, something like the following is, roughly, accurate:

(i′) If the Affective-Cognitive Theory is sound, "*X* is a worthy object of a positive dispositional emotion" is a necessary and sufficient condition for "*X* is intrinsically valuable."
(ii′) But it is always significant to ask "Is the worthy object of the positive dispositional emotion valuable?"
(iii′) Because (ii′) is always a significant question, the claim in (i′) cannot be true.

Put thus, even those who find the open-question argument persuasive may have doubts about its application to the Affective-

89 "The 'open question' argument is a genuine obstacle in any attempt to reduce values to natural properties. Once we know that an object is pleasant, desired, etc., we may still ask whether or not it is good." Risieri Frondizi, "Value as a Gestalt Property," p. 163. See Moore, *Principia Ethica*, pp. 15–16 (sec. 13).

Cognitive Theory. At the very least, by requiring that the object be *worthy* to the emotion, the point of (ii′) becomes somewhat obscure. To clarify it and regain the force of (ii), it would be necessary to distinguish "worthy *qua* appropriate to the emotion" from "worthy *qua* valuable." And I have argued against that distinction in §8.4. In any event, even in such a reformulated argument, the second step is problematic. The crux of Moore's argument is that even the most complete "natural" description of something leaves it open – in the sense of being appropriate and sensible – to ask whether it is also good. But recall our analyses of amusingness (§§10.1–2). Say I describe something as amusing – I found it to be amusing and believe that it is impersonally so, but then I ask "Is there anything good about it?" This seems an empty rather than an open question. It is certainly an odd one.[90] The very description of it as amusing in this way shows precisely what is good about it (see §6.2).

However, it is not my intention to rehearse familiar criticisms of the open-question argument.[91] Rather, I wish to pursue a related issue to which it points. Leaving aside the question of naturalism in ethics, the open-question test articulates a general worry about attempts to explicate one familiar notion (for example, value) in terms of another (for example, emotion): why do we have two distinct concepts when one will do, and why do we tend to think the concepts are different when the theory is telling us that they are in some sense the same? At least part of the intuitive force of the open-question test is that "goodness" is a distinct concept from "pleasure" or "emotion," and so we can always ask whether what can be described in terms of the latter is also appropriately conceived of in terms of the former. Now a theory that explicates one notion in terms of another in this way has two options: it can simply dismiss this intuition as ill-formed or can show how the conviction that the concepts are different is consistent with explicating one in terms of the other. I take this second route.

Let us begin by considering the nature of relational concepts. The most widely recognized relational concepts are those such as

90 See George Schrader, "The Status of Value," p. 198.
91 For discussions and criticisms, see e.g., Roger N. Hancock, *Twentieth-Century Ethics*, pp. 27–32; Mackie, *Ethics*, pp. 60–2; Frankena, "The Naturalistic Fallacy."

"to the left of" and "taller than." David Wiggins, however, suggests a rather more interesting case; in arguing that value is analogous to color concepts (§10.1), he insists that redness is not a relational property – "It is certainly not relational in the way in which "father of" is relational."[92] So let us take "father of," or, because it is somewhat simpler, "parent (of)" as our starting point. To explicate the concept (natural) "parent" we need to understand the relation *xRy*, where *x* and *y* are people and *R* is something like "begot or gave birth to." But – and this points to a difference between relational concepts such as "next to" and ones like "parent" – "parent" does not name or describe *xRy*: it refers specifically to *x* in the relation.[93] That is, although the concept of a parent cannot be understood without reference to *xRy*, "parent" is not itself a name for *xRy*. Moreover, "parent" is not the only concept the explication of which refers back to *xRy*; "offspring" is best understood as referring to *y* in *xRy*.

Wiggins is, of course, quite right that "value" (or, for that matter, "emotion") is not relational in the same way as is "father (of)"; the latter is at least much more obviously relational. Nevertheless, "parent" provides insights into "value" and "emotion." Recall that in Chapter II emotional states were analyzed in terms of an affective mode and a content, which often refers to an item in the world. Now, although it would perhaps be misleading to say that these states are relational, they do involve two elements, an affective mode and a content/object, which are indeed related in a certain way. Let us refer to this as [A(C)]. Picking up on the lessons derived from the analysis of "parent," we can see that emotion terms are not simply names for particular types of [A(C)], but rather refer primarily to the affective mode – "A" – in this complex. Emotion concepts thus focus primarily on the "feeling tone" of mental states, and tend to group together particular instances with respect to this variable. This is precisely why the Internal Sensation Theory appears so plausible at first sight: it is quite right that emotions are named largely in refer-

92 David Wiggins, "Truth, Invention, and the Meaning of Life," p. 349.

93 Anthony Kenny tells us that, like "most logicians," he holds that "in a genuinely relational proposition both terms are on an equal footing." *Action, Emotion, and Will*, p. 197. If so, I am concerned with quasi-relations: the important point is that a term can presuppose a relation but not itself name the relation.

ence to types of feeling states. The flaw in the internal sensation theory is in failing to recognize that emotion concepts cannot be analyzed simply in terms of affective mode.

The application of this to valuing is straightforward. Value terms focus on the content/object in [A(C)]. Our focus in value discourse is not chiefly on feeling states but types of objects and their properties. We might say that, whereas emotion discourse is inward looking, value discourse is outward looking. Moreover, there is no reason to expect a one-to-one relation between all value and emotion terms. Sometimes such a relation holds (for example, amused/amusing, hate/hateful, bored/boring, disgusted/disgusting), but our practical interests in classifying emotions and valuable things may well lead to much more complex relations. For instance, "beautiful" (or "noble" or "sublime") do not refer back to any particular affect nor, it would seem, to any specific complex of affects. Perhaps the perception of beautiful objects evokes a variety of affective states in people – for example, interested, joyous, and even sad. If so, "beautiful" is to be analyzed in terms of an array of affective states.

It is worth pointing out that this analysis of value concepts allows us to account for two widely held but opposing views: (i) that value concepts are inherently relational, and (ii) that when we call an object "valuable" we are not referring to relations but to the properties of objects.[94] As Mackie has remarked: "There is indeed a curious interplay of qualities and relations here."[95] We can now account for this: value ascriptions do indeed refer to objects and their properties and do not name relations, but the analysis of the nature of these properties refers back to (broadly construed) a "relation."

15.3 Anthropocentrism and the environment

The Affective-Cognitive Theory of value can be understood as, broadly interpreted, a "psychological theory" of value. It is psychological in the sense that ultimately the analysis of value con-

94 For examples of position (i), see Gracia, "The Ontological Status of Value," pp. 393–7; John R. Reid, "A Definition of Value"; Walhout, *The Realm of Values*, p. 58. For examples of position (ii), see Wiggins, "The Meaning of Life"; Frondizi, "Value as a Gestalt Property." See §10.1 of the present volume.

95 Mackie, *Ethics*, p. 56.

cepts and, in particular, value judgments, refers back to certain sorts of mental states of valuers. Psychological theories of value (again, very broadly conceived) are perhaps the most common in the recent history of axiology; the most famous Austrian and American value theorists of the twentieth century defend various versions of the psychological approach.[96] But, it is said, this is wrong: environmental objects can have intrinsic value, indeed a value that "is superior to humans in certain respects."[97]

It should be manifest that this objection does not apply to the Affective-Cognitive Theory. By rejecting the hedonistic thesis (§8.1), we departed from all theories according to which only certain sorts of psychological states have intrinsic value, with objects then only being capable of extrinsic value. The Affective-Cognitive Theory in no way precludes environmental objects or ecosystems from being rationally valued for themselves; a rational valuer may even see them as having greater intrinsic value than humans. It cannot be overemphasized that, on my account, to judge something to be, for instance, beautiful, is not necessarily to see it as instrumentally useful in bringing about any sort of mental state. The essence of intrinsic valuing is a certain type of intentional mental state; this mental state has no necessary foundation in beliefs about promoting agreeable experiences.

So, far from opposing ascriptions of intrinsic value to the environment, the Affective-Cognitive Theory has no difficulties embracing the qualities of environmental objects and systems to which environmental philosophers typically point as grounds of their intrinsic value. Richness,[98] complexity, diversity, and organic unity[99] are precisely those properties that evoke interest and

96 See Eaton, *The Austrian Philosophy of Values*; W. H. Werkmeister, *Historical Spectrum of Value Theories*. For some particular examples, see note 2, ch. II, in the present volume. Environmental philosophers such as Peter Miller are critical of this "psychological" foundation "of most contemporary accounts of value." The environmental argument against such "homocentric or psychocentric value theories" seems to be that, if all value is somehow founded on human beings and their psychological responses, then environmental objects only have an "instrumental" value insofar as they "service or provide spiritual sustenance for humans." Miller, "Value as Richness."

97 Miller, "Value as Richness," p. 113. For similar views, see Attfield, "The Good of Trees," e.g., p. 44; Charles Birch, "A Biological Basis for Human Purpose," p. 256.

98 See Miller, "Value As Richness."

99 Organic unity seems perhaps the best candidate for *the* general value-

fascination, and so ground intrinsic valuing.[100] But at this point a rather more subtle objection is raised by some environmentalists. Even if the Affective-Cognitive Theory does not attribute merely instrumental value to the environment, theories of this sort still strike some environmentalists as a sign of human arrogance. It seems to them to be "arbitrary and narrow" to depict value as "a gift of the spectator's mind." "We do not simply bestow value on nature; nature also conveys value to us."[101] Again: "Do we not value Earth because it is valuable, and not the other way round? Is it really just a matter of our late-coming interests, or is not Earth in some puzzling way an interesting, lively place even antecedently to the human arrival?"[102] I confess that I find this somewhat obscure. It is certainly right that things are not valuable simply because they are valued, but it does not seem strictly true that they are valued because they are "valuable," but rather because they are complex, useful, etc. But the real thrust of this argument, I think, is to insist that the Earth is not made interesting by the fact that we take interest in it; but, in fact, it was interesting before we arrived. Now it is no doubt true that taking an interest in the Earth does not confer the characteristic of being interesting on it; moreover, it is true that at least many of the features that make the Earth an interesting place were features of it before humans evolved. Were these features "interesting" before humans (or, let us say, valuers) arrived? This seems a moot question. What is clear is that, before valuers evolved, no interest was taken in these features, and no creature was capable of acting appropriately on this interest.

A significant amount of environmental ethics, I would thus

grounding property. Not only ecosystems and organisms, but art and even jokes might be said to be characterized by such "unity in diversity." Unified complexity interests us in many ways across many fields. But does it really account for the value of sexual pleasure or the disvalue of anger-provoking objects? The error here seems related to R. B. Perry's mistake in equating all valuing with interest (§8.1 of the present volume). For a strong argument in favor of value as organic unity, see Nozick, *Philosophical Explanations*, pp. 413ff.

100 According to Kenneth H. Simonsen, it is the wildness of nature, the knowledge that it was generated by forces independent of human design, which evokes "delight, wonder, astonishment, even awe from us." "The Value of Wildness," p. 259.

101 Holmes Rolston III, "Are Values in Nature Subjective or Objective?" pp. 132–8.

102 Rolston, "Values in Nature," p. 117.

like to suggest, confuses two quite distinct questions: (i) Does the value of the environment depend on its usefulness (however broadly construed) to humans or valuers? and (ii) Would the environment have value if there were no humans or valuers? My suggestion is that the answer to (i) is negative, but (ii) is unimportant.[103] It is unimportant because, if no valuers exist, no creatures capable of appreciating or appropriately responding to the value exist. The tendency to confuse these questions is nicely brought out by the frequent use of "last man" examples in environmental ethics:

> Suppose, a century hence, that in a tragic nuclear war each side has loosed upon the other radioactive fallout which sterilizes the genes of humans and mammals but is harmless to the flora, invertebrates, reptiles and birds. That last race of valuers, if they had a conscience still, ought not to destroy the remaining biosphere. Nor would this be for interest in whatever slight subjectivity might remain, for it would be better for this much ecosystem to continue, even if the principal valuers were taken out.[104]

The intuitive judgment – that the last valuer in his last moment of existence should not destroy the remaining ecosystem – is often taken as an argument against psychological accounts of value in general. But we can now see that the last man argument only causes difficulties for those who answer (i) *affirmatively* (that is, those who accept the hedonistic thesis). On the account I have offered, the last valuer has reason to care for and protect the remaining ecosystem until he dies, for that is what he intrinsically values. However, whether or not the ecosystem can sensibly be said to be value-able – worthy of being valued – in a world where it is impossible for it to be valued, strikes me as pointless. What is the point of asking whether something is the appropriate object of a valuing attitude when all possibility of valuing attitudes has ended?

---

103 I am not claiming that (ii) should be answered in the negative, but, rather, that it is quite literally a pointless question. In this respect, my position on "external value" is less critical than Eric Mack's in his "Moral Individualism," sec. III. Cf. Nagel, *The View From Nowhere*, p. 153.

104 Rolston, "Are Values in Nature Subjective or Objective?" p. 149. See also Attfield, "The Good of Trees," p. 45. "Last man" thought experiments seem problematic as a basis for objecting to psychological accounts of value: they attempt to eliminate the psychological factor – the reactions of humans – and then ask (the reader) what *his reaction* is to this situation. For a discussion of Moore's use of a similar thought experiment, see Aaron Ben-Zeev, "G. E. Moore and the Relation between Intrinsic Value and Human Activity," pp. 75–6.

TWO

A theory of moral justification

VI

Value and moral reasons

16 TWO RADICAL THEORIES

16.1 The orthodox view

In Part I, I defended five basic claims concerning the relation between, on the one hand, valuing and value judgments and, on the other, reasons for action, *viz.*:

(i) With very few exceptions, that one correctly values or disvalues *X* implies that one has reasons to act (§§9.2, 10.2).
(ii) That one soundly values *X* can provide one with reasons to act toward other things, persons, etc. in ways characteristic of valuing (§9.2).
(iii) One who soundly values *X* more than *Y* has reason to forgo promoting, protecting, or securing *Y* in order to promote, protect, or secure *X* (§§11.1, 14.1).
(iv) Sound impersonal value judgments provide one with reasons to act, unless one has grounds for concluding that one cannot grasp or appreciate the relevant value (§§10.3, 11.2).
(v) That another correctly values *X* (or grasps the value of *X*) does not necessarily imply that one has reason to promote or protect *X*, or to secure *X* for him or for oneself (§12).

Now the question arises as to whether (i)–(v) not only sum up the relation between value and reasons for action, but whether, indeed, it is also a summary of all our reasons to act. If we adopt what I shall call the *orthodox view* of value and reasons, (i)–(v) would seem to be a summary of all reasons for action, for on this view all reasons for action are concerned with promoting what is valued or is valuable. Rashdall, for example, insisted that reasoning was consequentialist in this way; "no better definition could be given of the irrational in conduct," he said, than the Kantian formula which maintains that one can have reasons to act that are unconcerned with the promotion of ends ("social or otherwise").[1] For Rashdall, in fact, our "respect" for reason itself derives from our conviction that rational conduct possesses "intrinsic value or goodness."[2] A number of contemporary philosophers agree that all practical rationality somehow derives from, or is identical with, value considerations. Thomas Nagel, for instance, tells us "that when a person accepts a reason for doing something he attaches value to its occurrence, a value which is either intrinsic or instrumental."[3] And E. J. Bond, in his *Reason and Value*, concludes that "for a reason to be genuine for an agent, it must be tied to a value that he himself could, given the right conditions, recognize as such, and consequently be motivated to pursue."[4]

It is, however, difficult to give a more precise formulation of the orthodox view. Bond's metaphor of a reason being "tied" to a value is consistent with an alternative view that I will defend later in this chapter. However, the crux of the orthodox view is, I think, captured thus:

(i) Alf has reason to ϕ if and only if ϕ-ing is itself soundly valued by him or promotes his sound values;[5]
(ii) Given the choice between ϕ-ing and ψ-ing, Alf has good reason to ϕ rather than ψ if and only if, all things considered, ϕ-ing better promotes his sound values.

I have already taken issue with one claim of the orthodox view in §9.2.3: promoting (or maximizing) what is valued is not, I suggested, the only appropriate response to valuing. One might also object, of course, that value judgments as well as values and valuings can ground reasons to act. But to take account of these objections would vastly complicate the analysis of the orthodox view while not, I suspect, significantly altering anything I want to say. As I have formulated it, the orthodox view is a familiar doctrine, and provides a useful point of departure for our discussion of value and reasons.

It is perhaps worth pointing out that on any plausible theory of value and reasons, clause (ii) easily follows from (i). To see this, assume that a fully rational agent, Alf, faces a choice be-

1 Hastings Rashdall, *The Theory of Good and Evil*, vol. I, p. 134.
2 Ibid., pp. 58–59. See §18.2 of the present volume.
3 Thomas Nagel, *The Possibility of Altruism*, p. 35.
4 E. J. Bond, *Reason and Value*, p. 90.
5 I assume here that Alf's value system is not rationally defective.

tween ϕ-ing and ψ-ing. Although both promote his (sound) values [hence, according to (i) he has good reason to do either], ϕ-ing better promotes his values, all things considered. However, let us deny clause (ii); Alf, let us say, has more reason to ψ than to ϕ. From whence could this reason derive? It cannot derive from comparative valuing because, *ex hypothesi*, ϕ better promotes his valuings. But, if so, it appears that a nonvalue reason is being considered, and that violates (i). One may perhaps try to defend a weaker version of the orthodox view, according to which any reason to act must include a value consideration but may also encompass nonvalue factors; on such a view, one might then have reason to ψ rather than to ϕ, even though one values the latter more. It is, one could say, a necessary condition for having a reason to act that the action promotes one's values [that is, clause (i) must be satisfied], but nonvalue considerations can also be constituents of this reason (for example, that the act is in accordance with duty). But surely this amounts to a repudiation of the orthodox view. In the end, it must come down to the claim that one can act contrary to one's value-promoting reasons to choose, and any "consideration" that leads one to do so is accurately described as a reason to act that is not concerned with promoting value. The only way to deny (ii) given (i) is to allow that, though one can determine which of two courses of action better promotes one's values, one has no reason to choose between them. One would then have reason to promote one's values, but not more reason to promote what one values more. And that seems counter-intuitive; it certainly renders valuings largely irrelevant in deliberation about action [feature (b), §1.1].

The orthodox view has very different implications for ethics and political philosophy depending on whether a theory endorses the agent-neutrality or agent-relativity of value reasons. Theories that accept both the orthodox view of value and reasons *and* the agent-neutrality of value reasons (§12.1) seem committed to some strongly consequentialist ethic. For, if all reasons for action concern promoting value, and if all such reasons are agent-neutral, then it would seem inescapable that one always has most reason to promote overall value. Not too surprisingly, then, those who embrace both the orthodox view and agent-neutrality typically have had to relax their assumptions about one or the other to avoid a full-fledged consequentialism. Samuel Scheffler thus seeks to mitigate the extreme intrusiveness of thoroughgoing consequentialism (§12.1) by relaxing the requirement of agent-neutrality, allowing an individual to give extra weight to his own conception of the good, and so discount the demands that other people's valuings make on him.[6] Thomas Nagel adopts a similar strategy in arguing that "the dominance of this agent-neutral conception of value is not complete. It does not swallow up or overwhelm the agent-relative reasons arising from those individual ambitions, commitments, and attachments that are in some sense chosen."[7] Alternatively, like David Lyons, one may insist on the limits of consequentialism by insisting that there are some reasons for acting – say, concerning fairness – that do not in any way reduce to ways to best promote utility, value, etc.[8] So Lyons distanced himself from thoroughgoing utilitarianism by rejecting the orthodox view of value and reasons.

However, we have found the case for agent-neutrality lacking (§12) and thus do not share the problems of Scheffler and Nagel with giving due weight to the personal point of view. Quite the contrary: the strong version of the agent-relativity of value reasons that I have defended focuses on each person's own point of view. But this leads to a very different sort of problem. If we assume strict agent-relativity of value reasons[9] and the orthodox view of value and reasons, we are confronted with the main problem of Hobbes's state of nature. Hobbes insists that, at least in the state of nature, value reasons are thoroughly agent-relative. Each has reason to promote what he desires or sees as good (these are essentially the same in Hobbes's eyes), and essentially only this. Hobbesian agents do not have reason to advance the de-

6 Samuel Scheffler, *The Rejection of Consequentialism*.

7 "But," he adds, "the admission of what I have called autonomous agent-relative reasons does not imply the possibility of deontological reasons." Thomas Nagel, "The Limits of Objectivity," p. 131.

8 David Lyons, *Forms and Limits of Utilitarianism*, ch. V. (I am not making any claims here about Lyons's more recent position.)

9 This is a more radical version of agent-relativity than I have defended. Impersonal value judgments, I argued, have a status that, if falling short of what most philosophers have in mind when they refer to agent-neutrality, certainly are to be distinguished from the sort of agent-relativity characteristic of valuings (see §§12.2, 15.1). Nevertheless, because (i) valuings, personal value judgments, and values are clearly the core of value-centered deliberation, and (ii) impersonal value judgments do not imply reasons to act if one has grounds for believing that one cannot appreciate the relevant value, I devote this and the next chapter to the problems posed by agent-relativity.

sires or values of others just because others desire, rightly value, etc. Indeed, in the state of nature, even the ways in which "good" and "evil" are employed are agent-relative: "these words . . . are ever used with relation to the person that useth them: there being nothing simply and absolutely so."[10] If one accepts both the strict agent-relativity of value reasons and, in addition, adopts the orthodox view of value and reasons, it becomes difficult to see how the anarchy of the state of nature can be avoided. If my only reasons to act are to promote what I value, and your only reasons to act are to promote your values, it is hard to see how we can rationally act on moral or political principles when doing so means that one must forgo promoting one's values.

Two traditional ways of solving this problem should be mentioned immediately. According to the first, let us call it the *morality is better than anarchy argument*, it is to the advantage of each and every person to live under a system of rules that regulates how each may go about promoting his values. Following Hobbes, the proponent of this argument can point out that it is most unlikely that one can successfully promote one's values in a state of anarchy in which no one pays any heed to rules and principles that would serve to order social life. So, says Kurt Baier (agreeing with Hobbes), "it will be clear to everyone that universal obedience to certain rules overriding self-interest would produce a state of affairs which serves everyone's interest much better than the unaided pursuit of it in a state where everyone does the same."[11] I shall consider Baier's argument in more detail a bit later on (§17.1), but for now it is enough to notice how difficult it is within the confines of the orthodox view to defend the rationality of complying with these rules when doing so does not best promote one's values. To be sure, as Hobbes and Baier would argue, Alf's aims are better promoted when everyone (including Alf) obeys moral principles or rules than in a state of nature in which no one pays any attention to them. But, at best, this can only be used to show that Alf typically has good reason

10 Thomas Hobbes, *Leviathan*, p. 48 (ch. 6).
11 Kurt Baier, *The Moral Point of View* (1958 edn.), p. 309. For other neo-Hobbesian arguments, see David Gauthier, *Morals by Agreement*, ch. 6; Gregory S. Kavka, *Hobbesian Moral and Political Theory*, esp. chs. 2, 9, 10; Loren Lomasky, *Persons, Rights, and the Moral Community*, ch. 4.

for following the rules, that is, clause (i) of the orthodox view is satisfied. It would be better still, at least as far as Alf is concerned, if everybody except him follows the rules, leaving him free to pursue his own values without restriction. Why shouldn't he cheat when he can get away with it? Admittedly, he may not want it to be known that he violates the rules, and he would not wish to flaunt his cheating; he would want to avoid punishment and avoid promoting disrespect for the rules. But if non-complying, *all things considered*, better promotes his values than complying, the orthodox view indicates that complying is irrational. To point out again that, after all, he has reason to comply is not enough, for he has better reason to not comply. To insist that compliance is rational because it does promote his values (in comparison with the state of nature), though it does so to a lesser extent than not-complying, is much the same as saying that it is rational for him to choose vanilla ice cream over chocolate because he likes vanilla, though he likes chocolate more and would, all things considered, enjoy it more in this case than vanilla. The choice is inconsistent with his reasons for choosing.

This is an important lesson. Moral and political philosophy provides numerous examples of attempts to justify some rule or principle on the grounds that it promotes a universal value without giving due consideration to problems of comparative value. To say that a universal value is furthered by some principle is not a strong argument that compliance is rational because, though universally valued, it may not be highly valued by many.[12] Indeed, Rokeach's study (§13.2) suggests that it is regarding the comparative ranking of values, and not whether they are simply accepted or rejected, that people's value systems differ.[13] This seems a particularly troublesome finding for the second traditional solution to our problem of compliance: the *generalized valuing of morality argument*, which relies on moral sentiments, a sense of justice, or a valuing of moral action. Even if we allow a psychological law such that, given human sociability, each will come to value being moral, all that can be established is that each has a good reason to act morally [that is, clause (i) of the orthodox view is satisfied]. But something stronger is needed: it must

12 This is well illustrated by public interest arguments. See S. I. Benn and G. F. Gaus, "The Liberal Conception of the Public and Private," pp. 44–7.
13 Milton Rokeach, "From Individual to Institutional Values," p. 49.

be shown that such action always, or at least typically (see §17.1), is valued more than any alternative action.

The most plausible version of this second argument is that which bases the motivation to act morally on altruistic emotions.[14] Such an argument is implied in Lawrence A. Blum's analysis of altruism. His account of altruistic emotions is especially interesting for us because it converges with the Affective-Cognitive Theory. He agrees (i) that one can have all the emotion-appropriate beliefs without experiencing the emotion, (ii) that emotions have a fundamental affective dimension, (iii) that emotions, attitudes, and values are intimately related, and (iv) that one can, rationally, pursue some endeavor that is of particular importance to one and this in a way that shows one need not be impartial between one's own concerns and those of others.[15] Consequently, when Blum describes a person as acting altruistically, it is essentially what I would characterize as acting on one's valuings aimed at promoting the good or welfare of another. Even Blum, however, is not a perfect exemplar of the position I wish to consider because he does not ground all reasons to act morally on such altruism, allowing some room for Kantian principled action.[16] (I shall argue later, however, that Blum overemphasizes the role of emotion vis-à-vis principled action in his analysis of friendship.) What we need to consider, then, is whether altruism could be the sole, or even fundamental, ground for rational moral action.

A number of considerations indicate that it cannot. Most obviously, to the extent the good or welfare of others is highly valued it is apt to be restricted to a fairly small number of people. Although utilitarians sometimes appeal to a sentiment of generalized benevolence,[17] strongly altruistic feelings involve personal attachments[18] and consequently are inherently nongeneralizable.

14 I stress that the altruism is *emotional* to exclude Nagel's argument for the possibility of altruism discussed in §12, which is better understood as a defense of the agent-neutrality of value-based reasons to act.

15 Lawrence A. Blum, *Friendship, Altruism, and Morality*. On (i) see pp. 173–7, 201–2; on (ii) see pp. 13, 179–86, 201; on (iii) see pp. 185–6; on (iv) see pp. 52–5, 64–6.

16 Ibid., pp. 7–9, 159–60.

17 See, e.g., J. J. C. Smart, "An Outline of a System of Utilitarian Ethics," p. 7.

18 See Derek Wright, *The Psychology of Moral Behaviour*, pp. 129–32.

Less obvious, but perhaps more interesting, is that studies indicate that altruism is not highly correlated with moral restraint, that is, resisting the temptation to benefit through violating moral rules.[19] And that, of course, is just the temptation confronting our potential noncompliers. In defense of an essentially altruistic theory of moral motivation, however, it has been pointed out that "individuals who scored high on measures of moral reasoning, as assessed by Kohlberg's dilemmas" also tend to be those engaged in helping – altruistic – behavior.[20] But allowing that an ability to reason about justice is related to altruistic behavior by no means implies that reasoning about justice, or moral reasoning in general, is itself altruistic. The reported correlation is consistent with the hypothesis that both reasoning about justice and altruistic behavior presuppose some common cognitive achievement. And there is indeed evidence to suggest that this is so. It is generally recognized that fundamental to Kohlberg's analysis of reasoning about justice (or morality) is the cognitive ability to take up the perspective of others (§§12.2, 17.4);[21] evidence also indicates that this ability is important in the development of altruism.[22] It thus is not surprising that those capable of complex reasoning about justice should also tend to be altruistic.

I thus see no compelling reason to accept the claim that a general tendency to altruism (or some other valuing of moral action) adequately accounts for the rationality of moral action. Both the arguments we have considered – that morality is better than anarchy and that acting morally is generally valued – are designed to show that there is no *compliance problem.* As I understand it, the compliance problem is the problem of how it can be rational to act morally even when such action does not, all things considered, best promote one's valuings. If one embraces the orthodox view

19 Ibid., pp. 142–3.
20 J. Phillipe Rushton, "Altruism and Society: A Social Learning Perspective," pp. 425–6, 433. For examples of Lawrence Kohlberg's dilemmas, see his "From *Is* to *Ought*" and "Justice as Reversibility."
21 See Lawrence A. Kurdek, "Perspective Taking as the Cognitive Basis of Children's Moral Development"; Dennis Krebs and Janet Gillmore, "The Relationship among the First Stages of Cognitive Development, Role-taking Abilities, and Moral Development." See also the references to Kohlberg in the previous note.
22 See Norman Buckley, Linda S. Siegel, and Steven Ness, "Egocentrism, Empathy, and Altruistic Behavior in Young Children"; Kurdek, "Perspective Taking," pp. 16ff.

of value and reasons to act, the answer must be, in one sense at least, simple: it can never be rational. *Ex hypothesi*, all reasons to act are value reasons, so moral action that does not, all things considered, best promote one's values cannot be rational. Because, then, those accepting the orthodox view cannot give any other answer, if they also accept the agent-relativity of value reasons, their effort must be directed at showing that moral action is rational *because* it best promotes one's values. Attempts to do this I shall describe as aiming at solving the *coordination problem*. That is, someone maintaining that value reasons are agent-relative and who also upholds the orthodox view will try to demonstrate the rationality of moral action by showing how action in accordance with moral rules or principles is rational for valuers who need to coordinate their actions in order to better promote their values. Thus, for example, Robert Axelrod's recent work has sought to demonstrate how those devoted solely to their own interests can rationally come to adopt a strategy that leads to coordinated outcomes in the interests of all.[23]

Such coordination problems are not my concern. Although they are doubtlessly important in various fields (for example, the analysis of international politics) they assume a fundamental role in the defense of morality as rational only if some version of agent-relativity is accepted along with the orthodox view. If, pace the orthodox view, we can provide a solution to the compliance problem – that is, we can demonstrate how it is rational to act morally even when doing so, all things considered, fails to best advance one's values – we no longer are committed to conceiving of rational moral behavior as a coordination problem. By rejecting the orthodox view of value and reasons, then, we can focus analysis on the compliance problem rather than coordination problems.

16.2 Simple Rationalism

Put that way, the task seems easy. All that is required is an alternative view that enables us to rationally act in a way that does not best promote our values. The orthodox view, however, is widely accepted for good reason: the tie between what a person

23 Robert Axelrod, "The Emergence of Cooperation among Egoists." See also his *The Evolution of Cooperation*.

cares for and what it is rational for him to do is deeply embedded in our very conception of a rational agent. Accounts of rational action that depart from the orthodox view would do well to keep this in mind; theories that insist on the intrinsic rationality of moral action but which are unable to tie such action to our concerns, values, etc. are apt to strike everyone but their proponents as intuitively suspect. R. B. Perry articulated the deep intuition informing consequentialism when he said: "It is certainly a doubtful compliment to the right to deny that it does not of itself do good."[24] But this intuition, I think, itself derives from yet a deeper one: action that does not aim at or achieve the good cannot possibly be rational. This latter deep intuition cannot be ignored. In this chapter, I aim both to show that its articulation by the orthodox view has radical and destructive implications and, further, that an alternative account captures the appeal of the intuition without these radical consequences.

Let us consider more carefully some of the difficulties attending a radical rejection of the orthodox view and, so, of the intuition that it articulates. The most radical rejection, I suppose, would insist that no reasons at all are value reasons, but that is clearly too farfetched. The most radical rejection that is both plausible and germane to our concerns I call *Simple Rationalism*:

> Independently of his value judgments, valuings, values, etc. any rational agent will acknowledge certain moral principles that he recognizes as providing him with reasons to act, reasons that always override (that is, are more important considerations in deliberation than) his value-based reasons to act.

Kant, I think, advocated such a rationalism. To call the moral imperative "categorical" is precisely to stress that its status is not in any way dependent upon the values, purposes, or ends of the agent. The agent can thus recognize it as an imperative even though he does not will anything else, and in this sense it is unconditional – that is, not a conditional presupposing a valuing.[25] "The categorical imperative . . . declares action to be of itself objectively necessary without making any reference to a purpose, i.e., without having any other end."[26] Kant thus rejects the claim that, in order to have a reason to act in accordance with the cat-

24 Ralph Barton Perry, *Realms of Value*, p. 107.
25 I am following Marcus George Singer, *Generalization in Ethics*, p. 222.
26 Immanuel Kant, *Foundations of the Metaphysics of Morals*, p. 32 (2nd sec.).

egorical imperative, one must desire, or value, acting morally or rationally: recognition of the categorical imperative itself necessarily leads any rational agent to acknowledge a reason to act. To possess freedom is to have the capacity to be determined by reason, independent of desire or natural instincts.[27]

Simple Rationalism is to be distinguished from deontology (see §22). According to Michael J. Sandel, "deontological liberalism" – the "liberalism of Kant" – maintains that the moral principles regulating social life are justified only if "they conform to the concept of *right*, a moral category given prior to the good and independent of it."[28] But this does not imply Simple Rationalism, or even a departure from the orthodox view. Sandel's own example of a "deontological liberal," John Rawls, is certainly no simple rationalist. In order for Rawls's principles of justice to be recognized as reasons to act, an agent must possess a "sense of justice" – a "desire to act in accordance with the principles that would be chosen in the original position." Furthermore, Rawls is clear that this sense of justice is linked to a person's value system or his conception of the good (§14.3).[29] It thus seems that, despite his commitment to deontological justification, Rawls embraces the orthodox view of value and reasons.

In many ways, Simple Rationalism is attractive, especially given the agent-relativity of values. If it can be established, what I have called the compliance problem admits of a straightforward solution: all rational agents, regardless of what they happen to value, will recognize a reason to act morally, and this will always override their agent-relative reasons to act. In order to defend such a solution, however, the simple rationalist must establish three claims:

(C1) Any rational agent will recognize certain moral principles.
(C2) Any rational agent will see that these imply reasons for action.
(C3) Any rational agent will be motivated to act on these reasons.

It seems doubtful that all three claims can be made; the argument that allows the simple rationalist to defend one, undermines the plausibility of at least one of the others.

Assume for the moment we grant (C1), in the sense that we

27 See ibid., pp. 78–9 (3rd sec.). See also W. D. Ross, *The Right and the Good*, pp. 157ff.
28 Michael J. Sandel, *Liberalism and the Limits of Justice*, p. 1.
29 See Rawls, *A Theory of Justice*, p. 312, sec. 86.

recognize moral principles to be a fact of social life; as some philosophers have argued, that "murder is wrong" is a linguistic and social fact. Consequently, any fully rational agent will believe that "murder is wrong." Moreover, philosophers have also contended that it necessarily follows from this belief that one has a reason not to murder:

> That a killing would be a murder is a reason for me not to perform it whether or not I actually refrain. If I should go ahead and commit murder, then my action is contrary to reason and properly described as unreasonable. . . . A murder is a wrongful killing, one that ought not to be performed . . . the classification is not made in terms of the wants, needs and interests of the prospective murderer, so the reason is not dependent on his wants, needs and interests.[30]

So (C1) and (C2) might in this way be defended. But, then, (C3) seems insupportable; that is, it cannot be shown that this defense of reasons to act morally is necessarily motivating. Recall what I earlier called *Strong Externalism*:

SE: "Alf recognizes that he has a moral obligation to ϕ" does not logically/conceptually imply "Alf is motivated to ϕ."

I will now be more specific. The Strong Externalism that grants Simple Rationalism's claims (C1) and (C2) but denies (C3) is:

SE(1): i) "Alf recognizes that he has a moral obligation to ϕ" implies
ii) "Alf recognizes that he has a reason to ϕ, but {i & ii} do not logically/conceptually imply
iii) "Alf is motivated to ϕ."

Philippa Foot points to this version of externalism when she says that "an agent may fail to be moved by a reason, even when he is aware of it."[31]

If SE(1) is sound, the simple rationalist claims (C1) and (C2) may be of no avail in solving what I have characterized as the compliance problem. Even if every rational agent accepted moral principle *M*, and recognized *M* as providing a conclusive reason

30 R. E. Ewin, *Co-operation and Human Values*, p. 127. His defense of (C1), that all will recognize these principles, depends on value arguments. However, although the justification of the basic moral principles turns on value considerations, his theory of reasons to act does not call on a valuing of the moral act. See his distinction between "reasons *inside* and reasons *for* the enterprise."

31 Philippa Foot, *Virtues and Vices*, p. 179. See also David A. J. Richards, *A Theory of Reasons for Action*.

to ϕ, it doesn't follow that anyone will be motivated to ϕ. Now the simple rationalist might object, and not without some cause, that this practical worry lies outside the competency of philosophical ethics. Insofar as philosophical ethics is a practical activity directed at altering what is done, it is aimed at humans conceived of as rational agents. Fully rational agents are always moved by, and only moved by, good reasons: to provide a rational agent with good reasons is thus necessarily to motivate him. Consequently, the focus of SE(1) – those who are unmoved by good reasons – is necessarily on nonrational agents.

There is certainly something to this. On the face of it, it is indeed puzzling that philosophers should be worried about how to motivate nonrational agents; that would seem the specialty of the psychologist, the demagogue, and, perhaps, the dramatist and the priest.[32] This is not to imply that SE(1) is necessarily false; those suffering from defects of rationality may well be able to recognize a reason in an intelligible enough sense without being motivated to act. Compulsives, for instance, are probably characterized by such a failure. The question, rather, is whether it should be a concern of philosophical ethics that some may be unmoved by sound reasons. Moreover, it is obscure how philosophical ethics could provide motivations of the required sort. For when philosophers try to motivate it is always through an appeal to some type of reason. William Frankena, at the close of his book *Ethics* confronts the question "Why should we be moral?" which, he says, could be a request for "motivation for adopting the moral point of view and otherwise subscribing to the moral institution or life." And, he says, it is "easy to see the form of an answer to a request" of this sort: "it will consist in pointing out the various prudential and non-prudential motives for doing what is right."[33] But pretty clearly these "motives" – "most of these are familiar or readily thought of"[34] – are just reasons of a different sort. The philosopher would not reply to the

32 "For we commonly think that wrong conduct is essentially irrational, and can be shown to be so by argument; and though we do not conceive that it is by reason alone that men are influenced to act rightly, we still hold that appeals to the reason are an essential part of all moral persuasion, and that part which concerns the moralist or moral philosopher as distinct from the preacher or moral rhetorician." Sidgwick, *Methods of Ethics*, p. 23.
33 William K. Frankena, *Ethics*, p. 114.
34 Ibid.

request by, say, conditioning the enquirer, but by providing him with yet more reasons, that is, self-interested ones.[35] But, if he just is not moved by reasons for action, the philosopher still cannot motivate him.

But this points to the significant philosophical issue raised by this version of Strong Externalism. SE(1), and the philosopher who advocates it, is especially concerned with *moral* reasons. Faced with doubts that moral reasons necessarily motivate, many philosophers have sought to motivate rational agents to be moral by providing them with other (for example, prudential) reasons. It would seem that moral philosophers have been particularly troubled as to whether otherwise rational people need be moved by recognition of moral reasons. This, of course, seems to contradict what I said in the previous paragraph, but no real contradiction is involved. Rational agents are, to be sure, necessarily motivated by good reasons, but the notion of a "rational agent" is not arbitrarily – stipulatively – defined so as to be necessarily moved by whatever a philosophic system designates as "a good reason." Our concept of a rational agent derives from our knowledge of humans (our only good example to date of a rational agent) and what sorts of considerations move humans who do not exhibit any manifest rational defect. (Rationality and the psychology of motivation are thus not so distinct as the previous paragraph suggested.) The difficulty with a good many purported "moral reasons" is that it is often unclear how such considerations would necessarily move our implicit model, a-human-without-any-rational-defect. And, if they would not, SE(1) poses a real worry for philosophical ethics.

The upshot of all this, then, is that if we are legitimately to dismiss SE(1) as a nonphilosophic problem, we must adopt a fairly rigorous criterion of what it is for something to be a reason. It must be acknowledged, I think, that any valid argument that some consideration is a reason to act must be plausibly able to claim that our implicit model, a-human-without-any-rational-

35 But cf. Marcus Singer's remark: "Yet, to give only prudential reasons, where one can give moral reasons, is it itself immoral. For it is essentially corrupting. It is, in the end, not really to give *reasons*, but only to give *motives*." *Generalization in Ethics*, p. 326. As I suggest in the text, this overlooks the philosophically problematic character of many moral reasons. In any event, it is puzzling why we are not to consider self-interested reasons as reasons.

defect, would be moved to act on the consideration, or at least take account of it in his deliberations (for one may rationally not act on a good reason to ϕ if there is better reason to refrain from ϕ-ing). Or alternatively, we might say that, if the consideration is really a reason, someone who ignores it in his deliberations is not a human-without-any-rational-defect: by ignoring the consideration, he shows for example, that he is inconsistent (see §18), ignores good evidence against his beliefs, ignores opportunities to promote what he (soundly) values, or is in some other sense obviously being crazy. Put simply, something is only a reason if ignoring it manifests an obvious defect of reason. This does not preclude arguments that only people of a certain sort (for example, those devoted to morality) would recognize it as a reason; it simply requires that, even for this limited claim to be sound, people-of-the-relevant-description-without-any-rational-defect would necessarily be motivated to act on the consideration. And, of course, this must be demonstrated in a manner that does not beg the issue by presupposing that it is a reason. That is, it cannot be argued that someone who ignored the proposed reason must be irrational because it is a reason to act, and anyone who ignores a reason to act is irrational. Because we already possess an implicit, though to be sure rough, model of what would move a nonrationally-defective human, this provides a rough, but by no means useless, benchmark by which to judge the intuitive plausibility of any claim that some consideration constitutes a reason to act.

Regrettably, these remarks are vague. It would be helpful if we had a clear and precise model of a nondefective agent, such that we could test any purported reason by asking "Would this reason move our model agent?"[36] But developing such a model would take us far afield here; I shall thus rely on a rougher and more intuitive test. Let us say that a test for *R* being a genuine reason for Alf to ϕ is that Alf's being unmoved to ϕ in the face of his recognition of *R* puzzles us and lead us to strongly doubt that Alf

36 Philosophers have tried to construct such models. Jean Hampton describes Hobbes's model of a nondefective agent in *Hobbes and the Social Contract Tradition*, pp. 38–42. Stanley Benn seeks to develop such a model in his *A Theory of Freedom*; I discuss his model (with which I largely agree) in my "Practical Reason and Moral Persons." See also Benn and Gaus, "Practical Rationality and Commitment."

understands the meaning of *R*, the nature of ϕ-ing or, alternatively, that we are led to conclude that he can appropriately be called "crazy" or "manifestly defective" (see §9.2.1).

It is the great strength of the orthodox view that it clearly and easily meets this test. If all reasons somehow presuppose, constitute or imply valuings, then "Alf recognizes a reason to ϕ" can (very roughly) be translated as (or it implies) "Alf values ϕ-ing (or its consequences)"; and it is indeed plausible to question the rationality of someone who is in no way moved to do that which he values doing. This, of course, is particularly clear given the Affective-Cognitive Theory of value. Remember that, when arguing that well-grounded (dis)valuings imply reasons to act, I considered what we would say about someone who recognized that he was afraid of a tiger, that his fear was entirely well-grounded, that running would remove the danger presented by the tiger, that he had no reason to refrain from running, yet he saw no reason at all to run (§9.2.3). That, I submit, really does seem crazy.

But adopting this more rigorous criterion of a reason for action does cause difficulties for Simple Rationalism. My suspicion is that the cost of allowing only reasons that meet the rough test I have sketched is that Simple Rationalism will be unable to establish either (C1) or (C2). Again, let us grant (C1), that all rational persons will recognize certain moral obligations or judgments as facts, but now we shall insist on a conception of a reason to act that avoids SE(1). Another variety of externalism now presents a challenge:

SE(2): i) "Alf recognizes that he has a moral obligation to ϕ" does not logically/conceptually imply
ii) "Alf recognizes that he has a reason to ϕ," and therefore (i) does not imply
iii) "Alf is motivated to ϕ."

Once the rationalist accepts a rigorous criterion of what it is to be a reason to act, the move from (C1) to (C2) becomes difficult. He can no longer insist, say, that anyone not defective in understanding will perceive that "ϕ is a murder" simply does constitute a reason for anyone to refrain from ϕ-ing. The prescriptivists provide a useful insight: an agent can reject such practical implications of moral concepts without exhibiting any rational flaw.[37] This, indeed, is the sort of externalist position that Foot typically has in mind, e.g. the man who admits that justice requires ϕ, but since he "does not care a damn" about justice,[38] he has no reason to ϕ. I am not insisting that such a man cannot be shown that he nevertheless has a reason to ϕ, but Simple Rationalism is committed to establishing that he possesses such a reason without any appeal to his value system. Given that restriction, it is not at all clear that Foot's externalist can be shown to be rationally defective.

Of course, one might say that the problem with Foot's externalist is that, though he can adequately employ moral language, and that allows him to identify ϕ as the just action, he has no commitment to justice, no sense of justice. In some sense, his lack of a sense of justice bars him from truly recognizing – grasping – his obligation, and that is why he does not acknowledge a reason (for him) to ϕ. That, to be sure, is the point. The problem is that it is very difficult to see how, in this rather strong sense of what it is to "recognize" a moral obligation, Simple Rationalism's claim (C1) can be made out. That is, if to recognize a moral obligation is to possess a sense of justice or devotion to the moral enterprise, then it seems false that any rational agent, independently of his values, necessarily will recognize moral principles in this way.

17 VALUE-GROUNDED RATIONALISM (I)

17.1 VGR and its paradox

The previous section did not attempt to provide conclusive arguments against either the orthodox view or Simple Rationalism. The aim, rather, was to point to some difficulties attending each, and by doing so arrive at some criteria for an adequate, or successful, theory of reasons to act morally. Given the nature of value-based reasons for action, the orthodox view renders it problematic how one could always, or even typically, have good reason to act on moral principles rather than one's valuings. Sim-

37 As Neil Cooper argues, specific moral concepts (e.g., "patriotic") are "rejectable" and general moral concepts (e.g., "good") are "reversible." *The Diversity of Moral Thinking,* ch. 7. See §8.3 in this volume.
38 Foot, *Virtues and Vices*, p. 130.

ple Rationalism solves that problem easily enough, but it is difficult to envisage a compelling response to the challenge of the Strong Externalist: how can we show that it is irrational to ignore moral reasons? We can avoid at least some of the problems confronting Simple Rationalism by adopting a more modest variety of rationalism. Call it *Value-Grounded Rationalism*:

> VGR: Given his valuings, any rational person will recognize moral principles as providing him with reasons to act, reasons that typically override (that is, are more weighty considerations in deliberation than) his simply value-based reasons for action.

Value-Grounded Rationalism relaxes two of Simple Rationalism's claims. Most obviously, it does not require that moral reasons always override nonmoral reasons for action. To be sure, if reasons to act morally were never recognized as more weighty than value-based reasons for action in fully rational deliberation, then in an important sense they would not be moral reasons at all; it is surely characteristic of the reasons implied by moral principles that sometimes – and I would venture, typically – they require a rational agent to put aside his own particular concerns and do the right thing.[39] Especially from the perspective of a theory stressing the agent-relativity of value-based reasons for action, this would seem to be the very *raison d'être* of morality: if the anarchy of each always acting on his own valuings is to be avoided, some reasons must be commonly accepted by rational agents to provide a basis for an ordered social life.[40] But, if these moral reasons were not generally more important than an individual's value-based reasons, they could not perform this function. However, this understanding of morality is not undermined by allowing that, at least in exceptional circumstances, fully rational agents may act on their valuations even when this means setting aside moral principles (see §29.2).

The second and more fundamental way in which this moderate rationalism departs from Simple Rationalism is in abandoning its claim that the recognition of reasons to act on moral principles

39 Cf. Ronald Dworkin's argument that, in order for *R* to be a right, it must outweigh at least some policy goals; if it does not, there seems little point in calling it a right. *Taking Rights Seriously*, p. 92.

40 See Baier, *The Moral Point of View* (1958 ed.), p. 309. Baier, however, seems to hold that it is essential to the nature of moral reasons that they always override reasons of self-interest.

is independent of what one values. This allows Value-Grounded Rationalism to employ a far wider range of arguments to show that any fully rational agent will recognize a reason to act morally [and, further, to show that the reason so defended is not subject to a philosophically legitimate challenge from SE(1)]. For example, at an earlier stage, Mrs. Foot endeavored to establish that "moral judgments necessarily give reasons for acting to each and every man" by showing it to be in each and every man's self-interest to be virtuous.[41] Similarly, as we have seen (§16.1), Kurt Baier seeks to answer the question "Why be moral?" by showing that each person's self-interest is advanced by a system of morality. Such arguments are abjured by the simple rationalist (or, at least, he asserts that he has no need for them). But what I have called Value-Grounded Rationalism relies on them; and, to that extent, it seems to offer a more fruitful path for those seeking a compelling alternative to the orthodox view.

But, if Simple Rationalism's problem is in showing how we have reasons to act morally (or why we are really irrational for ignoring them), the difficulty confronting VGR is in demonstrating how moral reasons could ever rationally override the reasons from which they derive. Say, following Baier or the early Foot, it is held that all rational agents will recognize a reason to act morally because it is in one's self-interest to do so. The very point of these reasons, however, is to (typically) override reasons of self-interest. So in this case our reason to act morally derives from considerations of self-interest, but it can override its own grounds such that one will act on the moral principles even when, *all things considered*, one could better promote one's values by violating it. All this sounds rather too much like Mill's characterization of a pedant, "who goes by rules rather than their reasons."[42] It does, indeed, seem like a sort of practical irrationality; if in such cases we act morally, "we should employ the means and the end will not follow."[43] Consequently, Mill cautions against relying on "even the plausible . . . absolute maxims of right and wrong" in such a way that one loses sight of the paramount good they are intended to promote: "The maxims may, as the rough

41 Foot, *Virtues and Vices*, p. xiii. See also her ch. VIII.
42 J. S. Mill, *A System of Logic*, bk. VI, ch. xii, sec. 2. I consider Mill's view in more depth in "Mill's Theory of Moral Rules."
43 Mill, *Logic*, bk. VI, ch. xii, sec. 3.

results of experience, be regarded as *prima facie* presumptions that what they inculcate will be found conducive to the ultimate end; but not as conclusive on that point without examination, still less as carrying an authority independent of, and superior to, the end."[44] Mill's argument presses Value-Grounded Rationalism back toward the orthodox view. If VGR is to succeed, it must establish precisely what Mill denies: that moral rules have an authority which, if not independent of the end, is certainly superior to it. Baier is aware of this problem:

> Moralities are systems of principles whose acceptance by everyone as overruling the dictates of self-interest is in the interest of everyone alike, though following the rules of a morality is not identical with following self-interest. If it were, there could be no conflict between a morality and self-interest and no point in having moral rules overriding self-interest. . . .
>
> But is it not self-contradictory to say that it is in a person's interest to do what is contrary to his interest? It certainly would be if the two expressions were used in exactly the same way. But they are not. We have already seen that an enlightened egoist can acknowledge that a certain course of action is in his enlightened long-term, but contrary to his narrow short-term interest. . . . For we are now considering not merely a single action but a policy.
>
> All the same, we must not make too much of this analogy. There is an all-important difference between the two cases. The calculations of the enlightened egoist properly allow for "exceptions in his favor." After all, his calculus is designed to promote his interest. . . . Moral rules are not designed to serve the agent's interest directly. Hence it would be quite inappropriate for him to break them whenever he discovers that they do not serve his interest. . . . [T]o say that following them is in the interest of everyone alike means only that it is better for everyone that there should be a morality generally observed than the principle of self-interest should be acknowledged as supreme. It does not of course mean that a person will not do better for himself by following self-interest than by doing what is morally right, when others are doing what is right.[45]

I quote at such length in order to capture not only Baier's argument, but also the sense that he is clearly wrestling with a paradox. And it does not seem that the paradox has been adequately resolved. For we are still confronted by the initial compliance problem: although, from Alf's perspective, it is better if everyone, including him, complies with moral or political principles

44 J. S. Mill, "Thornton on Labour and Its Claims," p. 659.
45 Baier, *The Moral Point of View*, abridged ed. (1965), pp. 154–7.

than if none comply, from Alf's perspective it is better still if everyone else complies, leaving him free to pursue his values unfettered by the constraints imposed by moral principles. He may try to persuade others to comply with moral rules regardless of the cost (in terms of their own valuings) – he may even try to move them to become Kantians – but, if he is fully rational, Alf should know better than to act in this Kantian way himself.[46]

Nevertheless, I think we can see that Baier really does go a long way toward an adequate account of reasons to act on moral principles. For our purposes, three of his claims are crucial:

(a) Moral rules are for the good of everyone.
(b) A person taking up the moral point of view acts in accordance with moral principles even when this does not, all things considered, advance his self-interest.
(c) Everyone has reason to adopt the moral point of view because accepting moral reasons as overriding reasons of self-interest promotes the self-interest of everyone alike.[47]

Claims (a) and (b) are, I shall argue, essentially sound. In Chapter 7, I defend claim (a), explaining in what sense, and why, moral rules must necessarily be for the good of all. Claim (b), of course, is the core of Value-Grounded Rationalism: one has reason to act morally even when it does not promote one's valuings.

---

46 Baier denies this in his "Rationality, Reason, and the Good." An ideally rational agent, Baier argues, would want to live in an equitable society, in which no such exceptions are made in his favor (p. 209). Baier thus maintains that Alf's violation of the moral rules "need not involve so gross a departure from the ideal of rationality as to involve irrationality. But it would not be in accordance with the idea of perfect rationality, that of flawless accordance with reason. For the fulfillment of such a hope [i.e., Alf's hope that the others will comply while he cheats] would involve making demands . . . on the socially disfavored [i.e., the compliers], which it would not be rational for . . . [Alf] to make, because it certainly would not be ideally rational for those on whom the demands are made to want to comply with them" (p. 209). Fully rational people, Baier insists, do not make demands on others that those others would be irrational to comply with. I believe that Professor Baier is entirely correct that Alf's problem here is that he cannot show others that their compliance is rational: he cannot justify to them the demand that they comply. But Baier has not shown why Alf is rationally committed to such justification. In itself, making demands on others with which they would not comply if they knew the whole truth (e.g., bluffs) is not, as far as I can see, necessarily any flaw in rationality. Only if Alf is committed to justifying himself is his inability to provide rational others with reasons to comply a rational fault.

47 Baier, *The Moral Point of View*. For claim (a), see 1958, pp. 200–4; 1965, pp. 100–6. For claim (b), see 1958, pp. 191–5; 1965, pp. 90–100. For claim (c), see 1958, pp. 308–15; 1965, pp. 91, 148–53.

However, (c), when conjoined with (b), raises precisely the paradox we have been considering: How can self-interest really lead one to accept a point of view which demands that one act in ways that, all things considered, are not in one's interest?

The problem is that Baier – and of course he is by no means unique in this regard – understands one's self-interested reason to take up the moral point of view as *instrumental*: taking up the moral point of view is characterized as a means to achieving one's self-interest. So long as the connection is conceived instrumentally, a value-grounded rationalist theory is open to Mill's criticism of employing the means where the end does not follow. An alternative, though, (and I will switch now from Baier's talk of self-interest back to our concern with value) is that one might be committed to taking up the moral point of view because it is foundational or central to one's value system. It will be recalled that in §14.2.2 I argued that a valuing could be central to a value system in the sense that "giving it up" or abandoning it would lead to the collapse or disintegration of the value system. And, significantly, a valuing that is important in this sense is not necessarily greatly valued *qua* highly comparatively valued. One may often incur the opportunity cost of not promoting it, even if it could not be rejected without great damage to one's value system. We have also seen how valuings depend on beliefs (§§5, 6, 10.4): a valuing is rationally flawed if a grounding belief is unsound. Consequently, if some belief, or cluster of beliefs, that grounds some central valuings is false or ill-grounded, the value system itself will be radically incoherent. The costs, then, of rejecting such a belief would, in terms of one's value system, be enormous.

In the remainder of §17, I shall argue that our value systems are indeed characterized by such a set of beliefs, articulating our conception of others as moral persons. In §§17.2–17.4, I look at ways of conceiving of others that fall short of seeing them as moral persons: to conceive of others in these ways, I maintain, would undermine the rationality of the value systems of all but the most unusual rational agents. §17.5 then examines the plausibility of alternative interpretations of moral action in terms of various sorts of habits or dispositions. All this concerns how all but the most unusual rational agents are, by virtue of their value systems, committed to conceiving of others. In §18, I take up the implications of this for one's conception of oneself, one's actions and one's judgments. Rational consistency, I argue, commits one to conceiving of oneself as a moral person and to acting according to this conception. Together, §§17 and 18 constitute a defense of VGR. With very few exceptions indeed, fully rational agents are committed to accepting Value-Grounded Rationalism – not, however, as a means to better promoting what they value, but because it is deeply embedded in their value systems.

17.2 Solipsism and egocentrism

Perhaps one might have no conception of others. That is, one could take the view that one's own perspective is the only perspective. We can at least imagine someone who believed that he alone was a valuer capable of agency; he would thus find himself sharing the world with outwardly, but deceptively, similar creatures, which, though being manikinlike replicas of himself, are neither valuers nor agents.[48] Or, even more radically, he could simply deny their reality claiming, say, that they are all characters in his ongoing dream.

From a psychological perspective, it is doubtful whether this combination of self-consciousness and failure to grasp the personhood of others is coherent. Piaget's study of the first year of life indicates that we all begin life with a sort of solipsistic outlook, and it is just because of this that babies are not aware of themselves as agents.

> The true solipsist feels at one with the universe, and so very identical to it that he does not even feel the need for two terms. . . . The true solipsist is entirely alone in the world, that is, he has no notion of anything exterior to himself. In other words, the true solipsist has no idea of the self. There is no self: there is the world. It is in this sense that it is reasonable to call a baby a solipsist: the feelings and desires of a baby know no limits since they are a part of everything he sees, touches, and perceives.[49]

The recognition of others as centers of consciousness distinct from oneself is fundamental to the development of one's own self-

48 Such a man would be essentially Stanley Benn's agent who conceives of himself as a "natural person" – he is aware of himself as an agent initiating events – but believes himself to be the only such being. "Freedom, Autonomy, and the Concept of a Person," pp. 118–19.
49 Jean Piaget, "The First Year of Life of the Child," p. 201.

consciousness. This was seen clearly by Hegel and Rousseau. One's conception of oneself is inherently social insofar as it is developed through seeing oneself in relation to, compared to, and reflected in the eyes of others. The child thus "discovers itself – comes to have more coherent, sophisticated, and realistic ideas about itself – in the process of learning how it appears to others, of drawing the implications of their behavior toward it, and in accepting or rejecting their ideas about it."[50] Consequently, if we aim to grasp what, if somehow he existed, the life and concerns of such a solipsist would look like, it would be entirely mistaken to imagine a sort of Robinson Crusoe who, though alone, conceived of himself as one of many humans. A much better model is Rousseau's savage in the *Second Discourse*, "without liaisons," "without speech," and possessing "only the sentiments and intellect suited to that state" and whose "intelligence made no more progress than his vanity."[51] Like Rousseau's savage, it seems impossible that our natural solipsist would develop any form of communication, for he has no one with whom to communicate. Again, as with Rousseau's savage, envy, vanity, and jealousy all would be impossible, for they too necessarily require a conception of others in some way like oneself. The vain need an audience, the envious someone with whom to compare themselves. Indeed, our solipsist would be even less recognizably human because Rousseau's savage at least possessed a primitive capacity for pity, vaguely recognizing others as being of its kind.

But what if we put aside these developmental concerns and consider instead a normal adult who, perhaps out of philosophic conviction, adopts the solipsistic outlook? Already equipped with self-consciousness and language, he would be far removed from Rousseau's savage. Our philosophic solipsist, however, would be committed to a wholesale revision of his language, his account of the behavior of replicants and the world in which he lives. All references to others as valuer-agents must be purged. Moreover, he would require some account of what his language was really about, what really was happening when, formerly, he thought he

50 This is John Plamenatz's description of Hegel's view. *Karl Marx's Philosophy of Man*, p. 94. I am drawing here on Benn, "Freedom, Autonomy, and the Concept of a Person," p. 119.

51 Jean-Jacques Rousseau, *Discourse on the Origin and Foundations of Inequality Among Men*, p. 137.

was communicating with others. But that is by no means all, for it is hard to see how anything but fragments of his former value system could be sustained. Valuings involving cooperation or competition with others, emotions presupposing the existence of others, striving after the recognition of others, all would be unsound. And we do not have to suppose particularly human-centered value systems to see the havoc that would result from embracing this conception of others. Even if, say, one was single-mindedly devoted to natural science, ridding oneself of the concept of others would undermine one's understanding of the scientific enterprise, the scientific tradition and the value of science. Alternatively, try to imagine what would remain of a thoroughgoing religious outlook if one came to embrace solipsism.

I shall not labor this further. To consistently adopt the solipsistic perspective would render most of one's current valuings unsound. As Stanley Benn says, "The cost . . . would be enormous."[52] Piaget depicts the solipsism of the baby as the most extreme instance of the egocentrism characteristic of children;[53] in contrast, what Piaget calls "adolescent egocentrism" is one of its mildest manifestations. The sort of personality I have in mind here accepts the existence of others' points of view, but confuses his own point of view with the objective point of view, or he assumes that all share his view.[54] The egocentric, then, believes that others value what he values, or at least would do so if they were rational because his values are objectively valid. According to Piaget and the Affective-Cognitive Theory, all such egocentrics suffer from a lack of objectivity. As I have already argued (§12.2), one who is objective can grasp that he is one valuer among others; he can take up the objective point of view as it is defined by the Affective-Cognitive Theory of value. Such a person has decentered – he has grasped that others have a distinctive point of view and can see in what sense theirs is on par with his own. Once he has achieved this modest level of objectivity, egocentrism is abandoned: he sees that others do not necessarily share his valuings, and he understands how the objective point of view as

52 Benn, "Freedom, Autonomy, and the Concept of a Person," p. 119.
53 Piaget, "The First Year of Life."
54 See Jean Piaget, "The Growth of Logical Thinking from Childhood to Adolescence," pp. 439–40. See also Jean Piaget, *Six Psychological Studies*, ch. 1; Jean Piaget, *The Moral Judgment of the Child*, p. 36.

defined by the Affective-Cognitive Theory takes account of, but is different from, his own point of view.

Egocentrism is objectionable because it is inconsistent with full acceptance of the Affective-Cognitive Theory of value. Put bluntly, egocentrism depends on, or implies, false claims. The egocentric maintains that others have reasons to act that they do not have because he insists that everyone necessarily shares his values (which they do not), or because he asserts that others are irrational for not doing so (which they are not), or because he holds that everyone has reasons to promote his valuings (which they do not). Once these claims are abandoned in favor of a more objective view of others and their reasons, egocentrism too is necessarily abandoned.

But what if the "egocentric" only claims that others are nonrationally defective for not sharing his values, for example, that they do not have affective sensibilities consistent with some character ideal? Well, from the objective point of view, we see that the others are rational to be unmoved by this criticism: a rational agent must admit that others have not been provided with any reason to do anything, and this even though they are fully rational. The externalist challenge to the criticism is entirely sensible: "What is this ideal to me?" (§§10.2, 16.2). If, then, the "egocentric" makes this sort of criticism of others in a way that is consistent with the Affective-Cognitive Theory, he is not purporting to provide others with reasons to act. And, if he refrains from claiming that his values necessarily provide others with reasons to act, he is not being "egocentric" in any way that is inconsistent with objectivity. It is entirely rational for anyone to criticize another's valuings or sensibilities, as long as one is cognizant that this criticism is tied to one's own valuational perspective, and is not validated from the objective point of view. Such criticisms are thus to be distinguished from those discussed in §10.4, which are indeed so validated.

17.3 Minimal objectivity

17.3.1 Viewing others as mere valuer-agents

Let us assume, then, that a person accepts the Affective-Cognitive Theory of value, and in so doing achieves a level of objectivity such that he understands that he is one valuer among others, each of whom occupies a distinctive valuational perspective that supplies him with reasons to act. Without abandoning his own "bias" for his own perspective vis-à-vis his own action, and without taking the perspectives of others to be on all fours with his own as far as his own deliberations are concerned (§12.1), achieving this level of objectivity allows him to see how in one sense it is intelligible to say that he is just one of many valuers and is not privileged or special. He thus steers a course between the Scylla of denying the distinctive importance his own point of view has *for him* and the Charybdis of denying the reality, and equal standing, of others' points of view. Now, let us further assume not only that everyone has achieved this level of objectivity, but also that everyone embraces the orthodox view of value and reasons. So, any given individual, Betty, will recognize that others value different things than does she, and, further, she holds that each valuer-agent, if rational, will act only to advance his own values, so other valuer-agents will not necessarily have any reason to advance Betty's valuings. Of course, in pursuing what they value, other valuer-agents may take account of Betty's valuings, and this for two reasons.

(i) If Alf, a mere valuer-agent, is to effectively threaten and manipulate Betty so as to better achieve what he values, he must take into account that he and she value different things. In contradistinction to the egocentric, who because he has unsound beliefs about the nature of others' valuings and/or their reasons to act is apt to blunder when attempting to manipulate others, our minimally objective valuer-agent is not wrong about these things. And, because manipulation will typically be an effective way for Alf to advance his values, he will often need to be alert to just what others value and what commitments to act they recognize.

(ii) The sort of person I am describing may have affection for others, aim at promoting their good, and help them to achieve what they value. It cannot be stressed enough that, as opposed to such theorists as Hobbes and Baier, my concern is not self-interest but the broader problem of agent-relative, value-based reasons for action. Now a mere valuer-agent not only can care for another, but he can be aware that the beloved cares for different things than does he. This again contrasts with the egocentric.[55]

55 It should be clear that an egocentric by no means need be egoistic. Ego-

The egocentric may also care for another, but because he is unable to grasp that others really do have distinctive points of view that legitimately differ from his own, the love will be one that seeks to impose its valuings on the beloved. "Just so do hungry and possessive parents . . . smother what they claim to love."[56] However, if one really does grasp that the beloved is a valuer and agent with a distinctive perspective, one could take on the project of promoting the beloved's values without smothering the beloved in this way (but see §17.3.3).

Nevertheless, though not necessarily self-interested, such people would not be very different from those populating Hobbes's state of nature. If all achieved only this level of objectivity, each would see that each has reason to act on his own valuings, but also that no rational agent has reason to take heed of the values of others, except in the two ways I have already mentioned. By recognizing no reasons to act except those that advance their own values, they are precisely the type of agents that raise the problem of compliance (§16.1). As I indicated at the beginning of this chapter, a good deal of moral and political philosophy has been devoted to showing that such agents can nevertheless rationally coordinate their actions. I make no attempt to review that large body of theory, so I shall certainly not claim that it cannot be done. I now want to argue, however, that it may not matter a great deal for moral and political philosophy whether or not the project can succeed, for (with the exception of a very small number of people) to entertain this conception of others or oneself is irrational. More precisely, to adopt it would render the value systems of very nearly everyone inconsistent. Because, then, philosophical ethics is aimed at presenting reasons to fully rational agents (§16.2), any philosophical ethics premised on the assumption that people entertain this conception of others or themselves is flawed, because it is a way conceiving of self or others that is irrational for almost all of us.

---

centrism is a way of looking at one's valuational perspective vis-à-vis others; it does not assume that one is in any way self-interested.

56 Benn, "Freedom, Autonomy, and the Concept of a Person," p. 120. Benn means this to be a description of (essentially) the minimal objectivist; my claim, however, is that it applies to the egocentric but not necessarily to the minimal objectivist.

17.3.2 The poverty of pure liberty: critical responses to others

Let us return to Hobbes's state of nature. We can, as I have already indicated, grant that the value systems of Hobbesians would tend toward egoism, and in this respect they would be quite unlike our mere valuer-agents, who may conceivably be altruistic. Nevertheless, the moral relations pertaining among mere valuer-agents would be essentially those informing Hobbes's state of nature. "The fundamental law of nature," Hobbes maintained, is that "Naturally every man has a right to everything."[57] As he understood it, a right "consisteth in liberty to do, or to forbear."[58] Elsewhere, he described this as our "*blameless liberty* of using our own natural power and ability."[59] Each, then, has a blameless liberty to do anything he must in order to promote his overriding concern: his self-preservation. Because it is rational for each to ensure his self-preservation, and because each has a blameless liberty to do whatever he must, no one can be said to be blameworthy or irrational when he promotes it, whatever the consequences to others. "It is therefore neither absurd nor reprehensible, neither against the dictates of true reason, for a man to use all his endeavours to preserve and defend his body and the members thereof from death and sorrows. But that which is not contrary to right reason, that all men account to be done justly, and with right."[60]

One who conceives of others as simply valuer-agents must grant that they possess such a blameless liberty to do what promotes their own values.[61] That is, one accepts that others only

57 Hobbes, *Leviathan*, p. 103 (ch. 14).

58 Ibid.

59 Thomas Hobbes, *The Elements of Law, Natural and Politic*, p. 71. (pt. I, ch. 14, sec. 6). Emphasis added.

60 Hobbes, *The Citizen*, p. 115 (ch. I, sec. 7). See also *Elements of Law*, p. 71 (pt. I, ch. 14, sec. 6).

61 The sort of liberty I have in mind is essentially Wesley Hohfeld's "privilege," that is, where "Alf is at liberty to ϕ" implies that Betty has no right that he shall not ϕ. See Hohfeld's "Some Fundamental Legal Conceptions as Applied in Judicial Reasoning," pp. 30ff. See also Joel Feinberg, *Social Philosophy*, ch. 4. For analyses of Hobbes's theory in terms of such liberties, see: D. D. Raphael "Human Rights, Old and New," pp. 55-9; Hampton, *Hobbes and the Social Contract*, pp. 51-5. Jeremy Waldron, however, resists this analysis in his "Introduction" to his (ed.) collection, *Theories of Rights*, as does Ian Shapiro in *The Evolution of Rights in Liberal Theory*, p. 41. See also Richard Flathman, *The Practice of Rights*, pp. 40–4.

have reason to do what advances their values; since *ex hypothesi* there are no reasons other than value-based, agent-relative reasons, no one is rationally defective for limiting himself to such reasons. But this undermines the point of blaming people for acting on such reasons. One might, to be sure, still insist on employing words such as "wrong," "blameworthy," "immoral," etc., even though they were not intended to provide others with reasons to act, being rather, as emotivists and some relativists would have it, only intended as gestures of disapproval made solely from the speaker's valuational perspective. But such uses undermine the point of discourse and practices centered on these notions. When we deem another's act wrong, or we blame him for what he has done, we presuppose that he could have rationally done otherwise. If fully rational, he would have recognized and acted upon the reason to refrain from the objectionable act; but he did not. To blame someone, to point out the wrongness of what he has done and to criticize him for it, while acknowledging that he was perfectly rational to do it – he had a reason to do it, he is not subject to any sound criticism that he is rationally flawed for not recognizing a reason to abstain, he was not lacking any relevant information, and given his (sound) values, you would have done the same – is so odd precisely because it misses the point of such censure. Hobbes, not the emotivists, is right here: if a fully rational agent will ϕ, there is no point in blaming him for ϕ-ing. He does indeed have a blameless liberty to ϕ. One might intensely dislike his ϕ-ing, think it disgusting, an outrage against the sensibilities of English-speaking peoples or whatever, but one must admit that one is unable to provide him with any reasons to refrain from ϕ-ing. And not because the agent fails to recognize good reasons when provided with them, or because he is ignorant about some relevant matter, but just because there are no good reasons for him not to ϕ.

Because, then, one must acknowledge the blameless liberty of others to act on their values without constraint, one's range of rational critical responses is greatly circumscribed. To be sure, as in Hobbes's state of nature, one can still engage in self-defense (including threats and preemptive strikes); one might even enter into alliances with others. But, if an ally defects to another camp, or itself preemptively strikes at you, your range of critical responses is limited to your own dislike and disgust, coupled with reprisals, deterrence, or counteralliances. But I do not want to suggest that mere valuer-agents must wage a war of all against all. Other valuer-agents might not only cooperate with you as an efficient way to promote their values, but they may directly value your welfare or the advancement of your values. So instead of a war of all against all, in which no one can complain if he is bested, one might enter into affectionate, benevolent relations. It is tempting to suppose that benevolence can be substituted for morality and blame-related practices: if one is loved, one can complain to the other if he or she fails to take account of your welfare. But benevolence is not a substitute for justice. Even if the other did love you, but somehow ignored you welfare, you have no special grounds for complaint.[62] Assuming that the ignoring was indeed irrational (which it need not be; see §17.3.3), you have no grounds for criticizing him that are not open equally to anyone. He is making a mistake and so is acting in a way that fails to best promote what *he* values, but this is the sort of practical error that anyone can point out to him. It is just like a mistake he might make in buying an inferior car or a forged masterpiece. He is not wronging you or denying you anything that is your due. In a fundamental sense, your position is that of a slave who has been ignored by his master. A slave may point out to his master how much he loves him, indeed how wonderful a slave he is but, nevertheless, the master owes him nothing and the slave has no basis for complaint.

In undermining the notions of wronging and blaming, the regime of pure liberty is too impoverished to sustain the rational use of a number of related concepts and practices. Punishment, for instance, is rendered impossible. "To punish is to hold responsible and to blame."[63] Of course one can still coerce others in order to shape their behavior and to promote some valued end, but this sort of "telishment"[64] does not rationally ground the concepts (and related practices) centered on guilt, exoneration, contrition, excuses, and justification, all of which are an essential part of our understanding of what punishment is about. This is so even if, as in Hobbes's state of nature, rules exist that are intended to guide behavior for the common benefit of all. For, al-

62 See J. R. Lucas, *On Justice*, pp. 3–4.
63 Ibid., p. 137.
64 This, of course, is John Rawls's term. "Two Concepts of Rules," p. 180.

though a person could certainly violate such rules, and even be penalized for doing so,[65] it would have to be accepted that the violator was blameless. He did no wrong to anyone; and no one has any grounds for complaint. Any rational agent in the shoes of the violator would have done the same (except, of course, if the violator miscalculated and the violation was indeed irrational).

In many ways, conceiving of others as mere valuer-agents implies that we must treat them in ways appropriate to mere objects. This becomes manifest when we observe that anger, but not indignation or resentment, would be an appropriate response to rule violations. According to the analyses of such philosophers as S. I. Benn, Thomas Nagel, David A. J. Richards, J. R. Lucas, Charles Fried, and John Rawls, indignation and resentment are not soundly grounded given this view of others.[66] Nagel, for example, writes of the egoist (though what he says applies to the view of others as mere valuer-agents in general), that he is disabled from regarding his "own concerns of being of interest to anyone else, except instrumentally or contingently upon the operation of some sentiment." Consequently, the egoist has no grounds for thinking that others necessarily have reason not to harm him, to refrain from injuring him, or whatever. "He is precluded from feeling resentment, which embodies the judgment that another is failing to act on reasons with which one's own needs provide him."[67] Richards extends this analysis. Resentment, he says, is an appropriate response if one believes that others have transgressed moral principles "in reference to oneself," and indignation is appropriate when third parties are wronged by such violation. In contrast to both, anger requires no belief that someone has been wronged, but only "some belief of frustration from another and the desire to strike back."[68]

Our analysis of emotions provides a rationale for this. We saw that emotions presuppose beliefs and contents; in order to be in

65 On the distinction between penalties and punishments, see John Kleinig, *Punishment and Desert*, pp. 23–34.

66 See Benn, "Freedom, Autonomy, and the Concept of a Person," pp. 120–1; Nagel, *The Possibility of Altruism*, pp. 84–5; Richards, *Reasons for Action*, pp. 250ff.; Lucas, *Justice*, p. 7; Charles Fried, *An Anatomy of Values*, pp. 56–7, ch. V; Rawls, *A Theory of Justice*, secs. 73, 74. See also P. F. Strawson, *Freedom and Resentment and Other Essays*, ch. 1.

67 Nagel, *The Possibility of Altruism*, p. 85.

68 Richards, *Reasons for Action*, p. 253.

a rationally nondefective emotional state *E*, one's state must not only be characterized by the relevant affect, it must also have an *E*-appropriate content, the state must be grounded in *E*-appropriate beliefs, and these beliefs must be sound (§6.1). Someone viewing others as mere valuer-agents cannot meet these conditions for resentment and indignation. Because the notions of blameworthiness, wrongdoing, wrongful harm, and violation of rights are unavailable, he is without the necessary grounding beliefs and appropriate content. So if he or his family is harmed (see §26.4) by another, he cannot rationally be indignant. Again, it is entirely on par with a piece of bad luck for him, like getting a flat tire on the way to work or getting hit by a falling tree when walking through the forest. Like the tire or the tree, the other cannot be said to have known better: the other had no reason, and was not rationally defective for not having such a reason, for refraining from the harm.

Of course, all these things might make him angry: one's emotional reaction to harm by others is thus reduced to a reaction appropriate to annoying or frustrating things. Some philosophers, however, have suggested that anger, along with effective deterrent/retaliatory action would be enough. It would certainly be enough to maintain one's negative valuation of harms; this is very much the sort of fall-back position that I had in mind in §10.4. And, so, it would be enough to ground reasons for action aimed at preventing the action or, perhaps but more dubiously, revenge.[69] But emotion terms, as we have seen, are not names for internal sensations (§3.1); it is surely not simply a matter of substituting the label "anger" for "resentment," leaving all else as it was before. Resentment and indignation are emotional states with certain sorts of contents based on certain sorts of beliefs, and this at least sets them apart from mere anger. Lucas explains the distinction thus:

> We are angry when we are hurt, but indignant when treated unjustly. We can be angry with enemies or rivals, but scarcely indignant. Indignation, which is the conceptually appropriate response to injustice, expresses, as its etymology shows, a sense of not being regarded as wor-

69 Revenge may be rational given certain sorts of anger, but I do not wish to pursue this controversial issue.

thy of consideration. Injustice betokens an absence of respect, and manifests a lack of concern.[70]

Resentment and indignation presuppose that one is located within a system of rights and duties which determine what is owed to you and to others. To demand that others respect you is to insist that they give you your due, and you can reasonably be resentful if they do not. It is not simply frustrating when someone ignores your rights: it is an affront. Replacing the emotions of resentment and indignation with simple anger is thus not calling the same thing by a different name. It is, rather, to acknowledge that one has no rational warrant to see the actions and interferences of others in this light. One would have to come to conceive of oneself as inhabiting a world in which people confront each other much as animals do: sometimes affectionate, sometimes hostile, sometimes indifferent, but never as rights-bearers owing each other respect. And, as I have been stressing, such an impoverished view would radically undermine our existing value systems.

To conclude: I have argued that denial that one has rights which provide rational others with reasons to act would so impoverish one's conception of others and social life that it is difficult to envisage anyone actually making the denial. Or, more accurately, if one now possesses the concept of others owing you certain respect, it is hard to see how one could have good grounds for purging yourself of it (see §§18.1, 18.4). This is not, however, the same as Alan Gewirth's argument that valuer-agents are necessarily inconsistent if they do not claim rights.[71] Pace Gewirth, it is not rationally incumbent upon all agents to claim rights; given a sufficiently impoverished outlook, one might entirely consistently embrace a regime of pure liberty. Hence, rational agents need not be moral persons.[72] Indeed, we will see in §17.4 that such agents may well exist. It is not, then, simply by virtue of one's status as a valuer and an agent, but by virtue of a value system deeply informed by notions of right, that most of us are committed to seeing ourselves as rights-holders and others as agents who can rationally act to respect these rights.

70 Lucas, *Justice*, p. 7. He puts the point rather too strongly. One can be indignant at an enemy if he acts beyond the pale.

71 See Gewirth, *Reason and Morality*, chs. II, III.

72 See R. M. Hare's criticism of Gewirth, "Do Agents Have to Be Moralists?"

17.3.3 The poverty of pure liberty: friendship

Rawls tells us, and we have seen, that resentment and indignation "invoke the concept of right."[73] As Fried has observed, this is "all rather juridical and cold."[74] But, he says, a similar analysis applies to love, friendship, and trust.

One who restricted himself to conceiving of others simply as valuers with only agent-relative value reasons to act could, as I have said, certainly come to take a liking to others and work to advance their good. Moreover, because such a person is not egocentric, he would not simply be imposing his values on others; he can genuinely grasp that their value systems might rationally differ from his own. But this sort of benevolence toward others, even if reciprocated, does not make for friendship. Friends, for example, must be able to count on each other and trust each other not to reveal confidences. Kant saw this clearly. What he called "moral friendship"[75] is the "confidence of two persons in revealing their secret thoughts and feelings to each other." But this sort of confidence is difficult for a person to come by; "hemmed in and cautioned by fear of the misuse others may make of this disclosure of his thoughts, he finds himself constrained to *lock up* in himself a good part of his opinions." However:

> If he finds someone understanding – someone who, moreover, shares his general outlook on things – with whom he need not be anxious about this danger but can reveal himself with complete confidence, he can air his views. He is not completely alone with his thoughts, as in a prison, but enjoys a freedom denied to him with the rank and file, with whom he must shut himself up in himself.

Kant goes on to point to the importance of being able to *trust* a friend, who is "bound not to share the secrets entrusted to him with anyone else, no matter how reliable he thinks him, without explicit permission to do so."

Keeping secrets, however, is only one aspect of the trust upon which friendship relies. A friend must be confident that the other will take his point of view into account, will treat him with due consideration and respect, and will resist any temptation to use

73 Rawls, *A Theory of Justice*, p. 484.
74 Fried, *Anatomy of Values*, p. 77.
75 Immanuel Kant, *The Doctrine of Virtue*, pp. 143–5. All references to Kant in this paragraph of my text are from these pages, which comprise sec. 47. Kant holds that perfect moral friendship is rare.

or exploit the friendship to promote other ends, no matter how dear. But, if the would-be friend is solely devoted to the promotion of his own values this confidence is undermined. Unlike lovers who may be able to suppose that the other values nothing as much as the beloved, and so no other valuings could ever be more weighty in deliberation than the welfare of the beloved, friendship does not rest on such an intensity.[76] Friends know perfectly well that they each have various aims and projects, some of which may matter more to them than the friendship itself. Yet they can trust each other not to use the friendship simply as a means to further these ends because they trust that the other will act fairly and in ways that seem reasonable to both. Those who are willing to sacrifice others to the pursuit of cherished projects are apt to find enduring friendship impossible. Such fanatics may, I suppose, have lovers of a sort, and they may certainly have allies, but they are not capable of genuine friendship.

This essentially Kantian understanding of (moral) friendship is, as Kant himself pointed out, to be distinguished from emotional friendship, a sweet feeling of "mutual possession that approximates to a fusion into one person."[77] In his *Friendship, Altruism, and Morality*, Lawrence Blum (see §16.1) has defended an essentially emotional conception of friendship. Although he allows the possibility of duties to friends,[78] his emphasis is on emotional attachment and identification. "In genuine friendship," he tells us, "one comes to have a close identification with the good of the other person."[79] And again: "We can say, in summary, that the moral excellence of friendship involves a high level of development and expression of the altruistic emotions of sympathy, concern, and care – a deep caring for and identification with the good of another from whom one knows oneself clearly to be other."[80]

I certainly do not wish to deny that friendship is rooted in emotion. One values the friend and cares for his good, and these are rooted in affects. Indeed, in one respect I wish to go further

76 Fried depicts friendship as a less intense and less significant sort of love. *Anatomy of Values*, p. 80.
77 Kant, *Doctrine of Virtue*, pp. 142–3 (secs. 46, 47).
78 Blum, *Friendship, Altruism, and Morality*, p. 58.
79 Ibid., p. 69.
80 Ibid., p. 70.

than Blum. Whereas he resists the suggestion that friendship is in any way based on extension of the self to include the good of the friend,[81] I see no reason to preclude what the quote from Kant in the previous paragraph suggests: that friendship leads to some extension of the self to, in a way, include the friend as part of you.[82] If, as I have argued (§14.2.3) personality is constituted by one's valuings, one's emotional attachments to others is indeed an extension of one's personality. This is not a particularly odd view; it is essentially the analysis of altruism and attachment advocated by psychoanalysis and related theories.[83] To be sure, this extension of the self becomes objectionable if it takes the forms of solipsism or egocentrism. But it need not; one can see one's self as inherently bound up with the promotion of another's welfare without losing sight of the fact that each is a center of valuing and an agent with differing reasons for action.[84] Neither does this necessarily lead to the variety of egoism that so worries Blum.[85] He is concerned that, if we see friendship as a sort of expansion of the self, acting in the interests of the friend will be simply a variety of self-interested action. (See my comments on self-realization theory in §14.3.) We need to keep clearly in mind two distinct, if ultimately related, notions of interests: (i) the things, resources, opportunities, etc. that benefit a person; and (ii) the concerns, values, commitments of a person. To employ Joel Feinberg's terminology, we can call the former "welfare interests" and the latter "ulterior interests."[86] Someone wholly devoted to his own welfare interests – what will benefit him – is perhaps selfish; more clearly, if all his ulterior interests (that is, values) concern his own sensual gratification and enjoyment, he is certainly selfish. But simply to pursue one's ulterior interests or values is not necessarily egoistic or selfish at all; indeed, as we have already seen, such pursuit could call for self-sacrifice (§14.3). That one is pursuing one of the things in which the self is interested is not to say one is being egoistic. One who pursues an (ulterior) interest

81 Ibid., p. 75.
82 I have argued that radical and unqualified separateness of persons is not a feature of modern liberalism in my *Modern Liberal Theory of Man*, p. 71.
83 See Wright, *The Psychology of Moral Behaviour*, p. 131.
84 See my discussion of Pritchard's criticism of T. H. Green's account of self-realization in *Modern Liberal Theory*, pp. 61–4.
85 Blum, *Friendship, Altruism, and Morality*, p. 75.
86 Feinberg, *Harm to Others*, pp. 38–45, 55–61.

in the good of a friend is not, then, being self-interested or selfish.

However, and here I fundamentally disagree with Blum, personal ties based simply on such emotional identification do not make for friendship. Or, rather, the friendships that would result would be characterized by jealousy, insecurity, and betrayal. If Alf can rely on Betty only because of the intensity to which she is committed to his good – her high valuation of him – all other people, in fact all other possible (ulterior) interests of Betty's, are Alf's competitors. And he is right to view them as competitors, for if she comes to love another more than him, he knows that she would be rational to sacrifice his good to the promotion of the other's. That is, she will forgo the opportunity to promote his welfare in order to promote the welfare of the other (§§11.1, 14.1). But more than that, even if Alf is valued more than any single other thing, if ψ is the act of promoting his welfare and ϕ is an alternative act that promotes most of her other values,[87] she may well still rationally be committed to ϕ-ing (§16.1). It is partly because of this that those in intense emotional relations are so subject to jealousy; they are not necessarily being irrational, but may well rightly perceive the advent of new valuings by the beloved as a real threat. If you are not first in the heart of the beloved, you can no longer rely on him or her to resist sacrificing your good for some greater good.

If friendships are exclusively, or I think even primarily, emotional, they will not only be intimate, but will also be prone to jealousy and instability. And indeed some are. But these are not, I think, the norm. Rather, we are friends with many with whom we are in various degrees intimate; new friends sometimes, but by no means typically (and not at all like lovers), displace the old; and not being first in the heart of the friend is no threat. All this is possible because friendship is informed – so deeply informed that it can easily be overlooked – by notions of respect, decency, and fairness. A friend would not sacrifice you to promote his interests (even if he is an assistant professor and the interest is tenure) because he recognizes what is due to you. This is not to say that he is consciously acting out of some conception of duty. As

87 The two-component theory of attitudes should be kept in mind here. See §8.2.

Kant stressed, friendship is an intimate union of love and respect,[88] and one's perceptions and actions are shaped by both. But if, as one who views others as mere valuer-agents must, one purges any notion that others can rationally act toward one out of respect, one will find oneself confronted by an alien conception of what it means to have a friend.

Thus far, I have allowed that love may simply be emotional, and so open (in a recognizable form) to a person who has only minimally decentered and who thus conceives of others as no more than valuers single-mindedly devoted to advancing their own values. The restricted nature of this love should now be evident. Passionate, romantic love is, I think, consistent with minimal decentering, as probably is the love of parents for their small children. But a mature love that persists in the face of changing valuings, commitments, and aging itself seems, like friendship, beyond his or her reach. For it relies on a trust in the other that is not threatened, or at least not easily, by changing interests and periods of intense commitment to various projects. Such love is informed by a deep sense of justice and rights, and it is this that provides the basis for enduring trust.[89] Unless, then, we have in mind the most passionate sort of love, it seems quite wrong to say that love is founded on an abandonment or renunciation of rights, and so is outside the sphere of justice.[90] It is no doubt true that loving relations are in serious trouble when disagreements about justice and rights arise within them. But this is by no means inconsistent with the importance of justice to the relation: if you become convinced that the beloved does not respect you, sympathy and love are apt to be undermined. By the time things get bad enough to complain that you are not being respected, the love is endangered. As John Kleinig observes, "[w]here people do love and care for each other, there is no need for recourse to

88 Kant, *The Doctrine of Virtue*, p. 140 (sec. 46).

89 It thus seems to me that justice and right action are much closer to the heart of trust than Annette Baier would have us believe. Despite his lack of a domestic life with the normal complications, Kant seems to have reached the crux of the matter. Cf. Baier, "Trust and Anti-Trust."

90 Martin P. Golding makes this claim concerning friendship and love. See his "Community and Rights." I criticize Golding's thesis in "On Community and Justice: A Reply to Professor Golding."

rights-talk, since what is due to the other will be encompassed within the loving or caring relationship."[91]

17.4 *Psychopathy*

I have tried to stress how thorough would be the transformation of a person's understanding of his relations to others if he came to see others as mere valuer-agents with an unlimited "blameless liberty" to do what best promotes their sound valuings. And, because so many of the things one values (including those values informing one's long-term projects, choice of occupation, and so forth) presuppose a conception of other persons and the type of social relations into which they enter, large parts of one's current value system would be rendered rationally unsound. I have focused on resentment, indignation, friendship, and love, but I hope it is clear that the ramifications of this change would go far beyond these. We would, for example, not only have to revise our conceptions of community and cooperative ventures, but even our notions of competition, rivalry, and conflict would be transformed, for nothing would be unjust. It is, indeed, difficult to underestimate the consequences of this change, but it is also difficult to imagine what such an outlook would really be like. It will, perhaps, help to bring home just how revolutionary would be the effects on our value systems to consider a real-life approximation to a conception of others as simply valuers and agents.

An obvious candidate is the Nazi. But I very much doubt whether the Nazis achieved anything like a thoroughgoing conception of the Jews as mere valuer-agents. Although they certainly denied the moral personality of the Jews in a multitude of horrendous ways, it seems very doubtful indeed that this was rational given the nature of their value systems. It seems manifest that the Nazis by no means purged their value systems of the assumption that Jews were moral persons, for they did not cease blaming them for their acts nor being indignant toward them. That is, although the Nazis typically acted in disregard of their conception of Jews as moral persons – persons able to take up and act upon the moral point of view – their view of things presupposed that the Jews were such persons. Bruno Bettelheim's own

91 John Kleinig, "Human Rights, Legal Rights, and Social Change," p. 46. See also Benn "Freedom, Autonomy, and the Concept of a Person," p. 120.

observations – as a prisoner in Dachau and Buchenwald – confirm this. Typical SS guards, for example, those who were not outright sadists, held a variety of beliefs about the evilness of the Jews, their own status as the Jews' victims, their wronging by the Jews, and the wrongness of their mistreatment of the Jews.[92] All these assume that Jews were not simply valuer-agents with a blameless liberty to act but moral agents who could be held accountable for their actions. Furthermore, even if the occasional Nazi did manage to so transform his value system as to remove any such assumption, this was only accomplished by appeal to a variety of unsound theories and false empirical claims that sought to provide a rationale for treating some people, but not others, as mere valuers. A rational value system based on the assumption that others are no more than valuer-agents cannot be grounded on such irrational theories.

A much better approximation to someone who rationally conceives of social life in these terms is the psychopath.[93] Although some psychiatrists have tried to reject the concept of psychopathy, it not only is generally recognized as necessary in clinical settings, but also recent empirical investigations confirm an identifiable cluster or constellation of traits that closely relate to the concept of psychopathy.[94] Psychopaths, who are often presented as a model of the amoralist, have been shown to possess a number of the characteristics I have been arguing follow from conceiving of others and oneself as mere valuer-agents. They seem, for instance, solely motivated by their own satisfactions and aims; the psychopath does not see the needs, aims, or values of others as themselves providing him with any reason to act.[95] Conse-

92 Bruno Bettelheim, *The Informed Heart*, chs. 4, 5, esp. pp. 225–31.

93 I am indebted to Stanley Benn for this point. See his "Freedom, Autonomy, and the Concept of a Person," p. 121, and his paper on "Wickedness," pp. 798–800.

94 See Robert D. Hare and David N. Cox, "Clinical and Empirical Conceptions of Psychopathy, and the Selection of Subjects for Research"; Daisey Schalling, "Psychopathy-related Personality Variables and the Psychophysiology of Socialization."

95 "Hobbes said: 'The wicked man is but the child grown strong.' The psychopath is like an infant, absorbed in his own needs, vehemently demanding satisfaction. The average child, by the age of two, compromises with the restrictions of his environment. He learns to postpone his pleasure and to consider his mother's needs as well as his own. The psychopath never learns this lesson; he does not modify his desires, and he ignores the needs of others." William McCord and Joan McCord, *Psychopathy and Delinquency*, p. 7. See also F. Kraupl Taylor, *Psychopathology*, pp. 173ff.

quently, psychopaths are unable to form lasting friendships, though they often charm people for short periods:

> Psychopaths sometimes behave with charm and spontaneity. They are thus able to manipulate other people to their own ends – but their relations with others are always a means to an end and never as ends in themselves. . . . They cannot form relationships of friendship, love or permanent attachment with other people. They are not concerned about the welfare or sufferings of others.[96]

Although the paradigmatic psychopath is indeed the sort of predatory and aggressive creature that populates Hobbes's state of nature, what has been called the "passive-parasitic type" achieves its aims by playing off the affection and sympathy of others.[97] (It is worth pointing out that these two types of psychopathy, the predatory and the parasitic, are very close to the two strategies I sketched in §17.3.2.) It would even appear that psychopaths can exhibit an easygoing sweet feeling for others, but, if something more interesting turns up, the object of this liking will be quickly forgotten.[98]

Psychopaths certainly can react angrily to others.[99] In fact, they have little tolerance for frustration.[100] It is, however, less clear whether they are resentful or indignant. Certainly these terms are employed to describe their reactions,[101] but at least some clinical evidence suggests that the "indignation" vanishes "at once and marvelously" as soon as it is perceived that it will not advance the psychopath's aims.[102] Although, when caught doing wrong, the psychopath will often protest of injustice – or, alternatively, promise to reform himself – his use of such discourse appears es-

96 Michael Argyle, *The Psychology of Interpersonal Behavior*, p. 219. See also Robert D. Hare, *Psychopathy: Theory and Research*, pp. 1–4.
97 See Hare, *Psychopathy*, p. 6.
98 See Hervey Cleckley, *The Mask of Sanity*, p. 70. Consider the following testimony of a psychopath: "I met a guy in a bar and he said that he wanted to pull some jobs in Florida; would I go along? I said 'O.K.,' but I forgot to tell my wife. She didn't know where I was but she took me back when I came home. It wasn't that I didn't like her – we get along O.K. I just had better things to do." McCord and McCord, *Psychopathy and Delinquency*, p. 16.
99 See, e.g., Cleckley, *The Mask of Sanity*, ch. 5.
100 Hare and Cox, "Clinical and Empirical Conceptions of Psychopathy," p. 12.
101 See ibid., p. 6; Schalling, "Psychopathy-related Personality Variables," pp. 97–9.
102 See, e.g., Cleckley, *The Mask of Sanity*, pp. 52, 67.

sentially manipulative.[103] On some views, the psychopath's genuine "emotional reactions are simple and animal-like, occurring only with immediate frustrations and discomfort."[104] What is fairly certain is that the psychopath does not see himself as having moral reasons to act. "If others get in the way it is their misfortune if they get hurt, and the psychopath feels no guilt or remorse."[105]

Psychopaths are philosophically interesting because, not being crazy or neurotic,[106] they at least approximate a rational amoralist. They really do seem to view others – and themselves – as no more than valuers seeking to advance their ends. Nevertheless, psychopaths are characterized by certain defects; someone upholding the viability of the conception of others as valuer-agents may thus be tempted to insist that it is these defects, and not the valuer-agent view itself, that is at the heart of the psychopathic personality. For one thing, it is widely held that psychopaths cannot take account of long-term considerations, acting primarily for immediate gratification. Psychopaths have thus been described as short-ranged hedonists.[107] It could well be maintained that it is this rational defect that is at the root of their ruthless and alien amoralism; as Hobbes would say, they suffer from "false reasoning," failing to see "those duties they are necessarily to perform towards others in order to their own conservation."[108] If the psychopath could act on his own long-term self-interest, we might conjecture, he would gain the benefits of cooperative behavior: if fully rational, he would act in accordance with moral rules. How-

103 Hare, *Psychopathy*, pp. 1–4.
104 See ibid., p. 6.
105 Wright, *The Psychology of Moral Behaviour*, p. 92. But cf. Marks's study reported in Hare, *Psychopathy*, pp. 18-19.
106 According to one research definition, psychopaths are characterized by five exclusions; that is, they are *not* characterized by "(i) mental retardation, (ii) organic brain syndromes or obvious brain damage, (iii) psychosis, (iv) neurosis, and (v) situational maladjustment. This definition conforms to the requirements of the International Classification of Diseases (ICD-8) and the classification of the American Psychiatric Association DSM-2." Eugene Ziskind, "The Diagnosis of Sociopathy," p. 49. Although his views on the responsibility of psychopaths differ from mine, Vinit Haksar also seeks to show that psychopaths are not insane in "The Responsibility of Psychopaths."
107 See Cathy Spatz Widom, "A Methodology for Studying Non-Institutionalized Psychopaths," pp. 73–4.
108 See Hobbes, *The Citizen*, p. 123n (ch. II, sec. 1). See also Hobbes, *On Man* in *Man and Citizen*, p. 48 (ch. XI, sec. 5).

ever, not all psychopaths act solely on short-ranged considerations. Some psychiatrists have employed the concept of a "complex psychopath," who is intelligent and able to effectively plan and execute plans in order to get what he wants.

> Whereas the simple psychopath can be seen as following a style of life based on the philosophy of Epicurus, or more correctly, on the philosophy attributed to Epicurus, the complex psychopath follows a style of life consonant with some tenets of Nietzsche and some teachings of Machiavelli. Historical figures like Nero, Cesare Borgia, Stalin and to a lesser degree Mussolini, were probably complex psychopaths.[109]

Moreover, a recent study of psychopaths who were not institutionalized failed to find any significant tendency to opt for immediate over delayed gratification.[110] Because most studies of psychopaths have been conducted on inmates of penal or mental institutions – that is, in some sense on unsuccessful psychopaths – the inability of psychopaths to plan may have been overestimated. It could well be that psychopaths able to act on long-term considerations only get caught less, not that they are any more cooperative.

More fundamental to psychopathy is the affective or emotional flatness that is always mentioned in any description of the psychopath.[111] The psychopath's emotional responses are very limited; he is particularly unloving,[112] unempathetic,[113] and seems to have difficulty experiencing anxiety or fear unless the danger is immediate.[114] Consequently, psychopaths have been described as affectively hollow.[115] It cannot be denied that this affective flatness gives the psychopath an alien quality, and it is surely at the root of his inability to form friendships. From the conceptual perspective, the psychopath's affective flatness makes him a flawed example of someone viewing others as no more than valuer-

---

109 See Silvano Arieti, *The Intrapsychic Self*, p. 257. See also Hare, *Psychopathy*, p. 7; Cleckley, *The Mask of Sanity*, chs. 18–24.
110 Widom, "Non-Institutionalized Psychopaths," p. 81.
111 Taylor describes psychopathy as "emotional psychopathy" – "a psychopathology of affect." *Psychopathology*, ch. 15.
112 This is emphasized by McCord and McCord, *Psychopathy and Delinquency*, pp. 13–14.
113 Widom, "Non-Institutionalized Psychopaths," pp. 79–80.
114 Hare, *Psychopathy*, pp. 5–7, 16–17. For analyses distinguishing types of anxiety in relation to psychopathy, see Charles D. Spielberger et al., "Dimensions of Psychopathic Personality: Antisocial Behavior and Anxiety"; Schalling, "Psychopathy-related Personality Variables," pp. 87ff.
115 Cleckley, *The Mask of Sanity*, p. 115.

agents. If you want to know how different you would be if you came to embrace this view of others, one thing you may want is a portrait of someone who is as much like you as possible, with only those things omitted that are rationally inconsistent with the view. And, because affective flatness is not conceptually required, you would have reason to reject the psychopath as a model. However, the psychopath is a more important model than this would indicate, because from a psychological perspective his defects may well be at the root of his impoverished conception of others. That is, if we wish to grasp not just what is rationally consistent with this view of others, but what sort of psychology gives rise to seeing others in this way, I think we can see that the psychopath is indeed a good model. Let me explain.

Hervey Cleckley, in his classic work on psychopathy, hypothesized that psychopaths suffer from "semantic dementia."[116] In his studies of psychopaths, Cleckley was most impressed by their ability to employ value and emotional language, at least in a superficially convincing way, without grasping just what it is all about. Of one case, for instance, he writes:

> He is unfamiliar with the primary facts or data of what might be called personal values and is altogether incapable of understanding such matters. It is impossible for him to take even a slight interest in the tragedy or joy of the striving of humanity as presented in serious literature or art. He is also indifferent to all these matters in life itself. Beauty and ugliness, except in a very superficial sense, goodness, evil, love, horror, and humor, have no actual meaning, no power to move him.[117]

This accords well with the Affective-Cognitive Theory. The psychopath, we can say, often possesses sound beliefs as to what grounds a judgment that something is disgusting, exciting, benevolent, or horrible, but the intentional affective states to which these judgments refer are quite beyond him (§10.1). His life can thus be understood on the model of a person with no sense of humor, who knows how to tell a joke in order to impress other guests at a party. In this sense, Cleckley seems quite right that the psychopath fails to grasp the point of value and emotional language.

---

116 Ibid., p. 406. See Hare, *Psychopathy*, pp. 5–6; Spielberger et al., "Dimensions of Psychopathic Personality," p. 30. For a brief critical appraisal of this general approach from a philosophic viewpoint, see Ronald D. Milo, *Immorality*, p. 62.

117 Cleckley, *The Mask of Sanity*, p. 59.

Now, as Cleckley goes on to notice, being incapable of grasping value – not just this or that value, but across almost the entire range of value – the psychopath cannot understand the place of value in the life of others.[118] He has great difficulty appreciating that there is more to value-based practices than he himself can grasp. "He can repeat the words and say glibly that he understands, and there is no way for him to realize that he does not understand."[119] He thus develops a machinelike conception of others, reflecting his own machinelike existence; because the psychopath has little in the way of driving purposes and grossly impoverished reactions, he naturally sees others in much the same light.

The point can be put somewhat differently. It seems relatively certain that psychopaths have great difficulty entering into the perspectives of others.[120] This has led some psychologists to describe them as being egocentric,[121] for as we have seen, in Piaget's thinking egocentrism is the state prior to decentering (§§12.2, 17.2). But this may be too hasty a conclusion. Typically, Piaget and Kohlberg are said to stress the way in which taking up the perspective of others is a distinctively cognitive achievement,[122] and, though it is certainly difficult to deny that they see decentering as cognitive, it is far less obvious that in their view it is thoroughly so. Some psychologists have introduced the notion of *affective perspective taking* – the ability to identify another's affective state. In comparison to cognitive perspective taking, this af-

---

118 Ibid.

119 Ibid. This, I think, is rather too strong. See §4.2.1.

120 Psychopaths' inability to role-play is well documented. See Hare, *Psychopathy*, pp. 7, 101–3. The relation between role-playing and empathy is explored in Schalling, "Psychopathy-related Personality Variables," pp. 97ff. See also §16.1 in this volume.

121 Wright, *The Psychology of Moral Behaviour*, p. 92.

122 See Kurdek, "Perspective Taking," p. 12. I suspect that this makes too little of the intimate link in Piaget's psychology between affective and cognitive development. If so, what I say in the text is not a radical departure from Piaget or, I think, Kohlberg. Cf., e.g., Kohlberg's remark that "Progressive educators stress the essential links between cognitive and moral development; they assume that moral development *is not purely affective* and that cognitive development is a necessary although not a sufficient condition for moral development." "Development As the Aim of Education," p. 54 (emphasis added). For a broad view of Piaget's social psychology that brings out the relations among affect, value, rationality, and taking account of differences in perspective, see Richard F. Kitchener, "Piaget's Social Psychology."

fective decentering has not been much examined,[123] but it seems reasonable to conjecture that it would be largely beyond psychopaths. We might expect, given Cleckley's semantic dementia thesis, that, because a psychopath can grasp that others are moved by different aims than is he, but is unable to grasp what it is like to entertain such values, he would not really be able to enter into their perspectives: his affective flatness limits his ability to decenter. This general account is consistent with the observation that a psychopath behaves like a salesman in all his social encounters.[124] A successful salesman must not be radically egocentric because he must not assume that his own values are the ones that move everyone. Rather, he needs to grasp that others' ends may be very different from his own, and he must pitch his appeal to their ends – what the customer longs for. This sort of decentering the psychopath can achieve, at least to some considerable degree, for he can indeed manipulate others.[125] But he cannot go beyond this to grasp what it really is to be the others. We might say that he correctly sees others as pursuing different ends than does he, but he cannot see what all the excitement is about; he sees others more akin to machines – each of which, to be sure, responds in different ways – than feeling agents.

All this is, of course, speculative, but not, I would venture, wildly so. It points to sound reasons to think that the psychopath's emotional flatness is at the root of his conception of others as machinelike competitors to whom he owes nothing. He, indeed, is apparently surprised when they are resentful of his incursions; on his model of humans, his actions are entirely reasonable.[126] So his failure to see others as more than mere valuer-agents may well be systematically related to his affective flatness and resulting "semantic dementia." Perhaps only some such affective failing is psychologically coherent with viewing others in this manner. It needs to be stressed that I am not backtracking

123 See Kurdek, "Perspective Taking."
124 Argyle, *The Psychology of Interpersonal Behavior*, p. 219.
125 It strikes me as implausible to argue that, just because the psychopathic *is* egocentric, he *can* manipulate others, e.g., "being unable to place himself in another person's position, the psychopath is able to manipulate others as he would any other object." Hare, *Psychopathy*, p. 7. Manipulating people requires insight into the fact that their motives and values differ from yours, and that goes beyond radical egocentricity.
126 Schalling, "Psychopathy-related Personality Variables," p. 97.

on my claim that affective deficiencies are not themselves rational flaws (§§6.3, 10.4, 11.2, 17.2). That the psychopath is affectively impoverished and, so, values very little is not necessarily a rational defect. My concern here, rather, is to suggest that, leaving aside all that one is rationally committed to giving up by seeing others as mere valuer-agents who owe one nothing, taking up this view may be psychologically impossible for very nearly all of us. Our best real-life model of one upholding such a conception of others, the psychopath, seems led to this view, and we might conjecture, sustains it, by an impoverished[127] valuational perspective we (nonpsychopaths) do not, and likely cannot, share.

17.5 Moral personality, habit, and reason

The conception of others as mere valuer-agents, I conclude, is both rationally and psychologically tied to grossly impoverished value systems. Unless one is already very much like a psychopath, one's valuings – or, we might say, one's way of life – is informed by a richer conception of others. We presuppose that others are not merely valuers pursuing their own aims, but moral persons. To conceive of them as moral persons is to suppose that they can transcend their own valuational perspectives to act morally. That is, our understanding of other humans and of social life is shaped by the conviction that others are capable of following a principle, a law, a *nomos*. We can feel indignation and resentment toward moral persons, trust them, and can be their friends because they are more than valuers single-mindedly devoted to their own perspectives. They can follow a *nomos*, taking up and acting on the moral point of view, even when this conflicts with what best promotes their valuings. Our underlying conception of moral personality is in this way deeply Kantian: we assume that others can act from duty and follow a law even if it thwarts their inclinations. A moral person – what Kant called the rational will – can be determined by duty.[128]

Perhaps, however, all this can be explained without abandoning the orthodox view, and certainly without accepting a Kantian

127 It is "impoverished" from our perspective: so much of what is valued *by us* is irrational from this perspective that we cannot help but see it as valuationally impoverished.
128 Kant, *Foundations of the Metaphysics of Morals*, pp. 29–31 (2d sec.).

conception of moral action. Recall my distinction between a coordination problem and the compliance problem (§16.1). A coordination problem, I claimed, was based on the assumption that a fully rational agent will always act so as to best promote his values: the problem then is to see under what circumstances coordinated action is rational. In contrast, the compliance problem assumes that, all things considered, an individual's moral action does not always best promote his values, and then asks how he could nevertheless have reason so to act. Now individual instances of the compliance problem might be seen in a broader framework as part of a coordination problem. Let us assume that, based purely on advancing our own agent-relative valuings, each person has reason not only publicly to embrace moral rules, but also agrees to take certain measures that would cause him to be psychologically disposed to follow the rules. Such a measure, for example, might help to create general confidence that the rules would be followed, and this would increase security, allow us to plan and rely on others, etc. But, an argument could run, it would also be a consequence of developing such a disposition that one will tend to comply with the rules even when the act of compliance does not best promote one's values. Indeed, that is the essential point of inculcating the disposition to comply. It might then be further claimed:

> (G1) If there is some motive that would be both (a) rational for someone to cause himself to have, and (b) irrational for him to cause himself to lose, then (c) it cannot be irrational for this person to act upon this motive.[129]

If so, then one solely devoted to pursuing his own values may nevertheless rationally act in particular instances in the ways that do not promote his values.

This argument depends on (i) principle G1 and (ii) a certain theory of rational dispositions or habits. Derek Parfit examines G1, and rejects it as unsound. However, let us grant G1; there is still reason to reject the proposal because it is based on a faulty theory of dispositions or habits. I argued in §7.2.3 that one acting rationally out of habit must be alert to cues that signify the inappropriateness of the habit in out-of-the-ordinary cases. Habits

129 Parfit analyzes this principle; I use his designation, G1. *Reasons and Persons*, p. 13.

and dispositions, to be sure, are useful insofar as they allow us to avoid information and decision-making costs, but it does not follow that these savings require that, as it were, we behave unintelligently. We can develop a disposition to ϕ, whether it be turning at a crossroad, tying our shoes in a certain way, or acting cooperatively, while still monitoring the environment for cues that the normal program is inappropriate. Even so simple a habit as putting on one's right shoe first will be inappropriate if one only wants to see if the left shoe pinches: someone who nevertheless had to start with the right could rightly be accused of acting without intelligence, that is, in a machinelike way. If this is so, then rational agents solely committed to their own valuings would not develop habits that typically led them to comply with moral principles when this is costly to their values. They would monitor the environment for cues that would indicate that compliance is inappropriate.

David Gauthier would disagree. "The just person," he writes, is disposed to act in accordance with the principles of morality even when this requires that he restrains his utility-maximizing actions.[130] Gauthier, following Hobbes, argues that each person gains if all agree to accept rules that constrain their utility-maximizing behavior. This, of course, is simply the morality is better than anarchy argument that we discussed earlier (§16.1). But Gauthier goes on to reply to Hobbes's "Foole," who believes that, though it is rational to make such agreements, it is also rational to break them when one can get away with it. "What the Foole challenges is [Hobbes's third law of nature] . . . requiring compliance, or adherence to one's covenants, for let it be ever so advantageous to make an agreement, may it not then be even more advantageous to violate the agreement made? And if more advantageous, then is it not rational?"[131] Gauthier argues that it is not more rational; a utility-maximizer, he holds, will do better to inculcate a "conditional disposition to base her actions on a joint strategy, without considering whether some individual [noncomplying] strategy would yield greater expected utility."[132]

130 David Gauthier, *Morals by Agreement*, p. 157.
131 Ibid., p. 161. On Hobbes's fool, see *Leviathan*, ch. 15. For other recent analyses of Hobbes's reply to the fool, see Hampton, *Hobbes and the Social Contract*, pp. 55–6, ch. 2; Kavka, *Hobbesian Moral and Political Theory*, pp. 137–56, 245–54, 378–84.
132 Gauthier, *Morals by Agreement*, p. 167.

The crux of Gauthier's reply to the fool turns on two claims: (i) the conditional nature of a just person's disposition to comply, and (ii) the assumption of translucency. According to (i), Betty, a just person, is not disposed to constrain her utility-maximizing behavior toward Alf if she knows that he employs an unconstrained utility-maximizing strategy. That is, if she knows that he breaks his agreements, she will not be disposed to keep hers with him. She is only disposed to keep her agreements with others who, like her, are disposed to constrain their utility-maximizing actions. (ii) In addition, Gauthier assumes that Alf is not opaque in respect to his dispositions – others can gain knowledge about them. If (ii) holds, Betty will be able to infer that Alf is unjust; and, if (i) holds, she will, on the basis of her inference, not act justly toward him. As a consequence, Gauthier argues that Alf's utility-maximizing projects will suffer because opportunities for successful cooperation based on just rules will not be available to him. So, in this sense, he will have outsmarted himself: by refusing to inculcate in himself a conditional disposition to act justly, his values are less well promoted than they would otherwise be.

A great deal depends here on just how "translucent" Alf is.[133] If others always know him for the cheater he is, then his opportunities for cheating will evaporate. If, on the other hand, they never can tell, he will be successful in his cheating. Discovering just what sort of fellow he is will have certain costs for Betty. As a rational utility-maximizer herself, she will not expend unlimited resources in uncovering his dispositions; she will incur costs doing so just as long as the expected utility of such knowledge exceeds the costs. It is here that Philip Pettit's distinction between foul dealing and free riding is relevant.[134] Roughly, a cheater who is a *foul dealer* lowers the utility of the cooperators below the baseline of universal defection. That is, if Alf is a foul dealer, cooperators such as Betty are made worse off by cooperating than they would be if they cheated too. Not only is the collective good

133 Translucency is a weakening of Derek Parfit's assumption of transparency. See *Reasons and Persons*, pp. 18–19. For a critical discussion of this assumption in Gauthier, see Edward F. McClennen, "Constrained Maximization and Resolute Choice," pp. 101–4.
134 Philip Pettit, "Free Riding and Foul Dealing." I am grateful to him for drawing my attention to the relevance of this distinction to Gauthier's argument.

not obtained, but they are disadvantaged by their cooperative behavior. Pettit's example here is an agreement to end a war of all against all by beating swords into plowshares. If everyone but Alf does so, his cheating will worsen their position vis-à-vis the state of nature, for now they will be at Alf's mercy.[135] In contrast, if he is a *free rider*, his cheating does not lower the utility of cooperators below the baseline. Although the cooperators would prefer that Alf too cooperates rather than free ride, they still achieve the collective good. They are not thus made worse off (vis-à-vis the baseline of universal defection) by their cooperative action.

A rational Betty will be more worried by foul dealers than by free riders. Foul dealers pose a threat to her; they make her worse off for cooperating. It will thus be rational for her to spend considerable resources finding out who is a foul dealer. On the other hand, free riders are, as Pettit says, "not so much injurious as irritating."[136] If there are a sufficient number of cooperators to achieve the collective good, it will not be rational for Betty to expend much in the way of resources trying to detect free riders. Consequently, at best all Gauthier shows is that it will typically be irrational to be a foul dealer, because others will expend considerable resources to detect foul dealers, and presumably somehow punish them when they are detected. But free riders are apt to get away with a great deal, at least when they find themselves lucky enough to live in a community of just people who are disposed to keep agreements. And, if my earlier discussion of rational dispositions was sound, even a just person like Betty should be alert to circumstances when she can get away with free riding and, indeed, foul dealing.

And that leads us back to our initial problem (§16.1): why should a rational agent comply when, *all things considered*, one could do better by cheating? But why suppose that agents are rational? If someone upholding the conception of others as mere valuer-agents could show that, *irrationally*, other people act morally out of habit or conditioning, then he could show that he is rational to trust them, rely on them, etc. Because people are creatures of habit, he can still count on them acting morally even when it runs counter to their own valuings. But, it may be in-

135 Hobbes, of course, would not agree.
136 Pettit, "Free Riding and Foul Dealing," p. 378.

sisted, this does not make such dutiful action rational, only predictable. This general orientation might claim to share something with learning-theory approaches to moral behavior, which stress the crucial role of conditioning and the formation of habits, though it goes beyond them by insisting that moral behavior is often irrational.

On first inspection, this may appear to provide the basis for friendships with mere valuer-agents. Because one can rely on one's friend to, irrationally, do the just or decent thing, trust could take root. But depicting friendship as the outcome of irrational habit hardly secures the possibility of friendship. Accepting this account of moral sacrifice (that is, acting morally even when this involves sacrificing one's values) would corrode friendship, for you would then understand that you can trust your friends because they are ignorant, stupid, or custom bound. Such insight breeds contempt. The friendships open to one would be very much like that of an insecure leader who surrounds himself with deputies who are only trusted because they are too dull to betray him. Admittedly, this does not imply that the irrational habit theory of moral sacrifice is inadequate as an explanation of trusting or friendly behavior; that acceptance of a theory of an activity undermines one's acceptance of the activity does not show the theory to be false. But it does demonstrate that it is not a virtue of the irrational habit account that it secures our friendship-centered practices. In any event, my arguments concerning critical reactions to others (§17.3.2) do not simply stress that, as a matter of fact, we rely on others to act morally or justly but, rather, that we suppose that they have good reason to do so. If it were simply a matter of relying on irrational habitual action, one might be surprised when they do the rational thing and best promote their values by disregarding one's "rights," but that would not be a ground for resentment or indignation. Putting all that aside, it seems simply wrong to characterize moral behavior as habitual in any straightforward sense. Social learning theorists themselves acknowledge that, except for very young children, moral judgments are complex.[137] And, as it is safe to say that moral reasoning often leads to moral action, it is hard to see how

137 See Gregory C. R. Yates and Shirley M. Yates, "Moral Reasoning in Young Children: A Review of Research into Intentionality and Implications for Education," esp. p. 161.

we can adequately conceptualize moral action as the outcome of habit in any straightforward sense. It seems a reasonably reflective activity.

To conclude: we not only assume that others can take up the moral point of view and act on it at a real cost to their values, but also that this is not simply habitual and, further, that it is rational. This, then, is what it is to see others as moral persons: persons who can rationally act from the moral point of view. This goes some way toward establishing Value-Grounded Rationalism (§17.1). According to VGR, given his valuings, any rational person will recognize moral principles as providing him with reasons to act that typically override in his deliberations his reasons to promote his values. We have thus far established that (excluding psychopath-like valuers), given his valuings, each must hold that rational others will recognize and act on such principles. What now needs to be done is to show that, given his commitment to seeing others in this way, each is also rationally committed to seeing himself as possessing moral personality.

18 VALUE-GROUNDED RATIONALISM (II)

18.1 Consistency and universalizability

My aim in this section is, then, to show that someone who conceives of others as moral persons cannot rationally deny that he too is a moral person. More specifically, I want to demonstrate how one is likely to be inconsistent by attributing moral personality to others but not to oneself. Inconsistency of belief is certainly the paradigmatic rational failing. Anyone who believes *p* and not-*p* is open to rational criticism; and anyone who ignores this inconsistency once it has been brought to his attention displays the most fundamental of all rational defects. It is the very core of our concept of a rational believer that he responds to the recognition of inconsistency in his beliefs by altering those beliefs to render them consistent. Recent challenges by proponents of deviant logics notwithstanding,[138] we do not know what to make of the claim that a rational believer might simultaneously hold two propositions the inconsistency of which he is aware: both

138 See, e.g., Graham Priest, "Contradiction, Belief, and Rationality."

cannot be true, and rational believers do not hold beliefs they know to be false.

Moral philosophers such as R. M. Hare and G. M. Singer have maintained that this fundamental notion of rational consistency grounds *universalization principles*. Hare indicates that the basic principle is:

> DU: If Alf describes *X* as Q, he is rationally committed to describing anything that is in relevant ways just like *X*, as Q.

Thus, as Hare says, "If I call a thing red, I am committed to calling anything else like it red. And if I call a thing a good *X*, I am committed to calling any *X* like it good."[139]

Let us call this a principle of *descriptive universalization*.[140] But DU is especially prone to the objection that it is trivial or vacuous;[141] everything depends on how "just like" is explicated. I propose to focus on a related, but more obviously nontrivial, nonvacuous, universalization principle:

> UR: If Alf describes *X* as Q just because *X* possesses trait *t*, then he is rationally committed to describing anything possessing *t* as Q.[142]

Thus, for instance, if *X* "is a racehorse because it has a certain pedigree and runs fast, then anything with a certain pedigree and runs fast is also a racehorse."[143] UR can, then, be understood as a version of descriptive generalization, where what constitutes "just like" is defined by the reasons that ground the judgment (description) that *X* is Q. UR, then, is a principle of *universalized reasons*. Something very much like this principle of universalized reasons seems endorsed by Hare, when he tells us that "to universalize is to give the reason."[144]

UR is indeed an implication of rational consistency. If *X*'s possession of *t* is the complete reason for describing *X* as Q, then it is certainly inconsistent to deny that *Y*, though also possessing *t*, is Q. As Singer, following Sidgwick, quite rightly says, "a reason

139 R. M. Hare, *Freedom and Reason*, p. 15. See §10.3 in this volume.
140 I borrow this term from Jann Benson, "Reflections on the Import of Universalizability in Ethics," pp. 226–7.
141 For a critical discussion of these charges, see ibid. For such a charge, see Don Locke, "The Trivializability of Universalizability."
142 See Benson, "The Import of Universalizability," pp. 227ff.
143 Ibid., p. 227.
144 Hare, *Freedom and Reason*, p. 5.

in one case is a reason in all cases – or else it is not a reason at all."[145] Put thus, it should be manifest that I have already defended UR in my argument for the principle of valuational consistency (§14.2.1). But it may still seem that organic-whole valuations pose difficulties for this demand for consistency. Because organic-whole valuations are rational, Alf might describe *X* as *Q* because it possesses *t* but refuse to deem *Y* as *Q* even though it too possesses *t*; *Y* might also be characterized by *s* and the set of traits {*s*, *t*} does not ground an accurate description of *Y* as *Q*. But, despite our initial impression, this sort of valuation does not constitute a violation of the principle of universalized reasons. After all, the difference in valuations between *X* and *Y* demonstrates that *X*'s possession of *t* was not the complete reason for describing it as *Q*; it was, rather, its possession of *t* in the absence of *s* that really grounded the description. Of course we may not always know beforehand that the possession of *t* is not the full grounds for characterizing something as *Q*; perhaps this was not realized until the combination {*s*, *t*} was encountered in *Y*. But this is only to say that we come to a more adequate understanding of our own judgments when we discover that possessing *t* is not sufficient for calling something *Q*. So, far from violating UR, it is the recognition that our initial descriptions of *X* and *Y* seem to violate it that leads us to refine them through organic-whole accounts so as to achieve the sort of consistency articulated by the principle of universalized reasons.

If, then, Alf is rationally committed to viewing others as moral persons, but rationally wants to insist that he is not a moral person, he must not run afoul of UR. He must, that is, take care not to describe others as moral persons simply by virtue of their possession of *t*, if *t* also characterizes him; for then he is rationally committed to describing himself as a moral person too. His first move in his attempt to rationally do so might be to insist that he has no reasons for calling others moral persons; being unable to specify any trait *t* that grounds his description, it is impossible to show that *t* also characterizes him. But clearly this will not do, for §17 has established precisely the trait that grounds the description of others as moral persons, namely, their capacity to put

145 Singer, *Generalization in Ethics*, p. 28. See Sidgwick, *Methods of Ethics*, p. 485.

aside their own valuative concerns and take up, and rationally act upon, the moral point of view. It is the assumption that others have such a capacity that grounds Alf's critical responses to their wrongdoing, including his indignation. And his trust in others is based on the assumption that they possess this rational capacity and, indeed, typically act from it. So he knows well enough what traits ground his description.

Given this, Alf's next move might be to appeal to organic-whole considerations. He might argue thus:

> (A) Yes, the capacity and tendency to act rationally from a moral point of view is the trait that grounds the ascription of moral personality to others. But when combined with the fact that *I* am *Alf*, this capacity does not ground moral personality.

For the moment, I leave aside the most obvious objection to his reply, that it relies on a bare difference in individuation. But, even if he could rely on such bare differences, it would be of no avail in (A). We are interested here in the capacity to act rationally from the moral point of view; if Alf admits he possesses such a capacity, it matters little whether or not he goes on to describe this as "moral personality."

Alf, then, must deny that he possesses such a capacity. He may thus hold:

> (B) It is rational for others to act morally, but not me. Just because I am Alf, I never have a good reason to put aside my valuative concerns and act from the moral point of view; just because others are not me (Alf), they do have such reasons.

This, I think, is indeed to misunderstand what a reason is. "The statement of a reason . . . ," Singer rightly says, "must imply a general rule or proposition."[146] If *R* is a reason for Alf, it must be the case that anyone just like him in every way except that he is not Alf will also have *R* as a reason. That is, it may be that only a very complex description of an agent and his circumstances shows that *R* is a reason for him, but it cannot be the case that *R* is particularly tied to Alf and necessarily to no one else simply because of the difference in individuation. In any event, Alf's reply (B) is tantamount to a violation of UR, for its effect just is to deny that the set of reasons for describing *X* as Q is a set of rea-

146 Singer, *Generalization in Ethics*, p. 24. See also Baier, *The Moral Point of View* (1958), pp. 92ff.

sons that could ground describing other things as Q. The considerations that lead Alf to describe $X_1 \ldots X_n$ as Q do not lead him to describe X_{n+1} as Q simply because he is X_{n+1}. When Alf views other valuer-agents, he describes them as able to rationally act on the moral point of view; but *just because* he is Alf he refuses to describe himself in that way.

If, then, Alf is going to show that, unlike others, he has no reason to act morally, he must establish that he differs from them in some way that goes beyond a simple difference in individuation. Assume, then, that he argues:

> (C) What is rational is what promotes that in which I see value. Hence, it is rational for others to act morally toward me and so put aside their own values, for that (at least usually) advances my valuings. But, on this criterion, it cannot be rational for me to do so.

Alf has finally avoided running afoul of UR. He is not relying on a *mere* difference in individuation; he has a theory of rational action that is linked to what he sees to be of value. It is not simply that he is Alf and others are not that grounds the difference in judgment; it is, instead, that his violations promote what he finds to be of value in a way that is not so regarding others' violations. But he has avoided violating UR only by embracing a false theory of rational action. He can, of course, use the word "rational" in any way he chooses, but we have established that others do not have a reason to promote his values considered simply as his values (§12). (C), then, is consistent with the principle of universalized reasons, but wrong.

Alf, perhaps, is a devoted amoralist living in a world of moralists. He may thus hold:

> (D) Others have reason to adopt the moral point of view because they are so devoted to the moral enterprise (they "go in" for morality). But I am not devoted to it; in fact, I don't give a damn about it. So I have no such reason.

As phrased, (D) is misleading. Alf is really arguing that others just highly value morality or acting morally. Presumably that is what he means by saying that they are "devoted" to it. But this is to imply that they are not putting aside their particular valuings and taking up the moral point of view, but only acting morally because it is one of their valuings. A valuing, Alf adds, he does not share. I have tried to demonstrate that this is an inadequate conception of the reasons we (for example, Alf) presume others have for acting morally. In §16.1 I, suggested some general difficulties with this approach, as articulated by the thesis that moral action is essentially altruistic. The upshot of §17.3 is that our critical reactions to others and friendly and (some types of) loving relations presuppose that others have reasons for acting morally that cannot be reduced to ways of best advancing their values. The understanding of the rationality of moral action informing (D) ignores all this. What if, however, Alf claims not just to be someone who does not go in for morality, but a sort of *Uebermensch*. He says:

> (E) The small men have their reason to act morally, but the overman will not be dragged under by it. He has no such reason.

Note first that, despite his efforts, Alf is not a very good Nietzschean. For our focus here is not the psychopath who, let us assume, makes no claims on others and acknowledges none on him. Rather, our concern is the valuer-agent who is committed to seeing others as moral persons, but who refuses to see himself in the same light. So Alf is quite willing to rely on the moral action of the small man, indeed even to demand it as his due. Consequently, his position is more akin to a slave owner's ethic, demanding compliance by the slave but rejecting any limits on his own pursuit of his values.

However, the real interest is not really whether Alf as a matter of fact acknowledges demands, but whether his rational deliberations about action solely concern his own comparative valuings, while other people can rationally act in ways that, all things considered, set back what they most highly value. Because, pace Nietzsche, the Affective-Cognitive Theory does not ascribe an objectively privileged status to any valuational perspective, and given that we have rejected any theory of rational action which holds that others necessarily have reason to advance Alf's valuings, it is hard to see any intelligible sense in which (E) is true. Alf must show that he is special if he is to make out his claim to be an *Uebermensch*, but our analysis of the objective point of view (§12) demonstrates that, though each person's own perspective is special to him, this does not imply reasons for others to act. And, from the objective point of view, no one's valuings are special, that is, superior to other sound valuings.

Of course, Alf might finally retreat to:

(F) Although, like others, in some sense I have reason to take up the moral point of view and act on it even at a cost to my own values, I am unable to recognize or act upon this reason.

But (F) acknowledges a defect in rationality. Alf is unable to recognize or act upon good reasons (reasons that meet the test sketched in §16.2). I have already argued that philosophic ethics is not concerned with motivating those who are defective in this way: our project is to demonstrate what reasons to act a fully rational agent will recognize and act upon.

I shall not pursue further strategies that Alf might employ to show that, unlike others, he does not possess moral personality. To be rational, any such claim must be consistent with (i) the principle of universalized reasons, (ii) the Affective-Cognitive Theory of value, including the account of the objective point of view and reasons for action, and, of course, (iii) it must not appeal to any false theories or unsound empirical generalizations. It is no easy task to meet all these conditions. Inconsistent or false, those seem to be Alf's options.

To sum up: I argued in §17 that, except for those with something like a psychopathic personality, a rational value system presupposes that others are capable of rationally transcending their particular value perspectives by acting morally. Unless we suppose that others possess such moral personality, our value systems are rationally unsound. In this section, I have tried to indicate how difficult it is for one consistently, and without departing from the Affective-Cognitive Theory of value, to ascribe moral personality to others but not to oneself. We thus have come very close to establishing Value-Grounded Rationalism, that is:

VGR: Given his valuings, any rational person will recognize moral principles as providing him with reasons to act, reasons that typically override (that is, are more weighty considerations in deliberation than) his simply value-based reasons for action.

I stress that I have only come close to establishing VGR because a rational agent capable of only minimal decentering will not recognize such reasons. However, with the exception of such agents entertaining this impoverished conception of others and the attending grossly impoverished value system, VGR is sound.

18.2 *The first objection: consistency as a value*

I now turn to several objections to my argument in support of Value-Grounded Rationalism. The first is that the argument assumes that we all value being consistent, and indeed that we all value it to a high degree. If we did not happen to value being consistent, recognizing that our value systems presuppose that others are moral persons would not lead us to see ourselves as moral persons. If one values other things more then being consistent – for example, living the life of an amoralist – one's value system will lead one to accept the inconsistency and continue to see oneself as lacking moral personality. If Alf did not happen to value consistency, he would not be worried that some of his replies violate UR.

This is, I suspect, the sort of objection that William A. Galston might press. In his *Justice and the Human Good*, he writes:

> Let us define theoretical rationality as the outcome of two imperatives: the avoidance of contradiction, and the provision of the most adequate possible basis or warrant for whatever we assert. These demands are nothing but the requirements for the attainment of knowledge. Theoretical rationality, then, is instrumental, and it loses its justification if the goal of striving for knowledge is rejected.[147]

This coheres well with Galston's rejection of all ethical and political theories that seek to avoid appeals to specific values; even appeals to rationality, if they are to matter to agents, are said to presuppose its value or worth.[148] So it would seem that, according to Galston, theoretical rationality loses its justification if one rejects the quest for knowledge. And, although Galston acknowledges that, from an external point of view, one would be judged irrational, internally no incoherence would be involved because the standard of theoretical rationality had been rejected.[149] Thus, it would seem that Galston allows that one may in some sense be coherent – not irrational – even though one does not take contradiction as a reason to alter one's beliefs.

I confess that this strikes me as more than a little odd. (It is especially surprising coming from an Aristotelian. It was Aristotle, after all, who suggested that someone who had no concern

147 William A. Galston, *Justice and the Human Good*, p. 91.
148 See William A. Galston, "Defending Liberalism." See also John Finnis, *Fundamentals of Ethics*, pp. 4ff.
149 Galston, *Justice and the Human Good*, p. 90.

for the law of contradiction cannot be distinguished from a vegetable.)[150] Galston, and those who endorse this general view, err in radically underestimating just how fundamental consistency of belief is to our understanding of any type of rationality or personality. It is hard, perhaps impossible, to imagine agents who freely held, and recognized themselves as holding, inconsistent beliefs. If we try to envisage people who really see contradiction as no constraint on their beliefs, we would have to concur with Aristotle that neither speech nor thought would be possible, for anything can be simultaneously true and false, and any utterance affirmed can be simultaneously denied.[151] At best, it remains obscure what it could mean to say that such people could be coherent in their own terms; it would be very much like the claim that schizophrenics are coherent in their own way – cognitive inconsistency seems to be a fundamental feature of schizophrenia.[152] The schizophrenic points to an insight: radical cognitive inconsistency undermines the possibility of any sort of minimally integrated personality. (See §14.2.3 on schizoid personalities.) Before we can talk of what a person values, and so whether he "accepts or rejects the quest for knowledge," we must be able to identify a continuing subject – a personality. But only by possessing significant theoretical rationality, that is, by recognizing inconsistency as a reason to alter belief, can a person arrive at a conception of himself as an agent in the world; indeed, without it he cannot think at all. And because theoretical rationality is logically more basic that the concept of a person as valuer, it is quite mistaken to explain the commitment[153] to the former in terms of the latter. Consistency, then, provides a reason to alter or accept beliefs quite independently of whether one values it or the quest for knowledge.[154] That *p* and *q* are inconsistent propositions is a reason not to believe both, a reason far more basic

150 Aristotle, *Metaphysics*, p. 742 (1008b 10–15).
151 Ibid.
152 Argyle, *The Psychology of Interpersonal Behavior*, p. 211. In fact, schizophrenics may not even be this irrational, because their "inconsistency" might be better described as a failure to recognize relations of transitivity.
153 Cf. Gewirth's remark that reliance on reason "is not a mere optional or parochial 'commitment' parallel to the commitments some persons may make to religious faith, aesthetic rapture, animal instinct, personal authenticity, national glory or tradition, or other variable objects of human allegiance." *Reason and Morality*, p. 22; see also pp. 196-8.
154 See W. H. Werkmeister, "Is Truth a Value?"

than value-based reasons to act. Moreover, because one's value system is grounded on belief (§5.4) and, further, because one's conceptions of oneself and of others are essentially matters of belief, rational valuer-agents will respond to inconsistency among such beliefs by correcting the beliefs on which their valuings depend, and so altering their valuings themselves. One may, I suppose, insist that consistency, or true beliefs, are matters of value, but values which it is rationally necessary for all to hold. But not only is this inconsistent with the Affective-Cognitive Theory, but it also seems to add nothing to the thesis that a rational valuer-agent necessarily sees inconsistency as a reason to alter belief. That is, in this context, to say that a rational agent necessarily values being consistent in his beliefs is just to say that consistency is a reason to alter beliefs. If so, I see no reason for bringing in reference to valuing.[155]

18.3 The second objection: the gap between belief and action

An objector may grant that a rational believer necessarily takes considerations of consistency as a reason to alter belief. But Value-Grounded Rationalism is about rational action, not rational belief. According to VGR, given his valuings, a rational agent recognizes *reasons to act* that typically override his reasons to advance his valuings. It is widely held, however, that theoretical and practical rationality are very different: consistency can yield a belief but not an action. For action, some motivator – typically a desire – is necessary. In part, this difference may be attributed to the alleged fishiness of the practical syllogism. Because an action is an event, not a proposition, it has no truth value, and cannot be the conclusion entailed by a set of premises.[156] Propositions entail only propositions. So the conclusion to a practical syllogism can be only a proposition about an action, not an action itself. Consequently, not acting on such a conclusion is not considered a failure of rationality in the same sense as not believing what is entailed by premises believed to be true. But consider:

(i) If *p*, then *q*;

155 Cf. my argument against desire as an "intentional want," in §7.2.3.
156 Passions, volitions, and actions, Hume asserted, cannot "be pronounced either true or false." *A Treatise of Human Nature*, p. 458. (bk. III, pt. I, sec. I).

(ii) p;
(iii) q;

yet (iii) does not entail anyone actually believing q.[157] Because one can hold on to a belief in the face of evident entailments, the best one can get from (i) and (ii) by way of belief is:

(iv) q is the rational thing to believe.

Rationality in belief is thus no more and no less a matter of logical necessity than is rationality in action. Just as a theoretical syllogism with true premises yields not a belief but a reason to believe, so does a practical syllogism with true premises yield not an action but a reason to act.

In §17, then, I argued that (psychopath-like valuers aside) we are committed to maintaining that others have reasons to act in certain ways regardless of whether acting in these ways is consistent with their comparative valuings. And in §18.1 I tried to show that we are committed to seeing ourselves as able to act rationally in a similar way. So the outcome of the argument is that we must see ourselves as having a reason to act that is not concerned with promoting what we most value. Having established that we have such a reason to act, no additional motivator is required. Just as a theoretical argument can show only that rational believers will accept the conclusion, so the practical argument needs only to show that rational agents will act in the specified way. It is not incumbent on either sort of argument to motivate believer/agents to be rational (§16.2).

18.4 The third objection: the instrumental interpretation

But it may be questioned whether I have actually shown that we have reasons to act from the moral point of view. All that has been shown, it might be thought, is that our value systems presuppose that others possess such reasons, and if we hold that they do, we are also committed to believing that we too have such reasons to act. It may be objected, though, that I have not demonstrated that anyone really *has* such reasons, only that we suppose that they do. But supposing something is so doesn't

157 See Michael H. Robins, "Practical Reasoning, Commitment, and Rational Action," p. 64.

make it so. If our value systems presuppose false beliefs, the appropriate response is not to believe the falsehood so as to maintain the internal consistency of the system, but to reject it along with all of the value system that rests upon it.

This is a powerful objection. It is surely right that, if we know that *p* is false, showing that our value systems would collapse if *p* were false doesn't make *p* true. More significantly, a rational believer-agent would still not have reason to believe *p*. As Bernard Williams has pointed out, belief is standardly truth-centered,[158] and that is why believing something just because one wants to believe it is an incoherent project. Someone who wants to believe *p* (for example, that his son, reported dead in an accident, is actually alive) really wants his belief to be true. He does not, and cannot, simply want that he believe it, for that would be to want to believe that something is true, knowing at the same time that one believed it only because one has so chosen, and choosing cannot make true what otherwise would be untrue. Admittedly, some motives for belief, such as social conformity, are nonstandard and non-truth-centered. Such motives, however, are parasitic on truth-centered ones; if the bulk of our beliefs were not truth-centered, those prompted by other interests could not be held as beliefs at all, that is, could not be held *as true*. These nonstandard cases involve a kind of self-deception: to believe the thing one wants to believe, one must hide from oneself that the grounding of one's belief is a non-truth-centered motive. So either through drugs, hypnosis, or repression one must forget one's motive for holding the belief – or at least take for granted that one's belief really is truth-centered.[159]

My argument in defense of Value-Grounded Rationalism is not at all like this: I have not maintained that we should accept VGR as means to render rational our value systems. Rather, I took as my starting point a widely accepted and prima facie plausible theory of rational action, what I called the orthodox view (§16.1). According to that theory of rationality in action, what is rational for Alf is the act, among those open to him, that best advances

158 See Bernard Williams, "Deciding to Believe."
159 This helps to explain why some forms of consequentialist ethics seem so counter-intuitive when they direct us to believe what is false but valuable. As Derek Parfit observes: "We would have to be made to forget how and why we acquired our new beliefs . . . " *Reasons and Persons*, p. 41.

what he values. But the upshot of the analysis of this chapter is that accepting this account of practical rationality undermines the rationality of our value systems. What starts out as a plausible doctrine – what is rational for you to do is what you most value doing – ultimately leads to the conclusion that your valuings are deeply irrational. For, as we have seen, our nonpsychopathic value systems presuppose that the orthodox view is false, that is, others have grounds for rational action other than doing what they most value doing, or what best advances their values. Now when deliberating whether to accept an account of a practical activity, one ground for embracing it is that it makes sense of the activity in which we are engaged. I have already allowed that a theory which condemns current practice as deeply confused or irrational could be sound, but I stressed that it is without this important pull on rational believer-agents (§1.3). In this context, the orthodox view is such a radically critical theory, not the intuitively appealing articulation of our current practice that its proponents suppose. Given all this, as rational-believer agents we have reason to reject the orthodox view: it is an inadequate account of rational action. Surprisingly, grasping the nature of our current practice of valuing leads us to reject the thesis that all rational action is aimed at securing or promoting what is most valued. Value-Grounded Rationalism, then, articulates the concept of practical reason upon which our valuational perspectives are based. It is to be embraced not as a way of making rational our otherwise irrational systems, but because it articulates our underlying concept of reason in action.

VII

Teleological and deontological justification

19 PUBLIC JUSTIFICATION

19.1 Moral personality and justification

In the previous chapter, I argued that, psychopathlike valuers aside, a rational valuer-agent must acknowledge the rationality of acting on moral principles even though such principles may require one to act in ways that, all things considered, do not best promote one's values. One must acknowledge the rationality of such action because one's value system presupposes that moral rules and principles provide others with such reasons to act and, further, because one who conceives of others as possessing moral personality in this sense is committed to acknowledging that he too is a moral person, that is, he possesses the capacity to act rationally on moral principles. As I have said, to conceive of self and others as moral persons, then, requires that one sees oneself and others as capable of following a *nomos*. We can feel indignant toward moral persons, trust them and be their friends, because they are more than valuers; they can follow a *nomos*.

Now this is an important conclusion: it establishes our deep commitment to the rationality of moral action, both in the sense that (i) we believe that others have reason to act morally, and (ii) each of us is rationally committed to acknowledging that he also has such reasons. Yet, though important, this conclusion upholds the rationality of moral action only at a general level. That is, I have argued that we nonpsychopathic valuers presuppose the rationality of moral action that does not, *all things considered*, best promote one's values. Consider now a more specific disagreement about the rationality of moral action. Assume that both Alf and Betty have come to accept the argument in favor of Value-Grounded Rationalism, but they disagree whether some particular moral rule or principle provides them both with a reason to act. Alf argues that the rule, say, against adultery provides both himself and Betty with moral reasons to abstain from infidelity. She rejects this. She sees no such reasons. The disagreement has moved from a general skepticism about the rationality of moral action per se to the rationality of acts dictated by certain moral rules, etc.

Because Alf accepts that moral action is rational, that is, a rational Betty would acknowledge reasons to refrain from adultery, his claim is sound only if she actually does possess such reasons, or would recognize such a reason if fully rational (see §9.2.2). Alf's supposing that a rational Betty has such reasons is not at all the same as her actually having reasons to act. He can be wrong. If his value system is fully rational, he will suppose that rational others have only the reasons to act morally that they really do possess. So a criterion for the rationality of Alf's morality-informed value system is that any moral claim *M* that he makes upon Betty rightly supposes that a rational Betty would have a reason to comply. We have already seen (§17.3.2) that the point of moral demands is undermined if fully rational others have no reason to comply.

It must, then, be the case that Alf is only rational to advance *M* as a moral claim (or demand) against Betty if a rational Betty is committed to accepting *M* as a reason for her to act. So for Alf to justify *M* to Betty is to show precisely this: that she either has a reason to comply with the demands made by *M* or would acknowledge such a reason if she had sound beliefs, values, and all the relevant information. From this it follows that a fully rational valuer who is also a moral person is one whose moral principles, rules, etc. can be *justified* to rational others. That is, rational others can be shown to be committed to these principles or rules, with this commitment implying reasons to act on them. To justify a principle to another is just to show that he has good reason to act on it, or would acknowledge such a reason if fully rational. In the absence of such a justification, a rational moral person (for example, Betty) can reject the principle as one to which she is not rationally committed, and so would not be irrational to ignore. And, of course, if she is right, Alf's supposition that she does have good reason to comply with it would be ill-grounded; it follows that indignation of his part over her violations, resentment, and so on all would be without good grounds (§17.3). So, if fully rational, our value systems presuppose that the moral principles on which we rely can be justified to others.

This justification must, moreover, supply what are reasons from *the other's perspective*. It will do no good to provide another with considerations that are reasons from your perspective but not from his. Our concern with justification derives from the presupposition that the other, if fully rational, would have good reason to act on the principle. Clearly, then, if I accept that a consideration is a reason for me and not for a fully rational you, it cannot enter into our justificatory argument. Consequently, given the Affective-Cognitive Theory of value and, in particular, the agent-relativity of value-based reasons to act (§12), I cannot cite my valuings (*qua* my valuings) as part of a justificatory argument aiming at showing that you have good reason to embrace a moral principle.

We are thus lead to confirm what is probably the dominant view of justification in moral theory:[1] to justify a moral theory or position is to provide reasons for accepting it which, Virginia Held adds, "a reasonable person ought to find persuasive."[2] However, her reference to what a reasonable person will find "persuasive" points to a tension in the notion of moral justification: on the one hand, it is held that justification is a matter of providing good reasons, yet, because moral justification seems to be essentially a practical matter, it also appears to have a persuasive function. That is, it ought to move people. It should be manifest that my concern here is to justify moral principles simply in the sense of showing that rational moral agents are committed to them: it is a presupposition of our value systems that rational others are committed to acting on justified moral principles, not that all others can be persuaded that they are so committed and will act accordingly. Equipped with the idea of a fully rational moral person, we have no need to refer to what he will be persuaded by; he will accept what he has reason to accept, and only what he has reason to accept. Philosophic ethics, then, aims to

1 For an alternative to this dominant view, see Carl Wellman, *Challenge and Response: Justification in Ethics*.
2 Virginia Held, "Justification: Legal and Political," p. 1.

justify by providing good reasons; it thus will necessarily "persuade" any fully rational agent.[3] Justificatory argument, then, is to be addressed to the others' *rational* perspective: the argument does not focus simply on what they *are* rationally committed to, but what reason to act they possess or would possess if they did not have false beliefs or inappropriate valuings (see §9.2.2). For most of this chapter, then, I will concern myself with moral justification among such rational agents; in §21.5, I shall consider justifications addressed to those with false beliefs or unsound values.

Our value systems, then, presuppose that rational others are committed to restraints on the pursuit of their values, that is, those restraints that can be justified to them. Each of us thus confronts a radical challenge: unless the morality on which one's value system relies can be justified to other rational moral persons, one's value system is rationally unsound. To presuppose in one's valuations moral demands that cannot be justified to rational others undermines the rationality of one's own value system. So, unless one entertains a system of valuings that is essentially psychopathic, one is rationally committed to maintaining that one's moral demands and expectations are justified. We thus have an answer to the challenge of William Galston's radical skeptic: "What do I care about rational justification?"[4] If I am right, one does indeed have a rational commitment to a justified morality.

19.2 Public morality and justification

19.2.1 Public and private morality

A fully rational moral agent, then, embraces a morality that provides good reasons to all rational moral persons upon whom it makes demands: it is a morality that can be justified to all whose value-promoting action it seeks to restrain. It is useful, I think, to conceive of a justified morality as falling into two parts: a public morality and a private morality.[5] The public morality is that

3 See Thomas C. Mayberry, "Morality and Justification," p. 210.
4 William Galston, "Defending Liberalism," p. 625. See also Henry B. Veatch, "The Rational Justification of Moral Principles," p. 218.
5 Cf. Stanley Benn's criticism in his "Private and Public Morality: Clean Living and Dirty Hands," pp. 155–9. My distinction between private and public morality is not that which moral philosophers typically have in mind.

part which specifies duties applying to anyone or everyone. Such duties do not refer to a specific person or persons but are (roughly) attributed to moral persons simply in virtue of their membership in a general class of persons.[6] As Sir George Cornewall Lewis said, "*Public*, as opposed to *private*, is that which has no immediate relation to any specified person or persons, but may directly concern any member or members of the community without distinction."[7] In contrast, then, one's private morality would be that part of one's moral code which essentially refers to a specific person or persons. Examples of public duties are abundant: for example, the duty of anyone not to murder, of anyone to refrain from lying, of anyone to assist those in need. However, uncontroversial cases of private morality are harder to come by. What are sometimes called "special duties" are not necessarily instances of private morality. Consider the duty of parents to see that their child is properly fed. This might seem like a private duty because it does not apply indiscriminately to all members of the public; it applies, we might say, only to a "section of the public," *viz.*, parents. Yet this too is a sort of public duty because it is a duty that applies to everyone within some specified boundary, that is, the class of parents.[8] I want to distinguish these sorts of special duties that apply only to a section of the public from those that are attributed only to specific persons. Someone may, for instance, hold that he has no general theory of duties that parents owe to their children, but he does believe that he has a duty to help his child in a particular way.[9] Such duties, which are essentially concerned with the relations between specific people, constitute what I will call one's private morality.

The crux of a public morality, then, is that it pertains to others as unknowns. One holds that anyone has a duty to refrain from injuring another, or that any parent must help his or her child. The core of publicness here is not that the duty necessarily ap-

"Public and private morality" usually refers to the distinction between the morality of public – that is, political – life and that of the private citizen.

6 The analysis of this section draws on S. I. Benn and G. F. Gaus, "The Liberal Conception of the Public and Private," pp. 31–8.

7 George Cornewall Lewis, *Remarks on the Use and Abuse of Some Political Terms* (London, 1832), as quoted by Brian Barry, *Political Argument*, p. 190.

8 It also has built into it an indexical: that parents are to help *their* children.

9 See Philip Pettit and Robert Goodin, "The Possibility of Special Duties." See their n. 1.

plies to each and every person – though many duties do – but rather that it applies to any moral person within some general class of moral persons. What is important about these duties is that one does not have specific knowledge of the person to whom one attributes the duty. He cannot be identified by name, as Tom, Dick, or Harry, and so, if the duty one attributes to him can be justified, it must be without resort to particular knowledge of that person. One is attributing this duty to any member of the public, or any member of some general subgroup of the moral community.

This notion of one's public morality has obvious affinities with the doctrine that moral rules and judgments must have a sort of generality, and cannot refer to specific persons. But I am not trying to define "morality" here, and I am certainly not seeking to criticize the idea of a private morality. The core insight of the idea of a private morality is that, within groupings in which people come to know each other as specifics, a rich texture of common valuings (including benevolent emotions) and shared moral intuitions may develop. And these may provide the foundation for the justification of network of rights and duties that are much more extensive than that which pertains to individuals in general. What we expect from our brothers and sisters – and this can be taken in either its narrow or wide sense – goes far beyond that which is owed to strangers. This is, perhaps, why philosophical discussions of the moral nature of love and friendship, or the obligations that family members owe to each other, seem either overly abstract or too legalistic and rule-bound.[10] If we try to capture the principles guiding the family as a social institution, we can provide those general regulative norms such as, for example, that parents are to educate their children or that family life should have some privacy vis-à-vis the political order. But this tells us little about the special demands that one's own brothers and sisters can legitimately make on one. Or, even more to the point, because intimate relations cannot withstand much in the way of overt demands (§17.3.3), private morality concerns what you perceive as the right thing to do in relation to them.

---

10 I have in mind here, e.g., Rawls's discussion of love in *A Theory of Justice*, pp. 486–88; Fried's analysis of love and friendship in *An Anatomy of Values*, pp. 77–80; John Finnis's account of friendship in *Natural Law and Natural Rights*, pp. 88, 141–4; and, indeed, my own analysis in §17.3.3.

A defense of a complete rational morality would have to justify not only those moral demands that strangers make on each other, but the special ones that family members and friends may rightfully assume in their intimate relations. Not only do we expect strangers to put aside their value-maximizing projects to treat others in ways consistent with respect, but we also expect family and friends to refrain from pursuing both indulgences and highly valued projects and act in a variety of ways that recognize the special status of other members of the association. It is certainly not enough to treat fellow family members and friends as one would a mere stranger.[11] Important as all this is, however, little useful can be said of a general nature about private morality. If Alf's private morality is to be justified by reference to the special shared values and concerns pertaining among those in the intimate associations in which he participates, we would not expect the content of his fully justified private morality to be identical with Betty's fully justified private morality. Contrast this to public morality. Public morality is, roughly at any rate, comprised of the rights and duties that strangers have in relation to one another. From the perspective of normative political philosophy, at least in large and diverse societies, public morality will be the focus of investigation. Whereas private morality is crucially dependent upon context, public morality is that which pertains among strangers or fellow citizens.[12] In the remainder of this book, then, I will be concerned only with public morality.

19.2.2 Public justification

A fully rational moral person accepts that the morality on which he relies must be justified to all on whom it makes demands. Furthermore, it is the defining feature of his public morality that it applies to the public at large. Again, all parts of it do not necessarily apply to everyone, for it may include duties of parents to their children, and not everyone is, or will be, a parent. But it

11 It might, of course, be argued that this is the realm of altruistic valuing rather than moral reasons (§16.1). I cannot pursue this issue here, but see my "Community and Justice."

12 Such morality may be called *Gesellschaft* morality insofar as it attributes general rights and duties to abstract moral persons. Eugene Kamenka, "What is Justice?" pp. 8–9. See also Martin Krygier, "Publicness, Privateness, and 'Primitive Law.' "

will apply to anyone of the relevant description.[13] I will say, then, that one supposes that one's public moral code must be publicly justified: if it is a rational code, it supposes that all rational moral persons will act on whatever duties it attributes to them. But, of course, all these other moral persons have their own moral codes; and, if they are rational, it must be true that rational others will act on them. So unless the codes are consistent, it follows that someone is somehow wrong or less than fully rational. To see this, consider once again Alf and Betty. According to his code, everyone has a duty to help another if the other is in danger and assistance will not injure or endanger the helper. Betty's code is more libertarian: one has no duty to help in these circumstances. Now Charlie, seeing Alf in danger, either has a moral reason to help or he does not, so either Alf or Betty is wrong. That is, either it is true or false that Charlie, as a member of the public, can be provided with reasons to accept a public moral code that includes the duty to assist Alf.

The upshot of this is that fully rational codes of public morality must be consistent. Yet consistent codes may still be different: Betty's code may be more comprehensive than Alf's, but, as long as his never contradicts hers, they are consistent. But if her code is sound throughout, then his code fails to recognize reasons for action (justified rights and duties) that rational others actually possess. Now moral codes are not mere expressions of wants, values, or aims: they are doctrines about the rational commitments of moral persons to act, even at a cost to their values. So a moral code is incomplete, and in that way flawed, if others have moral reasons to act that it does not recognize. So, if Alf's code was complete, it would be identical with Betty's. Fully rational and complete codes of public morality would thus be identical.[14]

A fully rational moral community (whatever the bounds of it may be; see §23.1) is thus committed to a shared public morality. This provides a rational, rather than a pragmatic, foundation for John Rawls's conception of public justification and the ideal of a

13 Drawing a distinction between general and specific descriptions obviously can lead to difficulties, but, though disputable, these distinctions are not arbitrary. Stanley Benn and I discuss the reasoning behind them in "The Liberal Conception of the Public and Private"; see esp. our discussion of the Charter's case. I return to the problem of the boundary of the public in §23.1.

14 Or, at the very least, extensionally equivalent. I remain unclear as to how much this difference would matter in practice.

public conception of justice. Rawls aims to publicly justify a public conception of justice. That is, the regulative aim of his theory of justice is to justify to all citizens a conception of justice that will provide a shared standard to resolve disputes and judge political institutions.[15] We can now see this aim in a new light. The ideal of a shared public morality is not simply a contingent aim or valuing that a community of persons might happen to entertain, and neither is it simply a practically important goal. If members of a community entertain any public moral code at all – and it is difficult to see how such a code can be avoided in a large and diverse society such as ours – they are necessarily committed to a publicly justified public morality, and we have seen that this will be a shared public morality. Fully rational moral persons must suppose that a rational morality that *applies to all* can be *justified to all*.

But it is only for fully rational moral agents that public justification necessarily leads to a shared public morality. For real agents in the real world, who are unable to construct sound justifications or who fail to respond to sound justifications,[16] some public morality could be publicly justified, yet actual individuals might still entertain different codes of public morality. And because of this, especially because justifications are not necessarily persuasive to less than fully rational persons, Rawls's practical aims for political philosophy are unlikely to be met. It is not at all likely that, as a matter of fact, we can resolve "fundamental disagreement over the just form of basic institutions within a democratic society under modern conditions."[17] This is no doubt to be regretted. But because our commitment to public justification is not pragmatic – it is not simply a means to achieve real public agreement – the commitment is not undermined by the likelihood that sound justification will not persuade everyone.

Yet in an important way Rawls is correct that moral justification is a practical problem.[18] Our concern is to show that rational

15 Rawls, "Kantian Constructivism," pp. 515–22, 567ff.

16 According to J. M. Rist, Aristotle believed that slaves could acknowledge an argument but not construct one. Hence, even Aristotelian slaves could be the target of a justificatory argument. "Aristotle: The Value of Man and the Origin of Morality," p. 3.

17 Rawls, "Kantian Constructivism," p. 518.

18 "[T]he justification of a conception of justice is a practical social task rather than an epistemological problem." Rawls, "Justice as Fairness," p. 224n.

others have reasons to act – to respond to our moral claims and demands. Our primary aim in justifying our public morality is not epistemic in the sense that we wish to propagate truth; the primary aim is practical insofar as we (as nonpsychopathic valuers) are committed to making moral demands that others act in this way or that, and only if we possess a publicly justified morality are our moral demands rational.

19.3 Contractualism

The statement of our justificatory problem points to a contractualist solution. We can envisage each moral person proposing a code of public morality, with each being committed to the supposition that fully rational moral persons will embrace the same code. So the aim of the parties to the agreement is to arrive at a shared code of public morality.

Contractualism is, I would venture, best understood as a method for publicly justifying the public moral code of a society.[19] Seen in this light, the idea of "consent" – or indeed "agreement" – is only heuristic. It is often suggested that the contractualist method is essentially voluntaristic;[20] people can be obligated to act in accordance with a moral duty or law only if they choose to so obligate themselves, and the contract (it is said) tries to show they would so choose. On this interpretation, it is not difficult to show that contractualism must fail to justify political or moral obligation.[21] But, if we suppose fully rational moral persons, what they will consent to is what they have best reason to adopt. The significance of consent is not any special quality of the consensual act that brings into being obligations, but rather as a way of determining what public morality can be justified to everyone.

This is not to say that only contractualist theories present public justificatory arguments. Although the form of contractualist theories stress public justification, nearly all arguments in the history of moral and political theory have sought to be public in this

For a discussion, see John Gray, "Contractarian Method, Private Property, and The Market Economy."

19 See T. M. Scanlon, "Contractualism and Utilitarianism."

20 See, e.g., Carole Pateman, *The Problem of Political Obligation*; Spencer Carr, "Rawls, Contractarianism, and Our Moral Intuitions."

21 See A. John Simmons, *Moral Principles and Political Obligation*, ch. III.

way.[22] A contractualist approach to public justification is particularly appropriate, however, when the parties' reasons for embracing or rejecting a proposed public morality are not necessarily identical. Suppose that all possible reasons that might justify a public morality were agent-neutral (§12.1). On this assumption, what would be a reason for Alf to accept the code would necessarily be a reason for Betty and everyone else to do so as well. So much follows from the claim that the reasons are neutral between agents. If this were so, the sound reasoning of one party is necessarily the sound reasoning of all others. Now, as T. M. Scanlon quite rightly recognizes, there is something about this that misconstrues the point of the contractualist thought experiment.[23] Contractualism aims at "judgmental harmony" resulting from a "genuinely interpersonal form of justification,"[24] but that seems unnecessary if the rational deliberations of all parties are necessarily identical. That is, the requirement of an interpersonal judgmental harmony would be, strictly speaking, otiose: if any one individual is correct about what he has reasons for accepting, all questions of "interpersonal justification" are necessarily settled. But, if, as I have argued, value-based reasons for action are strongly agent-relative, and valuings are divergent, then the contractualist approach is appropriate. For we are confronted with parties that (i) have divergent reasons for action, (ii) a rational commitment to a publicly justified public morality, and (iii) a commitment to the rationality of a shared public morality (that is, justification implies consensus on a shared public morality). We have, in short, parties with different perspectives committed to agreement on a public morality.

20 CONSTRAINED TELEOLOGY

20.1 Contractualism and teleology

It is a commonplace that contractualist theories must provide an account of the motivation of the parties to the original agreement. But on the interpretation of contractualism I have put for-

22 Nietzsche would appear to be an exception. I briefly discuss his critique of public justification in §28.2.4.
23 Scanlon, "Contractualism," pp. 119ff.
24 Ibid., p. 117.

ward, the question "What motivates the parties?" can be analyzed into several different questions: (i) What reasons do the parties have to justify themselves? (ii) What sorts of proposals do they have reasons to put forward? and (iii) What sorts of considerations justify a public moral code to others? Thus far, we have said something about (i) and (ii). I have explained why we are committed to justifying ourselves, and have suggested that the problem of justification can be best understood in terms of each endeavoring to justify a code of public morality. I now want to turn to consider the third and crucial question: What considerations can be advanced that justify a public morality to others? In this section, I wish to explore a powerful, though ultimately inadequate, theory: that the only reasons that are relevant for justifying public morality are value reasons.

David Gauthier's contractualist theory is a good example of this approach. He first characterizes value in terms of preference satisfaction, and then goes on to argue that morality can be understood as an agreement among those devoted to pursuing their own values to enter into a cooperative arrangement that benefits all, yet requires participants to sometimes act in ways that do not maximize their values (preference satisfaction).[25] I have already discussed Gauthier's proposed solution to the compliance problem (§17.5); what I want to stress in the present context is that according to him one justifies morality to another by showing that he too benefits, that is, his values are promoted by the possibilities for cooperation morality provides. Gauthier writes:

> If social institutions and practices can benefit all, then some set of social arrangements should be acceptable to all as a cooperative venture. Each person's concern to fulfill her own interests should ensure her willingness to join her fellows in a venture assuring her an expectation of increased fulfillment. She may of course reject some proposed venture as insufficiently advantageous to her when she considers both the distribution of benefits that it affords, and the availability of alternatives. Affording mutual advantage is a necessary condition for the acceptability of a set of social arrangements as a cooperative venture, not a sufficient condition. But we suppose that some set affording mutual advantage

25 David Gauthier, *Morals by Agreement*, esp. chs. I, II. For a similar theory, see James M. Buchanan, *The Limits of Liberty*. As Gauthier notes (p. 10), the basic structure of his theory shares much with Kurt Baier's *The Moral Point of View*. See Baier's claim (a), discussed in §17.1 of this volume.

will also be mutually acceptable: a contractarian theory must set out conditions for sufficiency.[26]

Gauthier's account of moral justification can be aptly described as a *constrained teleology*. I follow Michael J. Sandel's useful characterization of teleology as "a form of justification" in which first principles are derived in a way that presupposes "final human purposes or ends."[27] It is manifest that Gauthier's contractualism relies on just such a justificatory argument: only once we know the nature of human purposes or values can we derive principles of substantive right. Principles of right, or public morality, are justified through appeal to the values of actual people to whom the morality is to apply.

The suggestion that a contractualist theory is essentially teleological no doubt will seem strange, and this perhaps for at least two reasons. Firstly, it may seem that the notion of value upon which Gauthier relies is too general or vague to provide the basis of a teleology. As Sandel says, teleologies presuppose a "determinate" conception of the good.[28] Indeed, at least since Mill, teleology has been often associated with a doctrine that advocates a monism, or at least very limited plurality, of ends.[29] But, of course, a theory such as that of Hastings Rashdall's admits a wide array of ends, yet for all that is still teleological.[30] Even more to the point, perhaps the most widely accepted teleological theory today is a type of utilitarianism aiming at the overall maximization of the satisfaction of preferences. And, of course, Gauthier agrees that value is to be characterized in terms of preference satisfaction; so his conception of value is not more abstract or vague than, say, R. M. Hare's or John C. Harsanyi's.[31] But this raises the second point: Gauthier's account of value is thoroughly agent-

26 Gauthier, *Morals by Agreement*, p. 11.
27 Sandel, *Liberalism and the Limits of Justice*, p. 3. Sandel is characterizing deontology in this passage, contrasting it to teleology, and so the characterization of teleology is implied rather than explicit. For characterizations of teleology along similar lines, see Robert C. Olson, "Teleological Ethics"; William K. Frankena, *Ethics*, pp. 14–16.
28 Sandel, *Liberalism and the Limits of Justice*, p. 3.
29 See J. S. Mill, *A System of Logic*, pp. 950–1.
30 Hastings Rashdall, *The Theory of Good and Evil*, ch. VII.
31 R. M. Hare, *Moral Thinking*, pt. II; John C. Harsanyi, "Morality and the Theory of Rational Behavior," pp. 39–62. Cf. Gauthier's remark that both his theory and utilitarianism reject "any substantive conception of the good." *Morals by Agreement*, p. 341.

relative, and teleological theories are normally associated with an agent-neutral conception. Gauthier concurs with the utilitarian that practical rationality does indeed aim at maximizing value, but he insists that this value is agent-relative; Gauthier's analysis thus converges with our conclusion in §12.2 that universalistic theories such as utilitarianism presuppose much too strong a conception of practical rationality.[32]

What emerges from this is that Gauthier's teleology departs from our paradigm of a teleological theory – utilitarianism – not in its general characterization of value, but in the claim that value is agent-relative: what is of value to Alf, and what he has a reason to pursue, is the satisfaction of *his* preferences while Betty rationally values the satisfaction of *her* own preferences. Like the utilitarian, Gauthier maintains that what is right is that which promotes value, but because people rationally pursue divergent values their most favored principles of right may differ. In particular, Gauthier – and here he is characteristic of much contractualist thought – argues that each person must constrain his own effort to maximize value by acting on principles that can be justified to all.

Contractual arguments, then, can indeed be characterized as constrained teleologies. We can distinguish a necessary *formal constraint* that typically leads to a *substantive constraint*. The formal constraint is simply the requirement that a moral principle is sound only if it can be justified to others by showing them that it promotes their own values. Consider the perspective of Alf. Being a teleologist, he seeks to justify a public moral code by showing how it promotes what is of value. But, because he acknowledges the commitment to justify the code to others *and* because others, even though committed to teleological justification, will quite rationally evaluate the proposed public moralities in light of their own, differing, values, Alf finds himself committed to showing that the justified code advances valuings and values that he may not share. So he finds himself rationally committed to appealing to considerations in support of principles that, from his perspective, are not of value. (Or, more typically, things which are of less value in his value system than they are in others; see §§13.2, 14.3.) His teleological justification is thus formally

32 Gauthier, *Morals by Agreement*, pp. 7–8, 46ff., 52.

constrained by the need to appeal to considerations that are not, from his point of view, values.

It does not necessarily follow, however, that the final principles thus arrived at will reject a substantively teleological ethic such as utilitarianism. That is, the constrained teleological justification may endorse an unconstrained consequentialist normative ethics.[33] Rawls, for example, considers the possibility that some form of utilitarianism might be adopted by the parties to the original position, and a number of philosophers have argued that contractualism can indeed justify a utilitarian morality.[34] Whether or not contractors would agree to a utilitarian contract, it is clear enough that no theoretical barrier bars a contractual justification endorsing a utilitarian morality. If, for instance, it so happened that each person most valued the greatest happiness of the greatest number, it is easy to see how a contractual method could endorse some version of utilitarianism. But, unless some rather strong assumptions are made either about the conditions under which the parties deliberate or the nature of their values, the formal constraint is apt to yield a substantive constraint as well. In this case, *the constrained teleological justification will yield a public morality that from the perspective of each does indeed promote what is valued, but does not maximize the advancement of each person's values.* The extent to which the contractually justified moral principles promote any one person's values is constrained by the requirement that they also promote the (different) valuings of others. Put roughly, the resulting principles will be a compromise arising from a bargain: each will gain (in terms of the promotion of his values), but the extent of gain is constrained by the need to elicit the agreement of others. Unless otherwise specified, I shall employ the term "constrained teleology" to describe theories characterized by both the formal and substantive constraints.

---

33 This distinction between teleology as a justificatory method and consequentialism as a "first-order ethic" is Sandel's. *Liberalism and the Limits of Justice*, p. 3.

34 See Rawls, *A Theory of Justice*, pp. 161–75; Dennis C. Mueller, Robert D. Tollison, and Thomas D. Willett, "The Utilitarian Contract: A Generalization of Rawls' Theory of Justice," pp. 345–67; Dan W. Brock, "Contractualism, Utilitarianism, and Social Inequalities," pp. 33–43. But see also Scanlon, "Contractualism and Utilitarianism."

20.2 The common good

The notion of a constrained teleology allows us to clarify one of the most important, yet obscure, ideas in moral and political philosophy: the common good. Insofar as they are forms of constrained teleology, contractualist justifications, I claim, aim at a common good.

This may seem surprising. Contractualism is widely advocated today but the idea of the common good is generally out of favor.[35] Nevertheless, the relation between contractualism and the common good has been recognized. B. J. Diggs, for example, has argued: "Following Rousseau and Kant, there is a fundamental moral requirement that binds one, in matters that concern the common good, to seek a solution to which all can reasonably agree. . . . " And this, he indicates, is another way of framing Kant's idea of the "Original Contract."[36] But it is not simply that contractualism aims at reasonable agreement; when it takes the form of a constrained teleology, contractualism is a theory about the reasons for agreement. Agreement is rational because, from the perspective of each party, the contract promotes what is of value. Because such a contractualist argument seeks to provide a public justification by showing that the values of all are promoted by a certain code of public morality, it follows that a justified morality will be one that promotes the common good. This seemed, for example, to be Hobbes's position. As Jean Hampton writes, "Hobbes maintains that if there were some state of affairs that would be mutually advantageous for all people, this would be a 'common good,' an object that all people would cooperate in pursuing, insofar as it would further everyone's personal goals."[37] Rawls, whose contractualism otherwise shares little with Hobbes's agrees: "Government," he says, "is assumed to aim at the common good, that is, at maintaining conditions and achieving objectives that are similarly to everyone's advantage."[38]

So my claim is that, given constrained teleology, a public morality that failed to promote the common good could not be pub-

35 The main exception here is John Finnis. See his *Natural Law and Natural Rights*. Among Catholic philosophers the idea of the common good continues to be important.
36 B. J. Diggs, "The Common Good As Reason for Political Action," p. 293.
37 Jean Hampton, *Hobbes and the Social Contract Tradition*, pp. 241–2.
38 Rawls, *A Theory of Justice*, p. 233.

licly justified. To say that a morality does not promote the common good is just to say that, from the perspective of at least some people, it does not advance what they value. But if we employ constrained teleology, to justify is to advance value-based reasons in support of a morality. Consequently, if the code fails to adequately[39] advance what is valued by some rational moral persons, they cannot be provided with reasons to embrace it. And so it has not been justified to them.

Because the common good is the substantive criterion by which we justify a public morality, and because the public morality defines rights and duties, it follows that the common good determines what is just. Justice is (at least partially; see §22) defined by the common good. As Gauthier writes, "A just society is concerned only to enable each person to realize the greatest amount of her own good, on terms acceptable to all."[40] A just society, that is, is one based upon a public morality that advances the common good. The intimate relation between justice and the common good is fundamental to almost all conceptions of the common good. "The requirements of justice," writes John Finnis, "are the concrete implications of the basic requirement of practical reasonableness that one is to favour and foster the common good of one's own community."[41] Although the interpretation of the common good I have sketched here owes much more to the individualistic, contractualist tradition than to Aquinas,[42] the theme of relating justice to the advancement of the ends of all unifies the diverse theories of the common good. Even common good theories such as Gauthier's, which derive the common good from a compromise among individuals seeking to maximize the satisfaction of their preferences, do not simply aggregate individual goods a la utilitarianism.[43] Rather, the contract artic-

39 Just what is implied by "adequately" will concern us in what follows.

40 Gauthier, *Morals by Agreement*, p. 341.

41 Finnis, *Natural Law and Natural Rights*, p. 164. Cf. Thomas Aquinas, *Summa Theologica*, pt. II, first part, questions 90–96 (vol. 8); pt. II, second part, questions 47, 58–64, 79 (vol. 10).

42 This contrast is emphasized by some Catholic political theory. See, e.g., Franz H. Muller, "Comparative Social Philosophies: Individualism, Socialism, and Solidarism"; Heinrich A. Rommen, *The State in Catholic Thought*, ch. XIII, esp. pp. 314ff. See also Bruce Douglass, "The Common Good and the Public Interest"; Virginia Held, *The Public Interest and Individual Interests*, chs. 4, 5.

43 See Gauthier, *Morals by Agreement*, p. 341. For an interpretation of the

ulates a truly common good because (i) the public morality is acknowledged as promoting some good – though not necessarily the same good – from every valuational perspective, and (ii) the public morality must advance the values of everyone, and so does not sacrifice any individual to the aggregate or collective welfare.[44]

21 COMMON GOOD ARGUMENTS

Thus far, the discussion of the common good has been fairly abstract. My purpose has been twofold. First, I have sought to provide an alternative interpretation of contractualist justificatory theory, one that leads away from focus on consent toward constrained teleology and the common good. Secondly, I have endeavored to provide a general overview of an individualistic concept of the common good, because it may be somewhat alien to contemporary readers (especially as it bridges – or perhaps calls into question – Brian Barry's distinction between aggregative and distributive principles).[45]

It is now time to descend from these general concerns. A perennial objection to common good theories is that they are overly idealistic or unworkable. In the real world, where real and deep conflict is the norm, we are told that no common good is to be found. If so, and if we insist on the common good as the criterion of a justified public morality, we shall end up with nihilism, for no such justifications will be forthcoming. It would be an exag-

---

common good that does seem to have real affinities with utilitarianism, see Richard Taylor, *Good and Evil*, ch. 10.

44 See Aldo Tussi, "Anarchism, Autonomy, and the Concept of the Common Good," pp. 273–83. Even the Catholic interpretation, which is certainly less individualistic than the contractualist account I am offering, still insists that the individual person's good is not simply a function of the whole. See, e.g., Jacques Maritain, *The Person and the Common Good*, ch. 3.

45 See Barry, *Political Argument*, pp. 43ff., 202–6. See also his "Justice and the Common Good," pp. 189–93. His main normative thesis – that aggregate and distributive principles represent two independent and powerful ways of evaluating states of affairs and policies – is, I would venture, a consequence of the erroneous belief that some values are agent-neutral or provide agent-neutral reasons to act. If there were such values or reasons, then everyone would always have some reason to promote total value. But, if we abandon this picture, seeing that value-based reasons to act are essentially agent-relative, the aim of maximizing value leads directly to the question of whose values are to be maximized, and that in turn brings us to questions of justification and so to issues of fairness and justice.

geration, but not a radical one, to understand the rest of this book as a reply to this nihilistic challenge. I aim to demonstrate that the basic requirement of a rational morality can be met.

In this section, I explore four types of common good arguments. Although the first two may well be subject to the traditional criticisms, the latter two offer viable justificatory arguments.

21.1 Community of valuing

Let us concentrate on the two person case. Alf is committed to justifying his proposed code of public morality to Betty, and she is committed to justifying hers to him. In one case, the justificatory task is apt to be easy: if Alf and Betty value the same things. But this requires immediate clarification, for they may "value the same things" in two very different senses. Take first an obvious case where Alf and Betty appear to value the same thing, for example, wealth. But this apparent identity of valuing masks a conflict, for he values *his having wealth* while she values *herself being wealthy*. There is a common object of valuing, but the valuing also is of a state involving possession excluding others. I have in mind a different sense in which Alf and Betty may value the same thing: let us call it *community of valuing*.[46] If they share a community of valuing, then they really do value the same thing, with no implied indexicals that would ground competition or conflict. We might say, then, that they share values or ideals: all value the environment, national glory, civic culture, or whatever.

Such people would be like-minded, that is, they would care for the same things. Within such a group of like-minded valuers, common good arguments should be straightforward: the limiting case is where everyone values precisely the same things, for then whatever best promotes the valuings of anyone ipso facto best promotes the valuings of all. But, as Durkheim argued, this sort of "mechanical unity" – social unity grounded on sameness among individuals – is not characteristic of modern societies. Indeed, Durkheim maintained that the rise of personality – our in-

46 See R. B. Perry's discussion of community of interest in the *General Theory*, pp. 472ff.; F. C. T. Moore's analysis of "wills in concert" in his *Psychological Basis of Morality*, ch. 9. On community, values, and the common good, see also Arthur E. Murphy, "The Common Good"; W. H. Werkmeister, *Man and his Values*, pp. 205ff.

dividual qualities that distinguish us from others – undermines this sort of unity. Consequently, "[mechanical] solidarity can grow only in inverse ratio to personality."[47] So, within a modern, pluralistic society characterized by individualized personalities, we would not expect this pattern of argument to be dominant, for there may be little community of valuing. Moreover, even when such community is uncovered, little may follow for common good arguments. Alf and Betty may both value the environment, and indeed favor protection measures. But if he values economic growth more than the environment, he might still rationally reject her proposed environmental ethic, which places severe restraints on economic growth. As concluded earlier, we must beware of focusing only on the agreement in value judgment and in so doing ignoring differences in comparative valuations (§§14.3, 16.1).

I am not insisting that it is impossible to base common good arguments on a community of valuing in modern societies. It may reasonably be argued that the universal disvaluing of physical assault and murder provide the grounds for common good arguments justifying a moral code that prohibits them. But, although I have no wish to deny that a code may be thus justified, it is difficult to be confident. Some people, after all, *do* gain by murders. Many, indeed most of us, disvalue these things, but it is not at all clear that everyone does. And if some do not disvalue them, or, what is more likely, if they more highly value the activities that would be prohibited, then the code prohibiting them cannot be justified simply on the grounds of a community of valuings.

But this does not mean that justifications based on a community of valuing are impossible, for they play a crucial role in private morality (§19.2.1). People may, and often do, join together to promote some shared goal or ideal. Forming such an enterprise association, they are all characterized by a commitment to this ideal or goal and a comparative valuing that places this shared valuing above at least some other concerns (for example, they are willing to devote some time or resources to the pursuit of the aim).[48] And in some cases this commitment may be intense:

47 Emile Durkheim, *The Division of Labor in Society*, p. 129.
48 See S. I. Benn, "Individuality, Autonomy, and Community," pp. 47ff.; Lon Fuller, "Two Principles of Human Associations."

members of the enterprise may value their shared goal or ideal above nearly all else.[49] Within these enterprises, then, the justification of principles and policies will crucially depend on the appeal to the community of valuings. But, as Michael Oakeshott has maintained, despite attempts to transform them into enterprises, modern states and societies are not properly conceived thus.[50] They are, rather, characterized by an extremely wide diversity of comparative valuings, and this renders appeal to community of valuings a dubious foundation for the justification of a code of public morality.

21.2 Harmony

English liberalism in the late nineteenth and early twentieth centuries relied on common good justifications; and, for liberals such as T. H. Green and L. T. Hobhouse, common good arguments generally took the form of claims about the essential harmony of individual goods.[51] Like community of valuings, the idea of harmony needs clarification. Let us say that Alf's and Betty's valuings are harmonious if the public morality that best promotes his valuings is that which best promotes hers. This then, is a strong conception of harmony: what is best from his perspective is what is best from hers too.[52] It should be manifest that, in contrast to community of valuings claims, arguments from harmony are consistent with individual diversity of valuings: harmony arguments suppose that people value different things, the essential claim being that morality can be so structured as to maximally advance these diverse aims.[53] It is not difficult to imagine particular cases of pure harmony. Say Alf possesses a baseball bat but

49 For an account of one such intense community, see Bruno Bettelheim, *Children of the Dream*.
50 Michael Oakeshott, *On Human Conduct*.
51 See T. H. Green, *Prolegomena to Ethics*, bks. III, IV; L. T. Hobhouse, *The Rational Good*, esp. chs. IV, V. For discussions of Green's common good theory, see Henry Sidgwick, *Lectures on the Ethics of T. H. Green, Mr. Herbert Spencer, and J. Martineau*; Rashdall, *The Theory of Good and Evil*, vol. II, pp. 98–104; Geoffrey Thomas, *The Moral Philosophy of T. H. Green*, pp. 253–5. See also my *Modern Liberal Theory of Man*.
52 Some have advocated a very weak version of harmony, *viz.*, "negative" harmony as compatible or nonconflicting goods. See Perry, *General Theory*, pp. 513–14; Finnis, *Natural Law and Natural Rights*, pp. 138ff.
53 For an analysis from a very different perspective that arrives at some similar conclusions, see Moore, *The Psychological Basis of Morality*, ch. 8.

dislikes baseball (and has no other uses for a baseball bat) and Betty possesses a cricket bat though she dislikes cricket (and has no other use for the bat). Should it be the case that Alf is a devoted cricketer and Betty is an avid baseball player, a trade of bats will best advance the valuings of each.

Gauthier extends this reasoning to propose a general justification of the market. The concept of a perfectly competitive market, he claims, reveals "a structure in which divergent and seemingly opposed interests of different individuals *fully harmonize*."[54] Gauthier is entirely right in claiming that, if this is true, the market would be a zone free from moral constraints. For, if the market structure really does best promote the values of everyone, the problem of constraining value maximization does not arise. Strictly speaking, arguments from the harmony of values do not really justify moral constraints: they are, rather, arguments that some forms of interaction do not need to constrain value maximization. That Gauthier recognizes this clearly indicates that he is employing "harmony" in the strong sense I have proposed.

Care needs to be exercised in evaluating Gauthier's important claim. He does not claim that the operation of the market presupposes no constraints. "Before Smith's invisible hand can do its beneficent work, Hobbes' war of every man against every man must first be exorcised. And this . . . means that the ideal of free interaction which Smith celebrates is not natural but artificial, arising, for rational persons, only within a framework of agreed constraints."[55] As did the classical political economists, then, Gauthier distinguishes the "*conditions* of the market from its *operation*."[56] The conditions for the market include, for instance, private property and constraints on the use of force and fraud. These require independent justifications, and Gauthier does not contend that harmony arguments will suffice. But, once these conditions are provided, then Gauthier claims that the market harmonizes the efforts of each to maximize his values.

I have not captured the subtlety and sophistication of Gauthier's harmony-based justification of the market order. It is certainly one of the most powerful harmony arguments in moral

54 Gauthier, *Morals by Agreement*, p. 83 (emphasis added).
55 Ibid., p. 85.
56 Ibid., p. 94. On the classical economists, see my "Public and Private Interests in Liberal Political Economy, Old and New," pp. 186-95.

and political philosophy. Despite this, it seems to fail, and this for two reasons.

(i) To see the first problem, assume that Alf is a seller of oranges, and is willing to sell *q* quantity of oranges for any price greater than \$*m*.[57] Betty, a buyer, is willing to pay any price less than \$*n*. If $n > m$, then there is a range of bargains contained in the set *S*, where $m < S < n$. Because Alf does best as the bargain approaches *n* and Betty does best if the price approaches *m*, the final price which is best for him is not that which is best for her. Both, to be sure, gain by exchange, but their interests do not fully harmonize. This is precisely the feature of market transactions that radical economists have focused on, that is, the conflictual element in a market exchange.

Some might be tempted to argue that concentrating on this micro situation ignores crucial macro relations between price and supply. Overall, will not the seller supply the good until just the point where its marginal cost equals its marginal benefit?[58] But such optimality does not imply harmony. A particular buyer pays only for what the last unit (*l*) is worth; the difference in value between the worth of a $l - i$ unit and the price of the *l* unit accrues to the consumer. Figure 1 illustrates this familiar phenomenon of consumers' surplus.[59] In Figure 1, consumers purchase quantity *q* for price *m*; the hatched area CS indicates utility that consumers would pay for but do have to. Although economists often claim that the consumers' surplus is not achieved at the expense of the seller, this can be misleading. If it is intended to point out that both sellers and consumers gain, then it is certainly true. But, again, it is wrong if taken as a claim that harmony obtains. If sellers could redistribute CS from consumers to themselves they would: the *best* arrangement from the sellers' perspective would be to receive all of CS. And monopolists may be able to do so, requiring consumers to pay all that the good is worth to them.

(ii) Gauthier assumes in his analysis that "Each person's utility is strictly determined by the goods he consumes and the factor services he provides."[60] I shall have more to say later on about positing such limitations on the sorts of values that enter into jus-

57 I am adopting here Robert Nozick, *Anarchy, State, and Utopia*, pp. 63–4.
58 See Gauthier, *Morals by Agreement*, pp. 90ff.
59 For a standard treatment, see Paul Samuelson, *Economics*, pp. 438–40.
60 Gauthier, *Morals by Agreement*, pp. 86–7.

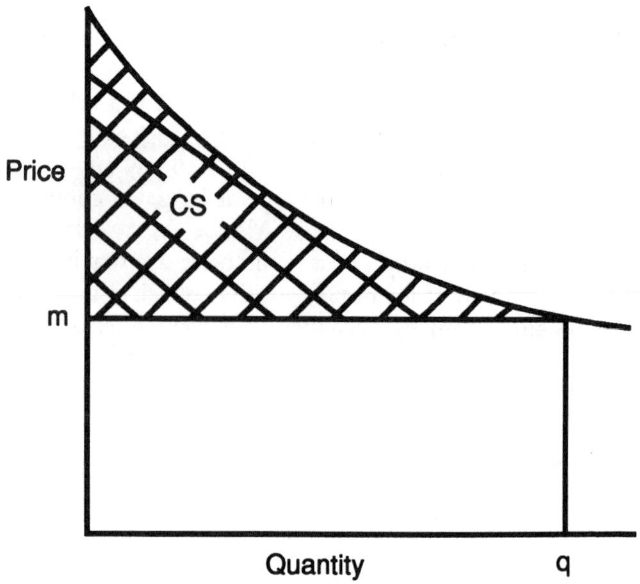

Figure 1.

tificatory argument (§22.1), but suffice it for now to note that it entirely misses the force of David Braybrooke's interesting objection to the market. Braybrooke upholds preferences (or values) opposed to the market and market relations:

> The dangers to justice include the danger of imposing market arrangements on people whose preferences at bottom disfavor having a market. How can those preferences be disregarded in favor of contrary preferences without prejudice – without unjustifiably discriminating against . . . [them] in the provision of things valued. If, as a species of injustice, this looks a bit *recherché*, it is only because it is commonly settled without attention, by prejudice.[61]

Such people upset any claim that the market *harmonizes* values. Even given a justification of the basic framework, important valuings of such people may be significantly set back by their participation in market relations.

61 David Braybrooke, "Preferences Opposed to the Market," p. 103.

21.3 *Compromise*

21.3.1 Rational compromise

It seems reasonable to conclude that, like community of valuings, harmony of valuings fairly rarely can justify elements of a public morality in plural societies. But this does not eliminate the possibility of common good arguments, for everyone's valuings may still be advanced even when they are not all best advanced. An arrangement may be justified on the grounds of its being a *compromise*: all gain, but each must give up something to elicit the agreement of the others. Compromise, as Martin Golding has noted, supposes a conflict insofar as each cannot get what he would most like. But it also requires some coincidence of interests or values: each, after all, does gain something from a compromise.[62] Compromise, then, can occur when the conditions for community of valuing and harmony are not met, yet some common good still exists. J. L. Mackie recognizes the importance of such compromise in the justification of moral principles. "We must," he says, "lower our sights a little and look not for principles which can be wholeheartedly endorsed from every point of view; but for ones which represent an acceptable compromise between different actual points of view."[63] Understood thus, we can see that the contractualist tradition has relied on such compromise in justifying morality.[64] As Rawls puts it, "the principles of justice are the result of a fair agreement or bargain."[65] And, if the justification is also teleological, the pact frames a compromise that articulates a common good.

The great difficulty with employing compromise arguments is to determine what, to use Mackie's word, is an "acceptable" compromise. A necessary condition for a proposal to be acceptable (or more accurately a reasonable compromise) is that it advances the values of all. But pretty clearly that is not sufficient. Assume that a variety of public moralities advance the values of everyone: call the set of such proposals *P*. Unless harmony ob-

62 Martin Golding, "The Nature of Compromise," pp. 3–25.
63 J. L. Mackie, *Ethics*, p. 93.
64 This is shown by Arthur Kuflik, "Morality and Compromise," pp. 55–64.
65 Rawls, *Theory of Justice*, p. 12. Cf. also his description of the contract as a "pact of reconciliation" (p. 221).

tains, for any proposed public morality *p*1 that is a member of *P*, some person will reasonably object that from his valuational perspective *p*1 advances his values less than some other member of *P*, and so he gives up too much if *p*1 is chosen. For any proposal, we must expect the less advantaged to claim that the proposal does not constitute a reasonable bargain. We thus require some criterion as to what constitutes a reasonable compromise.

Following John Harsanyi, Martin Golding makes a useful suggestion. It is plausible to suppose that a rational bargainer will not expect others to make larger concessions than he is willing to make.[66] The intuitive idea is straightforward.[67] In advancing *p*1 as a reasonable compromise to Alf, Betty is claiming that it is rational for him to accept *p*1. But if the two are equally rational bargainers,[68] Betty cannot claim that, though it is rational for Alf to accept the level of concession required by *p*1, she would never accept such a large concession. If they are equally rational, why should Alf rationally accept a level of concession that Betty sees as irrational? From this it follows that a rational Betty will not ask Alf to make a larger concession than she is willing to make.

As Golding notes, this points to a "50-50 split."[69] David Gauthier, however, develops this equal rationality intuition in another way that does not always lead to equal concessions. He focuses on society as a cooperative endeavor; given the existence of cooperative interaction that leads to gains – benefits that would not be available without the cooperation – he investigates what distribution of these gains would be agreed to by rational bargainers. Basic to his argument are the contrasts between what I will call one's *initial position*, one's *first proposal*, and one's *final concession*. One's initial position is what one brings into the bargaining situation; one's first proposal is the most one might claim. Gauthier writes:

66 Golding, "The Nature of Compromise," p. 15.
67 But not uncontroversial. For criticisms, see Thomas C. Schelling, *The Strategy of Conflict*, pp. 287ff.; Gilbert Harman, "Rationality in Agreement," pp. 6–8; Brian Barry, *Theories of Justice*, p. 20.
68 Describing each party as "an equally rational bargainer" does not imply "equal bargaining ability," a term that, as John Nash noted, "suggests something like skill in duping the other fellow. The usual haggling process is based on imperfect information, the hagglers trying to propagandize each other into misconceptions of the utilities involved." "Two-person Cooperative Games," p. 138. Brian Barry seems to ignore this in his criticism of the equal concession rule. *Theories of Justice*, p. 20.
69 Golding, "The Nature of Compromise," p. 15.

Each wants to get as much as possible; each therefore claims as much as possible. But in deciding how much is possible, each is constrained by the recognition that he must neither drive others away from the bargaining table, nor be excluded by them. Hence each person's claim is limited by the overall cooperative surplus, and more specifically by the portion of the surplus that it is possible for him to receive. To claim more would be to propose that others give up some of what they brought to the bargaining table. . . . [N]o rational person can expect others to do this.[70]

Lastly, one's final concession is the claim one advances in order to reach agreement, a claim that will typically be somewhere between one's initial position and one's first proposal. Now Gauthier measures the relative concessions each person makes in a bargain by comparing the utility of his initial position [call it U(ip)], the utility he would achieve if granted his first proposal [call it U(fp)], and the utility that he actually gets from his final concession [U(fc)]. So, a person's actual concession is the difference between the utility of his first proposal and the utility of his final concession [$U(\text{fp}) - U(\text{fc})$]. The magnitude of his complete concession would be the difference between his first proposal and his initial position; if his concession brings him back to his initial position, he concedes everything in the sense that he gains nothing from the cooperative endeavor. In such a complete concession, then, one would give up $U(\text{fp}) - U(\text{ip})$. Equipped with these two measures, Gauthier formulates the notion of the relative magnitude of a person's concession (RC): the proportion of the actual concession to the complete concession. That is:[71]

$$\text{(equation 3) RC} = \frac{U(\text{fp}) - U(\text{fc})}{U(\text{fp}) - U(\text{ip})}$$

We are now able to describe Gauthier's principle of *minimax relative concession*. Each person can be assigned, for any possible outcome of a bargain, a measure of relative magnitude of concession that will range between 0 and 1: if one makes no concession at all, that is, if one's first proposal is accepted, the relative magnitude of one's concession will be 0; if one's final concession is equal to one's initial position, the relative magnitude of concession will be 1. Gauthier argues that the bargainer whose "ratio

70 Gauthier, *Morals by Agreement*, pp. 143–4.
71 Ibid., p. 136. I have altered the names of some of these variables and have slightly changed the notation.

between cost of concession and cost of deadlock is less must rationally concede to the others."[72] This articulates the intuition that a rational bargainer confronting other rational bargainers will not expect others to make greater relative concessions than he is willing to make. So he will not suppose that a deadlock in negotiations would be broken by the concession of the other if that concession is of a greater relative magnitude than would be required of him, were he to break the deadlock by conceding. Whoever loses less by conceding (with this being measured by the relative magnitude of concession) would be irrational to expect others to concede; for, if he refuses the smaller concession, how can he expect equally rational others to grant a larger one? "Since each person, as a utility maximizer, seeks to minimize his concession, then no one can expect any other rational person to be willing to make a concession if he would not be willing to make a similar concession."[73] Consequently, a rational bargainer confronting other equally rational bargainers would acknowledge that the person of whom the lesser relative concession is required must concede.

> Extending this rule to bargaining among several persons, we claim that . . . given a range of outcomes, each of which requires concessions by some or all persons if it is to be selected, then an outcome [should] be selected only if the greatest or *maximum* relative concession it requires, is as small as possible, or a *minimum*, that is, no greater than the maximum relative concession required by every other outcome. We call this the principle of minimum-maximum, or *minimax relative concession*.[74]

21.3.2 Minimax relative concession and the theory of justification

If Gauthier's project succeeds, he shows that morality can be justified by appeal to a common good argument: morality can be understood as a rational compromise or bargain. Moreover, according to the principle of minimax relative concession, the commonsense notion of a reasonable or acceptable bargain can be formalized, and this in a way that does not apparently depend on intuitions about fairness or justice.[75]

---

72 Ibid., pp. 74–5.
73 Ibid., pp. 143–4.
74 Ibid., p. 137.
75 "The problem with this argument," Jules Coleman argues, "is that it ig-

In Chapter IX, I employ Gauthier's principle of minimax relative concession in my discussion of the social contract and the sort of public morality it endorses. As we will see, my interpretation of the principle differs significantly from that proposed by Gauthier; in particular, the characterizations of the initial bargaining position and each party's first (that is, best) proposal are radically different in Gauthier's and my account. For the moment, however, we can put aside these complications. In the context of the present discussion, the importance of Gauthier's principle it that is makes more precise our ideas about a common good based on compromise. Theories which insist that morality must work (in some sense) to the advantage of all are often confronted with a dilemma. If they insist that morality must work to maximum advantage of all (that is, harmony) they are unworkable, because no such harmony obtains. On the other hand, if it is good enough that morality provides some – however meager – advantage, then it is far too weak a requirement. And if the proponent of the common good insists that some fair compromise is required, it seems as if he is building on a hopelessly vague requirement. Gauthier's principle helps point the way toward a solution to these difficulties.

Several objections to my employing minimax relative concession should, however, be considered here. As I previously noted (§20.1), Gauthier proffers an account of value in terms of preference satisfaction, and I have rejected such accounts as inadequate (§7.2.4). Can we adopt Gauthier's principle of minimax relative concession while rejecting the account of value on which it is based? We can because we can adopt the concept of preference satisfaction as a way to describe rational choice in some circumstances without embracing it as a theory of value. To see this, assume that each individual, given his values, ranks, with respect to how well they promote his values, all the possible codes of public morality that might be proposed and that can

nores the potential unfairness of the initial positions." *Markets, Morals, and the Law*, p. 339. Brian Barry, however, has persuasively argued that theories such as Gauthier's, which seek to base justice on mutual advantage and self-interest, *aim* to build upon the unequal bargaining power in the initial, precontractual, situation. *Theories of Justice*, esp. Part I. However, as I hope will become clear in my argument in Chapter IX, I do not follow Gauthier in this regard; I endeavor to develop a description of the baseline position that is not open to Coleman's objection.

plausibly be said to advance the valuings of all. Call this ranking his preference ordering. Assuming the standard characteristics of completeness, transitivity, and asymmetry of preference/symmetry of indifference, we can generate from this an interval utility scale for each person ranging from 1 to 0.[76] The contractors' preferences, then, range over codes of public morality, and an interval "utility" scale provides an indirect measure of the extent to which each code advances one's values.

Here, and throughout this chapter, I have been referring exclusively to what "advances" or "promotes" one's values. But earlier (§9.2) I found inadequate the doctrine that the only reasons implied by valuings are maximizing reasons. It may thus seem that employing Gauthier's bargaining model commits us to embracing a flawed account of value-based reasons to act. Not so: my use of minimax relative concession does not require focusing on the maximization of values. Each person, we can say, evaluates each proposed code of public morality in the light of all his values and the reasons for action they imply, be they reasons to promote, protect, or respect. Each rational contractor thus asks: "In the light of these reasons and values, how does this public morality rank?" This evaluation, then, will yield the necessary preference ordering. Although for sake of simplicity I will continue to employ the language of "advancing" and "maximizing," the argument is consistent with a broader view of value-based reasons to act.

A third possible difficulty concerns Gauthier's reliance on the assumption of "non-tuisim." Following Wicksteed, Gauthier defines a non-tuistic motivated agent as one who is not interested in the purposes of the person with whom he is interacting. Wicksteed employed the notion of "non-tuisim" to show why economic science does not presuppose egoistic motivation. According to him, people enter into economic relations for the most selfish and the most altruistic reasons, and this wide range of reasons is entirely consistent with economic analysis. All economics supposes, he argued, is that when one enters a business transaction one is not concerned to promote the interests of the persons

76 All this is standard in the literature on preference and choice. For useful discussions, see S. I. Benn and G. W. Mortimore, "Technical Models of Rational Choice," esp. pp. 160–71; George Wright, *Behavioural Decision Theory*. See also Gauthier, *Morals by Agreement*, ch. II.

with whom one is then transacting. It is in this way that "[t]he specific character of an economic relation is not its 'egoism,' but its non-tuism."[77] However, when our concern is the contractarian justification of morality, which involves the justification of morality to all by each, non-tuism seems essentially the same as universal mutual disinterestedness; no one takes an interest in the satisfaction of anyone else's preferences.[78] Gauthier is explicit that this is the proper basis for the justification of morality. "Morals by agreement," he tells us, "have a non-tuistic rationale."[79] Indeed, as he sees it, to allow altruistic concerns to enter into the justification of morality would pave the way for exploitation. According to Gauthier, "the contractarian sees sociability as enriching human life; for him, it becomes a source of exploitation if it induces persons to acquiesce in institutions and practices that but for their fellow-feelings would be costly to them. Feminist thought has surely made this, perhaps the core form of exploitation, clear to us."[80] Gauthier does not, of course, seek to deny that people are often benevolently inclined, but he insists that altruistic concerns properly develop only on the basis of a non-tuistically justified morality.[81]

I shall return to this issue presently (§22.1), but it seems obvious enough that, if a teleological approach to justification is sound, we must be prepared to admit the full range of values. People do care deeply about others, and in some areas of social life these are the dominant relevant values. How could we, for instance, arrive at an adequate justification of the practice of friendship without appealing to the value friends place on each other's welfare?[82] If people do value the welfare of others far above their own, an appeal to this valuing in a justificatory argument is entirely appropriate. Or, as I have depicted the bargaining procedure here, in proposing his preferred code of public morality, an

77 Philip H. Wicksteed, *The Common Sense of Political Economy*, vol. I, p. 180. The relevant discussion is on pp. 170–83.
78 Gauthier distinguishes these on p. 87 of *Morals by Agreement*. The idea of mutual disinterestedness is described by Rawls in *A Theory of Justice*, p. 87.
79 Gauthier, *Morals by Agreement*, p. 328.
80 Ibid., p. 11. The claim is repeated on p. 351.
81 Ibid., pp. 327ff., ch. XI.
82 As Kant remarked, "friendship cannot be a union aimed at mutual advantage." *The Doctrine of Virtue*, p. 142 (sec. 46). If so, it seems misguided to justify it in terms of mutual advantage.

individual is to consider the full range of his sound values when determining whether it is best from his valuational perspective. Only by employing some theory of value according to which each most values leading his own life, and is most concerned with promoting his own private good, will it seem objectionable to admit such valuings. To be sure, liberal political philosophers have often employed such essentially private theories of "the good," which serve to circumscribe the range of values that matter in justification, but such limitations are no less objectionable for that.[83] If liberalism can only be justified by resort to such a truncated understanding of what values count, then we would have to conclude that it cannot really be justified.

Now it may well seem that the resort to the bargaining model itself implies some sort of non-tuism or mutual disinterestedness. Bargaining would seem to be a paradigm of an economic relation, and if, as Wicksteed said, economic relations suppose non-tuism, it would seem that employing the bargaining model commits us to some sort of non-tuism. It is important to distinguish (i) the values according to which people order the various proposed moral codes, and (ii) the bargaining between contractors as to which moral code is to be adopted. Regarding (i), I suppose an unlimited domain of sound valuings. When evaluating a proposed moral code, an individual can consider his valuing that others are successful in advancing their own values. One can ask, for instance: "If we adopt this moral code, will the valuings of those others be more likely to be advanced?"; if they are, and if one values that, one has some reason to support the code.[84] However, regarding (ii) we can insist on non-tuism. After having evaluated each proposed moral code in the light of one's complete value system, including all one's altruistic valuings, one's utility function in the bargaining situation is independent of the satisfactions of others' preferences (for moral codes). This version of

83 Kenneth Arrow notices and criticizes this aspect of liberal theory in his "Values and Collective Decision-making," pp. 222–3.

84 It is possible to create circles if one describes the negotiators in very narrow ways. Say Alf only values that Betty's values are furthered, while she only values that his are. So they each have only one value: that the other's single value is promoted. But real people's emotional lives are not so narrow: even if Alf cares deeply for Betty and she for him, they will have other values on which their altruism can get a foothold. There are many important and troublesome issues in moral theory; it is hard to see this as one of them.

non-tuism in no way implies that one cares most for one's own life or that moral principles that appeal to altruism are exploitative. All it supposes is that one is devoted to one's values and not (directly) to what others value. Consequently, once one has evaluated each proposed code with respect to one's values, one has taken into account all relevant considerations: no basis for further altruism exists.

21.4 Proceduralism

I have been arguing that a constrained teleology, aiming at the common good, can employ a notion of compromise: a justified moral code advances everyone's values, but not maximally. But surely sometimes it will not be possible for all to gain. In such cases, it appears that the common good fails as the criterion of justice. According to W. G. Runciman and Amartya K. Sen, the set of rules satisfying the requirement of the common good is a (proper) subset of the set of rules that satisfy the criterion of "social justice." Interpreting Rousseau's notion of the general will, they write:

> . . . the common good may be taken to be substantively embodied in what the general will wills: but the general will does not will anything which requires that any person should be a long-term loser. Although it may, of course, require him to forgo the pursuit of an individual advantage which, without forced collusion, would leave him in the end worse off. We may say, if you like, that the general will always fulfills the conditions of Pareto optimality, although it is not suggested thereby that Pareto optimality is a sufficient criterion of justice.[85]

A good example of a situation where this criterion seems inadequate to ground a judgment about justice is described in one of Lawrence Kohlberg's dilemmas:

> In Korea, a company of ten Marines was outnumbered and was retreating before the enemy. The company had crossed the river, but the enemy were still on the other side. If someone went back to the bridge and blew it up, the company could then escape. However, the man who stayed back to blow up the bridge would not be able to escape alive. The captain asked for a volunteer, but no one offered to go. If no one went back, it was virtually certain that all would die. The captain was the only person who could lead the retreat.

85 W. G. Runciman and Amartya K. Sen, "Games, Justice, and the General Will," pp. 557–8.

> The captain finally decided that he had two alternatives. The first was to order the demolition man to stay behind. If this man was sent, the probability that the mission would be accomplished successfully was 80 percent. The second alternative was to select someone by drawing a name out of a hat with everyone's name in it. If anyone other than the demolition man were selected, the probability that the mission would be accomplished successfully was 70 percent.
>
> Which alternative should the captain choose and why?[86]

Whatever should be done, it seems clear enough that no outcome advances the values of all, for at least one person will die. (Because no one volunteered for the dangerous mission, we can presume that no one has a value system such that sacrificing himself for the others would best advance what he values (see §14.3). If justice is not silent on such matters, then it would seem to follow that there is more to justice than constrained teleology can capture.

Now I shall shortly argue that justice does indeed extend beyond the common good, but not because of situations like this. That the outcome does not advance the valuings of all does not imply that common good justifications cannot be employed, for procedures relying on uncertainty may be justified by resort to the common good. Consider more carefully the position of the captain's Marines. Let us focus once again on the crucial two-person case, where one Marine is the demolition expert and the other is any other member of the company except the captain. Three obvious alternatives present themselves: no one goes (and both die), the inexperienced Marine goes (he dies, the other has a 70 percent chance of surviving), the demolition man goes (he dies, the other has an 80 percent chance of staying alive). It seems pretty clear that all three outcomes will be rejected by either one or both soldiers. But consider now the fourth alternative: a procedure to select a person to go back. *Ex ante*, such a procedure gives each person a possibility of advancing his values. We can imagine a range of such procedures, from those that will obviously result in a particular person being selected (for example, majority voting), to various procedures that employ a random element coupled with some bias ("Give the demolition man two chances of being selected, everyone else one") to a procedure in which each has an equal chance of being selected. I do not wish

86 Lawrence Kohlberg, "Justice as Reversibility," p. 206.

to consider here just what option would be selected (see §28.2). The important point is that each person could rank the expected utility of each procedure vis-à-vis the promotion of his value system. In the absence of agreement, let us say, everyone will die: so any procedure that gives one an expected utility of greater than certain death will improve upon the no-agreement point. So a procedure such as "the demolition man must go" will require a relative concession of 1 from the demolition man. He is certain to die, and so this constitutes no improvement over the no-agreement point. As we introduce randomizing procedures, and so give everyone a chance of surviving, the maximum relative concession – calculated in terms of expected utility – will decrease.

I will not pursue the complexities of this case. The important point is that compromise can be understood as essentially procedural.[87] On this view, given some procedure, whatever decision is reached constitutes a reasonable compromise. To be sure, giving each a chance of advancing his values is not the same as promoting each person's values. A procedure justified by a common good argument need not yield an outcome that satisfies the common good. But this does not imply that procedures cannot be justified by resort to the common good, but only that we need a rationale for determining whether the subject of a justification is to be an outcome or a procedure. Depending on what is justified by appeal to the common good, different results will emerge. Kohlberg's dilemma is so structured that the only possible justification must concern procedures: if one does not appeal to a justified procedure, nothing one does will be justified.

Justifications aiming at the common good are apt to differ depending upon whether they interpret the common good in a substantive or an essentially procedural manner. F. A. Hayek, for instance, presents an essentially procedural justification of a free-market order.[88] According to him, "[t]here is no need morally to justify specific distributions (of income or wealth) which have not

87 See Golding, "The Nature of Compromise," pp. 7–8.

88 Many readers are apt to think of Rawls's theory in this context, but the ways in which his theory is or is not procedural are complex indeed. See his "The Basic Structure as Subject." See also Robert Paul Wolff, *Understanding Rawls*, pp. 177–9. "I think it is clear," Wolff writes, "that there really is no genuine appeal to the notion of pure procedural justice in Rawls' full-scale version of his theory" (p. 177).

been brought about deliberately but are the outcome of a game that is played because it improves the chances of all."[89] Indeed, Hayek explicitly tells us that the "common good" is to be understood in terms of an "abstract order . . . which will increase everyone's chances as much as possible."[90] But, he adds, this does not preclude that some people will be losers. Thus, in contrast to Gauthier, who indicates that long-term losers are not sanctioned by the contractarian method,[91] Hayek's conception of the common good suggests that it is, at least for practical purposes, inevitable that some people will be overall losers in a fully justified social order.

It seems that we are confronted with two opposing interpretations of the common good: as that which actually advantages all and that which gives everyone a chance of advancing his values. In principle, both public moralities relying on procedural and nonprocedural compromise can be allowed in the contractual situation I have depicted. Each person, when evaluating whether a code advances his values, can perform the relevant expected utility calculations. It may well be that some codes employing risky procedures will nevertheless rank higher than proposals where the outcome is certain. To make the point more concrete, we can conjecture that some contractors would rank Hayek's free-market morality – even with its element of risk – higher than an ascetic morality in which it is certain how their values will fare. So there is no theoretical bar to advancing codes of public morality that rely heavily on procedures in which some people do, all things considered, lose out.

However, three further considerations indicate that such proposals are not apt to be embraced. (i) First, the contractors know just who they are, what their talents are, and the nature of their value systems. The contractual situation I have envisaged employs no Rawlsian "veil of ignorance." Hence, those who know that they will do badly under some procedure – for example, those who know they will lose out in the market – will score it very low. (ii) Secondly, if an outcome is to be procedurally justified, the procedure must actually have been employed. A procedure

89 F. A. Hayek, *The Mirage of Social Justice*, p. 117.
90 Ibid., p. 114.
91 Gauthier insists that justified morality benefits all. *Morals by Agreement*, p. 11.

such as that I have been considering justifies some outcome if it is a justified procedure and it has actually been employed. So, one cannot justify an outcome to those who lose out by showing that this outcome might have been generated by a reasonable procedure: it must actually have been produced by the justified procedure. (iii) Lastly, the procedure must be justified before the outcome has been generated. This is, I think, an implication of points (i) and (ii). To see this better, say that Alf, a follower of Hayek, seeks to justify the current distribution of income by showing that it is a consequence of a Hayekian public morality that promotes a procedural interpretation of the common good. But the losers know that they are losers because the procedure has already been employed; they will rank Alf's procedure at the bottom of their utility scale. Now Betty may try to advance the free-market cause in a more Nozickian way: "Let's start from scratch," she may say, "and henceforth employ the free market to distribute income." This is apt to fare better than Alf's proposal because no one knows that they are certain to be losers under Betty's proposal. But many people will have good grounds for expecting to lose and so they will still score her proposal pretty low.

Given (i), (ii), and (iii), it does not seem that proceduralism will loom large in the plausible proposals. A strongly procedural proposal would depict morality as a sort of ongoing lottery (ongoing because new players must be given their chance to win) that was at some prior time rationally accepted by the participants. I shall not further explore this rather exotic possibility. I shall take it that the main task of a contractual justification is to show that all do indeed benefit. Our aim, then, is to construct a rational morality – one we can show that rational moral persons have reason to embrace. If we can show that this morality advances their values in a way that articulates a fair compromise, we will have succeeded in that task. But none of this is a bar to justified public moralities employing procedures in some spheres. For instance, if a public morality justified conscription, then it may justify sending some and not others off to fight by employing a procedural argument: selecting through a lottery. So, although we have good grounds for doubting the justifiability of a public morality that is essentially a lottery, a public morality employing lotteries when some must be sacrificed seems plausible.

I wish to conclude this analysis of common good arguments by considering whether they must satisfy Bruce A. Ackerman's Neutrality condition, according to which "[n]o reason is a good reason if it requires the power holder to assert: (a) that his conception of the good is better than that asserted by his fellow citizens, or (b) that, regardless of his conception of the good, he is intrinsically superior to one or more of his fellow citizens."[92] Our analysis of value, public justification, and the common good all provide general support for the spirit of Ackerman's Neutrality condition: Alf cannot justify a moral demand on Betty (that is, a moral principle that purports that she has reasons to act at the cost of her values) by pointing out either (i) that it promotes valuings that she does not share, or (ii) that it is impersonally valuable, though she can have no access to such value. As I have already argued, neither (i) nor (ii) shows that a rational Betty is committed to acting (§§10.3, 12.1).

However, our analysis of valuing and reasons for actions indicates crucial departures from Ackerman's rather straightforward principle. Although it seems right to emphasize that one's sound valuings, *qua* one's sound valuings, do not provide others with reasons to act or to embrace moral principles, it does not seem right to insist that sound justificatory arguments cannot rest upon the claim that one's "conception of the good" is superior to another's. Two such claims of superiority are sound. Firstly, if something is impersonally valuable, and if Alf has reason to believe that Betty can appreciate it, then as an impersonal value judgment it does provide her with a prima facie reason to act even if it is not now valued by her, that is, is not part of her conception of the good. And it does not defeat this claim to say that she refuses to acknowledge her commitment to act. Our concern is what commitments to act a fully rational agent possesses, not what commitments actual agents recognize (see §16.2); so denying that one has a commitment does not destroy that commitment. Thus, pace Ackerman, if citizen Betty has a conception of the good that does not recognize the impersonal value of *V*, and if Betty has access to *V*, then Alf can provide Betty with a good justificatory reason even though it supposes that his con-

92 Bruce A. Ackerman, *Social Justice in the Liberal State*, p. 11.

ception of the good is better than hers (which, *ex hypothesi*, it is). That is, he might advance a common good argument to show that a public moral code can be justified to her because it promotes an impersonal value.

Secondly, Alf may claim that some of Betty's present valuings are unsound (§10.4) and so, whatever she may think, sound justifications cannot appeal to them. So if, say, she greatly disvalues the very possibility that others may be engaged in any sort of deviant sexual practices anywhere, Alf can intelligibly claim that her disvaluing is unsound, being a neurotic reaction and, so, premised on an inappropriate set of beliefs, or is based on false beliefs, or, perhaps, the content (that is, object) of the emotional state is inappropriate (§6.3). (Much depends here on the details of Alf's account.) If Alf is right, Betty's disvaluing is unsound, and is to be ignored in justificatory arguments. So (assuming that no other factors are relevant), that some code of public morality would prohibit these activities does not count as a reason for even Betty to embrace it. Alf's claim is, of course, highly contentious; it depends on a theory of neurosis and that in turn presumably depends on some sort of psychoanalytic theory. This is a point of absolutely fundamental importance: actual justificatory arguments rely on empirical claims, and these claims themselves are open to dispute. Alf will offer his psychoanalytic critique of Betty's adverse reactions to the sexual practices of others; and she will reply, perhaps criticizing the empirical soundness of his theory, perhaps arguing from within a psychoanalytic framework that his conclusions are unfounded. This makes justificatory arguments complex, often tentative, and it certainly shows that moral and political theory is not able to achieve any Euclidean-like deductive rigor in justifying a particular code of public morality. Whether or not particular valuings are sound, whether or not particular codes will advance or retard valuings, and how they compare to others in this way are all matters which depend on empirical claims that are open to dispute. Justificatory arguments then cannot achieve deductive certainty. This is not to say that moral and political philosophy has nothing to say on these matters; in the next two chapters, I shall advance arguments that aim to justify a certain sort of public morality. But that enterprise will depend on a number of empirical assumptions and its results will be tentative.

This position is challenged by John Rawls, who stresses that a justification must be public not simply in the sense that it is addressed to all (that is, aims to provide everyone with good reasons) but that the reasons advanced must be essentially noncontroversial (that is, they must be publicly recognized as reasons). Ways of reasoning relying on common sense and the well-established and noncontroversial methods and conclusions of science can be relied upon; philosophic and religious, (and I would think, psychoanalytic) doctrines open to dispute are thus ruled out of place in public justifications. And, consequently, because the soundness of conceptions of the good are likewise open to dispute, they are assigned "a public status analogous to religion."[93] Rawls's pragmatic concerns are evident here (§§2.4, 19.2): his aim really is to provide justificatory arguments that citizens of modern democracies actually can agree upon, and so form the basis for a public conception of justice. Let me reiterate: it seems wrong to understand philosophic ethics in this radically practical way. Ethics is practical, but only insofar as agents are rational, and so do what they have reason to do (§16.2). But, in providing reasons to act and to embrace moral codes, philosophic ethics need not, and properly does not, search for practical agreement on what particular considerations constitute good reasons. The problem as to what is a good reason for an individual will be resolved by the theory, and its conclusions may be both sound and, to some degree, surprising and contentious.

Rawls's pragmatic account thus does seem to imply something very much like Ackerman's Neutrality condition: from the perspective of public justification, individuals cannot base a justificatory argument on an appeal to superior valuations. But we now possess a theory of value, and in contrast to Rawls, I do not see its controversial character as disallowing it as a basis for public justification. So my defense of neutrality is very much circumscribed; indeed, it is probably better not to employ this problematic notion.

Might not it be argued, however, that Ackerman's neutrality is fundamental to true liberalism – that justifications ought to appeal to what a person values, even if this valuing is ultimately mistaken? Isn't it illiberal to insist that Betty's irrational valuings

93 Rawls, "Kantian Constructivism," p. 540.

do not count? It must be stressed – indeed, it cannot be stressed too much – that my concern at present is what values count in the *justification of morality*, not whether a person is to be accorded a moral right to pursue his unsound valuings. There is a tendency – illustrated by Ackerman's Neutrality principle – to equate liberalism's devotion to everyone's right to live according to his own valuings with a thesis that liberalism is so deeply skeptical about value claims that it cannot admit as relevant in justificatory discourse the distinction between what is truly valuable and what is merely valued. Indeed, this tendency is so strong that some readers may insist that my account forfeits all claims to be liberal simply because it admits such a distinction. Pretty clearly, I think that is wrong. That liberals treat, in a variety of normative and policy contexts, everyone's valuings as if they were equally sound, does not imply that they are equally sound, or that somehow liberalism is committed to an axiology or meta-ethics that ignores their inequality.[94] Equal liberty can be grounded on less skeptical theories of value and justification, as I hope to show in Chapters VIII and IX.

22 VALUE AND DEONTOLOGY

22.1 The problem of circularity

It is difficult to overestimate the attraction of teleology. To many philosophers, it is obviously the only sensible approach to ethics. In no small part, this is due to the attraction of the orthodox view of value and reasons (§16.1): if all rational action is aimed at promoting value, it will be difficult indeed to conceive of any reasonable justification of morality except that which shows it to advance value. But, even apart from the orthodox view of value and reasons, R. B. Perry's remark has a certain bite: "It is certainly a doubtful compliment to the right to deny that it does not of itself do good."[95] Even contractualist justification, I have argued, is typically teleological, though it is a constrained teleology demanded by the agent-relative character of value. In this section, I dispute the view that all moral justification is teleological. Moral principles, I shall argue, can be justified deontologically as well as

94 Cf. Joel Kupperman, *The Foundations of Morality*, pp. 82ff.
95 R. B. Perry, *Realms of Value*, p. 107.

teleologically. But, more than that, I want to suggest that the teleological justification of morality is only plausible when erected on a basis of deontologically justified moral principles.

Recall the discussion of §17.3. I argued at some length that disvaluing – as expressed in indignation and resentment – of certain sorts of acts and our valuing of friendship presuppose that others can act rationally in accordance with moral rules. More strongly, these valuings and disvaluings presuppose that the grounding moral rules are valid in the sense that they really do provide others with reasons to act. That is, such valuings are based on the belief that the rules provide rational others with reasons to act. Now suppose for a moment that, contrary to our presupposition, the rules fail to provide such persons with reasons to act. If so, then the relevant valuings are unsound. But I have just argued that only sound valuings are to be appealed to in a teleological justification (§21.5). And this raises the fundamental difficulty: any teleological justification that appeals to valuings such as friendship, mature love, indignation, or resentment must suppose that those values are sound. But that in turn implies that the relevant grounding moral rules are sound; consequently, the teleological justification presupposes the existence of a set of principles that cannot be justified teleologically. The thoroughgoing teleologist, then, aims to justify the code of public morality solely by showing that the code advances value. But valuings do not possess the requisite degree of priority and independence vis-à-vis principles of right for this project to succeed. Before the pure teleologist can determine whether he can appeal to the claim that a proposed code of public morality advances Betty's valuing of friendship he must determine whether her valuing is sound. And one of the things this involves is determining the soundness of her belief that friends are rationally committed to acting decently to each other whatever they value. So, before the pure teleologist's project can begin, he must determine the validity of these principles on nonteleological grounds, and that means the project fails before it can begin.

We can conceive of the teleologist's problem in terms of the need for a filtering device. The teleologist requires some way to filter irrational from rational values before he can apply his maximization calculation. But one of the things a filtering device would have to do is distinguish irrational from rational morality-grounded values. But for the teleologist this can only be decided after the maximization calculation has been applied. In short, what is required at the beginning of the argument can only be provided at the end. I shall call this the *problem of circularity*. This problem confronts any teleological theory: all such theories seek to explain the right in terms of promoting the valuable, yet the valuable often presupposes beliefs about what is right. The task that confronts any teleological account, then, is to respond to the problem of circularity in a plausible way. Theories that endeavor to remain purely teleological – either pure constrained or pure unconstrained teleologies – typically confront the problem in one of two ways, both of which undermine the plausibility of teleological justification.

The first, very familiar, response, is to let all valuings through the filter, that is, not to filter at all. This was Ralph Barton Perry's position.[96] Perry characterized value as the object of interest, and so it followed that, even if the interest was not well grounded, whatever was its object still was valuable. But we have seen that the Affective-Cognitive Theory of value distinguishes valuing from valuableness: a person can value that which is not valuable. And I have just argued that such unsound valuings should be excluded from public justification (§21.5).

The second familiar response is to drastically limit the values that enter into teleological justification. This second maneuver characterizes many constrained teleological justifications. Consider once again Kurt Baier's argument. Baier recognizes a wide range of value judgments and reasons for action, yet his justification of morality focuses on self-interest. That is, although he explicitly rejects egoism and its claim that reasons of self-interest are the only reasons that move people,[97] he nevertheless concludes that "Hobbes' argument is sound. Moralities are systems of principles whose acceptance by everyone as overriding the dictates of self-interest is in the interest of everyone alike."[98] So for Baier the range of values that enter into the justification of morality is properly limited to self-regarding considerations. He is not at all unique in this regard. As we saw, Gauthier appeals to non-tuism

96 R. B. Perry, *General Theory of Value*, p. 614.
97 This is especially clear in Baier's "Moral Reasons and Reasons to Be Moral," pp. 240ff.
98 Kurt Baier, *The Moral Point of View* (1958 ed.), p. 314.

(§21.3.2), and James Fishkin tells us that a personal life plan – which he takes as a fundamental justificatory category – is a "constellation of private-regarding wants and courses of action," that is, it concerns getting and doing things for oneself rather than others.[99] Like Baier, Fishkin realizes that many wants are not self-regarding, and indeed that to many people their most important wants are other-regarding. Nevertheless, Fishkin, too, focuses justification on this limited class of valuings.

Examples could easily be multiplied.[100] Basic to such approaches is the effort to limit the relevant values to those that concern only the agent's own plans, interest, or welfare. Under the influence of this way of thinking, liberal political theory and ethics becomes based on a self-centeredness. And, indeed, it is a self-centeredness of a fairly radical variety. If all appeal to values grounded on moral beliefs is to be avoided, then the advancement of friendship and mature love, for instance, are not legitimate considerations, presupposing as they do a network of rights and duties (§17.3.3). And, if friendship and such love form the grounding for other parts of our value system, affecting perhaps what jobs we prefer, our social life, our devotion to our family, and even our valuing of leisure activities, the set of values that are truly free from moral presuppositions may be very limited and not particularly significant.

22.2 *Deontological public justification*

Both teleological strategies I have sketched seem implausible. The first allows into the teleological argument all valuings, irrational as well as rational; the second restricts teleological justification to a self-regarding subset of our value systems. What is required for a plausible teleological justification is some nonteleological criterion by which to distinguish rational morality-grounded valuings from the irrational. Or, more simply, we need some criterion to evaluate the moral principles upon which those valuings rest.

One criterion is implicit in the claim that they constitute part of public morality. If Betty asserts that, say, telling the truth is a nonteleological principle of public morality, then she is claiming

99 James S. Fishkin, *Tyranny and Legitimacy*, p. 29.
100 See, e.g., Ronald Dworkin, *Taking Rights Seriously*, pp. 234ff.; Rawls, *A Theory of Justice*, pp. 13–14.

that any rational moral person, or any such person of some non-specific description, is committed not to lie, not because he values veracity and quite independently of whether the principle can be verified by the common good. This is a claim that can be evaluated. Betty is not simply saying that, given her valuings, she is rationally committed to refrain from lying, she is claiming that *any* moral person is so committed given his values. That is, given their value systems, Betty is claiming that others are always rationally committed to telling the truth.[101] Again, it must be stressed that they need not all actually agree with Betty, for they may fail to grasp the foundations of their own value systems: but, nevertheless, she is insisting that it is a presupposition.

This points the way toward a notion of deontological justification. To publicly justify a moral principle deontologically is to show that, by virtue of their value systems, each and every person is committed to this principle. This is a genuine form of public justification, for it aims to demonstrate that each person is rationally committed to acknowledging this principle because it is a foundation of his valuational perspective. To be sure, it is not sufficient to simply show that some moral principle is presupposed by some of a person's values. When cognizant for the first time that he presupposes a moral principle, a rational valuer-agent may decide to abandon this principle, and the values that rest on it because, say, it is at odds with his character ideal (§14.3). But, if the moral principle is truly foundational to his valuational perspective – not merely a presupposition of a small part of that perspective but of his whole outlook – then abandoning it will lead to the collapse of his value system. In such a case, one can only avoid the rational commitment to the principle at the cost of personal disintegration.

This type of justification is certainly not teleological: it does not aim to promote or maximize valuings. Rather, it justifies a moral principle by demonstrating that, given the sort of person one is, one is necessarily committed to it. However, the mode of justification I have been describing is not deontological if that is interpreted as "a form of justification in which first principles are derived in a way that does not presuppose any final human pur-

101 It must be remembered that this commitment can be overridden by other, conflicting, action commitments. See Benn and Gaus, "Practical Rationality and Commitment," pp. 259ff.

poses or ends, nor any determinate conception of the human good."[102] As I have understood it, deontological justification necessarily presupposes that individuals have "determinate conceptions of the good"; it is only by virtue of their possession of such "conceptions" that we can show they are rationally committed to certain principles. My use of "deontological" is, however, consistent with the way Rawls employs the term.[103] More importantly, the account of public deontological justification I have sketched shares much with Rawls's understanding of justification in political philosophy. According to him:

> Our hope is that there is a . . . sufficient sharing of certain underlying notions and implicitly held principles, so that the effort to reach an understanding has some foothold. The aim of political philosophy, when it presents itself in the public culture of a democratic society, is to articulate and to make explicit those shared notions and principles thought already to be latent in common sense.[104]

However, it must be stressed that, on the account of justification I have been developing, this only adequately captures the nature of deontological justification. Deontological justification is properly conceived as a search for consensus. Not, to be sure, the actual consensus that Rawls's recent writings endorse, but the consensus of rational valuer-agents who are moral persons, deriving from the commitments implied by their value systems. But not all justification is deontological. One way to publicly justify a moral principle is to show that it is foundational to the value systems of rational moral persons; another method is to show that it is part of a moral code that articulates the idea of the common good.

Understood thus, deontological justification provides a filter for teleological argument. For now some morality-based valuings can be rightfully included in the constrained teleological argument and others can be excluded. Valuings based on deontologically justified moral principles can enter into the teleological argument. Perhaps more importantly, we have a basis to judge various proposals that may be offered in the contractual negotiation. Say some proposal advances the values of all, but radically

102 Sandel, *Liberalism and the Limits of Justice*, p. 3. See also C. D. Broad, *Five Types of Ethical Theory*, p. 278.
103 See Rawls, *A Theory of Justice*, p. 30.
104 Rawls, "Kantian Constructivism," p. 518.

denies a basic moral principle on which all our value systems rest. This, I will argue in §27.2, is an immoral proposal, and is to be excluded from consideration in the contractual discussion.

The problem of circularity with which I began is thus mitigated. We can allow morality-based valuings into the teleological argument. But it still is true that some valuings grounded on moral principles, which may turn out to be sound, must be excluded. Consider someone who values liberal policies on the grounds of his belief that the social contract justifies liberal principles. It seems objectionable to allow this valuing to enter into the contractual deliberations; its rationality depends on the outcome of the deliberations and so it begs the question to include it as part of the data of the argument (I return to this problem in §27.1). Nevertheless, by allowing deontological justification, we have avoided both the arbitrary focus on self-regarding values and the irrationality of building justificatory argument on unsound valuings.

22.3 The rational commitment to both forms of justification

Let me pause here to consider a possible objection. It might be argued that, in a sense, my defense of deontological justification is too successful. Not only have I shown that teleological justification presupposes deontological justification, but, it could be argued, deontological justification totally displaces teleological justification. Consider: I have maintained that we are rationally committed to certain moral principles because they provide the foundations of our value system; to justify them deontologically is, then, to publicly demonstrate this rational commitment to all. Now suppose Alf proclaims that this exhausts his commitment to a justified morality; having shown all the moral principles to which he is already rationally committed, what more could be done? So, he says, he has no commitment to constrained teleological justification. Can we show that his commitment to public justification extends beyond deontological justification?

We can grasp the problem by posing it in terms of two interpretations of the argument in support of Value-Grounded Rationalism in §17. On one interpretation, all that is shown is that particular agents' value systems presuppose specific moral principles; consequently, if rational, these agents must embrace these specific principles or else abandon large parts of their value systems, transforming themselves into something akin to psychopaths. But an alternative interpretation is that we are committed to a more general conception of others and of ourselves; we are committed not just to particular moral principles but, in addition, to conceiving of ourselves and others as moral persons. As I argued in §17.3, we are committed to believing that others can take up the moral point of view and act according to reasons that transcend their own valuational perspectives.

This second, and more plausible, interpretation underwrites a more general commitment to public justification. For I have argued that our conception of others as moral persons deeply informs our valuational perspectives; we suppose in a variety of ways that they are capable of transcending their valuational perspectives to take up the moral point of view. Now, if we accept the first, narrow, interpretation, once deontological justification is exhausted no further moral principles can be justified. And if, as I shall argue in the next chapter is the case, it should turn out that deontological justification cannot get us very far – that is, not a great deal can be justified by rational consensus – the first interpretation would leave us generally confronting others not as moral persons who can justify themselves to each other, but as mere valuer-agents who have very little to say by way of justifying their activities to each other. That is, a purely deontologically justified morality could not sustain our conception of each other as moral persons. The constraints would be so abstract and minimal (as we shall presently see) that in most of our life we would be unable to see each other as moral persons. Because we are not simply committed to a list of moral principles, but to a conception of social life as life among moral persons, we are committed to a richer network of moral relations than can be sustained among those who embrace the bare demands of deontological morality erected on universal rational consensus. Alasdair MacIntyre's *After Virtue* has, I would venture, this much to teach us: ours is indeed a morally fractured culture in which consensus on a shared public morality is apt to be very thin indeed (see §29.3). But, although this does not mean that moral justification is impossible among us, it does indicate that deontological justification may be quickly exhausted.

Moreover, as we will see in Chapter VII, deontological morality is not only a thin thing, but it is also incomplete: it points beyond itself, presupposing that other forms of justification are available. One who embraced only what can be deontologically justified would find himself without a viable morality. Thus, some other form of justification is required to sustain moral life upon which our conceptions of others and ourselves are based. Unless we are to reject the lesson of all previous moral thinking, the required supplement is certainly teleological justification.

23 TWO REMAINING ISSUES

23.1 The boundary of the public

23.1.1 The subjects of justification and the objects of moral duties

The distinction between public and private morality raises several issues concerning boundaries. One such problem, the boundary between private morality and the public morality, has already been discussed (§19.2.1). A second boundary problem will be more familiar to readers acquainted with contractualist theory: Who is included within the public? Or, alternatively: To whom must we justify ourselves? Or, to employ T. M. Scanlon's formulation of the problem: "Who is to be included in the general agreement to which contractualism refers?" Given that Scanlon also conceives of contractualism as essentially an account of moral justification, his answer is of interest to us here: "morality applies to a being if the notion of justification to a being of that kind makes sense."[105] Scanlon advances three necessary conditions for being the subject of such a justification. (1) First, the being must "have a good, that is, that there be a sense in which things can be said to go better or worse for that being." (2) Because contractualism relies on judgments as to what it would be reasonable to accept (or reject),[106] we need to be able to make sense of comparative judgments as to how much various parties stand to gain or lose by accepting certain principles. So "in order

105 Scanlon, "Contractualism and Utilitarianism," p. 113. The subsequent quotations from Scanlon in this paragraph are all from pp. 113–14.
106 Scanlon proposes a criterion of contractualist justification that focuses on principles that none could reasonably reject, rather than on principles all could reasonably accept. Ibid., pp. 111–12.

for a being to stand in moral relation with us it is not enough that it have a good, it is also necessary that its good be sufficiently similar to our own to provide a basis for some system of comparability." (3) "One further minimum requirement for this notion [of justification to a being] is that the being constitute a point of view; that is, that there be such a thing as what it is like to be that being, such a thing as what the world seems like to it."

In Scanlon's eyes, these three conditions point to the capacity to feel pain as crucial in determining moral status: "a being which has this capacity seems to satisfy the three conditions . . . as necessary for the idea of justification to make sense."[107] Scanlon is aware, of course, that satisfying all these necessary conditions does not constitute sufficiency, but he seems wary of insisting on further conditions for sufficiency. In particular, he argues that it is "extremely implausible" to insist that the subjects of justification must be restricted to those "who have the capacity" to observe moral restraints. This, he indicates, would leave outside the protection of morality all those unable to act morally.[108]

Because we have placed contractualism in the wider context of a theory of value and justification, we can see that Scanlon goes astray on three points. (i) For reasons already explored (§§7.3, 14.3), it seems wrong to say that Alf's possessing a good is a necessary condition for having a justificatory argument directed to him. Beings that did not possess a good – that is, "a clear sense in which things can be said to go better or worse *for* that being"[109] – but which valued, could still be proper targets of justification. What is necessary is that the being possess a valuational point of view according to which the world can be evaluated as valuable or disvaluable; whether the world is evaluated in terms of how the being's own good progresses seems, for present purposes, irrelevant.

(ii) It should be clear that the set of beings that value cannot be the same as the set of beings to whom justification makes sense. Pace Scanlon, the justification of moral principles does only make sense when directed at moral persons, that is, those capable of acting morally. Mere valuer-agents, we have seen, would only have reason to act in order to advance their own valuings. And,

107 Ibid., p. 114.
108 Ibid., pp. 114–15.
109 Ibid., p. 113 (emphasis added).

that being so, how could we sensibly engage in the task of providing them with moral principles that imply reasons to put aside their value-based reasons to act? Thus, the justification of moral principles to pure psychopaths and animals really does not make sense.

(iii) Scanlon resists this conclusion because, I think, he fails to properly appreciate the distinction between (a) to whom must we justify ourselves? and (b) who are the beneficiaries of our moral duties? One reason he fails to do so is his acceptance of the common notion that a justificatory argument to some being must aim at showing that being's good is somehow advanced (that is, point (i) above). If justification is self-centered in this way, then those excluded from the contract are indeed liable to be unprotected. But, if it is the values and deontological commitments of moral persons that are relevant considerations, then there is no reason why the set of beings identified by our answer to (a) should be the same as that designated by the answer to (b). For instance, it seems plausible to hold that a basic deontological commitment of everyone in at least Western societies is to refrain from wantonly inflicting pain on other sentient beings. This is not to retract the earlier objection to Nagel (§12.1): that is, I am not claiming that one's disvaluing of pain provides one with reason to alleviate pain in whoever or whatever it may occur. Rather, my claim is that, as a matter of fact, anyone who is capable of moral personality is going to entertain judgments about the wrongness of cruelty that can be generalized to endorse this moral judgment. Again, this is to say neither that everyone will actually accept this judgment (for we may not accept what we have reason to) nor that no one enjoys being cruel.

Consider what it would be like for a person to entertain a value system that had no presumption that cruelty to any other *people* is wrong. Such a person would certainly be incapable of love or friendship; indeed, it is very likely that he would fail in affective decentering in the ways characteristic of psychopaths (§17.4). So it is likely that cruelty toward people is held wrong by all moral persons, being capable as they are of affective decentering. From this conviction, moral argument with a cruel moral agent could commence. In the ways in which we are all familiar, coherence and consistency considerations could be proffered to challenge the grounds of any attempt to limit the wrongness of cruelty to that inflicted against some sentient beings and not others. If it is terrible for a friend to writhe in agony, what makes it less terrible for a stranger? Is there no similarity between a stranger's pain and that of a dog? (The principle of valuational consistency will be employed here; see §14.2.1.) The arguments will be complicated, but the aim will be familiar: to undermine attempts to circumscribe the immorality of cruelty by showing them to be arbitrary or based on unsound data (for example, that animals do not possess feelings; see §4.2.2). The success of the argument cannot be guaranteed here, but at least in Western – or, perhaps, English-speaking – culture the shared understanding of human and, say, mammalian pain reactions indicates that the argument should be successful. Successful generalizations from neighbor to stranger, and from stranger to animals, has indeed characterized moral judgments of cruelty in the development of Western ethics. If I am right, then, a deontological argument can very likely be advanced to show the wrongness of cruelty to animals. Supplementing this essentially deontological tack, it can be argued that a deeper appreciation of animals as valuers will lead us to appreciate their impersonal value and why they matter.[110]

Much the same applies to psychopaths. As we have seen, the psychopath has no reason to justify himself to others (§17.4); on the other hand, others have no reason to justify themselves to him. Indeed, it would be pointless to do so, for, as I have been stressing, the practical aim of justifying a morality to others is to show that they have good reasons to embrace it, and so, act on it even at a cost to their own values. But *ex hypothesi* this cannot be true of the paradigmatic psychopath, for he cannot entertain any reasons but his own, narrow, value-based reasons to act. To be sure, we can give him prudential reasons to follow a moral code – we shall punish him if he does not – but prudential advice is not moral justification. The problem of compliance would again arise – he would be rational to disobey the rules when he could gain by doing so.

No doubt to many this will seem highly objectionable. It re-

110 See Mary Midgley, *Animals and Why They Matter*. Midgley's final appeal (ch. 13) is to the interestingness of animal life: in terms of our analysis, one of her (many) arguments upholds the intrinsic valuableness of animals. For Midgley's comments on, and criticisms of, contractualist thinking, see ch. 6, pp. 83ff.

calls what Hobbes said of he who remains outside the social contract, being "left in the condition of war he was in before; wherein he might be destroyed by any man whatsoever."[111] A contractualist such as Rawls accepts, I think, that in principle those without moral personality might be outside the bounds of justice, but adduces pragmatic reasons for not denying them the protections afforded by the principles of justice. We cannot go far wrong, he says, in supposing that all possess moral personality to some minimal degree. To withhold justice to some on this basis, he rightly points out, would be unwise. "The risk to just institutions would be too great."[112] Given that psychopathy manifests itself in various degrees, and, therefore, it is apt to be difficult to determine whether someone is entirely without the relevant capacity, this seems sound advice indeed.[113]

But, even if we could identify pure psychopaths, and even if we did exclude them from the public to whom the justification was addressed, it would not follow that they would be denied rights. Once we grasp that justifications are to appeal to values and deontological commitments rather than the good of the subjects of justificatory discourse, we can see that the question (a) "To whom must we justify ourselves?" is distinct from (b) "Who are to be protected by morality?" To be sure, to the extent that, as a matter of fact, moral persons do indeed only value their own well-being, the public code that can be teleologically justified will tend to equate classes (a) and (b). As far as teleological justification is concerned, everything depends on what is impersonally valuable, and what is soundly valued by those to whom moral principles can matter. And it is hard to see how any other sort of contractualist justification could make sense. The practical task is to show those who can be moved by moral principles that they have good reason to embrace some moral code: what they have good reason to accept is the only relevant issue. To address justifications to those who can take no cognizance of morality seems, quite literally, pointless. The protection of beings and entities that are not moral agents lies in showing that moral agents

111 Hobbes, *Leviathan*, p. 136 (ch. 15).
112 Rawls, *A Theory of Justice*, p. 506.
113 See Robert D. Hare, *Psychopathy*, pp. 11–12.

have reason to take account of them, not by insisting that they be included as parties to the contract.[114]

Failure to keep this point in mind is at the heart of one of the most serious difficulties in liberal theory: the status of children. Liberal arguments typically identify some trait *T*, for example, moral personality, as ground of moral citizenship. Those with *T* possess moral rights and duties, those without *T* do not. And, under almost all plausible accounts, young children, neonates, fetuses, etc. do not possess *T*, and hence seem outside the bounds of morality.[115] But this is a mistake.[116] The possession of moral personality is a necessary condition for sensible justificatory discourse, that is, discourse aiming at providing others with moral reasons to act. But this itself says nothing about who has rights. It makes little sense for me to try to justify moral demands to a neonate; it is entirely sensible for me to justify to other moral persons their duty to refrain from harming neonates.

23.1.2 Cosmopolitan vs. parochial morality

The relevant public to whom public justification is addressed will thus be restricted to moral persons. The possession of moral personality is, then, a necessary condition for justification. However, we have yet to consider whether it is also sufficient: does Alf's possession of moral personality show that Betty is committed to justifying herself to him? Or can the class of persons to whom Betty is committed to justifying herself be a proper subset of the class of persons to whom moral justification would be sensible? The question is whether it is rational for Betty to make moral claims on only some moral persons: in relation to other moral persons, she might advance no moral claims. We thus still face the problem: What are the bounds of the public to whom justification is directed?

Recall the principle of completeness introduced in §19.2.1. Given two codes M_1 and M_2, M_1 is superior to M_2 if it includes all the justified duties in M_2 and others as well. Now assume that

114 Robert Elliot argues for the inclusion of wolves in Rawls's original position in his "Rawlsian Justice and Non-Human Animals."

115 See, e.g., my comments on the status of children in Stanley Benn's theory. "Practical Reason and Moral Persons."

116 My colleague Loren Lomasky has also noted this, but his solution differs from mine. See his *Rights, Persons, and the Moral Community*, pp. 39–41, 153ff.

Betty accepts that all members of the public have a duty to help others, but she limits her public to her own national community. Along comes Alf, who is not a compatriot of hers but possesses a more cosmopolitan morality. What if he needs assistance; does she have a duty to provide it? However this question is answered, it needs to be stressed that this is not a matter of "choice": is not up to Alf to "choose" to include Betty in his moral community, and it is not open to her to "choose" to "opt out" of his moral community. Whether she has reasons to assist him turns on what sorts of reasons he can give a rational Betty. If he can show that a duty to assist is justified, then she has such a duty. And, if he can establish such a duty, then her code is incomplete. The question of boundaries to the moral community is then the outcome of what can be justified to whom, and so need not be a presupposition of a public justification.

Let me put the point in another way, which does not rely so heavily on the criterion of completeness. Some theorists of democracy have pointed out that *before* the democratic decision process can be applied there must be a decision as to the extent of the *demos*.[117] Democracy as a decision procedure thus presupposes a decision about boundaries. And a similar problem typically is thought to plague contractualism: who is to be party to the contract cannot, it is thought, be determined by the contract, but must be decided on independent grounds before contractual negotiation can commence. But, given the theory of justification, this is not a real problem. The contract is simply a device to allow us to consider what reasons can be given to others, and what reasons others can give to us, to embrace a system of duties. Just who can give us reasons, and to whom we can give reasons, is not a matter to be decided prior to and independently of the justificatory argument. It is an intrinsic part of it. If I, or anyone, can give reasons for a moral person to refrain from infringing certain liberties (see §24), then they do indeed possess such reasons. In this way, the bounds of the public is an outcome of the justificatory argument.

All this is, regrettably, rather abstract. My claim about boundaries is perhaps easier to grasp if we focus on the problem of

117 See Frederick G. Whelan, "Democratic Theory and the Boundary Problem."

whether morality is cosmopolitan or parochial. The analysis I have provided indicates that it is apt to have both a cosmopolitan and a parochial element. The parochial element derives from differences in the deontological basis. As I have argued, deontological justification is essentially a search for rational consensus among moral persons. Because the consensus stems from the common foundations on which people's value systems rest, it is not unreasonable to suppose that those in different cultures will share different foundational moral beliefs. And, if that is so, and if the deontological stage of justification constrains and shapes the constrained teleological, that is, contractual justification, then it will not be surprising if different cultures will have different publicly justified moralities. What can be justified within the moral community of Western individualists, I will argue, will be different from the morality that can be justified among, say, contemporary Balinese (§24.2), and one reason for this is that the deontological bases of the two communities differ. That is, Alf can show that his rational compatriot Betty is committed to acknowledging moral rule *M*, implying an action commitment to ϕ, which he may be unable to justify to Charlie, who lives in a very different culture. And this is not because Charlie has incomplete information or faulty beliefs or is in any way less than fully rational: it is because a fully rational Charlie is in no way committed to *M* and so really has no reason to ϕ.

Yet there still will be a cosmopolitan morality, and this for at least two reasons. Firstly, we have no reason to assume that the morality justified in Western pluralist societies will be parochial in the sense that outsiders are beyond the pale of moral constraint. Again, we must not confuse the specification of subjects of justification with the objects of moral duties. The point is that, within a certain culture, people may be able to justify to each other duties – including duties owed to those outside the culture – that could not be justified to those in other cultures. But, secondly, whenever any two moral persons confront each other, public justification is always possible. Regardless of their differing cultures, if Alf and Betty recognize each other as moral persons, they can make legitimate demands on each other based on the common good. Perhaps there will be no shared moral beliefs – that is, deontological justification will fail. But the common good remains as basis for justificatory discourse.

The picture that emerges is complex. Moral communities will exist at many levels of generality and richness, from the intimate associations that justify what I have called "private moralities" (§19.2.1) to cosmopolitan ethics. Indeed, the distinction between "private" and "public" moralities or "parochial" and "cosmopolitan" codes is, perhaps, better replaced by the idea of a continuum of moral communities, each based on a different deontological foundation and each leading to different notions of the common good. Because of this complexity, moral deliberation is apt to be fraught with tensions. Someone who lives most of his life in a tight-knit community may accept a morality that cannot be justified to the wider public. Furthermore, this morality and the more general public morality may point to different duties regarding, say, helping strangers. But if a stranger can show Betty – a person who is both the member of a tight-knit community and a more general public – that she has a reason to help him, then he has succeeded with his justificatory task. To be sure, she might have opposing reasons to do something else; but it must be kept in mind that she must justify herself to the stranger: she must provide considerations that are reasons from *his* perspective. Because of this, the moralities of smaller communities typically have no status when challenged before some wider public: what constitutes reasons within that group cannot be advanced as reasons to a more general public. So, in relations with outsiders, the parochial morality is rationally superseded by that which can claim to be rational to the wider group. We might say, then, that the account of public justification I have defended here both provides a place for parochial moralities while explaining why they must give way to more cosmopolitan demands.[118]

In the next two chapters, I focus on a public morality for those who share the culture of Western pluralism. This is not the most cosmopolitan level of justification, and so I do not rule out the possibility that it might be superseded by a yet more general level of moral demands. Nevertheless it makes sense to concentrate on this level. I think we can show that, even at this high level of generality, a strong case can be made for a common foundation that can be justified deontologically. Insofar as our primary concern is with the theory of justification rather then normative ethics, fo-

118 Must they *always*? Perhaps not. See my remarks in §29.2.

cusing on this level of morality sheds light on the idea of deontological justification. Furthermore, as members of this culture we have a practical interest in better understanding our own public morality, even if we should find that outsiders may make demands on us that supersede parts of our moral code.

23.2 Moral value

Before looking in detail at how this public morality might be justified, I wish very briefly to comment on a type of value that remained to be discussed at the close of Part I: moral value. It has been said that the notion of moral value is particularly troublesome for emotion-based theories of value.[119] Moral values, it has been said, (i) are agent-neutral, and (ii) do not necessarily delight the agent.[120] Consequently, philosophers such as James Fishkin insist on the distinction between, on the one hand, mere private values or "tastes" and, on the other, truly moral values.[121] Emotional theories such as the Affective-Cognitive Theory may be thought to focus solely on the former, and so entirely loose sight of the latter.

Let us first consider just what moral value, or a moral value, is normally thought to be. Under the sway of the orthodox view of value and reasons (§16.1), according to which all reasons to act must aim at the promotion of value, the idea of "moral value" is sometimes employed as a way to describe moral principles that generate impersonal reasons for action. Thus, for instance, E. J. Bond refers to "deontic moral values."[122] Once we recognize that not all reasons to act aim at promoting value, and further that there are indeed distinctively moral reasons to act, we need not depict all reasons as value reasons, and thus we can talk of deontic or moral reasons without bringing in value at all. And this seems sound, for the crux of deontic reasons is that we have them even if we do not particularly value the action. At the very least, nothing seems lost by omitting the idea of value: what is crucial is that some reasons to act do not vary from rational person to rational person and do not presuppose any direct affective re-

119 See John Laird's comments about the value of justice in *The Idea of Value*, p. 239.
120 See E. J. Bond, *Reason and Value*, pp. 64n, 90.
121 James Fishkin, *Beyond Subjective Morality*, pp. 21, 50, 140.
122 Bond, *Reason and Value*, pp. 64, 74, 77.

sponse to the relevant action or its outcome. If some philosophers insist on calling these "moral value" reasons, I see no real harm; on my account, however, they are nonvalue, but certainly moral, reasons.

So the theories of value and justification offered here in no way undermine moral reasons. Given that, is there any room for talk of moral values? The idea of a moral value is often used in reference to abstract notions such as "freedom," "equality," "charity," "truth," etc. These are obviously not rules or principles; they are abstract concepts that are instantiated in states of affairs. In this respect, they are just the sort of abstract values we examined in §13.1. Consequently, the Affective-Cognitive Theory can account for references to the moral values of people: they are values, and they are moral insofar as the object of the valuing is intimately bound up with acting morally. I take it that one who upholds the moral value of liberty believes that the infringement of others' liberty is wrong: to advance the moral value thus requires compliance with the principle. Yet the theory of rational moral action that I have offered – and this points toward its deontic and rationalistic character – does not require that everyone value the advancement of the right. Some love the right, but rectitude is all that rationality requires.

Are, then, moral values inherently agent-relative? A good case can be made that they are impersonally valuable. I have stressed that altruistic emotions are not a sufficiently firm basis on which to ground the rationality of moral action (§16.1), but altruism and morality are certainly intimately associated. Mankind, it seems clear, is characterized by sociability and altruism: we intrinsically enjoy, and take interest in, the life of our fellows, and have broad, if not universal, sympathies.[123] Morality accords well with this social nature; from one perspective at least, it is a manifestation of the love of humanity informed by respect. All this supports the conviction that our nature renders us well suited to a devotion to the moral enterprise: it holds out value to very nearly all of us. This idea can be put in yet another way: virtue, a love of the moral life, accords with our nature. If a morally virtuous person is one who does the right thing out of a love of the right, it seems certain that moral virtue is impersonally valuable.

123 See my *Modern Liberal Theory of Man*, chs. II, III.

Virtue nevertheless remains a derivative category in the account offered here. Ethical theories have traditionally been organized around one of three concepts: value, duty, and character.[124] The theories of value and justification defended in this book focus on the former two; both value and duty are fundamental, though intimately related, concepts. But the morality of character – virtue – is not on par with these. Some theorists, especially those influenced by Aristotelian ethics, conceive virtue as primary, thus understanding right action as that which a virtuous person would perform in a given situation. In these accounts, value and character are basic, for the virtuous person is one who loves the good, possesses the practical rationality necessary to perceive the goods at stake, and has the wisdom to make the proper choice. But, if virtue is not to be different for each person, an ethics of virtue requires some strongly agent-neutral conception of what is of value and of value-based reasons to act. Without proclaiming that such an account is impossible, it seems highly unlikely, especially in our plural, some might say fractured, Western culture.[125] For us, moral virtue seems manifested in valuing the moral enterprise, and this implies the primacy of the theory of value and, especially, right action.

124 See Lawrence Becker, *On Justifying Moral Judgments*, ch. II.
125 See Alasdair MacIntyre, *After Virtue*.

VIII

The state of nature

In the previous chapter, I examined the nature of moral justification and its relation to systems of value. Two main conclusions emerged. Firstly, the agent-relativity of value-based reasons to act points toward constrained teleological justifications – the mode of moral justification that characterizes contractualist argument. Properly understood, such justifications aim at demonstrating the existence of a common good that provides everyone with overriding reasons to act. Secondly, however, I argued that plausible teleological justifications presuppose deontological justifications. As we have seen, value systems presuppose moral beliefs; to try to justify these foundational moral beliefs teleologically, I maintained, either is circular or requires some objectionable specification as to what valuings count in moral justification.

In the next two chapters, I explore the implications of this analysis through a defense of a liberal understanding of public morality. The aims of these chapters are thus twofold. My overriding concern is to show that the theory of justification developed in the last two chapters is not so demanding that it precludes any justified morality. That is, I want to rebut the charge – heard, it seems, with increasing frequency – that modern ethics, relying on "subjectivist" theories of value, is essentially nihilistic. But, secondly, I wish to do this via the defense of an essentially liberal understanding of public morality. Hence, these chapters are explicitly normative.

24 THE RIGHT TO NATURAL LIBERTY

24.1 Deontology and the state of nature

As most contractualists have realized, some benchmark is necessary to determine what would constitute a reasonable contractual bargain. In the classic contract theories of Hobbes, Locke, and Kant, as well as in the contemporary theories of James Buchanan and David Gauthier, this benchmark is provided by a description of the state of nature.[1] It probably is right to say that to many critics the construct of the state of nature is the most objectionable part of the contractualist method. And it has long worried contractualists. " 'Tis often asked as a mighty Objection," Locke noted, "where are, or ever were, there any *Men in such a State of Nature*?"[2]

Nevertheless, some notion of the state of nature is necessary to contractualism. Our analysis of deontological and teleological justification allows us to interpret the concept of the state of nature and understand its place in contractual argument. *The description of the state of nature can be interpreted as articulating the justified deontological morality upon which the teleological argument, that is, the social contract, builds.* The story of the state of nature giving rise to an agreement thus mirrors our moral consciousness. It first characterizes our shared moral consciousness in terms of the moral constraints existing in the state of nature, and then builds upon this foundation a contractual (that is, constrained teleological) justification that promotes the values of all. An alternative account would be to allow two distinct sorts of arguments in "contractual negotiations": (i) arguments as to the basic moral principles we all agree upon, and (ii) arguments about what moral constraints and social arrangements advance the values of everyone. But this alternative story would obscure the logical priority of the deontological foundation. The claim is not simply that deontological and teleological arguments are distinct, but that the former sets the stage for the latter, chiefly by constraining acceptable arguments and defining the nature of the dispute leading to the bargain.

Understood thus, the idea of the state of nature is not open to the typical objections. It certainly does not describe any actual situation. Nor need it ask us to radically abstract from our current self-conceptions acting under a Rawlsian veil of ignorance. We are asked to explore our value systems and those of our fellows and determine to what moral principles we are all commit-

1 James M. Buchanan, *The Limits of Liberty*, chs. 1–2; Gauthier, *Morals by Agreement*, ch. VII.

2 John Locke, *Second Treatise of Government*, p. 294 (sec. 14).

ted before we can even sensibly talk of a morality that advances everyone's values; the next question, then, is whether there exists a more demanding moral code that, from each valuational perspective, is better. And if there is more than one code that everyone prefers to the basic deontologically justified morality, the question becomes which of these preferred alternatives is best from the perspective of the common good. It should be clear that this procedure is not particularly "ahistorical." The description of the state of nature derives from *our* examination of *our* value systems; by arriving at a description of the state of nature, we come to understand the shared foundations of our value systems. Describing the state of nature is thus an essentially self-reflective activity. It should also be stressed that the state of nature is not necessarily a state of moral anarchy. To be sure, it could turn out to be. If we discover no shared foundations, that is, if all deontological justification fails, then we may find ourselves committed to a contractualism along the lines proposed by James Buchanan. We would then find ourselves in a Hobbesian war of all against all, the rational value systems of each restricted to largely self-regarding considerations.[3] However, if significant deontological justification is successful – if, as Locke said, "The *State of Nature* has a Law of Nature to govern it, which obliges everyone,"[4] the nature of the contract will presumably be different.

24.2 *The justification of natural liberty*

In *The Second Treatise*, Locke wrote of man's "Natural Freedom." Basic to such freedom is that in the state of nature one is not subject "to the Will or Authority of any other Man."[5] Locke thus claims that all are naturally in "a *State of perfect Freedom* to order their Actions . . . as they see fit . . . without asking leave, or depending upon the Will of any other Man."[6] If such a claim can be made out, it would provide a point of departure for all subsequent moral and political theory. For, at least as I shall understand it, Lockean natural liberty implies that each is free to act as he wishes unless some justification can be advanced for re-

3 Buchanan, *The Limits of Liberty*, esp. ch. 1.
4 Locke, *Second Treatise*, p. 289 (sec. 6).
5 Ibid., p. 322 (sec. 54).
6 Ibid., p. 286 (sec. 4). I have omitted here Locke's claim that we are free to dispose of our property as we see fit. See §25.3 of this volume.

stricting that liberty. No one is naturally subject to the will of another; unless some justification can be given for interference, an agent's actions properly reflect his own purposes or values. If this can be established, it follows that justificatory ethics and political theory becomes devoted – as it is in liberal theory – to liberty-limiting principles. That is, moral and political theory would then aim at formulating those justified moral demands that can overcome the presumption of liberty by justifying interference with an agent's actions.[7]

Can such a presumption in favor of liberty be justified? Well, from the argument in §17, we know that, given the conditions for the rationality of emotions such as indignation and resentment, there is a clear consequence of *denying* that one possesses the right to natural liberty. Suppose that Alf totally repudiates the right to natural liberty; he is quite sure that he possesses no such right. It follows that he cannot reasonably experience resentment or indignation when Betty for no good reason at all stops him from doing what he intends to do. To be sure, in particular cases he may be able to ground a complaint on particular rights such as those to free speech and freedom of assembly.[8] But my concern now is not these politically important rights. Let us focus on Alf's mundane daily activities that need not call on any of these. In these daily activities, Betty may constantly push him aside as she goes about her business; or, even more perversely, she might decide to follow him around all day long as he goes about his business, with the aim of snatching up anything he reaches for, and making every effort to get in his way (as long as she does not violate any of his rights as specified by the Bill of Rights, or even, let us say, any of his legally defined rights). I venture that he will still be indignant. She is setting about thwarting his agency without being able to provide him with any justification for doing so; it is hard to imagine denying that this properly grounds indignation. But, more than that, it is hard to imagine a person

7 For analyses of liberalism that focus on the presumption in favor of liberty, see Joel Feinberg, *Harm to Others*, pp. 6ff.; S. I. Benn, *A Theory of Freedom*, chs. 5–6. For a criticism of this approach, see Joseph Raz, *The Morality of Freedom*, pp. 8–12.

8 My argument here points to an objection to Ronald Dworkin's claim that liberalism is devoted to a list of specific, important, rights to liberty, rather than a commitment to liberty in general. See his *Taking Rights Seriously*, ch. 12.

who fails to experience indignation or resentment at such affronts to his agency.

Most readers' favored counter-examples are likely to be drawn from contexts in which a background justification for such thwarting can be given. For instance, competitive games can require interference with another's actions, but this obviously presupposes a justification for the game itself. Market transactions are less clear: although the market depends on private property, and that certainly needs to be justified, many so-called "frustrations" in market competition are better described as decisions by others not to take up one's offers, and it is not clear that would constitute an infringement of one's right to natural liberty.[9] To constitute an effective counter-example, it is required (i) that the act of another clearly infringes one's freedom of action, (ii) the violation is intentional; (iii) there is no good reason to justify it; (iv) the agent interfered with experiences no resentment or indignation, has no tendency to complain that he has been wronged or that the other has reason to refrain from such actions, etc. To make the counter-example convincing, a fifth condition is also probably necessary: (v) that the interferer is a stranger. If one knows the interferer, especially if one has affectionate feelings towards him, it is all too possible that one's valuings are advanced by the interference: if one values the welfare of the interferer, or if one aims to please him, then his success may constitute a reason for one to accept the interference.

Yet any intuition can be denied (though, as should be clear by now, that is a long ways from rationally banishing it). It may help to better grasp the deeper grounding of the intuition. The right to natural liberty, I want to suggest, articulates the basic moral assumption of self-directed agents, an assumption so basic that it can only be denied by a sort of self-destructive act.

To see what a self-directed agent is, consider a contrasting sort of agent. Clifford Geertz has described Balinese social life as "at once a solemn game and a studied drama."[10] What is especially fascinating is that the main emotion helping to induce compliance with the demands of this drama is *lek* – a worry that one will not be able to play one's parts "with the required finesse."[11]

9 See here Bruce Ackerman, *Social Justice in the Liberal State*, ch. 6.
10 Clifford Geertz, "Person, Time, and Conduct in Bali," p. 400.
11 Ibid., p. 402.

Writes Geertz: "What is feared – mildly in most cases, intensely in a few – is that the public performance that is etiquette will be botched, that the social distance that etiquette maintains will consequently collapse, and that the personality of the individual will then break through to dissolve his standardized public identity."[12] The worry is thus that one may end up confronting individualized selves rather than stereotyped social roles. The social roles that define personality are thus designed to prevent the emergence of individualized selves in social relations. As Geertz notes, this leads to an illuminating paradox: "Balinese conceptions of personhood . . . are – in our terms anyway – depersonalizing."[13]

Those acquainted with Western analyses of personality will no doubt note the basic contrast: Western analyses typically identify the person with the individualized self. This, perhaps, reaches its extreme manifestation in the work of Carl R. Rogers, where the achievement of personhood is identified with the removal of masks and roles that prevent the emergence of "the real self underneath."[14] But the focus on the self or the autonomous ego as the core of personality is hardly unique to Rogers, and indeed it is fundamental to a large body of personality theory.[15] It even informs Erving Goffman's work. Like Geertz, he employs the dramaturgical method, depicting social interactions as a series of performances. But, despite the similarity in method, Goffman's conclusion is very different: he depicts the performances as vehicles for the self to manage self-presentation. Roles and performances allow us to direct and shape our self-revelations according to our self-images and plans, but they are not stereotyped scripts designed to prevent the possibility of self-revelations.[16] We might say, then, that in Western, pluralistic, societies, personhood is expressed through the available cultural resources, but it is not itself conceived to be a cultural artifact.

12 Ibid.
13 Ibid., p. 390.
14 Carl Rogers, "What It Is to Become a Person," p. 196.
15 For just a few examples, see: Heinz Hartmann, *Essays on Ego Psychology*, esp. "Comments on the Psychoanalytic Theory of the Ego": Karen Horney, *Neurosis and Human Growth*; Abraham Maslow, *Motivation and Personality*; Anthony Storr, *The Integrity of Personality*; Gordon W. Allport, *Pattern and Growth in Personality*.
16 See Erving Goffman, *The Presentation of the Self in Everyday Life*.

Let us use this contrast to develop two ideal types. For a *role-directed* conception of the person, I will say, agency is directed by culturally defined roles that are not devices or expressions of the self. In contrast, a *self-directed* person conceives of agency as an expression of the self, whether this requires overcoming roles (Rogers) or employing them (Goffman). I now proceed to my main claim: although a role-directed person can reject the right to natural liberty, a self-directed person cannot.

Consider first the role-directed person. *Prima facie*, it seems plausible that such persons might be committed to the principle:

> RD1: All interferences with the performances of another must be justified.

This would seem akin to the right to natural liberty. Just as self-directed persons would object to any interferences with their self-directed activity, role-directed persons would object to any interferences with their performances. Of course, even RD1 falls significantly short of the right to natural liberty because it only concerns interferences with one's performances. Still, it seems roughly analogous. But RD1 incorporates a presumption that action should reflect the intentions of the agent. Are role-directed agents committed to this presumption? Consider:

> RD2: All action must be justified by reference to the appropriate script.

This principle is free from the asymmetry of the right to natural liberty: not only interferences, but all action, must be justified by the relevant script. RD2 embodies no presumption that activity properly flows from the self, yet it seems appropriate for role-directed personalities. If the danger is that individuated selves may emerge, it is no less important that noninterfering action be justified by the appropriate stereotyped script. Activity is not to reflect the self but must conform to the self-containing scripts presented by the culture. Given such a view of the relation between self and action, the right to natural liberty seems out of place.

The right to natural liberty thus articulates the basic moral outlook of self-directed agents: activity rightly expresses the self. A self-directed agent who is also a moral person (for it is only this class of valuer-agents with whom we are now concerned) who rejected the right would be committed to allowing that another may take control of his activity, and this would be no cause of indignation. The self as director of action would thus be replaced by another self: one's activity becomes, strictly speaking, the expression of an alien self. Without complaint of wrongdoing, and in the absence of any justification, the self would thus allow another to supplant it as the source of action. But a self-directing moral person will resist this: the foundation of his conception of himself is that *his* activity properly is at *his* beck and call. For another self to subvert this tie and interpose itself between an agent's self and activity threatens self-direction, hence one's status as a person. And, because we are concerned here only with moral persons recognizing others as moral persons, the fundamental demand of self-directing moral persons will be that no one intervene in this intimate relation between the self and its activity without justifying the intervention to the self.

24.3 Two objections

24.3.1 The fear of freedom

It may be objected that, so far from being true that people necessarily see themselves as self-directed, much of the twentieth century can be described as a rush to renounce self-direction. Drawing on Eric Fromm, it may be argued that the rise of self-directed personalities out of the role-directed personalities of the Middle Ages has led to feelings of isolation and anxiety, and this in turn has led to mass movements in which people flee from freedom by subjugating themselves to some supreme authority.[17] I have no doubt that such flights have occurred; fascism represents perhaps the most extreme case, but the ways of escaping the rigors of an independent life are multifarious. However, great care needs to be exercised here, for the general idea of a self-directed life can be interpreted in a variety of ways. In particular, "self-direction" is often taken to be synonymous with the goal of "personal autonomy."[18] But personal autonomy is far more demanding than self-direction.[19] To be sure, typically the starting

17 Eric Fromm, *The Fear of Freedom*, esp. chs. III–IV.

18 I am assuming here that there is some widely agreed upon conception of personal autonomy. This may be an ill-grounded assumption. See Richard Lindlay, *Autonomy*.

19 For a careful analysis of the idea of autonomy and its relation to less demanding types of rational agency, see Benn, *A Theory of Freedom*, chs. 9, 10.

point of analyses of personal autonomy is indeed something very much like what I have called self-direction. Thus, for instance, Joseph Raz asserts that "A person who forces another to act in a certain way, and therefore one who coerces another, makes him act against his will. He subjects the will of another to his own and thereby invades his autonomy." In such a case, Raz adds, the person being coerced "is being treated as a non-autonomous agent, an animal, a baby, or an imbecile."[20] All this concerns what I have called self-direction. But proponents of autonomy typically expand this basic picture to describe a rich character ideal, that is, the sort of individual who forms plans, critically evaluates the social institutions and norms with which he is confronted, and takes responsibility for his own life and decisions.[21]

As should be obvious, self-direction in my sense is entirely possible without all this. Bruno Bettelheim, for example, argues that kibbutzniks have limited ability to arrive at opinions that fundamentally oppose their peers: their identification with the others is too intense for such critical autonomy.[22] But this is no reason to doubt that they are self-directing in the sense that I have suggested: it seems certain that a kibbutznik's activity is the expression of his self. Or again, Bettelheim's description of Jehovah's Witnesses in Nazi concentration camps indicates that they were consistently self-directed throughout, yet their apparent inability to rationally reflect on the soundness of their belief system would lead us to conclude that they were defective in personal autonomy.[23]

To oversimplify somewhat, we may say that the ideal of personal autonomy includes not only the insistence that action be self-directed, but goes beyond this to articulate a doctrine of the reflective and potentially nonconforming self. Certainly this is a demanding ideal: probably none of us live up to it all the time,

---

See also John Gray, "On Negative and Positive Freedom"; Richard Flathman, *The Philosophy and Politics of Freedom*, pp. 215ff.

20 Raz, *The Morality of Freedom*, pp. 154, 156.

21 See for example, Robert Young, *Personal Autonomy*, ch. 2; Richard Dagger, "Politics and the Pursuit of Autonomy," pp. 274ff. See also Raz's discussion referred to in the previous note.

22 Bettelheim, *The Children of the Dream*. For a less critical analysis of the kibbutznik personality, see Benjamin Beit-Hallahmi and Albert I. Rabin, "The Kibbutz As a Social Experiment and As a Child-rearing Laboratory."

23 Bruno Bettelheim, *The Informed Heart*.

and a great many consistently fail to achieve such a critically reflective self. Flights from the rigors of such selfhood are thus no doubt common enough. But a flight from self-direction is much harder to imagine, much less accomplish. What indeed would it be like to lose the sense that one's activity was self-directed?

One good example is the schizoid personality as it is described by R. D. Laing. According to Laing, the schizoid sees his activity controlled by a "false self" imposed by others; the "true self" is thus ineffective as a source of action. Schematically, we can say that instead of

$$(\text{self-activity}) \leftrightarrow (\text{other})$$

the situation is

$$(\text{self}) \leftrightarrow (\text{activity-other})$$ [24]

Moreover – and this recalls my contrast between Geertz's and Goffman's dramaturgy – Laing maintains that the schizoid, unlike the neurotic, does not use this "false self" as a vehicle for gratifying, or serving the aims of, the true self. Rather, the false self really is a reflection of the purposes of others. The false self thus acts according to a "stereotyped" script that the true self sees as fulfilling the aims of others.[25]

I am not claiming that flight from self-direction necessarily leads to a schizoid personality. But certainly abandoning self-direction entails, from our perspective at least, a very dramatic personality disturbance, such that we no longer can confidently describe the subject as a person, or possessing a personality. Bettelheim describes the "Muselmänner" – the walking corpses – of the concentration camps, "who came to feel that their environment was one over which they could exercise no influence whatsoever."[26] Having decided that agency was futile because the environment was unresponsive, agency was abandoned and the self withdrew. And Bettelheim indicates that infantile autism has similar roots.[27] In such cases where we witness an absence of self-

24 This is a slight modification of the schema presented by Laing in *The Divided Self*, p. 82.
25 Ibid., ch. 6.
26 Bettelheim, *The Informed Heart*, p. 151. I am indebted to Stanley Benn for impressing upon me the importance of Bettelheim's work in this regard. See Benn's *Theory of Freedom*, ch. 10.
27 Bettelheim, *The Empty Fortress*.

directed agency, personhood itself is in doubt, and this bears witness to just how fundamental is our conception of ourselves as self-directed.

None of this is inconsistent with my earlier suggestion that some cultures might be informed by role-directed conceptions of personality. In our pluralistic culture, in which the self has emerged and personality is characterized in relation to this self, the abandonment of self-direction without extreme disturbance seems impossible. It simply does not seem an option for self-directed persons to turn themselves into role-directed ones: having emerged as the source of activity, the self resists any attempt to dispose it.[28]

24.3.2 The inconsistency of moral personality and self-direction

Let me briefly consider a second, and much more radical, objection. John Charvet has argued that "the authentic self-determining" individual, who lies at the heart of human-rights theory, necessarily believes that his own subjective ends have ultimate value.[29] Such a self-determining individual will indeed demand liberty to pursue these ends. But Charvet insists that only an unlimited liberty, unconstrained by recognition of the rights of others, could satisfy this self. If, Charvet contends, one is restrained by the recognition of the rights of others (that is, one sees oneself as a moral person who can act on these rights), a second – moral – self is introduced, which is at war with the valuational self. And this suggests a picture much like that Laing presented: the valuational self sees the moral self as a false self imposed upon it and subverting its direction of action. And this seems to support those recent critics of liberal theory who insist that, ultimately, it relies on a schizophrenic conception of the person.[30]

It is certainly true that the conception of moral personality that

28 I am leaving aside here the question whether a cultural understanding of persons in terms of stereotyped roles is psychologically stable or damaging. For a critical analysis of the Balinese personality, see John W. Chapman, "Towards a General Theory of Human Nature." For a short discussion of Chapman's comparison of Western and Balinese personalities, see Christopher J. Berry, *Human Nature*, pp. 93–4.
29 Charvet, "A Critique of Human Rights," esp. pp. 31–8. See also his *A Critique of Freedom and Equality*, pt. I, esp. pp. 30–3.
30 See, e.g., Roberto Mangabeira Unger, *Knowledge and Politics*, chs. 1, 5.

informs liberal theory, and which I have defended in Chapter VI, allows that the greatest valuings of an individual may conflict with what morality demands. But allowing such a conflict in no way implies the liberal self is split or schizoid. Given the account of value and justification that has been developed here, we can grasp why the unity of the self is preserved even when value maximization and morality clash. Although what maximizes value can clash with what is moral, it is not the case that somehow value considerations and moral considerations are two independent subsystems of personality. Value systems themselves presuppose moral principles. If we value friendship and love, we are therefore committed to accepting certain moral rights and duties. And, as I have argued here, if we see ourselves as self-directing valuer-agents, then we are committed to accepting the right to natural freedom. The commitment to moral action is not the result of extraneous demands on the pursuit of value: it is the deep presupposition of the value system itself. Hence, our commitment to moral action is an expression of the deeper unity of the self.

The intimate relation of morality and value is thus one testimony to the unity of the valuational and moral personality. But there is another reason why the self does not see morality as alien. For, as I have insisted, moral demands must be justified to the agent, that is, reasons must be given to him, and that means that any considerations advanced must constitute reasons from his perspective (§19.1). This being so, even an interference to enforce a justified demand is not totally alien, for it always takes the rational moral and valuational self of he who is being interfered with as the relevant audience of the justification. Only to the extent that an agent is already split in such a way that his rational commitments diverge from his phenomenological self will morality confront him as an alien force.

24.4 On interpreting "liberty"

Thus far I have relied on an intuitive understanding of "liberty." A complete justification of the right to natural liberty would require an account of the nature of the freedom protected by the right. Some cases are clear: certainly restraining another by force or coercion calls for justification. But even these clear cases raise problems; although we are certain that coercive interference requires justification, we are considerably less sure just what constitutes coercion.[31] And this, of course, says nothing about the issue as to whether it is internal or external restraints that limit natural liberty, whether liberty is limited only by explicit restraints or also by the absence of resources to act or whether freedom is best understood as the absence of restraints or the nonrestriction of options. I cannot pursue all these issues. Because my main purpose is to exhibit the ways in which the theory of justification can be applied, rather than to defend a particular conception of public morality, these important issues can be left largely unresolved here. Nevertheless, it is important to grasp that the criteria for deciding on the favored interpretation of natural liberty will derive from the nature of the argument endorsing the right to natural liberty rather than from an analysis of ordinary language usages of "liberty" or even the concept of liberty. That is, the regulative concern in the interpretative analysis will be "What moral demands for liberty must a self-directive agent make?" rather than "What do we mean by 'liberty'?"

Given this, the favored conception of liberty will be *liberty as nonintervention* in the activity of the self. The essence of the case for the right to natural liberty is that a self-directing moral person will not accept as part of the natural order, and so requiring no justification at all, the authority of another such that the other controls its activity. So it is the intervention of another in the way one directs one's activities that raises the requirement to justify. This provides a fixed point that can orient us as we make our way through the complex concept that is "liberty." Without in any way denying that "intervention" is itself contentious and so in need of explication (see §25.1), this fixed point allows us to take positions on the various debates about the meaning of "liberty" that are nonarbitrary and make relatively little appeal to linguistic intuitions.

To see this better, consider Isaiah Berlin's argument in "Two Concepts of Liberty." Many contemporary philosophers are apt to dismiss his "two concepts thesis" on linguistic or narrowly semantic grounds. The point, however, is not whether propositions

31 The complexity of purported definitions of coercion testifies to this. See, e.g., Robert Nozick, "Coercion"; Peter Westin, " 'Freedom' and 'Coercion,' " pp. 558ff.

that ascribe negative and positive freedom fit the same linguistic schema,[32] nor is it the point that "freedom from" statements logically imply "freedom to" statements.[33] Berlin's thesis is not really about these matters, though he employed various distinctions such as "free from" versus "free to" to make his point. As he makes clear, Berlin is really contrasting two contending theories of freedom. One theory, he says, focuses on "How much am I governed?" and the other's concern is "By whom am I governed?"[34] As Berlin depicts the case for positive liberty – and this depiction is certainly true to much of what T. H. Green said in his famous lecture – the proponents of positive liberty start from a certain ideal of the rational self, and proceed (not without some foundation in ordinary usage) to characterize departures from this ideal as restrictions on freedom. Thus, for T. H. Green, someone who is dominated by certain sorts of appetites (for example, for alcohol) "may be considered in the condition of a bondsman who is carrying out the will of another, not his own."[35] Berlin contrasts this to a conception of freedom that focuses not on divisions within the self but on interpersonal relations. "By being free in this sense I mean not being interfered with by others. The wider the area of non-interference the wider my freedom."[36] It is absolutely fundamental to realize that Berlin's thesis is not that these two conceptions necessarily have different logical forms, but that they are based on different conceptions of human beings, value, and social life. And, Berlin wants to argue, the former theory – that of positive liberty – is based on a rationalism that is at odds with the theory of negative liberty. Hence, rather than being an extension of the theory of negative liberty, the doctrine of positive liberty has different roots and is actually subversive of the negative conception.

The discussion in the previous section certainly allows us to make *sense* of T. H. Green's doctrine. The self does indeed assert

---

32 For such a criticism, see Gerald C. MacCallum, "Negative and Positive Freedom." For an effective defense of Berlin, see Robert Kocis, "Reason, Development, and the Conflict of Human Ends," pp. 42–4.
33 See Joel Feinberg, "The Idea of a Free Man," pp. 3ff.
34 This is especially clear in the "Introduction" to *Four Essays on Liberty*, e.g., p. xlvii.
35 T. H. Green, "On the Different Senses of 'Freedom,' " p. 228.
36 Berlin, "Two Concepts of Liberty," p. 123.

a sort of sovereignty over its activity, and if, as is plausible, at least some neurotic impulses are understood as alien to the self, a self assailed by such impulses may indeed feel, as Green said, a bondsman.[37] So we may sensibly describe it as not free. Nevertheless, such freedom is *not* protected by the right to natural liberty. For the right to natural liberty is a claim that a moral person makes against other moral persons, insisting that they refrain from subverting his control over his activity without showing good reason. There are a multitude of ways that a self may lose control over its activity; but not all of them stem from the activities of other moral persons. The right to natural liberty is the basic claim that a self-directing moral person must make against other moral persons, that is, they not seek to subvert his sovereignty over his own activity.[38]

Let me immediately confront an obvious objection, one that plausibly leads from the claim to negative liberty to a sort of positive liberty. Why, it may be asked, will the self-directing moral person restrict himself to the claim that others not interfere: Why won't the self go beyond this to claim that other moral agents assist it in achieving self-mastery? This is a crucial point; understanding why one is not rationally committed to making this claim is necessary to distinguish my deontological case for natural liberty from those who would build liberalism on the pursuit of autonomy.[39] The crux of the answer is this: I have made no assumption that self-directing agents necessarily value their status as self-directing, nor that it is impersonally valuable in such a way that it provides all with reasons to act (§10.3). Let me explain.

The type of agent I have been analyzing is self-directing; such a person necessarily sees himself as deciding what he is to do, and he thus sees another's unjustified intervention as an affront. But this is not to say that he places any particular value on being self-

37 Cf. Freud's description of obsessional neurosis, in which the patient, confronted by alien impulses, "ends up in an ever-increasing degree of indecision, loss of energy and restriction of freedom." *Introductory Lectures on Psychoanalysis*, p. 299 (Lecture 17). But see my comments in §8.4.
38 The notion of sovereignty over one's activities is carefully explored by Joel Feinberg, *Harm to Self*, ch. 19.
39 See, e.g., Dagger, "Politics and the Pursuit of Autonomy"; Young, *Personal Autonomy*.

directed. Being self-directing is not necessarily valued – it is not a goal to be advanced – it is simply how he conceives of his relation to his own activity. And that is why he feels indignation when another claims sovereignty over his activity.

Consider Betty. Her value system may be such that there is little she really cares about. Being a sort of monomaniac, Betty (who is now blind) values the barren beauty of the dry center of Australia. But her agency does not play an important role in preserving or protecting this valuing. To be sure, threats confront the beauty of the dry center; atomic testing sites and mining operations have posed such threats in the past. So it might be said that Betty values her capacity for self-direction because she can defend the center against these threats. But she has read enough on the rationality of collective action for her to have pretty grave doubts that her agitation or direct action is going to outweigh the costs (in terms of physical tiredness, having to get herself moving, talking to people, etc.). And in contrast to many environmental activists, she does not enjoy political action or confrontation. Whether or not her valued desert is to be protected, she rightly concludes, has precious little to do with what she does. For her, agency is not of much value (see further §26.5).

Those who endorse a right to liberty by appeal to the value of agency (or personal autonomy) assume a particular type of value system. Such people value action, project-making, agency, and self-direction. For the argument to work, not only must everyone value these things, they must all place great value on them. As I have stressed, we must be wary of ignoring differences in comparative value. Even if Betty places some value on agency, she may be quite happy to give it up to protect her cherished desert. If the case for liberty is simply a constrained teleological argument about promoting what is of value, she can plausibly object that the liberal right to freedom does not meet the test of the common good. It is not, she may claim, a reasonable compromise: it gives pursuers of agency and autonomy almost all they want, and she gets something of little value, still unable to advance what she really values (but see §28.4). The point to remember is that, though everyone's value system implies reasons to act, this is not to say that each person's agency is an equally effective means to bringing about what is soundly valued. So those who value that which they cannot do much about will have far less value-based reasons than project-makers to insist on liberty.[40]

Some will surely object. Valuing, after all, seems inherently a practical activity, that is, one that leads to action. Indeed, recall my account of value conflicts in §14.1. We experience conflicts of values because we cannot promote all we value: for purposes of action we must choose one thing over another, we must incur the opportunity costs of putting one valuable thing aside as we pursue another. All this is true: I certainly do not wish to deny that valuing is practical in this way. But all this said, we need to distinguish (i) Betty's valuing of *X*, and her recognition that given this valuing certain actions are appropriate from (ii) Betty's valuing being a value pursuer, that is her valuing being a valuer-agent. The case for the right to liberty presupposes (i) but not (ii). And, it seems clear that (i) does not commit one to (ii), except insofar as one's agency is instrumental in advancing one's values. And, because this is so, one can embrace the right to natural liberty without embracing the value of agency, and so without being committed to those policies that promote this value, such as those aiming to make us into better (for example, more autonomous) valuer-agents.

My claim, then, is that our conception of ourselves as self-directing agents leads us to insist that no other, as it were, has equal right over our activity. We necessarily see ourself as having a privileged position vis-à-vis our own action. And this fundamental presupposition of our way of looking at the world grounds the right to natural liberty. Even if Betty does not have much use for agency, she will suppose herself to have this intimate relation to her activity. And because this does not suppose that agency is valued, the argument does not lend much support to a positive conception of liberty. If the basis of one's claim to natural liberty was that one valued self-direction, then one would also have grounds for claiming rights to additional instruments for achieving self-direction, for example, that others help one fight one's drug addiction. And this would be a convincing case that positive liberty really is simply an extension of the reasoning for negative liberty. But Berlin's general point is sound: the ar-

40 My colleague Loren Lomasky rejects this because he grounds rights on our status as project makers. See his *Persons, Rights, and the Moral Community*, chs. 2–4, esp. pp. 56–60.

gument for such positive liberty is not an extension of the case for negative liberty, but a very different argument that can be at odds with the case for negative freedom.[41]

25 PATERNALISM

The right to natural liberty articulates a moral asymmetry between an agent and an interferer. The agent does not have to justify his activity whereas the interferer must justify interference to the agent. This asymmetry between agent and interferer is, I have argued, fundamental to the self-conception of self-directed moral persons. And, because it is fundamental, it provides part of the deontological basis of our value systems and, so, is properly included in the description of the state of nature. But the right to natural liberty only places the onus of justification on would-be interferers; if a valid justificatory argument can be advanced, interference is morally justified. The remainder of this chapter and all of the next are devoted to the sorts of valid justifications that can be advanced. As we shall see, three categories of justificatory arguments can be proffered: (i) paternalist arguments, (ii) deontological arguments, and (iii) common good arguments. In this section, I explore paternalist justifications.

25.1 Paternalism and liberty

In his seminal essay on "Paternalism," Gerald Dworkin characterized paternalism as, roughly, "the interference with a person's liberty of action justified by reasons referring exclusively to the welfare, good, happiness, needs, interests, or values of the person being coerced."[42] So, for Dworkin, paternalism must (i) restrict liberty and (ii) do so in a coercive way. John Kleinig has argued, however, that both claims are dubious. "Paternalism," he says, "need not be either coercive or restrictive of liberty."[43] As counter-examples to the claim that coercion is necessary, he points out:

---

41 For a recent attempt to extend the case for negative liberty to include elements of the positive conception, see Richard E. Flathman, *The Philosophy and Politics of Freedom*. But note his appeal to the value of freedom in ch. 8.
42 Gerald Dworkin, "Paternalism," p. 20.
43 John Kleinig, *Paternalism*, p. 5. Cf. Gerald Dworkin, "Paternalism: Some Second Thoughts."

If Ruritania restructures its aid program so that needy citizens are given food, clothing, and free medical treatment instead of cash, their liberty to spend is limited though no coercion takes place. If the Outer Slobbovian Town Council seals off a dangerous track that is often used by motorists as a short cut, there is no coercion, though motorists' liberty of action is paternalistically limited.[44]

So, interfering with freedom need not involve coercion. Kleinig's objection to Dworkin's other condition (that paternalism involves interference with freedom) is based on a case presented by Bernard Gert and Charles Culver,

where a doctor lies to a mother on her deathbed when she asks about her son. The doctor tells her that her son is doing well, although he knows that the son has just been killed trying to escape from prison after having been convicted for multiple rape and murder. The doctor behaved paternalistically but did not attempt to control behavior, to apply coercion, or to interfere with liberty of action.[45]

If we accept Gert and Culver's analysis, it would seem that paternalistic acts do not necessarily confront the barrier posed by one's right to natural liberty, for paternalism does not necessarily interfere with liberty. And, if so, such nonliberty limiting paternalism does not stand in need of justification. Alf acting paternalistically (in this way) toward Betty would thus be, from the perspective of our theory, an expression of his agency *protected* by the right to natural liberty.

Kleinig, however, alerts us to the limited implications of Gert and Culver's example: it shows that paternalism need not constitute an interference with freedom of action, but that does not imply that freedom issues are irrelevant.

They [Gert and Culver] neglect to consider that other freedoms, such as freedom of thought and expression, and the freedom to be let alone, may be abrogated by paternalistic behavior in just those cases where no interference with liberty of action takes place. Although there is an obvious enough connection between these other freedoms and liberty of action, they are not reducible or rigidly tied to it. Doctors who deceive their patients are not simply violating a moral rule, as Gert and Culver suggest. *They are also imposing their will* (however well intentioned) *upon their patients*. They are being made to believe certain things.[46]

Kleinig thus suggests that in such cases the paternalist is impos-

---

44 Kleinig, *Paternalism*, p. 5.
45 Bernard Gert and Charles Culver, "Paternalistic Behavior," pp. 46–7.
46 Kleinig, *Paternalism*, p. 7 (emphasis added).

ing upon another. "The paternalist exercises some measure of control over some aspect of the life of another."[47]

The question for us, then, is whether such impositions – constraining liberty without interfering with liberty of action – require justification according to the right to natural liberty. The interpretive principle advanced in §24.4 must be our guide. The regulative consideration is not linguistic intuitions about "liberty," but whether the argument for freedom of action is appropriately generalized to include a presumption against such interference. And in one case at least the generalization does seem warranted. Assume a doctor, in the spirit of Gert and Culver's practitioner, misleads his patient in order to persuade him to undergo a treatment. The doctor, perhaps, systematically understates risks or adverse side effects of the proposed treatment, with the aim of inducing the patient to do what he might not if he were fully aware of the risks and consequences. In this case, the doctor is seeking to manipulate the deliberation (see §11.1.2) of the patient with the aim of inducing him to act in accordance with the values and/or decision of the doctor. The paternalizing self is imposing its view on another self, with the aim of controlling the action of the patient.[48] To be sure, rather than severing the nexus between self and its action as in overt interference, the paternalist is seeking to manipulate the deliberations of the self. But such manipulation is no less a challenge to self-directedness because of that. It remains true that the activity of the agent is being directed by another self: the difference is that in this case the alien self is rigging the choice situation in such a way that the agent will act in the way that the alien self wishes. Should an agent come to believe that all his actions were rigged in this way – that whatever he chose it was just what the puppet master wished him to choose – he would become disassociated from his own actions in much the same way as the schizoid.

If the argument from the necessary claim of self-directedness establishes a case for challenging those noncoercive paternalisms that do not directly interfere with freedom of action but manipulate deliberation about action, are we to conclude the argument has no force in Gert and Culver's case because the doctor is not

47 Ibid.
48 See Stanley Benn, "Freedom and Persuasion."

aiming at inducing *action* but only *belief*? We need to be careful here, for we do not want to commit the common error of inflating the notion of self-directedness into the ideal of personal autonomy (§24.3.1). Nevertheless, explicit attempts by others to manipulate one so as to conform to their view of the world certainly would seem to undermine self-direction. Should one come to discover the manipulation, one is apt to disassociate oneself from the imposed beliefs or values, viewing them as alien. One would be confronted with a version of the schizoid's view of a "false self" that had been imposed upon you, reflecting the values and outlooks of others.

25.2 *Is paternalism always justified?*

Following Kleinig's general lead, let us say that Alf acts paternalistically in regard to Betty if he, in order to promote her values, imposes upon her. And I have just argued that the case for natural liberty can plausibly be extended to provide a presumption against his act. He must justify himself to her. But on reflection this would seem to constitute no real barrier at all. Because Alf's paternalistic imposition will better advance Betty's values, it would appear that sound paternalist projects will always be justified. That is, if (i) to justify an imposition is to provide reasons for it that can be embraced from the perspective of the agent being imposed upon, and (ii) paternalist arguments show that the values of the agent being imposed upon will be better promoted than they would be without the imposition, then (iii) a sound paternalistic imposition will always be justified. Indeed, in contrast to interference on moral grounds, which shows that the interfered-with agent is morally required to put aside his value-maximizing projects and to act morally (§17.1), a paternalistic intervention aims to assist his value-maximizing projects. Conceived thus, an agent who opposes a sound paternalistic intervention seems manifestly irrational. The point is well made by Dan Brock:

> To resist interference would seem inconsistent with the assumptions of rational agency. And the same can obviously be said about the appeal to moral rights to block others from interfering in our action in ways that would better promote our good than would their not interfering; it seems perversely inconsistent with this conception of purposive, autonomous, and free action. Whether put in terms of rights or not, we have

on the one hand a conception of human action as seeking the agent's good, and on the other a deliberate refusal to permit the promotion of one's own good when it will be achieved by the paternalistic interference of another.[49]

Brock thus concludes that a right to act in ways that do not best promote one's values, aims, or purposes "appears paradoxical, if not a practical inconsistency."[50]

Brock's challenge is powerful: if as a rational valuer-agent you endeavor to promote your values in the best possible way, what reason could you have for objecting to paternalistic projects that do better for you than you can do for yourself? One plausible response is that one of the things you might value is doing things for yourself and making your own choices. But this is by no means a bar to paternalism; indeed, Robert Young has *based* his case for paternalism on preserving and protecting personal autonomy (§24.3.1). The aim of maximizing over her lifetime Betty's capacity to choose and act for herself may require paternalistic interferences in particular cases.[51] But, although the value of being a chooser seems a weak barrier against paternalistic interventions, the basic intuition is sound – that paternalistic justifications somehow do not take seriously our status as choosers. Instead of choice, however, let us focus on deliberation, something I have briefly discussed (§11.1.2). Now, as I argued, there is indeed a single correct answer to the question "Of the available courses of action, which best promotes Betty's valuings?" Not only Betty, but Alf too, can come to conclusions about that; and the paternalist is not wrong in supposing that Alf can be right and Betty can be wrong. But we have seen that the nature of the deliberative process regarding comparative value decisions is complex indeed, involving trade-off rates that are apt to be idiosyncratic to Betty (§11.1.1). As I stressed, these trade-off rates are one of the constituents of her character, and to a significant extent are matters of self-discovery. This in itself, I think, provides a strong challenge to Alf's paternalism, for it accords her decisions a privileged position vis-à-vis his concerning what course best promotes her valuings. But let us put this privileged

49 Dan Brock, "Promoting the Good," p. 248.
50 Ibid.
51 See Young, *Personal Autonomy*, esp. ch. 6. See also Fred D'Agostino, "Mill, Paternalism, and Psychiatry."

position aside. We can allow (counter-factually) that Alf's chances of being correct about what will best promote Betty's values are generally equal to her chances of being right. To erect a strong barrier to paternalism, we need only suppose (i) that disputes between paternalists and their targets will be typical, and (ii) their targets are self-directing agents. Let me explain.

Alf believes he knows what is best for Betty; she believes that she knows what is best for herself, and it is not what he believes. We have, then, an epistemological dispute. Each has deliberated as to what best promotes Betty's values, and each has reached a different conclusion. But because both Alf and Betty accept the Affective-Cognitive Theory of value, they both realize that such deliberations are prone to error; consequently, they both accept that their results are prone to error. Alf and Betty thus have an epistemological dispute, but there is no procedure for resolving it that can be justified to the other. We are assuming that Alf's and Betty's chances of being correct are about equal; so each is rational to be suspicious of the claims of the other to have reached the right conclusion. But their dispute is not a pure epistemological dispute, for it is also a practical dispute about what Betty should do. She must do *something*; she cannot wait until the epistemological dispute has been resolved. Alf and Betty thus need to resolve their practical dispute about what she should do, even though they cannot resolve the epistemological dispute upon which practical disagreement is founded.

The structure of Alf's and Betty's dispute mirrors the disagreements among Lockeans in the state of nature where (i) all accept a natural law that provides guidance about what is to be done, (ii) disputes arise about what this natural law requires, (iii) no rationally justified epistemological method can be found to resolve this dispute, but (iv) something must be done. We are thus confronted by an epistemological dispute (which concerns what is to be done), for which we have no justified method of resolution. Yet we are faced with a practical necessity that something must be done (hence, for purposes of action, one disputant must "win" even though the epistemological dispute remains unresolved given the absence of rational procedures). In Locke's state of nature, it will be remembered, the solution is to designate an umpire or "Judge."[52] One of the characteristics of such an umpire

52 Locke, *Second Treatise*, chs. III, IX.

is that, within some possible range of decisions *R*, a participant recognizes the umpire's decision as action-guiding, even if one believes it to be wrong. This much follows from the recognition that the umpire is a practical rather than an epistemological necessity: it is not crucial that we agree on the truth, but it is necessary that some one course of action is recognized as appropriate. The umpire, we can say, provides participants with reasons to act but not necessarily reasons to believe (that resolve the epistemological dispute). You may still legitimately believe that you are in the right even after the judge has found against you: what is required is that you accept the judgment as directive of action.

The question for Alf and Betty is "Who is to be the umpire?" It seems basic to the concept of a self-directed agent that one is accorded the role of judge or umpire over one's own activity. Again, this does not rely on the assumption that one is more likely to be correct, but, if there must be an umpire as to what action one's system of values calls for, self-directedness demands that it be oneself. To be a self-directing agent is not – as Brock sometimes almost seems to suggest – simply to deliberate about what action best promotes your values and then propose your answer as one of many in public discussion. In this way, practical deliberation is not like scientific deliberation. To assimilate the former to the latter radically splits the self from its activity; a self-directed agent necessarily supposes that *his* deliberations about *his* values provide *him* with grounds for *his* action.

Let us return to Alf and Betty. He is convinced that he is correct that a paternalistic imposition would greatly enhance the promotion of her values. Betty disagrees: she insists that some alternative course of action is better. Disagreement in itself, of course, should not paralyze Alf. In practical activity, one must often act on what seems best to one, even in the face of disagreement. But things are different if the activity is one over which Betty is umpire: for, as I have said, fundamental to being an umpire is that others accept your judgments as a reason to act (or refrain from acting), even if not a reason to believe. If, then, Betty is an umpire over her own value-based actions, it follows that as long as the outcome is within range *R*, Alf is to acknowledge that Betty's decision about what she should do "pre-empts" for *practical* purposes his.[53] Again, it must be stressed that her

53 I have benefited here from Raz's analysis in *The Morality of Freedom*, pt. 1,

role as umpire over her own activity does not resolve the epistemological dispute between her and Alf. He may continue to believe that he is right; indeed he may be. But it is also important to realize that Betty's practical decisiveness cannot totally be divorced from its epistemological basis. If she comes up with a decision that cannot plausibly be understood as an outcome of deliberation on her set of values, we can question whether she is a competent umpire (just as we can question the competency of a judge who gives irrelevant or wildly misguided decisions). Hence, it is only within some range *R* that Betty's decisions about what actions are best from valuational perspective are practically decisive for the rest of us.

This account of deliberation and agency allows us to make sense of the two intuitions that, Brock rightly says, are at the heart of rights-based analyses of paternalism:

> . . . first, that there is a wide array of choice and conduct that are only the agent's business, theirs alone to make and determine, even when others may be able to choose more wisely or interfere for their benefit – the intuition that might be expressed by the response, "you might be right, but it's my life, and so it's up to me to decide;" second, that there are some instances in which these choices are permissibly interfered with for the agent's good.[54]

The first concerns an agent's decisions within *R*; the second intuition focuses on decisions falling outside *R*. I have not, of course, provided any specification of *R*. And it will be very difficult as a practical matter to provide a general specification of what decisions lie outside the range of reasonable outcomes of the deliberative process (though, to be sure, we will be able to recognize particular crazy decisions when they confront us). As a general strategy, it seems far more fruitful to concentrate on flawed inputs and unsound deliberative processes rather than on irrational outputs. Thus, if Betty is known to base her reasoning on false beliefs, or if she was intoxicated when deliberating, or under duress, we have good grounds for questioning her competency as an umpire. (Compare the similar way in which we criticize judges: flawed inputs and unsound deliberative processes are much more effective criticisms than bad outputs.) And this

---

and Richard Friedman's excellent essay, "On the Concept of Authority in Political Philosophy."

54 Brock, "Promoting the Good," p. 246.

endorses the distinction between strong and weak paternalism, favored by many liberal political philosophers,[55] but criticized by Brock. Weak paternalism, let us say, is a paternalistic imposition on Betty supported by a sound claim that her deliberative processes or inputs are seriously flawed. My analysis provides no bar to, and indeed seems to endorse such paternalism, for it calls into doubt Betty's competency as a practical umpire over her activity. In contrast, strong paternalism seems ruled out. For a strong paternalist intervenes without claiming serious deliberative failure, but on the basis of the claim that the party has made the wrong practical decision. However, we have seen that it is the essence of practical umpireship in a realm of unresolved epistemological disputes that many may be convinced – often rightly – that the wrong decision has been reached, yet all have reason to be guided by that decision in their action.

26 ON FURTHER DESCRIBING THE STATE OF NATURE

26.1 Moral and political philosophy

It should be stressed that paternalistic interventions are not based on moral demands. As I said, the paternalist does not insist that the agent put aside his value-maximizing projects so as to act morally; the paternalist imposes on others in order to better promote their values. I now wish to consider the possibility of justified moral demands in the state of nature. On this issue, Locke, not a Hobbesian such as Buchanan, is right: "The *State of Nature* has a Law of Nature to govern it, which obliges everyone."[56] The extent of natural law will, I have argued, be determined by what can be deontologically publicly justified. A complete description of the state of nature will, then, be essentially a full account of the "law of nature," for this will provide the basis of the constrained teleological argument that characterizes the social contract.

I cannot provide such full description here. The more detailed a description becomes, the more controversial it will be. This, to

55 See, e.g., Joel Feinberg, "Legal Paternalism"; Michael D. Bayles, "Criminal Paternalism."

56 Locke, *The Second Treatise*, p. 289 (sec. 6). Cf. Buchanan, *The Limits of Liberty*, ch. 2.

be sure, is not a deep objection to the enterprise; I stressed in the last chapter that specific justificatory arguments are apt to be controversial. And certainly any theory as to the nature of our shared deontological morality is likely to be controversial, but, again, moral theory is not pragmatic in the sense that it searches for actual consensus among real (imperfectly rational) agents. But, although the controversial character of a complete description is not a deep theoretical concern, it suggests that in the present context an extended specification is apt to be unfruitful. If these matters are contentious, then adequate defenses of detailed descriptions must consider a variety of objections and counterproposals. And that leads one to suspect that adequate and useful defenses of particular descriptions of the state of nature will be complex and lengthy. A full description of our shared deontological morality is thus a major task of normative ethics, and cannot be usefully provided as a short discussion in a wider-ranging work such as this.

Does this mean that our sketch of a justified public morality has come to a rather abrupt halt because we are unable to provide an account of the deontological foundation on which contractual justification builds? Perhaps not. Assume we possess a basic description of the state of nature that includes some, but by no means all, of the deontologically justified public morality. And assume further that, given this basic description, a contractual argument is constructed justifying a certain code of public morality regulating the basic life of a society. Now these conclusions will be enlightening and useful to the extent they are *robust* with respect to further specifications of the state of nature. Contractual justifications are robust, let us say, if further specifications of the law of nature do not significantly affect the justifiability of the basic public morality. On the other hand, contractual justifications are *sensitive* to variations in the description of the state of nature if changes in the detailed specification of natural law significantly affect the justifiability of the core of public morality.

Robustness and sensitivity both possess a certain plausibility. If sensitivity holds, moral and political philosophy form a seamless web; the nature of the just state and society is part and parcel of the wider public morality and the justification of the former cannot be separated off from the latter. However, if robustness holds, normative political philosophy has considerable autonomy from ethics. A basic description of the state of nature incorporating, say, our basic beliefs about liberty and property, can provide the basis for a contract justifying the basic public morality that in turn justifies certain institutions, and this justification will not be undermined by further developments as to what can be deontologically justified. The contract tradition has supposed that political philosophy possesses considerable autonomy. Rawls, indeed, maintains that this is an essential part of contract theory. Contractualism, he says, must recognize the fundamental distinction between the principles of justice concerning the basic structure of society and the principles directly regulating individuals and associations; in his view, contractualism is committed to the priority of the justification of the former to the latter.[57] Thus, for instance, he tells us that we might imagine a sequence of contracts, dealing first with the basic structure and then other subjects, with the proviso that later agreements are to be somehow constrained by the earlier, more basic, ones.[58]

To be sure, Rawls is not explicitly concerned with the robustness of the contract argument in relation to the description of the state of nature (he has, in fact, little enthusiasm for the notion of the state of nature).[59] But his general concern is much the same as mine: to what extent are the terms of the social contract robust in relation to the further specification of the right? Now it seems at least reasonable to follow Rawls, and the contract tradition in general, is assuming significant autonomy for political philosophy. It would be more than a little surprising if the justification of the basic social structure was highly sensitive to fluctuations in what can be deontologically justified, or indeed the public morality generally. We typically suppose that significant movements in our shared public morality can occur without calling into question the justifiability of the basic characteristics of the social and political order. Significant changes in moral judgments concerning sexual relations or the ordering of family life may perhaps have implications for the justness of the basic structure, but it is not widely supposed they call into question its broad nature.

57 See Rawls, "The Basic Structure." His focus on political philosophy rather than moral theory is manifest in his most recent writings such as "Justice As Fairness: Political Not Metaphysical."
58 Rawls, "The Basic Structure," p. 50.
59 See ibid., p. 62. Contrast this to *A Theory of Justice*, p. 12.

I realize some may dissent here. Some feminists, for instance, are apt to see revisions in various moral judgments concerning family life as revolutionary, ultimately showing the oppressive nature of the liberal patriarchal structure. My assumption of the autonomy of political philosophy based on the robustness of the contractual argument is thus to some extent controversial. But, although I will proceed assuming robustness, this in no way precludes criticisms upholding the sensitivity of the contract to other aspects of morality. Once I have provided an account of the social contract, critics can then proceed by (i) deontologically justifying some moral principle in the state of nature and then (ii) demonstrating how inclusion of that principle in the state of nature invalidates the contractual argument I present in Chapter IX.

26.2 Property

26.2.1 Locke versus Rousseau

Even if we suppose considerable robustness for the contractual justification, we must possess some notion of a reasonable basic description of the state of nature. In various places, I have already suggested some additional features. I have pointed to an argument for the wrongness of cruelty (§23.1.1), and my basic argument concerning friendship presupposes that trust in, and fairness concerning, one's friends (§17.3.3) are fundamental deontological moral commitments. Moreover, I think it is very plausible indeed to include the principle that promises are to be kept. One of the most compelling justifications of promising points to the sort of personal obligations and thus bondings that it facilitates.[60] It is often said that, if we value personal relations in which we can bind our actions to the deliberations of another, we have reason to embrace the institution of promising. But this is, again, to take too instrumental a view. Rather, the proper perspective is that we do suppose the great importance of such relations, and the moral bindingness of promise-keeping is a presupposition of these valuings.

But we have yet to consider one issue that has divided contract theorists: the justification of property rights. According to

60 See Joseph Raz, "Promises and Obligation."

Locke, "The great and *chief end*... of Men's uniting into Commonwealths, and putting themselves under Government, *is the Preservation of their Property*. To which in the State of Nature there are many things wanting."[61] Locke, and contemporary Lockeans such as Nozick, would have us believe that property rights exist in the state of nature. For Locke, property is prior to the social contract. Recent interpretations of Locke have tended to dispute this rather straightforward understanding of him, stressing, for example, that he allows the legislature to "make Laws for the regulation of *Property* between the Subjects."[62] This is not the place to engage in detailed disputes concerning Locke scholarship; all I need to insist upon here is that in his theory the nature of the social contract is very much affected by the prior justification of rights to property in the state of nature. As the quote above illustrates, Locke's social contract is very much shaped by his endorsement of precontractual rights to property.

Contrast this to Rousseau. In the state of nature, as he sees it, one can only have mere possession; genuine property – not simply occupation but a claim to ownership – characterizes our departure from the state of nature,[63] and can only be justified by the social contract.[64] For Rousseau, then, property cannot be antecedent to political society. Given this, it is not very surprising that, whereas Locke stresses that the social contract aims to protect property, and prohibits the state from taking it without the subject's consent, Rousseau proclaims that "[t]he State, in relation to its members, is master of all their goods by the social contract."[65]

This contrast between Locke and Rousseau is, admittedly, highly stylized, but it serves to highlight the importance of property rights in any description of the state of nature. Given the central importance of questions of property and redistribution to current debates about the justice of our basic institutions, it is

61 Locke, *Second Treatise*, pp. 368–9 (sec. 124).
62 Ibid., p. 379 (sec. 139). I have greatly benefited from Stephen Buckle's *The Natural History of Property*. For some recent interpretations upholding the conventional nature of Lockean property rights in civil society, see James Tully, *A Discourse on Property*; John Christman, "Can Ownership Be Justified?"
63 Jean-Jacques Rousseau, *Discourse on the Origin of Inequality*, p. 141.
64 See Alan Ryan, *Property and Political Theory*, pp. 54ff.
65 Rousseau, *The Social Contract*, bk. I, ch. ix.

most doubtful that any contractual argument can be robust in relation to this aspect of the description of the state of nature. If Lockeans are right, the moral priority of property rights vis-à-vis the social contract is apt to limit the redistributive possibilities of the contractual public morality: people enter the negotiations with property rights. If Rousseau is right, the contractors need acknowledge no such restraints: property rights will then be whatever the contractors agree that they will be. Who, then, should we follow: Locke or Rousseau?

26.2.2 A quasi-Lockean case for property rights

If we focus simply on the right to natural liberty, Rousseau is vindicated: possession, but not exclusionary property rights, characterizes the state of nature. To see this, assume that Alf picks up an acorn in the state of nature. Is it his? Well, the right to natural liberty will protect him in his possession of it. As long as he is in physical possession, any attempt by Betty to take it from him would constitute an interference with his activity. Certainly any attempt to forcibly remove it from him would constitute such an interference, as would a nimble removal of it from his hand as he looked in the other direction. Indeed, even if he was using it in his activity without actually holding it, Betty's snatching it would be plausibly understood as an interference. According to the right to natural liberty, then, she would have to justify such interventions to him. So the right to natural liberty does help secure him in his possession of the acorn: the moral asymmetry between agent and interferer transfers to that between possessor and would-be remover. Again, I make no claim that Betty may not sometimes be able to meet this challenge. Perhaps she can present a paternalist justification that Alf is not the sort of person who can be trusted with acorns. My claim is simply that it is incumbent upon her to provide some justification.

It may be objected that any act whereby Alf gains possession of something can be interpreted as an interference with someone else's activity. When he picked up the acorn, he interfered with Betty insofar as that acorn was no longer available to her. And, if this is so, every act of possession is itself an interference standing in need of justification.[66] But my concern here is not to defend

66 This problem was suggested to me by Julian Lamont.

the possibility of such mere possession but to insist that, even if the right to natural liberty can ground a right of possession, the reasoning cannot be extended to justify exclusionary property rights. Indeed, as the objection suggests, the right to natural liberty is an obstacle to justifying ownership. Suppose Alf is cultivating, and constantly occupying, a small plot of land, such that it is reasonable to depict him as possessing it. He then makes the proclamation that Rousseau thought to be so momentous: Alf asserts that the land is his, even when he is not in physical possession of it. He owns it.[67] But this is to assert that others are excluded and cannot enter, and that implies demands upon them that seek to limit their liberty. The essence of ownership is to restrict the liberty of others in respect to that which is owned; but, according to the right to natural liberty, any such restriction must be justified to those being excluded. So the argument from the right to natural liberty does not lend itself to a transition from possession to ownership. At best, the right provides a foundation for continued possession, but it certainly is an obstacle to ownership.

If the right to natural liberty was the sole moral constraint in the state of nature, we would have to side with Rousseau rather than Locke: turning possession into property could only occur through the social contract. Lawrence Becker, however, advances a reconstruction of the Lockean argument for property that, I think, helps uphold the Lockean side in the debate. Becker alters the labor theory of property in a way that makes claims of desert fundamental.[68] The "notion of desert," he claims, "is a constituent of morality *per se*."[69] The crux of his thesis is that the concept of deservingness is a deep presupposition of the moral enterprise itself. People who act wrongly deserve blame; those who act in a worthy manner deserve praise. "To ask whether desert is an intelligible concept," says Becker, "is to call into question the whole enterprise of passing moral judgment on people for their

67 "The first person who, having fenced off a plot of ground, took it into his head to say *this is mine* and found people simple enough to believe him, was the true founder of civil society." Rousseau, *Second Discourse*, first sentence of pt. 2.
68 Jeremy Waldron criticizes this "common interpretation of Locke's theory." *The Right to Private Property*, p. 201.
69 Lawrence Becker, *Property Rights*, p. 49.

conduct."[70] Notice that his argument is precisely the sort required if desert principles are to be included in the description of the state of nature: the moral enterprise itself – hence all our morality-grounded valuings – suppose the validity of desert claims.

Some have charged that, at best, all Becker shows is that reward or praise, punishment or blame, can be deserved for moral or immoral acts.[71] But I think this is to miss the point. Becker's point – and it seems to me reasonable – is that our morality presupposes the sensibility of moral statements of the sort:

D: Alf deserves *X* because of some past act ϕ that he has performed.

That is, the concept of classifying people as deserving or undeserving because of some previous act of theirs is not a notion we are free to accept or reject: our morally informed outlook commits us to it.[72]

The question then becomes in what ways the variables *X* – the deserved benefit – and ϕ – the grounds of desert – are filled out. Becker believes that one deserves benefit (*X*) for adding value (ϕ) to the lives of others. Hence, he says, the "following principle must be sound by definition: A Person who, in some morally permissible way, and without being morally required to do so 'adds value' to others' lives deserves some benefit for it."[73] Becker insists that it is necessary that benefit accrue to others: "Deserving a benefit for producing something which only you profit from is a strange notion."[74] Becker thus advocates grounding desert on *contribution* rather than, say, *effort*; and, given the difficulties with effort-based accounts of desert, this may seem advisable.[75] But care needs to be exercised here. Consider the following two principles of desert:

D1: Alf deserves *X* because he has produced *X*.

70 Ibid.
71 See Christman, "Can Ownership Be Justified?" p. 167.
72 This is not to deny that some desert claims may ground a person's desert on his possession of some trait rather than some action he has performed. See George Sher, *Desert.*
73 Becker, *Property Rights*, p. 51.
74 Ibid., p. 55.
75 See David Miller, *Social Justice*, pp. 102ff. For the distinction between contribution-based and effort-based accounts, see also Michael A. Slote, "Desert, Consent, and Justice." But cf. Sher, *Desert*, ch. 4.

D2: Alf deserves *X* because he has contributed to the productive process and *X* is a suitable reward.

Becker – and this is the dominant position – sees D2 as the fundamental desert principle regarding economic systems and economic justice. Alf deserves *X* as a reward for contributing to the collective productive effort. But the intuition behind D1 is rather different, though the two are typically confused. David Miller, for instance, writes: "If we consider a state of nature, such as that constructed by Locke, we shall see how plausible is the view that when men produce in isolation from one another, and with land and raw materials in plentiful supply, they each deserve to retain whatever they can make by their own labor."[76] Miller depicts this desert claim as an instance of D2 (contribution); but, if *contribution* to the *social productive process* is the core grounding, why (as Miller rightly points out) is the intuition strongest under the assumption of isolated asocial production? The Becker-Miller account of the state of nature, I venture, is not really tapping D2 at all, but the different intuition that a person deserves what he produces or, as it used to be put, "the fruits of his labor." The reason why the intuition is strongest under the assumption of asocial isolated production is that we can easily identify what a particular person has produced himself (D1), not that we can identify his contribution to the lives of others. Miller, of course, is quite right that determining a person's desert in joint enterprises is far more difficult than in a state of nature, because what constitutes the "whole product of his labor" is difficult to determine.[77] But this in itself, I think, testifies that it is really D1 (production) rather than D2 (contribution) that he has in mind, for D2 requires proportionate *rewards* but not necessarily that a person receive the "whole product of one's labor."[78]

I propose, then, that D1 is an independent principle of desert. Some readers, however, simply deny this: they see no reason why a person deserves to own what he has produced. Apparently, these readers believe that one is not specially morally entitled to

76 Miller, *Social Justice*, p. 104.

77 Ibid.

78 Indeed, as Waldron points out, if the aim is to reward the worker for his contributions, it seems odd that we should give him the full value of his contribution. "He has added to the prosperity of society, but he gets to keep the extra he has added." So, in the end, only he benefits. *The Right to Property*, p. 205.

control what one has produced: that Betty has produced *X* does not provide her with a strong and special moral claim over *X* that Alf, Charlie, and Doris do not also have. To deny this intimate moral relation between the producer and what has been produced is, however, ultimately implausible. As Hegel and self-realizationist accounts of property have reminded us, insofar as we are both valuers and agents, we express ourselves in the world through our manipulation of it. To sunder the tie between what one has produced and control over it is, as Marx saw, alienating: "The *alienation* of the worker in his product means not only that his labor becomes an object, an *external existence*, but that it exists *outside him*, independently, as something alien to him, and that it becomes a power on its own confronting him."[79] A moral person who denies that he has some intimate moral claim to control his produce sees his activity as at his beck and call (as he claims a right to natural liberty), but his conception of his moral agency stops there: as soon as his action manifests itself in the creation of objects, he disclaims moral control. This does indeed seem profoundly alienating: a sharp distinction is supposed between one's activity (which one claims a right to direct) and the external embodiment of the activity (which one claims no rights to control). Locke's mixing metaphor, self-realizationist theories, and (in some moments) the early Marx all rightly saw such a sharp break as implausible.

Jeremy Waldron suggests a much more subtle criticism: granted that production and property seem to have some intimate connection, to claim that one deserves what one has produced does not tell us anything much about the nature of this link.[80] Waldron thus endorses a Hegelian over the Lockean account of this link. I cannot pursue this important issue here.[81] What is important for my purposes is that D1 acknowledges that the producer deserves to control the fruits of his labor in the sense that it is fitting and appropriate to accord him such control,[82] he has earned such control through his exertions, and to deny him such control is to do him an injustice. Hegelian, as well as Lockean, theory, I suspect, provides significant support for this understanding of D1.

79 Karl Marx, *The Economic and Philosophic Manuscripts of 1844*, p. 108.
80 Waldron, *The Right to Property*, p. 206.
81 See Appendix B for some remarks on the concept of desert.
82 See Joel Feinberg, "Justice and Personal Desert," pp. 56ff.

26.2.3 The problem of original acquisition

Quasi-Lockean property rights exist in the state of nature if three things are true. (i) It must be the case that the concept of desert is universally embraced in the state of nature. If, as I think is reasonable, the notion of desert is indeed basic to the moral endeavor, desert claims would be acknowledged prior to the social contract (that is, they are part of the deontological foundation). (ii) Secondly, it must be the case that valid desert claims provide moral reasons to act. If Alf can show a rational Betty he deserves *X*, he has provided her with (say) a reason to refrain from taking *X*, even if taking *X* would better promote her values.[83] (iii) Additionally, it must be true that one sound desert claim is that someone who produces something deserves to use and control that thing (within, to be sure, specific limits). Put simply, a worker deserves (in some sense) the fruits of his labor.

A defense of property rights grounded on D1 is not only quasi-Lockean, it is also Millian. "Private property, in every defense of it," said Mill, "is supposed to mean the guarantee to individuals of the fruits of their own labor and abstinence."[84] But Mill also added:

> When the "sacredness of property" is talked of, it should always be remembered, that any such sacredness does not belong in the same degree to landed property. No man made the land. It is the original inheritance of the whole species. . . . It is no hardship to anyone to be excluded from what others have produced: they were not bound to produce it for his use, and he loses nothing by not sharing in what otherwise would not have existed at all. But it is some hardship to be born into the world and to find all nature's gifts previously engrossed, and no place left for the newcomer.[85]

If we embrace Mill's claim that no one deserves the land – or, we might add, any natural resource – the desert/labor theory of property seems undermined. For, if the original appropriation of a natural resource – that is, exclusionary property rights over it – cannot be justified by desert claims, it would appear that very nearly all subsequent desert-based property rights are undermined. Say Alf takes possession of a tree, cuts it up into lumber,

83 See ibid., p. 60.

84 John Stuart Mill, *Principles of Political Economy*, p. 209 (bk. II, ch. ii, sec. 3). Becker points out the Millian connection in *Property Rights*, pp. 41ff.

85 Mill, *Principles*, p. 233 (bk. II, ch. ii, sec. 6).

and claims desert-based property rights over the chair he has produced. But Betty objects that he had no exclusionary rights over the tree in the first place: he never justified to *her* restricting her liberty by erecting such rights. To this, he may perhaps reply that he has mixed his labor with the tree; and, if he deserves the fruits of his labor, he also has exclusionary rights over that in which his labor is embodied. As far as I can see, however, Betty need not accept this. Alf's labor on the tree may be very much like Nozick's tomato juice in the ocean: by dumping it into what was not his, Alf lost his labor/tomato juice, rather than gaining the tree/ocean.[86] Betty wants the tree over which Alf has no exclusionary rights; and, though she acknowledges that he has a right to the fruits of his labor, she wants to use the tree. If he can remove the fruit of his labor from it, well and good; if not, then apparently he has lost it.

The intuitive appeal of desert-based theories of property begins to evaporate when we squarely face the problem of exclusionary rights over natural resources.[87] The typical response of Lockean-inspired theories are Lockean "provisos" that justify removing resources from the "common pool" when this does not worsen the situation of others.[88] And this in turn leads to complex compensation proposals or rather unconvincing arguments that Alf's extensive exclusionary rights over natural resources is never to the disadvantage of Betty, who possesses no such exclusionary rights.[89] Such problems arise, perhaps, because whatever the stated intentions of later theorists, they follow Locke in con-

86 Nozick, *Anarchy, State, and Utopia*, pp. 174–5. Will Alf be alienated? Perhaps. But such alienation appropriately seems the lot of one who expresses himself in that regarding which he cannot justify exclusionary rights.

87 John Christman apparently disagrees. Lockean provisos, he tells us, do not cohere well with desert-based accounts of property because the validity of desert claims is not "limited by the distribution of benefits generally." If one deserves it, one deserves it, whether or not it leaves as good and enough for others. But my argument is that the desert claim is undermined quite regardless of distributive issues because one had no exclusionary right over the resource. See Christman, "Can Ownership Be Justified?" p. 168.

88 See, e.g., Locke, *Second Treatise*, ch. V; Nozick, *Anarchy, State, and Utopia*, pp. 178ff.; Gauthier, *Morals by Agreement*, ch. VIII. See also John Bogart, "Lockean Provisos."

89 Cf. Locke's comparison of a "King of a large and fruitful Territory" in America and a "day Labourer in *England*." *Second Treatise*, p. 315 (sec. 41). Cf. the very similar argument of Adam Smith in *The Wealth of Nations*, vol. 1, p. 14. (bk. I ch. i).

ceiving of the state of nature as a condition in which people can exist – if only in our imaginations. As Locke said of the fruits of the earth, "[t]here must of necessity be a means *to appropriate* them some way or other before they can be of use, or at all beneficial to any particular Man."[90] If, it is thus reasoned, desert grounds property rights, there must be some account as to how these rights could function in the state of nature. After all, if they could not function at all, the inhabitants of the state of nature would starve!

This is clearly the road to error: the state of nature is but a phase in justificatory argument. The proper response to the problem of "original acquisition" is indicated by Mill. "The essential principle of property being to assure all persons what they have produced by their labor and accumulated by their abstinence, this principle cannot apply to what is not the product of labor, the raw material of the earth."[91] Desert-based property cannot in any significant way come into being until the problem of original acquisition has been resolved, and for that we must go outside desert-based rights. It does not seem, in fact, that any resolution of this difficult issue is possible within the state of nature; appeal must be made to the social contract. In the state of nature, then, people have *a right to a system of private property that recognizes the claims of desert.*[92] But, because the problem of acquisition of natural resources requires contractual justification, no significant property rights to particular things yet emerge.

26.3 Exchange

Mill believed that "all the reasons that recommend that private property should exist" also recommend that one should be able to alienate it, including free gifts and bequests.[93] But this is not obvious. If one gives away to another property that you deserve, it does not follow that he deserves it. Much the same applies to market exchanges, though, to be sure, they involve trades rather than free gifts. But if Alf deserves *X* and this grounds his exclusionary rights over *X*, and Betty deserves *Y*, and this grounds

90 Locke, *Second Treatise*, pp. 304–5 (sec. 26).
91 Mill, *Principles*, pp. 229–30 (bk. II, ch. ii, sec. 5).
92 This is a modification of a suggestion made by Alan Ryan, "Public and Private Property," pp. 226ff.
93 Mill, *Principles*, p. 226 (bk. I, ch. ii, sec. 4).

her exclusionary rights over *Y*, the desert-based argument does not obviously sanction free exchange. Does voluntary exchange somehow transform the situation such that Alf deserves *Y* and Betty *X*? It seems fairly obvious that a system of free exchange does not necessarily assure each person just what he deserves.[94]

We might depict the challenge this poses for a desert-based account of property in four claims:

(i) Alf's production of *X* justifies exclusionary rights over *X* because he deserves control, use, etc. of *X*.
(ii) Market transactions pass on exclusionary rights.
(iii) Market transactions do not pass on deservingness vis-à-vis a thing.
(iv) Market transactions presuppose transferring the rights over a thing without being able to transfer the grounding of the rights.

This would seem to illustrate Nozick's point: a pattern such as "to each according to his deserts" will be upset by free exchange.[95]

To see our way clear of this difficulty, we first must distinguish two claims:

DJ: Alf has a property right over *X* if and only if he deserves *X*.
PR: Alf's production of *X* grounds a desert-based exclusionary right of his over *X*.

The first claim is a desert-based conception of distributive justice: essentially it insists on a pattern that each gets what he deserves and only what he deserves. Betty's possessing *X*, which *ex hypothesi* she does not deserve, is precluded by DJ. But I have not endorsed DJ; I have argued for a desert-based property right (PR) which argues that Alf's deserving *X* justifies an exclusionary claim over *X*. No pattern exists to preserve: Alf has justified exclusionary rights. The fact that Betty may not deserve *X* is in itself no bar to her possessing property rights over it.

In itself, there is nothing particularly odd in the notion that Alf's possession of *X* might be warranted by his ϕ-ing, yet he can engage in some relation with Betty that passes on to her *X* even though she has never ϕ-ed. For instance, Alf might be warranted in believing in the current existence of Tasmanian tigers because he (and he alone) has seen one, but he may engage in a relation with Betty such that she comes to possess the belief

94 See Alan Buchanan, *Ethics, Efficiency, and The Market*, pp. 51–3. But cf. Riley, "Justice under Capitalism," p. 137.
95 Nozick, *Anarchy, State, and Utopia*, pp. 155ff.

without ever having seen one. The case is structurally similar to the transfer of desert-based property rights. If Alf had never seen a Tasmanian tiger, no firm beliefs in their existence would be warranted (assuming that all other sightings have been dismissed); but, once Alf's belief is warranted, he may legitimately pass it on to others. So too with property. Alf was able to justify his exclusionary property rights over *X* because he deserved it; once desert justified his exclusionary rights, no logical bar excludes relations that pass on the exclusionary right without the grounding he possessed. The history of a particular desert-based exclusionary right will trace it back through a multitude of exchanges to some deserving producer (just as the history of belief in Tasmanian tigers might be traced back to Alf's sighting).

So there is no logical barrier to transferring desert-based property rights without also transferring deservingness. But this only eliminates the objection to transferability; we have yet to provide any reason for accepting it. Of three plausible bases of property rights in the state of nature, I want to argue, the desert-based account I have given alone presupposes the intuitive notion of "ownership."

To see this, consider first contribution-based accounts (D2) a la Becker. Property rights, on this view, are a reward for contribution to the social productive process. Leaving aside that this tends to collapse into a view of social justice (DJ), it at best only sanctions limited transfer of property rights. A reward or an honor is not itself intrinsically transferable. A down-and-out actor can sell his Oscar statue; he cannot transfer his award for the best actor of 1926. To be sure, in order to render awards more beneficial to the recipient, we may allow one award to be exchanged for another, but nothing intrinsic to the notion of an award requires us to do so. Loyal members of the Party may be rewarded by receiving a dacha, but it may well be counter-productive to allow them to transfer it to others.

The second contrast is to a need-based account of property. Say, following Locke, one of the arguments for property is that God created mankind to flourish, and this means men *need* private property to live. Such an account may also place pretty severe limits on alienation: if people's needs are not always better advanced by alienation, then rights of transfer will not always be justified.[96] Such considerations often lie behind provision in kind, rather than in cash, of public assistance.

The argument I advanced in §26.2 supports, I think, the more direct intuition that people deserve to own what they have produced. Ownership is not a reward for social contribution or a way to serve needs; ownership of what one produced is, simply, fitting or appropriate. And, because my account posits this more direct tie, it supports appeal to something akin to what has been called "full ownership" – certainly including rights of exclusionary possession, to use, manage, consume, modify, destroy, and transfer the thing that one owns. The crux of my account, then, is not that property rights are a sort of reward for contribution or a way to satisfy needs, but that a person deserves to *own* what he has produced, and it is this which allows direct appeal to the concept of ownership. "The desert principle," Jonathan Riley rightly says, "holds that producers deserve to have exclusive control over the physical products of their own exertions."[97]

Conjoined with the defense of natural liberty in §24, this constitutes a limited justification of market relations. For given (i) that Alf has exclusionary property rights over *X* such that it is his, and (ii) that Betty has exclusionary property rights over *Y* such that it is hers, (iii) that each has rights of transfer over their property, then (iv) Charlie's refusal to recognize their post-exchange property rights constitutes a violation of their property rights, and (v) Charlie's demand that they refrain from engaging in the exchange constitutes an interference with their natural liberty and, so, *must be justified to them*. This is not to say that Charlie can never provide such justifications: the social contract may, for instance, protect him against externalities arising out of Alf and Betty's exchange. Nevertheless, the right to own and transfer along with the right to natural liberty yields a justification of market relations.

Let me stress the limits of this argument. It must be remembered that particular property rights in the state of nature have not been justified: the argument from desert established a right to a system of property rights that recognizes ownership over the

96 My thinking on these matters owes much to Stephen Buckle.
97 Riley, "Justice under Capitalism," p. 135. His account of a system of justified private property rights is very close to that defended here; however, he ultimately seems to endorse a version of DJ rather than PR.

fruits of one's labor. Thus, the justification for exchange is similarly contingent upon resolution of the problem of natural resources: no market exists in the state of nature. But what we do know is that a justified system of property will accommodate both the rights to private property and exchange. As constituents of the description of the state of nature, these desert-based principles articulate fundamental demands of justice that provide constraints on further, teleological, justification (see §27.2).

26.4 Harm

One of the obvious constraints on both the rights to natural liberty and property is the harm principle. Since the publication of Joel Feinberg's impressive *Harm to Others*, one cannot help but feel that anything one has to say on the subject is hopelessly incomplete and sketchy. One does not have to be particularly timorous to seek to avoid the impression of proposing an alternative to Feinberg's thorough analysis. Despite all this, I find that I do disagree fundamentally with his understanding of harm. Trying to explain why I do so will help, I think, the reader to better understand the role of the harm principle in the state of nature. And it does seem certain that some such principle will be included. Indeed, a great attraction of the harm principle is its intuitive force: how can we deny that a basic principle of public morality is that everyone has a moral reason to refrain from harming others? The harm principle, it seems, does not have to be justified: "no responsible theorist denies the validity of the harm principle."[98] Of course this does not really show it requires no justification, but it does suggest that its justification is based on our deep shared commitment to it.

But that said, Feinberg goes on to hold that, though all reasonable theorists accept that the harm principle provide *a* grounds for restraining liberty, "the liberal would prefer if possible to draw the line there, and deny validity to any other proposed ground of state interference."[99] Even taking into account Feinberg's restriction to state interference, this typical liberal project seems misconceived. The effort to show that only harm to others can justify interventions leads to ignoring the justifica-

98 Feinberg, *Harm to Others*, p. 14.
99 Ibid.

tion of other important interventions and, I think, adopting a confusing notion of harm.

The problem for this sort of liberal proponent of the harm principle is to show that all morally justified interventions in the lives of others can be depicted as cases of preventing harm to others. Now one easy way to do this is adopt the following characterization of harm:

H1: Alf harms Betty if he wrongs her or acts unjustly toward her.[100]

But this is clearly not an interesting version of the harm principle: the characterization of harm is entirely parasitic upon the concepts of wronging or unjust treatment. As far as I can see, the appeal to harm in H1 is otiose: the moral evaluation of Alf's act has been accomplished by saying that Betty was wronged or treated unjustly, and it is those notions that are really doing all the work. Contrast to this:

H2: Alf harms Betty if he sets back, thwarts, or defeats her interests.[101] To harm a person is, prima facie, to wrong her.

H2 seems a genuine harm principle, that is, it explains moral wrong in terms of harm rather than, as in H1, defining harm in terms of moral wrong. But, pretty clearly, a number of acts that are deemed as harms by H2 are not even prima facie wrong. Betty may turn down Alf's proposal of marriage in favor of Charlie's, and in so doing gravely set back Alf's interests, yet she is not obviously doing anything wrong. Or perhaps Alf is an escaped murderer about to board a plane for Paraguay, when Betty recognizes him and reports him to the police; again, she has set back his interests without wronging him. But H2 insists that both cases Betty has harmed Alf, but, if she did, it is in a way that does not imply even prima facie wrongness. One straightforward response is simply to say that harming is a necessary but not a sufficient condition for wrongdoing.[102] But Feinberg seeks a much more intimate tie between harming and wrongdoing, and so he defends:

H3: Alf harms Betty when Alf wrongfully sets back Betty's interests.[103]

---

100 See ibid., pp. 34–6.
101 Ibid., p. 33.
102 Mill, of course, suggests this in *On Liberty*, ch. v, paras. 2–3.
103 Feinberg, *Harm to Others*, p. 36.

This makes setback of interest necessary but not sufficient for a harm: also necessary is a judgment of wrongness. So on this view harm presupposes other moral evaluations (for example, wrong, unjust), but it conjoins to these the requirement that someone's interests are set back.

For Feinberg, then, the harm principle is not an alternative to a theory of justice or moral wrong: it operates on such theories, requiring that, in addition to their moral evaluation, interests must suffer before the state can coercively intervene. One odd consequence of this approach is that the harm principle cannot do the sort of work it seems most suited for. Say Alf is about to hit Betty over the head. On our intuitive understanding of the harm principle, the judgment "Alf is about to harm (that is, hurt) Betty" justifies intervention. But on Feinberg's H3, to show Alf harms Betty, it must first be shown that he has wronged her, so it cannot be shown that he wrongs her by showing that he harms her. Thus, we need some theory of rights, justice, or moral wronging before we can ever say that he harms her.

It seems that this gets things somewhat back to front. Intuitively, we wish to show that a wrong has been done by pointing to the harm, not vice versa. For all its faults, H2 captures the intuitive moral reasoning behind harm claims: that is, it justifies a conclusion that wrong has been done. (This inversion of the argumentative functions of "a harm" and "a wrong" may be inherent in the attempt to transform harm judgments from simply one type of moral judgment to the sole principle regulating intervention. Mill, for instance, suggests a similar inversion.)[104] This, of course, leaves us with Feinberg's worries about H2: What about harms that do not justify a judgment of moral wrongness? The problem, I think, is that complex notions such as harm just cannot be simply defined, and any attempt to do so will be too broad and/or too narrow. Feinberg's "setback of interest" seems a case in point: Betty certainly sets back Alf's interest, but for most of us his claim that her refusal harmed him will come as a surprise. (If she broke his heart in the process, that probably is a genuine harm.) Our clearest sense of harm is physical injury, and I suspect that a very large part of the intuitive appeal of the harm principle derives from this basic case. To be

104 See *On Liberty*, p. 75 (ch. IV, para. 3).

sure, there are certainly other sorts of genuine harms – including many of externalities generated by property holders in the course of their activities. However, I shall leave case by case discussions of harm to philosophers better qualified for such sensitive investigations. All that I wish to insist upon here is (i) when it is determined that Alf has harmed Betty, the onus of justification is met and interference with his action can be justified; and (ii) when the notion of harm is really doing work in our moral deliberations about justified interventions, the claim that Alf harms Betty justifies the claim that he has wronged her. Once it has been determined that he has acted unjustly or wrongfully, no moral bar to intervention remains (of course, there are various pragmatic concerns). Additional proof that interests have also been set back is quite unnecessary.

All this, I should note, concerns the way in which the harm principle is a guide for the justification of interventions. As a principle for guiding damages and compensations, something very much like Feinberg's harm principle H3 may be useful.[105] For, in determining if someone is to be compensated, we typically first wish to restrict ourselves to the set of wrongful acts, and then consider in some sense how much a person has suffered by being wronged. As a principle guiding compensation, then, I have no deep objections to some version of H3, but neither Mill nor Feinberg see the liberal harm principle in this way.

26.5 Needs

It has long been argued that claims of need override property rights. Even Locke thought so: "As *Justice* gives every Man a Title to the product of his honest Industry, and the Fair Acquisitions of his Ancestors descended to him, so *Charity* gives every Man a Title to so much of another's Plenty, as will keep him from extream want, where he has no means to subsist otherwise."[106] Moreover, as contemporary Locke scholars have noted, his notion of charity gives the needy a "Right to the Surplusage" of the "Goods" of the better off.[107] And it seems that Locke en-

105 See Judith Jarvis Thomson, "Government Regulation of Behavior."
106 Locke, *First Treatise*, p. 188 (sec. 42).
107 Ibid. I am again grateful here for Stephen Buckle's assistance. See his *History of Property*, ch. 3. See also Jeremy Waldron, "Enough and As Good Left for Others."

visages this right to surplusage as able to override another's property right. My analysis of the right to property and claims over natural resources is in the spirit of Locke. For, in endorsing the right to charity, Locke argues that if this right were denied, "no Man could ever have a just Power over the Life of another, by right of Property in Land or Possessions; since 'twould always be a Sin in any Man of estate, to let his Brother perish for want of affording him relief out of his Plenty."[108] I too have argued that no right to property could be fully justified unless exclusionary rights over land and resources can be justified; and this will require that the system of property rights advances the common good (see §28.5). So it seems sound to say that one person could not have a right to plenty based on a system of exclusionary property rights that do not advance the values of all. At this juncture, however, I wish to consider a different way in which a theory can be true to Locke's intuition: apart from the contractual argument, the sound claim that "Alf needs *X*" can justify infringing the property rights of Betty. I have argued that rights and desert claims are properly included in the description of the state of nature, but what of the third member of David Miller's triad – needs?

Consider the following conceptions of need:

N1: Needs are defined independently of value systems. There are some things that are needed by everyone quite independently of what a person values. There is some set of needs $\{n_1 \ldots n_i\}$ that pertains to all persons.

N2: Needs are defined relative to individual value systems. But the needs so defined intersect on the set $\{n_1 \ldots n_i\}$. These things are needed whatever a person values.

N3: Needs are defined relative to individual value systems. It is not assumed that the sets of needs thus defined intersect. The set of things needed by all people may be null.

N1 and N2 best support the intuition that needs generate moral claims on others (again, independently of the contractual argument), but the Affective-Cognitive Theory of value points toward N3, which provides a less firm foundation for needs claims in the state of nature.

Let us begin with N1. Assume we had some notion of basic human needs that all rational moral persons would recognize.

108 Locke, *First Treatise*, p. 188 (sec. 42).

One could say that Betty needed, say, adequate health care without making any reference to her value system. If such need claims could be upheld, they would form a part of the description of the state of nature. But it is not at all clear that the sorts of need claims generated by N1 can be justified. Recall Betty from §24.4: she is blind and her value system is focused on aesthetic and environmental concerns relating to her beloved dry center. For what does she need health care? To stay healthy, of course, but it is not clear why she should value health. To avoid the pain of disease? If she has a reason to avoid pain, why should she seek to be healthy rather than to obtain narcotics? Insisting that Betty needs something whether or not she has any use for it seems, in the end, to be reasserting an "objective" account of what is valuable that is divorced from her valuings, and this has already been rejected (§7.3).

David Braybrooke, as I understand him, would object that the possibility of exceptions does not undermine the validity of lists of basic needs. Exceptions may arise, but needs are defined relative to a general population. As Braybrooke sees it, "the standing of the . . . needs on the List will not be shaken, by the discovery of some exceptions, so long as the exceptions in any Reference Population are relatively infrequent."[109] Now in one respect this is certainly true: if one is developing a list of needs, describing the condition of a population and the goods and services they generally require, as a description of the general population the list will be accurate even if there are deviant individuals. But our concern is whether this list of needs can be deontologically publicly justified. And regarding public justification deviants are both important and, I think, apt to be troublesome for basic needs justifications along the lines of N1. Betty may object to the list of needs that *she* does not need these things; what *she* needs is that her beloved desert be saved. She cares little for her health or welfare; and she refuses to acknowledge that it is rationally incumbent upon her to seek these things when she does not value them. And she may ask: Why do the needs included in the list have a public standing denied to hers? Because they are "standard" in her "Reference Population"? But what is that to her? The list must be justified to her, even though she be a minority of one.

109 Braybrooke, *Meeting Needs*, p. 45.

But perhaps there are some things that are needed by every value system, that is, perhaps N2 holds. This, of course, is essentially Rawls's concept of primary goods.[110] This is not the place for a general critique of the theory of primary goods, but it should be stressed how much more plausible the idea becomes if we take as our starting point the notion of a "plan of life" or "projects." To focus on persons as the possessors of life plans immediately gives agency pride of place: people *pursue* projects and they *execute* life plans. And, once agency becomes the focal point of all conceptions of the good, the idea of a primary good becomes very plausible indeed. For we can identify the prerequisites for successful action: liberty, some level of resources, and health are rightly seen as fundamentally important whatever the particular direction one's agency takes. I do not wish to deny the importance of our conception of ourselves as agents; if we were not agents, we would not have reasons for action, whether valuational or moral. Furthermore, I too have based the right to free action on our self-understandings as agents (§24), and in some way it probably grounds the desert principle underlying property rights.[111] But my argument does not, as is the current practice in much ethics, equate "value systems," "what is valued," or even "conceptions of the good" with "projects" or "plans." We again return to the point I raised in §24.4: some people have far more reflective or passive values than do others. Although some value systems are true to the liberal vision of active pursuers of ends – people who not only know what they want but cherish the life of achievers and pursuers – others do not put action and the self at the center of their valuational outlook. These other types – who go almost unnoticed in contemporary liberal political philosophy – care deeply for certain things, and will act appropriately to promote or preserve them if possible, but often they can do little about the things they care for most. For such people, the pre-

110 For a recent statement of the theory of primary goods and the role they play in his theory, see Rawls's "Social Unity and Primary Goods." For an application of the idea of primary goods to a needs-centered theory, see Raymond Plant, Harry Lesser, and Peter Taylor-Gooby, *Political Philosophy and Social Welfare*, pp. 33–6.

111 Let me stress again that the argument for natural liberty does not suppose that everyone highly values liberty, action, or agency. It only supposes that we are all self-directed agents, and basic to being such an agent is that one supposes that one's activity is, as it were, naturally at one's own beck and call.

requisites of agency will have some value, but comparatively they may not rank high. If so, they will resist the liberal claim that securing such primary goods is fundamentally important to them.

But certainly the Affective-Cognitive Theory of value supports a concept of need along the lines of N3: given a particular value system, we can identify those things that are fundamental to promoting or protecting what is most valued. And these may plausibly be called one's needs. For Alf, an active, liberal pursuer of projects, these might be Rawlsian primary goods. Alf, perhaps, does not care about anything as much as being able to live his own life as he sees fit. But perhaps what Betty really needs is that mining be halted in her beloved desert. Are we willing to allow her to infringe property rights to satisfy her needs? Or, more precisely, can she employ this need as a reason that Alf must accept from his perspective as a reason for infringing his property rights? Although a justified public morality must reasonably promote her valuings as well as his, it seems counter-intuitive to say that her need to protect the dry center can be deontologically justified.

None of this establishes that some notion of need cannot be deontologically justified, that is, included in the description of the state of nature. Perhaps we are so committed to the notion of "basic needs" that it is simply a brute intuition that meeting them can always justify interferences with liberty and property, even if the person possessing such a need cares little about fulfilling it.[112] My aim here has been to suggest that our intuitions about needs are closely linked to theories of value; having rejected the sorts of theories of value that provide the best foundation for a strong appeal to needs as reasons to act, our intuitions about needs are apt to become confused. I shall not, however, further pursue the problem of the moral status of needs in the state of nature. As I suggested at the outset of this discussion, the argument in support of distributive justice (§28.5) does tie the justification of property rights to a requirement that all benefit, and

112 This may well be the moral force behind Braybrooke's list of needs; perhaps all the members of the reference population just do accept that certain things like health care are needs, and should be supplied. Perhaps Betty can be shown that her value system too rests on this supposition, even though she has no need for these things herself.

this will mean that the values of all must be advanced. It seems plausible to conjecture that most basic needs will be catered for at this stage of the argument. In relation to disputes about the place of need claims in the state of nature, it thus seems the social contract will be relatively robust (§26.1). Let us now turn to an analysis of contractual negotiation.

IX

The social contract

27 THE STATE OF NATURE AND THE SOCIAL CONTRACT

In the previous chapter, I proposed an account of the deontological foundations of our value systems. The right to natural liberty, extended to include a presumption against paternalistic interference, and the right to a system of private property are among the moral principles presupposed by the value systems of the self-directed moral persons that characterize our Western societies. I have not argued, of course, that all such self-directed agents will in fact acknowledge these moral principles, but it is indeed part of my thesis that any fully rational moral agent of the sort I have been describing would do so. Once again, it is important to grasp that philosophical ethics is only practical in this limited sense: it provides reasons for action, but it is neither necessarily persuasive nor does it aim to produce actual consensus (§16.2).

In this section, I explore three implications of this description of the state of nature for contractual justification. In section 28, I present the core of the contractual argument. I close in §29 with some general concluding remarks concerning the theory of justification and liberal political philosophy.

27.1 Irrational values

The analysis of the state of nature allows us to at least begin to identify the set of values that enter into the constrained teleological argument that constitutes the contractual justification (§20.1). As I have argued, only rational valuings are to enter into justificatory argument (§21.5); we can now allow into justificatory argument values that presuppose the moral right to natural liberty, the presumption against paternalism, prohibition of obvious harms, and the right to a system of private property. Thus, it is a legitimate argument in favor of a proposed code of public morality that it secures the rights to private property and natural liberty. In contrast, we will now disallow valuings that presuppose that natural liberty and private property are not fundamental moral rights. For example, we will reject the argument of a certain sort of conservative who may endorse a code of public morality because it recognizes the natural moral authority of the aristocracy over the masses. If we understand this claim to authority as presupposing that the masses possess no moral right to natural liberty, we must conclude that the conservative's valuing of this authoritarian morality is irrational.

Now it may seem that our conservative has an easy reply here: all he must do is to change the grounding of his valuing of this authoritarian order. Instead of grounding his valuing on the belief that an authoritarian public morality recognizes the natural authority of some over others, he can rescue his valuing by depicting it as a mere liking of such orders, not in any way founded on moral beliefs. And, because the appropriateness conditions for liking are very broad indeed (§6.1), the conservative's valuing very likely remains rational. But the force of this reply is blunted when we remember that people's valuings are caused by their grounding beliefs (§5.4.1); once we show someone that his valuings presuppose false beliefs, the valuing is typically undermined. Many disvaluings of a liberal order are, indeed, likely to be based on just such false moral beliefs; rational valuers who acknowledge the irrationality of their disvaluings are apt to abandon their ill-grounded disvaluings rather than change the grounds of their disvaluings.

However, even if the conservative does recast his valuing of an authoritarian order in terms of liking, he will still find himself with antiauthoritarian commitments. The deontological argument shows that, though he may possess some authoritarian valuings, he is also committed to the right of natural liberty. Because to reject this right would undermine his conception of himself, he has very strong reasons to acknowledge it. This does not mean that he must reject his authoritarian valuings; we have already seen that valuings can be rationally inconsistent in such ways (§14.1). However, his commitment to natural liberty does show that his value system is not thoroughly authoritarian; when we come to ask the question "Which public morality will best promote one's values?" our conservative will find himself with both authoritarian and liberal commitments.

27.2 Immoral proposals

It may seem that I have not taken a sufficiently strong approach to the conservative: if we have a right to natural liberty, then it would seem that an authoritarian moral code is necessarily ruled out. I have contended that the description of the state of nature articulates the basis for the contractual argument: it would thus seem to follow that establishing the right to natural liberty as part of the state of nature precludes any authoritarian order. Such a code is inherently immoral.

But I think this is too sweeping: certain sorts of nonliberal codes are consistent with the argument from the state of nature. That Alf possesses a right to natural liberty implies that any interference with his activity must be justified to him. But any moral code that is the outcome of the contractual argument is, *ex hypothesi*, publicly justified. Consequently, any restraints on action that are part of the justified moral code are consistent with the right to natural liberty; because the code is publicly justified – justified to each and every member of the public – the restraint has been justified, and so defeats the presumption against interference. At this point in the argument, then, I have by no means justified a liberal morality. If it could be shown that everyone's values are best promoted by a public morality that is based on a common conception of a virtuous life that requires such virtuous behavior from everyone,[1] the right to natural liberty would be respected.

Yet the idea of an inherently immoral code is not to be dismissed. Consider a strongly authoritarian proposal that the population should be divided into citizens and slaves; furthermore, the slaves must always be prepared to justify their every action in terms of how it satisfies their masters' instructions. Someone attracted to this order may advance the proposal that the contrac-

1 In this passage I am drawing on Ronald Dworkin's depiction of a conservative as one who "supposes that the good man would wish to be treated in accordance with the principles of a special sort of society, which I shall call the virtuous society." See "Liberalism," p. 198.

tors accept this structure, with the allocation of places being determined by lot. We need not consider whether contractors would accept this gamble (but see §21.4): it is an inherently immoral proposal. It is so because those who lose out would be committed to effectively renouncing their right to natural liberty. Henceforth, they have no right to have their activity directed by their self; their activity is to be the expression of the master's self. If self-directed agents must necessarily recognize each person's – including their own – right to natural liberty, then self-directed moral persons cannot rationally renounce this right in contractual justification. To do so would lead to the collapse of their value systems, but the point of contractual negotiation is to advance one's value system.

The divide between the permissible conservative code and the immoral authoritarian proposal is that between those proposals that place severe limits on the extent to which we direct our own activity and those that require renouncing the right to self-direction. This distinction, admittedly, cannot be made in a precise way, but it is nevertheless fundamental. It will help clarify it, I think, to relate it to the distinction between important and central valuings (§14.2.2). I have not claimed – indeed I have denied – that self-directed agency is highly valued by all. Some people may have values that are better advanced by placing severe limits on self-direction. Thus, Betty, our environmentalist (§24.4) may conclude that her all important environmental valuings will be better advanced in a highly traditional society in which economic innovation is discouraged; she may well sacrifice considerable self-direction to promote her environmental values. And because this is so, nonliberal public moralities can in principle be justified by the social contract. But, even if she does not highly value self-direction, this is different from renouncing it. If I am right about the disintegrating consequences on personality that such renouncing would bring about, it cannot be rational to give up this conception of oneself.

The upshot of this is that the right to natural liberty will not be renounced by rational contractors, though they can rationally agree to severe constraints on self-direction. Much the same applies to the right to a system of private property. If my reformulation of Becker's argument is correct (§26.2), the principle that one deserves what one has produced is basic to our moral outlook. To reject generally the claims of desert would undermine the moral enterprise, and thus all our morality-grounded valuings; and, if do we accept the concept of deservingness, I have maintained that we are committed to recognizing that a person deserves what he has produced. But this argument does not imply that rational contractors are necessarily committed to anything like the strong defense of private property advanced by Robert Nozick,[2] and this for at least two reasons. Firstly, I have argued that the description of the state of nature includes a right to a system of property rights that respects production as grounding title, but it does not endorse any particular property rights because the problem of acquisition of natural resources has yet to be solved. It is thus a matter of contractual argument as to what system of private property can be justified to all. Secondly, I have not argued that rational moral persons highly value a system of private property rights; it may be that the value systems of many could be advanced by a public morality that severely limits property rights.

But, again, the description of the state of nature does rule out some proposals as immoral. A proposal would be immoral if it entirely ignores the right to a system of private rights, that is, if it takes no cognizance of the justified claims of a worker that he has a particular claim to the fruits of his labor.

Consider, for example, Oliver Williamson's "Peer Group" system. In such a system of collective ownership, all the work stations in a production process are collectively owned by the workers, and reward is based on a nonmarginal product principle, for example, the workers are paid the average of the group product.[3] Now, in an economy in which Peer Ownership was the only option, it is plausible that some would have significant grounds for complaint that it violates their natural right to a system that gives one exclusionary rights over the fruits of one's labor. Mandatory participation in work organizations that reward on the basis of average performance very plausibly give others control over the fruits of the labors of those who contribute well above the mean.

The argument also casts doubt on the justifiability of market socialism (Yugoslav style), a form of work organization and own-

2 Robert Nozick, *Anarchy, State, and Utopia.*
3 Oliver E. Williamson, *The Economic Institutions of Capitalism*, pp. 217-18.

ership much in vogue today.[4] Worker-managed market socialist firms certainly can reward workers differently, recognizing the differential claims to the fruit of labor, but market socialism in effect expropriates the savings of workers invested into their firms.[5] If, as Mill claimed, one has a claim to the fruits of one's abstinence (§26.2.3), market socialism tends to systematically ignore this claim. Workers who have heavily invested in their firms, especially older workers, have no exclusionary rights to these funds, entirely losing them on leaving the firm.[6]

Nonmarket, that is, command economies, are also challenged by the argument from the state of nature. Many socialists have aspired to reward all according to the fruits of their labor, and we can at least imagine a command economy that sought to distribute income with this in mind (for example, according to marginal product).[7] But even if this desert-based claim informing quasi-Lockean property rights could be met in nonmarket systems, prohibition on market exchanges would infringe the right of transfer, as well as constituting an interference with natural liberty.

The argument thus points to a market system where people have exclusionary rights over the fruits of their labor. But must the system be capitalist? Robert Dahl thinks not; indeed, he indicates that "corporate capitalism" cannot be justified. "Whatever one may think of the validity of Locke's notion of labor as justifying private property," he says, "it cannot justify the ownership of a corporation by stockholders. For on Locke's justification only those who labor to produce goods and services, the workers and employees, would be entitled to own the goods and services produced by the firm."[8] If one adopts this view it would

4 See, e.g., Charles Lindblom, *Politics and Markets*, ch. 24. See also Buchanan, *Ethics, Efficiency, and the Market*, ch. 4.

5 It might be possible to create a bond scheme that could overcome this difficulty. See P. J. D. Wiles, *Economic Institutions Compared*, pp. 348–9.

6 Younger workers can receive the fruits of their investment through increased profitability. Hence the time horizon of workers is crucial in understanding the investment decisions of Yugoslav firms. See Erik G. Furubotn and Svetozar Pejovich, "Property Rights and the Behavior of the Firm in a Socialist State: The Example of Yugoslavia," pp. 239ff.

7 See Wiles, *Economic Institutions Compared*, ch. 11.

8 Dahl, *A Preface to Economic Democracy*, p. 78. Dahl rejects the Lockean treatment of property in favor of a more Rousseauean approach; that is, he rejects any claim to natural property rights that put moral constraints on what economic system the people may choose.

seem that a system of worker cooperatives – which, we must remember, was Mill's dream – is required by the argument.[9] Certainly a cooperative system is consistent with my argument, but it is not at all clear that corporate capitalism is precluded. Because we have rejected the desert-based conception of distributive justice (DJ) in favor of a desert-based theory of property rights including the power to transfer title (§26.3), Dahl's main claim – that those who do not labor cannot have justified title – can also be rejected.[10] Although I certainly have not demonstrated that it is impossible to show that in some way corporate capitalism is inherently immoral, it does seem (i) that any prohibition of capitalist acts between consenting adults is a violation of natural liberty and so stands in need of justification, (ii) that abolishing the right to transfer justified holdings is a violation of the right to property, and (iii) that those who do not produce have property rights under corporate capitalism is not inconsistent with the argument for quasi-Lockean property rights.

The social contract, I am claiming, cannot legitimately ignore this natural right. It may be thought that this claim rests on a confusion between a natural right and an indefeasible right. As Dahl points out, even if it can be established that we have a natural right to property, it does not follow that this right overrides other rights; so, in the interest of promoting these other rights, the right to property may be overridden.[11] But the idea of overriding a right, which is at home in discussion of particular cases, has very different implications when we are dealing with the construction of a public morality (and corresponding social institutions). Dahl is suggesting that in the design of basic social and economic institutions any natural right to property would be systematically overridden by the right of people to govern themselves in accordance with democratic processes. Presumably for Dahl this means that the natural right to property would be of no real consequence, for the preferred social structure would systematically override it in favor of advancing and respecting democratic

9 On Mill and cooperatives, see *Principles of Political Economy*, pp. 764–94 (bk. IV, ch. vii, secs. 5–7). Dahl, too, looks forward to a cooperative organization. See *A Preface to Economic Democracy*, esp. pp. 148ff.
10 Jonathan Riley would reject it for a different reason: that "long-run competitive rewards to labor *and* capital are justified by the principle of desert." "Justice under Capitalism," p. 139 (emphasis added).
11 Dahl, *A Preface to Economic Democracy*, p. 75.

values. But surely this is tantamount to rejecting the right to property. Unlike individual cases, where a right overridden one day may be respected the next, to systematically override a natural right in the design of social institutions is to ensure that it will never be respected. If it is indeed basic to our value systems that producers have claims to the fruits of their labor, a public morality that always ignored these claims in order to advance some valued outcome would, I think, be effectively rejecting the right. And if the right is foundational to the contractors' value systems, the public morality would be undermining the rational basis of the value systems it endeavors to promote.

The distinction between overriding a value (or a moral right) and giving it up, though sound and useful, tends to collapse if some value (or principle) is always overridden. Just as we may come to doubt the friendship of one who always has competing and overriding commitments to other concerns, so too will we come to doubt the commitment of a public morality that purports to recognize the claims of a producer to the fruits of his labor, but never is able to honor that claim because of competing commitments. If we have a rational commitment to acknowledging the claims of people to the fruits of their labor, there is something wrong with a public morality that never does so. It thus seems reasonable to impose as a condition on possible public moralities that they do not systematically override any natural right or duty, including the right to property. This condition – let us call it the *principle of minimal respect for natural rights and duties* – is consistent with considerable limitation of the right: I have excluded only economic systems that do not, as it were, take the right to property seriously. Thus, for instance, it seems to me that the economic system favored by Dahl, one composed of worker cooperatives, satisfies the principle,[12] as do some versions of corporate capitalism.

Of course, we may find that the principle of minimal respect for natural rights and duties cannot be met. Assume that further descriptions of the state of nature reveal other natural rights and duties and, further, suppose that it is shown that these additional rights and duties clash with, and indeed, override the right to property. (In this case, it would be shown that my description

12 See ibid., pp. 148ff.

was not robust in the sense discussed in §26.1.) Perhaps these alternative descriptions of the state of nature uphold a natural right to democratic government that systematically conflicts with the right to property. If so, then it may be impossible to meet the principle of minimal respect for natural rights and duties. But, even so, this would not necessarily justify ignoring the right. As Judith Thomson has argued, even if we are justified in violating a right, compensation may be owed.[13] And certainly if a public morality systematically but justifiably overrode natural rights compensation would be owed to those unable to exercise their natural rights.[14]

In what follows, I will assume that the natural rights to liberty and property can both be accommodated within the justified public morality. Adopting the principle of minimal respect for natural rights and duties does not make the theory utopian in the sense of depending on unrealistic or unduly optimistic claims.[15] It merely supposes that our moral world is not so wrought with conflict that some basic moral principles must be ignored in a justified public morality.

27.3 The state of nature as a baseline

One way to interpret the idea of an immoral proposal is one which, if accepted, would actually worsen the condition of some contractors vis-à-vis the state of nature. Recall Gauthier's condition that no one be driven away from the bargaining table (§21.3). An immoral proposal, we might say, drives some contractors away from the bargaining table as it asks them to give up rights that they have in the state of nature. That is, such proposals advocate that some leave the contractual negotiations with less than they brought in: the immoral proposal pushes them below the baseline defined as what contractors brought into the bargaining situation.

13 See her "Self-defense and Rights."
14 Robert Nozick adopts this general position; in his account of political society, some people are prohibited from exercising aspects of their natural right to liberty, and thus compensation is required. See *Anarchy, State, and Utopia*, ch. 4.
15 In the sense in which William A. Galston uses the term, however, I suppose that the theory presented here might well be called "utopian." See *Justice and the Human Good*, ch. 2. But cf. John Dunn, "The Future of Liberalism."

Like many analogies, this one is helpful up to a point, but then leads us astray. Teleological moral justification is not actually a bargain in which people enter with certain assets and intend to leave with more. Rather, constrained teleological arguments seek to justify a public morality by showing that it advances the values of all while at least minimally respecting the deontological principles on which those value systems are built. We must remember that the core of contractual theory is not consent or the striking of deals, but the notion of the common good (§20.2). The contractual analogy is a way to make this idea more concrete, but we must always be alert to cases in which the analogy is taking over and becomes misleading. And if we push very far the ideas of initial assets or being driven away from the bargaining table, we will indeed go astray. After all, people in the state of nature have no particular property rights, but only a natural right to a certain system of property rights. This does not seem a great asset, it may be reasoned, so perhaps they can be bought off easily, especially if our contractors do not highly value private property. By the time we arrive at such considerations, the contractual analogy has taken over; I shall employ the language of contractual negotiation where it is enlightening, but we must keep clearly before our minds that it is simply a way to shed light on the problem of a constrained teleological justification.

Let me express the point without resort to contractual language. Our concern in this chapter is to clarify our ideas as to what public morality truly advances the common good, that is, can be said to advance the values of all. I have already argued that, though there are a number of types of common good arguments, the most useful in the context of public justification in a society such as ours are compromise arguments (§21). Furthermore, I have adopted Gauthier's principle of minimax relative concession as a useful way to make more precise the idea of a rational compromise. So, to be more specific, our aim here is to employ the idea of minimax relative concession in order to sharpen our understanding of a morality based on a common good. As we have seen, minimax relative concession depends on measures of both the most that a person's values could be promoted [U(fp)], and the least that they could be promoted [(U(ip)]. Now the idea of immoral proposals allows us to identify both of these. No matter how much a public morality advances someone's values, it is to be excluded if it contains an immoral proposal. Thus, the best for anyone is the public morality among those proposed that best advances his values consistent with the principle of minimal respect for natural rights and duties. This, then, helps us identify *U*(fp); I hope to show that, rough as it is, it suffices for our purposes. I shall identify the lower boundary of possible solutions – the minimum acceptable outcome from anyone's perspective – as the public morality among those proposed that does least to advance one's values but is consistent with the deontologically justified public morality. This would constitute the greatest possible concession consistent with one's moral rights, giving one essentially what is required by the deontological morality.[16] So it defines *U*(ip).

Those familiar with Gauthier's analysis will realize just how far this characterization is from his. Not only is the substantive description of the upper and lower bounds different, but my definition of the variables is sensitive to the proposals put forward in a way in which his is not. However, as we are about to see, I shall advance some plausible assumptions that ensure that all possible options are considered. In any event, unlike Gauthier, I am not claiming to advance a general theory of rational bargains: it will suffice if the rough variables indicated here help sharpen our ideas concerning a morality based on rational compromise. I shall now try to show how they do.

28 IDEOLOGY AND COMPROMISE

28.1 Competing ideologies

Let us recall the problem of contractual negotiation. The aim is to settle on a code of public morality that advances the values of all and so satisfies the requirement of the common good. Such a

16 It is not precisely equivalent to Gauthier's total concession; that would seem more equivalent to an outcome which endorses only the morality that pertains in the state of nature. The problem is that the deontologically justified morality is necessarily incomplete: it justifies one's right to a system of property that recognizes production as a claim to title, but it does not solve the problem of original acquisition. Consequently, an outcome simply confirming the deontologically justified morality would not be moral: we must go beyond it if we are to actualize private property rights. This feature of the state of nature thus leads to complications for the application of the bargaining model.

public morality will be publicly justified because all rational moral persons are provided with good reasons for accepting it. Further, the idea of contractual negotiation points to compromise arguments, as opposed to arguments based on community of valuing, harmony, or proceduralism (§21). Each contractor, then, proposes a code of public morality that is best from his perspective (subject to the constraint prohibiting immoral proposals). The principle of minimax relative concession, I have argued, seems a plausible criterion of a rational compromise. But this does not take us very far in solving the problem of contractual negotiation. We can imagine an unlimited variety of public moralities that might be advanced: if we cannot somehow delimit the set of possible proposals, we will not be able to advance beyond this abstract description of the contractual problem.

Here, as in so many other places, Rawls provides an insight. In describing the alternatives to be considered in the contractual negotiation, he acknowledges that the ideal would seem to be to allow "all possible conceptions of justice."[17] But this would render the choice situation unmanageable. Rawls thus relies on a different procedure; the alternatives relevant in contractual negotiation are limited to a small list of traditional conceptions of justice. The problem of the contractors is thus redefined as the choice of one conception from this list. Rawls's procedure is not only a simplifying device to allow the contractual argument to proceed, however. He characterizes moral theory as "the systematic and comparative study of moral conceptions";[18] thus understood, his interest in moral theory recommends a focus on the main competing conceptions of justice.

At least for our purposes, however, the Rawlsian alternatives seem inappropriate. Given his interest in moral theory[19] – the comparative analysis of moral conceptions – his alternatives are fairly abstract moral theories rather than anything like competing moral codes. Classical utilitarianism, average utilitarianism, perfectionism, and intuitionism are the main alternatives to his two principles of justice.[20] Although some of these – for example, per-

17 John Rawls, *A Theory of Justice*, p. 122.
18 Rawls, "Kantian Constructivism in Moral Theory," p. 557.
19 See however Rawls's "Justice As Fairness: Political Not Metaphysical," esp. p. 224n, where he indicates that his concern is political philosophy rather than moral theory.
20 Rawls, *A Theory of Justice*, p. 123.

fectionism – may have determinate normative implications, others – such as the utilitarian theories – can *justify* nearly any set of rights and duties under given circumstances. And this suggests the somewhat odd character of the Rawlsian alternatives: they are essentially *justificatory* theories, but they are embedded in a contractual justificatory framework that undermines their justificatory force. For instance, utilitarianism is by no means simply a normative ethic; it is a justificatory theory, typically based on an agent-neutral conception of value-based reasons for action (§12.1), and it is this that grounds the normative universalistic claims of most[21] utilitarians. But in the context of contractual negotiation – which only has appeal once we have rejected strong claims of agent-neutrality – utilitarianism is cut off from its most plausible meta-ethical foundations. By the time we have posed the question whether rational contractors will adopt utilitarianism, we have already rejected much of the utilitarian case.

What is required, then, is a set of alternatives that (i) is more plausibly seen as each embodying a system of norms, and (ii) that can plausibly be cut off from their traditional justificatory basis and, so, be embedded in the contractual justificatory theory. If (i) is satisfied the alternatives are properly interpreted as articulating competing public moralities; if (ii) is satisfied, these alternatives remain of interest even when included within a contractual outlook aiming at public justification. Both conditions are reasonably satisfied by the traditional ideologies at the heart of political dispute during the last one hundred years: socialism, liberalism, and conservatism. All three ideologies are associated with a system of norms for regulating political life, much social life, a good deal of personal life, and the economic order. Indeed, ideologies are often characterized in terms of a body of norms; to Robert M. MacIver, for instance, an ideology "is a system of political, economic, and social values and ideas from which objectives are derived. These objectives form the nucleus of a political program."[22]

21 To be sure, this is not true of all utilitarians. R. M. Hare, for instance, seems to ground his theory on a universalization thesis (see §18.1 of this volume). And we have also seen that some utilitarians are prepared to accept the contractual method (see §20.1). R. B. Brandt, in fact, endorses something very much like my account of public justification. See *A Theory of the Good and the Right*, ch. X.

22 R. M. MacIver, quoted in William T. Bluhm, *Ideologies and Attitudes*, p. 3.

The term "ideology," all too often a source of confusion, is particularly suited to our purposes. To describe conservatism, liberalism, and socialism as "ideologies" is typically to see these doctrines as somehow simply expressions of individual value systems, and so unable to avail themselves of the claim of being "true."[23] The refrain "I have a social philosophy; you have political opinions; he has an ideology"[24] conveys, among other things, that, in contrast to me, my opponent has a mere ideology because his political opinions are ill-grounded. But, when applied less aggressively, especially when employed by those who are willing to describe their own political and social views as an ideology, the idea of an "ideology" indicates that none of the competing doctrine are true, but are matters of mere taste, preference, or whatever. The suggestion, then, is that we begin by conceiving contractual negotiations as the realm of competing ideologies. None of the alternatives has any claim to being true; each is to be seen simply as a public morality that express the value systems of some of our contractors. Of course, the ideology that is selected by the contractual argument then can rightly claim to be publicly justified, and thus better grounded than the competing views.

I am not claiming that the traditional theories of conservatism, liberalism, or socialism present themselves as mere expressions of individual value systems. Proponents of these theories all offer various grounds for embracing their political doctrine as the most adequate. Many of these claims are excluded by the theories of value and justification presented in this book. At least on one plausible interpretation, conservatism is based on a set of strongly agent-neutral values, centering on, say, nobility, honor, and social responsibility. Likewise, socialists such as R. H. Tawney have argued the case for socialism in a way that implies equality is an agent-neutral value that properly should regulate public policy.[25] Such arguments are excluded (see §§7.3, 12, 26.5). Thus, in some ways, the status of conservatism and socialism is akin to the sta-

23 The way in which theories of ideology lead to a skepticism about objective truth reaches perhaps its extreme manifestation in theories of "total ideology," in which it becomes hard to see just how any strong conception of truth, much less ethical truth, remains. See, e.g., Karl Mannheim, *Ideology and Utopia*, esp. ch. II.
24 See Clifford Geertz, "Ideology as a Cultural System," p. 194.
25 See Tawney, *Equality*.

tus of utilitarianism in Rawls's theory; in the context of a contractual negotiation based on the recognition of the essential agent-relativity of value and the commitment to public justification, these theories are far less powerful than if we allowed their traditional grounding claims. Instead of political doctrines claiming truth, they are mere ideologies. Yet my point is that conservatism and socialism are still of interest when considered in this light.

Clearly, the contractual justificatory method rules out less of the basis of liberalism; after all, contractualism is one of the main foundations of liberalism. To be sure, this can be exaggerated because modern liberal theory has made extensive appeal to perfectionism and to agent-neutral value.[26] Nevertheless, it must be acknowledged that in this sense the contractual device is not neutral among these ideologies. But I see no reason to strive after such neutrality; given the case for the contractual method, that an ideology coheres with it is a virtue of the ideology, not a criticism of the method. In any event, we shall see that the argument in favor of liberalism does not turn on this point.

28.2 The contractual argument in one-dimensional political space

It is not essential to the contractual argument that we provide specifications of the nature of each of our three ideologies. Rather, at least in the first phase of the argument, I shall rely here on the familiar idea of a left–right continuum in politics. Although political philosophers generally do not tire of insisting how inadequate is such a simple one-dimensional scale for capturing the important cleavages among political doctrines[27] (and I do not claim that they are wrong), the extent to which this simple spectrum dominates our political thinking is nevertheless striking. Factions within political parties, voters at elections, philosophers at APA meetings, and friends who have come to fisticuffs over a

26 See my *Modern Liberal Theory of Man*, pt. I.
27 Cf. Larry Siedentop's remark that "Nothing reduces the value of discussion about modern political thought more than the contrast commonly drawn between 'liberalism' and 'socialism.' That contrast has become *simplistic* and misleading." "Two Liberal Traditions," p. 153. See also Jan Narveson's "complaint about the use of the terms 'left,' 'right,' and 'center' in current political discussions." *The Libertarian Idea*, p. 10.

political controversy surprisingly often understand their disputes in terms of this simple political spectrum.

My aim, then, is not to specify the nature of conservatism, socialism, or liberalism. Each of these are tasks for entire books, and any thumbnail sketch would do little or nothing to clarify the intuitive ideas that all readers already possess. Rather, I wish to state formally the assumptions required by my argument.

28.2.1 Assumptions

(i) *Completeness.* I assume, as is standard practice, that all individual preference orderings are complete: that is, every individual orders all proposed public moralities.

(ii) *Inclusiveness.* All proposed public moralities can be placed on a scale of right–left ideologies. I shall relax this assumption later in the argument.

(iii) *Nonarbitrary end points.* I assume that our left–right political dimension has nonarbitrary endpoints because some conservative and some socialist proposals will be immoral. We have already considered such proposals in §27.2. Conservative proposals that violate the right to natural liberty, including the extension to the presumption against paternalism, are thus excluded. Thus, assuming inclusiveness, the furthest right is the conservative proposal that gives minimal respect to the natural right to liberty and the presumption against paternalism: to go any further to the right would then violate the constraints derived from the analysis of the state of nature. Thus, fascist proposals are certainly ruled out, as would be our slave society proposal. Moreover, all forms of conservatism that embody the presumption that strong paternalism toward some social group is the norm will also violate the principle of minimal respect for natural rights and duties.

Much the same applies to socialism. Socialist proposals that have no room for private property and the market are excluded: thus Marxist public moralities – understood in the traditional way, at any rate – will be beyond the pale. Certainly Soviet-type economies are to be excluded.[28] But forms of socialism akin to market socialism, with some provision that a worker has claims on his investment funds, seem allowed. Indeed, it might be

28 For an analysis of Soviet-type economies, see Wiles, *Economic Institutions Compared.*

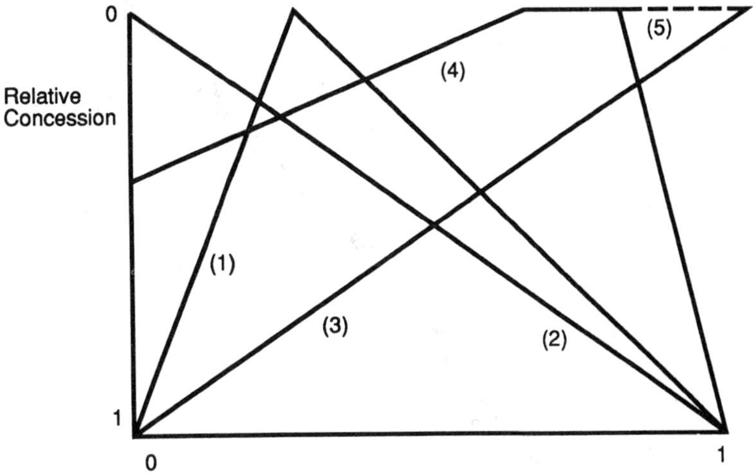

Figure 2.

maintained that my rejection of Yugoslav market socialism depended on the right to the fruits of one's abstinence, and that was not explicitly defended in the argument from the state of nature. So some may argue for the inclusion of market socialism as a part of a legitimate socialist public morality. Certainly nothing I say requires that market socialist proposals be excluded. Indeed, the formal argument does not depend on any particular limits, but it does require that the left–right political space have nonarbitrary end points.

(iv) *Number of alternatives*. To make the argument manageable, I assume that the contractors are selecting from among a moderate number of alternatives – say ten alternative public moralities. These alternatives range from the most radical (moral) conservative proposal to the most radical (moral) socialist proposal. I shall assume that these proposals are distributed evenly along the left–right spectrum.

(v) *Single-peakedness*. I assume that all preference curves are single-peaked. Figure 2 shows some basic types of single-peaked preference curves.[29] Allowing indifference at the top, curves can

29 I am following here William H. Riker, *Liberalism Against Populism*, p. 124. Figure 2 in the present volume draws on Riker's Figure 5-2, on p. 125.

be, for instance, (1) always running northeast to southwest; (2) always running northwest to southeast; (3) running southwest to northeast, and then turning southeast; (4) running southwest to northeast then going due east until it slopes down to the southeast; (5) just like curve (4), except it continues due east, never turning southeast.

The idea can be expressed in a more intuitive fashion if we think of the left–right spectrum in terms of a spatial analogy, following the analysis pioneered by Hotelling.[30] To do this, we must introduce some metric. As did Anthony Downs in his well-known theory of democracy, I will apply the spatial analysis to the left–right spectrum by assuming a linear scale; let us stipulate a scale running from zero to 1.[31] Given this, to say a contractor's preferences are single-peaked is to say that (i) if point x lies to the same side of the curve's peak as does y and (ii) if x is farther from the curve's peak than y, then (ii) it will never be the case that x is preferred to y and (iv) unless x and y are both at the top of the curve, it will always be true that y is preferred to x. Employing the spatial analogy, as we move away from the ideal point in any direction the alternatives are less desirable. One's first proposal, then, defines one's ideal position. Figure 3 provides an example of one contractor's preference curve. This figure depicts the preference curve of contractor Alf, a left-of-center contractor. To describe Alf as such is to say that his overall value system is best promoted by, say, a public morality that might be described as a weak socialism or, perhaps, a "Liberal Socialism."[32] So, in the contractual negotiations, Alf would propose his liberal socialism; if this public morality – depicted by s – were accepted, he would make no concession at all. Now, according to the condition of single-peakedness, the further we move away in any one direction from s, the less he likes it. As proposals move away from s, he prefers them less, and thus his relative concession increases.

We should distinguish single-peakedness from the stronger condition of symmetry.[33] If symmetry held, it would be the case

30 See Harold Hotelling, "Stability in Competition." For a useful graphical representation of Hotelling's analysis, see F. Zeuthen, "Theoretical Remarks on Price Policy."

31 Anthony Downs, *An Economic Theory of Democracy*, p. 115.

32 The phrase derives from L. T. Hobhouse, *Liberalism*, p. 90.

33 See James M. Enelow and Melvin J. Hinch, *The Spatial Theory of Voting*, pp. 8ff.

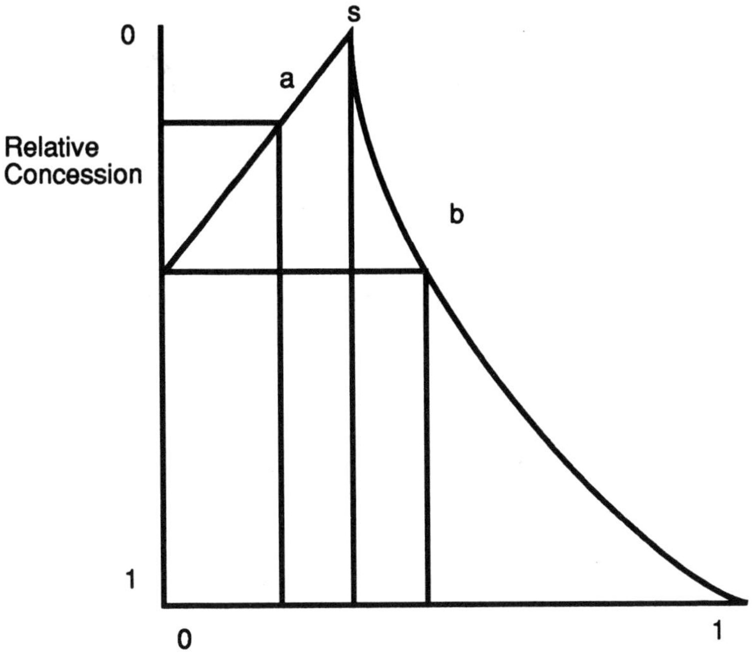

Figure 3.

that Alf would be indifferent between any two proposals precisely the same distance from s, such as a and b. But single-peakedness is a weaker condition: it allows that one's preferences may change at different rates depending on which side of one's ideal point one is traveling. For instance, in Figure 3 we see that Alf is a left-of-center contractor who much prefers ideologies of the left. Consequently, even though points a and b are equally distant from his ideal point, he prefers a to b. This is consistent with single-peakedness but violates symmetry. Roughly, symmetry holds that one's preferences are determined only by the distance any proposal is from one's ideal point; single-peakedness holds that one's preferences are determined by the distance from one's ideal point and the direction in which one is traveling.

(vi) *Exhaustiveness of preference structures.* I will assume that every possible preference curve that meets the conditions of completeness and single-peakedness is advanced. This, of course, allows for millions of variations. Figure 2 gives some indication of just how diverse are the preference functions that can satisfy the condition of single-peakedness.

The assumption of exhaustiveness of preference curves seems sound in the context of the social contract. Given that the public morality purports to regulate the life of societies containing many millions of people, it is not unduly strong to assume that, out of those millions, every possible preference structure will be represented. Indeed, not to assume the exhaustiveness of preferences would leave the argument open to the charge of being arbitrarily restricted to a certain set of preferences.

This assumption of exhaustiveness of preference structures can be usefully contrasted to the assumption of unrestricted domain as employed, say, by Arrow.[34] According to unrestricted or universal domain, if the social choice mechanism is to select from the set of options {x, y, z}, individual preference orderings can reflect any of the possible permutations. In this case, allowing for relations of both preference and indifference, individuals may order these three options in thirteen different ways.[35] The assumption of universal domain allows all thirteen profiles may be represented in the population. Now the assumption of exhaustiveness of preference curves is in one way akin to unrestricted domain: just as unrestricted domain allows all possible orderings, I am assuming that every possible complete and single-peaked preference curve exists. Yet, the assumptions I have made here violate Arrow's unrestricted domain. Single-peakedness imposes restrictions of the possible permutations of preference orderings.[36] So it is important to remember that I assume exhaustiveness only given the assumption of complete, single-peaked preference curves.

Taken together, these assumptions would seem to require that the contractors possess a tremendous amount of information.[37]

---

34 For a summary of Arrow's argument that brings out the importance of unrestricted domain, see his "Values and Collective Decision-making." For a short discussion of some criticisms of this assumption, see Amartya K. Sen, *Collective Choice and Social Welfare*, pp. 85–6.
35 See Riker, *Liberalism Against Populism*, pp. 115–17.
36 For useful discussions, see Sen, *Collective Welfare and Social Choice*, pp. 166–72; Riker, *Liberalism against Populism*, pp. 123–9.
37 David Braybrooke advances such a criticism against Gauthier's use of minimax relative concession. See Braybrooke's "Social Contract Theory's Fanciest Flight."

Surely, it may be objected, it is totally unrealistic to suppose that each contractor can rank every proposal with respect to how well it promotes his values. But all we need to suppose for the argument is that in a large and diverse society all – or even roughly all – the possible preference curves are represented. If that is so, no person actually needs to make any calculations. If we feel reasonably comfortable with the assumption that just about every possible political opinion is represented in Western societies that is (i) moral and (ii) single-peaked along the left–right spectrum, then (as we are about to see) no one is required to construct his own preference curve.

28.2.2 The median position result

Given these assumptions, it can be shown that the solution endorsed by minimax relative concession will always be the option nearest to median position on the left–right spectrum.[38] To see this, let us choose any preference curve; call it C. One of two things must be true about C. Either (1) C is a curve with its ideal point at the median on our left–right scale or (2) C is a curve with an ideal point that is not on the median. If (1) is the case, C endorses the median as the ideal solution; if all curves were like C, then minimax relative concession would adopt the median.[39] So assume that C is a curve that has an ideal point that is not on the median. For every curve C, there exists a mirror image curve, C′. Moreover, the intersection of C and C′ will occur at the median and will be the point of minimax relative concession. Figure 4 gives a graphic representation of this point. Point x is the intersection of the two curves between the two ideal points, i_c and $i_{c'}$. Now m, the projection of x on the left–right axis, identifies the compromise solution as defined by minimax relative concession. Any movement away from m increases the maximum relative concession. Point m is also the median point on the left–right axis.

38 To make the discussion less cumbersome, I shall henceforth refer to simply "the median" rather than "the option nearest to the median." It follows from the analysis, of course, that if none of the given options are precisely on the median, the maximum relative concession could always be decreased by introducing an option closer to the median.
39 If the curve has a plateau at the top, the contractor holds that the median is at least as good as any other alternative.

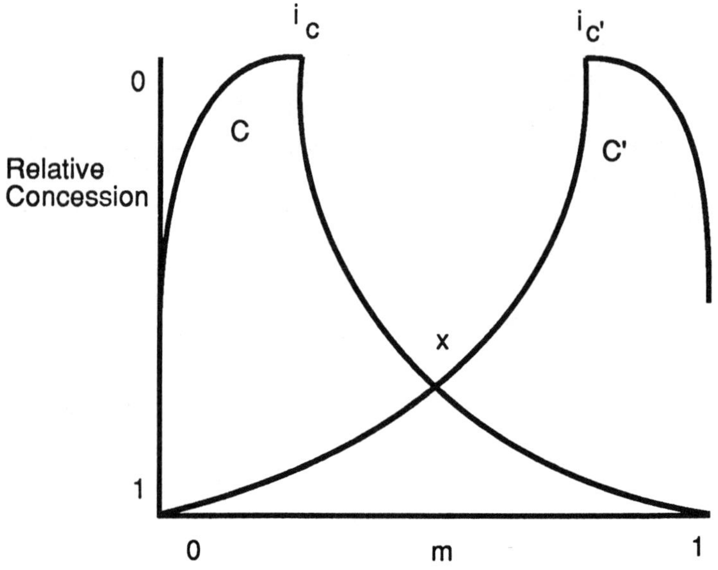

Figure 4.

To see why m, the projection of x on the horizontal axis, must always be the median, we need to put the argument slightly more formally.[40] The function of curve C can be described as f(a). For every curve C, we know (by virtue of the assumption of exhaustiveness of preference curves) that there exists a curve C′ with the function f(b) = 1 − f(a). The intersection of C and C′ will be at the point where f(a) = f(b). Solving algebraically, the intersection is at .5, that is, the median. Any departure from the intersection increases the relative concession of one mirror-imaged bargainer; hence, the median point is the point selected by minimax relative concession.

We can conclude, then, that for every curve there exists another curve such that minimax relative concession picks out the median as the rational compromise. Each possible preference curve has a mirror image; and, when each of these mirror images makes a bargain with its opposite, the median is always the compromise point.

The argument generalizes to all preference curves: given the as-

40 I am grateful to David Gow for his assistance with this argument.

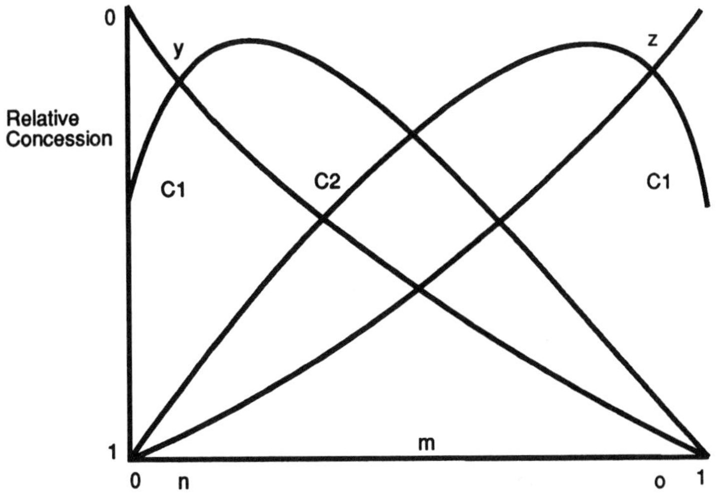

Figure 5.

sumption of exhaustiveness, the principle of minimax relative concession picks out, from the set of all possible preference curves, the median point on the horizontal axis. To see this better, consider Figure 5.

Consider first the preference curves C_1 and C_2. We can see that, once again, the principle of minimax relative concession picks out point y, the intersection between the two ideal points, as identifying the rational agreement point; its projection on the left–right axis is n, which is not the median point. We know, however, that there exist preference curves that are the inverse transformation of both of these curves. Hence, there must also exist curves C_1' and C_2'. Point z is their intersection, identifying point o as the rational bargain between these two curves. Our interest, however, is the rational bargain among all four, and once again we see it is point m, the median. We can see that the maximum relative concession will be increased by any movement away from m.

The important result, then, is that, given the assumptions detailed above, minimax relative concession will pick out the median point as the rational compromise solution. It must be stressed that this is not simply the claim that, given a metric scale, any departure from the median increases the distance from one end of the scale. I have not assumed that preferences are a simple linear function of distance from one's ideal point; if that were so, the median would be the obvious compromise. Rather, I have allowed that one's preferences may be a complex function of distance. For example, the argument allows that, in the eyes of some socialist, the liberal position may be only very slightly better than the conservative proposal, both being far inferior to any socialist proposal. But despite this, the argument picks out the median position as the compromise point.

28.2.3 The median voter result

Readers familiar with political science will recognize the similarity of my argument to the median voter result. Employing conditions somewhat different than I have assumed, it has been shown that in a majority contest the median voter's position cannot lose.[41] It will help clarify the nature of my argument to compare it briefly to the median voter result.

First, we must note that they are not extensionally equivalent, even under the conditions that I have specified. The median *voter* result relates to the voter – the person – who occupies the median position within the class of voters, arrayed over some space, such as the left–right spectrum. My result shows that minimax relative concession will pick out the median *position*. But the median position on the left–right spectrum need not be the position of the median voter. Indeed, my median position result is only extensionally equivalent to the median voter result when there are an equal number of contractors on both sides of the median, for example, if there is a normal distribution of contractors centered on the median position on the left–right spectrum. In this case, both the democratic procedure and minimax relative concession will select the median – or middle – position on the left–right spectrum.

This departure from the median voter result means that the contractual solution – unlike democratic politics – is not affected by the nature of the distribution of ideological loyalties in differing societies. For example, it is often claimed that American po-

41 For the proof, see Enelow and Hinch, *The Spatial Theory of Voting*, pp. 12–13. See also Downs, *An Economic Theory of Democracy*, ch. 8.

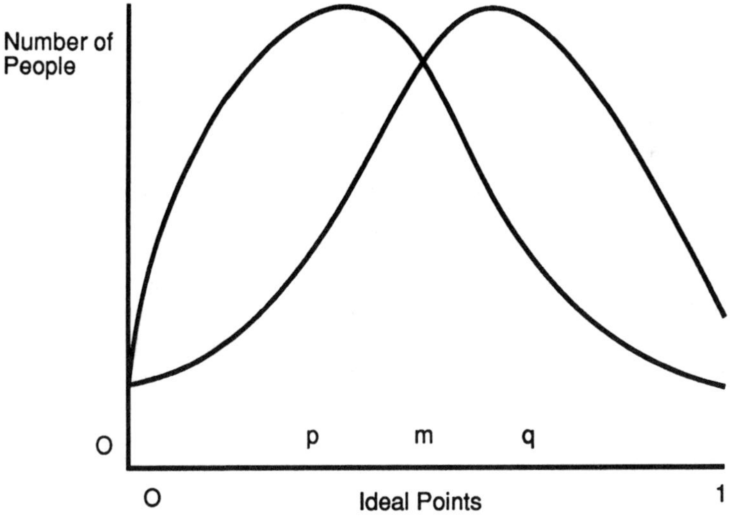

Figure 6.

litical culture is skewed to the right and at last some European political cultures are distributed about a more leftward position. Figure 6 illustrates this supposed difference. The median voter result selects position p as the democratic result in, say, a European democracy, and position q is identified as the median voter position in the American democracy. But, on my account, the contractual solution would not vary; as long as the assumptions detailed above were met, position m would continue to be the rational compromise solution for both political cultures.

But, this, it may be said, simply demonstrates the unreasonableness of the assumptions. Assume American society is indeed skewed to the right: indeed, let us say it is very skewed. Now Alf, a radical socialist, has the effect of bringing the rational compromise point much further out to the left than suits the great majority of the population. By justifying themselves to Alf, the population would be committed to embracing an ideology that is much further to the left than the overwhelming majority would like. Is it rational to suppose that the majority would take so seriously the value systems of a radical minority? Would it not be much better for the majority to exclude them, acknowledging only the demands of deontological justification? Care is required here; the issue is not the practical question whether we can expect the majority to take seriously the demands of justification; the issue, rather, is whether it is reasonable to hold that moral justification requires the majority to take so seriously the value systems of a few radicals.

To see our way clear of this problem, we must remember that our concern is the justification of a public morality among strangers (§19.2.1). If the right-leaning population was geographically distinct, say, and really did cover only a limited part of the available spectrum, then there is no bar to them justifying among themselves a different morality for their internal relations than pertains among them and outsiders. I have already considered this problem in §23.1.2. Here, my concern is a society of strangers skewed to the right but with a few individuals who occupy radical positions consistent with deontological morality. Need the majority justify their moral demands to this minority? Well, if they do not, they will have failed in their task of public justification, and so the minority among them will not be subject to any moral claims beyond what pertains in the state of nature. And, if I am right that this deontologically justified morality is apt to be rather thin and incomplete (§22.3), then the majority comes close to not interacting with the minority as moral persons. But more than that, the majority will be irrational: for the minority can offer them constrained teleological arguments justifying moral demands beyond bare requirements of deontological morality. As rational moral persons the majority are committed to acknowledging such demands, even if the majority might, in some sense, do better if they irrationally ignored them. Once again, the more cosmopolitan morality overrides the parochial viewpoint (§23.1.2.). It must be remembered that, in contrast to theories accepting the orthodox view of value and reasons (§16.1), justified moral reasons need not somehow claim to maximize one's values. That one could (in a way) do better by ignoring justified moral demands does not, much current moral philosophy notwithstanding, show such immorality to be rational.

28.2.4 Liberalism and the median position

My chief concern here is to defend the median position result rather than a specific characterization of the median position.

But, in the context of the traditional left–right political spectrum, it seems fairly clear that a public morality that can loosely be described as "liberal" is defended by the argument. To describe the nature of this liberalism in any detail would require that we first specify the end points of the left–right spectrum; we cannot give much of an idea of the nature of the median until we specify just what is the most extreme legitimate conservative proposal, and what is the most extreme legitimate socialist public morality. So we are not in a position to say a great deal about the debate within liberalism, between its more socialist- and conservative-inclining wings. All we can definitely say is that the most centrist version is rationally justified.

Many political theorists are apt to be dismayed by this argument; I have presented a philosophical defense of middle-of-the-road political ideologies. To make matters worse, I have defended them under that description! The variety of criticisms this invites can only be described as daunting; I shall make no effort to anticipate all of them here. Nevertheless, two lines of criticisms are almost certain, and I should like to at least clarify my position in relation to them.

The first is that I have done a disservice to liberalism; as I have presented it, liberalism is to be embraced just because it is a middle-of-the-road compromise. Some are apt to insist that this interpretation distorts the nature of liberalism. As Collingwood said long ago, liberalism "is no mere compromise; it has its own principles."[42] A great many liberals, who otherwise disagree, would endorse this: liberals as diverse as F. A. Hayek and John Dewey would certainly resist depicting liberalism as somehow an inherently middle-of-the-road or compromise theory not upholding a particular vision of its own.[43] More recently, William A. Galston has insisted that the liberal state cannot be justified successfully through a purely formal argument. The only successful route to a defense of liberalism, he maintains, is by appeal to distinctly "liberal virtues" and "liberal goals."[44] In short, this criti-

42 R. G. Collingwood, "Introduction" to de Ruggiero, *The History of European Liberalism*, pp. vii–viii.
43 Hayek explicitly rejects the view of liberalism as a "middle way." See the postscript "Why I Am Not a Conservative" to his *The Constitution of Liberty*, esp. pp. 398–9. John Dewey proclaimed in 1935 that "liberalism must now become radical." *Liberalism and Social Action*, p. 62.
44 William A. Galston, "Defending Liberalism," p. 621.

cism insists that liberalism, properly understood, offers an inspiring vision in its own right, and is only debased by justifying it as a compromise between competing ideologies.

Such criticism, I think, suggests that compromise is a pragmatic idea that is inconsistent with a principled understanding of liberalism. But I have tried to show that the notion of compromise, in the context of contractual theory, articulates an understanding of the common good; and the common good is a criterion of political right because it identifies what can be publicly justified to valuers with diverse aims. This ideal of public justification is at the heart of contractual liberalism. Indeed, the principled commitment to public justification in contractual liberalism runs deeper than the commitment to liberty itself; only if it can be demonstrated that rights to liberty are publicly justified will the contractualist liberal endorse them. For only those rights and duties that can be publicly justified are consistent with respecting the moral personhood of all. Consequently, that contractualist liberals will endorse a system of public morality by claiming that all could consent to it, or that it is a fair compromise among diverse points of view, is not evidence of the lack of principled commitment. It is, indeed, the demand of a principled commitment.

But a second sort of critic would hardly be appeased by this. The critic whom I am now imagining accepts this characterization of liberalism, but sees it only as testimony to the banal character of the liberal creed. Recall in this regard Nietzsche's polemic against egalitarian moralities in the first essay of the *Genealogy of Morals*. In the parable of the lambs and the birds of prey, he shows that he rejects the very idea of public justification. Understandably enough, the views of the birds of prey on the subject of lamb-eating are unacceptable to the lambs. But apparently the birds of prey would not think that this shows that the lambs are in any way rationally defective. The lambs could not be expected to accept the birds' views on lamb-eating, but that is not to say that they are ignoring good reasons, but only that lambs will be lambs. Thus, the birds of prey do not think the lambs are evil or wrong: "*We* don't dislike them at all, these good little lambs; we even love them; nothing is more tasty than a tender lamb."[45]

45 Frederick Nietzsche, *On the Genealogy of Morals*, p. 45 (first essay, sec. 13).

Nietzsche clearly thinks that the great mistake of birds of prey was to engage in any attempt to justify their actions to lambs; as much as anything, Nietzsche's parable is aimed at demonstrating to birds of prey the dangers of justificatory arguments with their quarry.

It may be thought that Nietzsche illustrates a particularly extreme view. But Nietzsche, I want to suggest, is the most plausible alternative to liberal justification.[46] Other arguments against the liberal banality of contractual justification are less polemical but also less rational, for they are, I think, typically based on the false claim that agent-neutral, value-based reasons can be provided to justify a social order pursuing a more noble or exalted goal. The interest of Nietzsche is that he refuses to make that false claim, and so is driven back to rejecting the very idea of public justification. Although that, too, ultimately proves very difficult to rationally sustain (§§17.3–4), it provides the soundest alternative to contractual negotiation leading to a liberal public morality.

28.3 The N-dimensional contractual argument

28.3.1 Arguments for multi-dimensional negotiation

I would anticipate that for many readers the most troublesome feature of the argument for the median position result is the limitation of contractual bargaining to one dimension. It does not seem particularly plausible to insist that all the relevant disagreements among the main ideologies, much less all the alternative public moralities, can be reduced to a simple left–right dimension. For example, the simple left–right spectrum has great difficulty distinguishing classical liberals from conservatives; both are apt to be strong defenders of private property, and so critics of socialism. But a reasonably sophisticated analysis would want to distinguish them in some way. Dispute about the nature of the correct public morality, in sum, is plausibly said to occur on a number of dimensions.

If we go beyond this general observation that disagreements about public morality are simply too complex to be analyzed in

46 Alasdair MacIntyre poses the question: "Nietzsche or Aristotle?" If *I* am right, the question is "Nietzsche or Liberalism?"; and, unless one is a psychopath (§17.4 in this volume), the answer must be the latter. *After Virtue*, ch. 9.

terms of a one-dimensional issue space, we can identify two rather more specific arguments in favor of a multi-dimensional analysis. The first derives from a study of political and moral theory: our traditional moral and political theories display cleavages along some familiar dimensions. As J. Roland Pennock has effectively argued, democratic political theories can be understood as differing along two dimensions: liberty-equality and individualism-collectivism.[47] And Jan Narveson has recently presented a "contractarian" analysis that points to the conflict between liberty and equality, and the possibility of an outcome that settles on a "mixture."[48] And the central debate in contemporary ethics between rights-based theories and utilitarianism can be understood in terms of a moral individualism/moral collectivism distinction.[49] The very familiarity of these dimensions attests to their usefulness in analyzing the differences between political and moral theories.

Of course, we can readily identify other dimensions: for example, government intervention versus laissez-faire; internationalist versus isolationist; noble versus ignoble. But we should be wary of greatly multiplying dimensions in an attempt to reflect all the disputes of political and moral life. In a world in which our contractors had perfect information as to how their value systems would fare under each alternative morality, it may be rational to view competing public moralities as no more than conjunctions of positions on a very large number of dimensions; each contractor would thus perform his utility calculations (§21.3) and construct an appropriate preference curve on each of the N-dimensions. But that is not the world we inhabit. Our concern here – as moral agents – is to reflect on the justification of public morality under conditions in which our knowledge of how individual value systems will fare under various public moralities is, to say the least, incomplete. In this world of uncertainty, ideologies help render our problem tractable.[50] They provide us with a general perspective on the nature of morality and public policy that

47 J. Roland Pennock, *Democratic Political Theory*, esp. chs. II–V.
48 See Jan Narveson, "Equality vs. Liberty: Advantage, Liberty."
49 I have suggested this. See "The Convergence of Rights and Utility," pp. 57–8.
50 I am, of course, indebted here to Downs, *An Economic Theory of Democracy*, ch. 7.

help us relate the broad nature of public morality to differing value systems. We may be quite unable to specify the complete code of public morality containing rules $r_1 \ldots r_n$ that best promotes Alf's values, but we may be sure that it will be a distinctively conservative, and certainly not a socialist, morality.

An argument, then, for restricting the number of dimensions is that a many-dimensional analysis would undermine our focus on competing ideologies, which makes our choice problem tractable. If we could specify every relevant dimension, we would have no need to consider ideologies.[51] However, the number of dimensions should not be restricted to those central to the traditional ideologies. The traditional ideologies – conservatism, liberalism, and socialism – arose in response to the issues central to the late nineteenth century, and so focus on those issues while ignoring others. Later issues, such as environmentalism, are not adequately captured by the traditional ideologies; thus Betty, our valuer who cares only about the preservation of the dry center of Australia (§24.4), would quite rightly protest any restriction of the public moralities to those traditional ideologies. She would propose an environmentalist code. So, although good reasons support restricting the number of dimensions to be considered, we must admit those new public moralities that claim to take seriously those dimensions that the traditional ideologies have ignored.

28.3.2 The set of all medians

N-dimensional analysis raises several problems. Because we are interested in minimizing the total relative concession over all dimensions, it seems that we need some way of aggregating the relative concessions that any given person, Alf, makes over the various dimensions. His total relative concession will be some function of his concession over all the dimensions. And this raises the problem of whether we should assume simple Euclidean space

51 This conclusion converges with two other sorts of analysis. According to John W. Chapman, political theories evince a coherent structure; rather than understanding a political theory as an amalgamation of positions on independent dimensions, he argues that a theory articulates a coherent view of the world. See his "Political Theory: Logical Structure and Enduring Types." It has been argued by Clifford Geertz that ideologies assist in making our social world more coherent. See his "Ideology as a Cultural System."

or adopt the more general assumption of Modified Euclidean Space.[52] Under simple Euclidean space, we would assume that for every person each dimension is equally important. This will simplify our analysis, but it is a very strong assumption. Most likely, different people will weight unequally the importance of the different dimensions. For example, from the perspective of Alf's value system, the question of environmentalism may not really matter at all. So his concession on the environmental dimension would seem to count very little toward computing his total concession. Perhaps for him the left–right dimension is dominant: that dimension should then be weighted most heavily in computing his total concession. But Betty may well weight the dimensions in the opposite way. So, for each person, the total concession will be a weighted sum of the concessions on each dimension. Thus, we can define the total concession (C_t) as:

$$\text{(equation 4) } C_t = \sum_{i=1}^{n} c_i \, w_i$$

where i is the dimension, c is the relative concession on that dimension and w is the weight of that dimension implied by the individual's value system. Because the concessions on each dimension are on a scale of 0 to 1, and the total concession must range from 0 to 1, it follows that the sum of weights for each individual must equal 1. It is important to remember that the sum of weights cannot exceed unity nor fall short of it because minimax relative concession does not suppose interpersonal comparisons of the intensity of preferences or importance of the dimensions.[53]

Given this, we can divide up the public into $n + 1$ groups. One group, presumably the largest, will be comprised of all those who do not put a weight of unity on any one dimension. For such people, then, at least two dimensions are of significance. The other n groups will be defined by those who, on any dimension i, place a weight of 1 on it, that is, they totally discount the others. At this point, we need to make an additional assumption:

(vii) *the exhaustiveness of preference structures for each of* n + *1 groups*. This seventh assumption extends the sixth to each of our

52 See here Enelow and Hinch, *The Spatial Theory of Voting*, pp. 15ff.
53 See Gauthier, *Morals by Agreement*, p. 155.

$n + 1$ groups. For each group, I assume, all possible preference structures are represented. Thus, for instance, among those who care only for the environmental dimension, the assumption of exhaustiveness holds, as it does for those who care only about the left–right spectrum, etc.

This may seem like an overly strong assumption: it assumes among those whose value systems render only one dimension salient, every possible preference structure is exhibited. Thus, our single-minded environmentalists will include those who care only about the environment, those whose value system is single-mindedly devoted to exploitation of the environment, as well as those who are wholeheartedly devoted to the middle. But, it may be thought, this surely is not plausible: those who care only about the environment will tend to have certain sorts of preference structures, for example, favoring the protection of the environment. However, two considerations point to the plausibility of the seventh assumption.

Firstly, it must be remembered that we are not directly concerned with the number of contractors who display a certain preference structure, but only whether there exists at least one preference structure of each possible type. Thus, it will be recalled that, in contrast to the median voter result, the median position result does not vary with respect to the skewness of the distribution. So this assumption does not deny that, say, among those who care only about the environment, most will be in favor of protecting it; it only asserts that there will always exist at least one preference structure of every type. Secondly, we must keep in mind that we are dealing with a very large number of contractors over a very small number of dimensions. I have already argued for a limited number of dimensions; I am thus assuming that we are considering negotiation involving a few rather than a large number of issue dimensions. So, when we reflect on the huge number of contractors and the small number of dimensions, the seventh assumption seems plausible.

Given this assumption, it can be shown that the minimax relative concession point will be the point defined by the medians of all dimensions. That is, the idea of a rational public morality points to the set of the median position points on all dimensions.[54] For each of the n groups who care solely about one di-

54 This set, of course, could contain inconsistent principles. For example, the

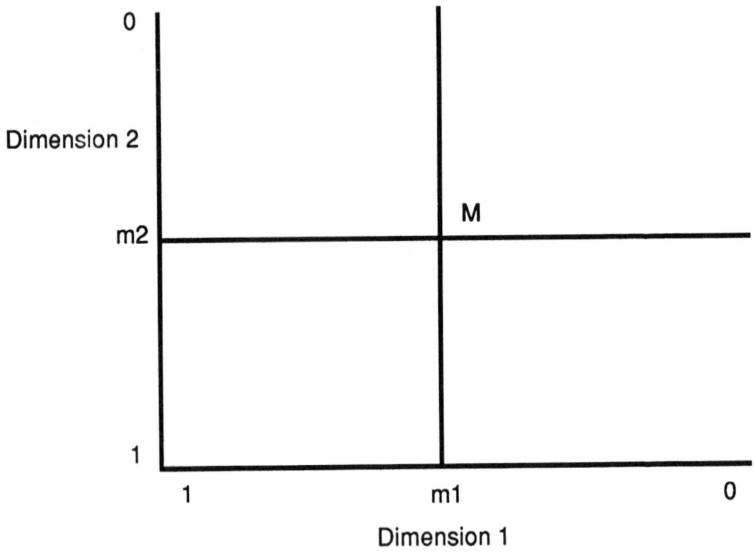

Figure 7.

mension, the argument from one-dimensional space shows that the median position will be selected by minimax relative concession. We also know that, for contractors who belong to such a group, their concession on this dimension constitutes their total concession because they weight this dimension at 1 (see equation 4). Let us now suppose that these groups of single-minded valuers confront each other in a bargain to determine the overall public morality on *n* dimensions. To enable us to graphically represent the situation, consider the two-dimensional case as depicted in Figure 7. It is helpful to think of the problem in terms of a two-stage agreement. The first stage of the contract was among those who care only about Dimension 1 or Dimension 2. Based

median environmental position may include policy prescriptions inconsistent with some personal liberties endorsed by the median position on the left–right dimension. I do not mean to suggest that the nature of a justified morality can somehow be mechanically produced by aggregating the prescriptions of the median positions; rather, the aim of the argument is to help clarify our notion of a reasonable compromise among millions of contractors with diverse ends. See my comments in the last three paragraphs of §28.

on this first stage, it is concluded that the median positions on Dimension 1 (D_1) is the minimax relative concession point for those whom $w(D_1) = 1$. Consequently, the vertical line up from m_1 represents the set of public moralities in which this lowest relative concession is maintained. Any public morality that is not on the vertical line from m_1 increases the maximum relative concession for this group. And, similarly, any departure from the horizontal line from m_2 increases the maximum relative concession for someone in the group for whom only D_2 is salient. Thus, only the intersection, point M, preserves the maximum relative concession of both groups at the level reached after the first (that is, intradimensional) negotiations. Any departure from M will increase the maximum relative concession of at least one person. This result generalizes to *n* dimensions.

Moreover, the result does not vary when we introduce the $n + 1$ group, that is, those who are concerned with all the dimensions. Assume that all the single-minded groups have deliberated and, based on the reasoning that I have advanced, the rational compromise point is identified as point M. Now suppose that Alf, for whom more than one dimension is salient, argues that M no longer satisfies minimax relative concession once his weighted relative concessions are calculated according to equation 4. His claim thus implies that point M requires that he grant a greater relative concession than any the single-minded contractors have given. Alf must be claiming that none of the previous contractors have conceded as much as he is asked to concede: if even one of these contractors concedes as much as him, his concession is not a greater relative concession.

We can see that Alf's claim cannot be true: at the very most, he concedes as much as one of the existing contractors who have already rationally accepted M. To see why this is so, let us take the largest concession Alf makes on any of the dimensions, and weight it by the sum of the weights he gives to all concessions, that is, give it a weighting of 1. For example, say that his biggest concession is on the environmental dimension. We take only this largest concession, and give it a weight of 1. Alf's total concession as defined by equation 4 cannot be larger than this; if on any dimension his concession is smaller than it was on the environmental dimension, his actual total concession will be less than we are assuming. If he makes this same magnitude of relative concession on every dimension, then this procedure will be identical with his actual concession. According to assumption (vii), we know that on whatever dimension he made his greatest concession, there was a single-minded person who made such a concession; and we also know that single-minded contractors give the dimension a weighting of 1. So, we know there was already a contractor who has made a total concession equal to Alf's, whose rational agreement point was M. So Alf's claim that his relative concession under M was greater than any of the single-minded contractors was false.

It is, then, impossible that any concession of the contractors in the $n + 1$ group will be larger than the relative concession already given by contractors in the n groups. And, because M was the point of minimax relative concession for them, it remains the point of minimax relative concession.

28.3.3 The antinomies of liberalism

Recently both supporters and critics of liberal theory have analyzed it in terms of its "antinomies."[55] Liberalism, it seems, is torn between individualism and collectivism, individuality and community, equality and liberty, interventionism and laissez-faire, capitalism and socialism. From one perspective, this shows the hopeless incoherence of liberal theory. Such critics are apt to see John Stuart Mill as the quintessential liberal: he is, we have been told, eclectic and ultimately inconsistent.[56] Others see these same tensions between opposites as the strength of liberalism, reflecting as it does the ambivalent character of human nature.[57] The contractual argument I have presented also indicates that liberalism's antinomies are the source of its moral justification. It is just because liberalism seeks to accommodate both the individualists and collectivists, socialists and capitalists, environmental-

55 See, for example, Edward Shils, "The Antinomies of Liberalism"; Roberto Mangabeira Unger, *Knowledge and Politics*. See also S. I. Benn and G. F. Gaus, "The Liberal Conception of the Public and Private."
56 For interpretations of Mill that tend to support this view, see R. J. Halliday, *John Stuart Mill*, e.g., p. 34; J. P. Anshutz, *The Philosophy of J. S. Mill*.
57 This is a central theme in the writings of John W. Chapman. See, for instance, his "The Moral Foundations of Political Obligation" and "Toward a General Theory of Human Nature." See also J. Roland Pennock, *Democratic Political Theory*.

ists and industrialists, that it lays claim to be the ideology justified by the social contract.

One of the remarkable characteristics of liberal theory as it has evolved in the last two centuries has been its ability to integrate new ideologies, albeit in a greatly modified form, within a revised liberal outlook. Although the founders of liberal theory were not feminists, socialists, or environmentalists, all these emerging ideologies are now part of the public morality of liberal society. To the enthusiastic proponents of these new ideologies, which often began as radical challenges to the moral legitimacy of liberal society, the ability of liberalism to accommodate a moderated form of their ideological claims has often been exasperating. To such radicals, it often seems that liberalism defeats challenges by co-opting and then taming them. Thus, for example, some socialists are apt to see the liberal state's welfare policies and mildly interventionist measures as an all too successful strategy to ensure that true socialism will never be implemented. On the other hand, to the opponent of these new ideologies, the contemporary liberal state has lost its way. Its moderating compromises with new challenges is seen as proof that it has abandoned true liberal principles. Or, alternatively, it is proof that liberalism has never been principled.

The argument I have presented does not justify compromising with every strong group pressing ideological claims. Indeed, the liberal must resist these claims when they seek to upset the justified public morality. Thus, not only those who strive to implement inherently immoral ideologies such as fascism, but also those who seek to ignore the demands of the contractual argument by reasserting defeated proposals, from conservatism to socialism, must be resisted. But the liberal conscience responds to appeals that the contemporary public morality neglects some question that is important to the value systems of some.

I have not, of course, justified here any specific public morality; indeed, I have only presented some general considerations that point to a liberal public morality, with its individualist-communalist, libertarian-egalitarian, socialist-conservative tensions. I have made no effort to identify the full set of relevant dimensions, so it cannot even be guaranteed that the justified public morality will be liberal. Perhaps on some dimension of political dispute, the median position is distinctly illiberal (I will consider that possibility more fully presently). It must be remembered that my chief concern here is to defend a contractual theory of justification, rather than a distinctly liberal solution. Nevertheless, a strong case is to be made that the median-point solution justifies a public morality that is in many ways akin to liberalism.

28.4 Equal liberty and antiliberal ideologies

My basic argument, then, has been for a median-point solution on all dimensions. Insofar as I have argued for a liberal public morality, it has been because liberalism occupies the middle ground on the crucial dimensions of contemporary political debate such as left-right, individualism-collectivism, libertarian-egalitarian. Now it may be argued that on one important dimension this surely cannot be right: the liberalism dimension. Liberals are radicals in their commitment to liberalism: no liberal would compromise with a despot. Consequently, the compromise point selected by the median result argument cannot be anything akin to liberalism. Indeed, this argument might be generalized to show that no ideology can be selected by the median result argument. Call the median point compromise on dimensions $n - 1$, ideology I. For the nth dimension, take the spectrum of I to anti-I. It follows that on the nth dimension the median cannot be I, for on the last dimension the compromise point would be the median between I and anti-I.

The general argument fails because it supposes that, for any solution I over $n - 1$ dimensions, it can be defeated by defining the nth dimension as having an end point at I. But not only are the dimensions not to be introduced sequentially, the dimensions of political dispute are not arbitrary. It certainly renders the idea of a contractual negotiation unhelpful if we choose dimensions arbitrarily or construct them with the sole aim of defeating some proposal. Our interest in justification is in deciding the preferred position among a number of public moralities or ideologies that compete for our allegiance. Unless the dimensions are firmly grounded in this way, the result of the contractual argument will be of little interest. So we have to require that the dimensions of dispute are indeed salient.

Although the general argument fails, the specific antiliberalism argument may still be sound. If we identify a liberalism-despotism dimension that meets the seven assumptions I have stated, then it is surely right that a liberal public morality could not be the outcome of contractual compromise. And indeed, given the number and spiritedness of recent criticisms and defenses of liberalism, it is not implausible to think that at least for some philosophers this is a salient dimension.

But we need to remember that placement of a person on a spectrum is not a matter of merely asking him; it is not, that is, a matter of mere preference. As I argued earlier (§21.3), one's preferences over ideologies are determined by the extent they promote one's value system. So to show that some people would place liberalism at the bottom of some dimension it is not enough that some people may detest the idea of a liberal public morality; that certainly shows that they disvalue it, but the issue here is the extent to which their total system of values is promoted or retarded by a liberal public morality.

Consider Rawls's argument for equal liberty. Contractors in the original position aim to promote their conception of the good. Not all these visions of the good are necessarily liberal; some may be based on religious convictions that are markedly illiberal. Alf, who is such a contractor, would prefer a regime that severely constrained the liberty of those who sought to pursue visions of the good at odds with his religious beliefs; his favored alternative thus might be a dogmatic and intolerant religious morality. On the other hand, the worst for him would be to be subjected to Betty's principles of justice. She favors an intolerant regime that seeks to root out all religious belief through persecution. Rawls's solution is to ensure equal liberty for all; in a sense, this is the second best alternative for a wide variety of contractors who advocate various opposing ideologies. His device, of course, is to require that the parties reason from behind a veil of ignorance; Alf does not know what his particular vision of the good is, so "[e]ven if he could get others to agree, he does not know how to tailor principles to his advantage."[58] Consequently, because he does not know whether he is dogmatic religious zealot or an intolerant atheist, he will be unsure whether to endorse an unequal liberty for either the religious zealot or the atheist. His reasoning thus leads him to accept a second-best solution: equal liberty for all.

58 Rawls, *A Theory of Justice*, p. 131.

Alf \ Betty	For me only	For both of us	For you only
For me only			1 0
For both of us		1>y>0 1>x>0	
For you only	0 1		

Matrix 1.

My argument in this book differs in many respect from that of Rawls. But he points to an important feature of the liberal principle of equal liberty: it can indeed be understood as a compromise between those intolerant ideologues whose values would best be promoted by a friendly intolerant morality but whose values would fare terribly under a hostile intolerant morality that would restrict their liberty. When such individuals rank the alternative public moralities, they will thus place first the regime of unequal liberty that favors them and place at the bottom those regimes that persecute them. A system of equal liberty will plausibly emerge as the compromise among such opposed dogmatists. Matrix 1 illustrates the bargaining between ideologues. Only solutions along the southwest-northeast diagonal are consistent, all other cells being blank. The numbers are relative concessions. So, in the far northeast cell, Betty concedes everything (relative concession = 1) and Alf gets all he wants (relative concession = 0). The far southwest cell reverses the situation. We know that the middle cell must be the point of minimax relative concession. Whatever the concessions x and y are, they are less than 1, and so the middle cell is rationally to be preferred to the other two possible cells.

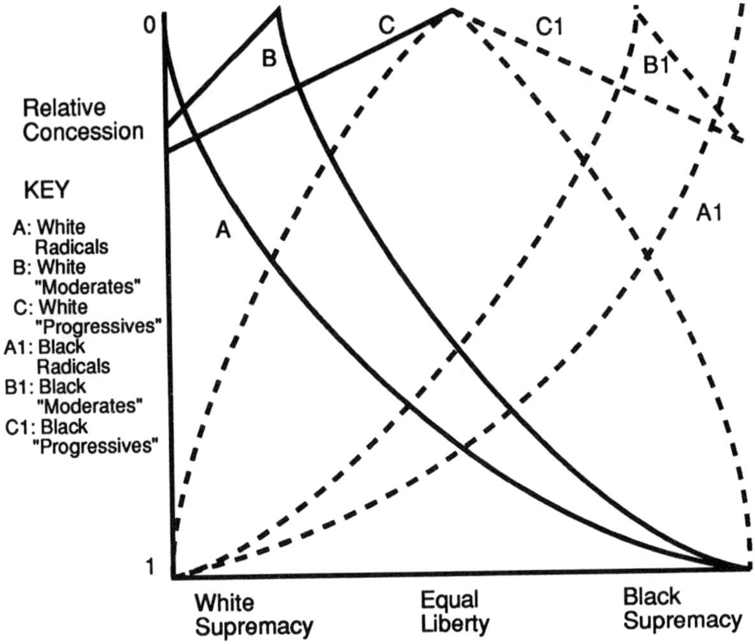

Figure 8.

As Russell Hardin remarks in his criticism of Gauthier's argument for minimax relative concession, generalizing from two-person to N-person bargaining is often problematic.[59] However, it is, I think, fairly obvious how the median position argument can be applied to this sort of case. Suppose that whites and blacks oppose each other in a racially divided society. Suppose further that both groups contain radicals, "moderates," and "progressives." The radicals would enslave the other group; the moderates would endorse some inequalities in their own group's favor; and the progressives uphold equal liberty as their ideal point. Figure 8 depicts the preference curves for the six groups. Notice that the argument does not require that the bargainers think that equal liberty is in some sense half as good as a system that is unequal in their favor. Even if to some of the radical ine-

59 Russell Hardin, "Bargaining for Justice."

galitarians equal liberty is not all that much better than victory by the opposing radicals, the median position argument still holds.

My claim, then, is that the contractualist tradition tends to see equal liberty as in some sense a compromise. In the context of the contractual argument, it is not the expression of the supreme liberal value, but the result of a rational compromise between those who would claim special advantages for themselves. Of course, my argument is consistent with some of the contractors being drawn toward a liberal position. Indeed, those who espouse liberal value systems will concede less than nonliberals in the contractual bargaining. *In this sense, then, the social contract is not neutral: it favors liberal values, and so those whose value systems are essentially liberal may concede very little.* Minimax relative concession, it must be remembered, does not demand equal concessions by all: it demands that the maximum concession be minimized.

It might be objected that everything depends on how one defines the relevant dimensions. Define it in terms of a liberalism-despotism dimension and liberalism is defeated; depict equal liberty as a sort of second best solution among competing intolerant proposals, and liberal liberty seems justified. It is indeed true that the justified public morality will differ depending on the salient dimensions. But this is not a matter of "defining" or "choosing." It is a matter of argument what are the salient dimensions within a society, and what is the best way of presenting arguments about equal liberty. William Galston, I suppose, would have us believe that the case for equal liberty is only sound if understood as an expression of distinctively liberal values;[60] if one is persuaded by this characterization, then one is indeed apt to see the principle of equal liberty as the extreme point on the liberalism-despotism dimension. But contractualists have argued for an alternative interpretation. The moral justification of equal liberty is that it is acceptable to all – though perhaps not wholeheartedly – because it allows each to pursue his own values.

28.5 *Distributive justice*

"Social justice," wrote Bertrand de Jouvenel, is "the obsession of our time."[61] Certainly it has amounted to something near an ob-

60 See Galston's "Defending Liberalism."
61 Bertrand de Jouvenel, *Sovereignty*, p. 139.

session in political philosophy in the years since the publication of *A Theory of Justice*. However, I shall offer nothing that amounts to a theory of social or distributive justice (for my purposes I shall not distinguish these). Nevertheless, the argument thus far has implications for the justification of economic systems and distributive arrangements. I shall conclude the analysis of contractual compromise by briefly highlighting these.

As I argued in §27.2, the argument from the state of nature limits the economic systems that can be justified: those that cannot recognize the rights to private property and exchange are excluded from contractual negotiation. This clearly rules out command economies, and I also have indicated that it poses real problems for market socialism modeled on Yugoslavia. I will not reiterate those problems here. I am thus assuming an economy with significant holdings of private property and market transactions. But thus far this excludes few of the proposals of distributive justice advanced in recent years. Nozick's minimal state, Gewirth's limited welfare state, and Rawls's more extensive redistributive state,[62] all seem consistent with the argument from the state of nature. And to complicate matters even more, as Gauthier sees it the principle of minimax relative concession endorses an essentially free-market liberalism.

Let us approach the problem by distinguishing two broad approaches in recent political theory to the problem of distributive justice. The first might be called the collective assets approach. At least from the time of L. T. Hobhouse, some liberals have argued for a redistributive state on the grounds that there exists a pool of assets, created by social cooperation that belongs to no one individual, but to the community as a whole. Wrote Hobhouse:

> Partly as a result of the organized efforts of society, but more largely through the mere fact of social life, and the tacit co-operation of many minds, society on the whole grows, the arts of life improve, population thickens. There is a total increment of wealth. What we take at first blush as the contribution of an individual to this growth is not his contribution alone. He absorbs from his society, he comes into a capital of organized knowledge and skill; he adds something to it but does not create it. The most individual production is largely a social production.[63]

62 For an excellent summary of these positions, see Chapman, "Justice, Freedom, and Property," pp. 289–304.
63 L. T. Hobhouse, *The Elements of Social Justice*, p. 162.

On this view, distributive justice concerns the distribution of the fruits of social cooperation. Thus, for example, Rawls tells us that contractors agree on principles of social justice that determine how "the greater benefits produced by their collaboration are distributed."[64] For those employing this approach, much depends on the relative magnitude of individual and collective assets. Rawls takes an extreme view, tending to depict all material assets and even individual talents and abilities as part of the collective pool of assets to be distributed in accordance with principles of justice.[65] Gauthier points to a very different division between individual assets and the fruits of cooperation; thus, though he too sees principles of justice as dividing the fruits of cooperation, his theory does not apparently have strong redistributive implications.[66]

The second approach is based on individual rights. Just as the first approach can lead either to a redistributive state or an essentially free-market society, so too can the second. In Nozick's hands, of course, a rights-centered account of distributive justice effectively precludes any significant redistribution. For him, there is no pool of collective assets to be distributed by the state; all assets take the form of individual holdings. Thus, in a now famous sentence, Nozick proclaims that "[t]hings come into the world already attached to people having entitlements over them."[67] But founding distributive justice directly on the idea of individual rights need not lead to a rejection of the welfare state; among many others, Alan Gewirth and Stanley Benn have defended the welfare state on the basis of rights arising out of an analysis of the demands of self-consistent agency and respect for persons.[68]

My argument from the state of nature suggests affinities with both approaches. On the one hand, I have endorsed a natural right to a system of private property that respects desert as a basis for ownership. This puts limits on the extent to which the

64 Rawls, *A Theory of Justice*, p. 4.
65 See ibid., pp. 101, 107, 179. See also Sandel, *Liberalism and the Limits of Justice*, pp. 77–82, 86–103.
66 Gauthier, *Morals by Agreement*, esp. chs. V, VII. Russell Hardin criticizes Gauthier on precisely this point in his "Bargaining for Justice."
67 Nozick, *Anarchy, State, and Utopia*, p. 160.
68 Gewirth, *Reason and Morality*, pp. 312–27; Benn, *A Theory of Freedom*, ch. 13.

wealth of those in a society can be seen as a collective asset to be distributed according to some formula. People do deserve to own what they have produced.[69] But it will be recalled that, in the state of nature, actual rights of private property could not be justified because the problem of the appropriation of natural resources had not been solved. Now it is not quite right to say that on my account these resources constitute a collective asset. I have made no claim that we are all joint owners of such resources.[70] Rather, my argument was that any claim to possess exclusionary property rights over resources would constitute an interference with the actions of others, and so must be justified to them. So, contractors entering the bargaining situation know (i) that the justified system must respect production as a grounds for ownership, and (ii) the exclusionary system of property rights must be justified to all.

The first constraint can be accommodated by understanding it as a criterion for excluding some proposals as immoral; I have already referred to this matter (§27.2). The second constraint can thus be interpreted in terms of a rational bargain; given all the systems of property rights that respect (i), which of them constitute a rational compromise? Let us assume that valid proposals range along a dimension of equal to unequal distribution along the lines suggested by John W. Chapman's gradient of theories of social justice.[71] At the egalitarian end of the dimension is the most egalitarian system of distribution that still respects individual claims to deserve what one has produced. Ronald Dworkin's proposal for an initial equality of resources may be close to the most egalitarian valid proposal.[72] From here, proposals might range from Rawls's difference principle, through Gewirth's

69 Hobhouse would not have denied this. See *The Elements of Social Justice*, ch. IX.

70 I thus do not assume that in the state of nature there is any "positive community" in which all individuals are joint owners of the natural resources. For a very useful analysis of the distinction between "positive" and "negative" community in state of nature accounts, see Buckle, *The Natural History of Property*, ch. 3.

71 Chapman, "Justice, Freedom, and Property." Some of the more egalitarian positions on Chapman's gradient are excluded by the argument from the state of nature.

72 See Dworkin, "What Is Equality? Part 2: Equality of Resources." For a similar proposal, see Hal R. Varian, "Distributive Justice, Welfare Economics, and the Theory of Fairness."

"supportive state," to Nozick's antiredistributive minimal state. Given such an egalitarian dimension, the median position result would apply, picking out, it seems, some form of moderately redistributive state.

To be sure, the argument is sensitive to the end points of the spectrum. According to the radical view, a distribution that is solely determined by the market mechanism will be exploitative: that is, it will not recognize the claims of workers to the fruits of their labor.[73] If this is so, then Nozick's proposal is immoral and must be excluded. On the other hand, perhaps I have underestimated how egalitarian a moral proposal can be; proposals for an initial equality of resources may not be as near the egalitarian end of the spectrum of moral proposals as I have supposed. If both these criticisms were accepted, the contractual argument would produce a much more egalitarian solution than I have suggested. But it should not be surprising that our judgments about the degree of equality demanded by the common good should be sensitive to our beliefs that certain arrangements do or do not violate fundamental moral principles. Debate as to whether a certain economic system is inherently exploitative, or whether it violates the natural right to a system of private property, will necessarily affect our judgment as to whether the degree of equality or inequality it entails is justifiable.

Again, it is not my aim to present a theory of distributive justice; I thus shall make no effort to resolve these perplexing and contentious issues. Rather, my aim has been to demonstrate how the theory of value and justification I have proposed will approach the problem of distributive justice, and to contrast it with some more familiar approaches. It does, however, seem that some sort of redistributive state based on private property and the market will be justified.

Let me conclude this section with an observation and an explanation. The observation is Aristotle's: "We must not expect more precision than the subject-matter admits of."[74] To quote Aristotle on this is to run the risk of sounding platitudinous, but, nevertheless, Aristotle is quite right; and because he is right some explanation of the preceding discussion is in order. The argument

---

73 See, e.g., Jon Elster, "Exploitation, Freedom, and Justice."

74 Aristotle, *Nichomachean Ethics*, translated by Sir David Ross (London: Oxford University Press, 1954), p. 2 [1094(a)19–(b)12].

in favor of the median position solution is intended to make more precise our intuitive idea of a reasonable compromise among contractors; and I have tried to show how such compromise is important given the theory of justification that I have developed in this book. In my argument I have made a number of assumptions, some of which – for example, that interval measures could be derived for each person's evaluations of the various codes of public morality – are demanding. But what is the point of this sort of precision: will we ever be able to evaluate moral codes by applying the relevant algorithm? And because most of us are properly skeptical that the justification of a morality could ever achieve such precision, why do we so often aim at precision in our analysis of moral theories? Isn't the search for such precision a perfect example of ignoring Aristotle's insight?

But recall Aristotle's own discussion of justice in the *Ethics*, which relied on notions of proportion and progression that are discussed in precise terms.[75] If an account of a practical activity like morals relies on a technical concept such as a proportion, or minimax relative concession, or a rational compromise, in evaluating the account we will want to know whether the theory really can sensibly employ the technical concept and whether strict application of the technical criterion would lead to very odd and counter-intuitive conclusions. Consequently, when evaluating the proposed account we may well assume, counter-factually, that a great deal of precision is possible, for assuming such precision may help us to better understand and evaluate a proposal. But it is all too easy to forget that, even if we accept the theory employing the technical term, our actual use of the theory, in arguing about the justifiability of competing moral theories, will not be able to achieve anything like this degree of precision. In actual arguments about morals, we employ criteria such as the maximization of preferences or the difference principle in a very tentative way; and so too will be the use of minimax relative concession and the median position argument.

A Frankenstein monster is a creation over which the creator loses control and which becomes, indeed, a threat to the creator. One is tempted to say that contemporary moral and political theory has spawned a good many such monsters. One need only

75 Ibid., pp. 106–25 [1128(b)35–1135(b)25].

compare the helpful insights into the nature of the individual and collective rationality that the prisoners' dilemma once seemed to offer and the all-too-often arid – and seemingly self-perpetuating – field of study that has emerged. The study of the prisoners' dilemma may not pose a dire threat to its creators, but it has often enough become a sort of distraction. I, of course, run a similar risk: many readers may be tempted to focus on the median position argument rather than the account of justification it is meant to illustrate. My concern is the nature of justification in morals, and I have developed a formal argument to show that the notion of the common good as compromise can be elaborated and clarified. But it is important that we not be distracted by the possibilities for formalization and precision. Our practical justifications will not achieve such precision; moreover, even should the median position argument fail as a solution to the problem of the contractors, the overarching idea, of a common good achieved through compromise, would remain. Let me stress that I am in no way denying the legitimacy of further detailed and precise analysis of either minimax relative concession or my median position argument. As I have said, such analysis may lead to insights into the strengths or weaknesses of the principles. It is, however, important to keep in mind that the formal arguments are only tools to help us better appreciate the nature of our justificatory task and the sorts of proposals that might be favored.

29 CONCLUDING REMARKS

29.1 A prolegomenon to political philosophy

I am all too aware of just how incomplete is my analysis of a public morality sanctioned by the common good. The analysis is incomplete in several respects. First I have only employed one sort of contractual argument: that based on the median position argument. It must be stressed that this is merely one mode of contractualist public justification upholding a common good. I certainly do not wish to suggest that this is the only sort of argument that may be used to make more concrete the demands of public justification and the common good. It is not implausible to object that some aspects of a public morality – for example, whether to include duties to assist others in need, what sorts of harms constitute a violation of rights, the moral duties to protect animals – cannot be usefully conceived in terms of N-dimensional public morality. That may be; if so, then another sort of argument would have to be advanced to show how the relevant duties can be justified by appeal to the common good. In this chapter, I have endeavored to provide some guidance as to the broad outline of the type of public morality that will be justified; it may well be that more specific problems demand a different approach.

The fundamental commitment of rational moral persons is to public justification: we necessarily presuppose that the moral claims we make on each other can be justified. The contractualist account that I have developed in these last two chapters is one way of articulating this commitment, and the median position argument is a way of making more precise the idea of a rational compromise upholding the common good. But it is worth stressing once again that the argument endorsing the commitment to public justification and the common good does not stand or fall with the more specific, detailed contractual analysis I have offered. Some may object to the principle of minimax relative concession and the claim that public moralities can be analyzed into dimensions such as I have described. I believe that my positions on these matters are reasonable, but they do have the status in my account of value and justification equal to the argument for a commitment to public justification. They are forays into normative ethics and political philosophy, intended as much to clarify the nature of the theory of justification as to sketch a defense of a normative ethic.

The analysis, then, is incomplete because it by no means fully explores the types of arguments that may be advanced to show that a public morality advances a common good. It is also incomplete in another and more obvious way: many of the most important issues of contemporary public morality have not been addressed. I have not, for instance, discussed the justification of democracy or the perplexing problems of international distributive justice. Regarding democracy, two types of public justifications have been advanced. Peter Singer has justified democracy on essentially procedural grounds; as he sees it, democratic procedures represent a fair compromise.[76] Although this certainly con-

76 See Singer, *Democracy and Disobedience*, p. 32.

stitutes a form of public justification based on the common good, William Nelson has insisted that procedural equality does not guarantee substantive justice.[77] My analysis of the types of common good arguments (§21) captures the appeal of both arguments from procedural and substantive justice, but it remains to sort out just what role each plays in the justification of democracy.

This book, then, is a prolegomenon to political philosophy. It has explored the theories of value, practical reason, and justification upon which an adequate political philosophy must be based. But the task of articulating that political philosophy, a task that at one stage I hoped to accomplish in this work, remains for the future.

29.2 The limits of justification

The analysis is incomplete in yet another way: I have not considered the limits of justification, and the possibility that one may have to act in unjustifiable ways in order to stay true to one's most basic values. In a criticism of Kantian morality in general, and Rawls's theory in particular, Bernard Williams argues that "[t]here can come a point at which it is quite unreasonable for a man to give up, in the name of an impartial good ordering of the world of moral agents, something which is a condition of his having any interest in being around in the world at all."[78] Williams argues that one's own valuational point of view may fundamentally clash with the moral point of view; in such cases, he says, the Kantian insistence that the thing to do is to act morally fails to recognize that real agents are devoted to specific projects that give a point to their life. To have a character is to be a particular sort of person who is devoted to certain ends and sees things in a certain light. The Kantian demand that one put aside these concerns to act in the manner required by an impartial morality ignores the character of real people, treating them as mere abstract moral persons.

Such conflicts – it may be appropriate to call them tragic conflicts – raise fundamental problems for theories of moral and practical rationality. I hope it is clear that the account I have of-

77 See William Nelson, *On Justifying Democracy*, ch. II.
78 Bernard Williams, "Persons, Character, and Morality," p. 14.

fered avoids both the extreme interpretation of objectivity that ignores the special place that one's values have for oneself (§12.1) and the abstract characterization of moral personality that so worries Williams. The theories of value and justification I have defended in this book aim to unite the valuational and moral points of view. Although they can conflict, the requirements of a justified morality are not alien demands intruding upon the valuational self (§24.3). The rational valuational self will understand that the commitment to morality is the basis of its character. Morality may demand that the cherished concerns of the valuational self be abandoned, but in a way this demand also arises from the valuational self.

Yet Williams's point still stands: in some cases, the demands of acting on a justified morality may undermine one's valuational perspective. Consider the possibility that one may have to justify oneself to others who share none of one's basic moral commitments (§23.1.2). One might still discover a common good that pertains between you and them, but this common good may not recognize one's right to natural liberty. But one's valuational perspective presupposes this right. In such a case, one is in a quandary: one's value system both provides one with a reason to act on the justified public morality, yet this morality would not accommodate moral beliefs foundational to one's perspective. In such cases, the integrity of one's value system could, conceivably, provide one with reason to violate the justified public morality.[79]

In such cases, whatever you do will leave your value system in tatters. Your value system rests on the supposition that you, like others, are a moral person and so can act in accordance with the demands of a justified public morality. For a rational moral person to renounce the demands of public morality will, as I have stressed, undermine the rationality of his value system. But in the case under consideration the justified public morality pays no heed to the principles upon which one's valuational perspective depends. So not only to reject, but to accept, the public morality undermines the rational basis of the valuational self. In such a moral and valuational catastrophe, a rational agent can do no more than to reconstruct his moral and axiological world; he

79 Recall my characterization of Value-Grounded Rationalism in §17, where moral reasons were said to at least "typically" override value-based reasons to act.

must see what can be salvaged and integrated into a new system of value.

29.3 Morality and value in a liberal society

A liberal morality can be publicly justified among those who entertain diverse and often competing values. Sometimes this is described as "liberal neutrality," but that is perhaps misleading. Because those with essentially liberal value systems concede relatively little in the contractual negotiation while those with illiberal values must concede the most, the contract is not usefully described as being neutral among competing value systems. Nevertheless, liberal public morality is publicly justified: rational self-directed valuers who are also moral persons are provided with good reason to embrace the liberal morality. And, furthermore, we have seen that the rationality requirement does not function to greatly circumscribe the things that may be valued: the Affective-Cognitive Theory of value allows a great variety of rational valuings. The claim, then, is that only such a liberal public morality is consistent with a sound theory of value and the demands of public justification.

Those who reject liberal morality are thus apt to take one of two strategies. Many proffer a theory of value that advances the strong agent-neutrality of reasons for action based on correct value judgments. So some insist that honor or other virtues provide all with a reason to act. A rational public morality will, these critics of "neutralist" liberalism maintain, give pride of place to these values. Because these value judgments provide reasons for all to act, they can enter into a public justification. The Affective-Cognitive Theory rejects these claims: although value judgments can provide prima facie agent-neutral reasons for action, this is insufficient as a basis for public justification of a morality.

The alternative strategy is Nietzsche's: to reject the commitment to public justification (§28.2.4). This, at least, is potentially a rational strategy. If one has a psychopathic value system, that is, a value system devoid of the commitment to a justified morality, then Nietzsche's alternative is the rational option. But most of us do not entertain such impoverished valuations, and it is dubious indeed that we could transform our view of the world so as to adopt such a system (§17.4). So Nietzsche suggests an interesting rational alternative, but it is one closed to most of us.

What remains for those who possess both a sound theory of value and a commitment to public morality is something like a liberal public morality. However, it is often charged that this sort of justificatory argument only serves to undermine liberal morality. As these critics understand it, the type of public justification I have presented here denies the possibility of political community based upon shared public values.[80] But, we are told, this association of abstract individuals committed to nothing but abstract principles of justice is an illusion. Real political communities are defined by a community of values.

One powerful reply to this familiar charge is that moral values arising out of a devotion to principles of right will indeed characterize the liberal community (§23.2). But the Affective-Cognitive Theory of value conjoined with the theory of public justification points the way to another reply. The theory of value I have defended does not deny that value judgments have a public status and can be right or wrong. Indeed, it is part of the Affective-Cognitive Theory that value judgments possess such a status. Within a community there will be right and wrong – if controversial – answers to what constitutes the beautiful, the noble, the demeaning. A community is thus constituted by a shared culture defined by publicly acknowledged value judgments. A liberal society will possess a public culture in which value judgments are "objective" in one sense of that confusing term.

A liberal theory need not – and will be faulty if it does – deny the reality of a culture characterized by such "objective" value judgments. If Alf asserts that Frank Lloyd Wright's Prairie Houses are not worth being valued, he is wrong; if he believes that billboards advertising the nearest gasoline station are generally beautiful, he will likewise be wrong. In his community with its shared culture, discourse about these issues makes sense, and disagreements will often be about who is right and who is wrong. A liberal public morality need deny none of this. It concerns itself with what principles can be publicly justified and so provide all with reasons to act. My claim in this book is that correct value judgments do not provide strongly agent-neutral rea-

80 See, e.g., Galston, "Defending Liberalism"; Sandel, *Liberalism and the Limits of Justice*; Sandel, "The Procedural Republic of the Unencumbered Self"; MacIntyre, *After Virtue*; Michael Walzer, "Liberalism and Separation." See also Amy Gutmann, "Communitarian Critics of Liberalism."

sons for action, and so cannot provide the basis for a public justification.

A community may be usefully understood as being characterized by a shared culture with public value judgments and a shared morality that can be justified to all. Both of these are endorsed by the theories of value and justification presented in this book. But, unlike many recent communitarian critics of liberalism, I have not depicted the public morality as simply a reflection of the value judgments constituting the culture of a society. The public discourse as to what reasons we all have to act in certain ways is not the same public discourse as that which asks what is of value and what is worthless. The two are, to be sure, related in subtle ways: it is only because we have value systems of certain sort that we are committed to the practical activity that is morality. But to communitarian critics this would not be enough: for them, morality can only be secure when it is an expression of the discourse about what is valuable. As I see it, the insight of liberal theory is that morality possess a limited autonomy vis-à-vis axiological discourse.

In one field, however, these two come particularly close together. In education, what is right to teach is intimately related to what is valuable. Liberal education can be seen in many ways, but surely one central aim is to expose a student to what is of value so that he can, if possible, come to appreciate its value. Liberal education, then, is not properly "value neutral" or simply concerned with "values clarification."[81] It aims at teaching what is rightly valued, yet is sensitive to the fact that this value may not be accessible to all. It thus introduces the student to that which is of value while at the same time it maintains the life of the community by acquainting the child with the public culture. Because a theory of what is valuable is required for an intelligent education, it is not surprising that contemporary liberal theories are often at a loss to defend a liberal education while upholding a "neutral" morality.[82] However, we now possess a liberal theory

81 For an introduction to this debate, see Kohlberg, "Indoctrination vs. Relativity in Moral Education"; Benson and Engeman, "Practical Possibilities in American Moral Education"; Bridger, "Values Education." See also Elliot "Curriculum, Morality, and Theories about Value."

82 Ackerman endeavors to wrestle with this problem given the constraints of his neutrality principle; the result is not, I think, a very appealing theory of

of value as well as a theory of right, and this allows for a community characterized by a shared public culture. And that, in turn, points the way toward an adequate liberal theory of education, a fundamental element of the normative liberal political philosophy to which this book is a prolegomenon.

---

liberal education. See his *Social Justice in the Liberal State*, ch. 5. I regret that I am not able to discuss here Amy Gutmann's recent *Democratic Education*; she and I concur in rejecting Ackerman's neutralism and the values-clarification approach (see her pp. 55–6), but she places considerable weight on the cultivation of a democratic character. See also Loren E. Lomasky, *Persons, Rights, and the Moral Community*, ch. 7.

Appendixes

Appendix A: Izard's DES Categories and Some Reliability Statistics

	Factor	*Item*	*Factor-Item Correlation*
I.	Interest	Attentive	.88
	(.76)	Concentrating	.79
		Alert	.87
II.	Enjoyment	Delighted	.81
	(.87)	Happy	.87
		Joyful	.86
III.	Surprise	Surprise	.83
	(.75)	Amazed	.85
		Astonished	.87
IV.	Distress	Downhearted	.86
	(.85)	Sad	.79
		Discouraged	.82
V.	Anger	Enraged	.74
	(.68)	Angry	.84
		Mad	.86
VI.	Disgust	Feeling of distaste	.86
	(.73)	Disgusted	.85
		Feeling of revulsion	.78
VII.	Contempt	Contemptuous	.89
	(.78)	Scornful	.90
		Disdainful	.84
VIII.	Fear	Scared	.88
	(.68)	Fearful	.90
		Afraid	.89
IX.	Shame/shyness	Sheepish	.73
	(.83)	Bashful	.87
		Shy	.88

	Factor	Item	Factor-Item Correlation
X.	Guilt	Repentant	.78
	(.77)	Guilty	.83
		Blameworthy	.80

Item-factor correlation for "state" instructions, $N = 259$; test-retest reliabilities for trait instructions given in parenthesis, $N = 63$. From: Izard, *Human Emotions*, p. 126. Used with permission of Plenum Publishing Company and C. E. Izard.

Appendix B: Desert and Value

In §26.2.2, I proposed that a production-grounded principle of desert (D1) is independent of contribution-grounded principles (D2). As I indicated, my proposal runs counter to what may be called the "accepted view" of economic desert, a view nicely summed up in J. R. Lucas's aphorism that "Desert . . . says 'Thank you.' "[1] The dispute between my proposal and the accepted view concerns the grounds of desert claims and, ultimately, the proper description of the deserved benefit. In order to bring out the contrast, I wish to examine a very simple model which, I think, often underlies the accepted view: let us call it the *reward* model. The crux of this model is that income or distributive shares are rewards for action that promotes some valued end.[2] Take a simple case: say we wish to spur economic growth, and it is determined that one way to do this is to reward people in declining industries who retrain. Henceforth, all those who undergo successful retraining will receive a cash grant. People who retrain then deserve their cash grant: the payment is not a simple forward-looking incentive because it rewards people on the basis of what they have already done. But the award structure – in which successful retraining is selected as a grounds for desert claims – has an incentive rationale.

If we operate with a reward model of economic desert, the principles of contribution and effort both make sense. It is easy to see why these traits might be rewarded: both encourage people

1 J. R. Lucas, *On Justice*, p. 209.
2 My thinking on these matters was spurred by Julian Lamont's "The Concept of Desert and Economic Desert," paper presented to the 1987 meeting of the Australasian Association of Philosophy.

to engage in activity that promotes economic growth. And, if we understand the grounds of desert claims in this way, we will also conceive of the thing that is deserved as a *reward* for a job well done. To give Alf what he deserves is, in effect, to congratulate him on a job well done and thank him for doing something that promotes some valued end. This reward model is powerful in economic thinking. And it makes sense of Becker's intuition that a person cannot deserve a reward for something that benefits him alone. Why would we want to encourage such behavior? If only he profits from it, why thank him for doing it?

I do not wish to deny that deserved benefits can sometimes be aptly described as rewards. What seems wrong is to suppose that all desert claims are ultimately claims for offered rewards. The reward model is, I think, inadequate as a general model of desert because it has great difficulty accounting for a fundamental characteristic of desert-based claims: the validity of Alf's desert-based claim is robust in relation to Betty's value system. That is, if he claims that he deserves X because he has ϕ-ed, the validity of this claim is not going to be highly sensitive to whether she values ϕ-ing, or whether ϕ-ing promotes a goal that she values. If deserved benefits are simply "thank yous," congratulations, or pats on the back, it would seem intelligible for Betty to insist that she does not go in for that activity, hence she has no reason to acknowledge Alf's claim for a reward. But the availability of this response would pretty radically undermine the function of desert claims as claims of justice: rather than achieving a level of impersonality that transcends differences in valuations, the validity of desert claims would be highly sensitive to these differences. Alf would then only have a desert-based claim to X because he has ϕ-ed in relation to those who value ϕ-ing, or value that which ϕ-ing produces.

Let me immediately consider two possible objections to this line of reasoning. (1) It might be argued that there is no reason why desert claims should not be sensitive in this way. If, as Lucas says, desert claims are forms of "thanks yous," they are based on debts of gratitude. And, of course, one only has a debt of gratitude when another has done something for which one should be grateful. So if Betty is not rationally grateful that Alf has ϕ-ed, she would be irrational to thank him. But this is to beg the question. To be sure, to the extent we are operating with an understanding of desert based on gratitude, we are only indebted when we have a reason to be grateful, but the issue here is whether such an understanding captures the ways in which desert claims function. And it seems clear that it does not.

(2) But it may be argued that reward models *can* capture the robustness of desert claims, focusing on the idea of institutional desert claims.[3] Desert claims, it is said, often derive from practices, and it is incumbent upon all participants in such practices to acknowledge them (though those outside the practice need not). That people who work extra hard deserve a reward simply is a constituent of our economic practice and institution. Unless one rejects that institutional arrangement, one must acknowledge the validity of the desert claim.

The idea of an institution, and the status of the claims it generates, is far too complex to be considered here. But obvious difficulties confront any attempt to make the idea of participating in a practice fundamental to the explanation of the robustness of desert claims: desert claims have significant robustness vis-à-vis whether one embraces an institution. Take a common example: "Alf deserves to win the prize because he is the best." Even if Betty places no value on the rewarding of prizes in, say, art, it still seems that he has a legitimate desert-based claim. Betty may sensibly say "I place no value on such competitions, but Alf deserves the prize nonetheless." Moreover, it often is unclear just what institution one must be committed to in order to accept a desert claim. If Betty accepts that coal miners deserve more pay, is this because she is committed to the institution of coal mining, the free economy, or the cooperative economic effort?

However, it may still be objected that I am making too much of the robustness of desert claims vis-à-vis value judgments. It is widely agreed that, if Alf deserves X by virtue of ϕ-ing, it must be the case that ϕ-ing is positively valued.[4] And surely, if Betty actually disvalues ϕ-ing – for example, if she hates it – she will not acknowledge it as the basis of a claim to some benefit, X. Certainly desert is a complex concept: it seems tied to value judgments, yet particular desert claims seem robust in relation to individual valuations. The Affective-Cognitive Theory of value,

3 See John Kleinig, *Punishment and Desert*, ch. III.
4 See, e.g., Kleinig, *Punishment and Desert*, pp. 61ff.; Miller, *Social Justice*, ch. III.

however, may help solve the puzzle of desert claims. A plausible suggestion is that, in order for ϕ to ground a desert claim, it must typically be the case that ϕ is impersonally valuable. But, in order for Betty to acknowledge that Alf deserves *X* because he has ϕ-ed, she need not value ϕ-ing. To borrow an example from John Kleinig, she may correctly assert that Alf "deserves good weather for his holidays. He's planned everything so carefully."[5] It does not follow that for Betty to sensibly say this she must value careful planning: she may well go in for spontaneity. But, still, it is probably right to say that it must be true that such planning is impersonally valuable: that is, it must be the case that it is the sort of thing it would be appropriate to value. Certainly it cannot be the case that planning is impersonally disvaluable.

Yet this seems to raise a problem. I have held that impersonal value judgments do not provide a person with a reason for action if the value is not accessible to him (§10.3). If this is so, might not it be that Betty's response to Alf's desert claim is on par with her response to impersonal value judgments she does not share? That is, she assents to them, but she does not see them as reasons to act. It is here that deservingness judgments – being judgments of justice – differ from value judgments. If Alf claims that he deserves *X* because he has ϕ-ed, he is claiming that *X* is due to him. Betty's reason for acting on this claim is not that she values ϕ-ing but rather that her value system is grounded on the presupposition that valid desert claims typically provide her with reasons to act.

In this respect, I think George Sher ties desert claims somewhat too closely to value. He writes that "although rights-claims and desert-claims both appear to provide answers to the single question 'Should person *X* have *Y*?' . . . a more discerning rendering of the question that desert claims generally answer is 'Is there something about person *X*'s constituting attributes or actions that would make it a good thing for him to have *Y*?' By contrast . . . when rights-claims appear to compete with desert claims, the question *they* typically provide answers is 'Are there at least some persons who have serious obligations to provide *X* with *Y*, to protect *X*'s possession of *Y*, or to refrain from preventing *X* from having *Y*?' "[6] But surely, if Alf claims that he

5 Kleinig, *Punishment and Desert*, p. 51.

6 Sher, *Desert*, p. 199. One is tempted to say here that in one sense at least

deserves *Y*, he is claiming much more than that because of constituting actions or attributes it would be good or valuable for him to have *Y*. He is saying that, in a just world, he would have *Y*. To be sure, and as Sher carefully explores, desert claims are puzzling insofar as often enough no one has any obligation to secure *Y* for Alf. If Alf is a hard-working author who deserves to succeed, it is not implied that anyone has a duty to see to it that Alf succeeds. Yet, even here desert claims often provide the basis for claims that others should act to secure justice. Consider Mill's remarks on the justice of society in 1852:

> . . . if the institution of private property necessarily carried with it as a consequence, that the produce of labour should be apportioned as we now see it, almost in inverse ratio to labour – the largest portions to those who have never worked at all, the next largest to those whose work is almost nominal, and so in a descending scale, the remuneration dwindling as the work grows harder and more disagreeable, until the most fatiguing and exhausting bodily labour cannot count with certainty on being able to earn even the necessaries of life; if this or Communism were the alternative, all the difficulties, great or small, of Communism would be but as dust in the balance.[7]

Granted, this may not entail an obligation of a particular employer to pay workers what they deserve – perhaps in the existing economic system that would only cause immediate ruin. But the charge that the system fails so miserably to accord workers their deserts is a powerful criticism that the system is unjust. And perhaps we all have an obligation to work to reform it. In any event, Mill's charge goes far beyond the claim that the workers are not getting something which, because of constituting actions or attributes it would be good or valuable for them to have: it claims that the system is fundamentally unjust.[8]

---

rights imply "serious obligations" because they are often tied closely to existing practices, which clearly require that certain people do specific things. In contrast, desert claims often are proffered as criticisms of practices or existing systems of rights (in this regard, consider the typical contrast between what one deserves and what one is entitled to). The conservative aspect of rights-based theories of justice is explored by David Miller in *Social Justice*.

7 J. S. Mill, *Principles of Political Economy,* bk. II, ch. i., §3.

8 Sher recognizes this on p. 205 of *Desert*; despite his general claim that desert is closely tied to value, he accepts that it is also tied to fairness and justice. My objection is that he seems too intent on tying desert to value, and separating it from obligation.

Bibliography

Abelson, Robert P., Donald R. Kinder, Mark D. Peters, and Susan T. Fiske. "Affective and Semantic Components in Political Person Perception." *Journal of Personality and Social Psychology* 42 (1982): 619–30.

Ackerman, Bruce A. *Social Justice in the Liberal State*. New Haven, Conn.: Yale University Press, 1980.

Allport, Gordon W. "Attitudes." In *A Handbook of Social Psychology*, edited by Carl Murchinson, pp. 798–844. New York: Russell & Russell, 1935.

Pattern and Growth in Personality. New York: Holt, Rinehart & Winston, 1961.

"Values and Our Youth." In his *The Person in Psychology*, pp. 155–70. Boston: Beacon, 1968.

Allport, G. W., P. E. Vernon, and G. Lindzey. *A Study of Values*. Boston: Houghton Mifflin, 1960.

Alston, William P. "Emotion and Feeling." *Encyclopedia of Philosophy*, II, pp. 479–86. New York: Macmillan and Free Press, 1967.

Anderson, Lynn R., and Martin Fishbein. "Prediction of Attitude from the Number, Strength, and Evaluative Aspects of Beliefs about the Attitude Object: A Comparison of Summation and Congruity Theories." *Journal of Personality and Social Psychology* 2 (1965): 437–43.

Anscombe, G. E. M. *Intention*, 2d ed. Ithaca, N.Y.: Cornell University Press, 1976.

"Modern Moral Philosophy." *Philosophy* 23: 1–19.

Anshutz, J. P. *The Philosophy of J. S. Mill*. Oxford: Clarendon Press, 1963.

Aquinas, Thomas. *Summa Theologica*, translated by the Fathers of the English Dominican Province. London: Burns, Oates, & Washburn, 1942.

Argyle, Michael. *The Psychology of Interpersonal Behaviour*, 3d ed. Harmondsworth, Eng.: Penguin Books, 1978.

Arieti, Silvano. *The Intrapsychic Self*. New York: Basic, 1967.

Aristotle. *Metaphysics*. In *The Basic Works of Aristotle*, translated by W. D. Ross and edited by Richard McKeon. New York: Random House, 1941.

Arnold, Magda. *Emotion and Personality*. New York: Columbia University Press, 1960.

Arrow, Kenneth. "Values and Collective Decision-making." In *Philosophy, Politics, and Society*, 3d series, edited by Peter Laslett and W. G. Runcimann, pp. 215–32. Oxford: Blackwell Publisher, 1967.

Asch, Solomon E. *Social Psychology*. New York: Prentice-Hall, 1952.

Attfield, Robin. "The Good of Trees." *Journal of Value Inquiry* 15 (1981): 35–54.
Audi, Robert. "Axiological Foundationalism." *Canadian Journal of Philosophy* 12 (March 1982): 163–83.
Axelrod, Robert. "The Emergence of Cooperation Among Egoists." *American Political Science Review* 75 (June 1981): 306–18.
The Evolution of Cooperation. New York: Basic, 1984.
Bagozzi, Richard P., and Robert E. Burnkrant. "Attitude Organization and the Attitude-Behavior Relationship." *Journal of Personality and Social Psychology* 37 (June 1979): 913–29.
"Attitude Organization and the Attitude-Behavior Relation: A Reply to Dillon and Kumar." *Journal of Personality and Social Psychology* 49 (July 1985): 47–57.
Baier, Annette. "Trust and Anti-trust." *Ethics* 96 (January 1986): 231–60.
Baier, Kurt. *The Moral Point of View: A Rational Basis of Ethics*. Ithaca, N.Y.: Cornell University Press, 1958; abridged edition, New York: Random House, 1965.
"Moral Reasons and Reasons to Be Moral." In *Values and Morals*, edited by Alvin I. Goldman and Jaegwon Kim, pp. 231–56. Dordrecht, Holland: Reidel, 1978.
"The Practice of Justification." *Journal of Value Inquiry* 9 (1975): 34–41.
"Rationality, Reason, and the Good." In *Morality, Reason, and Truth: New Essays on the Foundations of Ethics*, edited by David Copp and David Zimmerman, pp. 193–211. Totowa, N.J.: Rowman and Allenheld, 1984.
"What is Value?" In *Values and the Future*, edited by Kurt Baier and Nicholas Rescher, pp. 33–67. New York: Free Press, 1969.
Bakunin, Michael. "Federalism, Socialism, Anti-Theologism." In *Bakunin on Anarchy*, edited by Sam Dolgoff, pp. 102–47. New York: Vintage Books, 1971.
Barry, Brian. "Justice and the Common Good." In *Political Philosophy*, edited by Anthony Quinton, pp. 189–93. Oxford: Oxford University Press, 1967.
Political Argument. London: Routledge & Kegan Paul, 1965.
Theories of Justice. Berkeley: University of California Press, 1989.
Bayles, Michael D. "Criminal Paternalism." In *NOMOS XV: The Limits of Law*, edited by J. Roland Pennock and John W. Chapman, pp. 174–88. New York: Leiber-Atherton, 1974.
Becker, Lawrence C. *On Justifying Moral Judgments*. London: Routledge & Kegan Paul, 1973.
Property Rights. London: Routledge & Kegan Paul, 1977.
Bedford, Errol. "Emotions." *Proceedings of the Aristotelian Society* 57 (1956–7): 281–304.
Beit-Hallahmi, Benjamin, and Albert I. Rabin. "The Kibbutz As a Social Experiment and As a Child-rearing Laboratory." In *Annual Progress in Child Psychiatry and Child Development*, edited by Stella Chess and Alexander Thomas, pp. 292–309. New York: Brunner/Mazel, 1978.

Ben-Zeev, Aaron. "G. E. Moore and the Relation between Intrinsic Value and Human Activity." *Journal of Value Inquiry* 15 (1981): 69–78.
Benditt, Theodore. "Happiness." *Philosophical Studies* 25 (1974): 1–20.
Benn, Stanley I. "Freedom and Persuasion." *Australasian Journal of Philosophy* 45 (July 1967): 259–75.
"Freedom, Autonomy, and the Concept of a Person." *Proceedings of the Aristotelian Society* (1975–6): 103–30.
"Individuality, Autonomy, and Community." In *Community As a Social Ideal*, edited by Eugene Kamenka, pp. 43–62. London: Arnold, 1982.
"Personal Freedom and Environmental Ethics." In *Equality and Freedom: International and Comparative Jurisprudence*, II, edited by Gray Dorsey, pp. 401–24. Dobbs Ferry, N.Y.: Oceana Publications, 1977.
"Persons and Values: Reasons in Conflict and Moral Disagreement." *Ethics* 95 (October 1984): 20–37.
"Private and Public Morality: Clean Living and Dirty Hands." In *Public and Private in Social Life*, edited by S. I. Benn and G. F. Gaus, pp. 155–81. New York: St. Martin's, 1983.
"The Problematic Rationality of Political Participation." In *Political Participation*, edited by Benn et al., pp. 1–22. Canberra: Australian National University Press, 1978.
A Theory of Freedom. Cambridge: Cambridge University Press, 1988.
"Wickedness." *Ethics* 95 (July 1985): 795–810.
Benn, S. I., and G. F. Gaus. "The Liberal Conception of the Public and Private." In their *Public and Private in Social Life*, pp. 31–65. New York: St. Martin's Press, 1983.
"Practical Rationality and Commitment." *American Philosophical Quarterly* 23 (July 1986): 255–66.
"The Public and Private: Concepts and Action." In their *Public and Private in Social Life*, pp. 3–27. New York: St. Martin's Press, 1983.
Benn, S. I., and G. W. Mortimore. "Technical Models of Rational Choice." In their *Rationality and the Social Sciences*, pp. 157–95. London: Routledge & Kegan Paul, 1976.
Bennett, Jonathan. *A Study of Spinoza's Ethics*. Cambridge: Cambridge University Press, 1984.
Benson, G. C. S., and T. S. Engeman. "Practical Possibilities in American Moral Education." *Journal of Moral Education* 4 (October 1974): 53–9.
Benson, Jann. "Reflections on the Import of Universalizability in Ethics." *Philosophical Forum* 12 (Spring 1981): 225–37.
Bentham, Jeremy. *An Introduction to the Principles of Morals and Legislation*, edited by J. H. Burns and H. L. A. Hart. London: Athlone, 1970.
Berlin, Isaiah. "Does Political Theory Still Exist?" In *Philosophy, Politics, and Society*, 2d series, edited by Peter Laslett and W. G. Runciman, pp. 1–33. Oxford: Blackwell Publisher, 1962.
"Introduction" to his *Four Essays on Liberty*. Oxford: Oxford University Press, 1969.
"Montesquieu." *Proceedings of the British Academy* 41 (1955): 267–96.
"The Question of Machiavelli." *The New York Review of Books* 4 (November 1971): 20–2.

"Two Concepts of Liberty." In his *Four Essays on Liberty*, pp. 118–72. Oxford: Oxford University Press, 1969.
Berry, Christopher J. *Human Nature*. Atlantic Highlands, N.J.: Humanities, 1986.
Bettelheim, Bruno. *Children of the Dream*. London: Paladin, 1971.
The Empty Fortress: Infantile Autism and the Birth of the Self. New York: Free Press, 1967.
The Informed Heart: Autonomy in a Mass Age. New York: Free Press, 1960.
Birch, Charles. "A Biological Basis for Human Purpose." *Zygon* 8 (September-December 1973): 244–60.
Bluhm, William T. *Ideologies and Attitudes: Modern Political Culture*. Englewood Cliffs, N.J.: Prentice-Hall, 1974.
Blum, Lawrence A. *Friendship, Altruism, and Morality*. London: Routledge & Kegan Paul, 1980.
Bogart, John. "Lockean Provisos and State of Nature Theories." *Ethics* 92 (July 1985): 828–36.
Bond, E. J. "On Desiring the Desirable." *Philosophy* 56 (1981): 489–96.
Reason and Value. Cambridge: Cambridge University Press, 1983.
Boruah, Bijoy H. *Fiction and Emotion: A Study in Aesthetics and the Philosophy of Mind*. Oxford: Clarendon Press, 1988.
Bosanquet, Bernard. *The Principle of Individuality and Value*. New York: Kraus, 1968.
Psychology of the Moral Self. London: Macmillan, 1904.
Some Suggestions in Ethics. New York: Kraus, 1968.
Boulding, Kenneth E. "Prices and Values: Infinite Worth in a Finite World." In *Value and Values in Evolution*, edited by Edward A. Maziarz, pp. 31–46. London: Gordon and Breach, 1979.
Brandt, Richard B. "Some Puzzles for Attitude Theories of Value." In *The Language of Value*, edited by Ray Lepley, pp. 153–77. New York: Columbia University Press, 1957.
A Theory of the Good and the Right. Oxford: Clarendon Press, 1979.
Braybrooke, David. *Meeting Needs*. Princeton, N.J.: Princeton University Press, 1987.
"Preferences Opposed to the Market: Grasshoppers vs. Ants on Security, Inequality, and Justice." In *Liberty and Equality*, edited by Ellen Frankel Paul, Fred Miller, and Jeffrey Paul, pp. 101–14. Oxford: Blackwell Publisher, 1985.
"Social Contract Theory's Fanciest Flight." *Ethics* 97 (July 1987): 750–64.
Brentano, Franz. *The Origin of Our Knowledge of Right and Wrong*, translated by Roderick M. Chisholm and Elizabeth N. Schneewind. London: Routledge & Kegan Paul, 1969.
Psychology from an Empirical Standpoint, translated by A. C. Rancurello, D. B. Terrell, and L. A. McAlister. London: Routledge & Kegan Paul, 1973.
Bridger, Gale W., "Values Education: A Clarification." *Review Journal of Philosophy of Social Science* 5 (1980): 109–17.
Broad, C. D. *Five Types of Ethical Theory*. London: Routledge & Kegan Paul, 1930.

Brock, Dan W. "Contractualism, Utilitarianism, and Social Inequalities." *Social Theory and Practice* 1 (Spring 1971): 33–43.

"Promoting the Good." In *Paternalism*, edited by Rolf Sartorius, pp. 237–60. Minneapolis: University of Minnesota Press, 1983.

Brown, Robert. *Analyzing Love*. Cambridge: Cambridge University Press, 1987.

Buchanan, Alan. *Ethics, Efficiency, and the Market*. Oxford: Clarendon Press, 1985.

Buchanan, James M. *The Limits of Liberty*. Chicago: University of Chicago Press, 1975.

Buckle, Stephen. *The Natural History of Property*. Oxford: Clarendon Press, forthcoming.

Buckley, Norman, Linda S. Siegel, and Steven Ness. "Egocentrism, Empathy, and Altruistic Behaviour in Young Children." *Developmental Psychology* 15 (1979): 329–30.

Cadwallader, Eva H. "The Main Features of Value Experience." *Journal of Value Inquiry* 14 (1980): 229–44.

Campbell, James. "William James and the Ethics of Fulfillment." *Transactions of the Charles S. Pierce Society* 17 (Summer 1981): 224–40.

Cannon, Walter B. "The James-Lange Theory of Emotion." *Journal of Psychiatry* 39 (1927): 106–17.

Carr, Spencer. "Rawls, Contractarianism, and Our Moral Intuitions." *Personalist* 56 (Winter 1975): 83–95.

Carter, Robert Edgar. "Comparative Value Theory." *Journal of Value Inquiry* 13 (Spring 1979): 33–56.

Castañeda, Hector-Neri. "On the Ultimate Subjects of Value Predication." In *Value and Valuation*, edited by John William Davis, pp. 21–36. Knoxville: University of Tennessee Press, 1972.

Chaiken, Shelly, and Mark W. Baldwin. "Affective-Cognitive Consistency and the Effect of Salient Behavioral Information on the Self-Perception of Attitudes." *Journal of Personality and Social Psychology* 41 (1981): 1–12.

Chapman, John W. "Justice, Freedom, and Property." In *NOMOS XXII: Property*, edited by J. Roland Pennock and John W. Chapman, pp. 289–324. New York: New York University Press, 1980.

"The Moral Foundations of Political Obligation." In *NOMOS XII: Political and Legal Obligation*, edited by J. Roland Pennock and John W. Chapman, pp. 142–76. New York: Atherton Press, 1970.

"Political Theory: Logical Structure and Enduring Types." In *L'idee de philosophie politique*, vol. 6 of *Annals de philosophie politique*, pp. 57–96. Paris: Presses Universitaires de France, 1965.

"Toward a General Theory of Human Nature and Dynamics." In *NOMOS XVII: Human Nature in Politics*, edited by J. Roland Pennock and John W. Chapman, pp. 292–319. New York: New York University Press, 1977.

Charvet, John. *A Critique of Freedom and Equality*. Cambridge: Cambridge University Press, 1981.

"A Critique of Human Rights." In *NOMOS XXIII: Human Rights*, edited

by J. Roland Pennock and John W. Chapman, pp. 31–51. New York: New York University Press, 1981.
Chess, Stella. "The Role of Temperament in the Child's Development." *Acta Paedopsychiatrica* 34 (1967): 91-103.
Chisholm, R. M. *Brentano and Intrinsic Value*. Cambridge: Cambridge University Press, 1986.
"Intrinsic Value." In *Values and Morals*, edited by A. I. Goldman and J. Kim, pp. 121–30. Dordrecht, Holland: Reidel, 1978.
Christman, John. "Can Ownership Be Justified by Natural Rights?" *Philosophy and Public Affairs* 15 (Spring 1986): 156–77.
Cleckley, Hervey. *The Mask of Sanity*, 2d ed. St. Louis: C. V. Mosby, 1950.
Cohen, Brenda. "Positive Values." *Proceedings of the Aristotelian Society* supp. vol. 57 (1983): 17–35.
Cohen, Elliot. "The Epistemology of Value." *Auslegung* 5 (June 1978): 176–98.
Coleman, Jules. *Markets, Morals, and the Law*. Cambridge: Cambridge University Press, 1988.
Collingwood, R. G. "Introduction" to Guido de Ruggiero, *The History of European Liberalism*, translated by R. G. Collingwood. Boston: Beacon, 1959.
Collins, Clinton. "Comments on Philip G. Smith's Distinction between Intrinsic and Extrinsic Valuing." *Philosophical Studies in Education* (1981): 21–26.
Cooper, Neil. *The Diversity of Moral Thinking*. Oxford: Clarendon Press, 1981.
Crannor, Carl. "Toward a Theory of Respect for Persons." *American Philosophical Quarterly* 12 (October 1975): 309–19.
Dagger, Richard. "Politics and the Pursuit of Autonomy." In *NOMOS XXVIII: Justification*, edited by J. Roland Pennock and John W. Chapman, pp. 270–90. New York: New York University Press, 1986.
D'Agostino, Fred. "Mill, Paternalism, and Psychiatry." *Australasian Journal of Philosophy* 60 (December 1982): 319–30.
"The Method of Reflective Equilibrium." Unpublished paper.
Daniels, Norman. "Wide Reflective Equilibrium and Theory Acceptance in Ethics." *Journal of Philosophy* 76 (1979): 256–82.
Davidson, Donald. *Essays on Actions and Events*. Oxford: Oxford University Press, 1980.
Davis, Nancy. "Utilitarianism and Responsibility." *Ratio* 22 (1980): 15–35.
Davison, Ian. *Values, Ends, and Society*. St. Lucia, Australia: University of Queensland Press, 1977.
Dewey, John. *Democracy and Education*. New York: Free Press, 1944.
Liberalism and Social Action. New York: Perigee Books, 1980.
"Some Questions About Value." *Journal of Philosophy* 28 (1944): 449–55.
Reconstruction in Philosophy, enlarged ed. Boston: Beacon, 1948.
Diamond, Arthur M., Jr. "Stable Values and Variable Constraints: The Source of Behavioural and Cultural Differences." *Journal of Business Ethics* 1 (February 1982): 49–58.

Diggs, B. J. "The Common Good As Reason for Political Action." *Ethics* 83 (July 1973): 283–93.

Dillon, William R., and Ajith Kumar. "Attitude Organization and the Attitude-Behavior Relation: A Critique of Bagozzi and Burnkrant's Reanalysis of Fishbein and Ajzen." *Journal of Personality and Social Psychology* 49 (July 1985): 33–46.

Douglass, Bruce. "The Common Good and the Public Interest." *Political Theory* 8 (February 1980): 103–17.

Downs, Anthony. *An Economic Theory of Democracy*. New York: Harper and Row, 1957.

Dunn, John. "The Future of Liberalism." In his *Rethinking Modern Political Theory*, pp. 154–70. Cambridge: Cambridge University Press, 1985.

Durkheim, Emile. *The Division of Labor in Society*, translated by George Simpson. New York: Free Press, 1964.

Dworkin, Gerald. "Paternalism." In *Paternalism*, edited by Rolf Sartorius, pp. 19–34. Minneapolis: University of Minnesota Press, 1983.

"Paternalism: Some Second Thoughts." In *Paternalism*, edited by Rolf Sartorius, pp. 105–11. Minneapolis: University of Minnesota Press, 1983.

Dworkin, Ronald. *Law's Empire*. Cambridge, Mass.: Belknap Press of Harvard University Press, 1986.

"Liberalism." In his *A Matter of Principle*, pp. 181–213. Cambridge, Mass.: Harvard University Press, 1985.

Taking Rights Seriously. Cambridge, Mass.: Harvard University Press, 1978.

"What Is Equality? Part 1: Equality of Welfare." *Philosophy and Public Affairs* 10 (Summer 1981): 185–246.

Eaton, Howard O. *The Austrian Philosophy of Values*. Norman: University of Oklahoma Press, 1930.

Edwards, Rem B. *Pleasures and Pains: A Theory of Qualitative Hedonism*. Ithaca, N.Y.: Cornell University Press, 1979.

Ehrenfels, Christian. "The Ethical Theory of Value." *International Journal of Ethics* (now *Ethics*) 6 (1896): 371–84.

Ekman, Paul. "Biological and Cultural Contributions to Body and Facial Movement in the Expression of Emotions." In *Explaining Emotions*, edited by Amélie Oksenberg Rorty, pp. 73–101. Berkeley: University of California Press, 1980.

Ekman, Paul, Wallace V. Friesen, and Phoebe Ellsworth. *Emotion in the Human Face*. New York: Pergamon, 1972.

Elliot, Robert. "Curriculum, Morality, and Theories about Value." *Educational Philosophy and Theory* 14 (October 1982): 15–28.

"Rawlsian Justice and Non-Human Animals." *Journal of Applied Philosophy* 1 (1984): 95–106.

Elster, Jon. "Exploitation, Freedom, and Justice." In *NOMOS XXVI: Marxism*, edited by J. Roland Pennock and John W. Chapman, pp. 277–304. New York: New York University Press, 1983.

Enelow, James M., and Melvin J. Hinch. *The Spatial Theory of Voting*. Cambridge: Cambridge University Press, 1984.

Ewin, R. E. *Co-operation and Human Values: A Study of Moral Reasoning*. Brighton, Eng.: Harvester, 1981.
Ewing, A. C. "The Justification of Emotions." *Proceedings of the Aristotelian Society* supp. vol. 31 (1957): 59–74.
Feather, Norman. "Human Values and the Prediction of Action." In his *Expectations and Actions: Expectancy-Value Models in Psychology*, pp. 263–89. Hillsdale, N.J.: Lawrence Erlbaum, 1982.
Values in Education and Society. London: Collier Macmillan, 1975.
Feinberg, Joel. *Harm to Others*, vol. 1 of *The Moral Limits of the Criminal Law*. New York: Oxford University Press, 1984.
Harm to Self, vol. 3 of *The Moral Limits of the Criminal Law*. New York: Oxford University Press, 1986.
"The Idea of a Free Man." In his *Rights, Justice, and the Bounds of Liberty*, pp. 4–29. Princeton, N.J.: Princeton University Press, 1980.
"Justice and Personal Desert." In his *Doing and Deserving*, pp. 55–87. Princeton, N.J.: Princeton University Press, 1970.
"Legal Paternalism." In *Paternalism*, edited by Rolf Sartorius, pp. 3–18. Minneapolis: University of Minnesota Press, 1983.
"Sentiment and Sentimentality in Practical Ethics." *Proceedings and Addresses of the American Philosophical Association* 56 (September 1982): 19–46.
Social Philosophy. Englewood Cliffs, N.J.: Prentice-Hall, 1973.
Findlay, J. N. *Axiological Ethics*. New York: St. Martin's, 1970.
Meinong's Theory of Objects and Values, 2d ed. Oxford: Clarendon Press, 1963.
Values and Intentions. London: Allen & Unwin, 1961.
Finnis, John. *Fundamentals of Ethics*. Oxford: Clarendon Press, 1983.
Natural Law and Natural Rights. Oxford: Clarendon Press, 1980.
Fishbein, Martin. "Attitude and the Prediction of Behavior." In his *Readings in Attitude Theory and Measurement*, pp. 477–92. New York: Wiley, 1967.
"A Consideration of Beliefs and Their Role in Attitude Measurement." In his *Readings in Attitude Theory and Measurement*, pp. 257–66. New York: Wiley, 1967.
Fishbein, Martin, and Icek Ajzen. *Belief, Attitude, Intention, and Behavior*. Reading, Mass.: Addison-Wesley, 1975.
Fishbein, Martin, and R. Hunter. "Summation *Versus* Balance in Attitude Organization and Change." *Journal of Abnormal and Social Psychology* 69 (1964): 505–10.
Fishkin, James S. *Beyond Subjective Morality*. New Haven, Conn.: Yale University Press, 1984.
Tyranny and Legitimacy. Baltimore: Johns Hopkins University Press, 1979.
Flathman, Richard E. *The Philosophy and Politics of Freedom*. Chicago: University of Chicago Press, 1987.
The Practice of Rights. Cambridge: Cambridge University Press, 1976.
Foot, Philippa. *Virtues and Vices*. Berkeley: University of California Press, 1978.
Fortenbaugh, W. W. *Aristotle on Emotion*. London: Duckworth, 1975.

Frankena, William K. *Ethics*, 2d ed. Englewood Cliffs, N.J.: Prentice-Hall, 1973.
"The Naturalistic Fallacy." In *Perspectives on Morality: Essays by William K. Frankena*, edited by K. E. Goodpaster, pp. 1–11. Notre Dame: University of Notre Dame Press, 1976.
"Obligation and Motivation in Recent Moral Philosophy." In *Perspectives on Morality: Essays by William K. Frankena*, edited by K. E. Goodpaster, pp. 49–73. Notre Dame: University of Notre Dame Press, 1976.
Frankfurt, Harry G. "Freedom of the Will." In his *The Importance of What We Care About*, pp. 11–25. Cambridge: Cambridge University Press, 1988.
Freud, Sigmund. "On the Grounds for Detaching a Particular Syndrome from Neurasthenia under the Description 'Anxiety Neurosis.' " In *On Psychopathology*, edited by Angela Richards, pp. 33–63. Harmondsworth, Eng.: Penguin Books, 1979.
"Inhibitions, Symptoms, and Anxiety." In *On Psychopathology*, edited by Angela Richards, pp. 227–315. Harmondsworth, Eng.: Penguin Books, 1979.
Introductory Lectures on Psychoanalysis, translated by James Strachey. Harmondsworth, Eng.: Penguin Books, 1973.
New Introductory Lectures on Psychoanalysis, translated by James Strachey. Harmondsworth, Eng.: Penguin Books, 1962.
Fried, Charles. *An Anatomy of Values*. Cambridge, Mass.: Harvard University Press, 1970.
Friedman, Richard B. "On the Concept of Authority in Political Philosophy." In *Concepts in Social and Political Philosophy*, edited by Richard E. Flathman, pp. 121–46. New York: Macmillan, 1973.
Frijda, Nico H. *The Emotions*. Cambridge: Cambridge University Press, 1986.
Frondizi, Risieri. "Value as a Gestalt Quality." *Journal of Value Inquiry* 6 (Fall 1972): 163–84.
Fuller, Lon. "Two Principles of Human Associations." In *NOMOS XI: Voluntary Associations*, edited by J. Roland Pennock and John W. Chapman, pp. 3–23. New York: Atherton Press, 1969.
Furubotn, Erik G., and Svetozar Pejovich. "Property Rights and the Behavior of the Firm in a Socialist State: The Example of Yugoslavia." In their (eds.) *The Economics of Property Rights*, pp. 227–56. Cambridge, Mass.: Ballinger, 1974.
Galston, William A. "Defending Liberalism." *American Political Science Review* 76 (September 1982): 621–9.
Justice and the Human Good. Chicago: University of Chicago Press, 1980.
Garnett, A. Campbell. "Intrinsic Good." In *Value: A Cooperative Inquiry*, edited by Ray Lepley, pp. 78–92. New York: Columbia University Press, 1949.
Gaus, Gerald F. "On Community and Justice: A Reply to Professor Golding." *Bulletin of the Australian Society of Legal Philosophy* 9 (October 1985): 197–204.

"The Convergence of Rights and Utility: The Case of Rawls and Mill." *Ethics* 92 (October 1981): 57–72
"Mill's Theory of Moral Rules." *Australasian Journal of Philosophy* 58 (September 1980): 265–79.
The Modern Liberal Theory of Man. New York: St. Martin's, 1983.
"Practical Reason and Moral Persons." *Ethics* 100 (October 1989): 127–8.
"Public and Private Interests in Liberal Political Economy, Old and New." In *Public and Private in Social Life*, edited by S. I. Benn and G. F. Gaus, pp. 183–221. New York: St. Martin's, 1983.
"Subjective Value and Justificatory Political Theory." In *NOMOS XXVIII: Justification*, edited by J. Roland Pennock and John W. Chapman, pp. 241–69. New York: New York University Press, 1986.
Gauthier, David. *Morals by Agreement*. Oxford: Clarendon Press, 1986.
Geertz, Clifford. "Ideology as a Cultural System." In his *The Interpretation of Cultures*, pp. 193–233. New York: Basic, 1973.
"Person, Time, and Conduct in Bali." In his *The Interpretation of Cultures*, pp. 360–411. New York: Basic, 1973.
Gert, Bernard. "Introduction" to Thomas Hobbes, *Man and Citizen*, pp. 3–32. Garden City, N.J.: Doubleday, 1972.
The Moral Rules. New York: Harper & Row, 1973.
Gert, Bernard, and Charles Culver. "Paternalistic Behavior." *Philosophy and Public Affairs* 6 (Fall 1976): 45–57.
Gewirth, Alan. *Reason and Morality*. Chicago: University of Chicago Press, 1981.
Goffman, Erving. *The Presentation of the Self in Everyday Life*. Harmondsworth, Eng.: Penguin Books, 1971.
Golding, Martin. "The Nature of Compromise: A Preliminary Inquiry." In *NOMOS XXI: Compromise in Ethics, Law, and Politics*, edited by J. Roland Pennock and John W. Chapman, pp. 3–25. New York: New York University Press, 1979.
"Community and Rights." *Bulletin of the Australian Society of Legal Philosophy* 9 (October 1985): 185–96.
Gordon, Robert M. *The Structure of Emotions: Investigations in Cognitive Philosophy*. Cambridge: Cambridge University Press, 1987.
Gracia, Jorge J. E. "The Ontological Status of Value." *The Modern Schoolman* 53 (May 1976): 393–7.
Gray, John. "Contractarian Method, Private Property, and the Market Economy." In *NOMOS XXXI: Markets and Justice*, edited by John W. Chapman and J. Roland Pennock, pp. 13–58. New York: New York University Press, 1989.
"On Negative and Positive Liberty." *Political Studies* 28: 507–26.
Green, O. H. "Emotions and Beliefs." In *American Philosophical Quarterly Monograph No. 6: Studies in the Philosophy of Mind* (1972), pp. 24–40.
"The Expression of Emotion." *Mind* 79 (1970): 551–68.
Green, T. H. "On the Different Senses of 'Freedom' Applied to the Will and to the Moral Progress of Man." In *Lectures on the Principles of Political Obligation and Other Writings*, edited by Paul Harris and John Morrow, pp. 228–49. Cambridge: Cambridge University Press, 1986.

Lectures on the Principles of Political Obligation. In *Lectures on the Principles of Political Obligation and Other Writings*, edited by Paul Harris and John Morrow, pp. 13–193. Cambridge: Cambridge University Press, 1986.

Prolegomena to Ethics. Oxford: Clarendon Press, 1890.

Greenspan, Patricia. "A Case of Mixed Feelings: Ambivalence and the Logic of Emotion." In *Explaining Emotions*, edited by Amélie Oksenberg Rorty, pp. 223–50. Berkeley: University of California Press, 1980.

Griffin, James. "Are There Incommensurable Values?" *Philosophy and Public Affairs* 7 (1977): 39–59.

"Modern Utilitarianism." *Revue internationale de philosophie* 141 (1982): 331–75.

Grunberg, Ludwig. "Rationality and the Basis of the Value Judgement." *Journal of Value Inquiry* 12 (Spring 1978): 126–33.

Gutmann, Amy. "Communitarian Critics of Liberalism." *Philosophy and Public Affairs* 14 (Summer 1985): 303–22.

Democratic Education. Princeton, N.J.: Princeton University Press, 1987.

Liberal Equality. Cambridge: Cambridge University Press, 1980.

Guttman, Louis, and Edward A. Suchman. "Intensity and a Zero Point for Attitude Analysis." In *Readings in Attitude Theory and Measurement*, edited by Martin Fishbein, pp. 267–76. New York: Wiley, 1967.

Haksar, Vinit. *Equality, Liberty, and Perfectionism*. Oxford: Clarendon Press, 1979.

"The Responsibility of Psychopaths." *Philosophical Quarterly* 15 (1965): 136–45.

Halliday, R. J. *John Stuart Mill*. London: Allen & Unwin, 1976.

Hampshire, Stuart. *Freedom of the Individual*. London: Chatto & Windus, 1975.

"Morality and Conflict." In his *Morality and Conflict*, pp. 140–69. Oxford: Blackwell Publisher, 1983.

"Public and Private Morality." In his *Public and Private Morality*, pp. 23–53. Cambridge: Cambridge University Press, 1978.

Hampton, Jean. *Hobbes and the Social Contract Tradition*. Cambridge: Cambridge University Press, 1986.

Hancock, Roger N. *Twentieth-Century Ethics*. New York: Columbia University Press, 1974.

Hardin, Russell. "Bargaining for Justice." *Social Philosophy and Policy* 5 (Spring 1988): 65–74.

Hare, R. M. "Do Agents Have to Be Moralists?" In *Gewirth's Ethical Rationalism*, edited by Edward Regis, Jr., pp. 52–8. Chicago: University of Chicago Press, 1984.

Freedom and Reason. Oxford: Clarendon Press, 1963.

Moral Thinking. Oxford: Clarendon Press, 1981.

Hare, Robert D. *Psychopathy: Theory and Research*. New York: Wiley, 1970.

Hare, Robert D., and David N. Cox. "Clinical and Empirical Conceptions of Psychopathy, and Selection of Subjects for Research." In *Psychopathic Behavior: Approaches to Research*, edited by R. D. Hare and D. Schalling, pp. 1–21. New York: Wiley, 1978.

Harman, Gilbert. "Human Flourishing, Ethics, and Liberty." *Philosophy and Public Affairs* 12 (Fall 1983): 307–22.
"Rationality in Agreement: A Commentary on Gauthier's *Morals by Agreement*." *Social Philosophy and Policy* 5 (Spring 1988): 1–16.
Harris, Marvin. *Cows, Pigs, Wars, and Witches: The Riddles of Culture*. New York: Vintage Books, 1978.
Harrison, George J. "Values Clarification and the Construction of the Good." *Educational Theory* 30 (Summer 1980): 185–91.
Harsanyi, John C. "Morality and the Theory of Rational Behaviour." In *Utilitarianism and Beyond*, edited by Amartya Sen and Bernard Williams, pp. 23–62. Cambridge: Cambridge University Press, 1982.
Hart, H. L. A., and A. M. Honoré. *Causation in the Law*. Oxford: Clarendon Press, 1959.
Hart, Samuel. *Treatise on Values*. New York: Philosophical Library, 1949.
Hartmann, Heinz. *Essays on Ego Psychology*. London: Hogarth, 1964.
Hartmann, Nicolai. *Ethics*, translated by Stanton Coit. London: Allen & Unwin, 1932.
Hayek, F. A. *The Constitution of Liberty*. London: Routledge & Kegan Paul, 1960.
The Mirage of Social Justice, vol. 2 of *Law, Legislation, and Liberty*. London: Routledge & Kegan Paul, 1976.
The Political Order of a Free People, vol. 3 of *Law, Legislation, and Liberty*. London: Routledge & Kegan Paul, 1979.
Hayes, Edward C. "Social Values." *American Journal of Sociology* 18 (January 1913): 470–508.
Held, Virginia. "Justification: Legal and Political." *Ethics* 86 (1975-6): 1–16.
The Public Interest and Individual Interests. New York: Basic, 1970.
Henderson, T. Y. "A Substantial Theory of Value." *Journal of Value Inquiry* 7 (1973): 188–97.
Himmelfarb, Samuel, and Alice H. Eagly. "Orientations to the Study of Attitudes and Their Change." In their *Readings in Attitude Change*, pp. 2–49. New York: Wiley, 1974.
Hobbes, Thomas. *The Citizen*. In *Man and Citizen*, edited by Bernard Gert, pp. 87–386. Garden City, N.J.: Doubleday, 1972.
The Elements of Law, Natural and Politic, edited by Ferdinand Tönnies. London: Cass, 1969.
Leviathan, edited by Michael Oakeshott. New York: Collier, 1962.
On Man. In *Man and Citizen*, edited by Bernard Gert, pp. 35–85. Garden City, N.J.: Doubleday, 1972.
Hobhouse, L. T. *The Elements of Social Justice*. London: Allen & Unwin, 1922.
Liberalism. Oxford: Oxford University Press, 1964.
The Rational Good. New York: Holt, 1921.
Hohfeld, Wesley. "Some Fundamental Legal Conceptions As Applied in Judicial Reasoning." *Yale Law Journal* 23 (1913): 16–59.
Holmes, Robert L. "On Generalization." *Journal of Philosophy* 60 (1963): 317–23.
Horney, Karen. *Neurosis and Human Growth*. New York: Norton, 1959.

Hotelling, Harold. "Stability in Competition." *Economic Journal* 39 (1929): 41–57.
Hume, David. *An Enquiry Concerning the Principles of Morals*, 3d ed., edited by L. A. Selby-Bigge and P. H. Nidditch. Oxford: Clarendon Press, 1975.
A Treatise of Human Nature, 2d ed., edited by L. A. Selby-Bigge and P. H. Nidditch. Oxford: Clarendon Press, 1978.
Izard, Carroll E. *Human Emotions*. New York: Plenum, 1977.
James, Gene G. "Is Value a Gestalt Quality?" *Journal of Value Inquiry* 13 (Fall 1979): 207–23.
James, William. *The Principles of Psychology*. London: Macmillan, 1890.
Jouvenel, Bertrand de. *Sovereignty: An Inquiry into the Political Good*. Cambridge: Cambridge University Press, 1957.
Kamenka, Eugene. "What Is Justice?" In *Justice*, edited by Eugene Kamenka and Alice Erh-Soon Tay, pp. 1–24. London: Edward Arnold, 1979.
Kant, Immanuel. *The Doctrine of Virtue*, translated by Mary J. Gregor. New York: Harper & Row, 1964.
Foundations of the Metaphysics of Morals, translated by Lewis White Beck. Indianapolis: Bobbs-Merrill, 1959.
Kaplan, Morton A. *Justice, Human Nature, and Political Obligation*. New York: Free Press, 1976.
Kavka, Gregory S. *Hobbesian Moral and Political Theory*. Princeton, N.J.: Princeton University Press, 1986.
Kenny, Anthony. *Action, Emotion, and Will*. London: Routledge & Kegan Paul, 1963.
Kim, Jaegwon. "Supervenience and Nomological Incommensurables." *American Philosophical Quarterly* 15 (April 1978): 149–64.
Kitchener, Richard F. "Piaget's Social Psychology." *Journal for the Theory of Social Behaviour* 11 (1981): 253–77.
Kleinig, John. "Human Rights, Legal Rights, and Social Change." In *Human Rights*, edited by Eugene Kamenka and Alice Erh-Soon Tay, pp. 36–47. New York: St. Martin's, 1978.
Paternalism. Totowa, N.J.: Rowman and Allenheld, 1984.
Punishment and Desert. The Hague: Nijhoff, 1973.
Kocis, Robert A. "Reason, Development, and the Conflict of Human Ends: Sir Isaiah Berlin's Vision of Politics." *American Political Science Review* 74 (1980): 38-52.
Kohlberg, Lawrence. "Development As the Aim of Education." In his *Essays on Moral Development*, vol. 1: *The Philosophy of Moral Development*, pp. 49–96. New York: Harper & Row, 1981.
"From *Is* to *Ought*." In his *The Philosophy of Moral Development*, pp. 101–89. New York: Harper & Row, 1981.
"Indoctrination vs. Relativity in Moral Education." In his *The Philosophy of Moral Development*, pp. 6–23. New York: Harper & Row, 1981.
"Justice as Reversibility." In his *The Philosophy of Moral Development*, pp. 190–226. New York: Harper & Row, 1981.
Kohlberg, L., and R. Kramer. "Continuities and Discontinuities in Child-

hood and Adult Moral Development." *Human Development* 12 (1969): 93–120.
Kolnai, Aurel. "Aesthetic and Moral Experience: The Five Contrasts." *British Journal of Aesthetics* 11: 178–88.
"Contrasting the Ethical with the Aesthetical." *British Journal of Aesthetics* 11: 331–44.
"Dignity." *Philosophy* 51 (1976): 251–71.
Konner, Melvin. *The Tangled Wing: Biological Constraints on the Human Spirit.* New York: Holt, Rinehart & Winston, 1982.
Kothandapani, Virupaksha. "Validation of Feeling, Belief, and Intention to Act As Three Components of Attitude and Their Contribution to Prediction of Contraceptive Behavior." *Journal of Personality and Social Psychology* 19 (1971): 321–33.
Kraft, Victor. *Foundations for a Scientific Analysis of Value*, translated by Elizabeth Hughes Schneewind. London: Reidel, 1981.
Krebs, Dennis, and Janet Gillmore. "The Relationship among the First Stages of Cognitive Development, Role-taking Abilities, and Moral Development." *Child Development* 53 (August 1982): 877–86.
Krygier, Martin. "Publicness, Privateness, and 'Primitive Law.' " In *Public and Private in Social Life*, edited by S. I. Benn and G. F. Gaus, pp. 307–340. New York: St. Martin's, 1983.
Kuflik, Arthur. "Morality and Compromise." In *NOMOS XXI: Compromise in Ethics, Law, and Politics*, edited by J. Roland Pennock and John W. Chapman, pp. 38–65. New York: New York University Press, 1979.
Kupperman, Joel J. *The Foundations of Morality*. London: Allen & Unwin, 1983.
"Value Judgments." *Philosophy and Phenomenological Research* 42 (June 1982): 506–18.
Kurdek, Lawrence A. "Perspective Taking As the Cognitive Basis of Children's Moral Development: A Review of the Literature." *Merrill-Palmer Quarterly* 24 (January 1978): 3–28.
Laing, R. D. *The Divided Self.* Harmondsworth, Eng.: Penguin Books, 1965.
Laird, John. *The Idea of Value.* Cambridge: Cambridge University Press, 1929.
Larsen, Randy J., Ed Diener, and Robert A. Emmons. "Affect Intensity and Reactions to Daily Life Events." *Journal of Personality and Social Psychology* 51 (October 1986): 803–13.
Lee, Harold N. "Methodology of Value Theory." In *Value: A Cooperative Inquiry*, edited by Ray Lepley, pp. 147–66. New York: Columbia University Press, 1949.
Leventhal, Howard. "A Model of Emotion." In *Perception of Emotion in Self and Others*, edited by Patricia Pliner, Kirk R. Blankstein, and Irwin M. Spigel, pp. 1–46. New York: Plenum, 1979.
Lewis, C. I. *An Analysis of Knowledge and Valuation.* LaSalle, Ill.: Open Court, 1971.
Lindblom, Charles E. *Politics and Markets.* New York: Basic, 1977.
Lindley, Richard. *Autonomy*. London: Macmillan, 1986.

Locke, Don. "The Trivializability of Universalizability." *Philosophical Review* 77 (1968): 25–44.
Locke, John. *An Essay Concerning Human Understanding*, edited by Peter H. Nidditch. Oxford: Clarendon Press, 1975.
First Treatise of Government. In *Two Treatises of Government*, edited by Peter Laslett. Cambridge: Cambridge University Press, 1960.
Second Treatise of Government. In *Two Treatises of Government*, edited by Peter Laslett. Cambridge: Cambridge University Press, 1960.
Lomasky, Loren E. *Persons, Rights, and the Moral Community*. New York: Oxford University Press, 1987.
Loring, I. M. *Two Kinds of Values*. New York: Humanities, 1966.
Lucas, J. R. *On Justice*. Oxford: Clarendon Press, 1980.
Lycan, William G. *Judgement and Justification*. Cambridge: Cambridge University Press, 1988.
Lyons, David. *Forms and Limits of Utilitarianism*. Oxford: Clarendon Press, 1965.
Lyons, William. *Emotion*. Cambridge: Cambridge University Press, 1980.
McAlister, Linda. *The Development of Franz Brentano's Ethics*. Amsterdam: Rodopi, 1982.
MacCallum, Gerald C. "Negative and Positive Freedom." In *Philosophy, Politics, and Society*, 4th series, edited by Peter Laslett, W. G. Runciman, and Quentin Skinner, pp. 174–93. Oxford: Blackwell Publisher, 1971.
McClennen, Edward F. "Constrained Maximization and Resolute Choice." *Social Philosophy and Policy* 5 (Spring 1988): 95-118.
McCord, William, and Joan McCord. *Psychopathy and Delinquency*. New York: Grune & Stratton, 1956.
McDougall, William. *The Energies of Men*, 3d ed. London: Methuen & Co., 1935.
McDowell, John. "Aesthetic Value, Objectivity, and the Fabric of the World." In *Pleasure, Preference, and Value*, edited by Eva Schaper, pp. 1–16. Cambridge: Cambridge University Press, 1983.
"Are Moral Requirements Hypothetical Imperatives?" *Proceedings of the Aristotelian Society* supp. vol. 52 (1978): 13–29.
"Non-cognitivism and Rule-following." In *Wittgenstein: To Follow a Rule*, edited by Steven H. Holtzman and Christopher M. Leich, pp. 141–62. London: Routledge & Kegan Paul, 1981.
MacIntyre, Alasdair. *After Virtue*. Notre Dame: University of Notre Dame Press, 1981.
Mack, Eric. "Moral Individualism: Agent-relativity and Deontic Restraints." *Social Philosophy and Policy*, 7 (Autumn 1989): 81–111.
Mackie, J. L. *Ethics: Inventing Right and Wrong*. Harmondsworth, Eng.: Penguin Books, 1977.
MacLean, Paul D. "The Hypothalamus and Emotional Behavior." In *The Hypothalamus*, edited by Webb Haymaker, Evelyn Anderson, and Walle J. H. Nauta, pp. 659–78. Springfield, Ill.: Charles C. Thomas, 1969.
"Implications of Microelectric Findings on Exteroceptive Inputs to the Limbic Cortex." In *Limbic System Mechanisms and Automatic Function*,

edited by Charles H. Hockman, pp. 115–30. Springfield, Ill.: Charles C. Thomas, 1972.
"Psychosomatics." In *Handbook of Physiology – Section 1: Neurophysiology*, edited by John Field, pp. 1723–44. Washington: American Physiological Society, 1960.
"Some Psychiatric Implications of Physiological Studies on Frontotemporal Portion of Limbic System (Visceral Brain)." *Electroencephalography & Clinical Neurophysiology* 4 (November 1952): 407–18.
"Sensory and Perceptive Factors in Emotional Functions of the Triune Brain." In *Explaining Emotions*, edited by Amélie Oksenberg Rorty, pp. 9–36. Berkeley: University of California Press, 1980.
"The Triune Brain, Emotion, and Scientific Bias." In *The Neurosciences Second Study Program*, edited by Francis O. Schmitt, pp. 336–49. New York: Rockefeller University Press, 1970.
Mandler, George. *Mind and Emotion*. New York: Wiley, 1975.
Mannheim, Karl. *Ideology and Utopia*. London: Routledge & Kegan Paul, 1936.
Maritain, Jacques. *The Person and the Common Good*. London: Geoffrey Bles, 1948.
Marx, Karl. *The Economic and Philosophic Manuscripts of 1844*, translated by Martin Milligan. New York: International Publishers, 1964.
Maslow, Abraham. *Motivation and Personality*. New York: Harper & Row, 1954.
Matthews, Eric. "Objectivity, Values, and History." *American Philosophical Quarterly* 10 (July 1973): 213–21.
May, Rollo. "Values, Myths, and Symbols." *Review of Existential Psychology and Psychiatry* 13 (1974): 267–73.
Mayberry, Thomas C. "Morality and Justification." *Southern Journal of Philosophy* 6 (Winter 1968): 205–14.
Meinong, Alexius. *On Emotional Presentation*, translated by Marie-Luise Schubert Kalsi. Evanston, Ill.: Northwestern University Press, 1972.
Midgley, Mary. *Animals and Why They Matter*. Harmondsworth, Eng.: Penguin Books, 1983.
Wickedness. London: Routledge & Kegan Paul, 1984.
Mill, John Stuart. *Autobiography*. New York: Columbia University Press, 1924.
"Bentham." In *Collected Works of John Stuart Mill*, edited by J. M. Robson, vol. X, pp. 75–115. Toronto: University of Toronto Press, 1963.
On Liberty. New York: Appleton-Century-Crofts, 1947.
Principles of Political Economy. Fairfield, N.J.: Augustus M. Kelly, 1976.
A System of Logic. London: Longman's Group, 1947.
"Thornton on Labour and Its Claims." In *The Collected Works of John Stuart Mill*, edited by J. M. Robson, vol. IV, pp. 631–68. Toronto: University of Toronto Press, 1967.
Utilitarianism. Indianapolis: Bobbs-Merrill, 1957.
Miller, David. *Social Justice*. Oxford: Clarendon Press, 1976.
Miller, George A. *Psychology*. Harmondsworth, Eng.: Penguin Books, 1966.
Miller, Peter. "Value As Richness: Toward a Value Theory for an Expanded

Naturalism in Environmental Ethics." *Environmental Ethics* 4 (Summer 1982): 101–14.
Milligan, David. *Reasoning and the Explanation of Actions*. Brighton, Eng.: Harvester, 1980.
Milo, Ronald D. *Immorality*. Princeton, N.J.: Princeton University Press, 1984.
Mitchell, Dorothy. "Mill's Theory of Value." *Theoria* 36 (1970): 100–115.
Monro, D. H. "Utilitarianism." In *The Dictionary of the History of Ideas*, vol. IV, pp. 444–9. New York: Scribner, 1973.
Moore, F. C. T. *The Psychological Basis of Morality*. London: Macmillan, 1978.
Moore, G. E. "The Conception of Intrinsic Value." In his *Philosophical Studies*, pp. 253–78. London: Routledge & Kegan Paul, 1922.
Principia Ethica. Cambridge: Cambridge University Press, 1954.
Moore, Willis. "The Language of Values." In *The Language of Value*, edited by Ray Lepley, pp. 9–28. New York: Columbia University Press, 1957.
Morton, Adam. "Character and the Emotions." In *Explaining Emotions*, edited by Amélie Oksenberg Rorty, pp. 153–61. Berkeley: University of California Press, 1980.
Mueller, Dennis C., Robert D. Tollison, and Thomas D. Willett. "The Utilitarian Contract: A Generalization of Rawls' Theory of Justice." *Theory and Decision* (1974): 345–67.
Muller, Franz H. "Comparative Social Philosophies: Individualism, Socialism, and Solidarism." *Thought* 60 (September 1985): 297–309.
Murphy, Arthur E. "The Common Good." *Proceedings of the American Philosophical Association* 24 (September 1953): 3–18.
Nagel, Thomas. "The Limits of Objectivity." In *The Tanner Lectures on Human Values*, edited by Sterling M. McMurrin, vol. I, pp. 76–139. Cambridge: Cambridge University Press, 1980.
The Possibility of Altruism. Princeton, N.J.: Princeton University Press, 1979.
"Subjective and Objective." In his *Mortal Questions*, pp. 196–213. Cambridge: Cambridge University Press, 1979.
The View from Nowhere. New York: Oxford University Press, 1986.
Narveson, Jan. "Equality vs. Liberty: Advantage, Liberty." In *Liberty and Equality*, edited by Ellen Frankel Paul, Fred D. Miller, and Jeffrey Paul, pp. 32–60. Oxford: Blackwell Publisher, 1985.
"The How and Why of Universality." In *Morality and Universality: Essays on Ethical Universalizability*, edited by Nelson T. Potter and Mark Timmons, pp. 3–44. Dordrecht, Holland: Reidel, 1985.
The Libertarian Idea. Philadelphia: Temple University Press, 1988.
Nash, John. "Two-person Cooperative Games." *Econmetria* 21 (1953): 128–40.
Nelson, William. *On Justifying Democracy*. London: Routledge & Kegan Paul, 1980.
Nielsen, Kai. "Against Ethical Rationalism." In *Gewirth's Ethical Rationalism*, edited by Edward Regis, Jr., pp. 59–83. Chicago: University of Chicago Press, 1984.

Nietzsche, Friedrich. *On the Genealogy of Morals*, translated by Walter Kaufmann and R. J. Hollingdale. New York: Vintage Books, 1969.
Norton, David L. *Personal Destinies: A Philosophy of Ethical Individualism*. Princeton, N.J.: Princeton University Press, 1976.
Nowell-Smith, P. H. *Ethics*. Harmondsworth, Eng.: Penguin Books, 1954.
Nozick, Robert. *Anarchy, State, and Utopia*. New York: Basic, 1974.
"Coercion." In *Philosophy, Politics, and Society*, 4th series, edited by Peter Laslett, W. G. Runciman, and Quentin Skinner, pp. 101–35. Oxford: Blackwell Publisher, 1971.
Philosophical Explanations. Oxford: Clarendon Press, 1981.
Oakeshott, Michael. *On Human Conduct*. Oxford: Clarendon Press, 1975.
Oldenquist, Andrew. "Loyalties." *Journal of Philosophy* 79 (April 1982): 173–93.
Olson, Mancur, Jr. *The Logic of Collective Action*. New York: Schocken, 1968.
Olson, Robert C. "Teleological Ethics." *Encyclopedia of Philosophy*, edited by Paul Edwards. New York: Macmillan and Free Press, 1967.
Oppenheim, Felix E. *Political Concepts: A Reconstruction*. Oxford: Blackwell Publisher, 1981.
Parfit, Derek. *Reasons and Persons*. Oxford: Clarendon Press, 1984.
Parker, DeWitt H. "Discussion of John Dewey's 'Some Questions About Value.' " In *Value: A Cooperative Inquiry*, edited by Ray Lepley, pp. 243–4. New York: Columbia University Press, 1949.
Human Values. Ann Arbor, Mich.: George Wahr, 1944.
The Philosophy of Value. Ann Arbor: University of Michigan Press, 1957.
Pastin, Mark. "The Reconstruction of Value." *Canadian Journal of Philosophy* 5 (November 1975): 375–93.
Pateman, Carole. *The Problem of Political Obligation*. New York: Wiley, 1979.
Pennock, J. Roland. *Democratic Political Theory*. Princeton, N.J.: Princeton University Press, 1979.
Perry, Ralph Barton. *General Theory of Value*. Cambridge, Mass.: Harvard University Press, 1950.
Realms of Value. Cambridge, Mass.: Harvard University Press, 1954.
Pettit, Philip. "Free Riding and Foul Dealing." *The Journal of Philosophy* 83 (July 1986): 361–79.
"The Possibility of Aesthetic Realism." In *Pleasure, Preference, and Value*, edited by Eva Schaper, pp. 19–38. Cambridge: Cambridge University Press, 1983.
Pettit, Philip, and Robert Goodin. "The Possibility of Special Duties." *Canadian Journal of Philosophy* 16 (December 1986): 651–76.
Piaget, Jean. "The First Year of Life of the Child." In *The Essential Piaget*, edited by Howard E. Gruber and J. Jacques Vonèche, pp. 198–214. London: Routledge & Kegan Paul, 1977.
"The Growth of Logical Thinking from Childhood to Adolescence." In *The Essential Piaget*, edited by Howard E. Gruber and J. Jacques Vonèche, pp. 404–44. London: Routledge & Kegan Paul, 1977.
The Moral Judgment of the Child, translated by Marjorie Gabain. New York: Free Press, 1965.

Six Psychological Studies, translated by Anita Tenzer. New York: Random House, 1967.

Pitcher, George. "Emotion." *Mind* 74 (1965): 326–46.

Plamenatz, John. *Karl Marx's Philosophy of Man*. Oxford: Clarendon Press, 1975.

Plant, Raymond, Harry Lesser, and Peter Taylor-Gooby. *Political Philosophy and Social Welfare*. London: Routledge & Kegan Paul, 1980.

Prall, David. "A Study in the Theory of Value." *University of California Publications in Philosophy* 3 (1921): 179–290.

Price, A. W. "Varieties of Objectivity and Values." *Proceedings of the Aristotelian Society* 83 (1982-83): 103–19.

Priest, Graham. "Contradiction, Belief, and Rationality." *Proceedings of the Aristotelian Society* 86 (1985–6): 99–116.

Pugh, George Edgin. *The Biological Origin of Human Values*. New York: Basic, 1977.

"Values and the Theory of Motivation." *Zygon* 14 (March 1979): 53–82.

Quine, W. V., and J. S. Ullian. *The Web of Belief*, 2d ed. New York: Random House, 1978.

Quinn, Warren S. "Theories of Intrinsic Value." *American Philosophical Quarterly* 11 (April 1974): 123–32.

Radford, Colin. "How Can We Be Moved by the Fate of Anna Kerenina?" *Proceedings of the Aristotelian Society* supp. vol. 49 (1975): 67–80.

Rapaport, David. *Emotions and Memory*. New York: International Universities Press, 1950.

Raphael, D. D. "Human Rights, Old and New." In his *Political Theory and the Rights of Man*, pp. 54–67. Bloomington: Indiana University Press, 1967.

"Fallacies in and about Mill's *Utilitarianism*." *Philosophy* 30 (October 1955): 344–57.

Rashdall, Hastings. *The Theory of Good and Evil*. Oxford: Clarendon Press, 1907.

Rawls, John. "The Basic Structure As Subject." In *Values and Morals*, edited by Alvin I. Goldman and Jaegwon Kim, pp. 47–71. Dordrecht, Holland: Reidel, 1978.

"Justice As Fairness: Political Not Metaphysical." *Philosophy and Public Affairs* 14 (Summer 1985): 223–51.

"Kantian Constructivism in Moral Theory." *The Journal of Philosophy* 77 (September 1980): 515–72.

"Social Unity and Primary Goods." In *Utilitarianism and Beyond*, edited by Amartya Sen and Bernard Williams, pp. 159–85. Cambridge: Cambridge University Press, 1982.

A Theory of Justice. Cambridge, Mass.: Belknap Press of Harvard University Press, 1971.

"Two Concepts of Rules." In Samuel Gorovitz, ed., *Mill: Utilitarianism*, pp. 175–94. Indianapolis: Bobbs-Merrill, 1971.

Raz, Joseph. *The Morality of Freedom*. Oxford: Clarendon Press, 1986.

Practical Reason and Norms. London: Hutchinson, 1975.

"Promises and Obligation." In *Law, Morality, and Society*, edited by

P. M. S. Hacker and Joseph Raz, pp. 210–28. Oxford: Clarendon Press, 1977.
"Value Incommensurability: Some Preliminaries." *Proceedings of the Aristotelian Society* 86 (1985-86): 117–34.
Regan, Donald H. *Utilitarianism and Co-operation*. Oxford: Clarendon Press, 1980.
Reich, Ben, and Christine Adcock. *Values, Attitudes, and Behaviour Change*. London: Methuen & Co., 1976.
Reid, John R. "A Definition of Value." *Journal of Philosophy* 28 (1931): 637–89.
Rescher, Nicholas. *Introduction to Value Theory*. Englewood Cliffs, N.J.: Prentice-Hall, 1969.
Richards, David A. J. *A Theory of Reasons for Action*. Oxford: Clarendon Press, 1971.
Riker, William H. *Liberalism against Populism*. San Francisco: Freeman, 1982.
Riley, Jonathan. "Justice under Capitalism." In *NOMOS XXXI: Markets and Justice*, edited by John W. Chapman and J. Roland Pennock, pp. 127–62. New York: New York University Press, 1988.
Rist, J. M. "Aristotle: The Value of Man and the Origin of Morality." *Canadian Journal of Philosophy* 4 (September 1974): 1–21.
Robins, Michael H. "Practical Reasoning, Commitment, and Rational Action." *American Philosophical Quarterly* 21 (January 1984): 55–68.
Rohr, Michael David. "Is Goodness Comparative?" *Journal of Philosophy* 75 (1978): 494–503.
Rokeach, Milton. *Beliefs, Attitudes, and Values*. San Francisco: Jossey-Bass, 1968.
"From Individual to Institutional Values." In his *Understanding Human Values*, pp. 47–70. London: Collier Macmillan, 1979.
The Nature of Human Values. New York: Free Press, 1973.
Rolston, Holmes III. "Are Values in Nature Subjective or Objective?" *Environmental Ethics* 4 (Summer 1982): 125–51.
"Values in Nature." *Environmental Ethics* 3 (Summer 1981): 113–28.
Rommen, Heinrich A. *The State in Catholic Thought*. London: B. Herder, 1950.
Rorty, Amélie O. "Explaining Emotions." In her *Explaining Emotions*, pp. 103–26. Berkeley: University of California Press, 1980.
"Introduction" to her *Explaining Emotions*, pp. 1–8. Berkeley: University of California Press, 1980.
Rosen, Hugh. *Pathway to Piaget*. Cherry Hill, N.J.: Postgraduate International, 1977.
Rosenberg, Milton J. "An Analysis of Affective-Cognitive Consistency." In *Attitude Organization and Change*, edited by Milton J. Rosenberg and Carl I. Hovland, pp. 15–64. New Haven, Conn.: Yale University Press, 1960.
"Cognitive Structure and Attitudinal Affect." *Journal of Abnormal and Social Psychology* 53 (1956): 367–72.
Rosenberg, Milton J., and Carl I. Hovland. "Cognitive, Affective, and Be-

havioral Components of Attitudes." In *Attitude Organization and Change*, edited by Milton J. Rosenberg and Carl I. Hovland, pp. 1–14. New Haven, Conn.: Yale University Press, 1960.
Ross, W. D. *Foundations of Ethics*. Oxford: Clarendon Press, 1939.
The Right and the Good. Oxford: Clarendon Press, 1930.
Roupas, T. G. "The Value of Life." *Philosophy and Public Affairs* 7 (1978): 154–83.
Rousseau, Jean-Jacques. *Discourse on the Origin and Foundations of Inequality among Men*. In *The First and Second Discourses*, translated by Roger D. and Judith R. Masters. New York: St. Martin's, 1964.
The Social Contract, translated by Maurice Cranston. Harmondsworth, Eng.: Penguin Books, 1968.
Runcimann, W. G., and Amaryta K. Sen. "Games, Justice, and the General Will," *Mind* 74 (1965): 554–62.
Rushton, J. Phillipe. "Altruism and Society: A Social Learning Perspective." *Ethics* 92 (April 1982): 425–46.
Rycroft, Charles. *Anxiety and Neurosis*. Harmondsworth, Eng.: Penguin Books, 1970.
Ryle, Gilbert. *The Concept of Mind*. London: Hutchinson, 1949.
Sabini, John, and Maury Silver. "Emotions, Responsibility, and Character." In *Responsibility, Character, and the Emotions: New Essays on Moral Psychology*, edited by Ferdinand Schoeman, pp. 165–75. Cambridge: Cambridge University Press, 1987.
Sagan, Carl. *The Dragons of Eden*. New York: Random House, 1977.
Samuelson, Paul. *Economics*, 10th ed. New York: McGraw-Hill, 1976.
Sandel, Michael J. *Liberalism and the Limits of Justice*. Cambridge: Cambridge University Press, 1982.
"The Procedural Republic of the Unencumbered Self." *Political Theory* 13 (February 1984): 81–96.
Sankowski, Edward. "Responsibility of Persons for Their Emotions." *Canadian Journal of Philosophy* 7 (December 1977): 829–40.
Santayana, George. *The Sense of Beauty*. New York: Dover, 1955.
Sauerbach, Ferdinand, and Hans Wenke. *Pain: Its Meaning and Significance*, translated by Edward Fitzgerald. London: Allen & Unwin, 1963.
Savery, William. "A Defense of Hedonism." *International Journal of Ethics* (now *Ethics*) 45 (October 1934): 1–26.
Scanlon, T. M. "Contractualism and Utilitarianism." In *Utilitarianism and Beyond*, edited by Amartya Sen and Bernard Williams, pp. 103–28. Cambridge: Cambridge University Press, 1982.
Schachter, Stanley. "The Interaction of Cognitive and Physiological Determinants of Emotional State." In *Psychological Approaches to Social Behavior*, edited by Herbert Leigerman and David Shapiro, pp. 138–73. London: Tavistock, 1965.
Schachter, Stanley, and Jerome E. Singer. "Cognitive, Social, and Physiological Determinants of Emotional State." *Psychological Review* 69 (September 1962): 379–99.
Schalling, Daisey. "Psychopathy-related Personality Variables in the Psychophysiology of Socialization." In *Psychopathic Behaviour: Approaches to Re-*

search, edited by R. D. Hare and D. Schalling, pp. 85–106. New York: Wiley, 1978.
Scheffler, Samuel. *The Rejection of Consequentialism*. Oxford: Clarendon Press, 1982.
Scheler, Max. *Formalism in Ethics and Non-formal Ethics of Values: A New Attempt toward the Foundation of an Ethical Personalism*, translated by Munfred S. Frings and Roger L. Funk. Evanston, Ill.: Northwestern University Press, 1973.
Schelling, Thomas C. *The Strategy of Conflict*. Oxford: Oxford University Press, 1960.
Schrader, George. "The Status of Value." *Journal of Value Inquiry* 3 (Fall 1969): 196-204.
Scruton, Roger. *Art and Imagination*. London: Methuen & Co., 1974.
Searle, John R. *Intentionality*. Cambridge: Cambridge University Press, 1983.
Sen, Amartya K. *Collective Choice and Social Welfare*. San Francisco: Holden-Day, 1970.
"Rational Fools." In *Philosophy and Economic Theory*, edited by Frank Hahn and Martin Hollis, pp. 87–109. Oxford: Oxford University Press, 1979.
Sen, Amartya, and Bernard Williams. "Introduction" to their *Utilitarianism and Beyond*, pp. 1–21. Cambridge: Cambridge University Press, 1982.
Shapiro, Ian. *The Evolution of Rights in Liberal Theory*. Cambridge: Cambridge University Press, 1986.
Sher, George. *Desert*. Princeton, N.J.: Princeton University Press, 1987.
Sherif, Muzafer. *An Outline of Social Psychology*. New York: Harper & Bros., 1948.
Shibles, Warren. *Emotion*. Whitewater, Wis.: The Language Press, 1974.
Shields, Stephanie A., and Robert M. Stern. "Emotion: The Perception of Bodily Changes." In *Perception of Emotion in Self and Others*, edited by Patricia Pliner, Kirk R. Blankstein, and Irwin M. Spigel, pp. 85–106. New York: Plenum, 1979.
Shils, Edward. "The Antinomies of Liberalism." In *The Relevance of Liberalism*, edited by Zbigniew Brzezinski et al., pp. 135–200. Boulder, Colo.: Westview Press, 1978.
Sidgwick, Henry. *Lectures on the Ethics of T. H. Green, Mr. Herbert Spencer, and J. Martineau*. London: Macmillan, 1902.
The Methods of Ethics, 7th ed. Chicago: University of Chicago Press, 1962.
Siedentop, Larry. "Two Liberal Traditions." In *The Idea of Freedom*, edited by Alan Ryan, pp. 153–74. Oxford: Oxford University Press, 1979.
Simmons, A. John. *Moral Principles and Political Obligation*. Princeton, N.J.: Princeton University Press, 1979.
Simonsen, Kenneth H. "The Value of Wilderness." *Environmental Ethics* 3 (Summer 1981): 259–63.
Singer, Marcus George. *Generalization in Ethics*. New York: Knopf, 1961.
"The Generalization Principle." In *Morality and Universality: Essays on*

Ethical Universalizability, edited by Nelson T. Potter and Mark Timmons, pp. 47–73. Dordrecht, Holland: Reidel, 1985.
Singer, Peter. *Democracy and Disobedience*. Oxford: Oxford University Press, 1973.
Slote, Michael A. "Desert, Consent, and Justice." *Philosophy and Public Affairs* 2 (Summer 1973): 323–47.
Goods and Virtues. Oxford: Clarendon Press, 1983.
Smart, J. J. C. "An Outline of a System of Utilitarian Ethics." In J. J. C. Smart and Bernard Williams, *Utilitarianism: For and Against*, pp. 3–74. Cambridge: Cambridge University Press, 1973.
Smith, Adam. *An Inquiry into the Nature and Causes of the Wealth of Nations*, edited by Edwin Cannan. Chicago: University of Chicago Press, 1976.
The Theory of Moral Sentiments, edited by D. D. Raphael and A. L. Macfie. Indianapolis: Liberty Classics, 1982.
Smith, M. Brewster. "Personal Values in the Study of Lives." In his *Social Psychology and Human Values*, pp. 97–116. Chicago: Aldine, 1969.
Sousa, Ronald de. "The Rationality of Emotions." In *Explaining Emotions*, edited by Amélie Oksenberg Rorty, pp. 127–51. Berkeley: University of California Press, 1980.
Spielberger, Charles D., J. Kenneth Kling, and Stephen E. J. O'Hagan. "Dimensions of Psychopathic Personality: Antisocial Behaviour and Anxiety." In *Psychopathic Behaviour: Approaches to Research*, edited by R. D. Hare and D. Schalling, pp. 23–46. New York: Wiley, 1978.
Spinoza, Benedict. *Ethic*. In *Spinoza Selections*, edited by John Wild. New York: Scribner, 1930.
Spranger, Edward. *Types of Men: The Psychology of Ethics and Personality*, translated by Paul J. W. Pigors. Halle, Germany: Max Niemeyer, 1928.
Stevenson, C. L. *Facts and Values*. New Haven, Conn.: Yale University Press, 1963.
Stocker, Michael. "Psychic Feelings: Their Importance and Irreducibility." *Australasian Journal of Philosophy* 61 (March 1983): 5–26.
"Values and Purposes: The Limits of Teleology and the Ends of Friendship. " *Journal of Philosophy* 78 (December 1981): 747–65.
Storr, Anthony. *The Integrity of the Personality*. Harmondsworth, Eng.: Penguin Books, 1964.
Strawson, P. F. *Freedom and Resentment and Other Essays*. London: Methuen & Co., 1974.
Strongman, K. T. *The Psychology of Emotion*. London: Wiley, 1973.
Swinburne, R. G. "The Objectivity of Morality." *Philosophy* 51 (1976): 5-20.
Tawney, R. H. *Equality*. London: Allen & Unwin, 1964.
Taylor, Charles. "What Is Human Agency?" In *The Self*, edited by Theodore Mischel, pp. 103–35. Oxford: Blackwell Publisher, 1977.
Taylor, Gabriele. "Justifying the Emotions." *Mind* 84 (1975): 390–402.
"Love." *Proceedings of the Aristotelian Society* 76 (1976): 147–64.
Pride, Shame, and Guilt. Oxford: Clarendon Press, 1985.
Taylor, Kraupl. *Psychopathology*. Baltimore: Johns Hopkins University Press, 1979.
Taylor, Richard. *Good and Evil*. Buffalo: Prometheus Books, 1984.

Thalberg, Irving. "Emotion and Thought." *American Philosophical Quarterly* 1 (January 1964): 45–55.

Thomas, Alexander, and Stella Chess. *Temperament and Development*. New York: Brunner/Mazell, 1977.

Thomas, Geoffrey. *The Moral Philosophy of T. H. Green*. Oxford: Clarendon Press, 1987.

Thomson, Judith Jarvis. "Government Regulation of Behavior." In *Rights, Restitution, and Risk*, edited by William Parent, pp. 154–72. Cambridge, Mass.: Harvard University Press, 1986.

"Self-defense and Rights." In *Rights, Restitution, and Risk*, edited by William Parent, pp. 33–48. Cambridge, Mass.: Harvard University Press, 1986.

Thurstone, L. L. "The Measurement of Social Attitudes." *Journal of Abnormal and Social Psychology* 26 (1931): 249–69.

Tomkins, Silvan S. *Affect, Imagery, and Consciousness*. New York: Springer, 1962.

Trigg, Roger. *Pain and Emotion*. Oxford: Clarendon Press, 1970.

Tully, James. *A Discourse on Property: John Locke and His Adversaries*. Cambridge: Cambridge University Press, 1980.

Tussi, Aldo. "Anarchism, Autonomy, and the Concept of the Common Good." *International Philosophical Quarterly* 3 (September 1977): 273–83.

Unger, Roberto Mangabeira. *Knowledge and Politics*. New York: Free Press, 1975.

Urban, William Marshall. *Valuation: Its Nature and Laws*. London: Allen & Unwin, 1909.

Urmson, J. O. *The Emotive Theory of Ethics*. New York: Oxford University Press, 1968.

Varian, Hal R. "Distributive Justice, Welfare Economics, and the Theory of Fairness." In *Philosophy and Economic Theory*, edited by Frank Hahn and Martin Hollis, pp. 134–54. Oxford: Oxford University Press, 1979.

Veatch, Henry B. "The Rational Justification of Moral Principles." *Review of Metaphysics* 29 (1975): 217–38.

Waldron, Jeremy. "Enough and As Good Left for Others." *Philosophical Quarterly* 29 (1979): 319–28.

"Introduction" to his *Theories of Rights*, pp. 1–20. Oxford: Oxford University Press, 1984.

The Right to Private Property. Oxford: Clarendon Press, 1988.

Walhout, Donald. *The Good and the Realm of Values*. Notre Dame: University of Notre Dame Press, 1978.

Wall, Grenville. "Against Subjective Intrinsic Value." *Educational Philosophy and Theory* 10 (October 1978): 39–49.

Walzer, Michael. "Liberalism and Separation." *Political Theory* 12 (August 1984): 313–30.

Warnock, G. J. "On Choosing Values." *Midwest Studies in Philosophy* 3 (1978): 28–34.

Warnock, Mary. "The Justification of Emotions." *Proceedings of the Aristotelian Society* supp. vol. 31 (1957): 43–58.

Wavell, Bruce B. "The Rationality of Values." *Zygon* 15 (March 1980): 43–56.
Wellman, Carl. *Challenge and Response: Justification in Ethics.* Carbondale and Edwardsville, Ill.: Southern Illinois University Press, 1971.
Werkmeister, W. H. *Historical Spectrum of Value Theories.* Lincoln, Nebr.: Johnsen, 1970.
"Is Truth a Value?" *Southwestern Journal of Philosophy* 1 (Fall 1970): 45–49.
Man and His Values. Lincoln: University of Nebraska Press, 1967.
Westin, Peter. " 'Freedom' and 'Coercion': Vice and Virtue Words." *Duke Law Journal* 85 (1985): 541–93.
Weston, Michael. "How Can We Be Moved by the Fate of Anna Kerenina?" *Proceedings of the Aristotelian Society* supp. vol. 44 (1975): 81–93.
Whelan, Frederick G. "Democratic Theory and the Boundary Problem." In *NOMOS XXV: Liberal Democracy*, edited by J. Roland Pennock and John W. Chapman, pp. 13–47. New York: New York University Press, 1983.
White, Alan R. *Rights.* Oxford: Clarendon Press, 1984.
Wicksteed, Philip H. *The Common Sense of Political Economy*, edited by Lionel Robbins. London: George Routledge & Sons, 1946.
Widom, Cathy Spatz. "A Methodology for Studying Non-Institutionalized Psychopaths." In *Psychopathic Behavior: Approaches to Research*, edited by R. D. Hare and D. Schalling, pp. 71–84. New York: Wiley, 1978.
Wiggins, David. "Truth, Invention, and the Meaning of Life." *Proceedings of the British Academy* 62 (1976): 331–78.
Wiles, P. J. D. *Economic Institutions Compared.* New York: Wiley, 1977.
Willard, L. Duane. "Intrinsic Value in Dewey." *Philosophy Research Archives* 1, no. 1021 (April 1975): 55–77.
Williams, Bernard. "Conflicts of Values." In his *Moral Luck*, pp. 71–82. Cambridge: Cambridge University Press, 1981.
"A Critique of Utilitarianism." In J. J. C. Smart and Bernard Williams, *Utilitarianism: For and Against*, pp. 75–150. Cambridge: Cambridge University Press, 1973.
"Deciding to Believe." In his *Problems of the Self*, pp. 136–51. Cambridge: Cambridge University Press, 1973.
"Internal and External Reasons." In *Rational Action*, edited by Ross Harrison, pp. 17–28. Cambridge: Cambridge University Press, 1979.
"Persons, Character, and Morality." In his *Moral Luck*, pp. 1–19. Cambridge: Cambridge University Press, 1981.
Williams, Gardner. "Hedonic Individual Ethical Relativism." *Journal of Philosophy* 55 (1958): 143–53.
Williams, Robin M. "Change and Stability in Values and Value Systems: A Sociological Perspective." In *Understanding Human Values*, edited by Milton Rokeach, pp. 15–46. London: Collier Macmillan, 1979.
Williamson, Oliver E. *The Economic Institutions of Capitalism.* New York: Free Press, 1985.
Wilson, J. R. S. *Emotion and Object.* Cambridge: Cambridge University Press, 1972.
Wisdom, John. "God and Evil," *Mind*, 44 (January 1935): 1–20.

Wittgenstein, Ludwig. *Philosophical Investigations*, translated by G. E. M. Anscombe. New York: Macmillan, 1950.

Wolff, Robert Paul. *Understanding Rawls*. Princeton, N.J.: Princeton University Press, 1977.

Wright, Derek. *The Psychology of Moral Behaviour*. Harmondsworth, Eng.: Penguin Books, 1971.

Wright, Georg Henrik von. *The Varieties of Goodness*. London: Routledge & Kegan Paul, 1963.

Wright, George. *Behavioural Decision Theory*. Harmondsworth, Eng.: Penguin Books, 1984.

Yates, Gregory C. R., and Shirley M. Yates. "Moral Reasoning in Young Children: A Review of Research into Intentionality and Implications for Education." *Australian Journal of Education* 23 (1979): 153–70.

Young, Paul Thomas. "Feeling and Emotion." In *The Handbook of General Psychology*, edited by Benjamin B. Wolman, pp. 749–71. Englewood Cliffs, N.J.: Prentice-Hall, 1973.

Young, Robert. *Personal Autonomy: Beyond Negative and Positive Liberty*. London: Croom Helm, 1986.

Zeuthen, F. "Theoretical Remarks on Price Policy: Hotelling's Case with Variations." *The Quarterly Journal of Economics* 48 (1933): 231–53.

Zimmerman, David. "Moral Realism and Explanatory Necessity." In *Morality, Reason, and Truth: New Essays on the Foundations of Ethics*, edited by David Copp and David Zimmerman, pp. 79–103. Totowa, N.J.: Rowman and Allenheld, 1984.

Zimmerman, Michael J. "On the Intrinsic Value of States of Pleasure." *Philosophy and Phenomenological Research* 41 (September-December 1980): 16–45.

Ziskind, Eugene. "The Diagnosis of Sociopathy." In *Psychopathic Behavior: Approaches to Research*, edited by R. D. Hare and D. Schalling, pp. 47–54. New York: Wiley, 1978.

Index